Introduction

Welcome to 'Today's The Day', a unique book that takes an in-depth look into Newcastle United Football Club on each particular day, 365 days of the year (February 28-29 have been merged). The book lists on each day the playing record of the club, which includes all the goal times for and against the Magpies since their promotion to the Premier League. Every competitive game is listed, including Wartime League games and all the various Cup competitions United have been involved in over their 121-year history.

Substitute figures noted are included in totals given. All appearances and goals include all league and cup matches and other games, such as war, Charity Shield and Texaco Cup etc.

On each day where Newcastle has played at least five games (268 in all), statistics have been compiled to show the total matches and that day's success rate. The 267 days have then been ranked from the best day at number 1 to the worst day at 268. Where the success rates were the same for more than one-day goal difference and then, if needed, the number of goals scored were taken into account to separate the days.

The book includes birth and death dates of the players, with their personal career records, which United have used over the years, as well as any other news relating to the club and its personnel.

There is a selected 'Match of the Day' throughout the book covering every decade and almost every year since Newcastle's first Football league game in 1893 right up till the end of their last season 2002/03. Therefore whatever the age of the supporter, there will be a match report in this book which is treasured memory for you.

I hope you find your most memorable game and enjoy 'Today's The Day - Newcastle United Football Club'.

Acknowledgements

First of all I would like to thank Roger Marshall, Paul Burns, Linda Perkins, Chris Sweet and all at Britespot Publishing for all their help in making this book possible. Also, Nick Hingley for putting the artwork together and Iain Nannestad for assisting in the proof reading.

I would also like to thank Newcastle United FC official historian Paul Joannou who has helped with the proof reading and checking of the statistics within this book and has allowed me to take references from his previous titles 'Newcastle United: A Complete Record' and 'The Black 'n' White Alphabet'.

Research for the book has been aided greatly by the helpful and friendly staff at both Newcastle and Birmingham Central Libraries and I thank everyone for the efficient service they have provided during the year.

During a hectic summer I have worked tirelessly in collecting, checking, calculating and typing many hundreds of stats match reports and general trivia on Newcastle United FC and during this time I have been given tremendous support and help from family and friends Kevin and Josie, Margaret, Robert, Emma, Danny and Francesca, Alan and Carolyn Brettle, Clare, Anthony, Carol, Darren, Marcus and Samantha, Cate, Ken, Jack and Daniel, Lennie and Roy, Steve and Pete, Janet, Jess Hardman, Mike Lees and Ross Collins. I would also like to thank the teachers and staff at St. Thomas' CE Primary School, Great Colmore St, Birmingham.

For all their encouragement and well wishes thanks go to the management, staff and customers of The Raven public house, Weoley Castle, Birmingham. In particular my boss and colleagues Jim and Trudy Leach, James, Joanne, Sean and Christopher, Angela Parry, Sue Dunn, and Liz White. To the regular customers I would like to thank Paul and Lee Beesley, Steve Keating, Brian Callaghan, Mick and Sue, Haley, Paddy and Sheila Boyle, Peter Roberts, Sue Melville, Kim and Tony Hamilton, Dave Pollar, Paul and Nicky Roberts, Pauline, Ursula, and of course 'Geordie' John.

I would also like to acknowledge all the welcoming, useful information, and general friendliness shown towards me by Newcastle United fans on my two recent visits, my sincere hope is the Magpies continue to go from strength to strength as this, in my opinion, is what your support deserves.

Finally, to my wife Jennifer who has helped in every aspect with the book as well as keeping the house, myself, and our two children well kept. She has been an inspiration during some tough times when things inevitably go wrong and all without complaining or giving in. Without her during those times I think this publication had as much chance of getting finished as Sunderland winning the double, such was Jen's strength and commitment. My love and thanks go to Jen, and hopefully now I can get back to being a half decent husband and father again.

This book is dedicated to Jennifer, Morgan and Evelyn Henry

In memory of Richard Brettle and Craig Beesley

'Today's The Day' Newcastle United
A Britespot Publication

First Published in Great Britain by
Britespot Publishing Solutions Limited
Chester Road, Cradley Heath, West Midlands B64 6AB

© Britespot January 2004

ISBN 1 904103 24 3

Cover design and layout
© *Britespot Publishing Solutions Limited*

Printed and bound in Dubai, U.A.E.

Foreword

I am delighted to have been given the opportunity to write this foreword for "Today's the Day".

The format of the book is fascinating in that it chronicles the events as they happened on a particular day of the year in Newcastle United's long and distinguished history, and in doing so, it sets the book apart from the other excellent and meticulously researched historical reference books on the Club.

And for a club with such a long and proud tradition, interspersed with countless notable landmarks, this book is an ideal way for Magpie devotees to wallow in the wonderful nostalgia that is inextricably woven into the fabric that is Newcastle United.

From the foundation of the Club in the 1890s, the glory years of the Edwardian era when the Geordies were the undisputed kings of England, the Cup winning teams of the 20s, 30s and 50s through to the modern era, the book is a fascinating study of everything that is special about the Magpies - and much of it unique.

And for a youngster in the 1940s, who grew up watching such United legends as Jackie Milburn, Len Shackleton, Albert Stubbins and Charlie Wayman, I can without hesitation say that this was one of the golden periods for Newcastle United - when crowds flocked to football matches up and down the country in their thousands. Indeed there was no better place to be than on Tyneside in the immediate post war years, football was a religion and we simply couldn't get enough of it. To that end, for me, reading about the events of that period, over half a century ago, is almost as good as it gets.

I have always been intrigued about the history of Newcastle United, and what I would have given to have seen some of those olden day players in action, Bill McCracken, Colin Veitch and Hughie Gallacher to name but three. They are names etched firmly in the annals of the club, players who helped make the Club the focal point of the people of Tyneside.

As you are no doubt aware, my career in football has taken me away from Tyneside, both in my playing and managerial career, and whilst I have kept up to speed with all the major goings on at St. James' Park, there were inevitably many important and interesting historical details that passed me by. And that's the beauty of the book as it fills those gaps perfectly.

Newcastle United is a football club steeped in tradition, with tremendously loyal and passionate fans. This book is a tribute to each and every one of those supporters.

Sir Bobby Robson
December 2003

Month Introduction Images

January:	Sir Bobby Robson	June:	Joe Harvey sips champagne from the Inter-Cities Fairs Cup.
February:	Alan Shearer		
March:	Jimmy Nelson leads the Newcastle United team out to face Arsenal on March 19 1932.	July:	Craig Bellamy
		August:	Kevin Keegan
		September:	Malcolm Macdonald
April:	Bobby Moncur celebrates after the 1974 FA Cup Semi-Final victory.	October	Jermaine Jenas
		November:	Peter Beardsley
May:	Jackie Milburn	December:	St James' Park

January

, Division 2.
Lincoln City (h) 5-1   Att. 4,000
Bartlett (3), Thompson, Quinn
, Division 2.
Lincoln City (h) 4-2   Att. 4,000
Dickson, Willis, Thompson (2)
, Division 2.
Leicester Fosse (h) 1-0   Att. 7,000
Aitken
, Division 2.
Newton Heath (h) 2-0   Att. 16,125
Wardrope, Aitken
, Division 1.
Walsall (h) 2-1   Att. 16,000
Peddie, R. Allan
, Division 1.
Sunderland (a) 1-1   Att. 40,000
Orr
, Division 1.
Blackburn Rovers(a) 0-1   Att. 30,000
, Division 1.
Derby County(h) 2-0   Att. 30,000
Orr, Speedie
, Division 1.
Sheffield United (a) 1-1   Att. 20,000
Appleyard
, Division 1.
Everton (a) 1-0   Att. 40,000
Howie
, Division 1.
Chelsea (h) 1-0   Att. 30,000
Shepherd
, Division 1.
Sheffield United (a) 1-2   Att. 40,000
Stewart
, Division 1.
Liverpool (h) 0-0   Att. 30,000
, Division 1.
Manchester City (h) 0-1   Att. 20,000
, Division 1.
Sheffield Wed. (a) 1-2   Att. 11,000
King
, Division 1.
Aston Villa (h) 2-0   Att. 40,000
Smailes (2)
, Division 1.
Manchester United (h) 6-3   Att. 40,000
Seymour (2), Smailes, Harris (2),
Phillipson
, Division 1.
Oldham Athletic (h) 1-0   Att. 30,000
McDonald (pen)
, Division 1.
Aston Villa (h) 4-1   Att. 30,000
Seymour (2), McDonald, Harris
, Division 1.
Sheffield United (h) 0-0   Att. 20,000
, Division 1.
Burnley (h) 1-3   Att. 34,000
Urwin
, Division 1.
Leeds United (h) 1-0   Att. 51,343
Gallacher
, Division 1.
Blackburn Rovers (h) 0-2   Att. 40,000
, Division 1.
Aston Villa (h) 2-0   Att. 50,000
Starling, Wilkinson
, Division 1.
Aston Villa (h) 3-1   Att. 46,000
Lang, J.R. Richardson, Cape

continued opposite

January 1

Match of the Day from 1934

HAPPY NEW YEAR!

Magpies gain easy victory with record home win

Newcastle United began the New Year in style and in keeping with their impressive performance over the Christmas period when they notched up eighteen goals, conceding only eight. They had beaten Everton 7-3 at Goodison Park, and now it was the turn of the other Merseysiders to feel the full force of a Newcastle side which included six internationals.

It took only three minutes for Newcastle to open the scoring, despite the heavy going pitch. A cross from Lang found its intended target of England's inside-forward Jimmy Richardson who scored with ease.

Midway through the first half Taylor equalised for Liverpool, only for Newcastle to regain the lead straight away when Sammy Weaver got onto the ball and secured it in the net.

Before the half-time whistle went Liverpool were again given hope with another equaliser, this time courtesy of an own goal by Alec Betton. The crowd of 18,000 were beginning to think that they had seen most of the action for this game, certainly not expecting the events of the second half.

The last 45 minutes began with Newcastle again on the attack, and using all their skill and force to ensure their victory. Their tactics worked quickly, and they took the lead again with a superb shot from Richardson. With the score now 3-2 to the home side Liverpool began to lose their confidence. Newcastle took full advantage of this, and Richardson completed his hat trick, as did Sammy Weaver. Not wanting to be left off the scoresheet, wingers Boyd and Lang added a goal each, and along with Williams they ensured all the forwards had contributed to this record 9-2 win.

A hat trick for Sammy Weaver

Newcastle United
McPhillips, Nelson, Fairhurst, Bell, Betton, Murray, Boyd, Richardson, Williams, Weaver, Lang.
Liverpool
Scott, Steele, Done, Morrison, Bradshaw, McPherson, Nieuwenhuys, Taylor, Bush, Roberts, Hanson.

Toon News Extra

1900... Fog saves the Magpies

Newcastle's home game with Glossop fell victim to fog when the game was eventually abandoned after 72 minutes with United trailing 3-2. Newcastle who had just scored through MacFarlane were slowly getting back into the game but were hardly disappointed when it was called of by the referee with eighteen minutes remaining. A crowd of just 1,500 turned up at a freezing St. James' Park for the Division One league. When the game was rescheduled on March 14, the Magpies won by a late Peddie goal in the second half.

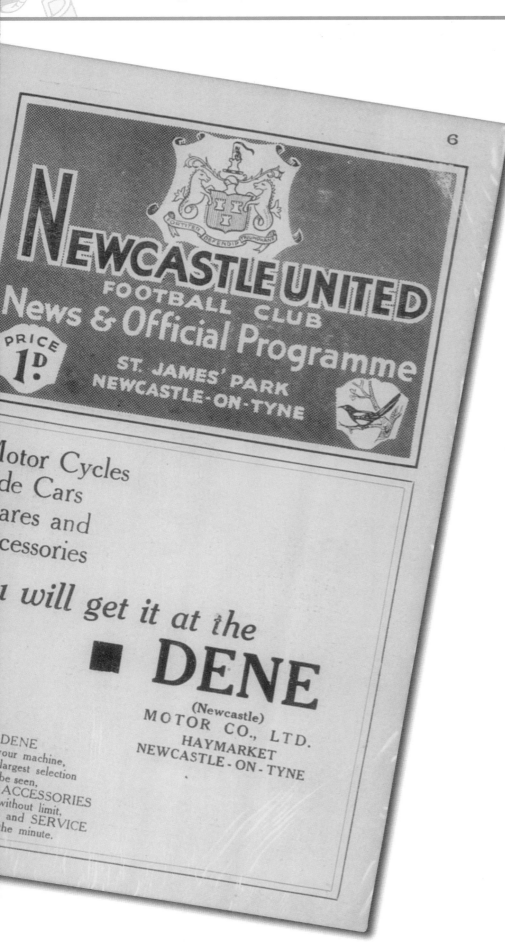

Played on this day

1934, Division 1.
Liverpool (h) 9-2   Att. 18,000
Boyd, Lang, J.R. Richardson (3),
Weaver (3), Williams

1935, Division 2.
Bury (h) 5-1   Att. 28,000
Bott (3), Pearson, Smith

1936, Division 2.
Plymouth Argyle (h) 5-0   Att. 20,000
Weaver (2, 1pen), J. Smith (2), Ware

1937, Division 2.
Bradford Park Ave. (h) 1-1   Att. 29,000
Leighton

1938, Division 2.
Manchester United (h) 2-2   Att. 40,088
Smith (2)

1944, Wartime.
Sunderland (a) 0-3   Att. 18,000

1946, Wartime.
Sheffield W. (h) 2-0   Att. 47,228
Hair, Wayman

1947, Division 2.
Nottingham Forest (h) 3-0   Att. 56,827
Bentley, Wayman, Woodburn

1948, Division 2.
West Bromwich A. (h) 3-1   Att. 61,301
Dodgin, Milburn (2)

1949, Division 1.
Preston North End (a) 1-2   Att. 37,000
Taylor

1953, Division 1.
West Bromwich A. (h) 3-5   Att. 48,944
Davies, Milburn, Mitchell

1954, Division 1.
Blackpool (h) 2-1   Att. 44,343
Milburn (2)

1955, Division 1.
Sheffield United (a) 2-6   Att. 32,000
Keeble, R. Mitchell

1957, Division 1.
Birmingham City (h) 3-2   Att. 29,383
Tait, Casey (2, 1 pen)

1966, Division 1.
Aston Villa (a) 2-4   Att. 19,402
Bennett (2)

1969, Inter Cities Fairs Cup 3rd round, 1st leg.
Real Zaragoza (a) 2-3   Att. 22,000
Davies, B. Robson

1972, Division 1.
Wolverhampton W. (a) 0-2   Att. 26,571

1973, Division 1.
Leicester City (h) 2-2   Att. 30,868
Tudor, Smith

1974, Division 1.
Arsenal (a) 1-0   Att. 29,258
Hibbitt

1980, Division 2.
Sunderland (h) 3-1   Att. 38,784
Cartwright, Shoulder (pen), Cassidy

1983, Division 2.
Carlisle United (h) 2-2   Att. 28,578
Keegan (2)

1985, Division 1.
Sunderland (h) 3-1   Att. 36,529
Beardsley (3, 1 pen)

1986, Division 1.
Everton(h) 2-2   Att. 28,031
Beardsley, Gascoigne

1987, Division 1.
Manchester United (a) 1-4   Att. 43,334
D. Jackson

continued next page

Played on this day

1988, Division 1.
　　Nottingham Forest (a) 2-0　Att. 28,583
　　Gascoigne, Mirandinha
1990, Division 2.
　　Wolverhampton W. (h) 1-4　Att. 21,937
　　Brock
1991, Division 2.
　　Oldham Athletic (a) 1-1　Att. 14,550
　　Quinn
1992, Division 2.
　　Southend United (a) 0-4　Att. 9,458
1994, Premier League.
　　Newcastle 2　　**Manchester City 0**
　　Cole 28, 45　　Att. 35,585
1997, Premier League.
　　Newcastle 3　　**Leeds United 0**
　　Shearer 4, 77
　　Ferdinand 87　　Att. 36,489
2003, Premier League.
　　Newcastle 1　　**Liverpool 0**
　　Robert 13　　Att. 52,147
　　Liverpool had Salif Dao sent off after 65
　　minutes.

Playing record for the day... 57 games,
Won 30, Drawn 10, Lost 17, GF 113, GA 84.
Todays success rate...61.40%.

Newcastle United's Andrew Griffin heads the ball
away from Liverpool's Vladimir Smicer on this day
in 2003.

January 2

Match of the Day from 1960

BATTLE OF THE UNITEDS

Ten-goal thriller ends in joy at St. James' Park

Most of Newcastle United's biggest crowd of the season, 57,200, watched with delight as the home side fought their way to victory over a determined Manchester United. Both teams battled it out on the pitch, and although Newcastle earned their win, it was no easy task. From the outset both teams were in attacking mode, and Newcastle proved to be the stronger side, taking the lead on just six minutes. A pass from White came to Hughes, whose shot sailed under Manchester United keeper Gaskell as he dived for the save. The home side were 1-0 up, and their confidence was just beginning to soar.

The second goal of the game came from White on sixteen minutes, who made an impressive run down the wing, past three of the opposition. He sent the ball to Eastham, who duly passed it back for White to shoot into the net over the keeper's head. Manchester United were not going to give in without a fight, and attempted to fight back. On 28 minutes Dawson ensured that his team was still in with a chance with a goal just squeezing in after hitting Keith's head and the underside of the crossbar.

With a minute to go before half time, Newcastle extended their lead with another goal from White. A pass from Stokoe gave him the opportunity to send in a smashing shot from eighteen yards, which he did with ease. The home side entered the half-time break 3-1 up, and still in fighting spirit.

Harvey made two great saves early in the second period, getting onto shots from Dawson and Viollet, and this summed up his performance in this match; determined and skilful.

With 54 minutes gone, Newcastle decided it was time to increase their lead yet again. White took up the easy challenge of completing his hat trick and didn't let his side down when Bell's shot hit the post and bounced straight to him. Manchester managed to get another goal back thanks to Quixall on 62 minutes, and with the score now 4-2 the fight was on again.

Newcastle were awarded a penalty on 67 minutes when Foulkes brought down Luke. Eastham did the honours and succeeded with ease. The next goal for the home side came when Allchurch passed the ball to Bell on 76 minutes. Bell managed to secure its place in the back of the net despite an impressive diving attempt at a save from Gaskell.

Next it was Manchester's turn for a penalty. Bell got his hand to the ball on 81 minutes, and the visitors were awarded the kick. Quixall took to the spot, and duly slotted the ball past Harvey, but it was more to do with saving face now than saving the match.

The final blow came on 87 minutes with a smashing header from Allchurch, still going strong despite having played the entire second half with his right thigh strapped up from an injury in the first half. This win for Newcastle went down in history, being Manchester United's heaviest defeat since the war.

Newcastle United

Harvey, Keith, McMichael, Scoular, Stokoe, Bell, Hughes, Eastham, White, Allchurch, Luke

Manchester United

Gaskell, Foulkes, Carolin, Goodwin, Cope, Brennan, Dawson, Quixall, Viollet, Charlton, Scanion

Referee Mr R Ryles (Sheffield).

Birthdays

Sam Russell born today in 1900.
Full-back 1920-1925, Apps 31. Goals 0.

Paul Stephenson born today in 1968.
Winger 1984-1988, Apps 71 (5 subs). Goals 1.

Sadly Missed

Charlie Mitten died on this day 2002, aged 80.
Manager 1958-1961.

James Collins died on this day 1900, aged 27.
Midfield 1892-1893 & 1895-1897, Apps 52.
Goals 1.

Played on this day

1894, Division 2.
 Middlesbrough Ironopolis (h) 7-2
 Law, Thompson, Willis (2), Quinn (2),
 Graham   Att. 3,000
1896, Division 2.
 Lincoln City (h) 5-0   Att. 5,000
 Aitken, Lennox (2), Stott, Collins
1897, Division 2.
 Lincoln City (h) 2-1   Att. 12,000
 Aitken, Smellie
1904, Division 1.
 West Bromwich A. (h) 1-0   Att. 16,000
 Orr
1905, Division 1.
 Notts County (h) 1-0   Att. 18,000
 Orr
1909, Division 1.
 Leicester Fosse (a) 4-0   Att. 15,000
 Higgins (2), Shepherd, Stewart
1911, Division 1.
 Everton (a) 5-1   Att. 40,000
 Randall, Shepherd (2), Stewart, Duncan
 An inspired second half by Newcastle as
 they come from 1-0 down at the interval
 to win 5-1 at Goodison Park.
1915, Division 1.
 Everton (a) 0-3   Att. 20,000
1922, Division 1.
 Liverpool (h) 1-1   Att. 43,000
 Harris
1926, Division 1.
 Bolton Wanderers (h) 5-1   Att. 35,000
 Gallacher (4), Urwin
1928, Division 1.
 Birmingham (h) 1-1   Att. 40,000
 Gallacher
1932, Division 1.
 Liverpool (a) 2-4   Att. 30,000
 Cape, Hutchison
1933, Division 1.
 Middlesbrough (a) 3-2   Att. 27,000
 Allen, Boyd, McMenemy
1937, Division 2.
 Sheffield United (h) 4-0   Att. 33,000
 Cairns, Mooney, Smith (2)
1939, Division 2.
 Chesterfield (h) 0-1   Att. 34,000
1943, Wartime.
 Middlesbrough (a) 7-3   Att. 3,000
 Stubbins (3), Short (2), Carr, Mullen
1954, Division 1.
 Manchester United (h) 1-2   Att. 56,034
 Broadis
1956, Division 1.
 West Bromwich A. (h) 0-3   Att. 50,768
1960, Division 1.
 Manchester United (h) 7-3   Att. 57,200
 Allchurch, White (3), Eastham (pen),
 Hughes, Bell
1965, Division 2.
 Huddersfield Town (h) 2-1   Att. 45,315
 McGarry (2)
1978, Division 1.
 Leeds United (a) 2-0   Att. 36,643
 Burns (2)
1984, Division 2.
 Barnsley (h) 1-0   Att. 29,842
 Waddle
1988, Division 1.
 Sheffield W (h) 2-2   Att. 25,503
 Goddard (2)

Continued next page

January 2

Played on this day

1989, Division 1.
Derby County (h) 0-1 Att. 31,079
1993, FA Cup 3rd round.
Port Vale (h) 4-0 Att. 29,873
Peacock (2), Lee, Sheedy

Playing record for this day is... 30 games,
Won 18, Drawn 4, Lost 8, GF 74, GA 40.
Success rate today... 66.67%.

NEWCASTLE UNITED FOOTBALL CLUB
ST. JAMES' PARK · NEWCASTLE

GROUND CAPACITY = 70,000
RECORD ATTENDANCE = 68,386

WE WELCOME TODAY—
MANCHESTER UNITED

Saturday, 2nd January, 1960 kick-off 3-0 p.m.

OFFICIAL PROGRAMME 3D

January 3

Match of the Day from 1981

GOALS AT LAST
Waddle ends goal drought at St. James' Park

Chris Waddle

Newcastle were today hoping for an end to the dry spell, the team having failed to score in five games. An FA Cup third round tie at home against Sheffield Wednesday, presented the ideal opportunity to break the run of misfortune and produce a convincing win.

The game started with both sides eager, but the team to show promise early on was Wednesday. Making only his fifth full appearance for them was Pearson who, at just seventeen years of age, certainly showed that he was indispensable in this match. However, Sheffield's early attacks amounted to nothing, and after thirteen minutes the game turned.

Newcastle keeper Carr sent a long goal kick which found its way to Chris Waddle. He took control of the ball and slammed the ball into the net past Bolder from fully 25 yards out to put the home side into the lead.

This had been the kick-start needed for both teams to step up the fight, and they rose to the challenge. The equaliser came in the 23rd minute with a shot from Pearson just avoiding the safe hands of Carr to reach the back of the net.

They were plenty of chances for the score to change. Curran missed a couple of golden opportunities for Wednesday, and McCulloch and Leman's attempts also failed to make the mark. The end of the first half came with the scores remaining level, and the fight still on.

The second period began in much the same way as the first one had ended. Both teams trying hard, and both just not getting it right. Then, on the hour it was Waddle who saved the day. A free kick was awarded to Newcastle and taken by Martin, Waddle got his head to the ball and nodded it home from twelve yards to put United 2-1 up.

Shortly afterwards there was an eight-minute period which saw three bookings. Newcastle's Boam, and Wednesday's Grant and Shirtliff all saw the yellow card for their offences, but that really signalled the end of the action. The Owls seemed to have given up, and didn't try to fight back. The game was over and Newcastle had won.

Newcastle United
Carr, Carney, P. Johnson, Martin, Boam, Halliday, Shinton, Trewick, Clarke, Wharton, Waddle.

Sheffield Wednesday
Bolder, Marshall, Grant, Smith, Shirtliff, Sterland, Pearson, J. Johnson, Leman, McCulloch, Curran.

Referee Mr. G. Peck (Doncaster).

Played on this day

1898, Division 2.
Loughborough Town (h) 3-1   Att. 4,000
Peddie, Ostler, Opponent (og)

1903, Division 1.
Stoke (a) 0-5   Att. 6,000

1910, Division 1.
Preston North End (h) 5-2   Att. 26,000
Shepherd (4), Opponent (og)

1911, Division 1.
Preston North End (h) 1-1   Att. 30,000
Wilson

1914, Division 1.
Everton (a) 0-2   Att. 25,000

1920, Division 1.
Oldham Athletic (h) 0-1   Att. 35,000

1925, Division 1.
Aston Villa (h) 4-1   Att. 28,000
Cowan (3), McDonald

1931, Division 1.
Grimsby Town (a) 2-2   Att. 10,000
Boyd, Hutchison

1942, Wartime.
Gateshead (h) 4-2   Att. 20,000
Balmer, Woollett, Stubbins, Short

1948, Division 2.
Luton Town (h) 4-1   Att. 64,931
Milburn (3), Stobbart

1953, Division 1.
Tottenham Hotspur (a) 2-3   Att. 52,648
Davies, Milburn

1959, Division 1.
Everton (h) 4-0   Att. 42,475
White (2), Allchurch (2)

1966, Division 1.
Sunderland (a) 0-2   Att. 54,668

1970, FA Cup 3rd round.
Southampton (a) 0-3   Att. 19,010

1976, FA Cup 3rd round.
Queens Park Rangers (a) 0-0 Att. 20,102

1981, FA Cup 3rd round.
Sheffield Wednesday (h) 2-1 Att. 22,458
Waddle (2)

1983, Division 2.
Bolton Wanderers (h) 2-2   Att. 23,533
Waddle, Martin

1987, Division 1.
Coventry City (h) 1-2   Att. 22,366
McDonald

2000, Premier League.

Newcastle 2	West Ham United 2
Dabizas 18	Lampard 84
Speed 65	Stimac 88
	Att. 36,314

Playing record for this day is... 19 games, Won 7, Drawn 5, Lost 7, GF 36, GA 33. Today's success rate... 50%.

Birthdays

Albert Craig born today in 1962.
Midfield 1987-1989, Apps 14 (5 subs). Goals 0.
Bruce Halliday born today in 1961.
Centre-half 1977-1983, Apps 38. Goals 1.

Sadly Missed

George Stobbart died on this day in 1995, aged 73.
Forward 1946-1949, Apps 72. Goals 22.

January 4

Played on this day

1896, Division 2.
Manchester City (a) 2-5   Att. 10,000
McKay, Lennox

1902, Division 1.
Blackburn Rovers (h) 0-3   Att. 12,000

1908, Division 1.
Sheffield Wednesday (h) 2-1 Att. 30,000
Appleyard (2)

1913, Division 1.
Oldham Athletic (h) 4-1   Att. 25,000
McDonald, Stewart, Higgins (2)

1930, Division 1.
Grimsby Town (h) 3-1   Att. 31,803
Gallacher, Hutchison, Scott

1936, Division 2.
Tottenham Hotspur (h) 1-4   Att. 35,000
Bott

1947, Division 2.
Swansea Town (a) 2-1   Att. 32,000
Shackleton, Wayman

1958, FA Cup 3rd round.
Plymouth Argyle (a) 6-1   Att. 40,000
Eastham (2), R. Mitchell, White (3)

1964, FA Cup 3rd round.
Bedford Town (h) 1-2   Att. 34,585
Anderson

1969, FA Cup 3rd round.
Reading (h) 4-0   Att. 41,255
Craig, Dyson, B.Robson, Scott

1975, FA Cup 3rd round.
Manchester City (a) 2-0   Att. 37,625
Nulty, Burns

1982, FA Cup 3rd round.
Colchester United (h) 1-1   Att. 16,977
Varadi

1986, FA Cup 3rd round.
Brighton & Hove A. (h) 0-2   Att. 25,112

1992, FA Cup 3rd round.
Bournemouth (a) 0-0   Att. 10,651

1994, Premier League.
Norwich City 1   Newcastle 2
Brown 4   Beardsley 20
                 Cole 80
                    Att. 19,564

1998, FA Cup 3rd round.
Everton 0   Newcastle 1
                 Rush 67
                    Att. 20,885

Playing record for this day is... 16 games,
Won 9, Drawn 2, Lost 5, GF 31, GA 23.
Today's success rate... 62.50%.

Match of the Day from 1994

COLE DOES IT AGAIN

Yet another goal from Andy Cole secures win at Norwich

It was a great game at Carrow Road today for both teams, showing the high quality of English football despite the national team being unable to qualify for the World Cup finals. A crowd of 19,564 turned out to watch this match, and they were rewarded with plenty of action, chances at goal and a real sporting atmosphere.

It took only five minutes for Norwich to take the lead after a six-yard shot from Mark Bowen managed to get past Newcastle keeper Hooper and into the net.

However, the equaliser for Newcastle always seemed to be on its way. There were lots of chances for both sides, but they always just missed the mark. Then on 21 minutes the score was brought to 1-1 when Peter Beardsley fired a shot from eight yards out. The ball went straight into the back of the net past Gunn, and became Beardsley's twelfth Premiership goal and the 200th goal of his career.

More attempts at goal followed from both sides and the action didn't lose pace in the second half. Both teams tried hard to add another goal to the score-sheet. For Norwich, Fox missed a great opportunity from just three yards and Newcastle keeper Mike Hooper had to pull off a save with his feet to stop a shot from Megson entering the net.

Just as it was beginning to look like a draw was inevitable, Andy Cole saved the day. His 79th-minute goal was his 28th of the season, and his 40th in 36 games, and it ensured a win for the visiting Toon Army.

Norwich City
Gunn, Newman, Culverhouse, Butterworth, Woodthorpe, Fox, Cook, Megson, Bowen, Ekoku, Sutton.

Newcastle United
Hooper, Robinson, Howey, Scott, Beresford, Lee, Clark, Elliott, Sellars, Cole, Beardsley.

Referee Mr T. Holbrook (Walsall).

200 career goals for Peter Beardsley.

Birthdays

Jimmy Fell born today in 1936.
Winger 1962-1963, Apps 53. Goals 17.

January 5

Match of the Day from 1991

WIN(D) FOR NEWCASTLE

Bad weather makes it difficult, but Newcastle struggle on

Steve Watson made his debut.

This FA Cup-tie against Derby County was almost postponed due to the strong winds at St. James' Park which interfered with play throughout this match.

Newcastle were expected to struggle in front of the crowd of 19,748 faced with adverse weather and First Division opposition. Toon had faced problems against sides in the Second Division, and now they had to face a top-flight team without McGhee and Scott. Making his home debut at just sixteen years was Stephen Watson, the youngest player to appear for Newcastle in the FA Cup.

There were plenty of chances from the outset. Brock's free kick just skimmed over the bar after 30 minutes, and Stimson sent a forceful shot from 25 yards which had Shilton making a diving save to keep out of the net.

It was in the 35th minute that Derby managed to get their first chance at goal. Francis produced a powerful shot, but it went straight to Burridge for the save. Before half-time another shot from Stimson scraped over the crossbar and the score remained at 0-0.

In the second half Newcastle were battling against the oncoming wind, and Quinn in particular stood out for his attempts at keeping up the fight and sending in shots to keep Shilton working hard.

After attacks from both sides the deadlock was finally broken on 61 minutes when a long ball from Anderson came to Quinn, who managed to get the ball into the net over Shilton.

Just two minutes later the score was 2-0 when a Derby free kick ended up in Watson's possession. Cross brought him down just outside the penalty area and the resulting free kick was taken by Dillon. He knocked the ball lightly to Stimson who slotted in a low ball past Shilton to win the game for Newcastle.

Newcastle United
Burridge, Ranson, Kristensen, Anderson, Stimson, Watson, Aitken, Dillon, Brock, Quinn, Sloan.
Derby County
Shilton, Sage, Kavanagh, Wright, Forsyth, Cross, Ramage (Gee 80), Harford, Pickering, Francis (Davidson 73), Saunders.
Referee Mr N. Midgley (Bolton).

Played on this day

1895, Division 2.
Burton Swifts (a) 3-5   Att. 3,000
Thompson, O'Brien, Graham
1901, Division 1.
Blackburn Rovers (h) 1-0   Att. 10,000
Peddie
1907, Division 1.
Birmingham (h) 2-0   Att. 26,000
Rutherford (2)
1924, Division 1.
Nottingham Forest (h) 4-0   Att. 28,000
Harris (2), Cowan (2)
1929, Division 1.
Sheffield United (h) 4-2   Att. 20,000
Boyd, Carlton, McCurley, Opponent (og)
1935, Division 2.
Brentford (a) 0-3   Att. 28,000
1946, FA Cup 3rd round, 1st leg.
Barnsley (h) 4-2   Att. 60,284
Hair, Stubbins, Milburn (2)
1952, Division 1.
Preston North End (h) 3-0   Att. 42,410
Foulkes, Milburn, G. Robledo
1957, FA Cup 3rd round.
Manchester City (h) 1-1   Att. 57,921
White
1974, FA Cup 3rd round.
Hendon (h) 1-1   Att. 33,840
Howard
1980, FA Cup 3rd round.
Chester (h) 0-2   Att. 24,548
1991, FA Cup 3rd round.
Derby County (h) 2-0   Att. 19,748
Quinn, Stimson
1997, FA Cup 3rd round.
Charlton Athletic 1 Newcastle 1
Kinsella 78   Lee 33   Att. 14,980
2002, FA Cup 3rd round.
Newcastle 2   Crystal Palace 0
Shearer 40
Acuna 76   Att. 38,089
2003, FA Cup 3rd round.
Wolverhampton 3 Newcastle 2
Ince 6   Jenas 40
Kennedy 28   Shearer 43 (pen)
Ndah 49   Att. 27,316

Playing record for this day is... 15 games,
Won 8, Drawn 3, Lost 4, GF 30, GA 20
Today's success rate... 63.33%.

Birthdays

Chris Hedworth born today in 1964.
Centre-half 1982-1986, Apps 10 (1 sub). Goals 0.

George King born today in 1923.
Centre-forward 1946-1948, Apps 2. Goals 0.

Bill Thompson born today in 1940.
Centre-half 1957-1967, Apps 89 (1 sub). Goals 1.

Played on this day

1894, Division 2.
Ardwick (h) 2-1 — Att. 1,200
Thompson, Graham
1900, Division 1.
Everton (a) 2-3 — Att. 5,000
Fraser, Peddie
1906, Division 1.
Birmingham (a) 1-0 — Att. 8,000
Gosnell
1923, Division 1.
Nottingham Forest (h) 1-0 — Att. 20,000
McDonald
1934, Division 1.
Leeds United (h) 2-0 — Att. 22,000
Weaver, Williams
1940, Wartime.
Leeds United (h) 3-0 — Att. 6,000
Moses, Gordon, Park
1945, Wartime.
Middlesbrough (h) 5-1 — Att. 17,000
Carr (4), Stubbins
1951, FA Cup 3rd round.
Bury (h) 4-1 — Att. 33,944
Milburn, G. Robledo, Taylor, Walker
1962, FA Cup 3rd round.
Peterborough United (h) 0-1 — Att. 42,782
1968, Division 1.
Stoke City (a) 1-2 — Att. 17,623
Davies
1973, Division 1.
Ipswich Town (a) 0-1 — Att. 19,609
1984, FA Cup 3rd round.
Liverpool (a) 0-4 — Att. 33,566
1985, FA Cup 3rd round.
Nottingham Forest (a) 1-1 — Att. 23,582
Megson
1990, FA Cup 3rd round.
Hull City (a) 1-0 — Att. 10,743
O'Brien

Playing record for this day is... 14 games,
Won 8, Drawn 1, Lost 5, GF 23, GA 15.
Today's success rate... 60.71%.

Match of the Day from 1906

UNITED EDGE BATTLE IN THE MUD

First home defeat for Brum by solitary Gosnell strike

In appalling conditions for football Newcastle ended Birmingham's undefeated home record for the 1905-6 season; they had also done the same to the Blues' neighbours Aston Villa just two months before. By kick off this afternoon the players were ankle deep in mud and water after overnight rain had turned into a morning downpour which threatened to postpone the match at the early morning inspection; referee Pearson giving the game the go ahead only at the second look at 1pm. This severely affected the attendance which was well below average, indeed at kick off just 8,000 were present.

It was Birmingham who got the early advantage after Wigmore won the toss and kicked off with the help of a strong wind behind them, this caused the United defence all sorts of trouble in the opening ten minutes. United, through some strong defending, held firm and midway through the half were settled enough to create pressure on the Birmingham goal; both McClarence and McWilliam having good efforts well saved by keeper Robinson. It was the pitch conditions however which were the only winner as passing became practically impossible in the Munk Street mud. The game was reduced to long balls in the hope defenders would slip, but forwards were having the greater difficulty in controlling the ball so the pattern of huge kicks by the backs continued from both sides.

Newcastle got of to a flying start in the second half forcing an early corner which was then headed narrowly wide by Orr. Still United continued to press forward and in the 48th minute they were in front 1-0. A hopeful ball played forward by Veitch was miskicked first by Wigmore then Hartwell. With acres of free space now, Gosnell ran on to the loose ball and made no mistake planting a firm shot past the keeper as he came off the goal line to narrow the shooting angle. The goal stung the home side into action and they swarmed forward dominating all the play in an exciting fifteen-minute period of pressure. However, after all this, still their best chance came from a dreadful sliced clearance from McCombie, the ball flying across his own goal beating Lawrence and missing the post by an inch or two. The muddy pitch meant tiredness soon set in, and the final twenty minutes were almost played at walking pace with no real threat to either goal, no doubt both sets of players already looking forward to their well earned dressing-room bath.

Birmingham
Robinson, Hartwell, Stokes, Beer, Wigmore, Cornan, Harper, Green, Mounteney, Wilcox, Anderson.
Newcastle United
Lawrence, McCombie, Carr, McWilliam, Veitch, Gardner, Gosnell, Orr, McClarence, Howie, Rutherford.
Referee Mr. J. H. Pearson (Crewe).

Toon News Extra

1912... Weather thwarts the Magpies at Bradford

Newcastle's Division One fixture at Valley Parade was abandoned after 52 mins due to a severe rain fall. Newcastle were level with Bradford 0-0 when play was stopped in front of a disappointed 8,000 crowd. The game was replayed on April 9 1912 and that game also finished with the sides level, this time at 1-1.

Birthdays

Bobby Shinton born today in 1952 .
Forward 1980-1982, Apps 49 (2 subs). Goals 10.

Sadly Missed

Eric Garbutt died on this day in 1997, aged 76.
Goalkeeper 1939-1951, Apps 54.
Albert Gosnell died on this day 1972, aged 91.
Winger & Team Trainer 1904-1910 & 1919-1921, Apps 125. Goals 18.
Ray Robinson died on this day in 1964, aged 69.
Winger 1919-1920, Apps 29. Goals 4.

January 7

Match of the Day from 1961

UNITED STROLL TO EASY CUP TIE VICTORY
Hat-trick for Duncan Neale in 5-0 romp

Newcastle eased into the FA Cup fourth round with an emphatic 5-0 win over the Londoners of Fulham. Despite the return from injury of star player Johnny Haynes, Fulham, still without their prime marksman Leggat, were never a match for a strong United side playing in front of a home crowd of 36,037 fanatical Geordies. On a rain swept and muddy pitch Newcastle dominated the game from the first to last whistle, taking the lead in the nineteenth minute through Neale's first goal of three in the afternoon. Such was United's dominance, and the quietness of the normally lively Haynes, that Neale played the game almost as a sixth United forward, becoming the first Newcastle half-back to complete a hat trick in 27 years. Newcastle made it 2-0 on 29 minutes when Allchurch finished a superb solo effort, strolling through the Fulham defence, sending Hewkins on his backside after being 'dummied', then curling a shot past the keeper from the edge of the penalty area. There was no stopping the black-and-white surge and it was becoming a case of exactly how many the Magpies would settle for, Neale's second goal making the score 3-0 after 32 minutes.

The second half was no different with Fulham unable to mount any attack to ease the pressure off their back four all afternoon. With just four minutes of the half gone Newcastle were 4-0 up when Woods reacted quickest in a goalmouth scramble to prod home the ball from barely a yard out. Uncharacteristically United then eased off and the visitors enjoyed a period of play when they actually put some passes together, and deep inside United territory too. Despite some nice neat play however, Fulham failed to test the home keeper at all and were punished again with five minutes of the game remaining. Neale scored to earn a fourth round tie against Stockport County at St. James' Park, and claim the first match ball of his career.

Newcastle United
Mitchell, Keith, McKinney, Neale, Thompson, Bell, Hughes, Woods, White, Allchurch, Scanlon.

Fulham
Hewkins, Cohen, Langley, Mullery, Lowe, Edwards, Key, O'Connell, Cook, Haynes, Chamberlain.

Malcolm Macdonald celebrates his birthday today.

Played on this day

1899, Division 1.
Everton (h) 2-2   Att. 15,000
Aitken, Stevenson
1905, Division 1.
Derby County (h) 2-0   Att. 20,000
Veitch, Gardner
1911, Division 1.
Oldham Athletic (h) 3-0   Att. 20,000
Shepherd, Stewart, Duncan
1922, FA Cup 1st round.
Newport County (h) 6-0   Att. 28,567
McDonald (2), Harris, Dixon (2), Mooney
1928, Division 1.
Tottenham Hotspur (a) 2-5   Att. 34,710
McKay, Hudspeth (pen)
1933, Division 1.
Liverpool (a) 0-3   Att. 25,000
1939, FA Cup 3rd round.
Brentford (a) 2-0   Att. 27,551
Clifton, Mooney
1950, FA Cup 3rd round.
Oldham Athletic (a) 7-2   Att. 41,706
Milburn (3), Mitchell, Walker (2),
Opponent (og)
1956, FA Cup 3rd round.
Sheffield Wednesday (a) 3-1 Att. 48,198
Curry, Keeble, Milburn
1961, FA Cup 3rd round.
Fulham (h) 5-0   Att. 36,037
Allchurch, Neale (3), Woods
1976, FA Cup 3rd round, replay.
Queens Park Rangers (h) 2-1 Att. 37,225
T. Craig (pen), Gowling
1978, FA Cup 3rd round.
Peterborough United (a) 1-1 Att. 17,621
Hudson
1989, FA Cup 3rd round.
Watford (h) 0-0   Att. 24,217
1996, FA Cup 3rd round.

Chelsea 1	Newcastle 1
Hughes 35	Ferdinand 90
	Att. 25,151

1998, Coca Cola Cup 5th round

Newcastle 0	Liverpool 2
	Owen 95
	Fowler 103
	Att. 33,207

A.E.T.
2001, FA Cup 3rd round.

Newcastle 1	Aston Villa 1
Solano 80	Stone 55
	Att. 37,862

Playing record for this day is... 16 games, Won 8, Drawn 5, Lost 3, GF 37, GA 19. Today's success rate... 65.63%.

Birthdays

George Bradley born today in 1917.
Defender 1938-1946, Apps 21. Goals 1.
Malcolm Macdonald born today in 1950.
Centre-forward 1971-1976, Apps 258 (1 sub).
Goals 138.

Sadly Missed

Albert McInroy died on this day in 1985, aged 84.
Goalkeeper 1929-1934, Apps 160.

January 8

Played on this day

1898, Division 2.
Manchester City (a) 1-1   Att. 20,000
R. Allan

1910, Division 1.
Blackburn Rovers (h) 4-1   Att. 35,000
Higgins, Shepherd (2), Howie

1921, FA Cup 1st round.
Nottingham Forest (h) 1-1   Att. 47,652
Harris
*Forest were drawn at home in the draw,
however after an agreement by both
clubs the match was switched to
St. James' Park.*

1927, FA Cup 3rd round.
Notts County (h) 8-1   Att. 32,564
Gallacher (3), McDonald (3), Seymour,
Urwin

1938, FA Cup 3rd round.
West Bromwich A. (a) 0-1   Att. 33,932

1944, Wartime.
Hartlepool United (a) 2-1   Att. 6,000
Stubbins (2)

1949, FA Cup 3rd round.
Bradford Park Ave. (h) 0-2   Att. 47,196

1955, FA Cup 3rd round.
Plymouth Argyle (a) 1-0   Att. 28,685
Keeble

1966, Division 1.
West Ham United (h) 2-1   Att. 31,754
Bennett, Suddick

1972, Division 1.
Coventry City (h) 4-2   Att. 25,875
Hibbitt, Tudor (2), Macdonald (pen)

1977, FA Cup 3rd round.
Sheffield United (a) 0-0   Att. 30,513

1983, FA Cup 3rd round.
Brighton & Hove A. (a) 1-1   Att. 17,711
McDermott

1994, FA Cup 3rd round.
Newcastle 2   Coventry City 0
Cole 21
Beardsley 76   Att. 35,444

1995, FA Cup 3rd round.
Newcastle 1   Blackburn Rovers 1
Lee 56   Sutton 30
                            Att. 31,721

2000, FA Cup 4th round.
Newcastle 4   Sheffield United 1
Shearer 5   Smith 17
Dabizas 47
Ferguson 59
Gallacher 69   Att. 36,220

Playing record for this day is... 15 games,
Won 8, Drawn 5, Lost 2, GF 31, GA 14.
Today's success rate... 70%.

Match of the Day from 1972

EARLY SHOCK INSPIRES NEWCASTLE
Sky Blues beaten 4-2 by rampant Newcastle

Despite a fifth minute goal by Billy Rafferty, Coventry soon found themselves trailing just two minutes later and were eventually swept aside 4-2 at St. James' Park today. Both sides were forced into late replacements, United gave young goalkeeper Martin Burleigh only his second senior start for the club in place of their experienced keeper Willie McFaul, the other change saw the return of Stuart Barrowclough on the wing. Coventry had to make do without their influential midfielder Mel Machin.

Coventry started in aggressive mood and forced the play from the outset. They took the lead after five minutes when Young's inswinging free kick was fumbled by Burleigh and Rafferty accepted an easy chance from close in, smashing the ball into the roof of the net. Coventry had scarcely finished congratulating themselves before United were level 30 seconds later. They swept through straight from the centre spot and Nattrass swung a fast low centre across a completely open goalmouth, Hibbitt nipping in from the left cracked the ball into the open net. In sensational style it was then 2-1 a minute later; Craig played through a long ball which Macdonald headed down for John Tudor. He wasted no time in volleying the chance into the net from fifteen yards. These three goals in the space of two minutes had the 25,875 crowd roaring their heads off, and with both defences looking wide open on the greasy surface there was no knowing what would happen next. After all these shocks play began to settle down a little with the sides beginning to get each other's measure. Then Rafferty again got the ball into the net, hooking it in from the edge of the area, but the linesman had flagged him offside.

Terry Hibbitt

In the 49th minute Newcastle were awarded a penalty when Nattrass, attempting to get round Blockley, was flattened by the defender. The ref had no hesitation with the decision and Blockley was lucky not to be cautioned, the kick was delayed over a minute before Nattrass hobbled back into the game. Macdonald gave Healey no chance with a powerful drive, bringing his twentieth goal of the season. Newcastle then wrapped up the game when John Tudor netted the home side a fourth goal in the 57th minute. Coventry, to their credit, continued to battle and some suspect keeping by the young United keeper gave them some heart. Twice he came and flapped at crosses he should have easily dealt with, the latter led to Blockley hitting the bar for the visitors. Coventry kept up the pressure and Dennis Mortimer added a second goal on 67 minutes after good work from Chilton. In the closing minutes Healey pulled off a magnificent save to deny Clark from scoring Newcastle's fifth from point-blank range, and the game finished 4-2.

Newcastle United
Burleigh, Craig, Clark, Nattrass, Burton, Howard, Barrowclough, Green, Macdonald, Tudor, Hibbitt. Sub: Reid

Coventry City
Healey, Smith, Cattlin, Mortimer, Blockley, Parker, Young, Carr, Chilton, Rafferty, St. John. Sub: Randell

Referee Mr. R. E. Raby (Leeds).

Birthdays

John Cowen born today in 1949.
Midfield 1967-1973, Apps 10 (4 subs). Goals 0.
Bobby Ferguson born today in 1938.
Left-back 1955-1962, Apps 12. Goals 0.

Gordon Hindson born today in 1950
Midfield 1968-1971, Apps 8 (1 sub). Goals 1.

January 9

Match of the Day from 1957

FIGHT TO THE END
Newcastle knock holders out of FA Cup in replay

Young schoolteacher Alec Tait, a part-time player, was brought into the squad for this FA Cup third round replay at Maine Road. The first match at St. James' Park had ended 1-1, and Newcastle had a lot of work to do today away from home to grab victory from the cup holders Manchester City.

It was a struggle to maintain their determination, but Newcastle proved that it's not over until the final whistle. Conditions were against them from the start. Cold weather and a muddy pitch made playing difficult, and it didn't take long for City to take the lead, albeit courtesy of an own goal from Bob Stokoe after six minutes whilst trying to send the ball to safety over the bar.

Newcastle may have been disheartened by this, and their hopes were knocked down further when a free kick was awarded to the visitors. The kick was taken, and it was Bobby Johnstone who got his head to the ball to put the side home side 2-0 up. Just one minute later and many would have said it was all over for United. McAdams passed the ball to Fagan and he slipped it past Simpson with ease. Just 30 minutes of the game gone and the visitors were 3-0 down.

However, the fighting spirit still hadn't left the Newcastle side, and they decided to pull together and give it their all. With the first half ending and still no comeback, most of the away crowd were beginning to admit defeat.

With less than a minute of the second half on the clock, United were given a ray of hope. A penalty was awarded for a foul on Bill Curry, and it was Tom Casey who stepped up to do the honours. His powerful shot flew past Bert Trautmann to reduce the lead to 3-1.

With twenty minutes to go, Newcastle lost Dick Keith through injury, but things were about to improve. After 74 minutes Tait added his name to the score-sheet when he took on, and beat, five opposition players to send a smashing ball into the net right past Trautmann.

Newcastle's hard fought game brought rewards on 86 minutes when a great header from Curry brought the scores level at 3-3. Extra-time wasn't going to be easy either, and this was clear when Manchester City regained the lead with another goal.

It didn't take long for United to accept the challenge again, and White managed to pull the scores level again shortly after. Just two minutes later and it was Newcastle who took the lead. It was White again who did the scoring, bringing the final score to 5-4. Despite Dyson hitting the post in a last ditch attempt, it was all over for Manchester City. Newcastle had fought to the bitter end, and won.

Manchester City

Trautmann, Leivers, Little, Barnes, Ewing, Paul, Fagan, McAdams, Johnstone, Dyson, Clarke.

Newcastle United

Simpson, Keith, Batty, Scoular, Stokoe, Casey, White, Davies, Tait, Curry, Mitchell.

Referee Mr F.B.Coultas (Hull).

Birthdays

Ralph Birkett born today in 1913.
Winger 1938-1941, Apps 66. Goals 15.
Paul Kitson born today in 1971.
Forward 1994-1997, Apps 49 (14 subs). Goals 14.
Franck Dumas born today in 1968.
Defender 1999-2000, Apps 7. Goals 0.

Sadly Missed

Billy Cairns died today in 1988, aged 75.
Centre-forward 1933-1944, Apps 113. Goals 67.

Played on this day

1914, FA Cup 1st round.
Sheffield United (h) 0-5   Att. 28,185

1920, FA Cup 1st round.
Crystal Palace (h) 2-0   Att. 15,000
Dixon, Hall

1925, FA Cup 1st round.
Hartlepool United (h) 4-1   Att. 36,632
Cowan, Harris, McDonald, MacKenzie

1931, FA Cup 3rd round.
Nottingham Forest (h) 4-0   Att. 34,219
Bedford, Hutchison (3)

1942, Wartime.
Sunderland (a) 2-2   Att. 12,000
Stubbins, Short

1948, FA Cup 3rd round.
Charlton Athletic (a) 1-2   Att. 53,428
Pearson

1976, Division 1.
Everton (h) 5-0   Att. 31,726
Gowling (3), Nulty, Nattrass

1981, Division 2.
Wrexham (a) 0-0   Att. 6,437

1989, FA Cup 3rd round, replay.
Watford (a) 2-2   Att. 16,431
Brock, Mirandinha
A.E.T.

1996, Coca Cola Cup 5th round.
Arsenal 2   Newcastle 0
Wright 44, 89   Att. 37,857
In an ill tempered game Newcastle had David Ginola sent off for violent conduct after an incident involving Arsenal full-back Lee Dixon.

1998, Premier League.
Sheffield Wed. 2   Newcastle 1
Di Canio 1   Tomasson 20
Newsome 51   Att. 29,446

Playing record for this day is... 11,
Won 4, Drawn 3, Lost 4, GF 21, GA 16.
Today's success rate... 50%.

Match of the Day from 1931

HUTCHISON'S HAT TRICK

Sudden burst of goals brings victory for United

The pitch at St. James' Park was heavy and soft for this game against Nottingham Forest, making it difficult for both teams to get going. Tired legs should have held back the players, but both sides brought out that extra effort needed to produce a great game.

Forest played exceptionally well, and the scoreline for this match does not reflect the determination and skill shown by the visitors. Simpson played notably well, although his aim on target was not good enough today, and German also kept Albert McInroy on his toes. His shots were all off target too, but together with Scott all three Forest players worked hard to worry the Newcastle defence.

Their skilful play served only to boost the fight in the home side, and an equal number of chances fell to Newcastle. Unfortunately Forest's defence was just as good and none of the shots threatened the goal, the visitors' McKinlay and Graham playing no small part in ensuring the ball didn't cross the line in the first half.

The second period began with no score, but things were about to change. Quick moving centre-forward Duncan Hutchison took advantage of two costly drops by Forest keeper Dexter, each one resulting in a goal for the home side. The score became 3-0 when Hutchison secured a hat trick with another strike and the score-sheet looked very different, very quickly.

The game looked as good as over, with Forest losing their will to fight. The dramatic change in the score had dealt them a huge blow, and tiredness was getting the better of them. Newcastle, however, had other ideas, and in the final minute another goal was added to the score with a super shot from Harry Bedford. The game ended with the score at 4-0 and despite the score even the home side were relieved it was over.

Newcastle United

McInroy, Nelson, Fairhurst, Naylor, Davidson, Weaver, Boyd, Bedford, Hutchison, Starling, Wilkinson.

Nottingham Forest

Dexter, Thompson, Barrington, McKinlay, Graham, Wallace, Scott, Stocks, Dent, German, Simpson.

"Hurricane Hutch"

Toon News Extra

1953... FA Cup tie abandoned

Just eight minutes play was possible in Newcastle's third round tie against Swansea at St. James' Park before fog sent the 63,499 crowd home very early, with the score 0-0. The game was played to a finish four days later and this time United stormed to a fine 3-0 win to progress to round four.

Birthdays

Paul Sweeney born in 1965.
Left-back 1989-1990, Apps 44 (9 subs). Goals 0.

Sadly Missed

Tony Whitson died on this day in 1945, aged 60
Left-back 1905-1919, Apps 146. Goals 0.

January 11

Match of the Day from 1978

POSH ARE BLOWN AWAY
United sail through to meet Wrexham in round four

One interested spectator summed up this game perfectly. In a post match interview Wrexham manager Aarfon Griffiths, in charge of United's next opponents, spent most of the time commenting on the weather, "The wind caused problems throughout the first half, the keeper was barely kicking the ball out twenty yards due to the gale, and it was bloody freezing in the stands." Not a vintage display by the Magpies against Third-Division Peterborough and Griffiths finished his piece by adding "Newcastle will be surprised by our standard of football, they will be in for a shock."

Peterborough's last visit to St. James' Park was back in 1962, and the visitors pulled off a surprise win. A repeat was still possible at the break after some hard resolute defending against a tremendous gale force wind which was against them throughout the first 45 minutes. However, during a mainly uneventful first half, it was the visitors who came the closest to scoring, but Slough's first-time effort from fifteen yards went inches too high.

Ironically, without the wind advantage, it was Newcastle who came out the stronger and within seven minutes they scored the all-important first goal. A good passing move put Hudson away and after running into the area he was rashly brought down by a sliding tackle from Carmichael. Tommy Craig stepped up and smashed his penalty kick against the underside of the bar before it bounced back into the roof of the net. This should have settled the home side, and allowed the goals to come flowing, but Peterborough with the second best defensive record in the Football League stuck to their task well. In the 74th minute Posh's influential playmaker Doyle went agonisingly wide with a volley from outside the penalty area. Then just seven minutes later, the visitors' full-back Lee overlapped to get behind the United defence and whack a shot from twenty yards which Carr acrobatically tipped over the bar. With Peterborough stretched, looking for the equaliser, United killed them off on a counter attack with four minutes of the game remaining. A neat one-two between Gowling and Burns split the Posh rear guard right open and this left Blackhall completely unmarked in the centre, taking the ball in his stride he took one touch before crashing in a fierce drive from 25 yards which flew over Barron's grasp and into the net. A decent sized crowd of 34,156 had deserved a finish of this quality and left the ground well satisfied in the end. Newcastle had progressed to round four with a 2-0 win.

Newcastle United
Carr, Nattrass, Barker, Cassidy, McCaffery, Blackhall, Hudson, Burns, Mitchell, Gowling, Craig.
Peterborough United
Barron, Hughes, Lee, Doyle, Turner, Ross, Slough, McEwan, Sargent, Carmichael, Robson.

Toon News Extra
1913... Cup run halted by snow

United's first round FA Cup tie lasted for just 45 minutes before snow caused the abandonment of the tie against Bradford City. The game at St. James' Park had attracted 15,928 fans and Newcastle had taken a 1-0 lead through a first half strike by George Wilson before the snow fell. The match was rearranged and played five days later and it was won by the Magpies 1-0, Wilson again on the score-sheet.

Birthdays

Lee Makel born today in 1973.
Midfield 1989-1992, Apps 14 (7 subs), Goals 1

Sadly Missed

Bobby Cowell died today in 1996 aged 73.
Right-back 1943-1956, Apps 409, Goals 0

Played on this day

1896, Division 2.
Grimsby Town (h) 1-5   Att. 5,000
Collins
1902, Division 1.
Stoke (a) 0-0   Att. 5,000
1908, FA Cup 1st round.
Nottingham Forest (h) 2-0   Att. 41,637
Appleyard, Rutherford
1919, Wartime.
Hartlepool United (h) 0-0   Att. 18,000
1930, FA Cup 3rd round.
York City (h) 1-1   Att. 38,674
Gallacher
1936, FA Cup 3rd round.
Walsall (a) 2-0   Att. 19,882
Connelly, J. Smith
1941, Wartime.
Grimsby Town (a) 0-4   Att. 3,500
Played at The Old Show ground, Scunthorpe.
1947, FA Cup 3rd round.
Crystal Palace (h) 6-2   Att. 43,183
Bentley, Pearson, Shackleton (2), Stobbart, Wayman
1958, Division 1.
Birmingham City (h) 1-2   Att. 34,825
White
The Magpies are forced into playing the last 34 minutes with ten men after Bob Stokoe leaves the field through injury.
1964, Division 2.
Charlton Athletic (a) 2-1   Att. 18,588
McGarry, Thomas
1969, Division 1.
Leicester City (a) 1-2   Att. 21,673
B. Robson
1971, FA Cup 3rd round.
Ipswich Town (h) 1-1   Att. 32,150
Mitchell
1975, Division 1.
Tottenham Hotspur (h) 2-5   Att. 39,679
T. Craig, Burns
1978, FA Cup 3rd round, replay.
Peterborough United (h) 2-0. Att. 26,837
T. Craig (pen), Blacknall
1986, Division 1.
West Bromwich A. (a) 1-1   Att. 9,106
Wharton
1992, Division 2.
Watford (a) 2-2   Att. 9,811
Kelly, Hunt
1997, Premier League.
Aston Villa 2   Newcastle 2
Yorke 39   Shearer 16
Milosevic 52   Clark 21
Att. 39,339

2003, Premier League.
West Ham United 2   Newcastle 2
Cole 14   Bellamy 9
Defoe 45   Jenas 81
Att. 35,048

Playing record for this day is... 18 games, Won 5, Drawn 8, Lost 5, GF 28, GA 30.
Today's success rate... 50%.

Played on this day

1895, Division 2.
    Woolwich Arsenal (a) 2-3.   Att. 5,000
    Thompson (2)
1901, Division 1.
    Stoke (a) 0-2   Att. 6,000
1907, FA Cup 1st round.
    Crystal Palace (h) 0-1   Att. 28,000
1921, FA Cup 1st round, replay.
    Nottingham Forest (h) 2-0   Att. 30,278
    Seymour, Harris
1924, FA Cup 1st round.
    Portsmouth (a) 4-2   Att. 26,422
    Seymour, Harris, J. Low, Gibson
    Portsmouth led 2-0 at half-time but went
    out after a dramatic four goal second half
    blitz by the Magpies.
1929, FA Cup 3rd round.
    Swindon Town (a) 0-2   Att. 17,689
1935, FA Cup 3rd round.
    Hull City (a) 5-1   Att. 23,000
    Bott (2), Cairns, Pearson, Opponent (og)
1946, Wartime.
    Huddersfield Town (a) 4-1   Att. 11,423
    Hair, Stubbins (2), Taylor
1952, FA Cup 3rd round.
    Aston Villa (h) 4-2   Att. 56,897
    Foulkes, Mitchell (2), G. Robledo
1957, Division 1.
    Manchester United (a) 1-6   Att. 44,911
    Milburn
1974, Division 1.
    Wolverhampton W. (a) 0-1   Att. 22,235
1980, Division 2.
    Chelsea (a) 0-4   Att. 32,281
1983, FA Cup 3rd round, replay.
    Brighton & Hove A. (h) 0-1   Att. 32,687
1985, Division 1.
    Everton (a) 0-4   Att. 32,156
1991, Division 2.
    Blackburn Rovers (h) 1-0   Att. 16,382
    Mitchell
2002, Premier League.
    Newcastle 3   Leeds United 1
    Duberry (og) 44   Smith 1
    Dyer 60
    Bellamy 87   Att. 52,130

Playing record for this day is... 16 games,
Won 7, Drawn 0, Lost 9, GF 26, GA 31.
Today's success rate... 43.75%.

Match of the Day from 1952

UNITED STEAL THE TIE AFTER SENSATIONAL COMEBACK

Late three minute burst shatters Villa

In all the classic cup-ties ever staged at St. James' Park there has never been a more dramatic three minutes of football as witnessed by the 56,897 crowd at this one. Villa had deservedly gone back in front at 2-1 with just nine minutes of the game remaining, then right out of the blue Newcastle suddenly burst into goal-scoring madness scoring three times in 180 seconds to win the tie sensationally 4-2.

The 'victory' Villa had fashioned was set up by their early dominance, they were far sharper and in many ways the better side, indeed, they will sit and wonder for weeks to come how on earth they lost this one. They got off to a storming start, the impressive Dixon scoring twice in the opening thirteen minutes. Newcastle gave themselves some hope when on a rare break away George Robledo unselfishly squared the ball to his partner Foulkes to tap in, this after a fine individual running dribble by the United left-half. The goal changed nothing and still Villa looked the more lively and dangerous, but for a linesman's quick flag Thompson would have put the visitors 3-1 up, but he was ruled offside after a consultation between the officials. Then, just before the break United keeper Simpson pulled off a magnificent reflex save to deny a close-range Gibson effort, the ball scooped up by his outstretched boot just enough to clear the crossbar. The half-time whistle went before the corner could be taken, Villa denied their fifteenth flag kick of the half, such was their superiority.

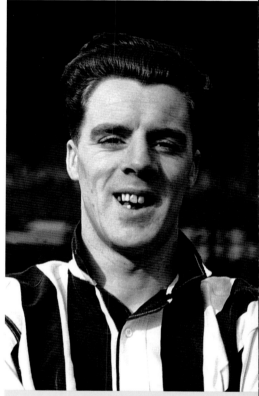

A brace today for Bobby Mitchell.

Newcastle fared a little better early on in the second period but only defensively, they never really applied any pressure to the Villa goal until the dramatic finish. So it was, with nine minutes remaining and Villa seemingly cruising, that disaster/jubilation struck. The United equaliser came from nothing, a desperate long ball was stopped by Thompson just outside his penalty area, his chipped pass to Lynn however was intercepted by Mitchell who struck the ball first time from 25 yards, the ball whizzing past the stationary keeper and into the top corner of the netting. This livened up the crowd, who, had been almost silent since kick off. A minute later Mitchell again picked up a long pass, rounding full-back Lynn and thumping in another thunderbolt, this time from just inside the penalty area, once again Villa keeper Martin got nowhere near it. Yet another minute later Milburn picked up a loose ball just inside his own half and dribbled forward, the Villa defence previously so solid, were now helplessly lost, Milburn got to within fifteen yards of the goal-line before squaring the ball to the unmarked George Robledo who couldn't miss. There was still time for Milburn to just miss a fifth United goal, his header from Mitchell's cross was fractionally too high. The full time whistle was greeted by some amazing scenes at St. James' Park, thousands poured onto the pitch to mob the black-and-white striped heros, who only ten minutes ago were out of the FA Cup third round. What a finish.

Newcastle United

Simpson, Cowell, McMichael, Harvey, Brennan, E. Robledo, Walker, Foulkes, Milburn, G. Robledo, Mitchell.

Aston Villa

Martin, Lynn, Parkes, Blanchflower, F. Moss, Dorsett, H. Smith, Thompson, Gibson, Dixon, Goffin.

Nolberto Solano (right) celebrates with Alessandro Pistone (far left), Alan Shearer (second left) and Duncan Ferguson (second right) after scoring the third goal.

Birthdays

Alex Cropley born today in 1951.
Midfield 1980, Apps 3. Goals 0

Stuart Robinson born today in 1959.
Winger 1975-1980, Apps 14(1 sub). Goals 3

Played on this day

1903, Division 1.
Sheffield Wednesday (a) 0-3 Att. 12,000
1914, Division 1.
West Bromwich A. (h) 3-3 Att. 18,200
Hardy, McDonald, Shepherd
1920, Division 1.
Oldham Athletic (a) 0-1 Att. 20,460
1923, FA Cup 1st round, replay.
Southampton (a) 1-3 Att. 20,060
Harris
1925, Division 1.
Arsenal (a) 2-0 Att. 30,000
Harris, Seymour
1931, Division 1.
Manchester United (h) 4-3 Att. 20,000
Bedford (2), Boyd, Hutchison
1942, Wartime.
Sunderland (h) 2-1 Att. 19,728
Stubbins, Short
1948, Division 2.
Brentford (a) 0-1 Att. 32,000
1953, Division 1.
Burnley (h) 0-0 Att. 49,366
1959, Division 1.
Tottenham Hotspur (h) 1-2 Att. 32,503
White
1970, Division 1.
Wolverhampton W. (a) 1-1 Att. 29,665
Guthrie
1976, Division 1.
Aston Villa (a) 1-1 Att. 36,389
Gowling
1981, Division 2.
Luton Town (a) 1-0 Att. 10,774
Harford
1996, FA Cup 3rd round, replay.
Newcastle 2   Chelsea 2
Albert 41   Wise 61 (pen)
Beardsley 63 (pen) Gullit 88
Att. 36,535
1998, Premier League.
Newcastle 2   Bolton Wanderers 1
Barnes 7   Blake 72
Ketsbaia 90   Att. 36,767
1999, Premier League.
Charlton Athletic 2 Newcastle 2
Bright 64   Ketsbaia 13
Pringle 90   Solano 55
Att. 20,043
2001, FA Cup 3rd round, replay.
Aston Villa 1   Newcastle 0
Vassell 50   Att. 25,387

Playing record for this day is... 17 games,
Won 5, Drawn 6, Lost 6, GF 22, GA 25.
Today's success rate... 47.06%.

Match of the Day from 1914

PATCHED UP UNITED EARN A POINT
Newcastle pegged back after leading 3-1

Newcastle's desperate bid to avoid the drop was given a morale booster thanks to the efforts of their reserves this afternoon against a strong West Bromwich Albion side. United's directors only managed to scrape together a team of eleven players literally hours before kick off such was the casualty list left over from their cup defeat at Sheffield Wednesday last week. This gave their latest acquisition, goalkeeper Bill Mellor, who signed from Norwich City in the week, his debut for the Magpies, lining up with no fewer than six regular Newcastle reserves. More problems for United lay in the appalling conditions due to the heavy rains over the last couple of days and this made the pitch a complete mud bath shortly after the start of play.

However, despite this, Newcastle, roared on by a good 18,200 fans in spite of the rain, made the better start, twice going close in the opening five minutes. But it was Albion who squandered the game's best chance when Bentley, who for once beat the tight offside trap marshalled well by Hudspeth, ran free into the area only to blaze his shot high over the bar with only Mellor to beat. Shortly after this let off a handball by Smith presented United with a great shooting chance from just outside the penalty area. From the free kick Hudspeth drove in a powerful shot which Pearson brilliantly turned round the post for a corner after a full-length dive. From the corner Low got up well to head the ball firmly goalwards but again Pearson sprang to tip his effort over the bar for another corner; from this the danger was cleared by the Albion defence. From Newcastle's next attack Hibbert beat Pennington with a lovely nutmeg and his shot from twenty yards just flicked the top of the bar with Pearson this time well beaten. Finally the goal United had threatened came on 25 minutes, a great pass from Shepherd put Low away and he raced between two defenders and slipped the ball past Pearson. The lead lasted just ten minutes as Albion equalised when Edwards took a fine pass from Jephcott in his stride to put the ball past the advancing Mellor from he acutest of angles. Newcastle were soon back in front however when McDonald, jumping for a header, flattened the Albion keeper allowing the ball to bobble into the empty net, despite the protests from Pennington the goal was allowed. Then, a minute before the interval, Newcastle broke again on the right wing with Douglas. His cross was met by Shepherd with a first-time volley which, although Pearson saved well, Hardy's quick reaction got him to the loose ball to score a simple goal to put United 3-1 up at half-time.

The second half resumed with Albion this time applying all the pressure against a quickly tiring Newcastle side. With just eleven minutes gone West Brom reduced the arrears to 3-2 with a fine long-range shot from their danger man Shearman. Now it was all Albion pressure and soon after Mellor had to save well from Shepherd as the ball came through a crowd of players only to be stopped a foot from the goal-line. Albion were then hampered with an injury to their other influential forward Jephcott who, although returning after a few minutes off the field, spent the last half an hour limping badly. Despite this the visitors became even more vigorous in attack and eventually got a deserved equaliser in the 77th minute when Bentley's superb shot from twenty yards flew past Mellor and into the top corner of the United net. Both sides to their credit still went out for a late winner after this and it was United who came closest with just two minutes of the game remaining, when first Shepherd then Hibbert had great close-range efforts magnificently saved by Pearson. In the last minute of the game there was tragedy for Albion forward Edwards when he collided accidentally with United's McDonald and suffered a nasty compound fracture of the right leg, an injury which will keep him out of action for the remainder of the season.

Newcastle United
Mellor, Whitson, Hudspeth, Hay, Low, Spink, Douglas, Hibbert, Shepherd, Hardy, McDonald.
West Bromwich Albion
Pearson, Smith, Pennington, Waterhouse, Deacey, McNeal, Jephcott, Edwards, Bentley, Morris, Shearman.

January 18

Match of the Day from 1982

UNITED THROUGH AFTER EXTRA TIME BATTLE
Grimsby next for the leg weary Magpies

Colchester fought back after being 2-0 down to take this thrilling third round replay into extra time. Newcastle then went another two goals in front in the extra half hour, but were pegged back again, and only a terrible miss by Adcock saved the tie going to a second replay.

Adcock, Colchester's promising young winger created three glorious chances early in the game, but they were woefully wasted by the Colchester forwards. Then, against the run of play, a quick break out led to Chris Waddle putting Newcastle in front 1-0. United full-back Wes Saunders then made it 2-0 with a freak goal out of nothing, his first goal for the club. His free kick from 25 yards hit a post, slid along the crossbar before dropping just over the goal-line. Just before the break Colchester deservedly reduced the score to 2-1 when Cook, their only survivor from that famous cup tie win over Leeds, scored a beauty, lobbing the ball over Carr as he advanced to the edge of the penalty area.

A disappointing second half then followed, the only highlight being Colchester's equaliser. During a prolonged spell of pressure United centre-half Carney handled in the area and Allinson smashed home the penalty kick.

In extra time United seemed to have won the game comfortably when goals from Brownlie, then moments later Varadi, put them 4-2 up. However they had to survive another thrilling Colchester comeback when Allinson converted his second spot kick of the night to make the score 4-3. In the dying seconds of the game a loose ball bobbled just as Adcock was about to shoot and the ball veered high and over the bar, a terrible miss from a mere seven yards out, it was Colchester's last chance too.

Colchester United

Walker, Cook, Rowles, Leslie, Coleman, Wignall, Wright, Adcock, Bremner, Osbourne, McDonough, Allinson.

Newcastle United

Carr, Brownlie, Saunders, Trewick, Carney, Haddock, Todd, Martin, Varadi, Wharton, Waddle.

Toon News Extra

1961... Magpies will not go on strike

The PFA led by Chairman Jimmy Hill today reached an agreement with the Football League and FA thus averting the threatened strike action called earlier. In the meeting with officials the maximum wage of $20 was scrapped and confirmation given that strike action by players from across the four divisions will now not go ahead.

Birthdays

Peter Beardsley born today in 1961.
Midfield 1983-1987 & 1993-1997, Apps 326 (4 subs), Goals 119.
Jeff Clarke born today in 1954.
Centre-half 1982-1987, Apps 134. Goals 5.
James Coppinger born today in 1981.
Forward 1998-2002, Apps 1 (1 sub). Goals 0.

Sadly Missed

Benny Craig died today in 1982, aged 66.
Full-back & Coach 1938-1982, Apps 122. Goals 0.
Duggie Livingstone died today in 1981, aged 82.
Manager 1954-1956.

Played on this day

1896, Division 2.
Woolwich Arsenal (h) 3-1 Att. 6,000
McKay, Stott, Miller

1902, Division 1.
Everton (h) 1-1 Att. 17,000
Roberts

1908, Division 1.
Bristol City (h) 2-0 Att. 30,000
McClarence, Soye

1913, Division 1.
Chelsea (a) 0-1 Att. 45,000

1919, Wartime.
Scotswood (a) 3-2 Att. 10,000
Donnelly, Tulthorpe, Brown

1930, Division 1.
Leicester City (a) 1-6 Att. 15,000
Hutchison

1936, Division 2.
Manchester United (a) 1-3 Att. 22,000
Ware

1947, Division 2.
Tottenham Hotspur (h) 1-0 Att. 62,873
Shackleton

1958, Division 1.
Chelsea (a) 1-2 Att. 37,327
White

1964, Division 2.
Grimsby Town (h) 4-0 Att. 23,681
Thomas (2), Anderson (2)

1969, Division 1.
Arsenal (h) 2-1 Att. 34,227
Davies, B. Robson

1975, Division 1.
Manchester City (a) 1-5 Att. 32,021
Macdonald

1982, FA Cup 3rd round, replay.
Colchester United (a) 4-3 Att. 7,505
Waddle, Varadi, Saunders, Brownlie

1986, Division 1.
Q.P.R. (a) 1-3 Att. 13,159
Gascoigne

1989, FA Cup 3rd round, 3rd replay.
Watford (a) 0-1 Att. 24,065

1992, Division 2.
Charlton Athletic (h) 3-4 Att. 15,663
Clark, Hunt, Brock
Newcastle led 3-1 at half-time

1995, FA Cup 3rd round, replay.
Blackburn Rovers 1 Newcastle 2
Sutton 75 Hottiger 58
Clark 85 Att. 22,658

1997, Premier League.
Southampton 2 Newcastle 2
Maddison 88 Ferdinand 14
Le Tissier 89 Clark 82
Att. 15,251

2003, Premier League.
Newcastle 2 Manchester City 0
Shearer 1
Bellamy 64 Att. 52,152
Alan Shearer's opening goal was timed at 10.5 seconds after kick off.

Playing record for this day is... 19 games, Won 9, Drawn 2, Lost 8, GF 34, GA 36.
Today's success rate... 52.63%.

Played on this day

1901, Division 1.
West Bromwich A. (h) 1-1   Att. 10,500
Peddie

1907, Division 1.
Everton (a) 0-3   Att. 45,000

1910, FA Cup 1st round, replay.
Stoke (h) 2-1   Att. 14,545
Higgins, Howie

1924, Division 1.
Tottenham Hotspur (a) 0-2   Att. 25,649

1929, Division 1.
Bury (a) 0-2   Att. 12,000

1935, Division 2.
Fulham (h) 1-1   Att. 25,000
Opponent (og)

1946, Wartime.
Huddersfield Town (h) 4-1   Att. 34,877
Stubbins (3), Milburn

1952, Division 1.
Burnley (a) 1-2   Att. 33,719
Milburn

1957, Division 1.
Arsenal (h) 3-1   Att. 46,815
Curry, White (2)

1959, FA Cup 3rd round.
Chelsea (h) 1-4   Att. 57,038
Eastham

1963, Division 2.
Plymouth Argyle (a) 2-0   Att. 11,940
Thomas, McGarry

1974, Division 1.
West Ham United (h) 1-1   Att. 27,217
Macdonald

1980, Division 2.
Orient (h) 2-0   Att. 20,954
Connolly, Barton

1991, Division 2.
Millwall (a) 1-0   Att. 11,478
Peacock

2002, Premier League.
Leicester City 0   Newcastle 0
Att. 21,354

Playing record for this day is... 15 games,
Won 6, Drawn 4, Lost 5, GF 19, GA 19.
Today's success rate... 53.33%.

Match of the Day from 1901

TITLE HOPES FADE AFTER WASTEFUL DRAW
Newcastle let vital home points slip away

This was a frustrating day for Newcastle. After wasting several great chances they took the lead and really should have gone on to a huge home win against relegation threatened Albion. Instead a lapse of concentration allowed the Midlanders back into the game and United then let several golden chances go begging. The result leaves Newcastle still in fourth place just six points behind leaders Liverpool leaves the title race wide open. It was a disappointing result against bottom of the table Albion.

Newcastle started well and looked as though they would sweep Albion away within the first half such was the pressure on the visitors' goal. Peddie had a great first-time shot brilliantly saved by Reader. Soon after that, however, came the first of many agonising misses which should have at least tested the keeper. First a shot by MacFarlane fizzed past the post by a mere fraction of an inch, then moments later Peddie, unmarked and inside the area, shot wildly wide when he had just the keeper to beat and plenty of time to place his shot more accurately. At the other end, Albion, try as they might to get forward, were having little joy from United's watertight defence superbly led by Dave Gardner. It seemed only a matter of time before United would score to open up the floodgates. This eventually happened amidst an almighty goalmouth scramble in the 37th minute, the ball reaching Peddie who this time took his time to chip over the three players left prone in the six-yard area and into the corner of the net. This should have been the platform on which to build a comfortable win, however, it was West Brom who responded better. Taking advantage of some slack play by Newcastle they had their best spell of the game right up until the half-time whistle.

Nothing much changed at the start of the second half and West Brom took full advantage of Newcastle's unwillingness to attack. Throwing men forward at every opportunity, with their First Division status at stake, they kept Kingsley in the United goal very busy. Albion got their deserved equaliser twenty minutes into the second half and fittingly it was set up and scored by the game's most influential player. Garfield, who had played so intelligently and skilfully on the Albion wing, was given the ball in his own half, but dribbled relentlessly forward towards the United goal. As the defence converged on him he sensationally hit a beautiful curling shot which flew past Kingsley before he had made up his mind where to dive. Newcastle had fallen to the sucker punch and although they tried to regain the lead the Albion defence gave nothing away. With six minutes remaining Adams managed to scramble away a chance to Fraser who slipped at the crucial moment trying to seal a desperately needed victory for Newcastle. It wasn't to be and the ball rolled tantalizingly past the wrong side of the post, United having to settle for a draw.

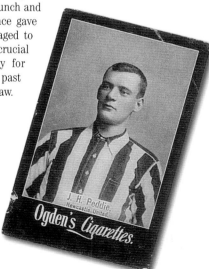

Newcastle United

Kingsley, Burgess, D. Gardner, Ghee, Aitken, Carr, A. Gardner, Peddie, Fraser, MacFarlane, Laidlaw.

West Bromwich Albion

Reader, Adams, Chadburn, Perry, Williams, Hadley, Roberts, Simmons, Stevenson, Wheldon, Garfield.

Birthdays

Ken Hodgson born today in 1942.
Winger 1959-1961, Apps 7. Goals 0.

Bobby Moncur born today in 1945.
Centre-half 1960-1974, Apps 361 (3 subs).
Goals 10.

January 20

Match of the Day from 1968

UNITED HAND OUT SKY BLUE HAMMERING
Season's first win on the road well worth the wait

This was Newcastle's first away win of the season, and it also completed the league double over a relegation threatened Coventry. The Sky Blues will need a tremendous improvement in results if they are now to avoid the drop. No one could accuse them of lack of effort today, however, in terms of possession they had as much as United, but were never as skilful or methodical. Coventry's defence was easily ripped apart, and their attacks were easily dealt with by a resolute back four led by Newcastle centre-backs McNamee and Moncur.

Newcastle looked to be in early trouble when Jim Iley went down suffering from an ankle injury after only eight minutes, after attention though, he was back in the game. Not so striker Albert Bennett who was led away by the physio just twelve minutes later with a serious knee injury and he was replaced by Jim Scott. The substitute then opened the scoring just eight minutes later, Burton crossing for Davies who skilfully nodded the ball into Scott's path and his well placed shot ended up in the bottom corner. Newcastle took full control and were denied by two wonderful saves by Glazier from Elliott and the impressive Scott. With half-time approaching Coventry drew level with a brilliantly taken first-time shot from Baker on the edge of the penalty area.

Coventry ran the opening fifteen minutes of the second half but couldn't beat the final obstacle, Marshall, who was having a great game between the posts. After the onslaught Newcastle got going again and new £67,500 signing Jackie Sinclair got his first goal for United in only his second game to put the Magpies back in front. Just two minutes later a corner taken by Iley was spectacularly headed in by a full-stretched dive from Tommy Robson, the game was now as good as over. The visitors added a fourth goal in the 82nd minute when Davies netted a well placed header past Glazier from Robson's perfectly floated free kick. Still Coventry gamely battled on and in the closing minutes Marshall again pulled off two superb saves to deny Gould, and Rees missed a sitter on the stroke of full time.

Coventry City
Glazier, Hill, Brock, Machin, Setters, Tudor, Hannigan, Barker, Gould, Gibson, Rees.

Newcastle United
Marshall, Burton, Clark, Elliott, McNamee, Moncur, Sinclair, Bennett (Scott 20), Davies, Iley, Robson.

Ollie Burton

Birthdays

Peter Garland born today in 1971.
Midfield 1992, Apps 3 (3 subs). Goals 0.
Jimmy Smith born today in 1947.
Midfield 1969-1976, Apps 179 (9 subs). Goals 16.
Graham Winstanley born today in 1948.
Centre-half 1964-1969, Apps 9(2 subs). Goals 0.

Sadly Missed

Bill McCracken died on this day in 1979, aged 95.
Right-back 1904-1923, Apps 444. Goals 8.

Played on this day

1894, Division 2.
Rotherham Town (a) 1-2   Att. 1,000
Wallace
1900, Division 1.
Derby County (a) 1-2   Att. 10,000
Stevenson
1906, Division 1.
Everton (h) 4-2   Att. 22,000
Orr, Appleyard, Howie, J.Rutherford
1912, Division 1.
Woolwich Arsenal (h) 1-2   Att. 10,000
Stewart
Newcastle are knocked of the league's pole position with this defeat, it's the first time since November that they have not topped the table.
1923, Division 1.
Chelsea (a) 0-3   Att. 30,000
1934, Division 1.
Derby County (a) 1-1   Att. 19,989
J.R. Richardson
1945, Wartime.
Gateshead (h) 2-4   Att. 11,688
Carr, Milburn
1951, Division 1.
Burnley (h) 2-1   Att. 40,666
Milburn (2)
1962, Division 2.
Huddersfield Town (h) 1-1   Att. 31,950
J. Wilson
1968, Division 1.
Coventry City (a) 4-1   Att. 33,760
Davies, T. Robson, Scott, Sinclair
1973, Division 1.
Crystal Palace (h) 2-0   Att. 24,676
Hibbitt, Nattrass
1990, Division 2.
Oldham Athletic (a) 1-1   Att. 11,190
McGhee
1993, Division 1.
Southend United (a) 1-1   Att. 8,246
Peacock
1996, Premier League.
Newcastle 2   Bolton Wanderers 1
Kitson 9   Bergsson 19
Beardsley 37   Att. 36,543
1998, Premier League.
Liverpool 1   Newcastle 0
Owen 17   Att. 42,791
2001, Premier League.
Leeds United 1   Newcastle 3
Keane 2   Solano 4 (pen)
                     Acuna 44,
                     Ameobi 86
                         Att. 40,005

Playing record for this day is... 16 games, Won 6, Drawn 4, Lost 6, GF 26, GA 24. Today's success rate... 50%.

January 21

Played on this day

1893, FA Cup 1st round.
Middlesbrough (h) 2-3   Att. 4,000
Thompson, Reay

1899, Division 1.
Stoke (h) 3-0   Att. 12,000
Peddie (2), Rogers

1905, Division 1.
Small Heath (h) 0-1   Att. 24,000

1911, Division 1.
Tottenham Hotspur (h) 1-1   Att. 22,000
Low

1922, Division 1.
Birmingham (a) 4-0   Att. 20,000
Dixon, Finlay, W. Low, Hudspeth (pen)

1928, Division 1.
Manchester United (h) 4-1   Att. 25,000
McKay, Seymour, Wilkinson (2)

1933, Division 1.
Leicester City (h) 2-1   Att. 20,000
Boyd, J.R. Richardson

1939, FA Cup 4th round.
Cardiff City (a) 0-0   Att. 42,060

1950, Division 1.
Manchester City (a) 1-1   Att. 42,986
Hannah

1956, Division 1.
Charlton Athletic (a) 2-0   Att. 34,414
Casey, Mitchell

1961, Division 1.
Manchester City (a) 3-3   Att. 19,746
Allchurch, White, Woods

1967, Division 1.
Nottingham Forest (h) 0-0   Att. 37,079

1976, League Cup Semi Final, 2nd leg.
Tottenham Hotspur (h) 3-1   Att. 49,902
Gowling, Keeley, Nulty
Newcastle won 3-2 on aggregate.

1978, Division 1.
West Ham United (a) 0-1   Att. 25,461

1984, Division 2.
Crystal Palace (a) 1-3   Att. 9,464
Beardsley

1987, FA Cup 3rd round.
Northampton Town (h) 2-1   Att. 23,177
Goddard, A. Thomas

1989, Division 1.
Charlton Athletic (h) 0-2   Att. 19,076

1995, Premier League.
Sheffield Wed. 0   Newcastle 0
   Att. 31,215

Playing record for this day is... 18 games,
Won 7, Drawn 6, Lost 5, GF 28, GA 19.
Today's success rate... 55.56%.

Match of the Day from 1976

WEMBLEY HERE WE COME

Newcastle knock out Tottenham in semi-final 2nd leg

An impressive crowd of 49,902 turned out for this cold, crisp evening match between Newcastle and Tottenham Hotspur. At stake was a place in the Football League Cup final at Wembley on February 28th, and Newcastle United had the bonus of being at home for this second leg of the semi final, the first having ended 1-1 at White Hart Lane.

It took just three minutes for Newcastle to take the lead when a long pass from Malcolm Macdonald came straight to Alan Gowling. He appeared to be offside according to the Tottenham defence, and therefore met no resistance when his shot went sailing into the goal past Tottenham keeper Pat Jennings. The flag was not raised for offside, and the goal stood.

The rest of the first period was full of determined play, but no real chances for either side. The second half began, and Newcastle increased their lead to 2-0 after a few minutes. A corner was awarded, and the kick was taken by Tommy Craig. It went high, and met perfectly with the head of an airborne Keeley who nodded it easily into the net.

The home side's lead was further increased on sixty-five minutes when a cross from Cassidy was left by Gowling and carried through to Nulty who put the ball into the net to secure Newcastle's place at Wembley.

On eighty minutes Tottenham pulled together all their efforts, and it paid off in the form of a goal from Don McAllister. It was too little too late for them, and the game ended 3-1 to United.

The Magpies reached Wembley where they met Manchester City, but sadly lost 2-1.

Newcastle United
Mahoney, Nattrass (Barrowclough), Kennedy, Nulty, Keeley, Howard, Burns, Cassidy, Macdonald, Gowling, Craig T.

Tottenham Hotspur
Jennings, Naylor, McAllister, Pratt, Young, Osgood, Coates, Perryman, Chivers, Duncan, Neighbour.

Referee Mr R Tinkler (Boston).

Newcastle United squad 1975-76: (back row, l-r) Mike Mahoney, David Craig, Jimmy Smith, Irving Nattrass, Alan Kennedy, Paul Cannell, Stewart Barrowclough, Malcolm Macdonald, Tommy Craig, John Tudor, Willie McFaul; (front row, l-r) Micky Burns, Geoff Nulty, Alex Bruce, Terry Hibbitt, Manager Gordon Lee, Tommy Cassidy, Pat Howard, Glen Keeley.

Match of the Day from 1907

UNITED STILL IN TITLE HUNT

Arsenal beaten in Rutherford and Orr's benefit game

Newcastle kept up the pressure at the top of the Division One championship race with a sound win over the Gunners today at St. James' Park. Indeed but for better finishing in the closing minutes the Magpies would have won this far more convincingly than the 1-0 scoreline they finished with. The fixture was officially made a benefit match for United winger Jackie Rutherford and midfielder Ronald Orr, who had clocked up over ten years service at St. James' Park between them. Ronald Orr made his debut against Blackburn Rovers in 1901 and went on to make 180 appearances for the club, scoring 70 goals, four of them in one game against Notts County not long after his debut. Jackie Rutherford made his debut in 1902 against Bolton Wanderers a game in which he scored one of his 94 career goals for the club, playing in a total of 336 games. He became one of the youngest ever scorers for Newcastle with his debut goal at just seventeen years of age. Both men were to figure prominently in this important game against Arsenal.

Over of 40,000 had crammed into Gallowgate by kick off and it was United, roared on by the above average crowd, who made the better start. Both defences were strong, and clear cut openings were few and far between as the half progressed. Eventually mistakes were made in the Gunners' defence, firstly by Cross who miscued his headed clearance, then Sharp who slipped when making a challenge on Appleyard who was left in the clear. Making good use of the free space he unselfishly laid the ball back for Howie to knock in a simple shot from six yards out. At half time the score remained 1-0 to the Magpies.

Heavy rain fell during the half-time break and conditions were tricky for the forwards at the start of the second period. Both defences looked comfortable, but it became increasingly noticeable that the Londoners were tiring towards the end of the game. In the last twelve minutes Arsenal's defence completely disappeared, allowing Rutherford a wonderful chance. Put clean through he had only Ashcroft to beat, and when the keeper then slipped over an empty net faced him, but somehow the usually consistent winger managed to roll the ball wide of the post when scoring seemed easier to do. In the dying minutes Howie presented Orr with another golden opportunity from ten yards out, but he snatched at his shot and the ball cleared Ashcroft's crossbar again without him having to make a save.

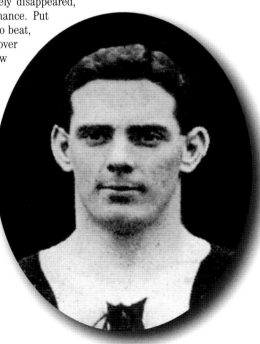

Jimmy Howie scored the only goal.

Newcastle United

Lawrence, McCracken, Carr, Gardner, Speedie, McWilliam, Rutherford, Howie, Appleyard, Orr, Brown.

Woolwich Arsenal

Ashcroft, Cross, Sharp, Bigden, Hynds, McEachrane, Garbutt, Coleman, Kyle, Statterthwaite, Neave.

Played on this day

Birthdays

John Gallacher born today in 1969.
Winger 1989-1992, Apps 37 (7 subs). Goals 8.

Played on this day

1894, FA Cup 1st round.
Sheffield United (h) 2-0 Att. 7,000
Wallace (2)

1900, FA Cup 1st round.
Reading (h) 2-1 Att. 11,259
Stevenson, Rogers

1906, Division 1.
Derby County (a) 1-2 Att. 7,000
McClarence

1912, Division 1.
Manchester City (a) 1-1 Att. 28,000
Lowes

1923, Division 1.
Chelsea (h) 0-0 Att. 15,000

1934, Division 1.
West Bromwich A. (h) 1-2 Att. 22,000
J.R. Richardson

1951, FA Cup 4th round.
Bolton Wanderers (h) 3-2 Att. 67,596
Milburn (2), Mitchell

1962, Division 2.
Leeds United (a) 1-0 Att. 17,209
Tuohy

1968, FA Cup 3rd round.
Carlisle United (h) 0-1 Att. 56,569

1973, Division 1.
Arsenal (a) 2-2 Att. 37,906
Macdonald, Smith

1979, FA Cup 4th round.
Wolverhampton W. (h) 1-1 Att. 29,561
Withe

1990, FA Cup 4th round.
Reading (a) 3-3 Att. 11,989
Quinn, McGhee (2)

1993, Division 1.
Luton Town (a) 0-0 Att. 10,237

2002, FA Cup 4th round.
Peterborough U. 2	Newcastle 4
O'Brien (og) 52	O'Brien 14
Farrell 69	McClen 43
	Shearer 84 (pen)
	Hughes 85
	Att. 13,841

Playing record for this day is... 14 games,
Won 5, Drawn 6, Lost 3, GF 21, GA 17.
Today's success rate... 57.14%.

Match of the Day from 1990

READING BOGEY CONTINUES
Six goal thriller ends in stalemate

In the history of the FA Cup few teams have had the same amount of success as Newcastle. Yet Reading drifting towards the relegation zone of the Third Division, were anything but overawed. Three times they looked to be beaten, three times they came back, the latest in stoppage time. Back in September, Reading had the better of the Magpies on the same ground in the Littlewoods Cup exploiting the same shaky defence which kept them in this fourth round tie, with all their goals coming from defensive lapses. As for Newcastle's play at the other end of the field, their finishing was razor sharp. Quinn and McGhee scored their goals, and excellent ones they were too. This was a thriller which had everything.

Quinn had put one header just wide of the post, when he next got the chance. This time it flew past the flailing right hand of Francis to give United a 27th minute lead. Yet Newcastle, indecisive at the back, failed to break down a Reading move just two minutes later which finished with Jones thumping in the equaliser. Next, United went ahead again when McGhee tucked in a low cross from Quinn. A minute before the interval, Reading were level for a second time, Quinn wasting all his productive good work by aiming an atrocious back pass to Burridge which was seized upon, and converted by Senior.

Midway through the second half the irrepressible McGhee gave Newcastle a further lead, this time with a simple finish. Ranson's drive was parried by Francis and the ball fell at his feet inside the six-yard box. By now referee Joe Worrall had hobbled off, having torn an achilles tendon. A linesman replaced him and it was for this stoppage that the time allowed for Reading's late equaliser was made. Gilkes playing his 150th game for the Royals, was astonishingly left unmarked just twenty yards from goal, and he rifled a drive into Burridge's left hand corner to earn the underdogs an unexpected replay.

Reading
Francis, Jones, Richardson, Gooding (Conroy 85), Hicks, Whitlock, Beavon, Tait (Leworthy 78), Senior, Gilkes, Moran.
Newcastle United
Burridge, Stimson, Ranson, Aitken, Scott, Kristensen, Gallacher, Sweeney, Quinn, McGhee, O'Brien (Dillon 56).
Referee Mr. J. Worrall (Warrington).

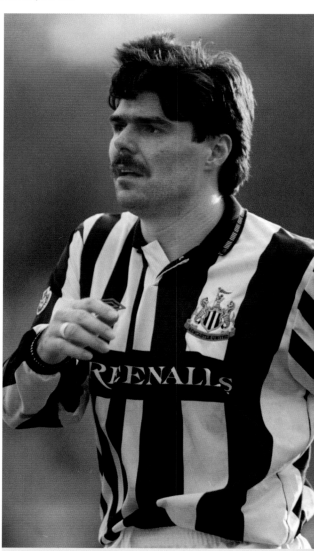

Mick Quinn

January 28

ANOTHER UNITED ROUT

Coventry's St. James' Park jinx continues

On a bone hard pitch, Newcastle roared into the FA Cup fifth round with this classy 5-0 hammering of Coventry. The Sky Blues hopes of ending a depressing 37-year record of failure at Gallowgate were dashed from the moment Micky Burns put United 1-0 up on 24 minutes. Further goals from Gowling, Macdonald (2), and Cassidy sent the 44,676 Geordie crowd home in delight and increased their hopes of a Wembley double of FA Cup and League Cup finals, a feat never before managed by any club. Newcastle, who have already booked their place in the League Cup final on February 28 against Manchester City, now they face Bolton Wanderers at Burnden Park in the next round of the FA Cup.

With a strong and bitterly cold wind blowing on their backs it was the visitors who started the livelier. Early pressure soon enabled Cross to rob Cassidy in the penalty area where he squared the ball to young Donal Murphy, but his deft side-footed shot cleared the crossbar by inches. A goal was all they lacked, and when after twenty minutes of convincing and clever play they still had nothing to show for their efforts, the tie quickly slipped away from them. The opening goal came at the other end, from a rare United attack. Coventry centre-half Alan Dugdale made a complete mess of a headed clearance and Gowling was allowed to seize the ball and play Burns in; taking the ball on the run he blasted a fierce shot into the far corner of King's net. Newcastle then added a second on 38 minutes with an equal amount of simplicity. Cassidy headed the ball forward to Macdonald, who in turn nodded it back for Gowling who placed a cool first-time volley past a helpless King. Coventry's defence was by now in total disarray but incredibly they got to the interval just the two goals down.

Coventry continued to hold out the United forwards for a further 25 minutes of the second half despite an injury to keeper King who started the half with a groin injury and his thigh heavily bandaged. Macdonald's first goal came on 70 minutes and was courtesy of a fine Tommy Craig pass. Helped by the slip of Coventry defender Jimmy Holmes, 'Supermac' was clear and finished with a thumping shot which flew into the roof of the net. Then just four minutes later Macdonald again gratefully accepted another defensive mix up as he fastened onto a header from Geoff Nulty to nudge the ball over the line from close range. It was becoming all too embarrassing and Cassidy grabbed United's fifth goal of the night right on the stroke of full time, with Coventry's players now looking completely broken and dejected.

Micky Burns

Newcastle United
Mahoney, Nattrass, Kennedy, Nulty, Keeley, Howard, Burns, Cassidy, Macdonald, Gowling, Craig.

Coventry City
King, Coop, Brogan, Powell, Dugdale, Holmes, Cartwright, Green, Cross, Murphy, Hutchison.

Played on this day

1899, FA Cup 1st round.
Glossop North End (a) 1-0   Att. 7,000
Peddie
1905, Division 1.
Manchester City (a) 2-3   Att. 35,000
Howie (2)
1911, Division 1.
Middlesbrough (a) 2-0   Att. 20,000
Randall, Stewart
1922, FA Cup 2nd round.
Preston North End (a) 1-3   Att. 33,000
Seymour
1933, Division 1.
Portsmouth (a) 0-2   Att. 13,000
1939, Division 2.
Southampton (a) 0-0   Att. 13,000
1947, Division 2.
Burnley (a) 0-3   Att. 25,309
1950, FA Cup 4th round.
Chelsea (a) 0-3   Att. 64,446
1956, FA Cup 4th round.
Fulham (a) 5-4   Att. 39,200
Casey, Keeble (2), Milburn, Stokoe
1967, FA Cup 3rd round.
Coventry City (a) 4-3   Att. 35,569
Davies (3), B. Robson
1976, FA Cup 4th round, replay.
Coventry City (h) 5-0   Att. 44,676
Gowling, Macdonald (2), Cassidy, Burns
1978, FA Cup 4th round.
Wrexham (h) 2-2   Att. 29,344
Bird, Blackhall
1995, FA Cup 4th round.
Newcastle 3   Swansea City 0
Kitson 41, 46, 72
Att. 34,372

Playing record for this day is... 13 games, Won 6, Drawn 2, Lost 5, GF 25, GA 23. Today's success rate... 53.85%.

Birthdays

Stuart Boam born today in 1948.
Centre-half 1979-1981, Apps 77. Goals 2.

Tony Nesbit born today in 1968.
Midfield 1985-1987, Apps 4 (3 subs). Goals 0.

January 29

1898, FA Cup 1st round.
Preston North End (a) 2-1   Att. 15,000
Peddie (2)
1921, FA Cup 2nd round.
Liverpool (h) 1-0   Att. 62,073
Harris
1927, FA Cup 4th round.
Corinthians (a) 3-1   Att. 56,338
McDonald (2), McKay
1936, FA Cup 4th round, replay.
Sheffield Wed. (h) 3-1   Att. 27,680
Bott (2), J. Smith
1938, Division 2.
Burnley (a) 1-2   Att. 9,000
Park
1944, Wartime.
Gateshead (a) 3-1   Att. 8,859
Woollett, Stubbins, Milburn
1955, FA Cup 4th round.
Brentford (h) 3-2   Att. 46,574
Curry, Hannah, R. Mitchell
1966, Division 1.
Nottingham Forest (a) 2-1   Att. 21,659
Suddick, Hilley
1969, FA Cup 4th round, replay.
Manchester City (a) 0-2   Att. 60,844
1972, Division 1.
Huddersfield Town (a) 0-0   Att. 12,829
1977, FA Cup 4th round.
Manchester City (h) 1-3   Att. 45,300
Gowling
1994, FA Cup 4th round.
Newcastle 1   Luton Town 1
Beardsley 65 (pen)   Thorpe 35
                     Att. 32,216

1997, Premier League.
Newcastle 4   Everton 1
Ferdinand 74   Speed 5
Lee 79
Shearer 83 (pen)
Elliott 90   Att. 36,143
2003, Premier League.
Tottenham H. 0   Newcastle 1
                     Jenas 90
                     Att. 36,084

Playing record for this day is... 14 games,
Won 9, Drawn 2, Lost 3, GF 25, GA 16.
Today's success rate... 71.43%.

Match of the Day from 1997

ASPRILLA ARRIVAL SPARKS COMEBACK
Late four-goal burst confounds Everton's troubled run

Looking to bounce back from their shock Cup defeat by Bradford City last week, Everton were inspired for an hour today at St. James' Park. This until the introduction of Faustino Asprilla who consigned them to a sixth successive league defeat, their worst sequence for 25 years, as Newcastle turned likely loss into improbable victory inside sixteen minutes. The difference between success and failure has never been highlighted more starkly than in this game and the visitors stunned the 36,143 crowd when Gary Speed struck a brilliant opening goal from 25 yards after just three minutes. The goal was certainly no fluke and it soon became clear that Everton meant business and had changed for the better. Whilst United's nervy young full-backs transmitted their uncertainty, Everton relished hunting for, and winning every ball. Even the loss of Craig Short, bleeding from a head wound, after 28 minutes did not upset their rhythmic stride and the signs looked ominous for the Geordies now looking anxiously on from the crowd.

Tino Asprilla

Then on 58 minutes Asprilla, significantly, made his first appearance in almost two months as a substitute replacing the tired looking Peter Beardsley. Suddenly the variety and potency of Newcastle's incisions soared and the aerial bombardment took on an imposing variety. With sixteen minutes of the game remaining, a Robbie Elliott free kick dropped to Les Ferdinand, who found the corner of the net with a neatly placed low drive, United were level. Six minutes later Asprilla created the second, wriggling away from David Unsworth on the right wing to send in an enticing cross to the far post where Robert Lee met the ball with a thundering volley from close range. The irrepressible Colombian then induced a foul from Claus Thomsen in the box, and Alan Shearer smashed in United's third goal from the penalty spot in the 83rd minute. United's stunning comeback was completed in stoppage time when Robbie Elliott, who appeared to kick the ball out of Paul Gerrard's hands, nicked a fourth goal to rub salt in to the Evertonians' wounds. Newcastle's manager Kenny Dalglish, who himself has witnessed his side giving away leads in their last two games, was delighted and summed up the mood felt by everyone after the game, he said: "Everton didn't deserve the scoreline of 4-1 but we are very grateful for it. To finish so well after starting so badly is a credit to everyone in the team."

Newcastle United

Hislop, Watson, Peacock, Albert, Elliott, Gillespie (Barton 86), Beardsley (Asprilla 58), Ferdinand, Shearer, Batty, Lee.

Everton

Gerrard, Short (Grant 28, Rideout 82), Watson, Unsworth, Barrett, Parkinson, Thomsen, Speed, Phelan, Stuart, Ferguson.

Referee Mr. M. Riley (Leeds).

Birthdays

Tommy Gaynor born today in 1963.
Centre-forward 1990, Apps 4. Goals 1.
Jimmy Woodburn born today in 1917.
Defender 1935-1948, Apps 96. Goals 8.

Sadly Missed

Bert Chandler died today in 1963, aged 66.
Right-back 1925-1926, Apps 36. Goals 0.

January 30

Match of the Day from 1974

HARVEY SENSING CUP GLORY

United ease into round five at last with a 3-0 win over Scunthorpe

Joe Harvey, who was the first skipper to lift the FA Cup in successive seasons back in 1951-52, saw his side confidently take their place in the fifth round of the competition today, as a manager. He, like everyone else around Tyneside, sensed another Wembley showdown in the final, and why not? This was the first time United had reached this stage of the competition since 1961. Newcastle's easy victory at the Old Showground over Scunthorpe now earns them a tie against Nottingham Forest in the next round.

Newcastle were eager to get that disappointing display in the first game out of their system, and set the record straight. From the kick off they were soon on the attack but failed to put an effort on target despite winning four corners in the opening six minutes. Then after just ten minutes they had the lead, and from that moment never looked back. A travesty of defensive errors, and one total miskick allowed a harmless pass from Tudor to bounce into the path of Stuart Barrowclough who made no mistake with his first-time shot just seven yards out. It was all Newcastle pressure, but Scunthorpe with a combination of desperate defending and a little luck, held out, and at the half-time interval the score remained 1-0.

The second half went pretty much the same way as the first with all the action in the Iron's half. Newcastle eventually settled the outcome in the 55th minute. This was when Malcolm Macdonald started showing again why there is no one better at snapping up goals. He had battled all through the game for his chance and from Jimmy Smith's teasing cross he was there to bury the ball in the back of the net from six yards out. With Newcastle in exhibition mode they simply delighted the enthusiastic crowd of 19,028 with some lovely football. A third goal was inevitable and it arrived in the 88th minute when Macdonald again got free of his marker to head home another superb right wing cross from man-of-the-match Smith.

Scunthorpe United

Barnard, Lynch, Wellbourne, Simpkin, Collard, Houghton, Collier, Pilling, Warnock, Davidson, Keeley. Sub: Money.

Newcastle United

McFaul, D. Craig, Clark, McDermott, Howard, Moncur, Barrowclough, Smith, Macdonald, Tudor, Hibbitt. Sub: Gibb.

Stewart Barrowclough

Played on this day

1897, FA Cup 1st round.
Aston Villa (a) 0-5   Att. 7,000
1904, Division 1.
Derby County (h) 0-0   Att. 16,000
1909, Division 1.
Sheffield Wed. (h) 1-0   Att. 33,000
Veitch
1915, FA Cup 2nd round.
Swansea Town (h) 1-1   Att. 30,005
McCracken (pen)
1926, FA Cup 4th round.
Cardiff City (a) 2-0   Att. 38,270
Seymour (2)
1932, Division 1.
West Ham United (h) 2-2   Att. 32,000
Weaver (2)
1935, Division 2.
Bradford Park Ave. (a) 3-1   Att. 5,000
Bott, Williams, Wilson
1937, Division 2.
Blackburn Rovers (a) 1-6   Att. 7,000
Park
1943, Wartime.
Leeds United (a) 2-7   Att. 2,000
Mullen, Carr
1954, FA Cup 4th round.
Burnley (a) 1-1   Att. 53,000
Broadis
1971, Division 1.
Burnley (a) 1-1   Att. 12,521
Barrowclough
1974, FA Cup 4th round, replay.
Scunthorpe United (a) 3-0   Att. 19,028
Macdonald (2), Barrowclough
1982, Division 2.
Norwich City (h) 2-1   Att. 14,492
Varadi, Mills
1988, FA Cup 4th round.
Swindon Town (h) 5-0   Att. 28,699
D. Jackson, Gascoigne (2, 1 pen), O'Neil, Goddard
1999, Premier League.
Newcastle 2   Aston Villa 1
Shearer 4   Merson 61
Ketsbaia 27   Att. 36,766
2002, Pemier League.
Tottenham H. 1   Newcastle 3
Iversen 17   Acuna 67
                     Shearer 69
                     Bellamy 78
                              Att. 35,798

Playing record for this day is... 16 games, Won 8, Drawn 5, Lost 3, GF 29, GA 27. Today's success rate... 65.63%.

Played on this day

1903, Division 1.
Notts County (a) 2-2   Att. 11,000
A. Gardner, Orr
1920, FA Cup 2nd round.
Huddersfield Town (h) 0-1   Att. 46,462
1925, FA Cup 2nd round.
Leicester City (h) 2-2   Att. 58,713
McDonald (pen), Cowan
1931, Division 1.
Bolton Wanderers (h) 4-0   Att. 10,000
Starling, Hutchison, Boyd (2)
1948, Division 2.
Leicester City (h) 2-0   Att. 51,675
McCall, Sibley
1953, FA Cup 4th round.
Rotherham United (h) 1-3   Att. 54,356
Keeble
1959, Division 1.
Manchester United (a) 4-4   Att. 48,777
Allchurch, McGuigan, White (2)
Newcastle trailed at half-time 4-1.
1970, Division 1.
Crystal Palace (h) 0-0   Att. 36,008
1976, Division 1.
Middlesbrough (a) 3-3   Att. 31,000
Gowling, Kennedy, Nattrass
1981, Division 2.
Bolton Wanderers (h) 2-1   Att. 19,143
Clarke, Martin
1987, FA Cup 4th round.
Preston North End (h) 2-0   Att. 30,495
Roeder, Goddard
1990, FA Cup 4th round, replay.
Reading (h) 4-1   Att. 26,658
McGhee (2), Quinn, Robinson
1993, Division 1.
Derby County (h) 1-1   Att. 27,285
O'Brien
2000, FA Cup 5th round.
Blackburn Rovers 1 Newcastle 2
Jansen 25   Shearer 20, 79
                             Att 29,946
2001, Premier League.
Chelsea 3   Newcastle 1
Zola 37   Bassedas 23
Poyet 62
Grokjaer 79   Att. 35,108

Playing record for this day is... 15 games,
Won 6, Drawn 6, Lost 3, GF 30, GA 22.
Today's success rate... 60%.

UNITED PUT THE RECORD STRAIGHT

Reading bundled out of the FA Cup after emphatic 4-1 victory

Newcastle brushed aside the spirited challenge of Reading at St. James' Park today to move swiftly into the fifth round of the FA Cup, where they will enjoy home advantage again against troubled Manchester United. Newcastle dominated this entertaining and sporting fourth round replay from first whistle to last and should have had the luxury of a much bigger margin of victory at the end. Reading, hoping to gain entry to the FA Cup fifth round for the first time in 55 years played as well as can be expected, but were simply outclassed by their higher league opponents. The result, and the manner in which it was earnt, finally made up for the humiliation suffered last September when the same side beat Newcastle to put them out of the Littlewoods Cup.

Newcastle cheered on by a 26,658 crowd got off to a flying start, openings for both Quinn and Dillon were made, but incredibly squandered in the opening five minutes. Newcastle however got the inevitable breakthrough after eleven minutes when McGhee, who scored twice in the 3-3 draw at Elm Park, side-footed home Aitken's low cross from the right. Nine minutes later the crowd was treated to an uncanny action replay. Aitken the Scottish captain who recently joined United from Celtic, again cut a swathe through the Reading defence before crossing accurately for McGhee to convert, this time with a simple header.

Mark McGhee

Reading's decision to throw caution to the wind after the interval, commendable though it may have been, did little to disrupt Newcastle's flow. The Magpies' one moment of genuine concern came in the 57th minute when Aitken limped away from the field and was replaced by Bradshaw. With just nineteen minutes of the game remaining the home side added a third, Quinn bagging his 25th goal of the season to put Newcastle firmly in command at 3-0. Reading still gave their all and were rewarded with a deserved consolation goal in the 87th minute when Senior headed in from a corner. In the second minute of injury time Robinson completed the scoring for Newcastle.

Newcastle United
Burridge, Ranson (Robinson), Stimson, Aitken (Bradshaw), Scott, Kristensen, Gallacher, Dillon, Quinn, McGhee, Sweeney.
Reading
Francis, Jones, Richardson, Gooding, Hicks, Whitlock (Conroy), Beavon, Tait, Senior, Gilkes, Moran (Wood).
Referee Mr. R. Nixon

Birthdays

Ron Greener born today in 1934.
Centre-half 1951-1955, Apps 3. Goals 0.

February

February 1

1896, FA Cup 1st round.
Chesterfield (a) 4-0   Att. 5,000
Wardrope (2), Aitken, Thompson

1902, Division 1.
Small Heath (h) 2-0   Att. 13,000
Veitch, Carr

1908, FA Cup 2nd round.
West Ham United (h) 2-0   Att. 47,285
Appleyard (2)

1913, FA Cup 2nd round.
Hull City (a) 0-0   Att. 18,250

1919, Wartime.
Durham City (a) 2-0   Att. 10,000
Booth (2)

1930, Division 1.
Huddersfield Town (a) 0-2   Att. 15,000

1932, FA Cup 4th round, 2nd replay.
Southport (n*) 9-0   Att. 19,350
Lang, McMenemy, Cape (2), Weaver,
Boyd, J.R. Richardson (3)
Played at Hillsborough, Sheffield.
Newcastle's record Cup victory (to date).

1936, Division 2.
Fulham (a) 1-3   Att. 30,000
Ware

1941, Wartime.
Middlesbrough (h) 6-2   Att. 4,500
Duns, Herd, Birkett, Stubbins (3)

1947, Division 2.
Barnsley (h) 4-2   Att. 40,182
Bentley, Shackleton, Stobbart, Wayman

1958, Division 1.
Sunderland (h) 2-2   Att. 47,739
Curry, Tait

1961, FA Cup 4th round.
Stockport County (h) 4-0   Att. 48,715
Allchurch, White, Woods (2)

1964, Division 2.
Preston North End (a) 0-3   Att. 18,982

1975, Division 1.
Middlesbrough (h) 2-1   Att. 42,514
Macdonald, Burns

1986, Division 1.
Coventry City (h) 3-2   Att. 16,785
Wharton, Beardsley, Allon

1992, Division 2.
Oxford United (a) 2-5   Att. 5,872
Scott, Peacock (pen)

1995, Premier League.
Newcastle 2   Everton 0
Fox 74
Beardsley 80 (pen)   Att. 34,465

1998, Premier League.
Aston Villa 0   Newcastle 1
Batty 58
   Att. 38,266

Playing record for this day is... 18 games,
Won 12, Drawn 2, Lost 4, GF 46, GA 22.
Today's success rate... 72.22%.

SOUTHPORT RESISTANCE IS SHATTERED

Record 9-0 win for United in quest for Wembley

After two stalemates and 270 minutes of football Newcastle have finally seen off the plucky resistance of Southport. United now face Leicester City at St. James' Park on February 13th in the fifth round of the FA Cup, their Wembley dream still intact. (indeed, they went all the way beating Arsenal 2-1 in the final on April 23.) United made one change for this second replay at Hillsborough, Sheffield, Jackie Cape coming in to lead the forward line in place of the injured Jack Allen. Southport for the third time remained unchanged and at full strength, a crowd of 19,350 were present for the kick off making a combined total of 89,515 spectators over the three games.

Although Southport made a determined effort in defence led by Vincent and Robinson they could not hold Newcastle in this form, and once the first goal went in it opened up the floodgates. The Magpies deserved to win by such a margin for they completely outclassed their opponents in every area, only some stubborn defending preventing further goals early on. United then scored four goals inside seven minutes just before half time through Cape, Boyd, Richardson and Lang to put the tie well out of Southport's reach.

Newcastle continued to dominate play in the second half now sensing a huge win and they raced to establish a new record cup win. United's forwards did what they pleased almost entirely throughout the half. At the other end keeper McInroy had one shot to deal with when he saved comfortably from Dobson on the hour mark. However, despite being so one sided there was plenty of good football played. But it was the goals Newcastle accumulated after the break which made the game, and they were scored by Richardson (2), to complete his first hat-trick of the season, Cape, McMenemy, and Weaver, who got the record-breaking ninth goal. To such an extent did Newcastle gain a mastery control of the game, they hardly missed the loss of goal-scorer McMenemy who had to leave the field after 79 minutes through injury. Without doubt, on this showing, it will take some side to put the Geordies out of this year's FA Cup.

Newcastle United
McInroy, Nelson, Fairhurst, MacKenzie, Davidson, Weaver, Boyd, J.R. Richardson, Cape, McMenemy, Lang.

Southport
Middleton, Little, Robinson, Seagrave, Vincent, Holmes, Bell, McConnell, Waterston, Cowen, Dobson.

Jimmy Richardson

2003... Riverside postponement, frustration turns to anger.

Newcastle's scheduled Premiership fixture away at Middlesbrough which was called off late last night caused anger amongst the Toon Army this afternoon. Newcastle who had won in midweek against in form Spurs had gone second in the table, and were about to face a Boro' side minus some of its star players. The match was postponed after overnight snow on Thursday but anger surrounded the decision as to why it was possible for Third Division side Hartlepool play their home league match against Torquay which went ahead this afternoon despite being within thirteen miles of the Riverside Stadium.

Hugh Cameron born today in 1927.
Winger 1951-1952, Apps 2. Goals 0.

Rob Lee born today in 1966.
Midfield 1992-2002, Apps 381 (12 subs).
Goals 56.

Match of the Day from 1970

FREEZING FRIDAY

Two pitch inspections, but Newcastle manage a win

A crowd of 32,054 had turned out to watch this match, the first ever to be held on a Friday evening at St. James' Park. Two pitch inspections were needed before the game got the go ahead, and as soon as play started it became clear what had caused the concern. The pitch was causing great problems for the players, the frost and ice making skids, slips and slides inevitable. It was no surprise to the crowd that it took a little while for the match to really get started. Players had to adjust their game accordingly and build up their confidence given the state of the field.

The ball bounced awkwardly, slowed down and sped up at the wrong times and was generally unpredictable, which made it even harder for the players to judge what was going to happen next.

The first chance of the game fell to Newcastle when Elliott had a great opportunity to score, but his shot just scraped over the crossbar. Next it was Albion's turn, and Astle was the best man to try his luck. His eighth minute attempt was also too high to enter the goal, and the scores remained frustratingly level.

Just one minute later and Albion should have taken the lead. Hope passed to Brown, who slammed a shot goalwards. The ball beat Newcastle keeper McFaul but rebounded off the goal post to stay in play.

Attacks from the Newcastle side were just as determined, but their attempts were kept at bay by the adequate Albion defence. A powerful shot from Dyson could have changed the score but the ball, despite making it past the defence, just skimmed the angle of the goal, missing by a fraction of an inch.

Half time was just two minutes away when Newcastle sent themselves into the lead with a cracking shot from Dyson. The move started with a clearance from McFaul which fell to Davies who sent the ball through to Dyson. He snaked through the Albion defence and beat goalkeeper Cumbes with a fierce low shot to put the home side one goal up at the interval.

The second half began with a change for United when Craig, still suffering from a knock in the first half, was replaced by Thomson. The inspiration was still there for the home side and the attempts at furthering the scoreline were plenty. The Albion defence had to work hard to keep out many of the shots, but they rose to the challenge and managed to keep the ball out of the net. A superb shot from Dyson had Cumbes making a full-length diving save, and he managed to get the ball away from goal.

In the 72nd minute Albion made an attempt at a comeback with a lovely shot which beat McFaul, but bounced off the post for the second time. This proved to be the final stab at levelling the scores, the pitch having taken its toll on the players. It was too late for Albion to get back into the game and Newcastle had done enough to ensure the win on this freezing Friday night.

Newcastle United
McFaul, Craig (Thomson), Clark, Gibb, McNamee, Moncur, Robson, Smith, Davies, Elliott, Dyson.
West Bromwich Albion
Cumbes, Fraser, Wilson, Brown, Talbut, Kaye, Cantello, Suggett, Astle, Hartford, Hope. Sub: Hughes.

Sadly Missed

Tom Curry died on this day 1958, aged 63
Wing-half 1912-1919, Apps 248, Goals 5.
Tom was Manchester United's first-team trainer
when he died tragically in the Munich air crash.

Played on this day

1897, Division 2.
  Manchester City (h) 3-0   Att. 9,000
  Wardrope (2), Aitken
1904, FA Cup 1st round.
  Bury (a) 1-2   Att. 12,635
  Templeton
1909, FA Cup 2nd round.
  Blackpool (h) 2-1   Att. 32,137
  Howie, Rutherford
1915, FA Cup 2nd round, replay.
  Swansea Town (a) 2-0   Att. 15,000
  King, Pailor
1924, FA Cup 2nd round, replay.
  Derby County (h) 2-2   Att. 50,393
  Harris, Cowan
1926, Division 1.
  West Ham United (h) 4-1   Att. 28,000
  Cowan, Gallacher (2), Seymour
1932, Division 1.
  Sheffield Wednesday (a) 0-2 Att. 14,000
1937, Division 2.
  Bury (h) 1-3   Att. 22,000
  Leighton
1943, Wartime.
  Sunderland (a) 3-3   Att. 12,000
  Carr, Short, Stubbins
1954, Division 1.
  Tottenham Hotspur (a) 0-3   Att. 35,798
1960, Division 1.
  Burnley(a) 1-2   Att. 26,998
  Allchurch
1965, Division 2.
  Preston North End (a) 0-2   Att. 18,961
1970, Division 1.
  West Bromwich A. (h) 1-0   Att. 32,054
  Dyson
1971, Division 1.
  Chelsea (h) 0-1   Att. 34,336
1978, FA Cup 4th round, replay.
  Wrexham (a) 1-4   Att. 18,676
  Burns
1982, Division 2.
  Cambridge United (a) 0-1   Att. 5,092
1988, Division 1.
  Wimbledon (a) 0-0   Att. 10,505
1999, Premier League.
  Leeds United 0   Newcastle 1
                      Solano 63
                      Att. 40,202

Playing record for this day is... 18 games,
Won 6, Drawn 3, Lost 9, GF 22, GA 27.
Today's success rate...41.67%.

Played on this day

1903, FA Cup 1st round.
Grimsby Town (a) 1-2   Att. 6,000
McColl

1906, FA Cup 2nd round, replay.
Derby County (h) 2-1   Att. 28,257
Appleyard, J. Rutherford

1914, Division 1.
Bolton Wanderers (h) 4-3   Att. 35,000
G. Wilson (2), Shepherd (2, 1pen)

1920, Division 1.
Bradford City (a) 0-1   Att. 25,000

1925, Division 1.
Nottingham Forest (h) 4-1   Att. 21,000
Harris (2), McDonald, Urwin

1931, Division 1.
Liverpool (a) 2-4   Att. 35,000
Hutchison, Wilkinson

1942, Wartime.
Rotherham United (a) 1-2   Att. 3,000
Robson

1953, Division 1.
Stoke City (h) 1-2   Att. 31,426
G. Robledo

1959, Division 1.
Wolverhampton W. (h) 3-4   Att. 42,377
Eastham (2 pens), White

1976, Division 1.
Derby County (h) 4-3   Att. 45,770
T. Craig (pen), Macdonald, Nulty,
Opponent (og)

1981, Division 2.
Queens Park Rangers (h) 1-0 Att. 20,404
Waddle

1987, Division 1.
Luton Town (h) 2-2   Att. 22,437
P. Jackson, Goddard

1998, Premier League.
Newcastle 0   West Ham United 1
                   Lazaridis 16
                   Att. 36,736

Playing record for this day is... 13 games,
Won 5, Drawn 1, Lost 7, GF 25, GA 26.
Today's success rate... 42.31%.

NAILBITING FINISH, JOY FOR UNITED

Unlucky Derby so close but Newcastle hold out in thriller

Although over 45,000 partisan Geordies were undoubtedly delighted with Newcastle's win, there would no doubt be an awful lot of them who felt sorry for Derby County today. Derby put so much into this memorable match, refusing to acknowledge defeat right up to the final whistle, and yet went away with nothing. Manager Dave MacKay, still stunned half an hour afterwards said "I can hardly believe that we played so well and yet lost, but full credit to Newcastle for taking their chances". His opposite number, the newly named Manager of the Month, Gordon Lee quipped, "If we have many more games like this I'll be dead at 45, and I'm already 41 now."

After a first half of skilful yet rarely exciting football, dominated by the defenders, the game really burst into life in the second half. At that point Newcastle were leading 1-0, through an own goal by Colin Todd, who back headed a Tommy Craig free kick over his keeper and into the roof of the net.

It was 2-0 after 50 minutes as Derby's defenders failed to mark Newcastle skipper Geoff Nulty as he raced in to head an Alan Gowling cross into the net. Derby fought back immediately and Powell reduced the deficit with a fine headed goal following a cross from Leighton James after 56 minutes. Powell then spoiled his day by pulling down Craig in the penalty area just seven minutes later; it was Craig who got up to send the keeper the wrong way with a neatly placed penalty. Still there was no hint of what was to come, even when Charlie George made the score 3-2 in the 66th minute. Newcastle were coasting on that slender lead when suddenly with just seven minutes of the game remaining, the match burst into frenzied activity, with the one of most exciting finishes ever seen at St. James' Park. Bruce Rioch started it off when an Archie Gemmill cross bounced off his knee for a fortunate equaliser for Derby. Just one minute later, and six minutes from time, Malcolm Macdonald raced in to the goalmouth to head home another superb cross from Craig. There was still more nail biting action for the Newcastle supporters to endure though, Macdonald set up Gowling with an open goal but somehow the United forward miskicked and the ball was sliced agonisingly wide. At the other end Keeley headed a goal-bound shot from James off the line, this seconds after a fantastic acrobatic save from the United keeper to deny George. Finally, with the crowd now pleading for that final whistle, Davies who had come on as sub for Francis Lee after an hour's play, had a shot cleared off the line by Kennedy. Seconds later the final whistle sounded to a huge sigh of relief, and a tremendous roar round the ground, the crowd having witnessed a game that will be talked about for years to come.

Newcastle United
Mahoney, Nattrass, Kennedy, Nulty, Keeley, Howard, Burns, D. Craig, Macdonald, Gowling, T. Craig.

Derby County
Moseley, Thomas, Nish, Rioch, McFarland, Todd, Powell, Gemmill, Lee (Davies), George, James.

Manager of the Month for January 1976, Gordon Lee.

Birthdays

Joe Butler born today in 1943.
Left-back 1960-1965, Apps 4. Goals 0.
Ossie Park born today in 1905.
Centre-half 1924-1931, Apps 43. Goals 0.

Sadly Missed

Billy Foulkes died on this day 1979, aged 52.
Midfield 1951-1954, Apps 68, Goals 9.
Cam Theaker died on this day in 1992, aged 79.
Goalkeeper 1938-1947, Apps 81.

February 8

FOREST FROZEN OUT BY BRILLIANT BEARDSLEY

Two-goal strike a timely reminder for Robson's England

Two superb goals from Newcastle United's in-form striker, Peter Beardsley, proved enough to swamp sad Nottingham Forest at a snowbound City Ground today. Beardsley, who is being tipped in many quarters for a place in Bobby Robson's England World Cup squad, was clearly out to impress and made the most of some slack Forest defending.

Beardsley struck twice in the space of six minutes during the second half as Forest struggled to come to terms with the severe wintry conditions. His first goal, which was his 50th for the Magpies, came in the 66th minute when he lobbed Forest keeper Steve Sutton after delightfully controlling a splendid through ball from promising Newcastle midfielder, eighteen-year-old Paul Gascoigne. Six minutes later, Beardsley struck again as he burst through the Forest middle and beat off the challenge of Brett Williams and Des Walker. He darted through into the area and chipped the advancing Sutton with outlandish audacity.

Forest had struggled throughout and gave no indication of their recent good form which had seen them climb to sixth place in the First Division with four consecutive league victories. They were sluggish in defence, struggled to put decent passing moves together and rarely tested Martin Thomas in the Newcastle goal. Their only ray of hope come with nine minutes of the game remaining, when right out of the blue, Colin Walsh unleashed a devastating curler from 25 yards straight into Thomas's right-hand corner. It was Walsh's seventh goal in six games and sparked off something of a late revival for the home side. But try as they might, they could not penetrate the obstinate Newcastle defence again, and could have no complaints about the 2-1 result.

Newcastle United

Thomas, Anderson (McDonald), Bailey, McCreery, Clarke, Roeder, Stephenson, Gascoigne, Cunningham, Beardsley, Wharton.

Nottingham Forest

Sutton, Fleming, Williams, Walker, Metgod, Bowyer, Carr (Campbell), Webb, Clough, Davenport, Walsh.

Paul Gascoigne

Birthdays

Dave Hamilton born today in 1919.
Winger 1939-1946, Apps 10. Goals 2.
Clarence Acuna born today in 1975.
Midfield 2000-present day, Apps 59 (15 subs). Goals 7.

Sadly Missed

Frank Hudspeth died on this day 1963, aged 72.
Left-back 1910-1929, Apps 482, Goals 38.

Played on this day

1895, Division 2.
Manchester City (a) 0-4   Att. 3,500
1901, FA Cup 1st round.
Middlesbrough (a) 1-3   Att. 16,000
Aitken
1907, Division 1.
Bury (h) 3-2   Att. 25,000
Brown, Howie, Rutherford
1921, Division 1.
Chelsea (h) 1-0   Att. 40,000
Smailes
1924, Division 1.
Huddersfield Town (h) 0-1   Att. 25,000
1927, Division 1.
Manchester United (a) 1-3   Att. 25,402
McDonald
1929, Division 1.
Manchester United (h) 5-0   Att. 40,000
Lang, Gallacher (3, 1pen), Urwin
1935, Division 2.
Norwich City (a) 0-2   Att. 16,000
1952, Division 1.
Fulham (a) 1-1   Att. 46,000
G. Robledo
1957, Division 1.
Preston North End (h) 1-2   Att. 43,086
Milburn
1974, Division 1.
Coventry City (h) 5-1   Att. 27,371
Tudor, Macdonald, Bruce,
Opponents (2 ogs)
1980, Division 2.
Wrexham (a) 0-1   Att. 13,299
1985, Division 1.
Manchester United (h) 1-1   Att. 32,555
Beardsley
1993, Division 1.
Portsmouth (a) 0-2   Att. 21,028
1994, FA Cup 4th round, replay.
Luton Town 2   Newcastle 0
Hartson 16
Oakes 77
Att. 12,503
2002, Premier League.
Newcastle 3   Southampton 1
Robert 24   Pahars 39
Shearer 29, 45 (pen)   Att. 51,857
2003, Premier League.
Newcastle 1   Arsenal 1
Robert 53   Henry 35
Att. 52,157

Playing record for this day is... 17 games,
Won 5, Drawn 3, Lost 9, GF 23, GA 27.
Today's success rate... 38.24%.

Match of the Day from 1974

COVENTRY CRUSHED

Sky Blues star in their own nightmare with 2 own goals

It was a day of complete contrasts between the North and Midlands today. Newcastle recorded their biggest win of the 1973-4 season, Coventry crashed to their heaviest defeat. Newcastle in a polished classy display, made the most of their good fortune. The Midlanders, for the most part, looked second best but were blighted by bad luck, culminating in two unfortunate own goals. The win sets up United's FA Cup clash against West Brom nicely, with all the confidence a team needs for a cup-tie away from home. Coventry, with this defeat, have plenty of unwanted problems ahead of their fifth round tie at home to QPR next week.

The visitors started well enough, indeed they should have gone ahead on 27 minutes when David Cross, after a brilliant run by Les Cartwright, was presented with one of the best chances of the match. Cross's shot hit the foot of the post as Iam McFaul came out of goal and Newcastle breathed again. A goal then would have been a confidence booster for Coventry but instead they went behind rather unluckily just before the interval when Pat Howard, following up, hit a ball hard, low and probably wide of the target from twenty yards. The ball struck Coventry centre-half Craven's foot and flashed into the top corner of the net. This was tough on keeper Bill Glazier who had played brilliantly, making two great full-length saves earlier to deny both Malcolm Macdonald and John Tudor.

A slip by Alan Dugdale, who failed to intercept Tommy Cassidy's pass to Macdonald, led to Newcastle's second goal after 48 minutes. Macdonald centred and although Tudor missed the ball, Alex Bruce, United's £150,000 buy from Preston, scored his first goal for the club in his second game. After 65 minutes Bruce was replaced by Stuart Barrowclough with the intention of exploiting the tiredness now sweeping through the Sky Blues back four. His pace proved too much for Coventry debutant Peter Hindley who was given a torrid time by the young winger. In the 71st minute Barrowclough raced down the wing and centred hard and low and Dugdale, attempting to intercept, could only crash the ball past his own goalkeeper. Then, after 79 minutes, Terry Hibbitt completed good build-up work by Macdonald and Barrowclough by crossing to the far post for Tudor to head a fourth goal. Macdonald completed Coventry's misery in the 83rd minute when he followed up and netted after Glazier had stopped, but failed to hold, a blistering drive from the flying Barrowclough. A minute later Alderson headed a consolation goal from Cross's centre but by this time the Sky Blues looked a well beaten and demoralised side.

Newcastle United
McFaul, Craig, Clark, Gibb, Howard, Moncur, Bruce (Barrowclough 65), Cassidy, Macdonald, Tudor, Hibbitt.
Coventry City
Glazier, Hindley, Holmes, Mortimer, Craven, Dugdale, Cartwright, Alderson, Cross, Carr, Hutchinson.

Alex Bruce

Sadly Missed

Harry Brown died on this day 1934, aged 50.
Midfield 1906-1907, Apps 25. Goals 10.
Arthur Metcalf died on this day in 1936, aged 46.
Midfield 1909-1912, Apps 12. Goals 2.

Charlie Spencer died on this day in 1953, aged 53.
Centre-half 1921-1928, Apps 175. Goals 1.

February 10

ASPRILLA LEADS THE UNITED FIGHTBACK
Surprise substitute inspires the Magpies

He arrived late in the day, wearing gloves, his team trailing. Within eleven minutes he had inspired another dramatic win for Newcastle, a victory which will have a significant influence on the race for the Premiership title. A seventh successive defeat was harsh on Middlesbrough and especially on their own latin gem, Juninho, but Asprilla's introduction to English football was the stuff of fantasy. The 26-year-old Colombian was supposed to have been watching the game from the stands, but Kevin Keegan surprised everyone by naming the new signing from Parma amongst the substitutes at the last minute. The first signs didn't inspire much confidence either, running out for the pre-match warm up Asprilla headed towards the Boro' players until he was steered in the right direction by the home side's coaching staff.

The inevitable frenzy of the opening spell produced an equally inevitable rash of errors. Newcastle gradually mustered a little order from the mayhem and Steve Watson might have done better than glance a header, from Beresford's centre, beyond the angle of bar and post. Newcastle's composure was in complete contrast to Boro's nervousness. Even when they won possession, the home side surrendered it again too easily, hitting the ball forward in desperation, only to find black-and-white shirts. Middlesbrough's optimism was raised in the most unlikeliest manner, Juninho outjumping Peacock which put Barmby in the clear. The end shot was blasted at Beresford's arm but the appeals for the penalty were rightly rejected. Boro', and Juninho in particular, had caught fire and after 36 minutes the boy from Brazil forced his team ahead. He drilled in a low cross from the left and Beresford, under pressure from Wilkinson, bundled it over the line.

Three times early in the second half Barmby might have extended Boro's advantage, and twice Peter Beardsley was crowded out at the other end. Then after 67 minutes, Asprilla was sent on for Gillespie, instantly running into an uncompromising tackle from Jamie Pollock. Undeterred, and after some attention by the physio, Asprilla then got up to create the equaliser just seven minutes later, his skill and cross providing a simple heading opportunity for Watson. In the 78th minute Newcastle went in front, Ferdinand's shot carried no venom yet somehow squirmed beneath the body of keeper Walsh. Newcastle held out to claim their first top-flight victory over Middlesbrough away from home since 1953.

Middlesbrough

Walsh, Cox, Morris, Vickers, Pearson, Barmby, Pollock, Whelan, Stamp, Juninho, Wilkinson.

Newcastle United

Srnicek, Barton, Beresford, Peacock, Clark, Lee, Albert, Gillespie (Asprilla), Ferdinand, Watson, Beardsley.

Referee Mr. S. Dunn (Bristol).

1894, FA Cup 2nd round.
Bolton Wanderers (h) 1-2   Att. 10,000
Crate
1906, Division 1.
Nottingham Forest (a) 1-2   Att. 7,000
Gosnell
1912, Division 1.
West Bromwich A. (a) 1-3   Att. 25,000
Lowes
1923, Division 1.
Cardiff City (a) 0-5   Att. 18,000
1934, Division 1.
Sheffield Wednesday (h) 0-0 Att. 14,169
1940, Wartime.
Hartlepool United (h) 3-0   Att. 4,333
Stubbins (2), Pearson
1945, Wartime.
Hartlepool United (h) 4-1   Att. 15,467
Stubbins (4)
1951, FA Cup 5th round.
Stoke City (a) 4-2   Att. 48,500
Milburn, Mitchell, G. Robledo (2)
1962, Division 2.
Southampton (h) 3-2   Att. 30,564
Thomas, Kerray, Neale
1968, Division 1.
Arsenal (a) 0-0   Att. 36,996
1973, Division 1.
Coventry City (h) 1-1   Att. 23,051
Barrowclough
1990, Division 2.
Portsmouth (a) 1-1   Att. 14,204
Quinn
1996, Premier League.
Middlesbrough 1   Newcastle 2
Beresford (og) 37   Watson 74
Ferdinand 78
Att. 30,011
Faustino Asprilla United's new £7.5 million striker from Italian side Parma makes his debut.

Playing record for this day is... 13 games, Won 5, Drawn 4, Lost 4, GF 21, GA 20. Today's success rate... 53.85%.

1900... Saints cup tie snowed off
Southampton 0 Newcastle United 0

Abandoned after 50 minutes, with a crowd of 10,000 present at the Dell. This game was rescheduled for February 17th and produced a 4-1 win for the Saints.

Keith Dyson born today in 1950.
Forward 1967-1971, Apps 98 (6 subs). Goals 26.
Dave Elliott born today in 1945.
Midfield 1966-1971, Apps 90 (4 subs). Goals 4.

Mike Hooper born today in 1964.
Goalkeeper 1993-1996, Apps 30 (2 subs).

Played on this day

1899, FA Cup 2nd round.
Liverpool (a) 1-3   Att. 7,000
Peddie

1905, Division 1.
Sheffield United (a) 3-1   Att. 15,000
Gosnell, McClarence, Opponent (og)

1911, Division 1.
Notts County (a) 2-2   Att. 10,000
Randall, Stewart

1920, Division 1.
Everton (h) 3-0   Att. 20,000
Robinson, Smailes (2)

1922, Division 1.
Arsenal (h) 3-1   Att. 30,000
Harris (2), McDonald

1924, FA Cup 2nd round, 2nd replay.
Derby County (n*) 2-2   Att. 17,300
Seymour, Hudspeth (pen)
Played at Burnden Park, Bolton.

1925, Division 1.
Bury (a) 0-0   Att. 6,000

1928, Division 1.
Blackburn Rovers (a) 0-1   Att. 10,000

1933, Division 1.
Huddersfield Town (a) 0-4   Att. 11,000

1939, FA Cup 5th round.
Preston North End (h) 1-2   Att. 62,327
Cairns

1956, Division 1.
Everton (a) 0-0   Att. 35,653

1961, Division 1.
Leicester City (a) 3-5   Att. 26,449
Allchurch, White (2)

1967, Division 1.
Everton (h) 0-3   Att. 31,214

1970, Division 1.
Southampton (h) 2-1   Att. 30,738
Davies, Smith

1984, Division 2.
Grimsby Town (h) 0-1   Att. 28,633

1989, Division 1.
Coventry City (a) 2-1   Att. 16,577
Hendrie, Mirandinha (pen)

1995, Premier League.
Newcastle 2   Nottingham Forest 1
Fox 47   Lee 74
Lee 73   Att. 34,471

2001, Premier League.
Charlton Athletic 2   Newcastle 0
Svensson 37
Bartlett 43   Att. 20,043

Playing record for this day is... 18 games,
Won 6, Drawn 4, Lost 8, GF 24, GA 30.
Today's success rate... 44.44%.

AT LAST, VICTORY OVER THE SAINTS
Fifth meeting this season ends in victory for United

Having already drawn three games (one league, two Inter Cities Fairs Cup) and suffered a humiliating 3-0 defeat in the FA Cup at the Dell, Newcastle finally gained some comfort today with a closely fought win over the Saints of Southampton. The visitors were up against it this time at St. James' Park being forced to start without their influential schemer Ron Davies and captain Terry Paine, both through injury.

Wyn Davies

Newcastle started shakily and were almost punished for their bad start after just ten minutes. A good move by the Saints allowed a shooting chance for Channon his effort rebounded of Moncur and fell invitingly for Saul. The return shot from seven yards beat McFaul but struck the underside of the bar, bounced down on the line and was eventually booted clear by the relieved McNamee. Southampton's route-one game was working well and the pacy Jenkins on the wing was getting the better of both full-backs as United continued to struggle. Then, against the run of play, Newcastle went ahead 1-0 in the 28th minute. A free kick taken by Robson was headed on by Wyn Davies, seemingly straight into the hands of keeper Martin. But up popped Jimmy Smith the £100,000 signing from Aberdeen, to nod the ball over Martin for his first goal in thirteen games for United. From this point on it was a different game. Now Newcastle thwarted the danger of the Saints' midfield. Fisher and Gabriel so dominant early on, were simply nowhere to be found. Roared on by their noisy 30,738 crowd United surged forward but by half-time had failed to increase their one-goal advantage.

The second half started notably with long airborne passes which worried the Saints' defence, and although Jenkins' pace countered this on occasions it was Newcastle who went 2-0 up after 79 minutes. Clark's long centre across the box was headed down and just inside the post by Wyn Davies, the unfortunate Martin slipping as he tried desperately to get across and keep it out. In the game's final minute Southampton gained a deserved consolation goal when striker Mick Channon seized on another rebound off Moncur to place the ball into an empty net.

Newcastle United
McFaul, Gibb, Clark, Elliott, McNamee, Moncur, Robson, Smith, W. Davies, Thomson, Dyson (Ford 69).
Southampton
Martin, Kirkup, Byrne, Fisher, McGrath, Gabriel, Stokes, Channon, Saul, Walker, Jenkins.

February 12

FIRST HALF BLITZ SEES OFF LIVERPOOL
Tudor, Macdonald, and Barrowclough on target

Newcastle's eager forwards overwhelmed a jittery Liverpool defence at a rain swept St. James' Park today. Despite the weather, a good crowd of 38,115 turned out to see a fabulous United performance in the first half which set up a good 4-1 victory. The win takes Newcastle up to eleventh place in the First Division table and denies their opponents the opportunity to go top of the league. Newcastle hit three goals in the first 22 minutes from John Tudor, Malcolm Macdonald, and Stuart Barrowclough. The lead could have been even more decisive by half-time such was United's overall first-half dominance.

Tudor, back after a three-match absence, scored the first after seven minutes with a close range drive. Then Macdonald stabbed in a right-foot shot in the fourteenth minute. Newcastle full of confidence, swept through for a third goal in the 22nd minute. Craig provided a telling pass, and Barrowclough timed his run perfectly to take the ball in his stride and shoot past keeper Clemence. Liverpool, who had hoped for victory to take them to the top of the table, attempted a revival through Hall, Toshack and Cormack all of whom should have beaten McFaul from Thompson's crosses. But back came Newcastle, and Macdonald and Nattrass might have increased the Magpies' lead before the half-time break.

Liverpool at last managed a goal in the 66th minute when Hall headed through from Heighway's corner. Their comeback however, was short-lived, Newcastle scoring their fourth goal just five minutes later. The goal was the result of some sloppy midfield play by Liverpool and allowed Smith to thread a pass to Macdonald who ran through and beat the advancing Clemence with a crisp low shot into the corner. Smith, whose skill had contributed much to Newcastle's sparkling performance, was then booked for a high and clumsy challenge on Liverpool's Callaghan in the 72nd minute.

Newcastle United

McFaul, Nattrass, Kennedy, Smith, Keeley, Howard, Barrowclough, Nulty, Macdonald, Tudor, Craig.

Liverpool

Clemence, Neal, Lindsay, Thompson, Cormack, Hughes, Keelan, Hall, Heighway, Toshack, Callaghan.

Played on this day

1898, FA Cup 2nd round.
Southampton (a) 0-1   Att. 14,000
1902, FA Cup 2nd round.
Sunderland (h) 1-0   Att. 23,000
Orr
1910, Division 1.
Manchester United (h) 3-4   Att. 30,000
Wilson, Higgins (2)
A disastrous second half for Newcastle after leading comfortably 3-0 at half time.
1921, Division 1.
Huddersfield Town (h) 1-0   Att. 45,000
Smailes
1927, Division 1.
Sheffield United (a) 1-2   Att. 40,000
Seymour
1938, Division 2.
Coventry City (a) 0-1   Att. 20,957
1944, Wartime.
Middlesbrough (h) 4-1   Att. 14,857
Stubbins (3), Opponent (og)
1955, Division 1.
Chelsea (a) 3-4   Att. 50,667
Keeble (2), Milburn
1966, FA Cup 4th round.
Sheffield Wednesday (h) 1-2 Att. 39,495
Suddick
1972, Division 1.
Manchester United (a) 2-0   Att. 44,983
Tudor, Barrowclough
1975, Division 1.
Liverpool(h) 4-1   Att. 38,115
Tudor, Macdonald (2), Barrowclough
1994, Premier League.
Wimbledon 4   Newcastle 2
Earle 9   Beardsley 50 (pen),
Blissett 26   90 (pen)
Fashanu 55
Holdsworth 63   Att. 13,358
2000, Premier League.
Newcastle 3   Manchester U. 0
Ferguson 26
Shearer 76, 86   Att. 36,470

Playing record for this day is... 13 games, Won 6, Drawn 0, Lost 7, GF 25, GA 20. Today's success rate... 46.15%.

NEWCASTLE UNITED

10ᵖ

FIRST DIVISION

VERSUS
LIVERPOOL

ST. JAMES' PARK
WED., 12th FEB., 1975
KICK-OFF 7.30 p.m.
VOL. 3, No. 20

Birthdays

Mick Harford born today in 1959.
Centre-forward 1980-1981 & 1982, Apps 19 (1 sub). Goals 4.

Played on this day

1904, Division 1.
Notts County (h) 4-1   Att. 16,000
Orr (2), Appleyard, Howie

1905, FA Cup 1st round, 2nd replay.
Plymouth Argyle (n*) 2-0   Att. 11,570
Orr (2, 1 pen)
Played at Manor Ground, London.

1909, Division 1.
Preston North End (a) 1-0   Att. 10,000
Anderson

1915, Division 1.
Manchester City (h) 2-1   Att. 18,000
King, Hibbert

1924, FA Cup 2nd round, 3rd replay
Derby County (h) 5-3   Att. 32,496
Seymour, Harris (3), Cowan

1926, Division 1.
Arsenal (a) 0-3   Att. 40,000

1932, FA Cup 5th round.
Leicester City (h) 3-1   Att. 43,354
Allen, Lang, Weaver

1937, Division 2.
Leicester City (a) 2-3   Att. 25,000
Cairns, Smith

1943, Wartime.
Sunderland (h) 2-3   Att. 20,500
Stubbins, Short

1954, Division 1.
Burnley (h) 3-1   Att. 29,114
Broadis (2), Milburn

1960, Division 1.
Leeds United (h) 2-1   Att. 16,148
Hughes, White

1965, Division 2.
Ipswich Town (h) 2-2   Att. 29,459
Suddick, Anderson

1971, Division 1.
Huddersfield Town (a) 1-1   Att. 15,580
Smith

1982, Division 2.
Cardiff City (h) 2-1   Att. 15,129
Varadi, Trewick

1988, Division 1.
Norwich City (h) 1-3   Att. 21,068
Gascoigne

1991, FA Cup 4th round.
Nottingham Foest (h) 2-2   Att. 29,231
Quinn, McGhee

1993, FA Cup 5th round.
Blackburn Rovers (a) 0-1   Att. 19,972

Playing record for this day is... 17 games,
Won 9, Drawn 3, Lost 5, GF 34, GA 27.
Today's success rate... 61.76%.

A RESULT AT LAST!

Newcastle finally end cup-tie deadlock to beat Rams

Newcastle entered this tie against Derby warily, and a little weary. This was the fourth attempt by these two sides to reach a conclusion to their FA Cup second round tie. So far this tie had been played at the Baseball Ground, Gallowgate and Burnden Park, and all had ended 2-2. Newcastle had won the toss of a coin, and therefore chose to play this game at St. James' Park, where a crowd of 32,496 turned out to watch the drama unfold.

It seemed from the outset that this would be Derby's day. Despite the absence of their star winger George Thornwell, Randolph Galloway managed to score twice for the Rams, putting them well into the lead quite early on.

It was an anxious wait to see if Newcastle had the fight left in them to stage a comeback, but the wait was not a long one. Within the space of 24 minutes, ace centre-forward Neil Harris scored a hat-trick, bringing United from two goals down to 3-2 in front.

It was eight minutes into the second half when the Magpies extended their lead, Seymour doing the honours, but Derby had not given up yet. In the 60th minute Harry Storer kept them in with a chance with a fine goal. the Rams were still fighting hard to stay in the game, and their efforts almost paid off, but luckily this was one match that wasn't going to include extra time.

The win was secured by a wonderful goal from Willie Cowan, bringing the final score to 5-3.

With 420 minutes of football in four games, this cup-tie is still the longest tie involving Newcastle United, and one of the longest in the history of the FA Cup. For Newcastle it was worth the wait. The Magpies made it to Wembley, where they won the trophy with a 2-0 win over Aston Villa.

Newcastle United
Mutch, Hampson, Hudspeth, Mooney, Spencer, Gibson, Low, Cowan, Harris, McDonald, Seymour.
Derby County
Olney, Chandler, Crilly, McIntyre, Thoms, Plackett, Keetley, Whitehouse, Galloway, Storer, Murphy.
Referee Mr. J.T. Howcroft (Bolton).

Charlie Spencer

Birthdays

Geoff Nulty born today in 1949.
Midfield/Centre-half 1974-1978, Apps 127.
Goals 14.

February 14

BATTLING BOLTON FORCE A REPLAY

Late drama at Burnden Park, United held 3-3

History and nostalgia were buried in stirring fashion at Bolton today by a match which quite simply demands to rank among the most climactic ties of its day. Apart from goals it had extreme contrasts of style, it had stamina, character, will and manliness and it deserved no end other than the heady ovation it received from the 46,880 crowd. The contrast was in the very flavour of the opponents, the stronger brew of bludgeoning aerial persistence which has carried Newcastle already to one final (this season), against the more varied and technically more skilful ground play of Bolton Wanderers.

The pulse raced from the first goal, after five minutes, to the last, six minutes from time. Peter Thompson, the former Liverpool winger, twice sent Macdonald the wrong way with matador's hip-swerves, then sent a pin-point cross to the far post with such accuracy that big Sam Allardyce had barely to stoop to nod in the opening goal. But although Bolton dominated the first half, Macdonald won it for Newcastle. His first goal, the equaliser on 32 minutes, was made by Cassidy's perceptive through ball which beat the offside trap for the United centre-forward to score easily with a left-foot shot inside the area. The second, a minute before half-time, was extraordinary, Craig took a throw out on the left, Macdonald, 25 yards out with his back to goal allowed the ball one bounce, half turned and with his unfavoured right-foot, volleyed the ball over Siddall before the keeper had even thought about moving for it. Perfect execution, audacious speculation, and although Macdonald naturally doesn't admit it, probably a little good fortune.

Bolton's effective response was less spectacular, coming just six minutes after the restart. A deft touch by Gary Jones sent the ball over Mahoney's head after Greaves' shot had caused a melee in the United goalmouth. Yet once more the sway of the match was wrestled from the home side by Cassidy, who began a four-man move with passes which proved Newcastle could link together on the ground and ended with what everyone thought was the winning goal for Gowling after 81 minutes. But final it was not allowed to be. Within a minute, Paul Jones outjumped everyone to head in Greaves' corner to send this memorable tie into a replay at St. James' Park on February 18.

Bolton Wanderers

Siddall, Ritson, P. Jones, Allardyce, Dunne, Greaves, Reid, Byrom, Whatmore, G. Jones, Thompson.

Newcastle United

Mahoney, Nattrass, Howard, Keeley, Kennedy, Cassidy, Nulty (Barrowclough 61), Craig, Burns, Gowling, Macdonald.

Referee Mr. B.J. Homewood (Sunbury-on-Thames).

1903, Division 1.
Middlesbrough (a) 0-1   Att. 20,000
1914, Division 1.
Chelsea (a) 1-0   Att. 35,000
Shepherd
1920, Division 1.
Bradford City (h) 0-1   Att. 45,000
1923, Division 1.
West Bromwich A. (h) 2-0   Att. 10,000
Seymour, J. Clark
1925, Division 1.
Liverpool (a) 1-1   Att. 35,000
Clark
1931, Division 1.
Middlesbrough (h) 0-5   Att. 35,000
1942, Wartime.
Rotherham United (h) 1-3   Att. 6,000
Woollett
1953, Division 1.
Manchester City (a) 1-2   Att. 24,898
Milburn
1976, FA Cup 5th round.
Bolton Wanderers (a) 3-3   Att. 46,880
Gowling, Macdonald (2)
1981, FA Cup 5th round.
Exeter City (h) 1-1   Att. 36,984
Shoulder
1987, Division 1.
Queens Park Rangers (a) 1-2   Att. 10,731
Goddard
1998, FA Cup 5th round.
Newcastle 1   Tranmere Rovers 0
Shearer 22   Att. 36,675
1999, FA Cup 5th round.
Newcastle 0   Blackburn Rovers 0
                               Att. 36,295

Playing record for this day is... 13 games, Won 3, Drawn 4, Lost 6, GF 12, GA 19. Today's success rate... 38.46%.

Kevin Keegan born today in 1951.
Forward & Manager 1982-1984 & 1992-1997,
Apps 85. Goals 49.

February 15

1896, FA Cup 2nd round.
Bury (h) **1-3**   Att. 14,250
Thompson
1902, Division 1.
Sheffield Wednesday (h) **2-1** Att. 15,000
Roberts, Veitch
1908, Division 1.
Manchester City (h) **1-1**   Att. 27,000
Willis
1913, Division 1.
Manchester City (h) **0-1**   Att. 35,000
1930, FA Cup 5th round.
Brighton & Hove A. (h) **3-0** Att. 56,469
Gallacher (3)
1936, FA Cup 5th round..
Arsenal (h) **3-3**   Att. 65,484
Pearson, J. Smith (2)
1939, Division 2.
Nottingham Forest (a) **0-2**   Att. 7,000
1941, Wartime.
Rochdale (h) **1-2**   Att. 4,385
McIntosh
1947, Division 2.
Southampton (h) **1-3**   Att. 50,516
Pearson
1969, Division 1.
Southampton (a) **0-0**   Att. 22,213
1975, Division 1.
Burnley (h) **3-0**   Att. 40,602
Macdonald (2), Barrowclough
1992, Division 2.
Blackburn Rovers (a) **1-3**   Att. 19,511
Kelly

Playing record for this day is... 12 games,
Won 3, Drawn 3, Lost 6, GF 16, GA 19.
Today's success rate... 37.50%.

Match of the Day from 1936

UNITED HELD AFTER SIX-GOAL THRILLER
Late United pressure not enough to beat Arsenal

A crowd of 65,484 people paid £4,430 for the privilege of seeing the Magpies take on the mighty Arsenal today, and every spectator must have felt he was given his money's worth. It was a game packed with excitement and one which will live long in the memories of those fortunate to get into St. James' Park, for thousands were turned away an hour before the kick off. It was not a game of brilliant football, but both sides put in so much effort and determination to win, the crowd were kept thoroughly thrilled in this typically tense cup-tie atmosphere. Although six goals were scored, it was the defences of both sides who took the honours of the day. In particular the brave and heroic Arsenal back line which stood up to the Newcastle attack as they lay siege on the visitors goal in the later stages of the second half.

It was the Londoners who started the better, but the Arsenal attack found the home full-backs and Davidson at centre half in great form. Something a little special was needed to crack such a tight unit and this was found by Arsenal after nine minutes. A nice run from James, who had had shaken off two defenders when turning sharply on the wing, sent him free and with enough time to pick out his team mate Hulme who was left with a simple shot from six yards out. Stung into action Newcastle hit back just four minutes later when Smith converted Pearson's cross to the far post with a powerful header. Arsenal continued to look the better side and in centre-forward Bowden, deputising for Drake, they had the best player on the field. Newcastle however kept themselves in the game by marshalling the Gunners' threat very well, on another day Arsenal may well have wrapped up this tie by half-time. With the interval approaching the visitors went back in front with a well-taken goal by Bastin, this was just reward for his, and the team's efforts during the first half.

Tommy Pearson

The second half was a complete contrast, now it was Newcastle and their forwards Smith, Connelly and Pearson looking the livelier, and Arsenal's back line were now at full stretch to contain them. Newcastle gained their second equaliser ten minutes into the half when Smith rose again to head in a corner taken by Bott. The goal galvanised the whole ground, and roared on by their noisy crowd Newcastle went in search of a winning goal. The enthusiasm and dash of the Magpies went unrewarded as a result of some desperate defending by Arsenal who were now pegged back deep in their own half, almost overrun by the intense pressure. However, it was the visitors through Bowden who exploited this cavalier attacking by gaining the advantage again in the 75th minute. A long clearance was charged down by Bowden who raced clear and chipped the ball over the advancing dive from keeper Tapken. The goal did not deter United and they continued to pile forward relentlessly, now looking to save the game. With nine minutes remaining they deservedly forced the tie into a replay at Highbury when a fine solo effort from Pearson put them level for the third time in the game.

Newcastle United
Tapken, Richardson, Garnham, Gordon, Davidson, Weaver, Bott, Ware, Smith, Connelly, Pearson.
Arsenal
Wilson, Male, Hapgood, Crayston, Sidey, Copping, Hulme, Bastin, Bowden, James, Beasley.

Sadly Missed

Andy Aitken died today in 1955, aged 77.
Half-back 1895-1906, Apps 349. Goals 41.

Match of the Day from 1974

UNITED END ALBION'S DREAM

Newcastle too good for Albion and march on to Wembley

A huge crowd of 42,699 turned out to watch this FA Cup tie against West Bromwich Albion at the Hawthorns. From the outset it looked likely that Newcastle would win this match and place themselves in the quarter finals of the competition. Albion, though, were keen to reproduce another promotion and FA Cup double having achieved this particular feat in 1931.

All the opening chances fell to the visiting side, and Albion were in despair at their lack of good play. Eighteen minutes into the game Newcastle had a stroke of bad luck that turned out to be a blessing in disguise. Terry Hibbitt was injured and had to leave the field of play. His replacement for the rest of the match was substitute Jim Smith. This change brought about an immediate effect on Newcastle. Smith's first touch of the ball almost resulted in the opening goal of the game. He fired his shot just a little too high and it scraped the woodwork as it skimmed over the crossbar.

Twelve minutes later and the elusive first goal arrived for Newcastle. It was Smith who provided the cross for Malcolm Macdonald, and he managed to get his head to the ball and score his twentieth goal of the season.

This lead gave Newcastle a big advantage over an already struggling Albion team. The Midlanders had hoped desperately for the first goal to be theirs, but when the visitors took the lead the home side became deflated.

The second half was to bring more misery for Albion. On 47 minutes Tudor mistimed his shot, but luck was on the side of the Magpies and the rebound fell to Barrowclough who made no mistake in hitting the back of the net past a flailing Latchford in the Albion goal.

Just three minutes later and the fate of the two sides was sealed. A lovely cross from Cassidy set the ball up well for Tudor to get his head to it and nod it into the goal to put Newcastle three goals ahead.

McFaul didn't have a completely easy ride in the Newcastle goal. He had to make two great saves from shots by Alan Glover and Tony Brown, but there was no other real threat for him to worry about.

It would be a huge uphill struggle for Albion to attempt a comeback at this late stage, and they didn't seem to be up for the challenge. Macdonald again made it through the Albion defence, and actually shot the ball into the back of the net, but for some reason the referee decided the goal would not stand and Albion were given a free kick instead. The kick amounted to nothing, and the disallowed goal didn't really affect Newcastle's resolve. They had already won the match easily and were on their way to the quarter finals for that infamous battle with Nottingham Forest.

West Bromwich Albion

Latchford, Nisbet, Wilson, Cantello, Wile, Robertson, Johnston, T. Brown, Shaw, Hartford, Glover.

Newcastle United

McFaul, Craig, Clark, McDermott, Howard, Moncur, Barrowclough, Cassidy, Macdonald, Tudor, Hibbitt (Smith 18).

Birthdays

Christian Bassedas born today in 1973.
Midfield 2000-2003, Apps 33 (8 subs). Goals 1.

Sadly Missed

Eddie Connelly died on this day in 1990, aged 73.
Midfield 1935-1938, Apps 30. Goals 9.

Played on this day

1895, FA Cup 2nd round.
Aston Villa (a) 1-7   Att. 9,000
Thompson
1901, Division 1.
Derby County (a) 1-1   Att. 7,000
Peddie
1907, Division 1.
Manchester City (a) 1-1   Att. 35,000
Brown
1924, Division 1.
Notts County (a) 0-1   Att. 10,000
1929, Division 1.
Leeds United (a) 0-0   Att. 20,000
1935, Division 2.
Swansea Town (h) 5-1   Att. 9,000
Cairns (3), Imrie, Murray
1946, Wartime.
Barnsley (a) 3-1   Att. 16,900
Wayman, Hair, Milburn
1952, Division 1.
Wolverhampton W. (a) 0-3   Att. 42,000
1957, Division 1.
Luton Town (a) 1-4   Att. 21,003
Milburn
1970, Division 1.
Liverpool (a) 0-0   Att. 38,218
1974, FA Cup 5th round.
West Bromwich A. (a) 3-0   Att. 42,699
Tudor, Macdonald, Barrowclough
1977, Division 1.
Manchester City (h) 2-2   Att. 28,954
Burns (2)
1985, Division 1.
Chelsea (a) 0-1   Att. 21,806

Playing record for this day is... 13 games, Won 3, Drawn 5, Lost 5, GF 17, GA 22. Today's success rate... 42.31%.

Malcolm Macdonald

February 17

Played on this day

1894, Division 2.
Rotherham Town (h) 4-0   Att. 6,000
Wallace, Crate, Quinn, Graham

1900, FA Cup 2nd round.
Southampton (a) 1-4   Att. 8,000
Peddie

1912, Division 1.
Sunderland (h) 3-1   Att. 45,000
Anderson, Lowes, Stewart

1932, Division 1.
Bolton Wanderers (h) 3-1   Att. 25,000
Cape, Lang, Weaver

1945, Wartime.
Darlington (h) 3-1   Att. 19,899
Taylor, Pearson, Stubbins

1951, Division 1.
Sheffield Wednesday (h) 2-0   Att. 47,075
G. Robledo, Taylor

1962, Division 2.
Luton Town (a) 0-1   Att. 9,040

1973, Division 1.
Wolverhampton W. (a) 1-1   Att. 22,147
Hibbitt

1979, Division 2.
Leicester City (a) 1-2   Att. 15,106
Nattrass

1999, Premier League.
Newcastle 4   Coventry City 1
Shearer 19, 75   Whelan 18
Speed 55
Saha 58   Att. 36,352

2002, FA Cup 5th round.
Newcastle 1   Manchester City 0
Solano 59   Att. 51,020

Playing record for this day is... 11 games,
Won 7, Drawn 1, Lost 3, GF 23, GA 12.
Today's success rate... 68.18%.

Match of the Day from 1999

SHEARER BRACE SINKS COVENTRY

Sky Blues' St. James' Park misery continues

Just to underline his importance to England's cause no matter who picks the team, Alan Shearer scored twice as Newcastle once again made light work of Coventry City, taking their tally to nine goals over the Midlanders in two Premiership matches. As at Highfield Road back in September, Gordon Strachan's side made the mistake of taking an early lead, and then suffered the consequences. A convincing win for United and their manager Ruud Gullit now takes the Magpies into the top half of the Premiership table, and a position of regional prominence, above Middlesbrough. The victory was dominated by the performances of Gullit's two Englishmen in the United side, such has been the change on Tyneside since the departure of Kevin Keegan two years ago. One, Steve Howey, gave a solid defensive show whilst Shearer began his side's comeback with a superb individual goal.

The Sky Blues made the perfect start when Noel Whelan reacted quickest to Darren Huckerby's cross from the left, controlling the ball on his chest and beating Shay Given. The lead lasted less than a minute thanks to Shearer. Taking Louis Saha's pass in his stride, he outpaced two defenders beating Magnus Hedman with an emphatic right-foot shot.

Newcastle went ahead in the 55th minute when Gary Speed ran on to Shearer's pass to prod the ball under Hedman. Four minutes later the unmarked Saha headed home Nolberto Solano's corner at the near post. The two-goal margin had a soporific effect on the match, though George Boateng's challenge sent Stephen Glass to the dressing room on a stretcher nursing his right knee. The only surprise about Shearer's second goal, his thirteenth of the season, was that he passed on responsibility for a direct free kick to Dietmar Hamann. The German produced a venomous shot which was brilliantly parried by Hedman, but the ball fell loose to Shearer and he accepted the easiest of chances, a yard out in front of an open goal.

Newcastle United
Given, Charvet, Dabizas, Howey, Domi, Hamann, Solano, Speed (Barton 86), Glass (Brady 67), Shearer, Saha (Ketsbaia 77).

Coventry City
Hedman, Nilsson, Shaw, Konjic, Burrows, Boateng, Soltvedt (Clement 68), McAllister, Froggatt, Huckerby (Aloisi 76), Whelan.

Gary Speed fires in Newcastle's second goal.

Birthdays

Jack Smith born today in 1915.
Centre-forward 1934-1938, Apps 112. Goals 73.

Sadly Missed

John Alderson died today 1972, aged 80.
Goalkeeper 1913-1919, Apps 1.

February 18

UNLUCKY STOKE OUSTED BY UNITED

Defeat is harsh for game performance by City

If poor old Stoke had possessed the finishing power of their opponents, and more significantly enjoyed a little piece of the large slice of Newcastle's luck, then this tie may have been a far different story. Stoke's only mistake was severely punished on the stroke of half-time, then they endured the loss through injury to Wilshaw, their best player, after the break. Add to this a harshly awarded penalty which was not even appealed for by the 46,253 crowd, and the visitors had every right to feel aggrieved. Newcastle, however, played well for their victory with goals from Scanlon, Allchurch, and McKinney's penalty that set up the 3-1 result. The Magpies now face Sheffield United at St. James' Park on March 4th in the FA Cup 6th round.

A keenly fought match for much of the first half was finally rewarded with a goal right on the last whistle when Stoke's reliable defence made a terrible error. A bad pass and an unfortunate slip allowed Scanlon to pounce, within a split second he had controlled the ball, raced into the area and blasted a low shot into the bottom corner from a slight angle. As the teams left the field it was noticeable that Wilshaw, the Stoke forward who had been a thorn in the United side much of the game so far, was limping badly after a challenge near the end of the half. He didn't failed to reappear for the restart, and Stoke's hopes of getting back in the game were now looking desperate.

Without Wilshaw the visitors' threat was minimal, it also allowed the Newcastle midfield and forwards more time and space to cause their own trouble. With ten minutes of the second half gone a shot by Scanlon came back off the post and straight to the feet of Allchurch, he couldn't quite believe his luck, tapping the ball into the empty net for a simple 2-0 lead. The tie was as good as won now for United, but for anyone who had doubts, Stoke were finished when McKinney whacked in a third from the penalty spot eight minutes later. It was a harsh decision by the referee, and one had to feel for the Stoke players who had made such a fight of the game. A shot from Allchurch must of been travelling 100 mph when it struck a defender's arm in the penalty area, then as the game continued the Stoke players looked back in total disbelief to see the referee pointing to the spot. Even the crowd fell silent wondering exactly what play had been stopped for. Without further explanation, and Stoke obviously too stunned to argue, McKinney placed the ball neatly on the spot then lashed it into the roof of the net; game over. To their credit the Potters never gave in after this and got a deserved consolation goal fourteen minutes from time through a fine strike from King. Then in the last minute following more pressure from the ten men, Bentley struck the bar with a rasping shot from outside the penalty area.

Newcastle United

Mitchell, Keith, McKinney, Neale, Thompson, Bell, Hughes, Woods, White, Allchurch, Scanlon.

Stoke City

O'Neill, Wilson, Allen, Howitt, Andrews, Skeels, Bentley, Asprey, King, Ratcliffe, Wilshaw.

Birthdays

Sir Bobby Robson born today in 1933.
Manager 1999-Present day.

Keith Gillespie born today in 1975.
Winger 1995-1998, Apps 147 (26 subs). Goals 14.

John Ryan born today in 1962.
Left-back 1983-1984, Apps 31. Goals 1.

Paul Dalglish born today in 1977.
Forward 1997-1999, Apps 13 (5 subs). Goals 2.

Jermaine Jenas born today in 1983.
Midfield 2002-present day, Apps 53 (15 subs). Goals 7.

Sadly Missed

Robert Bradley died today in 1934, aged 27
Right-back 1927-1929, Apps 1. Goals 0.

Played on this day

1899, Division 1.
Bury (h) 2-0   Att. 16,000
Peddie (2)

1905, FA Cup 2nd round.
Tottenham Hotspur (a) 1-1   Att. 19,013
Howie

1911, Division 1.
Manchester United (h) 0-1   Att. 45,000

1928, Division 1.
Bolton Wanderers (h) 2-2   Att. 28,932
McCurley, Urwin

1933, Division 1.
Sheffield United (h) 2-0   Att. 8,000
Betton, J.R. Richardson

1939, Division 2.
Tranmere Rovers (a) 3-0   Att. 9,155
Clifton, Stubbins, Gordon

1950, Division 1.
Stoke City (a) 0-1   Att. 28,000

1956, FA Cup 5th round.
Stoke City (h) 2-1   Att. 61,550
Curry, Mitchell

1961, FA Cup 5th round.
Stoke City (h) 3-1   Att. 46,253
Scanlon, Allchurch, McKinney (pen)

1967, FA Cup 4th round.
Nottingham Forest (a) 0-3   Att. 45,962

1976, FA Cup 5th round, replay.
Bolton Wanderers (h) 0-0   Att. 52,760

1981, FA Cup 5th round, replay.
Exeter City (a) 0-4   Att. 17,668

1984, Division 2.
Manchester City (a) 2-1   Att. 41,767
Beardsley, Keegan

1990, FA Cup 5th round.
Manchester United (h) 2-3   Att. 31,805
McGhee (pen), Scott

1991, FA Cup 4th round, replay.
Nottingham Forest (a) 0-3   Att. 28,962

2003, Champions League, Group A.
Bayer
Leverkusen 1   Newcastle 3
Franca 25   Ameobi 5, 15
     LuaLua 32
     Att. 22,500

Playing record for this day is... 16 games,
Won 7, Drawn 3, Lost 6, GF 22, GA 22.
Today's success rate... 53.12%.

Played on this day

1898, Division 2.
Luton Town (a) **1-3**   Att. 3,500
R. Allan

1910, FA Cup 3rd round.
Blackburn Rovers (h) **3-1**   Att. 54,772
Higgins, Howie, Rutherford

1921, FA Cup 3rd round.
Everton (a) **0-3**   Att. 54,205

1927, FA Cup 5th round.
Southampton (a) **1-2**   Att. 21,408
McDonald (pen)

1936, FA Cup 5th round, replay.
Arsenal (a) **0-3**   Att. 62,391

1938, Division 2.
Nottingham Forest (h) **3-1**   Att. 17,000
Bowden, J.R. Richardson, Imrie (pen)

1944, Wartime.
Darlington (h) **2-0**   Att. 12,500
Stubbins (2, 1 pen)

1949, Division 1.
Manchester City (a) **0-1**   Att. 48,624

1955, FA Cup 5th round.
Nottingham Forest (a) **1-1**   Att. 25,252
Milburn

1966, Division 1.
Northampton Town (a) **1-3**   Att. 14,541
Iley

1972, Division 1.
Everton (h) **0-0**   Att. 29,584

1977, Division 1.
Manchester United (a) **1-3**   Att. 51,828
Nulty

1983, Division 2.
Oldham Athletic (h) **1-0**   Att. 20,689
McDermott

1995, FA Cup 5th round.
Newcastle **3**   Manchester City **1**
Gillespie 18, 64   Rosler 29
Beresford 34   Att. 33,219

1994, Premier League.
Blackburn Rovers **1** Newcastle **0**
May 76   Att. 21,269

Playing record for this day is... 15 games,
Won 5, Drawn 2, Lost 8, GF 17, GA 23.
Today's success rate... 40%.

Match of the Day from 1995

TWO-GOAL GILLESPIE PROVES HIS WORTH
Awesome display from the new boy helps beat City

Kevin Keegan was adamant when the furore over the sale of Andy Cole was at its most intense, that the £7 million deal would prove a good piece of business for Newcastle United. The performance of Keith Gillespie today indicated that the manager's confidence was not misplaced. The label of makeweight was almost an insult to Gillespie, already a full Northern Ireland international and regarded by Alex Ferguson as one of the most exciting prospects to emerge from Manchester United's flourishing production line of outstanding teenagers. His value in the part-exchange record transfer was put at £1 million, but he is already worth much more than that. His contribution to an eventful FA Cup fifth round tie against Manchester City did most to thrust Newcastle into the quarter finals for the first time in nineteen years.

Though Gillespie's first goal for his new club was highly controversial, he thoroughly deserved that crucial twentieth minute breakthrough. The second a 65th minute tap in, finally broke City's resistance. Gillespie, twenty years old yesterday, was denied a hat-trick when another effort unfortunately struck the inside of a post. His mesmerising dribbling eventually led to the withdrawal of his marker, David Brightwell, and sapped the morale of the other City players so eager to ease the pressure now on manager Brian Horton.

Horton must have thought the fates were against him when his frantic touchline protests against the opening goal were rejected by referee Ashby, who had judged that Newcastle striker Paul Kitson was not interfering with play when flagged offside. That allowed Gillespie to make a suspect challenge on Brightwell and force the ball into the City penalty area where Andy Dibble had adequate time to make a routine clearance. Instead the keeper, a late replacement for the injured Tony Coton, hesitated on the ball and Gillespie charged it down and nodded it over the line.

Gillespie's second came after the influential Peter Beardsley danced round Alan Kernaghan and chipped the ball to the far post where the hapless Brightwell wanted more time to clear than the winger was prepared to concede. In between John Beresford, formerly on the Maine Road payroll but released by Billy McNeil, restored Newcastle's advantage with the second fluke goal of the afternoon ten minutes before the interval. The United full-back was clearly trying to chip towards Paul Kitson at the far post but the ball looped over a disbelieving Dibble and into the corner of the net. That was a cruel blow for City who had fought back to parity five minutes earlier through Uwe Rosler. That also owed much to eccentric goalkeeping, this time by Pavel Srnicek, who dropped Peter Beagrie's corner allowing Rosler to swivel and drive the ball into the roof of the net.

Newcastle United
Srnicek, Hottiger, Howey, Peacock, Beresford, Venison, Gillespie, Lee, Fox, Beardsley, Kitson.

Manchester City
Dibble, I.Brightwell, Curle, Kernaghan, D.Brightwell (Foster 74), Summerbee, Gaudino, Flitcroft, Beagrie, Quinn (Mike 84), Rosler.

Referee Mr. G. Ashby (Worcester).

Keith Gillespie is mobbed after scoring against Manchester City.

Birthdays

Ray Blackhall born today in 1957.
Right-back 1973-1978, Apps 47 (14 subs). Goals 2.

Sadly Missed

Bob Benson died today in 1916, aged 33.
Right-back 1902-1904, Apps 1. Goals 0.

February 24

SOLID SECOND HALF SEES OFF WOLVES' THREAT

Elliott and Robson add to the midlanders' problems

Newcastle United swept away a sound defensive display by Wolves in the second half today, and stretched their unbeaten home league record to 21 games. Wolves on the other hand, have solved one problem only to run slap into another at St. James' Park, and this result puts them in real danger of dropping back into Division Two. For the past few week Wolves have needed to tighten up their defence. This they did against a confident Newcastle side, only to find their attack was completely ineffective. Derek Parkin, who became Britain's costliest full-back when he moved from the Second Division to the First Division for £80,000, looks as though he may well be going back again next season.

Despite all this, Wolves' first half performance was better than many they have given in recent weeks and they might have been ahead by the interval. Wilson had the ball in the net in the sixteenth minute only to have the effort disallowed for a foul by Dougan on United keeper Gordon Marshall. Then David Woodfield was denied a goal with a spectacular overhead kick which was cleared off the line by the alert Frank Clark. But the best move of the half involved Knowles, Bailey and Thompson which set up a superb volley from Kennedy, which flashed past the United post by inches. The half time score of 0-0 was a real credit to the visitors resolve after their numerous problems of late which have seen them slide down the table.

Any hopes the Wolves had of gaining a point, though, were dashed early in the second half. Just five minutes after the restart Dave Elliott, from the right-hand edge of the penalty area, turned beautifully to hammer in a left-foot shot which beat Phil Parkes and flew into the top right-hand corner of the net. Newcastle, who have not been beaten at St. James' Park in the League for just over a year, looked likely to keep that impressive record going further. Wolves' lack of thrust in attack finally piled so much pressure on their defence that they cracked again four minutes from time. Ollie Burton booted a hopeful ball forward from well inside his own half and Parkin committed himself to a tackle on Tommy Robson but, on the greasy surface, he mistimed the challenge. Robson was left to charge forward completely alone and put the ball into the inviting empty net.

Newcastle United

Marshall, Burton, Clark, Elliott, McNamee, Moncur, Sinclair, Scott, Davies, B. Robson, T. Robson.

Wolverhampton Wanderers

Parkes, Parkin, Thompson, Monro, Woodfield, Holsgrove, Kenning, Knowles, Dougan, Bailey, Wilson.

Sadly Missed

Joe Harvey died on this day in 1989, aged 70.
Defender & Manager 1945-1955 & 1962-1989,
Apps 281. Goals 13.

Played on this day

1894, Division 2.
Grimsby Town (h) 4-1   Att. 4,000
Crate, Thompson, Quinn, Jeffrey.

1906, FA Cup 3rd round.
Blackpool (h) 5-0   Att. 34,405
Orr (2), Appleyard, Gardner,
Opponent (og)

1909, FA Cup 3rd round, replay.
West Ham United (h) 2-1   Att. 36,526
Anderson, Shepherd (pen)

1912, Division 1.
Preston North End (h) 1-0   Att. 25,000
Hay

1934, Division 1.
Arsenal (h) 0-1   Att. 35,000

1945, Wartime.
Darlington (a) 3-2   Att. 8,920
Stubbins, Carr (2)

1951, FA Cup 6th round.
Bristol Rovers (h) 0-0   Att. 63,000

1962, Division 2.
Charlton Athletic (a) 1-1   Att. 16,935
Allchurch

1968, Division 1.
Wolverhampton W. (h) 2-0   Att. 35,431
Elliott, T. Robson

1973, Division 1.
Norwich City(a) 1-0   Att. 26,411
Macdonald

1979, Division 1.
Sunderland (h) 1-4   Att. 34,733
Connolly

1982, Division 2.
Sheffield Wednesday (h) 1-0 Att. 19,174
Varadi

1990, Division 2.
Sheffield United (a) 1-1   Att. 21,035
Morris (og)

1993, Division 1.
Bristol Rovers (h) 0-0   Att. 29,372

1996, Premier League.
Manchester City 3   Newcastle 3
Quinn 16, 62   Albert 44, 81
Rosler 77   Asprilla 71
                    Att. 31,115

1999, FA Cup 5th round, replay.
Blackburn Rovers 0 Newcastle 1
                    Saha 37
                    Att. 27,483

2001, Premier League.
Newcastle 0   Manchester City 1
                    Goater 61
                    Att. 51,981

2002, Premier League.
Sunderland 0   Newcastle 1
                    Dabizas 64
                    Att. 48,290

Playing record for this day is... 18 games,
Won 10, Drawn 5, Lost 3, GF 27, GA 15.
Today's success rate... 69.44%.

February 25

Played on this day

1899, Division 1.
Preston North End (h) 2-1   Att. 15,000
MacFarlane, Peddie (pen)
1905, Division 1.
Preston North End (h) 1-0   Att. 20,000
Appleyard
1911, FA Cup 3rd round.
Hull City (h) 3-2   Att. 46,531
Shepherd (2), Veitch
1922, Division 1.
Blackburn Rovers (h) 2-0   Att. 25,000
J. Low, Woods
1928, Division 1.
Sheffield Wednesday (a) 0-0 Att. 20,000
1939, Division 2.
West Ham United(h) 2-0   Att. 30,000
Pearson (pen), Cairns
1950, Division 1.
Burnley (h) 0-0   Att. 30,032
1954, Division 1.
Charlton Athletic (a) 0-0   Att. 13,441
1956, Division 1.
Arsenal (h) 2-0   Att. 50,822
Curry, Milburn
1961, Division 1.
Aston Villa (h) 2-1   Att. 21,275
White (2)
1967, Division 1.
Arsenal (h) 2-1   Att. 27,463
Davies, Hilley
1970, Division 1.
Chelsea (a) 0-0   Att. 35,341
1978, Division 1.
Ipswich Town (h) 0-1   Att. 22,264
1981, Division 2.
Cardiff City (a) 0-1   Att. 4,235
1984, Division 2.
Cardiff City (h) 3-1   Att. 27,964
Waddle, Keegan (2, 1 pen)
1995, Premier League.
Newcastle 3   Aston Villa 1
Venison 31   Townsend 40
Beardsley 55, 66   Att. 34,637

Playing record for this day... 16 games,
Won 10, Drawn 4, Lost 2, GF 22, GA 9.
Today's success rate... 75%.

Match of the Day from 1995

IN TOON BEARDSLEY SINKS VILLA
Vintage display from the 'old' master

On the face of it, this looked like a regulation home win, indeed it was, the 3-1 scoreline could in fact been greater if not for the brilliance of Villa keeper Mark Bosnich. But, the 34,637 crowd at St. James' Park would have to concede the game was a far closer contest, but for one man. The fundamental difference between third-place Newcastle and the now relegation-threatened Villa side, was Peter Beardsley. Even at 34 you wouldn't bet against Beardsley having a major impact for England in next year's European Championship finals. His first goal was a perfect illustration of clinical finishing, his second was sheer magic, certainly too mesmerising for the two people with the closest view, Gary Charles and Paul McGrath. Beardsley would have had a well-deserved hat-trick but for a spectacular save by Bosnich who also produced a moment of brilliance to keep out a Darren Peacock header. If there was ultimately no argument about the outcome, the undisputed fact is that for nearly an hour Villa were the more enterprising side. Only in the later stages, when Keith Gillespie and Ruel Fox cut loose down the flanks, did the Midlanders look vulnerable defensively.

All Villa lacked during their imposing opening was the killer touch to finish off some cultured approach play which frequently had the Magpies chasing shadows. Even Barry Venison's 32nd minute strike, his first goal for the club, failed to throw Villa out of their stride. An Andy Townsend equaliser four minutes before half-time was stunning enough to warrant inclusion in the BBC's Goal of the Month competition, and Villa looked at this stage perfectly capable of claiming a point.

In the second half however, the threat of Dwight Yorke and Ian Taylor was snuffed out easily by Peacock and Beresford at the heart of United's defence. The supply of crosses from the impressive Steve Staunton dried up thanks to Steve Howey's eagerness after the half-time 'talking to' by Kevin Keegan. This left Townsend battling to stem the flow of United's increasingly menacing runs from midfield as the game progressed and in the end it became an impossible task. Once Beardsley had inflicted his damage in the 55th and 66th minutes, there was no way back for the visitors, and Newcastle, in the end, might have won by a far greater margin.

Newcastle United
Srnicek, Hottiger, Howey, Peacock, Beresford, Venison, Fox, Lee, Kitson, Beardsley, Gillespie.
Aston Villa
Bosnich, Charles, Ehiogu, McGrath, Teale (Atkinson 85), Staunton, Townsend, Taylor, Yorke, Johnson, Saunders.
Referee Mr. P. Don (Middlesex).

Ruel Fox

Birthdays

Bill Paterson born today in 1930.
Centre-half 1954-1958, Apps 27. Goals 2.

Match of the Day from 2003

SHEAR BRILLIANCE

Hat-trick hero Shearer keeps hopes up for Newcastle

Newcastle had made Champions' League history in the run up to this match against Bayer Leverkusen. They are the first team to lose their first three ties in the first stage and yet still qualify for the next round.

Newcastle had beaten Leverkusen just eight days previously and were hoping to secure this victory to add another three points to their total.

Alan Shearer was in the side for this tie, and it was a good job too. He was crucial to play right from the outset, and it took just five minutes for the striker to make his presence felt. A centre from Gary Speed sailed over the head of Cris, and was perfectly placed for Shearer to get his head to the ball and send it straight into the back of the net.

Just five minutes later Cris had possession of the ball, but his carelessness proved costly. He lost the ball to Shearer who sent it through to Shola Ameobi. He came through the defence unchallenged and sent the ball goalwards. It was thumped away from goal by Leverkusen keeper Butt, and came to Cris. He failed to keep control, and the ball fell to Shearer again who finished the move with a sure shot into the net from just two yards.

Before this match Shearer had never scored from open play in the Champions League. Two penalties were all he had managed, and only one of those was for Newcastle, the other being for Blackburn. Now he was on a hat-trick, and seemed to be unstoppable in his ability to be in the right place at the right time.

It was debatable as to whose side Cris was on in this match, and Leverkusen seemed to have similar worries. He was substituted after 30 minutes, and Newcastle felt they had lost a friend.

Newcastle keeper Shay Given was lucky not to have been shown the red card after his needless tackle on Franca. However the Danish referee decided that Leverkusen had not lost a goalscoring opportunity, and therefore the Newcastle keeper got away without even a stern word.

Shortly afterwards Leverkusen were given the opportunity to get back into the game, and perhaps gain some justice for the decision of the referee not to punish Given for felling Franca. A penalty was awarded and swiftly taken by Olivier Neuville, but it was certainly not a good night for the German team. Shay Given anticipated the kick well and saved the penalty, much to the frustration of the Leverkusen fans.

Shearer ensured the win for Newcastle with the completion of his fifteenth career hat trick. It was his third hat-trick for Newcastle and the goal came in the form of a penalty. Thomas Kleine had pulled Kieron Dyer, and the resulting kick brought the score to 3-0.

Leverkusen pulled a goal back in the 64th minute with a lovely shot from Marko Babic, this being only the seventh goal Newcastle had conceded in seven games. Then a fine chance from Kleine amounted to nothing when his header hit the bar from a corner.

Shearer had the opportunity to equal Marco van Basten and Simone Inzaghi's record of being the only players to score four goals in a Champions League tie, but it wasn't to be. However, this didn't disappoint the Newcastle fans too much. They had won 3-1, and that was good enough for them.

Newcastle United
Given, Griffin, Caldwell, Bramble, Bernard, Kerr (Viana 82), Dyer (Solano 70), Speed, Robert, Ameobi, Shearer (LuaLua 81).

Bayer Leverkusen
Butt, Preuss, Kleine, Cris (Zivkovic 30), Placente, Ramelow (Babic h/t), Kaluzny, Neuville (Brdaric 62), Basturk, Simak, Franca.

Referee Mr. B. Larsen (Denmark).

Played on this day

1898, Division 2.
Lincoln City (h) 3-0 — Att. 10,000
Wardrope (2), Smith

1910, Division 1.
Sheffield Wednesday (h) 3-1 — Att. 8,000
Shepherd, Howie, McWilliam

1913, FA Cup 3rd round, replay.
Liverpool (h) 1-0 — Att.39,769
Hudspeth (pen)

1921, Division 1.
Middlesbrough (h) 2-0 — Att. 40,000
Smailes, Aitken

1927, Division 1.
Liverpool (a) 2-1 — Att. 34,000
Seymour (2)

1936, Division 2.
Charlton Athletic (a) 2-4 — Att. 15,000
J. Smith, Imrie (pen)

1938, Division 2.
Aston Villa (h) 2-0 — Att. 47,782
Cairns, Park

1944, Wartime.
Darlington (a) 2-8 — Att. 5,000
Stubbins (2)

1955, Division 1.
Sunderland (h) 1-2 — Att. 62,835
Milburn

1966, Division 1.
Stoke City (h) 3-1 — Att. 26,201
Suddick (2), Hilley

1972, Division 1.
Southampton(a) 2-1 — Att. 18,884
Macdonald (pen), Barrowclough

1977, Division 1.
Tottenham Hotspur (h) 2-0 — Att. 30,230
Gowling, Burns

1983, Division 2.
Fulham (a) 2-2 — Att. 14,277
McDermott, Varadi

1989, Division 1.
Middlesbrough (a) 1-1 — Att. 24,385
O'Brien

2000, Premier League.
Sheffield Wed. 0   Newcastle 2
Gallacher 11
Shearer 86
Att. 29,212

2003, Champions' League, Group A.
Newcastle 3   Bayer Leverkusen 1
Shearer 5, 11,   Babic 73
36 (pen)   Att. 40,508

Playing record for this day is... 16 games, Won 11, Drawn 2, Lost 3, GF 33, GA 22. Today's success rate... 75%.

February 27

Played on this day

1902, FA Cup 3rd round, replay.
Sheffield United (a) 1-2   Att. 20,000
McColl
1904, Division 1.
Wolverhampton W. (a) 2-3   Att. 5,000
McColl, Howie
1909, Division 1.
Manchester City (a) 2-0   Att. 25,000
Jobey, Stewart
1911, Division 1.
Liverpool (a) 0-3   Att. 8,000
1915, Division 1.
Sheffield United (a) 0-1   Att. 15,000
1924, Division 1.
Huddersfield Town (a) 1-1   Att. 6,000
Seymour
1926, Division 1.
Sunderland (a) 2-2   Att. 36,000
Mordue, Urwin
1932, FA Cup 6th round.
Watford (h) 5-0   Att. 57,879
Allen (3), Boyd, J.R. Richardson
1943, Wartime.
Gateshead (a) 6-2   Att. 9,500
Carr (2), Stubbins (4)
An amazing scoring season continues for Stubbins. This is his sixth hat trick of the season, and his goals scored total now stands at 31.
1954, Division 1.
Wolverhampton W. (a) 2-3   Att. 38,592
Broadis, Milburn
1960, Division 1.
Arsenal (a) 0-1   Att. 47,657
1965, Division 2.
Bury (h) 2-3   Att. 33,923
Suddick, Anderson
1971, Division 1.
Manchester United (a) 0-1   Att. 41,902
1982, Division 2.
Derby County (a) 2-2   Att. 12,257
Waddle, Varadi
1988, Division 1.
Chelsea (h) 3-1   Att. 17,858
Mirandinha (2), Gascoigne
1991, Division 2.
Brighton & Hove A. (h) 0-0   Att. 12,692

Playing record for this day is... 16 games,
Won 4, Drawn 4, Lost 8, GF 28, GA 25.
Today's success rate... 37.50%.

Match of the Day from 1988

UNITED'S RECOVERY CONTINUES

Chelsea's problems increase after two penalty misses

Newcastle's steady push up the First Division table continued in dramatic fashion today at St. James' Park. United were a worrying eighteenth place in the table at the start of November, but having now won six games from fourteen they have climbed up to a more respectable eleventh place. A crowd of 17,858 witnessed an amazing game that had everything. As well as three United goals to cheer there was a controversial goal from the visitors, two penalty saves from United keeper Gary Kelly, and a sending off for Newcastle's Kenny Wharton.

Mirandinha found his scoring touch again, his first goal since New Year's Day giving United an early lead. The Brazilian then scored his twelfth of the season to put United 2-0 up after 31 minutes. Chelsea, without a win since October, were then given some hope when awarded a penalty eight minutes later for handball. Micky Hazard took the kick but Kelly guessed correctly diving to his right to push the ball out for a corner.

Chelsea battled well despite their troubles and probably deserved their huge slice of luck in the 67th minute when Kevin Wilson, a mile offside, reduced the deficit to just the one goal, this after being introduced as a sub for Roy Wergerle just seconds earlier. The hope of a point soon disappeared however when Paul Gascoigne drove in Newcastle's third after 73 minutes, but Chelsea refused to lie down. Just three minutes later Pat Nevin skipped clear of the United defence with only Wharton close to him. As the Chelsea winger entered the area Wharton clearly pulled him back by the shirt. To make matters worse for the Newcastle full-back he then slung the ball at the prostrate Nevin and referee Harrison had no option but to send the Newcastle man off. This time the spot kick was left to Kevin Wilson, who decided to place the ball to Kelly's left, once again the keeper guessed correctly and smothered the ball in his chest. The ten men saw out the remaining fourteen minutes without further trouble or incident, and registered another important league win, their hopes of a top ten finish now looking very likely.

Newcastle United
Kelly, McDonald, Wharton, McCreery, P. Jackson, Roeder, Cornwell, Gascoigne, Goddard, Mirandinha (D. Jackson 81), O'Neill (Craig 78).
Chelsea
Freestone, Clarke (Hall 55), Dorigo, Pates, McLaughlin, C. Wilson, Nevin, Hazard, Dixon, West, Wergerle (K. Wilson 66).
Referee Mr. P. Harrison (Oldham).

Two goals for Mirandinha.

Birthdays

Stan Anderson born today 1934.
Right-half 1963-1965, Apps 84. Goals 14.
Tony Bell born today 1955.
Goalkeeper 1973-1975, Apps 2.

Sadly Missed

Billy Lindsay died on this day in 1933, aged 60.
Right-back 1898-1900, Apps 62. Goals 1.

Match of the Day from 1951

UNITED IN THE SEMIS

Bristol Rovers' lengthy Cup run is all over in the first half

This FA Cup sixth round replay looked as if it was all going to go wrong for Newcastle. The team, and supporters had travelled quite a distance for the tie against Bristol Rovers who were definitely favourites to win.

The early advantage, and most of the chances at goal, fell to Rovers, and it was no surprise to anyone when they took the lead on fifteen minutes. It all started from an attack by Newcastle which was stopped in its tracks. The ball fell to Bradford who came straight through the centre and sent it on to Pitt. Bush delivered the pass and Lambden managed to get his head to it, but a great diving save from Fairbrother kept the ball out of the net..

However, by thumping the ball away from the net the Newcastle keeper inadvertently sent it straight to Bradford who was waiting to slam it straight back goalwards, only this time it was out of reach and crossed the line to give the home team the lead.

Things were beginning to slip away from Newcastle, but the team managed to find new strength almost straight from the restart. Team captain Joe Harvey got onto the ball and took it through to the penalty area. He sent it to Taylor who shot the ball hard. The deflection off Bamford in defence sent the ball into the back of the net to bring the scores level.

Just seven minutes later United brought themselves into the lead. A smashing shot from Crowe from the edge of the box sailed straight through the tangle of limbs to find the only space between Hoyle and the post. The ball hit the back of the net to everyone's surprise and the score was 2-1.

It took only five more minutes for Newcastle to seal the game. Taylor had possession of the ball and he sent it through to Milburn whose shot had no trouble beating the keeper and landing in the net.

Despite Rovers having the vast majority of possession in the second half there were no real attempts at goal from either side. Newcastle may have been put off by the number of home players taking to defence, sometimes up to eight, but they didn't really need to try that hard. The game was already won, and United would face Wolves in the semi-finals at Hillsborough on March 10th.

The Magpies went on to lift the trophy at Wembley beating Blackpool 2-0.

Bristol Rovers
Hoyle, Bamford, Fox, Pitt, Warren, Bush, Bradford, Lambden, Roost, Watling, Sampson
Newcastle United
Fairbrother, Cowell, Corbett, Harvey, Brennan, Crowe, Walker, Taylor, Milburn, G. Robledo, Mitchell.

Birthdays Feb 28

Arthur Bottom born today 1930.
Inside-right 1958, Apps 11. Goals 10.
Jamie Scott born today in 1960.
Midfield 1976-1980, Apps 10 (1 sub). Goals 0.
Kevin Todd born today in 1958.
Forward 1981-1983, Apps 11 (3 subs). Goals 3.

Sadly Missed Feb 28

Dick Keith died on this day in 1967, aged 33.
Right-back 1956-1964, Apps 223. Goals 2.

Played on this day

Games marked with asterix (*), denote games played on February 29.

1903, Division 1.
Wolverhampton W. (h) 2-4   Att. 16,000
Andy Gardner, Alex Gardner
1914, Division 1.
Manchester United (a) 2-2   Att. 25,000
Hibbert, Shepherd
1920, Division 1.
Bolton Wanderers (h) 0-1   Att. 40,000
1923, Division 1.
Cardiff City (h) 3-1   Att. 11,000
Harris, McDonald, Seymour
1925, Division 1.
Cardiff City (a) 0-3   Att. 25,000
1931, Division 1.
Sheffield United (h) 1-0   Att. 30,000
Hutchison
1936, Division 2.*
Norwich City (h) 1-1   Att. 4,000
Imrie
1942, Wartime.
Middlesbrough (h) 1-1   Att. 8,000
Short
1948, Division 2.
West Ham United (a) 2-0   Att. 30,000
Milburn, Thompson
1951, FA Cup 6th round, replay.
Bristol Rovers(a) 3-1   Att. 30,724
Crowe, Milburn, Taylor
1953, Division 1.
Wolverhampton W. (h) 1-1   Att. 46,254
G. Robledo
1955, FA Cup 5th round, replay.
Nottingham Forest(h) 2-2   Att. 38,573
Keeble, R. Mitchell
1959, Division 1.
Leicester City (a) 1-0   Att. 24,362
Eastham
1964, Division 2.*
Swindon Town (h) 4-1   Att. 23,565
Suddick, Cummings, Hilley, Burton
1970, Division 1.
Tottenham Hotspur (h) 1-2   Att. 34,827
McNamee
1973, Division 1.
Derby County (h) 2-0   Att. 34,286
Tudor, Macdonald
1975, Division 1.
West Ham United (a) 1-0   Att. 33,150
Macdonald
1976, League Cup Final.
Manchester City (n) 1-2   Att. 100,000
Gowling
Played at Wembley Stadium, London
1981, Division 2.
Oldham Athletic (a) 0-0   Att. 5,887
1987, Division 1.
Wimbledon (a) 1-3   Att. 6,779
Beardsley
1990, Division 2.
Bournemouth (h) 3-0   Att. 15,163
Anderson, Quinn (2)
1992, Division 2.*
Port Vale (a) 1-0   Att. 10,321
Watson
1993, Division 1.
Tranmere Rovers (a) 3-0   Att. 13,082
Lee (2), Kelly
1995, Premier League.
Ipswich Town 0   Newcastle 2
Fox 12, Kitson 38
Att. 18,639

continued next page

Played on this day

Games marked with asterix (*), denote games played on February 29.

1998, Premier League.
    Everton 0   **Newcastle 0**
                                   Att. 37,972

1999, Premier League.
    Newcastle 1   **Arsenal 1**
    Hamann 77   Anelka 36
                                   Att. 36,708

Playing record for this day is... 26 games, Won 12, Drawn 8, Lost 6, GF 39, GA 26. Today's success rate... 61.54%.

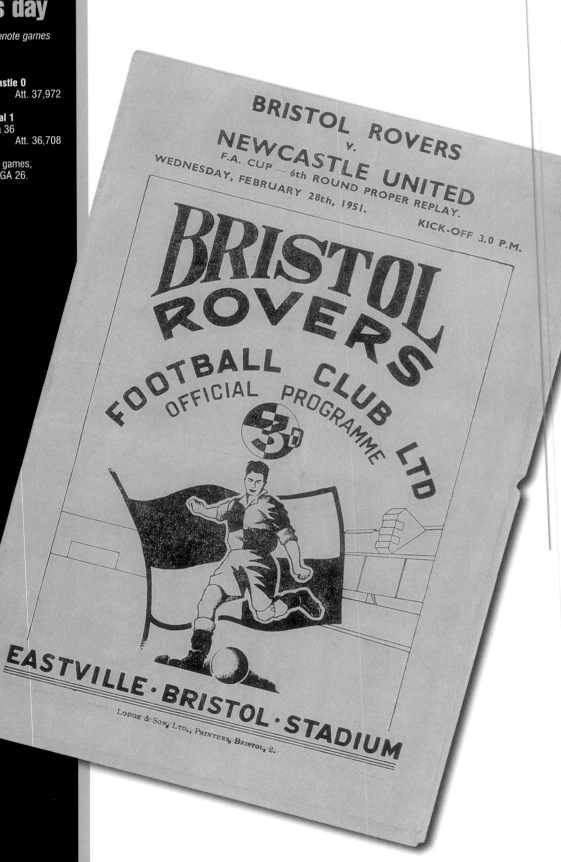

BRISTOL ROVERS
v.
NEWCASTLE UNITED
F.A. CUP — 6th ROUND PROPER REPLAY.
WEDNESDAY, FEBRUARY 28th, 1951.
KICK-OFF 3.0 P.M.

BRISTOL ROVERS

FOOTBALL CLUB LTD

OFFICIAL PROGRAMME

3d

EASTVILLE · BRISTOL · STADIUM

LODGE & SON, LTD., PRINTERS, BRISTOL, 2.

March

Played on this day

1902, Division 1.
Bolton Wanderers (h) 4-1   Att. 12,000
Roberts (2), Rutherford, McColl
1913, Division 1.
Everton (h) 2-0   Att. 25,000
Shepherd, Stewart
1919, Wartime.
Darlington F. Albion (h) 0-2 Att. 23,000
1924, Division 1.
Everton (a) 2-2   Att. 30,000
McDonald, Cowan
1930, FA Cup 6th round.
Hull City (h) 1-1   Att. 63,486
Lang
1939, Division 2.
Tottenham Hotspur (h) 0-1 Att. 18,500
1941, Wartime.
York City (a) 1-1   Att. 4,000
Duns
1947, FA Cup 6th round.
Sheffield United (a) 2-0   Att. 46,911
Bentley (pen), Milburn
1952, Division 1.
Huddersfield Town (h) 6-2 Att. 51,394
Mitchell (2), G. Robledo, Milburn (3, 1 pen)
1958, Division 1.
Aston Villa (h) 2-4   Att. 40,135
R. Mitchell (pen), Bottom
1969, Division 1.
West Ham United (a) 1-3   Att. 26,336
Davies
1980, Division 2.
Watford (h) 0-2   Att. 23,091
1986, Division 1.
Arsenal (h) 1-0   Att. 22,085
Roeder
1988, Division 1.
Southampton (a) 1-1   Att. 13,380
O'Neill
1997, Premier League.
Newcastle 0   Southampton 1
Le Tissier 56
Att. 36,446
2003, Premier League.
Newcastle 2   Chelsea 1
Hasselbaink (og) 31 Lampard 37
Bernard 53   Att. 52,157

Playing record for this day is... 16 games,
Won 6, Drawn 4, Lost 6, GF 25, GA 22.
Today's success rate... 50%.

Match of the Day from 2003

CHELSEA THWARTED BY WILY ROBSON
Champions' League qualification now looking good

When Sir Bobby Robson warmly shook Claudio Ranieri by the hand at the end of their intriguing battle of minds, he did so with a feeling of immense satisfaction after overcoming a kindred spirit. Ranieri had boldly sought to outwit his managerial counterpart with a series of changes that saw Chelsea's attacking reinforcements swarm towards the Newcastle goal in the last quarter of this gripping encounter. The Chelsea boss made some brave and significant changes not just like for like, but real tactical changes, which tested the resolve of Newcastle and their boss Robson in particular.

Jonathan Woodgate battles with Jimmy Floyd Hasselbaink.

Chelsea were victims of the prudent new world that is St. James' Park, a place once synonymous with caution to-the-wind, cavalier attacking play. Now under the wily and respected charge of Robson things are a little more cautious, but they gain the results when needed. Robson rightly commented after the game, "All good teams in the past have known there will be big games when just to win will be a fine performance. In the big games you can't knock your opponents over. You have to learn how to win 2-1. By defending well encouraging teams to come at you and sticking one man in attack you can hit them on the counter. That's the beauty of the game. The Chelsea manager had thrown everybody forward, they had Zola, Cole, Gudjohnsen, Hassebaink, and Zenden all surging forward in the later stages, Robson countered this supremely by playing six defenders during the same period.

With a modicum of luck Chelsea, despite this, would have secured a point but for a freak own goal by Hasselbaink after 31 minutes. A goal down it was always difficult for the Blues but they gained a deserved equaliser through Frank Lampard's smart first-time shot inside the area eight minutes before half time.

The winning goal came just eight minutes into the second half and was fittingly scored by man-of-the-match Olivier Bernard with an exquisite finish which was worthy of such a game of this importance. Newcastle then matched Chelsea's late surge and held out for the three points which now makes them favourites to claim a top-three finish in the Premiership, and with it Champions' League qualification. The game was summed up well by Chelsea's stand-in skipper John Terry who said afterwards, "You can see why Newcastle are so high in the League. They're a very good side with some exceptional players. Jonathon Woodgate will make a difference. He's without doubt one of the best central defenders in the country. Any team would like to have him in their side".

Newcastle United

Given, Hughes, O'Brien, Woodgate, Bernard, Solano (Griffin 79), Dyer (Ameobi 88), Speed, Viana (Bramble 72), Shearer, Bellamy.

Chelsea

Cudicini, Melchiot, Gallas, Terry, Babayaro (Cole 77), Gronkjaer (Zola 67), Morris, Lampard, Stanic (Zenden 67), Hasselbaink, Gudjohnsen.

Referee Mr. J. Winter (Stockton-on-Tees).

Birthdays

Diego Gavilan born today in 1980.
Midfield 2000-present day, Apps 8 (6 subs).
Goals 1.

Sadly Missed

Tommy Pearson died on this day in 1999, aged 84.
Winger 1933-1948, Apps 279. Goals 62.

Match of the Day from 1970

RAMSEY IMPRESSED BY SUPERB UNITED
Newcastle destroy the Hammers 4-1

Sir Alf Ramsey, England's team manager, probably travelled up to Tyneside to look at West Ham's established international players, but after today's performance, he must have left with a notebook full of Newcastle names after an emphatic show by the Magpies at St. James' Park.

It took Newcastle only eight minutes to pierce a West Ham defence that was stretched to the limit for almost the entire game, and young Peter Grotier had to show all his skill in the visitors' goal to keep the score down. Wyn Davies, Newcastle's Welsh international centre-forward who has been out of touch for so long, started the execution with a typical header when he rose above Bobby Moore to nod David Craig's free kick home from eight yards. That was just the beginning. A new look Newcastle much more confident than the timid team beaten by Spurs three days ago, carved a dozen scoring chances as Grotier defied gravity in a fantastic display to keep them at bay. Robson and Foggon could each have scored hat tricks; even United centre-half McNamee got forward to glide a beautifully timed header just inches over the bar. Despite this, Newcastle and their 27,726 crowd were stunned after 28 minutes when West Ham equalised, but nevertheless it was a worthy effort from Eustace. Redknapp supplied the right-wing cross, which McFaul misjudged. McNamee then headed the ball out, but only as far as Eustace and the former Sheffield Wednesday player calmly shot the ball home via a post. Newcastle, however, stormed back and in the 40th minute Robson converted Dyson's flick to cap a brilliant performance.

The second half was almost embarrassingly one-sided as West Ham strove desperately, but unsuccessfully to make their presence felt. Newcastle could have had another six, but they had to be satisfied with just two more goals. In the 74th minute Robson and Dyson combined to buffer the West Ham defence, and the latter made no mistake with his drive after Robson had beaten three defenders. With two minutes remaining Foggon crowned a glorious return to the team by side-footing the ball home from the most absurd angle possible to wrap up an incredible United display.

Alan Foggon

Newcastle United
McFaul, Craig, Craggs, Gibb, McNamee, Moncur, Robson, Smith, Davies, Foggon, Dyson.

West Ham United
Grotier, Bonds, Howe, Peters, Stephenson, Moore, Redknapp, Lindsay, Hurst, Eustace, Sissons.

Played on this day

1901, Division 1.
Notts County (a) 1-3   Att. 4,000
A. Gardner.

1907, Division 1.
Preston North End (a) 2-2   Att. 12,000
Gosnell, Howie

1912, Division 1.
Sheffield Wednesday (h) 0-2   Att. 22,000

1932, Division 1.
Blackburn Rovers(h) 5-3   Att. 20,000
Allen (2), Boyd, Lang, J.R. Richardson

1935, Division 2.
Manchester United (a) 1-0   Att. 16,000
Pearson

1938, Division 2.
Stockport County (a) 3-1   Att. 8,000
Bowden (2), Park

1946, Wartime.
Everton (a) 1-4   Att. 59,000
Milburn

1955, FA Cup 5th round, 2nd replay.
Nottingham Forest(h) 2-1   Att. 36,631
Monkhouse (2)

1957, Division 1.
Manchester City (a) 2-1   Att. 25,229
R. Mitchell, White

1963, Division 2.
Sunderland (a) 0-0   Att. 62,420

1968, Division 1.
Sheffield Wednesday (a) 1-1   Att. 24,762
T. Robson

1970, Division 1.
West Ham United (h) 4-1   Att. 27,726
Dyson, Foggon, Davies, Robson

1974, Division 1.
Leeds United (a) 1-1   Att. 46,611
Barrowclough

1977, Division 1.
Leeds United (h) 3-0   Att. 33,714
Burns, Oates, McCaffery

1985, Division 1.
Watford (h) 3-1   Att. 24,875
Cunningham, Reilly, Megson

1991, Division 2.
Leicester City (h) 2-1   Att. 13,575
McGhee, Sloan

2002, Premier League.
Newcastle 0   Arsenal 2
Bergkamp 11
Campbell 41
Att. 52,067

Playing record for this day is... 17 games, Won 9, Drawn 4, Lost 4, GF 31, GA 24. Today's success rate... 64.71%.

Birthdays

David Ford born today in 1945.
Winger 1969-1971, Apps 31 (3 sub). Goals 3.
John Kelly born today in 1913.
Centre-forward 1933-1935, Apps 5. Goals 1.

Alex Reid born today in 1947.
Midfield 1971-1973, Apps 26 (10 subs). Goals 0.

March 3

Played on this day

1900, Division 1.
Wolverhampton W. (a) 1-1   Att. 8,000
Peddie
1906, Division 1.
Middlesbrough (a) 0-1   Att. 20,000
1923, Division 1.
Blackburn Rovers (h) 5-1   Att. 30,000
Harris (3), Seymour (2)
1934, Division 1.
Sunderland (a) 0-2   Att. 32,358
1945, Wartime.
Hartlepool United (a) 1-2   Att. 9,523
Carr
1951, Division 1.
Derby County (a) 2-1   Att. 25,999
G. Robledo, Walker
1956, FA Cup 6th round.
Sunderland (h) 0-2   Att. 61,474
1962, Division 2
Bury (h) 1-2   Att. 25,853
Thomas
1976, Division 1.
Stoke City (h) 0-1   Att. 38,822
1979, Division 2.
Charlton Athletic (h) 5-3   Att. 14,998
Connolly, Shoulder (2, 1 pen), Martin,
Mitchell
1982, Division 2.
Leicester City (a) 0-3   Att. 12,497
1984, Division 2.
Fulham (a) 2-2   Att. 12,290
Beardsley, Keegan
1990, Division 2.
Barnsley (h) 4-1   Att. 18,999
Anderson, Scott, Aitken, McGhee (pen)
2001, Premier League.
Everton 1   Newcastle 1
Unsworth 82 (pen)   Unsworth (og) 47
   Att. 35,779

Playing record for this day is... 14 games,
Won 4, Drawn 3, Lost 7, GF 22, GA 23.
Today's success rate... 39.29%.

Match of the Day from 1923

HARRIS & SEYMOUR SEE OFF ROVERS

A brace in the first half and a hat-trick in the second half

A good crowd of 30,000 witnessed another brilliant performance by the Magpies today, totally thrilled by the six great goals, five of which came from the home side. The result leaves Newcastle now unbeaten at St. James' Park in nine league and cup games and keeps the pressure at the top of the league, United still holding on to the outside chance of winning the championship. This was Newcastle's third successive win and bar far the most convincing, their second-half display had to be seen to be believed, and they could have easily ended up with a score in double figures.

The game started at a cracking pace both sides, playing some wonderful open football both eager to get forward and put pressure on their opponents' goal. In the opening few minutes Harris gave a glimpse of what was to come for the Newcastle supporters with a belting shot from 25 yards which skimmed the cross bar. At the other end Hodkinson and Longmuir threatened the home goal, but their danger was eventually subdued by some inspired defending by Hudspeth and Mooney, who were as much responsible for the win as Newcastle's brilliant forwards. Midway through the first half the game opened up for United as they hit two quick goals both of which came from the boot of Seymour. The first was a sweetly hit volley from the edge of the penalty area, the other moments later, a tap-in from Aitken's cross to the far post. Blackburn refused to lie down and came back just before half time, reducing the deficit to one goal when Longmuir headed in a corner.

The second half was almost entirely played out in the Blackburn half, as Newcastle swept away their opponents. A hatful of chances went begging due to wasted opportunities and brave goalkeeping, but eventually United got the goals they had threatened to score.

Stan Seymour

Neil Harris, not often a hero, answered his critics with an absolutely marvellous display of finishing. Inside a quarter of an hour he netted his eleventh, twelfth and thirteenth goals of the season. A hat-trick for the player, and probably his best set of finishes for the club. For the Newcastle fans who were present at the game, they were certainly by far the most memorable.

Newcastle United
Bradley, Hampson, Hudspeth, Curry, Spencer, Mooney, Low, Aitken, Harris, McDonald, Seymour.
Blackburn Rovers
Davis, Rollo, Wylie, Healless, Reilly, McKinnell, Hodkinson, Longmuir, Dawson, McKay, McIntire.

Birthdays

Stewart Mitchell born today in 1933.
Goalkeeper 1953-1963, Apps 48.

March 4

Match of the Day from 1911

VISITORS BURY'D BY FIVE GOALS
Newcastle deserve easy victory at home

This home tie against Bury drew a crowd of 12,000, all expecting a bit more of a fight from Bury. Anderson, Metcalf, Willis and Finlay were all included in Newcastle's line up due to absences for injuries and international duties.

From the start United were in control of play. All attacking moves came from the home side, and there was no comeback from Bury at all. There were plenty of chances at goal for Newcastle, and because of the difference between the two teams it didn't matter much when the ball failed to cross the line. The Magpies knew that the next chance would not be far away, and the more attempts that were made at goal, the more likely it was that one would go in sooner or later.

That was exactly what happened for the home side. Randall was having another shot at goal, and this time it was meant to be. The ball sailed over the line past the Bury keeper to put Newcastle 1-0 up.

The score didn't stay the same for long. Skill and determination started to pay off further when Higgins added another goal just two minutes later. Bury were lacking in force and confidence, and everything Newcastle did seemed to add to their struggle. Just before the break Hibbert and Beney both missed open goals for Bury, but this didn't surprise the visiting supporters.

The game entered half-time with the score at 2-0 to Newcastle.

The start of the second half brought about no surprises. United still had the upper hand, and Bury were still weak and outplayed.

The only real surprise that the fans had was the fact that the lead wasn't larger. The Magpies were attacking at every opportunity, and they also had the ability and skill to create those opportunities.

It was Randall who increased the lead further, adding another easy shot to his tally of goals. Newcastle were in danger of becoming overconfident, their total control of play was beginning to make them careless. Many easy chances were missed due to players being too sure they would score.

Bury were trodden down further when Newcastle raised their score to 4-0. It was Stewart who managed to get the ball over the line past the keeper, and he did it with ease.

Shortly afterwards Metcalf brought Newcastle's tally to five with a superb shot hurtling into the net, and still the attacks were coming.

However, Newcastle's run had ended, and although it was too late for Bury to make an impact on the game they still had time to secure one goal. It was Hibbert who finally managed to attack well enough to break through the defence and put the ball past the home keeper.

The final score was 5-1, and the win was thoroughly deserved by Newcastle United.

Newcastle United
Lawrence, McCracken, Whitson, Higgins, Willis, Finlay, Rutherford, Metcalf, Stewart, Randall, Anderson.
Bury
Raeside, Fenner, Millington, Jarvis, Dewhurst, Bullen, Birnie, Lomas, Hibbert, Beney, Walker.

Birthdays

Len Walker born today in 1944.
Defender 1963-1964, Apps 2. Goals 0.
Billy Wright born today in 1931.
Winger 1958-1959, Apps 5. Goals 3.

Kenny Dalglish born today in 1951.
Manager 1997-1998.

Played on this day

1898, Division 2.
Darwen (a) 3-1 Att. 2,000
Peddie (3)

1910, FA Cup 4th round.
Leicester Fosse (h) 3-0 Att. 52,544
Wilson, Shepherd, Howie

1921, Division 1.
Middlesbrough (a) 0-0 Att. 38,000

1927, Division 1.
Everton (h) 7-3 Att. 45,000
Gallacher (3), McDonald, McKay,
MacKenzie, Seymour

1930, FA Cup 6th round, replay.
Hull City (a) 0-1 Att. 32,930

1932, Division 1.
Manchester City (a) 1-5 Att. 28,000
Allen

1938, Division 2.
Bradford Park Ave. (a) 0-2 Att. 12,000

1949, Division 1.
Sunderland (h) 2-1 Att. 58,250
Milburn, Robledo

1955, Division 1.
Portsmouth (a) 1-3 Att. 54,055
Keeble

1960, Division 1.
Fulham (h) 3-1 Att. 33,993
Allchurch, Eastham, White

1966, Division 1.
Sunderland (h) 2-0 Att. 52,051
Suddick (2)

1977, Division 1.
Liverpool (a) 0-1 Att. 45,553

1983, Division 2.
Crystal Palace (a) 2-0 Att. 10,239
Waddle, Varadi

1988, Division 1.
Everton (a) 0-1 Att. 25,674

1994, Premier League.
Sheffield Wed. 0
Newcastle 1
Cole 88 Att. 33,153

2003, Premier League.
Middlesbrough 1
Newcastle 0
Geremi 62 Att. 34,814

Playing record for this day is... 16 games,
Won 8, Drawn 1, Lost 7, GF 25, GA 20.
Today's success rate... 53.13%.

Match of the Day from 1960

UNITED'S TABLE CLIMB CONTINUES

Early set back but Newcastle claim the points

If only Newcastle's 1959-60 season had started at the end of September, it seems a distant memory away now but the fact remains United lost five of their opening nine league games. Battling back from the relegation zone the Magpies are now firmly established in the top ten and looking to further improve their position with ten games of the season still remaining. Today Newcastle showed all the new qualities that have continued their impressive improvement. A goal down early on they simply came back confidently to overcome their dangerous opponents from London. United were also keen to avenge that desperately unlucky 4-3 defeat at Craven Cottage earlier in the season, they did so in the end very convincingly.

Fulham were in front to an excellent goal through Bentley after just four minutes before most of the Newcastle side had even touched the ball. The Londoners then continued to dominate as United struggled to get out of their own half, and after the opening quarter of an hour a hectic disappointing afternoon seemed to be the only outcome for the Magpies and their watching supporters. Fulham were hogging all the possession, with Johnny Haynes dictating most of their forward moves and Langley a powerful general in defence was preventing any threat to the visitors' goal, but

Ivor Allchurch

much of their work lacked directness and punch, and shots at the Newcastle goal were all too few and far between. This gave United hope and the tide started to turn midway through the first half culminating in an equalising goal for George Eastham, his seventeenth of the season. With the crowd now relishing every moment Newcastle surged forward and with eight minutes left before the interval they took the lead through Ivor Allchurch's powerfully placed header.

The second half was completely controlled by Newcastle, even Haynes hardly got a look in and it was only a matter of time before United would add to their half-time lead. Their third goal came just after the hour mark and settled the game, a brilliant move involving half the United team ended with a back-heeled pass from Mitchell on to the on-rushing Len White who smashed in his 22nd goal of the ever improving campaign. At the final whistle 33,993 happy Geordies left St. James' Park wondering just how high United will climb this First Division table, a top five position is now a real possibility.

Newcastle United
Harvey, Keith, McMichael, Bell, Stokoe, Mitchell, Hughes, Eastham, White, Allchurch, Mitten.
Fulham
Macedo, Cohen, Langley, Lawler, Lampe, Low, Key, Cook, Bentley, Haynes, Leggatt.

Birthdays

Keith Kennedy born today in 1952.
Left-back 1968-1972, Apps 1. Goals 0.

Sadly Missed

Frank Brennan died on this day in 1997, aged 72.
Centre-half 1946-1956, Apps 349. Goals 3.

March 6

Match of the Day from 1993

CHAMPS BATTER BRENTFORD

Premiership bound Newcastle in another awesome victory

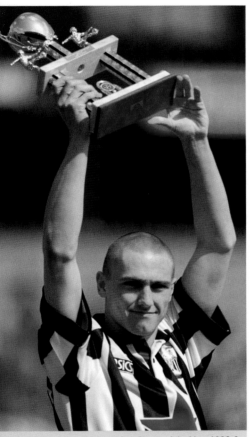

Lee Clark, Barclays Division One Player of the Year 1992-3.

The aim of the Newcastle chairman Sir John Hall, to make The Magpies one of the top three clubs in the UK may still look a little extravagant at this stage. But the hope of his manager, Kevin Keegan, a man more used to realities, that the club will be among the top six in England, looks feasible, it could even happen next season. The destruction today of Brentford was frightening, even their goal was scored by a Newcastle player, an own goal by the unfortunate Kevin Scott. Lee Clark, the twenty-year-old midfielder, was at the centre of things from the start and sustained his exceptional form throughout. His display was brilliant and surely he should be considered for the full England squad. He is by far the best thing to come out of St. James' Park since Paul Gascoigne. Newcastle's opening pressure, in which Kelly had two half-chances, was interrupted when Bennett attempted to catch Srnicek off his line, but the United keeper was not deceived and tipped the ball over the bar, albeit at full stretch. The important opening goal came from a corner taken by Clark on 24 minutes. The kick led to a scramble, Kelly was first to get a proper kick at the ball which took it over the goal-line. Brentford's keeper Graham Benstead then pulled off a fantastic save a minute before the interval to keep the score down to just the one goal.

In the second half however, The Bees found it impossible to thwart the swarm of United pressure. From a Beresford free kick, just three minutes after the restart, Clark flicked the ball on for Paul Bracewell to score with a scorching low drive from fifteen yards. At the other end Blissett went close with a header, but this apart it was one-way traffic. Clark strode through a static defence to add Newcastle's third goal after 55 minutes. Then just two minutes later came the moment centre half Scott will want to forget, a cross from Manuel seemed harmless enough until he diverted the ball past the shocked Srnicek who could do nothing to stop it going in. Newcastle soon regained their momentum and Lee headed in Stimson's cross to make the score 4-1 after 74 minutes. The irrepressible Clark got the final goal eight minutes from time with a well deserved individual effort. Between the final two goals came a remarkable shot from Rob Lee which would have been a candidate for goal of the season, from 70 yards he lobbed the advanced keeper, the ball bouncing once before hitting the back of the net. Incredibly this was disallowed after the referee had blown for offside against Brentford, and ironically the free kick went in Newcastle's favour.

Newcastle United

Srnicek, Venison, Howey (Neilson 77), Scott, Beresford, Lee, Bracewell, O'Brien, Stimson, Clark, Kelly.

Brentford

Benstead, Bates, Westley, Millen, Statham, Bennett, Radcliffe(Dickens 68), Manuel, Stephenson, Blissett, Allon.

Referee Mr. I. Hendrick (Preston).

Sadly Missed

Wilfred Feeney died on this day in 1973, aged 62.
Midfield 1930-1932, Apps 4. Goals 1.

Played on this day

1897, Division 2.
Walsall (h) 2-0   Att. 6,000
Connell, Ostler (pen)
1909, FA Cup 4th round.
Sunderland (h) 2-2   Att. 53,353
Rutherford, Wilson
1915, FA Cup 4th round.
Chelsea (a) 1-1   Att. 58,000
Goodwill
1920, Division 1.
Blackburn Rovers(h) 0-0 Att. 35,000
1922, Division 1.
Blackburn Rovers (a) 2-0 Att. 20,000
Harris, Seymour
1926, Division 1.
Huddersfield Town (h) 0-2 Att. 57,000
1933, Division 1.
Wolverhampton W. (a) 1-1 Att. 16,000
McMenemy
1937, Division 2.
Plymouth Argyle (a) 1-1 Att. 19,000
Imrie
1943, Wartime.
York City (h) 3-2   Att. 19,989
Short, Stubbins, Carr
1948, Division 2.
Bury (h) 1-0   Att. 56,444
Milburn
1954, Division 1.
Aston Villa (h) 0-1   Att. 36,847
1965, Division 2.
Portsmouth (a) 2-1   Att. 19,399
Cummings, Robson
1976, FA Cup 6th round.
Derby County (a) 2-4   Att. 38,362
Gowling (2)
1982, Division 2.
Barnsley (h) 1-0   Att. 18,784
Varadi
1993, Division 1.
Brentford(h) 5-1   Att. 30,006
Kelly, Bracewell, Clark (2), Lee
2002, Premier League.
Liverpool 3   Newcastle 0
Murphy 32, 53
Hamann 75   Att. 44,204

Playing record for this day is... 16 games,
Won 7, Drawn 5, Lost 4, GF 23, GA 19.
Today's success rate... 59.38%.

Played on this day

1896, Division 2.
Loughborough Town (a) 0-1   Att. 2,000
1903, Division 1.
Liverpool (a) 0-3   Att. 15,000
1908, FA Cup 4th round.
Grimsby Town (h) 5-1   Att. 44,788
Appleyard (3), Gardner, Opponent (og)
1925, Division 1.
Preston North End (h) 3-1   Att. 20,000
Cowan, Harris, Low
1931, Division 1.
Leeds United (a) 0-1   Att. 10,000
1936, Division 2.
Doncaster Rovers (a) 2-2   Att. 14,000
Pearson, J. Smith
1953, Division 1.
Charlton Athletic (a) 0-0   Att. 33,222
1956, Division 1.
Cardiff City (a) 1-1   Att. 42,000
Curry
1959, Division 1.
Preston North End (h) 1-2   Att. 31,962
White
1962, Division 2.
Middlesbrough (a) 0-3   Att. 21,023
1963, FA Cup 3rd round.
Bradford City (a) 6-1   Att. 13,605
McGarry (2), Thomas, Hilley, Hughes (2)
1964, Division 2.
Northampton Town (a) 2-2   Att. 11,440
Suddick, Cummings
1981, Division 2.
West Ham United (a) 0-1   Att. 26,274
1987, Division 1.
Aston Villa (h) 2-1   Att. 21,224
Cunningham, Beardsley
1990, Division 2.
Hull City (h) 2-0   Att. 20,684
McGhee (2, 1 pen)
1992, Division 2.
Brighton & Hove A. (h) 0-1   Att. 24,597
1999, FA Cup 6th round.
Newcastle 4   Everton 1
Ketsbaia 21, 73   Unsworth 57
Georgiadis 61
Shearer 81   Att. 36,584
*A new gate receipts record for St. James'
Park is set with £830,270 taken this
afternoon.*

Playing record for this day is... 17 games,
Won 6, Drawn 4, Lost 7, GF 28, GA 22.
Today's success rate... 47.06%.

Match of the Day from 1999

KETSBAIA PUTS UNITED WEMBLEY BOUND

Spurs or Barnsley next for Cup specialists Newcastle

Beaten finalists last year, Newcastle vigorously thrust their way past relegation threatened Everton and into the FA Cup semi finals. United's victory was in the end well deserved, but was less convincing than the score suggests, and the draw made soon after today's game sets up a possible repeat of last years final against Arsenal at Wembley. It is said on these occasions that the result is all that matters. This Cup-tie epitomised that maxim, a bad sanded pitch, passed by a late inspection, a wet and windy afternoon, and a match error-strewn until Newcastle eventually took command after an hour's play. Tyneside's fanatical supporters left the ground not reflecting on the quality of the performance, only the four goals which have yet again given this football crazy city an excuse to celebrate and speculate again. The tide of enthusiasm amongst the Toon Army is unceasing, yet with the score at 1-1 after 60 minutes, none would have predicted such a comfortable victory.

The game was a scrappy affair early on with few opportunities for either side. Newcastle's dominant defence helped curb any threat from Everton, whilst the performance of Alan Shearer at the other end made Everton's defensive task all the more simple. At times the England centre-forward lacked support and United suffered for it. Despite this however it was Newcastle who took a fortunate lead after 21 minutes when Ketsbaia's drive from the edge of the penalty area, when put through by Maric and Lee, was deflected by Materazzi and the ball skidded past Myhre and into the bottom left-hand corner. Newcastle then, much to the annoyance of manager Gullit, sat back on the lead, allowing Everton back into the game.

A half-time 'roasting' did little to change United in the second half. So it was with just reward when David Unsworth, with the United defence retreating yet again, cracked home a left-foot drive from outside the box on 57 minutes. At last, this seemed to galvanise everyone in black and white, and a resurgent Newcastle started to compete again, they had "woke up" according to Gullit in his post-match summary. Shearer now looked dangerous with support and it was he who won the free kick which ultimately brought about the winner seven minutes later. From the free kick, some 28 yards out on the right, Dietmar Hamann, who had been the outstanding figure in midfield, struck a low drive that was parried by Myhre. The ball rolled towards goal where Materazzi, attempting to clear on the goal-line, only steered the ball into the path of the lunging Georgiadis. Newcastle were back in front and from this point onwards were on top of their game also. Another goal, Ketsbaia's second, wrapped up the tie in the 73rd minute and Shearer completed the scoring with a thundering strike after Ketsbaia unselfishly set up the England leader who lashed the ball past Myhre from the edge of the box for one of the goals of the season.

Newcastle United
Given, Barton, Howey, Dabizas, Domi, Solano, Hamann, Lee, Maric (Georgiadis), Shearer, Ketsbaia.

Everton
Myhre, Weir, Watson, Materazzi, O'Kane, Grant, Hutchinson, Unsworth, Barmby, Jeffers, Cadamarteri.

Referee Mr. G. Barber (Surrey).

Robert Lee shoots despite the attentions of Danny Cadamarteri.

Birthdays

Andy Griffin born today in 1979.
Defender 1998-present day, Apps 96 (13 subs).
Goals 3.

March 8

Match of the Day from 1952

MAGPIES WIN 'BATTLE OF THE GIANTS'

United look Wembley bound after famous win

Dubbed by the media as the "Battle of the Giants" this game was played between twice League Champions Portsmouth and FA Cup holders Newcastle, both clubs currently in the top five of the First Division. A massive 44,699 expectantly awaited kick off including a contingent of 8,000 travelling down from Tyneside. They were treated to a real classic cup-tie, a memorable game which was perfectly illustrated by the amazing performance of United forward Jackie Milburn. One newspaper reporter said of him afterwards, "A dazzling display, rarely has a centre-forward been so deadly in the face of stern opposition and Milburn's drive and skill, time after time split the Pompey defence." Milburn was to comment on his own game as "One of the best, if not the best match I've played in."

Newcastle started this FA Cup sixth round tie in disastrous style, a goal down after just three minutes through a header from Portsmouth's Belgian star Marcel Gaillard. Newcastle however soon settled and began to get the better of their south coast opponents as the half wore on. The visitors were unlucky to be denied what seemed a clear-cut penalty when Foulkes was floored as he was about to shoot from a mere six yards out. Justice was finally done when Milburn nipped in and scrambled the ball over the line during a five-player melee in the Pompey six yard box. The equaliser was bitter-sweet for United as during the goal celebrations it became clear Milburn had injured himself and he left the field before play was restarted.

A huge sigh of relief came from the travelling fans when Milburn appeared for the second half and this seemed to galvanise everyone in black and white. All the pressure came from United and once again referee Griffiths upset the Geordies on 59 minutes when he disallowed what seemed a good goal from George Robledo. A minute later it was Milburn again exacting justice for United when he lobbed the ball over the keeper's head to put United 2-1 in front. Now it was Portsmouth's turn to be aggrieved by the officials when a linesman failed to spot a handball by Cowell. As the Pompey players appealed Simpson lost concentration dropped the ball and gifted Duggie Reid an equaliser. Two minutes later Cowell again blocked a shot, this time with his boot, whilst on the goal line to deny Harris. Newcastle seemed to be losing their grip but in the last quarter they again took control and swept Pompey away with two great goals. The first, and what proved to be the winner was probably Milburn's finest goal of his career, and it completed a superb hat-trick. Forced wide on the left with Froggatt, Ferrier and Dickinson closing on him, he hit a 30-yard drive from an acute angle which flew past goalkeeper Butler and into the roof of the net. In the 88th minute George Robledo wrapped the tie up for United and sent the thrilled visiting fans home celebrating another possible dream final at Wembley.

Portsmouth
Butler, Gunter, Ferrier, Scoular, Froggatt, Dickinson, Harris, Reid, Henderson, Phillips, Gaillard.

Newcastle United
Simpson, Cowell, McMichael, Harvey, Brennan, E. Robledo, Walker, Foulkes, Milburn, G. Robledo, Mitchell.

Referee Mr. B.M. Griffiths (Newport).

A Jackie Milburn hat trick secures a semi-final place.

Birthdays

George Georgiadis born today in 1972.
Midfield 1998-1999, Apps 13 (5 subs). Goals 1.

David Beharall born today in 1979.
Defender 1997-2002, Apps 6 (2 subs). Goals 0.

March 9

1895, Division 2.
  Crewe Alexandra (a) 1-2 Att. 2,000
  Hedley
1901, Division 1.
  Preston North End (h) 3-5 Att. 17,000
  Heywood, Peddie, Aitken
1907, Sheriff of London Shield.
  Corinthians (n) 5-2 Att. 30,000
  Rutherford, Appleyard, Brown (2),
  Opponent (og)
  Played at Craven Cottage, Fulham.
  This competition was the forerunner to
  the FA Charity Shield which started during
  the 1907-08 season.
1910, Division 1.
  Bradford City (a) 3-3 Att. 10,000
  Stewart (2), Shepherd
1912, Division 1.
  Bury (a) 1-2 Att. 10,000
  Stewart
1929, Division 1.
  Sunderland (h) 4-3 Att. 66,275
  Gallacher (2, 1pen), Urwin, Opponent (og)
1935, Division 2.
  Port Vale (h) 1-2 Att. 23,000
  Pearson
1940, Wartime.
  Huddersfield Town (h) 3-5 Att. 6,000
  Scott, Moses, Pearson (pen)
1957, Division 1.
  Bolton Wanderers (h) 4-0 Att. 34,073
  Davies, Milburn, Scoular, White
1963, Division 2.
  Leeds United (h) 1-1 Att. 29,575
  Hilley
1974, FA Cup 6th round.
  Nottingham Forest (h) 4-3 Att 54,500
  Tudor, Moncur, McDermott (pen), Craig
  Match declared void by F.A.
1977, Division 1.
  Ipswich Town (h) 1-1 Att. 33,820
  Nattrass
1985, Division 1.
  Nottingham Forest (a) 0-0 Att. 17,425
1991, Division 2.
  Watford (a) 2-1 Att. 10,018
  Anderson, Quinn
2002, FA Cup 6th round.
  Newcastle 1   Arsenal 1
  Robert 52   Edu 14 Att. 51,027

Playing record for this day is... 14 games,
Won 4, Drawn 5, Lost 5, GF 30, GA 28.
Today's success rate... 46.43%.

Match of the Day from 1974

THE GAME THAT NEVER WAS
Pitch invasion forces replay

The crowd of 54,500 who turned up to watch this game were unaware that it would turn out to be one of the most infamous in the history of the FA Cup. It was the sixth round, and a seemingly easy ride for First Division Newcastle against a struggling Second Division Nottingham Forest. However, things were not going to go quite as smoothly as United would have hoped.

It took just minutes for Bowyer to put Forest into an early lead, and then a corner was awarded to Newcastle. It was taken quickly, and the ball found Craig who slotted the ball home past Forest keeper Barron. With half time approaching it looked as if the score would remain 1-1, but the visitors had other ideas. O'Kane got onto the ball and managed to smash it into the net from fully twenty yards out to put Forest a goal ahead.

The start of the second half seemed to reinforce Forest's determination when Newcastle's Pat Howard was sent off for arguing against a penalty decision awarded for Craig's foul on McKenzie. The referee's decision stood, and it was Lyall who stepped up to take the kick, after waiting for things to calm down on the pitch, and coolly netted to increase Nottingham's lead to 3-1.

It seemed to be all over for United and the crowd made it worse when some of the Newcastle fans invaded the pitch. With an hour of the match played, the referee took the players off the pitch for eight minutes whilst order was restored by the police.

Play resumed, and despite being down to ten men Newcastle had recovered their fighting spirit. In the 68th minute Forest's Barron

John Tudor dives to power home the equalising goal.

took a push at Macdonald, and Newcastle were awarded a penalty. McDermott came to the spot to do the honours, and he duly found the net.

It was only three minutes later when the score was brought to 3-3. Tudor dived to get his head to Hibbitt's low cross, and the force was enough to send the ball past Barron.

It looked like a draw was inevitable until the final minute of play. A cross from Tudor was headed back to Bobby Moncur by Macdonald. Moncur slammed the ball hard and it sailed into the net giving Newcastle the lead in the dying seconds. Final score 4-3.

All seemed rosy for Newcastle until it emerged that a complaint had been made by Nottingham Forest claiming that the pitch invasion had altered the pattern of play. This claim was upheld by the FA, and the result of this game was erased from the records and a replay ordered. There were two replays at Goodison Park, and it was by the skin of their teeth with a goal from Macdonald, that United made it through to the semi finals. They went on to make it to Wembley for the final where they took on Liverpool but lost 3-0.

Newcastle United
McFaul, Craig (Kennedy), Clark, McDermott, Howard, Moncur, Barrowclough, Smith, Macdonald, Tudor, Hibbitt.
Nottingham Forest
Barron, O'Kane, Winfield, Chapman, Serella, Robertson, McKenzie, Lyall, Martin, O'Neill, Bowyer
Referee Mr. G. Kew (Amersham).

Sadly Missed

George Jobey died on this day in 1962, aged 76.
Midfield 1906-1913, Apps 53. Goals 2.

March 10

Match of the Day from 1928

OH, WHAT A GAME!
10 Villans, 11 Heroes, and 12 goals in thriller

A truly amazing game of open attacking football finished at 5pm this afternoon and 25,000 spectators filed out of St. James' Park having witnessed one of the greatest games ever played at the famous old stadium. It finished a truly spectacular 7-5 win for the home side after they had led 7-2 with just thirteen minutes to play. The visitors having lost their keeper Olney through injury (and with no subs back in 1928, played with ten men) pegged the score back with three quick goals and finished the game by the stronger team, indeed Newcastle were grateful to hear the final whistle sound at the end. Both sides left the field to a rousing reception by a cold but thoroughly thrilled crowd.

The game kicked off in a blizzard and the snow caused havoc when either side attempted to play any sort of neat football. The long kick upfield being the only worthwhile tactic in the opening ten minutes, then the sun came out to the relief of everyone. It was United, without their inspirational centre-forward Hughie Gallacher (serving a two month suspension) who started the better. Jonathan 'Monte' Wilkinson, Gallacher's replacement, was leading the attack brilliantly and almost gave United a perfect start after being set up by the equally influential Seymour early on. However when this pair swapped roles moments later United were a goal up, Wilkinson's perfect through ball hammered home by Seymour. After some unconvincing displays of late, the Magpies were now eager to get forward and score. So they did, further goals from Tom McDonald, Jock McCurley and Wilkinson quickly put the game seemingly out of Villa's reach at 4-0, and all within the first half hour's play. To their credit Villa, although under severe pressure, never looked totally out of the game and pulled a goal back through Cook then Pongo Waring poached a second for the visitors just before the half-time interval.

The second half started more evenly with fantastic end-to-end attacking football, and it was Newcastle who scored an all important fifth goal on the hour mark through McCurley, this his second of the game. United were again rampant and Wilkinson in particular was superb up front. He scored his second goal soon after to make the score 6-2, then completed his hat-trick with a thunderbolt from outside the penalty area to wrap the game up for the home side. Then came that devastating spell of football by Villa in the final thirteen minutes in which Waring again, then Dorrell and York found the back of home keeper Wilson's net. Newcastle were stunned by the ten-man visitors, but held on for the final couple of minutes of injury time, the anxious crowd cheering their every move, what a game!

Newcastle United
Wilson, Maitland, Evans, Harris, Park, Gibson, Urwin, McCurley, Wilkinson, McDonald, Seymour.
Aston Villa
Olney, Smart, Brittleton, Gibson, Milne, Moss, York, Cook, Waring, Walker, Dorrell.
Referee Mr. E. Wood.

Jonathan 'Monte' Wilkinson

Birthdays

Pavel Srnicek born today in 1968.
Goalkeeper 1990-1997, Apps 188 (2 subs).

Played on this day

1899, Division 1.
Nottingham Forest (h) 0-1   Att. 18,000
1905, Division 1.
Wolverhampton W. (h) 3-0   Att. 20,000
Appleyard, Rutherford, McWilliam
1908, Division 1.
Preston North End (h) 0-0   Att. 17,000
1922, Division 1.
Bolton Wanderers (h) 2-1   Att. 30,000
Curry, Harris
1930, Division 1.
Burnley (a) 3-0   Att. 10,000
Cape, Devine, Lang
1933, Division 1.
Sheffield Wednesday (h) 3-1   Att. 33,000
Allen (2), McMenemy
1939, Division 2.
Sheffield Wednesday (h) 2-1   Att. 29,000
Frost, Scott
1944, Wartime.
Hartlepool United (h) 3-0   Att. 26,110
Stubbins (2, 1 pen), Woodburn
1950, Division 1.
Derby County (h) 2-1   Att. 40,784
Mitchell, Corbett (pen)
1959, Division 1.
Portsmouth (a) 5-1   Att. 19,404
Eastham (pen), Curry (3), Taylor
1961, Division 1.
Manchester United (h) 1-1   Att. 28,867
Scanlon
1967, Division 1.
Manchester United (h) 0-0   Att. 38,203
1970, Inter Cities Fairs Cup 4th round, 1st leg.
R.S.C. Anderlecht (a) 0-2   Att. 30,000
1972, Division 1.
Arsenal (h) 2-0   Att. 33,907
Macdonald, Smith
1978, Division 1.
Manchester United (h) 2-2   Att. 25,825
McGhee, Burns (pen)
1989, Division 1.
Queens Park Rangers (h) 1-2 Att. 21,665
Ranson
2000, Premier League.
Newcastle 1   Watford 0
Gallacher 59
Att. 36,433
2003, Champions League Phase 2, Group A.
Internazionale 2   Newcastle 2
Vieri 46   Shearer 42, 49
Cordoba 60   Att. 53,459

Playing record for this day is... 18 games,
Won 10, Drawn 5, Lost 3, GF 32, GA 15.
Today's success rate... 69.44%.

Match of the Day from 1959

EASY RIDE FOR UNITED

Newcastle have no trouble with win in Portsmouth

A crowd of 19,404 turned out to watch this Division One league match against Portsmouth. It turned out to be a real disappointment for the home fans, and a great win for the travelling Newcastle supporters.

The Portsmouth defence was rendered useless by the quick thinking forwards in the Newcastle team. The strikers, being a little too eager to score and shooting without really being ready, were the only reason that Newcastle's score wasn't far higher.

Surprisingly it was Portsmouth who almost took the lead early on when Barnard sent a shot goalwards, only for it to be cleared from right under the crossbar by McMichael.

Eight minutes further into the game and Newcastle deservedly went into the lead. Eastham sent a short pass to Curry who avoided the half-hearted attempts of a tackle from Hayward. Then he simply had to dart round the Portsmouth keeper Brown, who had come out from his line, to flick the ball into an empty net. It was an easy task, and one which Curry did without fault to put Newcastle a goal ahead.

With just a minute to go before half-time, United extended their lead with a penalty. It was Portsmouth's new signing from Wolves, Ron Howells, who brought down Eastham well within the box, and Eastham duly stepped up to the spot to effortlessly send the ball sailing into the net.

The second half started with a renewed Portsmouth side. The interval seemed to have served them well, and they came out with fighting spirit. However, they seemed to be too hard, and Saunders had two good chances at goal, which were both missed due to a lack of patience and concentration.

Newcastle scored their third goal thanks to a lovely shot from right-winger Taylor, and that signalled the end for Portsmouth. What fight they had left in them was soon gone after this, and the Magpies knew they had won.

Despite this, Newcastle didn't give up trying, and their efforts paid off again. Two more smashing goals from Curry secured his hat-trick in this match, and brought United's tally of goals to five.

A late spurt from Saunders for Portsmouth resulted in a goal, but it wasn't enough to lift spirits. The home fans were relieved to see the end of this game, but for the visiting supporters it was worth the long journey. Final score 5-1.

Portsmouth
Brown, Morrison, Gunter, Howells, Hayward, Dickinson, Barnard, Newman, Saunders, Harris, Dougan
Newcastle United
Harvey, Whitehead, McMichael, Franks, Scoular, Mitchell, Taylor, Allchurch, Curry, Eastham, White.

Bill Curry

Birthdays

John Brownlie born today in 1952.
Right-back 1978-1982, Apps 136 (1 sub). Goals 3.

Tommy Casey born today in 1930
Midfield 1952-1958, Apps 134. Goals 10.

March 12

Match of the Day from 1994

KEEGAN'S MEN IN SEVENTH HEAVEN

Goals, without Cole, galore in United super show

Who said Newcastle are toothless when Andy Cole is not his usual predatory self? Two goals apiece from Peter Beardsley, bringing up his 200th for the club, Lee and Watson, along with one from Ruel Fox dispelled this particular Southern-orientated myth. United today have probably never enjoyed such goalscoring fun, not even in their five-a-side practise games in training. The embarrassment from Swindon's camp was complete by the fact their keeper Fraser Digby had such a good game. He made significant saves throughout probably preventing a Newcastle score in double figures. The visitors, grimly glued to the bottom of the Premiership, are now certainly heading for relegation, in stark contrast to last season when they were promoted with United.

Newcastle took just twelve minutes to open up the Swindon defence through a harshly awarded penalty, this after Taylor was adjudged to have brought down Beardsley. The England international, fresh from winning his 50th cap recently, got up to send Digby the wrong way with his spot kick. The score was doubled five minutes later when Lee, having collected a superb pass from Sellars, shrugged off the attention of two defenders to plant a crisp rising shot beyond the keeper's reach. Swindon offered little during the game but their one moment in the first half came soon after when Srnicek made a splendid reflex save from McAvennie's point-blank header.

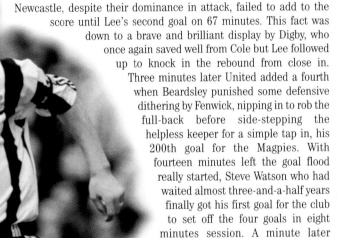

Newcastle, despite their dominance in attack, failed to add to the score until Lee's second goal on 67 minutes. This fact was down to a brave and brilliant display by Digby, who once again saved well from Cole but Lee followed up to knock in the rebound from close in. Three minutes later United added a fourth when Beardsley punished some defensive dithering by Fenwick, nipping in to rob the full-back before side-stepping the helpless keeper for a simple tap in, his 200th goal for the Magpies. With fourteen minutes left the goal flood really started, Steve Watson who had waited almost three-and-a-half years finally got his first goal for the club to set off the four goals in eight minutes session. A minute later Swindon replied with a consolation goal, albeit a wonderfully struck free kick from Moncur which Srnicek got a hand to, but couldn't hold. Then Watson proving his first strike was no fluke grabbed a second goal two minutes later with another powerful first-time shot which gave Digby no chance. Newcastle wrapped up the scoring six minutes from time with another goal, this time by Ruel Fox. He converted an inch perfect cross from Beresford with a well timed diving header.

Newcastle United
Srnicek, Robinson, Venison, Elliott, Beresford, Watson, Lee, Sellars, Fox, Cole, Beardsley.

Swindon Town
Digby, Nijholt, Fenwick, Taylor, Horlock, Moncur, Ling, Bodin, (Gooden h/t), Scott (Hammond 78), Fjortoft, McAvennie.

Referee Mr. M. Reed (Birmingham).

Peter Beardsley reached his 200-goal milestone today.

Played on this day

1898, Division 2.
Luton Town (h) 4-1   Att. 15,000
Wardrope, Harvey (3)
1904, Division 1.
Middlesbrough (a) 3-1   Att. 15,000
Appleyard, Howie, Rutherford
1910, Division 1.
Bury (h) 2-2   Att. 20,000
Wilson, Waugh (pen)
1913, FA Cup 4th round, replay.
Sunderland (h) 2-2   Att. 56,717
McTavish, Veitch
1921, Division 1.
Blackburn Rovers (h) 1-2   Att. 44,000
Hudspeth (pen)
1927, Division 1.
Blackburn Rovers (a) 2-1   Att. 40,000
Gallacher (2)
1932, FA Cup Semi Final.
Chelsea (n) 2-1   Att. 36,709
Allen, Lang
Played at Leeds Road, Huddersfield
1938, Division 2.
West Ham United (h) 2-2   Att. 22,000
Docking, J.R. Richardson
1949, Division 1.
Wolverhampton W. (a) 0-3   Att. 40,000
1952, Division 1.
Chelsea (a) 0-1   Att. 42,948
1955, FA Cup 6th round.
Huddersfield Town (a) 1-1   Att. 54,960
White
1960, Division 1.
Bolton Wanderers (a) 4-1   Att. 24,648
Eastham, Mitten (2), White
1966, Division 1.
Burnley (a) 0-1   Att. 16,257
1969, Inter Cities Fairs Cup 4th round, 1st leg.
Vitoria Setubal (h) 5-1   Att. 57,662
Davies, Foggon, Gibb, B. Robson (2)
1977, Division 1.
Norwich City (h) 5-1   Att. 27,808
T. Craig, Gowling, Oates, McCaffery (2)
1983, Division 2.
Leeds United (h) 2-1   Att. 24,543
Waddle, Keegan (pen)
1991, Division 2.
Middlesbrough (a) 0-3   Att. 18,250
1994, Premier League.
Newcastle 7   Swindon Town 1
Beardsley   Moncur 77
12 (pen), 70
Lee 17, 67
Watson 76, 79
Fox 84   Att. 32,219
1995, FA Cup 6th round.
Everton 1   Newcastle 0
Watson 66   Att. 35,203

Playing record for this day is... 19 games, Won 9, Drawn 4, Lost 6, GF 42, GA 27. Today's success rate... 57.89%.

Played on this day

1897, Division 2.
Blackpool (a) 1-4   Att. 3,000
Smellie
1909, Division 1.
Bury (a) 1-1   Att. 15,000
Opponent (og)
1911, FA Cup 4th round.
Derby County (h) 4-0   Att. 59,700
Shepherd, Stewart, Rutherford,
Willis (pen)
1915, FA Cup 4th round, replay.
Chelsea (h) 0-1   Att. 49,827
1920, Division 1.
Blackburn Rovers (a) 0-2 Att. 25,000
1926, Division 1.
Birmingham (a) 1-1   Att.30,000
Urwin
1929, Division 1.
Aston Villa (h) 2-1   Att. 35,000
Gallacher (2)
1937, Division 2.
Coventry City (h) 4-2   Att. 12,000
Imrie, Pearson, Smith (2)
1943, Wartime.
York City (a) 0-2   Att. 11,385
1948, Division 2.
Southampton (a) 2-4   Att. 28,000
Milburn, Sibley
1954, Division 1.
Huddersfield Town (a) 2-3 Att. 25,710
Milburn, Monkhouse
1963, FA Cup 4th round.
Norwich City (a) 0-5   Att. 34,770
1965, Division 2.
Norwich City (h) 2-0   Att. 41,441
Cummings, Robson
1971, Division 1.
Ipswich Town (a) 0-1   Att. 17,060
1976, Division 1.
West Ham United (h) 2-1 Att. 33,866
T. Craig (pen), Macdonald
1982, Division 2.
Rotherham United (a) 0-0 Att. 16,905
1993, Division 1.
Swindon Town (a) 1-2   Att. 17,574
Kelly
1999, Premier League.
Newcastle 1   **Manchester United 2**
Solano 16   Cole 25, 51
                         Att. 36,776

Playing record for this day is... 18 games,
Won 5, Drawn 3, Lost 10, GF 23, GA 32.
Today's success rate... 36.11%.

Match of the Day from 1911

DERBY HUMBLED BY CUP HOLDERS UNITED
Newcastle in great form victorious by 4-0

For an incredible sixth time in seven years cup specialists Newcastle United have qualified for the FA Cup semi finals. In front of a huge 59,700 crowd at St. James' Park today, the cup holders dismissed Second Division Derby County by four goals to nil in one of the finest displays of football that have ever characterised the greatest club cup competition in the world. Still flushed with their sensational win over Everton, fourth-placed in the First Division, Derby journeyed to Tyneside, not entirely without hope of an upset, aiming to succeed where both Nottingham Forest and Hull City had failed. Unfortunately for them, they caught Newcastle in supreme form. Individually and collectively the Magpies gave a brilliant exposition of football which thrilled those fortunate to have witnessed the game. The Rams were completely outplayed by United and they thoroughly deserved their passage into the semi finals where they will now face Chelsea in Birmingham on March 25th.

Derby made a reasonable start but their efforts to force the game were hampered by some below average finishing. Their forwards were tenacious without ever being dangerous, well marshalled by a strong steady defence led by Wilf Low and Dave Willis. Low in particular was first class and probably the best player on the field. Newcastle were not long gaining the measure of their opponents, and after 25 minutes play Albert Shepherd netted his 31st goal of the season, his seventh in this year's FA Cup competition, to put United in front. The free-scoring United centre-forward tricked two Derby defenders on the edge of the penalty area before turning to hit a powerful drive which flew past keeper Scattergood, giving him absolutely no chance of stopping it. Newcastle settled and an inevitable second goal came just before the interval when Jackie Rutherford finished off a fine four-man move from close range, and the score remained 2-0 at the break.

The second half was a complete Newcastle United exhibition game, full of great football which had the crowd thrilled by their every move. Derby for their credit never relaxed their efforts where another team may have suffered a landslide loss. United added their third goal of the game through Jimmy Stewart's thumping header from inside the six-yard box. Then, inside the final ten minutes, Willis wrapped up the rout with a penalty, and the crowd relished the fact, United had cruised into another semi final.

Newcastle United
Lawrence, McWilliam, Whitson, Veitch, Low, Willis, Rutherford, Stewart, Shepherd, Higgins, Wilson.
Derby County
Scattergood, Atkin, Flanders, Garry, Barbour, Blackshaw, Grimes, Bloomer, Bentley, Bauchop, Barnes.

Jackie Rutherford

March 14

Match of the Day from 1951

TWO IN TWO MINUTES STRIKE PUTS UNITED INTO FINAL

Wolves rocked by Mitchell and Milburn

Frank Brennan

Having won their way to Wembley again, to face Blackpool conquerors of Birmingham in the other semi-final replay, Newcastle now have a real chance of landing the Cup and League double. This feat has not been repeated since Aston Villa's accomplishment 55 years ago. Newcastle are now six points behind the League leaders Tottenham Hotspur but have three games in hand over the Londoners. In an odd twist to today's game, Newcastle now face Blackpool for League points at Bloomfield Road this coming Saturday (March 17) this a real Cup Final preview. After an enthralling game which kept every spectator thrilled United overcome Wolves 2-1 in the semi final replay at Leeds Road, Huddersfield. The only regret by most fans on either side, paying record gate receipts of £7,635, was that this game could not have been the final itself. Wolves deserved runners-up medals for their performance and the game was more than worthy of a Wembley setting.

Newcastle were slightly the better side in the opening quarter of an hour but a lack of incisiveness in the penalty area prevented them turning this advantage into goals. Instead they paid the penalty when Wolves drew first blood in the fifteenth minute. Walker accepted a pass from Mullen and ran on to within fifteen yards of goal before sweetly hitting a shot across Fairbrother and into the bottom corner of the net. All the time Newcastle were improving, however, and this setback didn't deter them at all. They carried on as they started throwing men forward whenever they could in a bold onslaught on the Midlanders' goal. This paid off in dramatic fashion just after the half hour mark when the Magpies struck twice in as many minutes play. In the 32nd minute Taylor cleverly beat two opponents and made the perfect opening for Jackie Milburn to put Newcastle level at 1-1. Just two minutes later, with the Magpies supporters still celebrating, they went ahead, Milburn delaying his pass perfectly before sliding the ball left for Bobby Mitchell to run on and hit first time into the roof of the net.

Wolves now had to come from behind, and the second half was largely dominated by their desperate attacking. However in the 64th minute Mitchell scored what everyone in the ground thought was a legitimate third goal for United only for the referee to disallow the effort for offside. Wolves never gave up trying for the equaliser. They threw attack after attack at the Newcastle goal and at times every one of their players except keeper Williams was well in the United half. During this period Hancock continually menaced Newcastle once hitting the crossbar with a spectacular shot from twenty yards. But for all their efforts Fairbrother kept them out aided by the heroic defending of Cowell, Corbett and Brennan, particularly in the final quarter of an hour when Wolves forced four corners in succession. But there was no further score in this palpitating game and United now pass on to Blackpool and Wembley on April 28.

Newcastle United
Fairbrother, Cowell, Corbett, Harvey, Brennan, Crowe, Walker, G. Robledo, Milburn, Taylor, Mitchell.

Wolverhampton Wanderers
Williams, Short, Pritchard, Russell, Shorthouse, Wright, Hancocks, Walker, Swinborne, Dunn, Mullen.

Birthdays

Graham Oates born today in 1949.
Midfield 1976-1978, Apps 43 (10 subs). Goals 3.

Steve Harper born today in 1975.
Goalkeeper 1991-present day, Apps 55 (3 subs).

Played on this day

1896, Division 2.
Notts County (a) 1-0   Att. 5,000
Aitken

1900, Division 1.
Glossop North End (h) 1-0   Att. 6,000
Peddie

1903, Division 1.
Sheffield United (h) 0-0   Att. 20,000

1906, FA Cup 4th round, replay.
Birmingham (h) 3-0   Att. 39,059
Appleyard (2), Howie

1908, Division 1.
Bury (h) 3-0   Att. 25,000
Appleyard (2), Howie

1914, Division 1.
Preston North End (a) 1-4   Att. 18,000
Shepherd

1923, Division 1.
West Bromwich A. (a) 1-2   Att. 5,520
Harris

1925, Division 1.
Burnley (a) 3-1   Att. 12,000
Harris (2), McDonald

1931, Division 1.
Blackpool (h) 0-2   Att. 20,000

1936, Division 2.
Bury (h) 3-0   Att. 14,000
Connelly (2), J. Smith

1942, Wartime.
Sheffield United (a) 0-0   Att. 7,000

1951, FA Cup Semi Final, replay.
Wolverhampton W. (n) 2-1   Att. 47,349
Milburn, Mitchell
Played at Leeds Road, Huddersfield

1953, Division 1.
Arsenal (h) 2-2   Att. 51,618
Mitchell, G. Robledo

1959, Division 1.
Manchester City (a) 1-5   Att. 25,417
White

1964, Division 2.
Sunderland (h) 1-0   Att. 27,341
McGarry (pen)

1970, Division 1.
West Bromwich A. (a) 2-2   Att. 19,641
Dyson, Robson

1973, Texaco Cup Semi Final, 1st leg.
Ipswich Town (h) 1-1   Att. 22,531
Macdonald

1981, Division 2.
Preston North End (h) 2-0   Att. 12,015
Harford (2)

1992, Division 2.
Swindon Town (h) 3-1   Att. 23,138
Kelly, Peacock, Quinn

1998, Premier League.
Newcastle 0   Coventry City 0
    Att. 36,762

Playing record for this day is... 20 games, Won 10, Drawn 6, Lost 4, GF 30, GA 21. Today's success rate...65%.

March 15

Played on this day

1902, Division 1.
Wolverhampton W. (h) 3-1   Att. 7,000
Veitch, Rutherford (2)
1913, Division 1.
Blackburn Rovers (h) 0-1   Att. 18,000
1919, Wartime.
Scotswood (h) 2-2   Att. 12,000
Booth, Cooper
1924, Division 1.
West Bromwich A. (h) 1-1   Att. 20,000
Harris
1930, Division 1.
Sheffield Wednesday (a) 2-4   Att. 10,000
Devine, Weaver
1941, Wartime.
Sheffield Wednesday (a) 0-2   Att. 1,371
1952, Division 1.
Portsmouth (h) 3-3   Att. 62,870
Milburn, Mitchell, G. Robledo
1958, Division 1.
Leicester City (h) 5-3   Att. 33,840
Bottom (2), White (3)
1975, Division 1.
Ipswich Town (a) 4-5   Att. 23,450
Tudor (2), Macdonald (2)
1977, Division 1.
Stoke City (a) 0-0   Att. 12,708
1978, Division 1.
Birmingham City (h) 1-1   Att. 19,493
Nattrass
1980, Division 2.
West Ham United (h) 0-0   Att. 25,474
1986, Division 1.
Ipswich Town (h) 3-1   Att. 19,451
Beardsley, Whitehurst, Gascoigne
1989, Division 1.
Nottingham Forest (a) 1-1   Att. 20,800
Brock
1997, Premier League.
Newcastle 4   Coventry City 0
Watson 12
Lee 45
Beardsley 76 (pen)
Elliott 87   Att. 36,571
2003, Premier League.
Charlton Athletic 0 Newcastle 2
                     Shearer 33 (pen)
                     Solano 49
                     Att. 26,728
*Alan Shearer nets the winner on his 200th
Premier League appearance.*

Playing record for this day is... 16 games,
Won 4, Drawn 7, Lost 5, GF 31, GA 25.
Today's success rate... 53.12%.

Match of the Day from 1997

ASPRILLA MAGIC WRECKS COVENTRY
Colombian thrills the Toon Army in superb show

Faustino Asprilla supplied the inspiration as Newcastle stormed to a 4-0 win against Premiership strugglers Coventry at St. James' Park today. The Colombian international laid on first-half goals for Steve Watson and Rob Lee to put United firmly in command. In the second half his trickery and pace led to the dismissal of one man, and almost the dismissal of another as Newcastle hit two more goals to leave the crowd of 36,571 thoroughly entertained. Asprilla's display deserved a goal and he was desperately close when a beautifully curled free kick struck a post, this would have capped a magnificent day for the crowd favourite. Kenny Dalglish had been forced into using Asprilla and Beardsley to lead United's attack following the withdrawal of England strikers Alan Shearer and Les Ferdinand through injury. Coventry, who have now lost a fourth successive Premiership visit to Tyneside, were also short of regular first-teamers Noel Whelan and Paul Williams.

Marcus Hall, who was a late replacement in the visitors' side, almost gave Coventry a perfect start inside a minute. Only a terrific defensive block by Rob Elliott inside the penalty area saved them. Then Asprilla's menace started to swing the game and it was clear Coventry's chance had gone for good. Asprilla was the provider when Watson fired Newcastle into a twelfth minute lead with his first goal of the season. The Colombian's neat flick opened up Coventry's defence and Watson steadied himself before sliding his close-range shot under Ogrizovic's dive. The visitors gained some heart when Shaka Hislop dropped Paul Telfer's cross and this left a great chance for Kevin Richardson, but the United keeper redeemed himself and saved the follow up header. Darren Peacock then prevented Huckerby scoring on his return to St. James' Park with a superbly timed sliding tackle. Then Hislop again kept United in front when he pulled off a fantastic reflex save to deny Gary McAllister's diving header. On the stroke of half-time United then went 2-0 ahead. Asprilla put Lee through but his initial hesitancy allowed Richardson to get back and cover. A neat turn on the edge of the box created room for a crisply hit low shot which beat Orizovic's full-length dive.

Coventry were then further hampered by the early dismissal of Brian Borrows in the second half. Again Asprilla skipped clear of the Sky Blues defence and as he was about to chase into the area the half-time substitute for Evtushok sent him flying with a clumsy tackle. Referee Ashby immediately sent Borrows off, and from the free kick, Asprilla curled the ball round the wall and onto the post with the keeper nowhere near it. Moments later Asprilla was bundled over again this time inside the box, but to everyone's surprise Dublin, who had been booked earlier, escaped further punishment. Beardsley stepped up to smash in the penalty and Coventry were dead and buried. Peter Beardsley then turned goal provider four minutes from time with a pass to Warren Barton. His cross evaded Ogrizovic and Robbie Elliott made no mistake with the empty net facing him.

Newcastle United
Hislop, Watson, Elliott, Batty, Peacock, Albert, Lee (Clark 76), Ginola, Asprilla (Gillespie 76), Beardsley, Barton.
Coventry City
Ogrizovic, Shaw, Richardson, Jess, Breen, McAllister, Telfer, Hall, Evtushok, (Borrows h/t), Dublin, Huckerby.
Referee Mr. G. Ashby (Worcester).

Sadly Missed

Sandy Higgins died on this day in 1939, aged 53.
Midfield 1905-1919, Apps 150. Goals 41.

March 16

Match of the Day from 1907

UNITED ALMOST PAY THE PENALTY
Newcastle claim victory despite two missed spot kicks

There was vast interest in this game at St. James' Park today and a crowd of 48,000 were present at kick off. The Villa were hoping to end their North-East bogey having taken just four points from a possible five matches against Middlesbrough, Sunderland, and Newcastle. United's interest lay entirely on their pursuit of the League title and to maintain their unbeaten home record over the 1906-07 season.

In drizzling rain and a muddy pitch Newcastle got off to a cracking start, and in only their second attack took the lead after three minutes. Appleyard set up Rutherford with a neat chip inside the area but his header bounced off the cross bar, Appleyard then raced in to prod the ball over the line. Soon after Villa had the ball in the net, a challenge by Cantrell on keeper Lawrence seemed to be legitimate but when Millington put the loose ball in he found, for some unseen reason, that the goal had been disallowed, probably for the original challenge but no one appeared to appeal at the time. It was tough on Villa who were starting to get into the game but worse was to follow for them in the tenth minute when United doubled their lead. A smart interchange of passing between Howie and Brown left Appleyard with another simple tap-in from close range, his second of the game. Just four minutes later Villa pulled themselves back in the contest when McWilliam fouled Hall inside the area and this time the referee's decision went the Midlanders' way, Hall picked himself up to blast the penalty past Lawrence. Villa were now on top and Newcastle were having problems dealing with Bache, Hampton and Cantrell all of whom got in half chances without hitting the target. At last United broke on the counter attack and Rutherford beat the offside trap to race clear only to be pulled down by Logan. Another penalty was awarded, but this time George, the Villa keeper, guessed correctly to push out Rutherford's kick. Logan then made amends for the foul by blocking Rutherford's follow-up shot, out for a corner. Still Villa continued to dominate play and should have equalised just before half time when Lawrence, under pressure from Hampton's challenge, dropped the ball, but the Villa forward then put his shot wide of the open goal. Newcastle then landed the killer blow for the visitors on the stroke of half-time, Gosnell, after beating Millington, raced down the right wing sending in a beautifully flighted cross for Rutherford, his volley going in via the keeper's hand then post.

Despite the late goal it was Villa again who started the better in the second half, but some great defending by Gardner and McWilliam saw United weather the onslaught until the tide turned briefly on 55 minutes. Newcastle broke again with the ever dangerous Appleyard, who beat his man Miles to go clear, but again Logan came across and bundled him over just as he was about to shoot. This time United called on Veitch to take the penalty but again George pulled off a fantastic save at the foot of his right-hand post to deny Newcastle a second time from the spot. Boosted by their keeper's heroics the visitors launched an attack on their left wing through Millington. He centred for Cantrell to head Villa back in the game on the hour mark. The final half hour was seen out by the Newcastle defence in which McWilliam was outstanding. At the final whistle the score remained 3-2 and United took two more precious points towards the Championship.

Newcastle United
Lawrence, McCracken, Carr, Gardner, McWilliam, Veitch, Rutherford, Howie, Appleyard, Brown, Gosnell.
Aston Villa
George, Logan, Miles, Codling, Buckley, Greenlaugh, Halt, Bache, Hampton, Cantrell, Millington.
Referee Mr. McQueen (Liverpool).

Played on this day

1895, Division 2.
Bury (h) 1-0   Att. 4,000
Thompson
1898, Division 2.
Manchester City (h) 2-0   Att. 17,000
Peddie, Aitken
1901, Division 1.
Wolverhampton W. (a) 0-1   Att. 5,000
1907, Division 1.
Aston Villa (h) 3-2   Att. 48,000
Appleyard (2), Rutherford
1912, Division 1.
Middlesbrough (h) 0-1   Att. 35,000
1929, Division 1.
Huddersfield Town (a) 1-2   Att. 12,000
Cunningham (pen)
1935, Division 2.
Barnsley (a) 1-2   Att. 14,511
Wilson
1939, Division 2.
Norwich City (a) 1-1   Att. 7,764
Clifton
1940, Wartime.
Bradford Park Ave. (a) 1-2   Att. 3,000
Moses
1946, Wartime.
Bolton Wanderers (h) 3-4   Att. 38,517
Stubbins (2), Wayman
1955, FA Cup 6th round, replay.
Huddersfield Town (h) 2-0   Att. 52,449
Keeble, R. Mitchell
1957, Division 1.
Leeds United (a) 0-0   Att. 33,000
1963, Division 2.
Swansea Town (a) 0-1   Att. 8,000
1968, Division 1.
Leeds United (h) 1-1   Att. 46,075
T. Robson
1974, Division 1.
Chelsea (a) 0-1   Att. 24,207
1976, Division 1.
Arsenal (a) 0-0   Att. 18,424
1991, Division 2.
Bristol City (h) 0-0   Att. 13,578
2002, Premier League.
Newcastle 2   Ipswich Town 2
Robert 60   M. Bent 50, 63
Shearer 88   Att. 51,115

Playing record for this day is... 18 games,
Won 4, Drawn 6, Lost 8, GF 18, GA 20.
Today's success rate...38.89%.

Birthdays

Alan Gowling born today in 1949.
Forward 1975-1978, Apps 123 (1 sub). Goals 52.
Billy Wilson born today in 1943.
Defender 1960-1962, Apps 1. Goals 0.

Sadly Missed

Billy Hibbert died on this day in 1949, aged 64.
Midfield 1911-1920, Apps 159. Goals 50.

Played on this day

1900, Division 1.
Liverpool (a) 0-2   Att. 18,000
1906, Division 1.
Wolverhampton W. (a) 2-0   Att. 9,000
Gosnell, J. Rutherford
1913, FA Cup 4th round, replay.
Sunderland (h) 0-3   Att. 49,754
1915, Division 1.
Chelsea (h) 2-0   Att. 5,000
Finlay (2)
1923, Division 1.
Bolton Wanderers(a) 0-1   Att. 25,000
1928, Division 1.
Sunderland (a) 1-1   Att. 40,071
McDonald
1934, Division 1.
Sheffield United (a) 0-4   Att. 25,000
1937, Division 2.
Nottingham Forest (h) 3-2 Att. 4,000
Smith, Rogers, Imrie (pen)
1945, Wartime.
Gateshead (a) 3-0   Att. 14,300
Stubbins (3)
*Stubbins nets his second consecutive
hat-trick after his four goals last week
against Middlesbrough.*
1951, Division 1.
Blackpool (a) 2-2   Att. 30,000
Milburn, G. Robledo
1956, Division 1.
Blackpool (a) 1-5   Att. 23,740
Keeble
1962, Division 2.
Scunthorpe United (h) 2-1 Att. 37,931
Thomas, Day
1964, Division 2.
Swansea Town (a) 1-0   Att. 9,000
Anderson
1971, Division 1.
Everton (h) 2-1   Att. 22,874
Tudor, Moncur
1973, Division 1.
Manchester United (a) 1-2 Att. 48,426
Nattrass
1984, Division 2.
Middlesbrough (h) 3-1   Att. 30,421
McDermott, Beardsley, Keegan
1990, Division 2.
Ipswich Town (h) 2-1   Att. 20,554
Quinn (2)
2001, Premier League.
Newcastle 1   Middlesbrough 2
Cort 60   Boksic 28, 33
                           Att. 51,751

Playing record for this day is... 18 games,
Won 9, Drawn 2, Lost 7, GF 26, GA 28.
Today's success rate... 55.56%.

Match of the Day from 1906

UNITED WIN AT WOLVES

Newcastle take the win after end-to-end struggle

It was Wolves who won the toss in this Division One tie in front of a crowd of 9,000, and the home side began with the full intention of winning hands down. Newcastle had other ideas, and in the opening minutes they had gained their first free kick. It was taken quickly, but James managed to get to the ball for Wolves and stop it reaching danger.

Wolves then decided it was their turn for an attack, and a promising move was started with another free kick, sent from Bettelley to Pedley. McCracken stopped him in his tracks, and in the next minute Wolves won a corner from an attempt at goal from Wooldridge. The ball was sent into the box, and the all-important touch went to Smith who tried to beat the Newcastle keeper. Lawrence was able to get his hand to it and thumped the ball away from goal to stop the shot.

Next it was Newcastle's turn for a free kick. This time it was sent too wide, and missed the goalmouth by a long way.

Another attempt from Pedley for Wolves was blocked by Carr, and a shot from Gosnell was saved by Wolves' keeper Baddeley.

Despite the movement of the ball from one goal to the other, and then back again, it was Newcastle who had most possession in this match. Play seemed to be in their favour throughout, and they just needed some luck in order to take advantage of the situation. That luck was not forthcoming in the first half, and there were plenty more chances at goal for both teams.

A fine save from Lawrence stopped Wolves from scoring, and the action was repeated by Baddeley, keeping out the Newcastle forwards. With strenuous efforts from both sides, and still no score on the sheet, play entered half time.

The second period began in full swing with a tremendous shot by Rutherford which was kept out of the net by Wolves' keeper Baddeley with a full-length diving save. Newcastle were on the attack, and they were not going to give up yet. Another shot by McClarence was saved by Baddeley, but Wolves were beginning to tire.

The deadlock was finally broken by Gosnell with a lovely run, beating the entire Wolves defence before flicking the ball into the net with Baddeley given no hope of getting his hand to it. Newcastle were leading, and they intended to keep it that way. Another goal was needed to ensure the win, but it was Wolves who were now in attacking mode.

A good chance for the equaliser was ruined when Breakwell totally ruined his shot at goal, and it turned out to be the last real chance the home side got to get back into the match.

The final score was settled when Rutherford took advantage of an opening in the Wolves defence and slipped through to catch Baddeley off guard. He shot the ball high into goal, and the Wolves' keeper had no chance to save. The score was 2-0, and despite their best efforts to make a comeback, Wolves were out of the game.

Wolverhampton Wanderers
Baddeley, Jones, Bettelley, Williams, Lloyd, James, Layton, Breakwell, Wooldridge, Smith, Pedley.
Newcastle United
Lawrence, Carr, McCracken, McWilliam, Aitken, Liddell, Gosnell, McClarence, Hardinge, Howie, Rutherford.
Referee Mr. McQueen (Liverpool).

Birthdays

Pat Heard born today in 1960.
Midfield 1984-1985, Apps 36. Goals 2.
Jock McCurley born today in 1906.
Midfield 1927-1930, Apps 45. Goals 8.

Sadly Missed

John Carr died on this day in 1948, aged 72.
Left-back 1897-1922, Apps 278. Goals 5.

March 18

Match of the Day from 1970

BRAVE FIGHTBACK NOT ENOUGH

Newcastle out on away goals rule despite impressive win

The holders, Newcastle United, are out of this year's European Inter Cities Fairs Cup. They defeated Anderlecht, of Belgium, 3-1 today at St. James' Park, but as they lost the first leg 2-0 the tie ended 3-3 on aggregate leaving United out due to the visitors' solitary strike scored just two minutes from the end of the game.

Roared on by the 59,309 crowd, Newcastle were out for an early goal, and it came after just four minutes. A free kick by Clark was headed down by Davies to Robson, who neatly flicked his header over the advancing keeper. In an eventful opening spell Robson was then booked seven minutes later for a clumsy charge on the Anderlecht keeper Trappeniers. Man of the match, Robson capped a marvellous performance by netting an all-important second goal for United to put the tie level after twenty minutes, and make amends for his earlier rush of blood. A long ball out of defence by Gibb was brilliantly controlled by Robson who after taking one stride smashed a terrific 30-yard thunderbolt which flew past the helpless Trappeniers before he could move. Newcastle continued to create plenty of opportunities throughout the half but at the interval had to be content with a 2-0 lead.

With the strong wind now at their backs, Anderlecht started to turn up the pressure on the United goal. McFaul, the Newcastle keeper, took an early knock and spent the remainder of the game limping quite badly. But despite the setback the United defence managed to cover adequately to keep Anderlecht out. Indeed, as the half wore on it was Newcastle who looked the more likely to add a third goal. With five minutes of the game remaining they did just that and St. James' Park erupted. Another well taken free kick by Moncur dropped cleverly into the goalmouth and as the ball bobbled about, Dyson nipped in to tuck a close-range shot into an empty net. As Newcastle celebrated a thrilling win however, Anderlecht went on the attack and three minutes later had the ball in United's net. A cross-field pass by Mulder should have been intercepted by Burton, who had had a great game, but the United defender missed this one and it left Nordahl in the clear to race on and crack in a left-foot shot past McFaul. The game petered out in almost silence after such wild scenes of jubilation but at the final whistle United's players were given a tremendous reception by the fans for their fight.

Newcastle United
McFaul, Craig, Clark, Gibb, Burton, Moncur, Robson, Dyson, Davies, Guthrie, Foggon.
Anderlecht
Trappeniers, Heylens, Martens, Nordahl, Velkeneers, Kralunda, Desanghere, Devrindt, Mulder, Van Himst, Puis.

Toon News Extra

1901... St. James' Park...Home of English football!

In the first international staged at Newcastle's home ground St. James' Park, England emphatically beat Wales this afternoon 6-0. It was a great debut for Newcastle's first England capped player, goalkeeper Matt Kingsley, who kept a clean sheet in a great all round team performance.

Birthdays

Reg Evans born today in 1939.
Winger 1956-1959, Apps 4. Goals 0.
Charlie Woods born today in 1941.
Midfield 1959-1962, Apps 30. Goals 10.

Temuri Ketsbaia born today in 1968.
Midfield 1997-2000, Apps 109 (52 subs). Goals 14.

Played on this day

1899, Division 1.
Bolton Wanderers (a) 0-0   Att. 5,000
1905, Division 1.
Bury (a) 4-2   Att. 18,000
Appleyard (3), Aitken
1911, Division 1.
Aston Villa (h) 1-0   Att. 15,000
Shepherd
1914, Division 1.
Burnley (h) 3-1   Att. 15,000
Douglas, Goodwill, Hibbert
1922, Division 1.
Oldham Athletic (h) 1-1   Att. 30,000
Harris
1939, Division 2.
Fulham (a) 1-1   Att. 19,941
Clifton
1944, Wartime.
Darlington(a) 0-2   Att. 12,835
1950, Division 1.
West Bromwich A. (a) 1-1   Att. 33,469
Houghton
1967, Division 1.
Blackpool (h) 2-1   Att. 30,568
B. Robson (2)
1970, Inter Cities Fairs Cup 4th round, 2nd leg.
R.S.C. Anderlecht (h) 3-1   Att. 59,309
Dyson, Robson (2)
With the scores level on aggregate 3-3, Newcastle lost on the away goals rule.
1972, Division 1.
Liverpool (a) 0-5   Att. 43,899
1974, FA Cup 6th round.
Nottingham Forest (n) 0-0   Att. 40,685
Played at Goodison Park, Everton.
1975, Division 1.
Arsenal (a) 0-3   Att. 16,540
1978, Division 1.
Chelsea (a) 2-2   Att. 22,777
McGhee, Burns (pen)
1996, Premier League.
Newcastle 3   West Ham United 0
Albert 21
Asprilla 55
Ferdinand 65   Att. 36,331
1997, UEFA Cup Quarter Final, 2nd leg.
A.S. Monaco 3   Newcastle 0
Legwinski 42
Bernarbia 50, 67   Att. 18,500
Newcastle lost 4-0 on aggregate.
1998, Premier League.
Newcastle 1   Crystal Palace 2
Shearer 77   Lombardo 14
                   Jansen 23
                   Att. 36,565

Playing record for this day is... 17 games, Won 6, Drawn 6, Lost 5, GF 22, GA 25.
Today's success rate... 52.94%.

March 19

Played on this day

1902, Division 1.
Nottingham Forest (a) **2-0**   Att. 20,000
Pattinson, Aitken

1904, Division 1.
Liverpool (h) **1-1**   Att. 20,000
Howie

1910, Division 1.
Tottenham Hotspur (a) **4-0**   Att. 30,000
Stewart (2), Howie, Rutherford

1921, Division 1.
Blackburn Rovers (a) **3-3**   Att. 25,000
McDonald, Smailes, Harris

1924, Division 1.
Notts County (h) **1-2**   Att. 10,000
McDonald

1927, Division 1.
Sunderland (h) **1-0**   Att. 67,211
Gallacher

1932, Division 1.
Arsenal (a) **0-1**   Att. 57,516

1936, Division 2.
Leicester City (a) **0-1**   Att. 10,000

1938, Division 2.
Southampton (a) **0-1**   Att. 20,000

1949, Division 1.
Arsenal (h) **3-2**   Att. 55,248
Harvey, Mitchell, Robledo

1955, Division 1.
Wolverhampton W. (a) **2-2**   Att. 36,614
Milburn (2)

1958, Division 1.
Preston North End (a) **1-2**   Att. 24,793
White

1960, Division 1.
Luton Town (h) **3-2**   Att. 29,269
Eastham, White (2)

1966, Division 1.
Chelsea (h) **0-1**   Att. 35,118

1977, Division 1.
West Bromwich A. (a) **1-1**   Att. 23,780
Barrowclough

1983, Division 2.
Burnley (a) **0-1**   Att. 13,900

1986, Division 1.
Oxford United (a) **2-1**   Att. 10,052
Gascoigne, Beardsley

1988, Division 1.
Arsenal (a) **1-1**   Att. 25,889
Goddard

1994, Premier League.

West Ham United 2	Newcastle 4
Breacher 67	Lee 34, 73
Martin 81	Cole 69
Att. 23,132	Mathie 90

1995, Premier League.

Newcastle 1	Arsenal 0
Beardsley 89	Att. 35,611

2000, Premier League.

Everton 0	Newcastle 2
	Hughes 79
Att. 32,512	Dyer 87

2003, Champions League.

Newcastle 0	Barcelona 2
	Kluivert 60
Att. 51,883	Motta 74

Playing record for this day is... 22 games,
Won 9, Drawn 5, Lost 8, GF 32, GA 26.
Today's success rate... 52.27%.

Match of the Day from 1994

UNITED'S PASSPORT TO EUROPE
Emphatic win at Upton Park sets up UEFA Cup spot

In a match which leapt dramatically to life in the final quarter, Cole, Lee and Mathie scored goals in front of an ecstatic travelling Toon Army to give United three more valuable league points. Newcastle began the day in third spot and kept the same side that hammered Swindon 7-1 a week ago. Their goal is a UEFA Cup place and their chances after this performance today are now looking very good. Europe would be the next logical step for United boss Kevin Keegan. After all, his story has been one of success breeding more success since he left Scunthorpe for Liverpool almost 23 years ago.

It was West Ham who made the better start today and Chapman got in two headers which should have troubled Srnicek more, but on both occasions the keeper merely watched the ball roll harmlessly wide of goal, Cole's effort, at the other end, from Fox's cross was a little nearer. The Hammers were helped by Beardsley being second best for the first half an hour, but he sprang into action with a delightful through ball which put Lee in the clear only for his shot to be deflected wide. With half time approaching Newcastle came on strong, gaining their deserved reward, a goal from Rob Lee on 34 minutes. As the ball fell to him, on the edge of the area, Lee hit a crisper and more accurate shot at goal. Whether this strike would have gone in directly we'll never know but the ball took a nasty deflection of Potts and left keeper Miklosko well beaten.

Beardsley began the second half with a superb 40-yard run and Newcastle continued to pass the ball neatly, with Venison cool at the heart of their defence. For West Ham, Martin continued to stand out as their best player helped by some clever play by Holmes, Chapman and Marsh. It was from the latter's telling pass that West Ham stole an equalising goal twelve minutes into the half. An arrowing long cross-field ball left Breaker completely open on the right wing enabling him to cut inside and plant a hard, low drive into the far corner of Srnicek's goal. Now, there was all to play for, and against the run of play at this stage, it was Newcastle who burst into action with two quick and devastating goals. The first of them, after 69 minutes, was down to the lightning instincts of Cole. Fox centred from near the by-line and Cole, his boot raised, nipped in just ahead of Martin and Potts to steer United back in front. Four minutes later Newcastle scored a third goal and again it was from another sweet move, Beardsley fed Cole and he in turn put Lee free to run on and blast the ball past the shell-shocked Miklosko. To their credit the home side never gave up and nine minutes from time Martin headed in Bishop's free kick from close range. Then in the last minute of the game Beardsley and Cole combined again to set up Mathie with a simple chance close in to complete the scoring at 4-2.

West Ham United
Miklosko, Breaker, Potts, Martin, Rowland, Marsh, Butler, Bishop, Holmes, Chapman, Morley (Boere 80).
Newcastle United
Srnicek, Robinson, Venison, Elliott, Beresford, Fox (Mathie 80), Watson (Neilson 22), Sellars, Cole, Beardsley, Lee.
Referee Mr. K. Morton (Bury St Edmonds).

Rob Lee

Birthdays

Warren Barton born today in 1969.
Right-back 1995-2002, Apps 220 (27 subs).
Goals 5.
Darren Bradshaw born today in 1967.
Centre-half 1989-1992, Apps 47 (7 subs). Goals 0.

Sadly Missed

Jimmy Scoular died on this day in 1998, aged 73.
Midfield 1953-1961, Apps 272. Goals 6.

March 20

Match of the Day from 1993

COUNTY DEMOLISHED BY KELLY'S HEROES
Awesome Newcastle set up another memorable win

Newcastle extended their lead at the top of Division One by completing a league double over Notts County at St. James' Park today. When the sides last met in December, Newcastle were victors by 2-0, today the winning margin was doubled thanks largely to a magnificent attacking display by the Magpies in the second half. The win also allayed any doubts about Kevin Keegan's side's potential after last week's shock defeat at Swindon, and the disappointing draw at home to Charlton the previous week.

Some great defending coupled with County's early eagerness in midfield helped keep the score down to a respectable 1-0 at the half-time break. Only one lapse was made in the 32nd minute allowing Robert Lee to net his eleventh goal of the season. The significant breakthrough though virtually guaranteed Newcastle's win as their defence never looked anything but comfortable against the County forwards, the visitors ending the half without a shot of any note on target.

In the second half Newcastle took full control but the score threatened to stay the same due to some terrible early finishing. Good chances fell to both Lee Clark and David Kelly, who both missed the target when shooting from inside the penalty area. Kelly however soon made amends for his miss when he converted a great run and cross by Lee after 56 minutes. Just five minutes later Kelly, after good approach play by Andy Cole and Lee Clark, headed in United's third goal from inside the six-yard box, this his 23rd goal of the season. Newcastle completed their scoring in the 69th minute with a tremendous strike from Cole, his first for the club since his record £1.75 million transfer from Bristol City. Put through by man-of-the-match Lee Clark, Cole controlled and turned in one movement before lashing the ball into the corner from just inside the area. On this form Cole and Newcastle can expect many more opportunities, and goals, as there seems no match for the sheer brilliance of their forwards, this second half showing was simply awesome.

Newcastle United
Srnicek, Venison, Beresford, Bracewell, Scott (Peacock), Howey, Lee, Cole, Kelly, Clark (Robinson), Sellars.
Notts County
Cherry, Short, Johnson (Slawson), Thomas, Cox, Walker, Lund, Draper, Wilson, Devlin (Williams), Smith.

Birthdays

Dave Beasant born today in 1959.
Goalkeeper 1988-1989, Apps 27.
Wyn Davies born today in 1942.
Centre-forward 1966-1971, Apps 216. Goals 53.

Silvio Maric born today in 1975.
Striker 1999-2000, Apps 31 (14 subs). Goals 2.

Played on this day

1896, Division 2.
Manchester City (h) 4-1   Att. 12,000
Wardrope, Thompson, Collins, Lennox

1903, Division 1.
Grimsby Town (a) 0-1   Att. 4,000

1908, Division 1.
Birmingham (a) 1-1   Att. 20,000
Howie

1914, Division 1.
Tottenham Hotspur (a) 0-0   Att. 20,000

1925, Division 1.
Leeds United (h) 4-1   Att. 19,000
Harris (2), McDonald (2)

1931, Division 1.
Portsmouth (a) 2-1   Att. 17,000
Bedford, Lang

1934, Division 1.
Manchester City (a) 1-1   Att. 14,000
Leighton

1936, Division 2.
West Ham United (a) 1-4   Att. 40,000
Wilson

1942, Wartime.
Preston North End (h) 4-4   Att. 8,000
Short (3), Stubbins

1953, Division 1.
Derby County (a) 2-0   Att. 19,741
G. Robledo (2)

1959, Division 1.
Arsenal (h) 1-0   Att. 32,774
Curry

1970, Division 1.
Stoke City (h) 3-1   Att. 28,485
Davies, Robson (2, 1 pen)

1973, Anglo Italian Cup, Group Stage.
Bologna (h) 1-0   Att. 15,220
Gibb

1974, FA Cup 6th round, replay.
Nottingham Forest (n) 1-0   Att. 31,373
Macdonald
Played at Goodison Park, Everton

1981, Division 2.
Shrewsbury Town (a) 0-1   Att. 4,975

1987, Division 1.
Manchester City (a) 0-0   Att. 23,060

1990, Division 2.
Bradford City (a) 2-3   Att. 10,364
McGhee (pen), Aizlewood (og)

1992, Division 2.
Grimsby Town (a) 1-1   Att. 11,613
Sheedy

Playing record for this day is... 18 games,
Won 8, Drawn 6, Lost 4, GF 28, GA 20.
Today's success rate... 61.11%.

Match of the Day from 1974

AT LAST!
UNITED COMPLETE CUP-TIE VICTORY

Long running Forest saga ended by solitary Macdonald strike

Malcolm Macdonald, after a series of squandered chances, finally confirmed Newcastle's right to a place in the FA Cup semi finals much to the relief of everyone connected with the club. Just as this highly controversial tie was entering its fourth hour Macdonald struck the goal which ended Forest's resistance, so Newcastle who were forced to replay a tie they had won twelve days ago because of crowd trouble, are back on course for cup glory. Predictably, the third episode of this cliffhanger again produced moments of high drama and controversy before it was decided. Forest had a cleverly worked goal from a first-half free kick disallowed for the flimsiest of technical infringements. Then, as tension reached fever pitch, up popped Macdonald to make amends for the hatful of opportunities he missed in the first replay, and in this game too.

Newcastle's noisy legion of the Black-and-White Army had only a twenty second wait before Macdonald's finishing nerve was tested in the Goodison Park cauldron. Straight from the kick off Newcastle cut through Forest's defence and David Craig's cross found Macdonald unmarked only two yards away from an open goal. But Macdonald looked more like a Sunday league amateur than England's next centre-forward as he misjudged the height of the cross which struck him in the face and bounced agonisingly wide. Then came the moment of controversy Forest fans will never forget, ironically, for them, in the thirteenth minute of the game. Paul Richardson shaped to take a free kick on the edge of the Newcastle penalty area, but stepped over the ball and pushed it back into the path of Ian Bowyer; his shot pierced the defensive wall and flew past United keeper Iam McFaul. But the referee ordered the kick to be retaken. At the time it looked as though he had penalised Forest because Newcastle's Terry Hibbitt had broken from the defensive wall and moved within ten yards of the ball. However, referee David Smith explained later, "I blew for ungentlemanly conduct against Richardson. I have been told to watch this sort of gamesmanship, his action of jumping over the ball and running at the wall disturbed Newcastle's concentration. In fact, I had blown the whistle before the ball was struck into the net". Either way, after all that has gone on between these sides during this epic struggle, the decision seemed very harsh indeed.

After this Newcastle wrestled almost full control as Forest felt consigned to defeat but it then became a case of whether United would actually put the ball in the net themselves. Finally the chance arrived which Macdonald could not refuse and the tie was effectively over on 30 minutes. A huge goal kick from McFaul was headed on majestically by Jimmy Smith and Macdonald, after charging through two clumsy challenges, raced through to slip the ball wide of Forest keeper Jim Barron and into the corner of the net. Newcastle were through and now meet Burnley at Hillsborough on March 30th.

Newcastle United
McFaul, Craig, Kennedy, McDermott, Clark, Moncur, Cassidy, Smith, Macdonald, Tudor, Hibbitt.
Nottingham Forest
Barron, O'Kane, Winfield, Chapman, Serella, Richardson, McKenzie, Lyall, Martin, O'Neil, Bowyer.

Birthdays

Malcolm Allen born today in 1967.
Midfield 1993-1995, Apps 13 (1 sub). Goals 7.

Helder born today in 1971.
Defender 1999-2000, Apps 12. Goals 1.

March 26

Match of the Day from 1910

'BANANA SKIN' SWINDON SAFELY SIDE-STEPPED

Newcastle reach FA Cup final for the fourth time

This was a game which held tremendous interest for football fans around Britain today at White Hart Lane. Newcastle, the favourites, had just to see off the sole surviving team from the Southern League, Swindon Town, to reach the FA Cup final for a fourth time. Such was the interest 33,000 fans were present at kick off, paying £2,200 in gate receipts, many having travelled from Tyneside. As the teams ran out there was a significant difference in vocal greetings with the Newcastle supporters having the upper hand over the Wiltshire club. The game however, played in stifling sunshine, was largely a scrappy affair with Newcastle always comfortable against the workmanlike battlers from Swindon. In the end the favourites overcame the underdogs without too much trouble and now meet Barnsley in the final on April 28.

Newcastle created the first of a the scoring opportunities in the opening half. After five minutes a cross from Wilson found the unmarked Higgins, but his header was badly directed and Skiller, the Swindon keeper, was able to watch the ball roll wide. At the other end Whitson had to react quickly to kick clear a goalbound strike by Fleming. The flow of the game was forever being halted by a series of needless free kicks by a fussy referee, but he was right to stop the game for several minutes when Rutherford and Walker clashed heads following a Wilson corner for United. Neither side really got going during this period of play midway through the half, but on the half-hour mark the Swindon goal came under a brief siege following another free kick. Veitch lobbed the ball into the area which Skiller failed to catch and Bannister, then Kay, both cleared shots off the goal-line as the Swindon keeper frantically tried to gather the bobbling ball which was eventually belted wide by Stewart from another close-range shot. With half time approaching Swindon almost took a surprise lead when Lawrence flung himself full length to deny Silto what would have been a spectacular strike from 30 yards out. Then there was another scramble in which Walker made three consecutive goal-line blocks, the latter from Rutherford's stinging volley rebounded off the full-back's backside and ballooned over the bar.

The second half started with a collision between Lavery and United half-back Veitch, which caused a prolonged delay whilst both men received attention from the physios, but both soon returned to the game. Veitch played a major part in United's breakthrough goal on 65 minutes. His inch perfect free-kick was missed in the air by Bannister and Fleming, and this allowed a simple chance for Rutherford at the far post. He made no mistake with a cracking low drive into the corner of Skiller's goal. Within a minute United killed the game with a second goal which deflated the Swindon resistance. It was a great move between Rutherford and Howie with the latter running free into the area, as the keeper came out to close him down, Howie then squared the ball to Stewart to hammer home in front of the unguarded net. The final moments were played out at virtual walking pace as the afternoon's sunshine took its toll on the 22 players' stamina, both sides at the end glad to hear the final whistle.

Newcastle United
Lawrence, McCracken, Whitson, Veitch, Low, McWilliam, Rutherford, Howie, Stewart, Higgins, Wilson.
Swindon Town
Skiller, Kay, Walker, Tout, Silto, Bannister, Wheatcroft, Jefferson, Fleming, Brown, Lavery.

Birthdays

Harry McMenemy born today in 1912.
Midfield 1931-1937, Apps 149. Goals 37.

Played on this day

1897, Division 2.
Burton Swifts (h) 2-1   Att. 4,000
Blyth, Lennox

1901, Division 1.
Bolton Wanderers (h) 3-0   Att. 16,000
Heywood, MacFarlane, A. Gardner

1909, FA Cup Semi Final.
Manchester United (n) 0-1   Att. 40,118
Played at Bramall Lane, Sheffield.

1915, Division 1.
Oldham Athletic (a) 0-1   Att. 7,836

1920, Division 1.
Notts County (a) 0-0   Att. 15,000

1937, Division 2.
Fulham (h) 1-1   Att. 10,000
Smith

1943, Wartime.
Leeds United (h) 4-5   Att. 8,403
Diamond, McCormack, Stubbins (2)
Newcastle won the tie 7-6 on aggregate.

1946, Wartime.
Bradford Park Ave. (a) 3-5   Att. 9,397
Stubbins (2, 1 pen), Milburn

1948, Division 2.
Nottingham Forest (a) 0-0   Att. 30,000

1954, Division 1.
Cardiff City (a) 1-2   Att. 20,000
Monkhouse

1959, Division 1.
West Ham United (a) 0-3   Att. 35,000

1963, Division 2.
Grimsby Town (h) 0-0   Att. 27,884

1964, Division 2.
Leeds United (h) 0-1   Att. 55,039

1965, Division 2.
Swansea Town (h) 3-1   Att. 28,634
Penman (3)

1967, Division 1.
Stoke City (a) 1-0   Att. 17,802
B. Robson

1970, Division 1.
Sunderland (a) 1-1.   Att. 51,950
Smith

1971, Division 1.
Derby County (h) 3-1   Att. 26,502
Dyson, Foggon (2)

1974, Division 1.
Manchester City (a) 1-2   Att. 21,590
Cassidy

1976, Division 1.
Coventry City (a) 1-1   Att. 14,144
Bird

1982, Division 2.
Chelsea (h) 1-0   Att. 26,994
Waddle

1989, Division 1.
Sheffield Wednesday (h) 1-3   Att. 31,010
Mirandinha (pen)

Playing record for this day is... 21 games,
Won 6, Drawn 6, Lost 9, GF 26, GA 29.
Today's success rate... 42.86%.

Match of the Day from 1971

UNITED IMPROVEMENT CONTINUES
Derby assistance is welcomed by Newcastle fans

Although it seems a long time ago now, Newcastle's 1970-71 season looked to be one of struggle after the opening month in August. In the relegation zone back then, United now are looking likely to finish in the top ten. Today's win over Derby, who are no easy target, was as convincing as any this season, and proof again that the gloomy days are long gone. Newcastle who deserved their win thus extended their unbeaten home record to four games, three of which have been victories. Derby will argue about their lack of fortune, but the truth is Newcastle completely outplayed them and the winning margin could and should have been greater.

The Derby defenders fell back so quickly that they got themselves into some dreadful tangles and their forwards preferred to stand around and wait for passes rather than move into the vast spaces at St. James' Park. Newcastle moved with slick efficiency, lightening speed and superb skill at all times. The contrast over the whole ninety minutes was that stark. Newcastle went a goal ahead in the very first minute after the kick off. A fierce low cross into the box aimed for Alan Foggon was horribly, and unintentionally, deflected by Dave Mackay into the net. Then another 'who claims it' dilemma happened twenty minutes later when Ron Webster, under pressure from John Tudor, did exactly the same thing to Foggon's shot from inside the penalty area. The siege toward the Derby goal at this point was relentless, but some good defending, and better luck, enabled the visitors to reach half-time without being behind by a cricket score.

The second half started with a short spell of pressure by Derby as Newcastle relaxed, much to the annoyance of the 26,502 partisan crowd. During this time John O'Hare came close with two well struck efforts on goal which were both brilliantly saved by Iam McFaul. One felt at this stage it wasn't going to be Derby's day at all. The pressure didn't quite last long enough, however, and on 55 minutes Derby inflicted yet another goal on themselves. Under no pressure, the normally sound and reliable, John Robson, mis-hit a back-pass which fell woefully short of his keeper. This was easily intercepted by Foggon who rounded the stranded keeper and slipped the ball into the empty net. In the last minute Kevin Hector managed to put the ball in from close range following a scramble in the Newcastle six yard box to give Derby some consolation. But by this time the Rams looked a truly well beaten side and could have no complaints about the result.

Newcastle United
McFaul, Craggs, Clark, Gibb, McNamee, Moncur, Foggon, Tudor, Dyson, Smith, Young.

Derby County
Boulton, Webster, Robson, Todd, McFarland, Mackay, McGovern, Wignall, O'Hare, Hector, Gemmill.

Sadly Missed

Colin Gibson died on this day in 1992, aged 68.
Winger 1948-1949, Apps 24. Goals 5.

Matt Kingsley died on this day in 1960, aged 85.
Goalkeeper 1898-1904, Apps 189.

March 28

Match of the Day from 1908

FULHAM'S DREAM IS OVER

Minnows are simply no match for red hot champions

League newcomers Fulham, the minnows who have surprised and delighted everyone in their quest for FA Cup glory have gone out in a blistering semi final to the mighty League Champions, by an emphatic 6-0 scoreline. The conquerors of both Manchester sides in earlier rounds were simply torn apart by a strong Newcastle team full of internationals, they turned the second half into an exhibition game for the 45,571 packed Anfield crowd.

United went into the game without Scottish International Peter McWilliam, a late fitness test ruling him out with an ankle injury. Due to an overnight downpour, it was the Magpies who got the better of a slippery pitch. Fulham's staunch resistance held out for half an hour when a clumsy tackle by Morrison sent Gardner sprawling. From the free kick Appleyard rose in the box to plant a firm header past Skene in the Fulham goal. This opened up the game with Fulham now looking for an equaliser, but within minutes they found themselves 2-0 down. Again the goal was provided by a cross from Rutherford who had skipped clear of the Londoners' defence down the right wing. This time Appleyard threw his marker with a clever feint and Howie followed up unmarked to tap in from seven yards. The Magpies continued to dominate the game but at half time were still just the two goals in front, although realistically this was streets ahead of their opponents.

The threatened rout materialised in the second half with the now slow and demoralised Fulham side being punished for every mistake they made. Gardner added a soft third goal when put through by a terrible miscued pass from Ross, the Fulham full-back. United's fourth was far more classy, Rutherford slipping the ball between two defenders before running on to hit a first-time shot which flew past the keeper before he had moved. Things then got worse for Fulham keeper Skene, Appleyard flattened him with a combination of shoulder and boot when challenging for a cross from Howie's corner kick. Although clearly groggy, the keeper saw out the remaining twenty minutes but any chance now of a Fulham comeback was effectively over. United added a fifth goal when Howie's close-range cross shot went in via the far post, then Rutherford completed the scoring with a fine individual goal. Collecting the ball wide on the right wing he beat two defenders before cutting into the penalty area, and as Skene came out to narrow the angle the flying winger delightfully chipped the ball over his head and into the back of the net to leave the score 6-0.

Newcastle went onto meet Wolves in the final at the Crystal Palace, but were unfortunately beaten by the Midlanders 3-1 (see April 25).

Fulham
Skene, Ross, Lindsay, Collins, Morrison, Goldie, Hogan, Dalrymple, Harrison, Millington, Mouncher.
Newcastle United
Lawrence, McCracken, Pudan, Gardner, Veitch, Willis, Rutherford, Howie, Appleyard, Speedie, Wilson.
Referee Mr. J.T. Howcroft (Bolton).

Toon News Extra

1979... Match abandoned

Newcastle's Second Division fixture with Wrexham at St. James' Park was halted at half-time when heavy rain made playing conditions impossible. A crowd of just 7,152 were present and the score stood at 1-1 when play was stopped. Newcastle's goal was scored by Tommy Cassidy. The fixture was replayed on the 8th May 1979 and Newcastle won 2-0.

Sadly Missed

Andy McCombie died on this day in 1952, aged 76.
Right-back & Trainer 1904-1950, Apps 131. Goals 0.

Played on this day

1902, Division 1.
Grimsby Town (a) 0-3   Att. 8,000
1903, Division 1.
Aston Villa (h) 2-0   Att. 20,000
McColl (2)
1908, FA Cup Semi Final.
Fulham (n) 6-0   Att. 45,571
Appleyard, Gardner, Howie (2),
Rutherford (2)
Played at Anfield, Liverpool.
1921, Division 1.
Oldham Athletic (a) 0-0   Att. 16,801
1925, Division 1.
Birmingham (a) 1-1   Att. 36,000
Harris
1931, Division 1.
Sunderland (h) 2-0   Att. 38,000
Bedford (2)
1936, Division 2.
Sheffield United (h) 3-0   Att. 22,000
Connelly, J. Smith, Weaver
1942, Wartime.
Sheffield United (h) 1-6   Att. 9,000
Stubbins
1953, Division 1.
Blackpool (h) 0-1   Att. 41,205
1959, Division 1.
Luton Town (a) 2-4   Att. 20,878
Allchurch, Hughes
1970, Division 1.
Nottingham Forest (a) 2-2   Att. 21,360
Dyson, Robson
1981, Division 2.
Chelsea (h) 1-0   Att. 17,297
Halliday
1984, Division 2.
Leeds United (h) 1-0   Att. 31,222
Opponent (og)
1987, Division 1.
Southampton (h) 2-0   Att. 22,717
Goddard, Gascoigne
1993, Division 1.
Birmingham City (h) 2-2   Att. 27,087
Cole, Lee
1998, Premier League.
Southampton 2   Newcastle 1
Pearce (og) 69   Lee 46
Le Tissier 85 (pen)   Att. 15,251

Playing record for this day is... 16 games,
Won 7, Drawn 4, Lost 5, GF 26, GA 21.
Today's success rate... 56.25%.

yed on this day

Division 1.
Stoke (h) 1-0   Att. 30,000
Rutherford
Division 1.
Tottenham Hotspur (h) 3-0   Att. 20,000
Higgins (2), Hibbert
Division 1.
Liverpool (a) 2-2   Att. 3,000
Hall, King
Wartime.
Middlesbrough (h) 0-1   Att. 35,000
FA Cup Semi Final.
Manchester City (n) 2-0   Att. 50,039
Harris (2)
Played at St Andrews, Birmingham.
Division 1.
Portsmouth (a) 0-2   Att. 18,000
Division 1.
Leicester City (a) 2-4   Att. 25,000
Allen, Weaver (pen)
Wartime.
Middlesbrough (h) 3-0   Att. 12,397
Birkett, Duns, Gilholme
FA Cup Semi Final.
Charlton Athletic(n) 0-4   Att. 47,821
Played at Elland Road, Leeds.
Division 2.
Barnsley (a) 1-1   Att. 30,247
McCall
Division 1.
Derby County (a) 1-1   Att. 16,029
Hannah
FA Cup Semi Final.
Blackburn Rovers(n) 0-0   Att. 65,000
Played at Hillsborough, Sheffield.
Division 1.
Luton Town (h) 3-2   Att. 16,775
Bottom, Davies, White
Division 1.
Coventry City (h) 2-0   Att. 26,750
B. Robson (pen), McNamee
Division 1.
Leeds United (a) 1-1   Att. 41,225
Nulty
Division 1.
Manchester City (h) 2-2   Att. 20,256
Bird, Kennedy
Division 2.
Bristol Rovers (h) 3-1   Att. 18,975
Withe (2), Cassidy
Division 1.
Everton (a) 0-1   Att. 41,116
Division 2.
Sunderland (h) 1-0   Att. 30,306
Kelly
Premier League.

Newcastle 3	Norwich City 0
Cole 45, Lee 50	
Beardsley 70	Att. 32,228

Premier League.

Newcastle 6	Everton 2
Shearer 13	Ferguson 6
Cort 15, O'Brien 59	Alexandersson 34
Solano 71, 73	
Bernard 88	Att. 51,921

record for this day is... 21 games,
, Drawn 6, Lost 5, GF 36, GA 22.
success rate... 61.90%.

A FRIDAY NIGHT PARTY

Toon Army treated to a six goal feast over Everton

Friday nights are made for revelling on Tyneside and the local heroes of Newcastle United certainly got the party going on this occasion. Given a real cutting edge by Kieron Dyer's rapier thrusts from midfield and the broadsword of Alan Shearer in attack, United ripped apart a decent Everton side at a jubilant St. James' Park. After five games without a win, this was the ideal tonic for the Toon Army to savour as they saw their side glide five points clear of Leeds and six ahead of Chelsea in the chase for the fourth Champions' League place. The scoreline, though, hardly reflects that Everton, much more confident and organised under David Moyes' leadership, were deservedly level 2-2 at the half time interval. This was their new manager's first defeat after two straight victories and a general improvement in form.

A series of Newcastle misjudgements led to Everton opening the scoring. Scarcely five minutes had elapsed when Pistone's long throw was headed out by O'Brien but only to Ferguson, whose lofted shot was misread by Given. The United keeper palmed the ball up but with insufficient force to clear the bar and it dropped over the line rather apologetically. Ferguson, wearing new boots, had not even had a chance to tie the laces up. But then Newcastle showed their counter attacking class just seven minutes later. A quick throw by Robert sent Shearer racing in from the left, exploiting the poor covering of Stubbs and Pistone, before placing a firm, low shot past Simonsen. Two minutes later St. James' Park was in full cry. Robert outpaced Alexandersson and curled in a wonderful cross that Cort met on the half volley with the outside of his right foot, giving Simonsen no chance. But Newcastle's defenders were then guilty of being too generous to their guests, Distin's dithering allowing Alexandersson to prod an equaliser past the exposed Given on 34 minutes.

In the second half a much stronger United were just too much for Everton, fourteen minutes in O'Brien toe-poked the Magpies ahead from a goalmouth scramble before Solano, the poacher from Peru, struck twice within the space of three minutes. Dyer having exchanged passes with Shearer, outstripped Pistone and cut the ball back to Solano who scored with ease. Jenas, who exuded class throughout, then dribbled forward before sliding a perfect pass through for Solano again to supply the simple finish. Everton were on the ropes, brutalised by Newcastle's swift combinations. The knockout blow was delivered when LuaLua sprinted 60 yards and cut the ball back for Bernard to hammer in United's sixth goal two minutes from time.

Alan Shearer scores Newcastle's first goal of the game.

Newcastle United
Given, Hughes, O'Brien, Dabizas, Distin, Solano, Dyer (Acuna 77), Jenas, Robert (Bernard 73), Cort (LuaLua 73), Shearer.
Everton
Simonsen, Hibbert (Watson 29), Weir, Stubbs, Pistone (Blomquist 73) Alexandersson, Gemmill, Gravesen, Unsworth, Radzinski (Chadwick 73), Ferguson.
Referee Mr. G. Poll (Tring).

Birthdays

Ian Davies born today in 1957.
Left-back 1979-1982, Apps 82 (1 sub). Goals 4.
Steve Guppy born today in 1969.
Winger 1994, Apps 1 (1 sub). Goals 0.

Sadly Missed

Tom Mather died on this day in 1957, aged 69.
Manager 1935-1939

Match of the Day from 1974

SUPERMAC SEALS SEMI SHOWDOWN

Battling Burnley beaten after brave fight at Hillsborough

Newcastle overcame a great fight from Burnley today to march relentlessly on their way to another FA Cup showdown at Wembley, this time against Liverpool. To reach this stage United had taken eight games and scored seventeen goals to overcome their opponents, an odd collection of the amateur and the uneasy, who provided them plenty of thrills. Even today they were made to hang about for an hour on the fringe of a match at times dominated entirely by Burnley. But then came Malcolm Macdonald with the first of two decisive goals to supply another recovery and in the end the Magpies had deserved a chance to add to their great FA Cup history.

But in that first hour, we must not forget, Burnley had shown all the qualities of a young team on which time and thought had been lavished. Jimmy Adamson's team have achieved a high place in the league and performed magnificently in the cup, all this with a squad of players numbering just fifteen, three of when are just eighteen years of age. In the end the memory will recall the conviction of Newcastle's play and those two notable contributions from Macdonald, and, it must be said, the influence of the United crowd. The Newcastle supporters roaring their Geordie chants with vigour and timing made Hillsborough's stands tremble and the head swim. The vast terrace at one end looked like an Alpine mountain after a thin snowfall, as thousands of white scarves amongst the black waved a welcome to the team. However it was Burnley who came out to dominate the start. As the crowd's noise died, Newcastle were looking troubled. James was darting about with ease down the left, Dobson and Collins patrolled the midfield and alertly set up moves which were frightening for anyone in black and white. At the back Fletcher and Casper were solid and sound; things looked ominous in the opening quarter. A Waldron header then another from Dobson moments later almost broke the deadlock for Burnley but Newcastle and McFaul's goal remained intact. United's main creator, Hibbitt a man who usually gives the impression of being able to find space in a telephone kiosk, was made to look a mere fringe figure and was deprived of targets for any of his passes. At half-time Newcastle left the field relived to be still in a goalless game.

The second half started with a booking for Noble, after he had committed just one too many risqué fouls for the referee to take. Suddenly Newcastle looked more confident and Hibbitt helped Smith find a gap in which to feed Tudor. His shot, struck well and goalbound, was brilliantly saved by Stevenson and from nowhere United were the much stronger team. In the 65th minute Macdonald wrestled with Waldron to race clear into the area. His shot on the run was parried by the keeper but Supermac, not to be denied, stayed on his feet and whacked in the loose ball with Stevenson still prostrate. It was all United now; a header from Tudor, then a fine shot from distance by Smith came close before the inevitable second goal. Another long ball by Hibbitt set up a chase for Macdonald and Thomson again, but this time the Burnley defender was left for dead, Macdonald was left with a one-on-one with Stevenson and he finished with a thumping drive close in. The game ended with a late flurry by Burnley in which McFaul pulled off a wonder save to stop Casper's volley, then Noble headed against the crossbar. Newcastle held out and gained another memorable cup-tie win.

Burnley

Stevenson, Noble, Waldron, Thomson, Newton, Dobson, Nulty, Collins, Casper, Fletcher, James.

Newcastle United

McFaul, Craig, Moncur, Howard, Clark, McDermott, Cassidy, Hibbitt, Macdonald, Smith, Tudor.

Referee Mr. G. W. Hill (Leicester).

Birthdays

John Hope born today in 1949.
Goalkeeper 1969-1971, Apps 1.
John Mitten born today in 1941.
Winger 1958-1961, Apps 10. Goals 3.

Sadly Missed

Ron Williams died on this day in 1987, aged 80.
Centre-forward 1933-1935, Apps 36. Goals 14.

Played on this day

1901, Division 1.
Liverpool (a) 0-3 Att. 10,000
1907, Division 1.
Bristol City (h) 3-0 Att. 40,000
Howie, Rutherford (2)
1912, Division 1.
Tottenham Hotspur (h) 2-0 Att. 15,000
Hibbert, Peart
1923, Division 1.
Oldham Athletic (a) 0-0 Att. 19,149
1929, Division 1.
Birmingham (a) 0-0 Att. 30,000
1934, Division 1.
Middlesbrough (h) 1-1 Att. 36,000
Weaver
1935, Division 2.
Bradford City (a) 3-3 Att. 8,000
McMenemy, Bott, J. Richardson
1937, Division 2.
Aston Villa (a) 2-0 Att. 65,000
Smith (2)
1946, Wartime.
Preston North End (a) 1-3 Att. 10,000
Hamilton
1955, FA Cup Semi Final, replay
York City (n) 2-0 Att. 59,239
Keeble, White
Played at Roker Park, Sunderland.
1956, Division 1.
Manchester United (a) 2-5 Att. 58,748
Keeble, Stokoe
1957, Division 1.
Everton (a) 1-2 Att. 29,775
Opponent (og)
1959, Division 1.
West Ham United (h) 3-1 Att. 20,911
Allchurch, Keith, Taylor
1963, Division 2.
Luton Town (a) 3-2 Att. 7,281
Fell, Thomas, Suddick
1964, Division 2.
Leeds United (a) 1-2 Att. 40,105
Iley
1970, Division 1.
Burnley (h) 0-1 Att. 33,264
1974, FA Cup Semi Final
Burnley(n) 2-0 Att. 55,000
Macdonald (2)
Played at Hillsborough, Sheffield.
1985, Division 1.
Sheffield Wednesday (a) 2-4 Att. 26,525
Beardsley (pen), Waddle
1991, Division 1.
Swindon Town (a) 2-3 Att. 9,309
Peacock, Quinn

Playing record for this day is... 19 games,
Won 7, Drawn 4, Lost 8, GF 30, GA 30.
Today's success rate... 47.37%.

March 31

Played on this day

1902, Division 1.
Sunderland (a) 0-0 Att. 35,000
1906, FA Cup Semi Final.
Woolwich Arsenal (n) 2-0 Att. 19,964
Veitch, Howie
Played at the Victoria Ground, Stoke.
1909, Division 1.
Middlesbrough (h) 1-0 Att. 45,000
Allan
1923, Division 1.
Huddersfield Town (a) 0-2 Att. 8,000
1928, Division 1.
Burnley (a) 1-5 Att. 15,000
Wilkinson
1934, Division 1.
Leicester City (a) 2-3 Att. 17,920
Allen, Pearson
1945, Wartime.
Darlington (a) 3-0 Att. 15,796
Wayman, Carr (2)
1951, Division 1.
Fulham (a) 1-1 Att. 30,000
Walker
1956, Division 1.
Wolverhampton W. (a) 1-2 Att. 31,940
Keeble
1961, Division 1.
Sheffield Wednesday (h) 0-1 Att. 42,181
1962, Division 2.
Rotherham United (h) 1-0 Att. 21,865
Thomas
1973, Division 1.
Leicester City (a) 0-0 Att. 18,712
1975, Division 1.
Queens Park Rangers (h) 2-2 Att. 29,819
Tudor, Macdonald
1976, Division 1.
Leeds United (h) 2-3 Att. 32,685
T. Craig (pen), Gowling
1979, Division 2.
Oldham Athletic (a) 3-1 Att. 6,329
Withe, Shoulder (pen), Nattrass
1982, Division 2.
Crystal Palace (h) 0-0 Att. 22,151
1984, Division 2.
Swansea City (h) 2-0 Att. 27,329
Beardsley, Wharton
1986, Division 1.
Sheffield Wednesday (h) 4-1 Att. 25,714
Stephenson, Gascoigne, Beardsley,
Whitehurst
1990, Division 2.
Brighton & Hove A. (h) 2-0 Att. 18,742
Gallacher, Quinn
1992, Division 2.
Wolverhampton W. (a) 2-6 Att. 14,480
Quinn, Peacock
1998, Premier League.
Wimbledon 0 Newcastle 0
Att. 15,478

2001, Premier League.
Bradford City 2 Newcastle 2
Wetherall 8 Cort 25, Acuna 77
Blake 10 (pen) Att. 20,160

Playing record for this day is... 22 games,
Won 8, Drawn 7, Lost 7, GF 31, GA 29.
Today's success rate... 52.27%.

Match of the Day from 2001

NO DEFENCE IN BRADFORD DRAW

Early errors prove costly, United in two goal comeback

Newcastle have now gone 26 games without keeping a clean-sheet and even with the introduction of centre back Andy O'Brien for an emotion testing debut against his old club they continued to look soft touches. But, for this fact, United would have won easily; they came back into the game they were never really out of despite their defence, and ironically it was then poor finishing which prevented them from taking all three points.

Bradford, surely doomed to relegation from the Premiership, breached the Newcastle rearguard twice in the first eight minutes and 21-year-old O'Brien was directly responsible for the first goal. Defending Gareth Whalley's seventh minute corner kick, the Republic of Ireland Under-21 international allowed himself to be outjumped by his former defensive partner, David Wetherall, whose thundering header was deflected past Shay Given in the United goal by Aaron Hughes. Then within two minutes and with the home fans still celebrating, it was 2-0. Robert Lee, playing in his 700th senior match of his career, collided with Robert Molenaar and referee Paul Taylor, to the disbelief of the travelling Toon Army, pointed to the spot. Robbie Blake converted the penalty. The decision didn't just anger the fans; the normally calm Newcastle boss Bobby Robson was infuriated and continued his animated protest long after play had restarted. To their credit the United players rallied in fine style with Wayne Quinn in particular making deep inroads down the left flank from where he put over a stream of teasing crosses. From one of these Carl Cort contrived to direct his header downwards so powerfully that the ball bounced amazingly over a gaping open goal on 23 minutes. However, just two minutes later, the £7 million signing from Wimbledon, who has only recently returned to action after recovering from a knee injury, made no mistake when nodding firmly past Gary Walsh from another expert delivery from Quinn.

If only Cort could have kept his composure in two further instances, Newcastle would surely have wrapped up a remarkable comeback with a convincing victory, instead they were forced to settle for a point. Just after the restart he wasted Warren Barton's excellent through ball by mistiming his shot which the in form Walsh managed to push just wide of the post. Newcastle, enjoying a purple patch by this time, then equalised thanks to Chilean midfielder Clarence Acuna's point-blank header from a beautifully flighted Nolberto Solano cross. At this point, with thirteen minutes to play, it looked likely United would go on and win the game. However Cort, from close range when it seemed easier to score, managed to put another header over the bar in the 87th minute.

Bradford City
Walsh, Jacobs, Molenaar, Wetherall, McCall, Locke (Hall 36), Jess, Whalley, Ward, Blake (Grant 89), Carbone.

Newcastle United
Given, O'Brien, Barton, Hughes, Lee, Speed, Quinn, Solano (Gallacher 81), Acuna (Bassedas 84), Cort, Ameobi.

Referee Mr. P. Taylor (Cheshunt, Hertfordshire).

Sadly Missed

John Finlay died on this day in 1933, aged 40.
Midfield & Trainer 1909-1930, Apps 173. Goals 9.

Tom Smith died on this day in 1993, aged 70.
Centre-half 1941-1952, Apps 155. Goals 0.

We're on our way to Wembley! Bobby Moncur celebrates after the defeat of Burnley in the 1974 FA Cup Semi Final at Hillsborough.

April

Played on this day

April 1

Match of the Day from 1904

APRIL FOOLS IN MANCHESTER

Newcastle manage lucky win against Manchester City

This Division One match saw Newcastle United travelling to Manchester to play City in front of a crowd of 25,000. Newcastle knew this game would be a struggle, but just how difficult was yet to be seen. It was a very hard match, but luck was on their side.

From the start though, the crowd needed convincing that Newcastle would be victorious in this game. Their play was nowhere near the standard of that of City, and within minutes of the start this showed itself in a goal for the home side. It was Turnbull who put City into the lead with a lovely shot, making the most of his skill.

However, Newcastle's first piece of luck was just about to arrive, and the equaliser was not far away. A corner was awarded, and the ball landed perfectly for Orr. He slammed the ball into the back of the net past the City keeper Edmundson.

For a long while after this it looked like City would regain their lead, but despite outplaying United right until the half-time whistle, they failed to score again.

The second half began in much the same way. City were by far the better team, but they lacked the finishing needed to add another goal to the scoresheet. The attacks were coming in to the Newcastle goal frequently and from all angles, but amazingly all failed to hit the target.

The crowd were resigned to a draw, and the visitors felt lucky to have done that well. What is certain is that no one in the ground was prepared for what happened next.

Ronald Orr

With just four minutes left on the clock, Newcastle had another burst of luck. Howie spotted an opening in the City defence, and took full advantage of his opportunity. He got his head to the ball, and sent it flying into the goal to give Newcastle the lead. Time was ticking by and the whole City team was in despair.

It wasn't over yet though, and Newcastle weren't be content until the win was secure. With sixty seconds remaining, Appleyard managed to add a third goal for the Magpiese, sending the score to 3-1.

Newcastle beat City at home that season too, albeit thanks to another visit from Lady Luck.

Manchester City
Edmondson, McMahon, Burgess, Frost, Hynds, Holmes, Meredith, Livingstone, Gillespie, Turnbull, Booth.
Newcastle United
Watts, McCombie, Carr, Gardner, Aitken, Veitch, Rutherford, Howie, Appleyard, Orr, Birnie.

Birthdays

John Bailey born today 1957.
Left-back 1985-1988, Apps 42 (1 sub). Goals 0.
Ian Baird born today 1964.
Centre-forward 1984-1985, Apps 5 (1 sub). Goals 1.
Steve Watson born today in 1974.
Right-back 1989-1998, Apps 263 (43 subs).
Goals 14.

Sadly Missed

Trevor Hockey died on this day in 1987, aged 43.
Winger 1963-1965, Apps 56. Goals 3.
George Robledo died on this day in 1989, aged 62.
Midfield/Forward 1949-1953, Apps 166. Goals 91.

April 2

Match of the Day from 1952

NEWCASTLE SET NEW FA CUP RECORD

Magpies make it FA Cup final number nine after Rovers victory

FA Cup holders Newcastle United have qualified again for the Wembley final, where they will meet Arsenal on May 3rd, this for a record ninth time. As a matter of historical fact too, this is only the second time since the 1900s a side has reached a final the following year as current holders of the FA Cup. Today's win over Blackburn at Leeds United's Elland Road ground was watched by almost 54,000 thrilled fans who were kept waiting until five minutes before time to see the winning goal, scored by Bobby Mitchell from the penalty spot.

However, in the opening 45 minutes Newcastle looked anything but champions, four times they missed simple chances to break the deadlock, and all fell to the same forward, George Robledo. The most glaring of these were after just four minutes. When put clean through from a long clearance the normally steady marksman raced into the area and with the open goal in front of him blazed the ball high over the bar from fifteen yards. The unfortunate striker then went on to miss another three good opportunities, all from close-range headers, all within the opening twenty minutes. The tension at this stage was unbearable for the thousands of travelling Geordies, who were in a state of disbelief as the chance of putting the game out of Blackburn's reach seemed to be slipping away. The Rovers slowly, and, for the Newcastle supporters worryingly, got into the game and came agonisingly close themselves with shots by Quigley and Nightingale. But some strong brave defending, in which McMichael for United was outstanding, saw the first half remain tantalisingly goalless.

The second half started with much better football from both sides but, rather ironically, the opening goal came from a Newcastle error. A ball from Harvey, trying an ambitious cross field pass, was intercepted by Quigley who now had a free run at goal some 40 yards out. For a moment it seemed Rovers would take the lead but Quigley tired and Brennan, chasing back with twenty yards to make up, slid in and took the ball away magnificently. With the ball at his feet he continued to run with it towards the Rovers goal before laying a perfect pass to Milburn on the right. He majestically beat Eckersley, and there was George Robledo, this time making no mistake with a close-range header. Newcastle were ahead and the pendulum, it seemed, at last had swung. Not quite, Blackburn came back like terriers refusing to admit defeat. Nightingale and Crossan, backed tirelessly by Campbell and Clayton, not yet eighteen years of age, set up attack after attack to bring the best out of Brennan, Cowell and McMichael. With twelve minutes left Blackburn were level, Wharton's beautiful cross was headed down by Crossan and Quigley belted his volley into the roof of Simpson's net. It was anybody's game again with surely the next goal the winner, and both sides attacked at every opportunity. With just five minutes of the game left Milburn sent over another cross which George Robledo won in the air again. His header was strong and goalbound, and was stopped by the hands of Crossan, who was back covering for the off-the-field Gray. With the tension now at fever pitch the cool handed Bobby Mitchell placed the ball on the spot and duly drove it past Elvy to put Newcastle into the record books.

Blackburn Rovers

Elvy, Gray, Eckersley, Campbell, Kelly, Clayton, Glover, Crossan, Quigley, Nightingale, Wharton.

Newcastle United

Simpson, Cowell, McMichael, Harvey, Brennan, E. Robledo, Walker, Foulkes, Milburn, G. Robledo, Mitchell.

Sadly Missed

Ian Mitchell died on this day in 1996, aged 49.
Winger 1970-1971, Apps 5 (2 subs). Goals 1.

Played on this day

1898, Division 2.
Gainsborough Trinity (h) **5-2** Att. 12,000
Smith (2), Peddie (3)
1904, Division 1.
Blackburn Rovers (h) **2-1** Att. 20,000
Orr, Veitch
1910, Division 1.
Notts County (a) **2-2** Att. 8,000
Shepherd, Liddell
1915, Division 1.
Tottenham Hotspur (a) **0-0** Att. 18,000
1920, Division 1.
Burnley (a) **0-1** Att. 30,000
1921, Division 1.
Derby County (h) **0-1** Att. 35,000
1924, Division 1.
Everton (h) **3-1** Att. 12,000
Seymour, Harris, Gibson
1926, Division 1.
Burnley (a) **0-1** Att. 30,000
1927, Division 1.
Bury (h) **3-1** Att. 20,000
Clark, McDonald, McKay
1929, Division 1.
Arsenal (a) **2-1** Att. 25,000
Cunningham, Lang
1930, Division 1.
Birmingham (h) **1-1** Att. 30,000
Devine
1932, Division 1.
West Bromwich A. (a) **1-2** Att. 20,000
Allen
1934, Division 1.
Middlesbrough (a) **0-1** Att. 15,000
1938, Division 2.
Plymouth Argyle (a) **1-2** Att. 22,000
Pearson
1945, Wartime.
Sunderland (h) **0-3** Att. 13,000
1949, Division 1.
Blackpool (h) **3-1** Att. 62,672
Milburn (2), Robledo
1952, FA Cup Semi Final, replay.
Blackburn Rovers (n) **2-1** Att. 53,920
Mitchell (pen), G. Robledo
Played at Elland Road, Leeds.
1955, Division 1.
Charlton Athletic (a) **1-1** Att. 24,918
Hannah
1956, Division 1.
Manchester United (h) **0-0** Att. 37,395
1960, Division 1.
Blackpool (h) **1-1** Att. 32,152
Mitten
1969, Division 1.
Tottenham Hotspur (a) **1-0** Att. 22,528
Horsfield
1977, Division 1.
Birmingham City (a) **2-1** Att. 20,283
T. Craig (pen), Barrowclough
1980, Division 2.
Notts County (h) **2-2** Att. 22,005
Shoulder, Cassidy
1983, Division 2.
Grimsby Town (h) **4-0** Att. 20,202
Varadi (2), McDonald, Keegan
1988, Division 1.
Luton Town (h) **4-0** Att. 20,565
O'Neill (3), Goddard
2002, Premier League.

Aston Villa 1	Newcastle 1
Crouch 26	Shearer 3

Att. 36,59

Playing record for this day is... 26 games, Won 11, Drawn 8, Lost 7, GF 41, GA 28. Today's success rate... 57.69%.

April 3

Played on this day

1896, Division 2.
Burslem Port Vale (h) 4-2   Att. 8,000
McDonald (2), Collins, Opponent (og)

1897, Division 2.
Walsall (a) 2-0   Att. 4,000
Aitken, Smellie

1899, Division 1.
Liverpool (a) 2-3   Att. 12,000
Stevenson, Higgins

1909, Division 1.
Nottingham Forest (h) 1-1   Att. 22,000
Allan

1911, Division 1.
Sheffield United (a) 0-0   Att. 8,000

1915, Division 1.
Manchester United (h) 2-0   Att. 12,000
Hibbert (2)

1920, Division 1.
Sheffield Wednesday (h) 1-1   Att. 20,000
Phillipson

1926, Division 1.
Cardiff City (h) 0-1   Att. 25,000

1931, Division 1.
Huddersfield Town (h) 1-1   Att. 35,000
Lindsay

1937, Division 2.
Burnley (a) 3-0   Att. 9,400
Cairns, Docking (2)

1943, Wartime.
Middlesbrough (a) 1-2   Att. 3,000
Stubbins

1948, Division 2.
Bradford Park Ave. (h) 2-0   Att. 50,367
Stobbart, Woodburn

1953, Division 1.
Middlesbrough (h) 1-0   Att. 48,434
Hannah

1954, Division 1.
Manchester City (h) 4-3   Att. 27,764
Milburn (2, 2 pens), Monkhouse, Davies

1961, Division 1.
Sheffield Wednesday (a) 1-1   Att. 35,273
Woods

1963, Division 2.
Charlton Athletic (h) 3-2   Att. 30,360
Penman, Hilley, Suddick

continued opposite

Match of the Day from 1996

THE PREMIERSHIP GAME OF THE DECADE
Millions vote Anfield thriller the most memorable ever

Asked to vote for the Premiership game of the decade in 2003, millions of football fans nationwide had no doubt, today's game at Anfield in 1996. It was the match which put Liverpool back in the title hunt and broke the hearts of second-placed Newcastle, and their magnificent travelling Toon Army. The game began, finished and was filled in its intervening minutes with a level of football that seemed impossible to maintain. Robbie Fowler, scored the first of his two goals after 98 seconds and Stan Collymore, got his second of the game ten seconds into the additional time required by referee Mike Read. Between such savage blows Newcastle roused themselves to a level of football few sides in the country would have had the gall to expend across a ground with Anfield's intimidating reputation. But Kevin Keegan's side know no other way. For Liverpool, and their boss Roy Evans, this was their last chance, knowing defeat would consign them to merely watching Newcastle and Manchester United slug it for the Premier League title.

Liverpool's first passing movement spoke volumes of their resurgence this season. From deep inside their own half they linked first-time passes, Redknapp's cross field ball unsettling Watson, who was caught between two players. The pressing Jones knocked the ball forward to Collymore, who seemed pegged to the touchline but he managed to cross for Fowler to ghost in and head wide of Srnicek. Newcastle's response was emphatic, and in the tenth minute, Asprilla having rode a flimsy challenge by Ruddock, slid the ball across the area for Ferdinand to turn and shoot through the arms of keeper James. The recovery was completed and embellished just four minutes later with a peach of a goal, Ferdinand releasing Ginola to accelerate past McAteer, keep his nerve and slip the ball under the advancing James. United were then denied a clear-cut penalty when Barnes compounded the error of gifting the ball away to Asprilla, chased back and tripped him in the area.

The second half proved as unrelenting as the first, Fowler side-footing MacManaman's cross past Srnicek after 55 minutes, only to watch Lee put Asprilla away for a chance the Colombian cooly accepted two minutes later. Many sides would not have had the courage to come back from that, but Liverpool had everything at stake, they simply had no choice. McAteer was always a threat down the right wing and his 68th minute cross was so devilish no defender could read it as Collymore nipped in to poke in the equaliser. A draw would not have suited either side, but it would have been the preferred natural conclusion to any neutral in this memorable game. But on came Rush to combine with Barnes in a series of one-touch passes before Barnes fed Collymore, alone in one half of the Newcastle area, and the rest is history.

Liverpool
James, Jones (Rush 84), McAteer, Wright (Harkness h/t), Collymore, Barnes, Scales, Redknapp, McManaman, Fowler, Ruddock.

Newcastle United
Srnicek, Beresford, Howey (Peacock 82), Batty, Watson, Albert, Beardsley, Lee, Ferdinand, Ginola, Asprilla.

Referee Mr. M. Reed (Birmingham).

Birthdays

Tommy Lang born today in 1906.
Winger 1926-1934, Apps 230. Goals 58.
Tom Patterson born today in 1927.
Winger 1950-1952, Apps 2. Goals 0.

Sadly Missed

Joe A. Wilson died on this day in 1984, aged 73.
Midfield 1933-1936, Apps 30. Goals 5.

Joseph W. Wilson died on this day in 1996, aged 85.
Centre-half 1927-1930, Apps 1. Goals 0.

Clockwise from top:
Rob Lee is involved in a chase with Steve McManaman.
Tino Asprilla celebrates after scoring Newcastle's third goal.
David Ginola battles with Jason McAteer.

April 3

Played on this day

1965, Division 2.
  Derby County (a) 3-0   Att. 19,668
  Knox, Hilley, Iley
1968, Division 1.
  Leicester City (h) 0-0   Att. 33,932
1971, Division 1.
  Blackpool (a) 1-0   Att. 14,637
  Foggon
1972, Division 1.
  Derby County (a) 1-0   Att. 38,119
  Cassidy
1974, Division 1.
  Stoke City (a) 1-2   Att. 16,437
  Tudor
1976, Division 1.
  Queens Park Rangers (h) 1-2 Att. 30,145
  Gowling
1982, Division 2.
  Charlton Athletic (a) 1-0   Att. 6,357
  Waddle
1990, Division 2.
  Plymouth Argyle (h) 3-1   Att. 16,528
  Quinn, McGhee (2, 1 pen)
1993, Division 1.
  Cambridge United (a) 3-0.   Att. 7,925
  Howey, Kelly, Cole
1996, Premier League.
  Liverpool 4   **Newcastle 3**
  Fowler 2, 55   Ferdinand 10
  Collymore 68, 90   Ginola 14
                         Asprilla 57
                                    Att. 40,702
  Voted the best game ever played in the
  history of the Premier League in April
  2003.
1999, Premier League.
  Derby County 3   **Newcastle 4**
  Burton 8   Speed 11, 24
  Baiano 22 (pen)   Ketsbaia 39
  Wanchope 90   Solano 60
                                    Att. 32,039

Playing record for this day is... 27 games,
Won 15, Drawn 6, Lost 6, GF 49, GA 29.
Today's success rate... 66.67%.

April 4

- **Division 1.**
  Burton Swifts (h) 5-0   Att. 7,000
  Wardrope (2), Thompson (2), Stott
- **Division 1.**
  Nottingham Forest (a) 2-3   Att. 4,000
  Alex Gardner (2)
- **Division 1.**
  Sheffield United (h) 2-1   Att. 20,000
  Appleyard, Hardinge
- **Division 1.**
  Everton (a) 0-2   Att. 10,000
- **Division 1.**
  Aston Villa (a) 3-1   Att. 20,000
  Shepherd (2), G. Wilson
- **Division 1.**
  West Bromwich A. (h) 0-1   Att. 25,000
- **Division 1.**
  Blackburn Rovers (a) 0-1   Att. 12,000
- **Division 2.**
  Nottingham Forest (a) 2-1   Att. 5,000
  Bott, Ware
- **Wartime.**
  Gateshead (a) 0-4   Att. 3,000
- **Division 2.**
  Birmingham City (h) 2-2   Att. 57,259
  Bentley, Milburn
- **Division 1.**
  Aston Villa (h) 0-1   Att. 38,543
- **Division 1.**
  Chelsea (a) 2-1   Att. 40,218
  Mitchell (2)
- **Division 2.**
  Manchester City (a) 1-3   Att. 15,450
  Thomas
- **Division 1.**
  Chelsea (a) 1-1   Att. 42,078
  B. Robson (pen)
- **Division 1.**
  Manchester United (h) 5-1   Att. 43,024
  Smith, Davies, Robson (3, 2 pens)
- **Anglo Italian Cup, Group Stage.**
  Como (a) 2-0   Att. 3,000
  Moncur, Tudor
- **Division 1.**
  Coventry City (a) 0-0   Att. 22,135
- **Division 2.**
  Preston North End (h) 4-3   Att. 12,167
  Connolly, Withe, Shoulder, Barton
- **Division 2.**
  Watford (a) 0-0   Att. 10,986
- **Division 2.**
  Derby County (a) 1-2   Att. 19,779
  Waddle
- **Division 1.**
  Leicester City (h) 2-0   Att. 23,360
  Wharton, Goddard
- **Division 1.**
  Derby County (a) 1-2   Att. 18,591
  O'Neill
- **Division 2.**
  Tranmere Rovers (h) 2-3   Att. 21,125
  Brock (2)
- **Premier League.**
  Newcastle 0   Chelsea 0
      Att. 32,218

...g record for this day is... 24 games,
...9, Drawn 5, Lost 10, GF 37, GA 33.
...'s success rate... 47.92%.

Match of the Day from 1914

NEWCASTLE JUST TOO STRONG
Experimenting Villa are well beaten by United

Having had their cup run ended by Liverpool last week and their last remaining hope of the championship dented by Preston three days ago, Villa decided to give some of their fringe players a chance against mid-table Newcastle today. United took full advantage and deservedly picked up only their third away victory of the 1913-14 season, this being by the biggest margin too. With such a disappointing week for the home fans to endure they decided to stay away en masse, a crowd of just 20,000 were present at Villa Park almost half their season average.

Villa, despite the six first-team changes, were the better side early on and, but for a very dubious offside decision on Edgley, would have taken the lead. The Villa left-winger received the ball inside the area completely unmarked, having timed his run almost to perfection. This good fortune seemed to galvanize the Newcastle side and within minutes only a brilliant clearance from Lyons prevented Wilson from putting the Magpies ahead. The game was now end-to-end attacking football, and despite the small crowd, there was plenty of enthusiasm. A good interchange of passes between Wallace and Whittaker, sent the former, charging into the area for a shot which United keeper Mellor expertly tipped round the post at full-stretch. At the other end Anstey made just as important a save from Shepherd's first-time volley just fifteen yards out; this effort however was flicked over the bar by the Villa keeper. With just four minutes of the half remaining Newcastle then got the important breakthrough. Villa's defence was caught out by a quick counter attack led by Grey, his long ball to Wilson was beautifully controlled, then, after a short dribble into the box, he finished with a fierce rising shot into the roof of the net.

A goal down, Villa then found themselves handicapped by the sun in their eyes during the second half. But even this failed to stop their constant will to attack; twice they were thwarted by some desperate defending early on in the half. A volley from Wallace was headed clear by Veitch off the line. Moments later the ever dangerous Wallace dribbled into the box again only for a brave and timely challenge by Hudspeth to stop him before he got his shot in. However, on his next attack, Wallace, who had got round McCracken, saw his cross into the centre stopped by the hands of the United right-back. It was Wallace who beat Mellor, although the keeper got a hand to the ball, from the penalty spot to earn a well deserved goal for the Villa forward. Newcastle responded magnificently, when the signs at this stage looked ominous. With ten minutes of the game remaining Shepherd tricked Lyons into slipping over, after a superb long ball from McCracken, and chased into the area to fire in a well placed cross shot past Anstey. Three minutes later United wrapped up the league points when a clever ball from Hibbert fell to Shepherd inside the box and the striker made no mistake for his second goal of the game. Villa never gave up and in the last few minutes Wallace again come close, then Smart almost squeezed the ball in but his shot hit the side netting with spectators thinking it had gone in.

Aston Villa

Anstey, Lyons, Weston, Morris, Harrop, A. McLachlan, Wallace, Whittaker, J.McLachlan, Smart, Edgley.

Newcastle United

Mellor, McCracken, Hudspeth, Veitch, Grey, Finlay, Douglas, Hibbert, Shepherd, Wilson, Goodwill.

Referee Mr. T.P. Campbell (Blackburn).

Birthdays

George Hope born today in 1954.
Centre-forward 1971-1975, Apps 6. Goals 1.

Sadly Missed

Jimmy Hay died on this day in 1940, aged 59.
Midfield 1911-1919, Apps 149. Goals 8.
Arthur Turner died on this day in 1925, aged 47.
Winger 1903-1904, Apps 13. Goals 1.

April 9

Match of the Day from 1924

UNITED HAND OUT INSTANT REVENGE
4-1 defeat is put right at snowbound St. James' Park

Just hours before kick off a sudden and heavy snowstorm fell, and together with the failing light it seemed inevitable the referee would postpone the game without hesitation. Incredibly however, the falling snow ceased and the light improved enough for an earlier than scheduled start which took everyone on Tyneside, it seemed, by total surprise. Still, although well below average, a crowd of 8,000 were present when Newcastle kicked off.

The conditions were soon creating an exciting but scrappy game between the two sides. The snowbound pitch made gaining any secure foothold very difficult, and accurate passing nigh on impossible, but for the large part the game was tremendously entertaining. With the lack of intricate skill the game produced much more honest endeavour, indeed it was a credit to all 22 players that the thrilling pace of the game was maintained for 90 minutes. Newcastle took a long time to settle and should have been a goal down after eleven minutes, Islip taking far too long to steady himself when presented with a golden chance from close range which was eventually cleared by Mutch. Almost immediately United wasted a great chance of their own when Clark headed wide of an open goal from Aitken's superb cross from the right. It was the ever impressive Aitken however, who produced a replica inch-perfect centre for Thompson to make absolutely no mistake with his header on 24 minutes, and United had the all-important first goal. But back came Birmingham with a deserved equaliser just eight minutes later, this after a magnificent double save from the unfortunate Mutch. The United keeper was on his knees and could do nothing about Bradford's close-range toe-poke goal. This after his breathtaking stop from first Harvey, then an equally brilliant stop to deny the eventual goalscorer whose follow up volley was scooped out from the foot of the post.

After the half-time interval the pace of Birmingham's winger Linley, whose goal and play had set up United's hammering just four days ago, started to look ominous again. He was giving Hampson several yards start yet still outpacing the troubled United full-back. But the big difference today was the marshalling of Bradford, who had scored twice at Birmingham. He was kept relatively quiet by the much improved defenders Low and Mooney. This helped United soak up the early second half pressure enabling them to counter attack with devastating consequences just after the hour mark. Aitken, who had been the thorn in the side from Birmingham's point of view, slipped a fabulous ball for Mitchell who turned his marker on the edge of the penalty area and beat Tremelling with a crisp low drive into the corner of the net. But for the odd moment, this killed off the visitors' threat, and Newcastle could have sewn up the game in the latter stages with two great chances that fell to Clark and Aitken. United's decision to rest their FA Cup final team, only four were present today, was vindicated by their overall deserved victory, and revenge, for the United fringe players, was very sweet indeed.

Newcastle United
Mutch, Hampson, Hudspeth, MacKenzie, W. Low, Mooney, Aitken, Keating, Thompson, J. Clark, Mitchell.
Birmingham
Tremelling, Ashurst, Womack, Dale, Cringan, Hunter, Harvey, Crosbie, Bradford, Islip, Linley.

Played on this day

1898, Division 2.
Leicester Fosse (a) 1-1 — Att. 6,000
Peddie
1904, Division 1.
Nottingham Forest (a) 0-1 — Att. 10,000
1906, Division 1.
Liverpool (a) 0-3 — Att. 18,000
1910, Division 1.
Middlesbrough (a) 1-1 — Att. 10,000
Duncan
1912, Division 1.
Bradford City (a) 1-1 — Att. 18,000
Hibbert
1913, Division 1.
West Bromwich A. (a) 0-1 — Att. 10,000
1921, Division 1.
Bolton Wanderers (a) 1-3 — Att. 25,000
McDonald
1924, Division 1.
Birmingham (h) 2-1 — Att. 8,000
Mitchell, Thompson
1927, Division 1.
Birmingham (a) 0-2 — Att. 30,000
1930, Division 1.
Bolton Wanderers (a) 1-1 — Att. 6,000
Gallacher
1932, Division 1.
Sunderland (h) 1-2 — Att. 45,000
Lang
1938, Division 2.
Fulham (h) 1-2 — Att. 12,000
Pearson
1949, Division 1.
Derby County (a) 4-2 — Att. 24,076
Harvey, Robledo (2), Sibley
1955, Division 1.
Sheffield Wednesday (h) 5-0 — Att. 40,883
Davies (2), Hannah, R. Mitchell, White
1960, Division 1.
Blackburn Rovers (a) 1-1 — Att. 22,100
Eastham
1966, Division 1.
Blackburn Rovers (h) 2-1 — Att. 21,607
Hilley, Robson
1969, Division 1.
Sheffield Wednesday (h) 3-2 — Att. 25,973
Arentoft, Dyson, Horsfield
1977, Division 1.
Leicester City (h) 0-0 — Att. 32,300
1983, Division 2.
Blackburn Rovers (h) 3-2 — Att. 17,839
Waddle, Varadi, Opponent (og)
1986, Division 1.
Aston Villa (h) 2-2 — Att. 20,435
Whitehurst, Gascoigne
1988, Division 1.
Queens Park Rangers (h) 1-1 — Att. 18,403
O'Neill
1994, Premier League.
Manchester City 2   Newcastle 1
Walsh 31   Sellars 19
D. Brightwell 48   Att. 33,774
2000, FA Cup Semi Final.
Chelsea 2   Newcastle 1
Poyet 17, 72   Lee 66
                    Att. 73,876
Played at Wembley Stadium, London.

Playing record for this day is... 23 games, Won 6, Drawn 8, Lost 9, GF 32, GA 34.
Today's success rate... 43.48%.

April 10

1897, Division 2.
Burton Wanderers (h) 3-0   Att. 6,000
Aitken, Smellie (2)

1903, Division 1.
Derby County (h) 2-1   Att. 25,000
Templeton, Roberts

1909, Division 1.
Sunderland (a) 1-3   Att. 30,000
Shepherd

1914, Division 1.
Blackburn Rovers (h) 0-0   Att. 40,000

1915, Division 1.
Bolton Wanderers (a) 0-0   Att. 15,000

1926, Division 1.
Sheffield United (a) 3-4   Att. 25,000
McDonald, Hudspeth (2, 1pen)

1928, Division 1.
Birmingham (a) 2-0   Att. 25,000
Wilkinson (2)

1936, Division 2.
Hull City (h) 4-1   Att. 16,000
Pearson, Connelly (2), Weaver (pen)

1937, Division 2.
Southampton (h) 3-0   Att. 12,000
Cairns, Livingstone, Pearson

1943, Wartime.
Middlesbrough (h) 4-0   Att. 8,811
Dixon, Carr, Stubbins (2)
Newcastle won the tie 5-2 on aggregate.

1946, Wartime.
Bolton Wanderers (a) 1-0   Att. 9,386
Pearson

1948, Division 2.
Cardiff City (a) 1-1   Att. 50,000
Stobbart

1954, Division 1.
Portsmouth (a) 0-2   Att. 26,604

1965, Division 2.
Swindon Town (h) 1-0   Att. 32,503
Hilley

1971, Division 1.
Leeds United (h) 1-1   Att. 49,699
Tudor

1973, Texaco Cup Semi Final, 2nd leg.
Ipswich Town (a) 0-1   Att. 18,627
A.E.T (score at 90 minutes 0-0)
Newcastle lost 2-1 on aggregate.

1974, Division 1.
Burnley (h) 1-2   Att. 30,168
Macdonald

1976, Division 1.
Wolverhampton W. (a) 0-5   Att. 20,083

1979, Division 2.
Burnley (a) 0-1   Att. 7,851

1982, Division 2.
Leicester City (h) 0-0   Att. 25,777

1991, Division 2.
Oxford United (h) 2-2   Att. 10,004
Hunt, Melville (og)

1993, Division 1.
Wolverhampton W. (a) 0-1   Att. 17,244

Playing record for this day is... 22 games,
Won 8, Drawn 6, Lost 8, GF 29, GA 25.
Today's success rate... 50%.

Match of the Day from 1928

NEWCASTLE BACK TO WINNING WAYS
Wilkinson brace lifts United at St. Andrews

After three successive defeats and without a win in four games Newcastle were on the slide down the First Division table. Lying in eighteenth place after having been top in October, United suddenly remembered how to win at last with a solid, if not spectacular, performance in Birmingham today. Hard to believe, but this was Newcastle's first victory outside St. James' Park for five months, the victory however was well timed, the Magpies moving up the First Division table seven places.

Both sides had to make adjustments to their line-ups due to injury. Newcastle's noticeable absentee was Gibson, his place going to Evans. Birmingham's problems were slightly worse, they were short of first-team regulars Crosbie and Cringan, but, they also had the boost of having Womack back after an absence of thirteen games.

Injury troubles however, continued to hamper the home side's game just half an hour after kick off when Randle, who had been playing well, was badly hurt. With no substitutes allowed the full-back was moved to the left wing, where he limped throughout the remainder of the half. Newcastle soon took advantage of the accident and produced their liveliest spell of attacking football for weeks. A great ball from Gallacher gave Wilkinson the perfect shooting chance inside the area but his blockbuster struck the bar. Following up came Seymour with a brave lunging shot which Tremelling did brilliantly well to push out for a corner kick. During the stop it became clear Seymour was badly hurt in the collision with Barton and he was still off the field when McDonald took the corner. His flag kick was perfect and up rose Wilkinson to head United into the lead. Just after this Birmingham's problems were further compounded when Barton left the field injured, another victim of the goalmouth scramble earlier. With the home side still down to ten men, and effectively just nine, Newcastle hit them with a sucker punch second goal, right on the stroke of half time. A long ball by Maitland into space was chased by Wilkinson and on the first bounce he lobbed the ball over the advancing keeper Tremelling for a fantastic finish.

Unfortunately for Birmingham the break failed to improve the condition of Barton and they played the first ten minutes of the half a man short. The other casualty, Randle, was able to resume his more familiar position in defence, and Barton took over the left-winger's role when he returned. These accidents could not be used as a defence for the Blues defeat however. Newcastle were worthy winners having exploited Birmingham's weakness to an extent that a fully-fit eleven would not have stopped. In the remainder of the second half Newcastle stroked the ball about with confidence displaying the qualities they had when heading the league earlier in the season. For all this there were very few scoring chances for either side, indeed very few half chances either. But the result will hearten the Newcastle supporters once again, their team is now back to winning ways at last!

Birmingham
Tremelling, Womack, Randle, Liddell, Barton, Leslie, Briggs, Firth, Bradford, Curtis, Bond.
Newcastle United
Burns, Maitland, Evans, Harris, Park, Curry, Urwin, Gallacher, Wilkinson, McDonald, Seymour.

Birthdays

Andreas Andersson born today in 1974.
Forward 1998-1999, Apps 32 (7 subs). Goals 4.

April 11

Match of the Day from 1908

NEWCASTLE 3, LIVERPOOL 1
The Magpies take the win in benefit match

A crowd of 30,000 attended for this Division One game at home against Liverpool. This was also a benefit match for Bill Appleyard and Frank Watt, the club secretary.

The game started in Newcastle's favour, and stayed that way throughout the entire game. In fact they totally outplayed Liverpool.

The visitors' defence was fairly strong, and they managed to hold out the Newcastle forwards to some extent. However, the first goal was inevitable, and Newcastle then just had to keep up the pressure and wait for their opportunities

The first goal came thirteen minutes into the game, and it was Howie who penetrated the defence well enough to beat the Liverpool keeper and slam the ball into the back of the net.

One goal was not enough to secure the win, though, so United maintained their efforts and kept attacking. There was not much defending for the Newcastle team to do as Liverpool didn't seem to have much possession of the ball. When they did get hold of it, they rarely threatened and there was no danger to the Newcastle goalkeeper.

Bill Appleyard

Twenty three minutes into the match Duncan sent a lovely ball to Wilson, who managed to score Newcastle's second goal with ease.

The rest of the first half was played out in much the same way, with Newcastle totally in control of the game. The second half began with renewed vigour for the Magpies and just nine minutes after the restart Jobey extended the lead to three goals with a superb shot, well placed to beat the Liverpool keeper.

This seemed to kick-start the Reds into action, but even then it was not enough to produce an impact on the game. With their forwards making the odd attempt at scoring it seemed only right that they should contribute a consolation goal.

It came for the visitors on the hour mark, and it was ex-Newcastle star Ronald Orr who beat his old teammates to put the ball into the back of the net.

Newcastle United
Lawrence, McCracken, Pudan, Gardner, Veitch, Willis, Duncan, Howie, Jobey, Speedie, Wilson.
Liverpool
Doig, West, Rogers, Chorlton, Berry, Bradley, Goddard, Robinson, Hewitt, Orr, Griffen.

Played on this day

1898, Division 2.
Loughborough Town (a) 1-0   Att. 2,000
Campbell
1903, Division 1.
Bury (h) 1-0   Att. 18,000
Turner
1908, Division 1.
Liverpool (h) 3-1   Att. 30,000
Howie, Jobey, Wilson
1914, Division 1.
Middlesbrough (h) 1-0   Att. 30,000
Shepherd
1925, Division 1.
Tottenham Hotspur (a) 0-3   Att. 23,144
1931, Division 1.
Manchester City (h) 0-1   Att. 20,000
1936, Division 2.
Swansea Town (h) 2-0   Att. 12,000
Connelly, J. Smith
1942, Wartime.
Middlesbrough (a) 3-2   Att. 2,500
Woollett, Howden, Hart
1950, Division 1.
Huddersfield Town (a) 2-1   Att. 37,700
Houghton, G. Robledo
Played at Elland Road, Leeds.
1951, Division 1.
Portsmouth (h) 0-0   Att. 32,222
1952, Division 1.
Middlesbrough (h) 0-2   Att. 59,364
1953, Division 1.
Manchester United (h) 1-2   Att. 39,078
Mitchell
1955, Division 1.
Everton (h) 4-0   Att. 45,329
R. Mitchell (2), Milburn (2)
1959, Division 1.
West Bromwich A. (a) 2-2   Att. 22,000
Curry (2)
1964, Division 2.
Bury (h) 0-4   Att. 20,001
1966, Division 1.
Everton (a) 0-1   Att. 32,598
1981, Division 2.
Cambridge United (h) 2-1   Att. 11,013
Shoulder, Opponent (og)
1987, Division 1.
Oxford United (a) 1-1   Att. 10,526
Goddard
1990, Division 2.
West Bromwich A. (h) 2-1   Att. 19,471
Anderson, Quinn
1992, Division 2.
Ipswich Town (a) 2-3   Att. 20,673
Peacock (2)
1998, Premier League.
Arsenal 3   Newcastle 1
Anelka 41, 64   Barton 79
Vieira 72   Att. 38,102
1999, FA Cup Semi Final.
Newcastle 2   Tottenham Hotspur 0
Shearer 109 (pen), 118   Att. 53,609
A.E.T. Played at Old Trafford, Manchester.

Playing record for this day is... 22 games, Won 12, Drawn 2, Lost 8, GF 30, GA 27. Today's success rate... 59.09%.

April 12

yed on this day

Division 2.
Burslem Port Vale (h) 1-2   Att. 3,000
McNee
Division 2.
Burton Swifts (a) 0-3   Att. 2,000
Division 2.
Small Heath (a) 0-1   Att. 5,000
Division 1.
Sheffield United (a) 0-1   Att. 7,837
Division 1.
Everton (h) 3-0   Att. 30,000
Stewart (2), McCracken (pen)
Division 1.
Notts County (h) 0-0   Att. 12,000
Wartime.
Durham City (h) 2-0   Att. 15,000
Hagan, Opponent (og)
Division 1.
Chelsea (h) 2-1   Att. 20,000
Seymour, Keating
Division 1.
Aston Villa (a) 0-2   Att. 35,066
Wartime.
Sheffield United (h) 4-0   Att. 20,000
Short, Duns (2), Birkett
Trailing 2-0 from the first leg of this war cup-tie, Newcastle go into half time at St. James' Park level at 0-0. After the break a remarkable resurgent Magpies destroy United with a four goal blitz within twenty minutes late on, enabling them to go through 4-2 on aggregate.
Division 2.
Plymouth Argyle (a) 1-0   Att. 32,500
Shackleton
Division 1.
Manchester City (h) 1-0   Att. 46,645
G. Robledo
Division 1.
Arsenal (h) 3-3   Att. 43,221
Curry, White, Stokoe
Newcastle comeback from 3-1 down at half time.
Division 2.
Huddersfield Town (h) 1-1   Att. 49,672
McGarry
Division 1.
West Bromwich A. (h) 2-2   Att. 40,308
ley, T. Robson
Division 1.
Manchester United (h) 2-0   Att. 46,379
Foggon, B. Robson (pen)
Division 1.
Manchester City (h) 0-0   Att. 29,148
Division 1.
Everton (h) 0-1   Att. 29,585
Division 1.
West Bromwich A. (a) 0-2   Att. 17,053
Division 2.
Fulham (a) 0-1   Att. 7,152
Division 2.
Sheffield Wednesday (a) 1-2   Att. 29,917
Barton
Division 1.
Birmingham City (h) 4-1   Att. 20,334
Beardsley (2), Anderson, Whitehurst
Division 1.
Watford (h) 3-0   Att. 16,318
O'Neill, Wharton, Tinnion
Premier League.
West Ham 2   **Newcastle 1**
Wanchope 60, 89   Speed 48
   Att. 25,817

Match of the Day from 1986

TEN MEN GIVE BRUM A HAMMERING

Beardsley brilliance the key in 4-1 win

Newcastle's brilliant striker Peter Beardsley showed all his England qualities today as he almost single-handedly dismantled Birmingham at St. James' Park. The Blues simply had no answer to his class and now face the certainty of Second Division football next season. All this despite the second half sending off of Newcastle's Paul Gascoigne at a time when they led by just a single goal. In the end United mauled their opponents who, bar the performance of Robert Hopkins, offered very little.

Newcastle were ahead after just fourteen minutes, a short ball was played to Beardsley who slipped through two tackles and then hit a low superbly placed shot past David Seaman. At this point United should have gone on to score more but some crude Birmingham tackling seemed to put off any unnecessary urgency. Despite the rough play only two of the visitors had been cautioned by the interval and both for dissent, Wright and Kuhl the guilty men.

Birmingham started better in the second half but always lacked the penetration required to beat United's defence. In the midst of this bright spell by the visitors Gascoigne clashed with City's most productive player Hopkins, and was immediately sent off. The incident however seemed to spur on Newcastle rather than aid Birmingham's slim hopes of a much needed win. The backlash started nine minutes later and it was the ever impressive Beardsley who again supplied the ammunition shooting his team into a 2-0 lead. It was an unbelievable goal too. Forced wide by the Blues defence he managed to squeeze the ball in from an amazingly acute angle between Seaman and the post. A minute later Beardsley was denied what would have been a fabulous hat-trick when his fierce volley struck the very same post with Seaman well beaten again. Birmingham then picked up their third booking after a nasty tackle by Handysides sent Stevenson crashing to the ground. The same player moments later created Birmingham's goal on 78 minutes, sending in a low curling cross which Hopkins hit on the run straight at Martin Thomas, but, the rebound fell kindly for a second shot into an empty net. The fight back was short lived, 62 seconds by the clock, and Whitehurst combined with Anderson for the United full-back to restore their two-goal lead. Then two minutes from time Whitehurst made no mistake with a simple strike inside the area to give Newcastle a well deserved fourth goal, and Blues left dejected and relegated.

Newcastle United

Thomas, Anderson, Bailey, McCreery, Clarke, Roeder, Stephenson, Gascoigne, Whitehurst, Beardsley, McDonald.

Birmingham City

Seaman, Ransom, Dicks, Smalley, Wright, Kuhl, Hagan, Clarke, Frain, Handysides, Hopkins.

Sadly Missed

Billy Reid died on this day in 1923, aged 47.
Midfield 1899-1900, Apps 4. Goals 1.

April 12

CASTLE UNITED

v BIRMINGHAM CITY

12th APRIL, 1986
Kick-off 3.00 p.m. Volume 9 No. 21

MATCH SPONSORED BY:

DAIRY CREST

April 13

yed on this day

Division 2.
Newton Heath (h) 3-0 — Att. 4,000
McNee, Thompson, Milne
Division 1.
Manchester City (h) 0-0 — Att. 16,000
Division 1.
Sheffield United (h) 3-0 — Att. 16,000
MacFarlane, Carr, Ghee
Division 1.
Bolton Wanderers (h) 2-0 — Att. 15,000
McColl (2)
Division 1.
Bury (a) 4-1 — Att. 18,000
Gosnell, Veitch (pen), Howie, . Rutherford
Division 1.
Sheffield United (h) 0-0 — Att. 30,000
Division 1.
Sunderland (h) 1-0 — Att. 40,000
Higgins
Division 1.
Liverpool (h) 1-1 — Att. 15,000
Hibbert
Division 1.
Manchester City (a) 1-0 — Att. 30,000
Shepherd
Division 1.
Sheffield United (a) 2-1 — Att. 20,000
McDonald (2)
Division 1.
Bolton Wanderers (a) 0-1 — Att. 10,000
Division 2.
Southampton (a) 0-2 — Att. 9,000
Division 2.
Hull City (a) 3-2 — Att. 6,000
Pearson, J. Smith, Imrie (pen)
Wartime.
Leeds United (h) 1-1 — Att. 22,991
Milburn
Division 1.
Wolverhampton W. (a) 0-2 — Att. 22,335
Division 1.
Burnley (h) 1-0 — Att. 27,229
Sinclair
Division 1.
Manchester United (a) 0-1 — Att. 44,751
Division 1.
Queens Park Rangers (h) 1-0 — Att. 21,733
Reilly
Division 2.
Oldham Athletic (h) 3-2 — Att. 16,615
Peacock, Hunt, Brock
Premier League.
Sheffield Wed. 1 — Newcastle 1
Pembridge 57 — Elliottt 35
Att. 33,798
Premier League.
Newcastle 2 — Barnsley 1
Andersson 40 — Fjortoft 50
Shearer 86
Att. 36,534
Premier League.
Derby County 2 — Newcastle 3
Christie 46 — Robert 73
Morris 53 — Dyer 76
LuaLua 90
Att. 31,031

record for this day is... 22 games,
, Drawn 5, Lost 4, GF 32, GA 18.
success rate... 70.45%.

Match of the Day from 2002

KNOCKOUT DERBY

Shearer injured as Newcastle overturn a two-goal lead

This Premiership clash against Derby at Pride Park was played out in front of a crowd of 31,031, many of whom watched in amazement as the game unfolded. Derby were struggling to stay in the Premier League, having lost four consecutive games prior to this one, and were praying for a win. A draw would not be good enough to keep them safe, and they had a hard fight on their hands to beat Newcastle who, in contrast, were doing well near the top of the table.

The first half was played out with both teams trying for a goal early on. All efforts proved to be fruitless, and Derby were beginning to think they were in with a chance. However, no matter how hard each team tried to beat the other's defence, they failed. The entire first half passed without incident, and the crowd were becoming agitated. Derby needed the win, and Newcastle were a little surprised that they had not achieved anything either.

The restart saw a dramatic change in the pace, and the first goal was not far away. It came just one minute into the period, and it was Derby who had broke the deadlock. Higginbotham sent a lovely ball which came to Branko Strupar, who chested it down and knocked it to Lee Morris. He then passed Aaron Hughes in the Newcastle defence and flicked the ball back to Malcolm Christie who had the easy job of pushing it over the line to put the home side into the lead.

The relief was almost tangible, and even more so when, just seven minutes later, Derby's lead was doubled. Newcastle keeper Andy Oakes made a fine save from an attempt by Alan Shearer, then a cross from Barton fell to Morris who sent the ball into the net with a little help from the well-placed post.

Derby were starting to feel comfortable in their lead, and Newcastle were unable to make a comeback. They decided to bide their time, sure that their chance would come. Before any more attempts at goal were made, Shearer clashed heads with Robert Lee. Both men were injured and bleeding, Shearer needing stitches to his nose and Lee having his head bandaged. Jenas was brought on in place of Shearer, while Lee managed to play on for seven minutes before being replaced by Evatt.

The incident sparked the start of the Newcastle revival, and the visiting crowd were in for a treat. On 73 minutes a free kick was taken by Robert from 30 yards, and without any help it sailed into the goal past a bewildered Oakes. Newcastle had managed to pull a goal back, and they were now in fighting spirit. It took just three minutes for their next goal to arrive, and it was Kieron Dyer who added his name to the score-sheet. His goal was deemed to be offside by Derby, but the referee disagreed. Protests from Higginbotham and Riggott served only to get their names written down in the ref's book, and manager John Gregory was ordered to take a seat in the stands for making his complaints known. His concerns were well founded, as later television footage showed that Derby were right. Dyer had indeed been offside when Gary Speed gave him the ball.

However, the goal stood and Newcastle were now level. Derby lost their spirit after this, and Newcastle were more than ready to take advantage of their lack of heart. Attempts at goal from Robert and Jenas bounded off the woodwork, and there was even a shot from Derby that could have changed the scores again. An easy strike from Ravanelli was fluffed, and Derby gave up hope.

Newcastle sealed their win in the final minute when Lua Lua, brought on in place of Cort, decided that now was the time to score his first goal in 37 Premiership appearances. It was welcomed heartily by the Newcastle supporters, but a kick in the teeth for Derby.

This win brought Newcastle into fourth place in the table, with three points more than Chelsea and a game in hand.

Derby County
Oakes, Barton, Riggott, HIgginbotham, Boertien, Jackson, Lee (Evatt 81), Kinkladze, Morris (Elliott 90), Christie (Ravanelli 65), Strupar.

Newcastle United
Given, Hughes, O'Brien (Bernard 66), Dabizas, Distin, Solano, Dyer, Speed, Robert, Shearer (Jenas 73), Cort (LuaLua 59).

Referee Mr. R. Styles (Hampshire).

Newcastle United

Fairbrother, Cowell, Craig, Harvey, Brennan, Dodgin, Houghton, Stobbart, Milburn, Woodburn, Walker.

Sheffield Wednesday

McIntosh, Westlake, Swift, Whitcomb, Turton, Cockcroft, Marriott, Quigley, Jordan, Froggatt, Woodhead.

Referee

Mr. H. Trenholm (Stockton)

NEWCASTLE UNITED

ASSOCIATION FOOTBALL CLUB

Newcastle Utd. v. Sheffield W.

FOOTBALL LEAGUE FIXTURE

SAT. APR. 17th, 1948

K.O. 3-15 P.M.

HOT OXO

A BEEFY DRINK MADE IN A MOMENT

You can obtain an Excellent Meal at a Moderate Price at any of

Carricks

CAFES

Branches throughout the North

Head Office :
47 GREY STREET, NEWCASTLE, 1

The Big Five—

Teams of Experts cover ALL the games and ALL the sport ONLY through the North's Own Papers

NEWCASTLE JOURNAL
EVENING CHRONICLE
SUNDAY SUN
WEEKLY CHRONICLE
SPORTING MAN

Have your copies ON ORDER

Mortgages arranged at 4%

The UNIVERSAL BUILDING SOCIETY

36 Grey Steet, Newcastle-on-Tyne

Secretary:—H. Spoor

Buy your Home the UNIVERSAL WAY

OFFICIAL PROGRAMME

(No. 44)

TWOPENCE

April 18

Played on this day

1903, Division 1.
Blackburn Rovers (a) 1-3   Att. 8,000
McColl
1908, Division 1.
Sunderland (h) 1-3   Att. 50,000
Howie
1914, Division 1.
Sheffield United (a) 0-2   Att. 17,000
1924, Division 1.
Bolton Wanderers (a) 1-0   Att. 20,000
J. Low
1925, Division 1.
Bolton Wanderers (h) 0-1   Att. 8,000
1928, Division 1.
Everton (a) 0-3   Att. 28,266
1930, Division 1.
Liverpool (h) 3-1   Att. 40,000
Gallacher, Hill, Weaver
1931, Division 1.
Leicester City (a) 1-3   Att. 12,000
Bedford
1933, Division 1.
Aston Villa (a) 0-3   Att. 25,000
1936, Division 2.
Southampton (a) 3-1   Att. 9,000
J. Smith (2), Ware
1938, Division 2.
Norwich City (a) 1-1   Att. 22,575
Imrie (pen)
1942, Wartime.
Middlesbrough (h) 3-1   Att. 4,500
Woollett, Stubbins, Short
1949, Division 1.
Middlesbrough (a) 2-3   Att. 43,000
Milburn, Mitchell
1951, Division 1.
Bolton Wanderers (h) 0-1   Att. 39,099
1953, Division 1.
Portsmouth (a) 1-5   Att. 27,835
Keeble
1955, Division 1.
Manchester United (h) 2-0   Att. 35,569
Hannah, White
1959, Division 1.
Leeds United (h) 2-2   Att. 19,321
Allchurch, Curry
1960, Division 1.
Sheffield Wednesday (a) 0-2   Att. 33,332
1964, Division 2.
Scunthorpe United (a) 0-2   Att. 6,433
1973, Division 1.
Manchester City (a) 0-2   Att. 25,156
1979, Division 2.
Notts County (h) 1-2   Att. 12,017
Withe
1981, Division 2.
Derby County (a) 0-2   Att. 14,139
1987, Division 1.
Manchester United (h) 2-1   Att. 32,706
Roeder, Goddard
1992, Division 2.
Millwall (h) 0-1   Att. 23,821
1998, Premier League.
Manchester U. 1   Newcastle 1
Beckham 38   Andersson 11
   Att. 55,194

Playing record for this day is... 25 games,
Won 6, Drawn 3, Lost 16, GF 25, GA 46.
Today's success rate... 30%.

Match of the Day from 1936

UNITED WIN AT THE DELL
Newcastle deserve win against Southampton

Newcastle United travelled to The Dell today to meet Southampton in this Division Two match. 9,000 had turned out to watch the game on a spring day, and the home side were confident of a win. It had been a long trip for Newcastle, and they were hoping that they had the energy to give a good game and hopefully take the points home.

Southampton showed promise from the start, but when it came down to scoring goals, they lacked the finishing skills needed to convert their efforts.

Newcastle, on the other hand, had enough patience to bide their time and shoot with confidence. Therefore it was expected that they should be the first to score today. They did just that with a great shot from Smith, sending the ball rocketing past Scriven in the Southampton goal to put the visitors into the lead.

The second goal of the game also fell to Newcastle, and it was Smith again who was the one to beat the Southampton defence and slot the ball home. The half-time interval arrived with Newcastle two goals ahead, leaving Southampton with a lot of catching up to do.

The interval must have been good for Southampton, and they came out revived and more determined. Shots were fired at the Newcastle goal from all angles, and the visiting keeper had to pull off some super saves. He managed this with skill and confidence, and kept the ball out of the net during this barrage of attacks.

Despite this fierce attacking period from Southampton, it was Newcastle who added another goal to the score-sheet. Ware got hold of a lovely pass and sent it powerfully into the net for their third.

Bill Imrie

It was getting late now, and Southampton were running out of time to make their comeback. They started their fight with a nice goal from Watson who finally managed to get the ball past Tapken.

However, it wasn't enough for the home side, and the game ended with a 3-1 win for Newcastle.

Southampton
Scriven, Adams, Sillett, Henderson, McIlwaine, King, Neal, Tully, Watson, Holt, Fishlock.
Newcastle United
Tapken, Fairhurst, Johnson, Gordon, Bullock, Imrie, Ware, Wilson, Smith, Connelly, Pearson.

Sadly Missed

Stan Barber died on this day 1984 aged 75.
Midfield 1925-1928, Apps 1. Goals 0.

April 19

Match of the Day from 1997

ASPRILLA/SHEARER MENACE KEEPS UNITED IN EURO HUNT

Colombian magic inspires United to 3-1 win over Derby

Man-of-the-match Faustino Asprilla walked off the St. James' Park pitch today to a standing ovation from the Toon Army, but it was the work rate of Alan Shearer that did the most to unhinge an unhappy Derby County defence. Not that such an observation will concern Kenny Dalglish, now firmly established as successor to Kevin Keegan whose last away game in charge, ironically, was a successful visit to the Baseball Ground, Derby. Six matches without defeat and Liverpool's decline have fuelled Newcastle hopes of finishing second in the Premiership and claiming a place in the European Champions' League rather than the lesser prize of a place in the UEFA Cup next season.

United were never in any serious danger of losing once they nullified a goal in only 33 seconds when a shoddy response from Steve Watson and Darren Peacock to Gary Rowett's long ball enabled Dean Sturridge to nick in and beat the cruelly exposed Shaka Hislop. Newcastle's equaliser on twelve minutes was more than a little fortunate and kick-started a totally miserable afternoon for Derby keeper Russell Hoult. He was clearly furious with himself for allowing Robbie Elliott's swirling corner to be turned into the net, rather than round the post under no apparent pressure at all. After this the Shearer-Ferdinand-Asprilla triangle started to probe and menace the hard pressed Derby defence with the Colombian, only recently restored to the attack, a real threat throughout. To their credit Derby went in at half time level at 1-1.

Just seven minutes into the second half Les Ferdinand, with his nineteenth goal of an injury-disrupted season, was well rewarded for his brave diving header from a wickedly teasing cross from Elliott to put United in front. Then another calamity for Hoult made it 3-1 after 75 minutes. Shearer's effort in the game had deserved a goal but his shot from 30 yards seemed, at the time, a little optimistic until Hoult misread the swerving ball and in it went for the England striker's 27th of the season. A performance like this could not have come at a worse time for Hoult who was hoping to be named in Glen Hoddle's England squad to face Georgia, the announcement coming 24 hours later.

For United, and in particular Asprilla, they had a brilliant day summed up by Dalglish after the game: "He worked hard and his contribution was immense, when he's on this form you never know what he's going to do next." Nor do his team-mates, but Asprilla is clearly appreciated by the St. James' Park faithful, who now face the kind of cluttered championship run-in that confronts title favourites Manchester United. Newcastle have four games in eight days with the first three away, but on this form their players will be relishing the task.

Newcastle United
Hislop, Watson, Elliott, Peacock, Beresford, Barton, Batty, Lee, Asprilla, (Gillespie 85), Ferdinand, Shearer.
Derby County
Hoult, Laursen, Rowett, McGrath, C.Powell (D.Powell h/t), Van Der Laan (Solis 75), Trollope, Asanovic, Dailly, Sturridge, Ward (Wanchope h/t).
Referee Mr. D. J. Gallagher (Banbury)

Played on this day

1902, Division 1.
Nottingham Forest (h) 3-0   Att. 12,000
Roberts, Rutherford (2)
1913, Division 1.
Manchester United (a) 0-3   Att. 17,000
1919, Wartime.
South Shields (h) 1-1   Att. 40,000
Little (pen)
1924, Division 1.
Chelsea (a) 0-1   Att. 30,000
1927, Division 1.
Huddersfield Town (a) 0-1   Att. 45,049
1930, Division 1.
Leeds United (h) 2-1   Att. 30,000
Gallacher (2)
1935, Division 2.
Bury (a) 2-0   Att. 17,000
Bott, Murray
1941, Wartime.
Preston North End (a) 0-2   Att. 23,000
1946, Wartime.
Manchester United (h) 0-1   Att. 47,493
1947, Division 2.
Leicester City (h) 1-1   Att. 36,739
Wayman
1952, Division 1.
Derby County (a) 3-1   Att. 18,940
Harvey, Keeble, Prior
1957, Division 1.
Chelsea (h) 1-2   Att. 30,708
White
1958, Division 1.
Bolton Wanderers (a) 1-1   Att. 19,284
White
1965, Division 1.
Bolton Wanderers (a) 1-1   Att. 15,762
Cummings
1969, Division 1.
West Bromwich A. (a) 1-5   Att. 23,087
B. Robson
1972, Division 1.
Leeds United(h) 1-0   Att. 42,164
Macdonald
1975, Division 1.
Stoke City (a) 0-0   Att. 32,302
1976, Division 1.
Sheffield United (a) 0-1   Att. 18,906
1980, Division 2.
Swansea City (h) 1-3   Att. 14,314
Shoulder (pen)
1986, Division 1.
Chelsea (a) 1-1   Att. 18,970
Anderson
1988, Division 1.
Watford (a) 1-1   Att. 12,075
Anderson
1997, Premier League.

Newcastle 3	Derby County 1
Elliott 12	Sturridge 1
Ferdinand 52	
Shearer 75	Att. 36,550

2003, Premier League.

Fulham 2	Newcastle 1
Legwinski 69	Shearer 39
Clark 86	Att. 17,900

Playing record for this day is... 23 games, Won 6, Drawn 7, Lost 10, GF 24, GA 30. Today's success rate... 41.30%.

Birthdays

Ron Guthrie born today in 1944.
Left-back 1963-1973, Apps 66 (6 subs). Goals 2.

Sadly Missed

George Mathison died on this day 1989 aged 79.
Midfield 1926-1933, Apps 22. Goals 0.

April 20

yed on this day

Division 2.
Burslem Port Vale (a) 0-2 Att. 2,000
Test Match
Stoke (h) 2-1 Att. 17,000
Smith, Harvey
Division 1.
Manchester City (a) 1-2 Att. 18,000
Peddie
Division 1.
Bolton Wanderers (a) 2-4. Att. 5,000
Orr, Veitch
Division 1.
Middlesbrough (a) 1-2 Att. 20,000
Higgins
Division 1.
Aston Villa(a) 0-2 Att. 20,000
Division 1.
Sheffield Wednesday (h) 2-1 Att. 20,000
Gallacher (2, 1pen)
Division 2.
Bolton Wanderers (h) 1-3 Att. 28,000
Leach
Wartime.
Bradford Park Ave. (a) 0-2 Att. 5,208
Wartime.
Sunderland (a) 0-1 Att. 39,000
Division 1.
Preston North End (h) 3-3 Att. 38,681
Davies, Hannah, Milburn
Division 1.
Aston Villa (h) 1-2 Att. 28,453
R. Mitchell
Division 2.
Derby County (h) 3-0 Att. 33,138
Fell (pen), Hale, Thomas
Division 2.
Bury (h) 1-3 Att. 25,017
McGarry
Division 1.
Blackpool(a) 1-1 Att. 12,446
Suddick
Division 1.
Fulham (a) 0-2 Att. 21,612
Division 1.
Birmingham City (h) 1-1 Att. 34,066
Robson
Division 2.
Grimsby Town(h) 1-1 Att. 13,170
Shoulder
Division 2.
Rotherham United (h) 4-0 Att. 18,523
McDermott, Varadi, Keegan, Wharton
Division 2.
Blackburn Rovers (a) 1-1 Att. 19,196
Trewick
Division 1.
Liverpool (a) 1-3 Att. 34,733
McDonald
Division 1.
Everton (a) 0-3 Att. 43,576
Division 2.
Ipswich Town (h) 2-2 Att. 17,638
Stimson, Quinn
Division 2.
Derby County (a) 1-4 Att. 21,363
Peacock
Premier League.
Newcastle 3   Charlton Athletic 0
Speed 22
LuaLua 46, Shearer 89 Att. 51,360
Alan Shearer's 200th Premier League goal.

record for this day is... 25 games,
Drawn 6, Lost 14, GF 32, GA 46.
success rate... 32%.

SHEARER'S 200 NOT OUT

Speed and LuaLua also on the mark in 3-0 win

It took some doing to upstage Lomana Lua Lua's first goal in front of the Toon Army, not least because of the six backward somersaults which followed, but Alan Shearer managed it with just a minute of time remaining with his 200th Premiership goal. The crowd had groaned with despair just minutes earlier when Lua Lua, making his first start for United, played Shearer through with an impudent back heel and the former England captain failed to thread the ball through keeper Dean Kiely's legs. It seemed that his chance of reaching the milestone in this game had gone. But Shearer is nothing if not a trier and that wholehearted commitment came to his rescue as he slotted home a pass from Gary Speed. It was as if the crowd had willed it by sucking the ball into the net.

Gary Speed scores the first goal despite pressure from Athletic's Luke Young.

Charlton, one would have thought with nothing to play for, could have afforded to be a bit more adventurous. They started the game with a dull 3-6-1 formation from which they only deviated in the last quarter, by then they were a well beaten side and it was all too late. They may well have been in trouble as early as the eighth minute when their on-loan Portuguese international, Jorge Costa, blatantly nudged the ball back to Kiely, but referee Mike Dean, failed to spot the most obvious infringement of the entire 90 minutes. In the absence of Craig Bellamy, LuaLua provided a much more lively foil for Shearer's craft than Carl Cort, who surprisingly was not even on the subs' bench. Even so, if a goal was going to come, set-pieces seemed the most likely means, thanks to the negative approach by visiting boss Alan Curbishley. So, sure enough on 21 minutes a corner by Nolberto Solano enabled Speed to brush aside the challenge of Luke Young and power home an unstoppable header, his sixth goal in an injury-interrupted season.

It took just a minute of the second half to produce the biggest roar at St. James' Park this afternoon, and probably more than a few other afternoons also, as LuaLua struck United's second. The man from the Democratic Republic of Congo had gone 36 games, all as a sub, without scoring until his late goal at Derby last week. He celebrated that one with an impressive backward somersault, but this time he would have impressed a panel of Olympic gymnastic judges with a superb repertoire of backward flying arched loops which surely would have warranted a 9.9 in anyone's book. The goal was taken a little less spectacularly, turning neatly in the penalty area to lash the ball first time into the corner past a motionless Kielly. With the game won all eyes turned to Shearer to wrap up a perfect end, the patient crowd were well rewarded and Newcastle collected another impressive home win.

Newcastle United

Given, Hughes, O'Brien (Dabizas 70), Distin, Elliott, Solano (Jenas 78), Dyer, Speed, Robert (Bernard 78), Shearer, Lua Lua.

Charlton Athletic

Kiely, Young, Rufus, Costa, Konchesky, Stuart, Kinsella, Parker (Lisbie 73), Robinson, Johanson, Euell (Fortune 90).

Referee Mr. M. Dean (Heswall, Wirral).

Birthdays

Shay Given born today in 1976.
Goalkeeper 1997-present day, Apps 228 (1 sub).

Jimmy Wilson born today in 1942.
Winger 1959-1962, Apps 13. Goals 2.

April 21

Match of the Day from 1934

WOLVES ARE WALLOPED
Four goals in eleven minutes destroys the Wanderers

Newcastle without a win in twelve successive league games suddenly and emphatically put the record straight against Wolverhampton Wanderers today. United's poor current form had been the catalyst to their losing their First Division status; despite this win they will be playing in the Second Division next season for the first time since 1898. Wolves, were left stunned by the result, especially as they had beaten United twice already this season in league and cup, the latter only last January. Despite the gloom around St. James' Park the game attracted an above average crowd of 26,000 for the game, the goals and the result being a just reward for those loyal Newcastle fans.

United almost took the lead from their very first shot on target in the second minute. Wolves' keeper Weare, making his senior debut, was very fortunate to stop a stinging free kick by Murray with his knees. On their next attack eight minutes later, Williams squandered a great chance when he completely miskicked the ball when set up by a clever pass from Boyd, all this whilst Weare was grounded at the other side of the goal. At the other end a good move by Shaw, Jones, and Barrowclough released Hartill on the left wing, he dangerously beat Fairhurst to chase into the area, but a magnificently timed tackle by Nelson put an end to the threat on goal. After twenty minutes Newcastle's attacking domination was finally rewarded when Williams, making amends for his earlier error, took a pass from McMenemy in his stride and blasted the ball into the top corner from just inside the penalty area. With the visitors now penned into their own half Newcastle hit a second just five minutes later. McMenemy won a free kick just outside the area and this was smashed in off the post by Imrie. Wolves were now being completely overrun by United and it was only another two minutes before they conceded a self-inflicted third goal. A woefully short back pass from Smalley was chased down by the alert Richardson who made no mistake with a precise low-placed shot past the stranded keeper. What a tonic these goals were to the Newcastle supporters, they hadn't had this much to cheer for weeks and were now revelling in their side's complete domination of the game. Incredibly United then hit a fourth goal inside eleven minutes after a quickly taken free kick. With the fouled Williams still grounded, Boyd quickly squared to Imrie who cracked it home from eighteen yards. A shell-shocked Wolves side to their credit never gave up their attacking style though, and they were rewarded with a goal seven minutes before the interval, albeit a fortuitous one. A great ball from Phillips put Clayton away and his cross from the right was deflected into the net by United keeper McPhillip's sliced attempt to clear. Then, just before half time Boyd put the ball into the Wolves' net only for the effort to be ruled marginally offside.

Despite a promising start by Wolves in the second half it was United who grabbed a fifth and final goal after 59 minutes. Newcastle, after a series of crosses into the box from either wing, suddenly had one handled by the desperate Smalley and the resultant penalty was emphatically smashed in by Imrie to complete his match-ball winning hat-trick. Newcastle continued to pile on the pressure and, but for brave keeping by Weare, would have scored many more goals in the second half. He brought off wonderful saves to deny Lang, Richardson and Williams all within quick succession midway through the half. His stunning save from Lang was almost given the loudest cheer of the day by the now thoroughly thrilled St. James' Park crowd whose patience throughout the season was well rewarded this afternoon.

Newcastle United
McPhillips, Nelson, Fairhurst, Imrie, Davidson, Murray, Boyd, Richardson, Williams, McMenemy, Lang.
Wolverhampton Wanderers
Weare, Lawton, Shaw, Smalley, Nelson, Richards, Phillips, Clayton, Hartill, Jones, Barrowclough.
Referee Mr. S.F. Rous (Watford).

Sadly Missed

Jackie Rutherford died on this day in 1963, aged 78.
Winger 1902-1913, Apps 336. Goals 94.

Played on this day

1900, Division 1.
Stoke (h) 2-2   Att. 12,000
Peddie, A. Gardner
1906, FA Cup Final.
Everton (n) 0-1   Att. 75,609
Played at The Crystal Palace, London.
1919, Wartime.
Harlepool United (a) 1-6   Att. 12,000
Hibbert
1923, Division 1.
Stoke (h) 1-0   Att. 15,000
Spencer
1924, Division 1.
Aston Villa (a) 1-6   Att. 40,000
J. Clark
1928, Division 1.
Arsenal (h) 1-1   Att. 25,000
Seymour
1930, Division 1.
Liverpool (a) 0-0   Att. 20,000
1934, Division 1.
Wolverhampton W. (h) 5-1   Att. 26,000
Williams, J.R. Richardson, Imrie (3, 1pen)
1945, Wartime.
Bolton Wanderers (a) 0-3   Att. 26,000
1951, Division 1.
Manchester United (h) 0-2   Att. 45,209
1956, Division 1.
Chelsea (h) 1-1   Att. 24,322
Milburn (pen)
1962, Division 2.
Sunderland (a) 0-3   Att. 57,666
1969, Division 1.
Wolverhampton W. (h) 4-1   Att. 24,986
Davies, B.Robson (2), Sinclair
1973, Division 1.
Liverpool (h) 2-1   Att. 36,810
Tudor (2)
1979, Division 2.
Fulham (h) 0-0   Att. 11,924
1986, Division 1.
West Ham United (a) 1-8   Att. 24,735
Whitehurst
1990, Division 2.
Plymouth Argyle (a) 1-1   Att. 11,702
McGhee
1999, Premier League.
Sheffield Wednesday 1   Newcastle 1
Scott 52   Shearer 45 (pen)
      Att. 21,545
2001, Premier League.
Sunderland 1   Newcastle 1
Carteron 67   O'Brien 78
      Att. 48,277
2003, Premier League.
Newcastle 1   Aston Villa 1
Solano 37   Dublin 69
      Att. 52,015

Playing record for this day is... 20 games,
Won 4, Drawn 9, Lost 7, GF 23, GA 40.
Today's success rate... 42.50%.

April 22

1899, Division 1.
Sunderland (h) 0-1   Att. 22,000
1905, Division 1.
Sunderland (h) 1-3   Att. 30,000
Veitch
Newcastle played the final 65 minutes with just ten men after Alex Gardner was carried off with a broken leg (this in the days when no substitutes were allowed).
1911, FA Cup Final.
Bradford City (n) 0-0   Att. 69,800
Played at The Crystal Palace, London
1922, Division 1.
West Bromwich A. (a) 2-1   Att. 25,000
Curry, Harris
1933, Division 1.
Blackburn Rovers (h) 2-1   Att. 12,500
Allen, Dryden
1936, Division 2.
Blackpool (a) 0-6   Att. 7,935
1939, Division 2.
Swansea Town (h) 1-2   Att. 14,000
Clifton
1944, Wartime.
Sunderland (h) 5-2   Att. 12,106
Stubbins (3), Milburn, Opponent (og)
1946, Wartime.
Manchester United (a) 1-4   Att. 39,173
Wayman
1950, Division 1.
Manchester United (h) 2-1   Att. 52,203
Milburn, Walker
1957, Division 1.
Chelsea (a) 2-6   Att. 20,795
Milburn, White
1959, Division 1.
Bolton Wanderers (h) 2-0   Att. 17,451
Curry, Taylor
1961, Division 1.
Bolton Wanderers (h) 4-1   Att. 18,820
Tuohy, McGuigan, Keith, McKinney (pen)
1967, Division 1.
Sheffield Wednesday (a) 0-0   Att. 25,007
1972, Division 1.
Chelsea (a) 3-3   Att. 33,000
Tudor (2), Macdonald
1978, Division 1.
Queens Park Rangers (h) 0-3   Att. 13,463
1989, Division 1.
Luton Town (h) 0-0   Att. 18,636

Playing record for this day is... 17 games, Won 6, Drawn 4, Lost 7, GF 25, GA 34. Today's success rate... 47.06%.

Match of the Day from 1922

NEWCASTLE U-TURN
United come back from 1-0 down to take victory

Newcastle United entered this Division One game against West Bromwich Albion with the advantage over their opponents. West Brom were having a bad run, as they did at the start of the season, and Newcastle should have had no problem winning convincingly. The game was played out in front of a crowd of 25,000.

The first goal of the game came for Albion. The ball was cleared from the goal-line and came to Jones, who let it flow on to Davies who flicked it into the net with his first shot. The goal took Newcastle keeper Bradley by surprise, and the rest of the side were a little taken aback too. They were not expecting such good play from the home side.

The rest of the first half saw equal play from the two teams, but the defences stood strong and no more goals were added to the score-sheet.

The second half began with Newcastle by far the better team. Albion seemed to have lost all their stamina and fight, and they appeared less solid than in the first half.

This pleased Newcastle greatly and it wasn't long before their forwards managed to break through the weak Albion defence. Goalkeeper Pearson was well beaten by a lovely shot on target by Harris, forcing its way into the net. This goal levelled the scores, and gave Albion a worrying warning of what was to come if they didn't snap out of their lacklustre performance.

The home side didn't heed the warning, and so it was inevitable that Newcastle would score again. It was Curry who saw his chance and leapt through the Albion defence to shoot the ball powerfully in the net. Newcastle had come from behind to deservedly take the lead from Albion, a team who normally have no trouble against the Magpies.

Two late shots by Morris and Davies gave Albion a chance of getting back into the game, but their efforts failed to reach the target and that didn't give the home side much to pin their hopes on.

United kept up the pressure on the Albion defence and keeper, but none of their attempts were destined for the back of the net. The game ended with the score 2-1, a great comeback from the Newcastle side.

West Bromwich Albion
Pearson, Smith, Pennington, Richardson, Bowser, McNeal, Jephcott, Jones, Davis, Morris, Gregory.
Newcastle United
Bradley, Russell, Hudspeth, Curry, Spencer, Mooney, J. Low, Smailes, Harris, McDonald, Mitchell.

A. SMAILES

Sadly Missed

Jackie Bell died on this day 1991, aged 51
Midfield 1956-1962, Apps 117. Goals 8.

April 23

Match of the Day from 1932

ALLEN DOUBLE WINS THE CUP FOR UNITED
Controversial equaliser, then Newcastle take control

This was a great final, with plenty of incident, in front a 92,298 crowd paying record gate receipts of £24,688. Arsenal, having taken the lead through a goal from John, were pegged back by a crushing equaliser five minutes from the interval in the most controversial circumstances. In making his cross Richardson appeared to pull the ball back from beyond the touchline and this caused the Arsenal keeper to momentarily stop. As the ball came across the area Allen had the simple task of hammering the ball into the net. The referee, who was in a good position to see the incident, had no hesitation in awarding the goal. Although there was a slight protest from keeper Moss, much to their credit, the Arsenal team immediately walked back to the centre circle to restart play. The disappointment was clearly visible within the Arsenal ranks and Newcastle then went on to claim the only goal in the second half and thus received the FA Cup from the King.

The game got off to a slow start with very few goalscoring chances. Arsenal were having most of the possession but were able to do little in the way of threatening a tight Newcastle defence. At the other end the United forwards also had little sight at goal but this was more to do with the lack of service from their midfield The first real opportunity of the game went to Arsenal when a bobbling ball inside the area was eventually struck by Bastin from ten yards but his shot was tipped over the bar by McInroy's instinctive dive. The Gunners' next attack produced the opening goal on twenty minutes. A great run by Hulme from inside his own half took him deep inside United territory. From his cross three Newcastle defenders, Fairhurst, Nelson and Davidson all jumped blocking the view of their keeper. Behind

United's Jack Allen (left) fires the controversial equalising goal.

was the incoming John who got there before the trio to steer his header down and past McInroy. With a goal lead Arsenal continued to dominate until the half hour mark when United suddenly started to stir from their slumber. Five minutes before half-time Newcastle struck their dubious equaliser and the final was once again anybody's game.

It was Newcastle who looked more lively and dangerous in the second half. Within minutes Boyd raced clear again and was sent sprawling in the penalty area by Roberts, but, this time it was United's players and supporters who looked amazed by the decision given by referee Harper; no penalty was awarded. The winning goal came after 70 minutes when Weaver sent a long ball up the centre to Boyd, who, charging in from the right wing, controlled neatly and timed his short pass to Allen to perfection. Allen took the ball round the defender and as Parker and Moss came to narrow the angle he placed a lovely shot into the far corner of the net from just inside the penalty area. Arsenal were stung into action but Newcastle's confidence was growing by the minute. However, with just twelve minutes of play remaining, Arsenal were given the game's best chance. A deflected cross from Lambert fell to the feet of Jack but with an open goal in front of him he only managed to screw the ball wide.

Arsenal
Moss, Parker, Hapgood, Jones, Roberts, Male, Hulme, Jack, Lambert, Bastin, John.
Newcastle United
McInroy, Nelson, Fairhurst, MacKenzie, Davidson, Weaver, Boyd, Richardson, Allen, McMenemy, Lang.
Referee Mr. W.P. Harper (Worcester).

Birthdays

Darren Huckerby born today in 1976.
Forward 1995-1996, Apps 2 (2 subs). Goals 0.

Sadly Missed

Matthew McNeil died on this day 1977, aged 49.
Centre-half 1949-1951, Apps 11. Goals 0.

Played on this day

1898, Test Match.
Stoke (a) 0-1   Att. 20,000
1910, FA Cup Final.
Barnsley (n) 1-1   Att. 76,980
Rutherford
Played at the Crystal Palace, London.
1921, Division 1.
Arsenal (a) 1-1   Att. 30,000
King
1927, Division 1.
West Ham United (a) 1-1   Att. 30,000
Seymour
1928, Division 1.
Sheffield United (a) 1-1   Att. 16,000
Gallacher
1932, FA Cup Final.
Arsenal(n) 2-1   Att. 92,298
Allen (2)
Played at Wembley Stadium, London.
1938, Division 2.
Chesterfield (h) 3-1   Att. 16,000
Mooney (2), Park
1949, Division 1.
Liverpool (a) 1-1   Att. 43,488
Mitchell
1952, Division 1.
West Bromwich A. (h) 1-4   Att. 31,188
Prior
1955, Division 1.
Bolton Wanderers (h) 0-0   Att. 48,194
1958, Division 1.
Manchester United (a) 1-1   Att. 28,393
White
1960, Division 1.
Nottingham Forest (a) 0-3   Att. 28,066
1962, Division 2.
Derby County (a) 2-1   Att. 10,745
Allchurch, Thomas
1963, Division 2.
Charlton Athletic (a) 2-1   Att. 12,341
Suddick, McKinney
1966, Division 1.
Sheffield United (h) 0-2   Att. 25,733
1975, Division 1.
Arsenal (h) 3-1   Att. 21,895
Bruce, Macdonald, T. Craig
1977, Division 1.
Queens Park Rangers (a) 2-1 Att. 20,544
Barrowclough, Nattrass
1983, Division 2.
Charlton Athletic (h) 4-2   Att. 20,567
McDermott, Varadi (2), Wharton
1984, Division 2.
Carlisle United (h) 5-1   Att. 33,458
Waddle, Beardsley (2), Keegan (2)
1988, Division 1.
Charlton Athletic (a) 0-2   Att. 7,482
1994, Premier League.

Newcastle 3	Oldham Athletic 2
Fox 19	Jobson 43
Beardsley 56	Sharp 57
Lee 63	Att. 32,214

2000, Premier League.

Newcastle 2	Leeds United 2.
Shearer 24, 48	Bridges 12
	Wilcox 17
	Att. 36,460

2002, Premier League.

Blackburn Rovers 2	Newcastle 2
Gillespie 28	Shearer 63, 71
Cole 67	Att. 26,712

Playing record for this day is... 23 games,
Won 9, Drawn 9, Lost 5, GF 37, GA 33.
Today's success rate... 58.70%.

Played on this day

1901, Division 1.
Sunderland (h) 0-2   Att. 20,000
1906, Division 1.
Stoke (h) 5-0   Att. 12,000
Orr, Howie, J. Rutherford (2), Veitch
1909, Division 1.
Blackburn Rovers (a) 4-2   Att. 7,000
Allan, Rutherford (3)
*The win gains Newcastle their third
League Championship win in five years
with two games of the season to play.*
1915, Division 1.
Notts County (a) 0-1   Att. 10,000
1920, Division 1.
Manchester City (a) 0-0   Att. 25,000
1926, Division 1.
Everton (a) 0-3   Att. 15,000
1937, Division 2.
Bradford City (h) 2-0   Att. 10,000
Rogers, Smith
1943, Wartime.
Huddersfield Town (h) 2-2   Att. 14,000
Carr, Stubbins
1948, Division 2.
Tottenham Hotspur (a) 1-1   Att. 44,164
Sibley
1954, Division 1.
Chelsea (a) 2-1   Att. 46,991
Mitchell, White
1965, Division 2.
Manchester City (h) 0-0   Att. 35,600
*Newcastle finish the season promoted as
Division Two champions.*
1971, Division 1.
West Ham United (h) 1-1   Att. 22,790
Tudor
1974, Texaco Cup Final.
Burnley (h) 2-1   Att. 36,076
Macdonald, Moncur
1976, Division 1.
Tottenham Hotspur (a) 3-0   Att. 29,649
Macdonald (2), Burns
1982, Division 2.
Grimsby Town (h) 0-1   Att. 14,065
1991, Division 2.
West Ham United (a) 1-1   Att. 24,195
Peacock
1999, Premier League.
Wimbledon 1   Newcastle 1
Hartson 24   Shearer 18
    Att. 21,172

Playing record for this day is... 17 games,
Won 6, Drawn 7, Lost 4, GF 24, GA 17.
Today's success rate... 55.88%.

Match of the Day from 1909

CHAMPS AGAIN!

Rutherford and Allan secure victory and Championship

A crowd of 7,000 turned up to see this match at Blackburn Rovers. Newcastle had the distinct advantage over their opponents with a full strength team to boast, whereas Blackburn were playing with more than a few reserves in their side.

The first attacks of the game came from Rovers, and they caused a lot of worry for the Newcastle defence. left-back Jack Carr was fortunately on hand to take the strain and keep the defensive line strong. Then a free kick was awarded to Newcastle and was swiftly taken, but the shot lacked enough power and fell to Blackburn keeper Ashcroft who saved with relative ease. Ten minutes into the game Blackburn took the lead with a powerful shot from Davies beating the Newcastle keeper; but then the scoreline was destined to remain unaltered for quite a while. Despite many attempts from both sides, the ball just wouldn't cross the goal-line, and the first half ended without further incident.

The second period began in much the same way, both teams having a good go at breaching the opposition defence. For a further fifteen minutes nothing was going to give. Then after 60 minutes of play Newcastle scored the equaliser. Rutherford got into position and received the ball with perfect timing. His shot slammed into the net giving Ashcroft no chance to make the save. The next goal also came Newcastle's way and it was Rutherford again who took the credit. It was a great ball, well placed and thoroughly deserved. With Rutherford now wanting to complete his hat-trick, the game stepped up a gear. Rovers pulled a goal back and the pressure was on again.

However, Newcastle were up for the challenge and the attacks increased at both ends of the pitch. Rutherford, trying hard for his third of the game managed to find an opening, his shot was perfectly aimed to whizz past a bewildered Ashcroft to secure his hat-trick.

There was one more goal to come, and by now Rovers were a little deflated. Both teams had played well but Newcastle had gained the upper hand. Allan secured the result for the visiting side, and in doing so also assured them of their third League Championship win in four years with two games left of the season to play.

Blackburn Rovers

Ashcroft, Cowell, Suttie, Walmsley, Chapman, Stevenson, Bracegirdle, Cameron, Davies, Kyle, Anthony.

Newcastle United

Lawrence, McCracken, Carr, Willis, Veitch, McWilliam, Rutherford, Howie, Allan, Stewart, Anderson.

1908. Newcastle United J.C. 1909.

Birthdays

Stuart Pearce born today in 1962.
Left-back 1997-1999, Apps 52 (1 sub). Goals 1.

April 25

Match of the Day from 1903

UNITED SPOIL IT FOR SUNDERLAND
Newcastle win and stop Sunderland taking title

This derby game against Sunderland was played at St. James' Park in front of a crowd of 26,500. The visiting side were desperate for a victory, and hoping it would be today. Just one more win would secure their second successive championship win, and who better to beat than their local rivals Newcastle?

United had other ideas though, and there was no way they would give in easily to allow Sunderland the joy of a victory and the title.

Both teams were in attacking mode, and the first chance of the day fell to Templeton, but his shot was cleared by Doig. Hewitt forced Watts into making a save, and both teams were stepping up the pressure.

Colin Veitch

Two great chances were missed for Newcastle when Turner failed to take advantage of the opportunities, and at the other end Watts again had to pull off a fine save to keep a shot from Bridgett out of goal.

Templeton had the next effort, but his eagerness meant he sent the ball too high and it sailed over the crossbar. Half time arrived and Sunderland were becoming agitated. They were expecting an easy ride to enable them to take the title and Newcastle were playing so well the visitors were frustrated.

The second period started with both sides focused on their game. The deadlock was broken by Newcastle just three minutes later when a great move from Appleyard and Gardner enabled them to get through the Sunderland defence and create an opening for McColl. He relished the opportunity and scored with ease, putting the home side into the lead.

Sunderland were reeling, and gathered themselves together quickly to try to make a comeback. They went all out on the attack, but Newcastle keeper Watts was up to the challenge and saved well.

A fine ball from Appleyard just failed to hit its target, but now Newcastle were by far the better team. Sunderland changed their tactics in the hope of confusing the United side and slipping through to score but they failed miserably and began to panic.

Newcastle managed to keep the ball out of danger, and in doing so robbed Sunderland of the glory that could have been theirs today.

Newcastle United
Watts, Aitken, Agnew, McWilliam, Veitch, Carr, Turner, Alex Gardner, McColl, Appleyard, Templeton.
Sunderland
Doig, Watson, Rhodes, Farquhar, Barrie, Jackson, Hogg, Robinson, Miller, Hewitt, Bridgett.

Birthdays

Wilfred Bott born today in 1907
Winger 1934-1936, Apps 44. Goals 15.

...yed on this day

Division 1.
Bury (a) 0-4   Att. 3,500
Division 1.
Sheffield Wednesday (a) 3-1   Att. 12,000
Orr (pen), Howie, McWilliam
Division 1.
Preston North End (a) 0-0   Att. 5,000
Division 1.
Aston Villa (a) 0-3   Att. 8,000
FA Cup Final, replay.
Bradford City (n) 0-1   Att. 66,646
Played at Old Trafford, Manchester
Division 1.
Aston Villa (h) 2-3   Att. 20,000
Higgins, Veitch
Wartime.
Darlington F. Albion (a) 4-0   Att. 4,000
Ramsay (3), Wilson
FA Cup Final.
Aston Villa (n) 2-0   Att. 91,695
Seymour, Harris
The first all ticket Cup Final, played at Wembley Stadium, London.
Division 1.
Derby County (a) 1-3   Att. 10,093
Devine
Wartime.
Preston North End (h) 0-0   Att. 29,931
Wartime.
Gateshead (h) 3-1   Att. 4,148
Stubbins, Carr, unknown
Division 2.
Chesterfield (a) 0-1   Att. 14,800
Division 1.
Aston Villa (h) 6-1   Att. 36,852
Brennan, Davies (2), Hannah, Milburn,
Mitchell
Division 1.
Leeds United (h) 1-2   Att. 32,594
R. Mitchell
Division 1.
West Ham United (h) 1-0   Att. 38,863
Opponent (og)
Division 1.
Birmingham City (h) 1-2   Att. 24,787
Macdonald
Division 1.
Norwich City (h) 2-2   Att. 7,986
Burns, Kennedy
Division 2.
Queens Park Rangers (a) 1-2   Att. 11,245
Ferguson
Division 1.
Manchester City (h) 3-1   Att. 23,479
Clarke, Roeder, Whitehurst
Premier League.
Sunderland 0   **Newcastle 1**
         Solano 43 (pen)
             Att. 45,067

...record for this day is... 20 games,
Drawn 3, Lost 9, GF 31, GA 27.
...success rate... 47.50%.

UNITED RIDE THE STORM TO LIFT THE CUP

Late goals from Cowan and Seymour, bring glory

In one of the finest FA Cup finals ever played, and by far the wettest, Newcastle United saw out the storm of Aston Villa pressure to stun their Midland opponents with two goals in the last twenty minutes to bring them their second victory in the competition. This final will live long in the memory of the 91,695 fans who were privileged to be at Wembley Stadium today, especially those who travelled from Tyneside to witness Newcastle's first Cup triumph since 1910 when they beat Barnsley.

On a wet Wembley pitch, mastering ball control and having the superior fitness was always going to be critical. In the early stages it was Villa who had the advantage, but Newcastle would show they had the upper hand later on. Although Villa began to swarm forward in numbers, the United defence seemed to anticipate their every move with a Northern canniness and scoring opportunities were thus reduced to a minimum. However, as the game progressed, so did Villa's threat to the United goal, but they found one huge obstacle in their path, which proved their ultimate undoing, Newcastle's keeper Bradley, who at the last moment had been forced to take over the jersey left by first-team regular Mutch due to injury. On the day, Mutch would have been hard pressed to overshadow the performance from Bradley, indeed it's doubtful whether he would have merely equalled it. His saves were made with remarkable coolness given the circumstances of the game and the prize at stake. Two Capewell headers, Walker's shots and

W. Cowan.

another half volley from Kirton inside the penalty area were all confidently and cleanly kept out, keeping United in the tie. When Bradley failed to hold on to the ball cleanly, three times from Walker's powerful drives, his incredible agility in appalling conditions was lightning quick, too quick for Capewell who was denied time after time the chance to charge any rebound home.

With an hour gone Villa's onslaught seemed to be fizzling out. United, bar the odd half chance, had hardly contributed to this absorbing game at all, apart from defending as if their lives depended on it. At this point it seemed even the players were settling down for the extra half hour's football, such was the stalemate. This is also the point at which Newcastle's superior fitness kicked in, which proved fatal for Villa. Newcastle won possession on the halfway line and surged forward. Harris taking the ball whilst his team mates ran in zig zag pattern just in front so to hold off any challenge from the man with possession. United had reached the penalty area and Harris let fly with a superb shot which Villa keeper Jackson did well to push away. But the keeper could do little to stop Cowan who raced in to smash the loose ball into the back of the net. United had the all-important first goal. Villa were physically spent; they had thrown their best at Newcastle all afternoon without reward and now they had just twenty minutes to find an equaliser. With five minutes remaining Dorrell swung in a terrific cross which Capewell and Kirton, for some unknown reason, both challenged for. It was an easy chance for a lone forward to head in, but whoever got their head to the ball first on this occasion put it high over the bar. Within seconds United had restarted play with the goal kick and raced upfield where the ball was suddenly whipped across into the box and Seymour struck a fantastic volley which proved an unstoppable shot. United had clinically done in twenty minutes what Villa threatened to do in 70: hit the back of the net twice to wrap up the game.

Aston Villa
Jackson, Milne, Smart, Mort, Moss, Blackburn, Dorrell, Walker, Capewell, Kirton, York.
Newcastle United
Bradley, Hampson, Hudspeth, Mooney, Spencer, Gibson, J. Low, Cowan, Harris, McDonald, Seymour

April 27

Match of the Day from 1994

FORTY FOR COLE

Andy Cole seals club record in 5-1 win over Villa

Aston Villa travelled to St. James' Park tonight for this Premiership clash which saw Andy Cole establish a club record with his fortieth goal of the season. The match began with Villa on top form, and it was just eleven minutes into the game when the Midlanders took the lead. Beinlich was the man to score, whilst Newcastle's centre-half Darren Peacock seemed to take a step back and let him through, worrying the home supporters at this early stage.

However, the Tynesiders didn't have to worry for long. Bracewell equalised just four minutes later with a superb 25-yard strike, and the game was level again.

Newcastle immediately began to take control of the game, and the visiting side lost their confidence bit by bit and cracks began to show in their defence.

Peter Beardsley was brought down inside the penalty area by Staunton after 23 minutes, and he stepped up to the spot to take the kick which sailed into the net past Spink in the Villa goal to put the home side a goal ahead.

Then with half time approaching, Newcastle furthered their lead with the goal that everyone was waiting for. After 41 minutes Sellars sent the ball through to Cole, who tempted the Villa goalkeeper off his line. Cole then passed Spink with ease and slotted the ball into the far corner of the net for his record-breaking fortieth goal of the season. The crowd went wild and now with Newcastle two goals ahead it looked like it was to be all downhill for Villa.

Andy Cole

In the second half Villa's troubles were increased when Teale was carried off injured and to be replaced by Daley. The position of right-back did not suit the sub, and therefore the Villa defence was easier to penetrate. Beardsley seized the opportunity presented to him, and his second goal was hammered into the net after 66 minutes with a powerful 25-yard shot which put Newcastle three goals ahead.

It was all over after 79 minutes when Sellars slotted home the fifth goal for Newcastle, and with the score 5-1, the visiting Midland side were well defeated.

Newcastle United

Srnicek, Venison, Peacock, Neilson, Beresford, Fox, Lee, Bracewell (Watson 70), Sellars, Cole (Mathie 88), Beardsley.

Aston Villa

Spink, Barrett, Teale (Daley 51), Ehiogu, Staunton, Houghton, Richardson, Townsend, Farrell (Breitkreutz 70), Fenton, Beinlich.

Played on this day

1901, Division 1.
Bury (h) 0-0   Att. 9,000
1910, Division 1.
Aston Villa (a) 0-4   Att. 25,000
1912, Division 1.
Blackburn Rovers (a) 1-1   Att. 10,000
Peart
1929, Division 1.
Derby County (a) 2-1   Att. 13,355
Chalmers (2)
1932, Division 1.
Blackpool (h) 2-2   Att. 32,000
Boyd, McMenemy
1935, Division 2.
Oldham Athletic (a) 2-3   Att. 3,638
Wilson, Weaver (pen)
1940, Wartime.
Bradford Park Ave. (h) 3-0   Att. 9,470
Clifton (3)
1946, Wartime.
Sunderland (h) 4-1   Att. 29,564
Milburn, Brown, Pearson, Stubbins
1955, Division 1.
Cardiff City (h) 3-0   Att. 19,252
Hannah (2), McMicheal
1963, Division 2.
Rotherham United (a) 1-3   Att. 9,384
McGrath
1968, Division 1.
Tottenham Hotspur (h) 1-3   Att. 30,281
T. Robson
1974, Division 1.
Burnley (a) 1-1   Att. 21,340
Macdonald
1985, Division 1.
Southampton (h) 2-1   Att. 20,845
Reilly, McDonald
1991, Division 2.
Charlton Athletic (a) 0-1   Att. 7,234
1994, Premier League.
Newcastle 5   Aston Villa 1
Bracewell 15   Beinlich 10
Beardsley
23 (pen), 66
Cole 41
Sellars 79   Att. 32,217
2002, Premier League.
Newcastle 3   West Ham United 1
Shearer 41   Defoe 20
LuaLua 53
Robert 66   Att. 52,127

Playing record for this day is... 16 games, Won 7, Drawn 4, Lost 5, GF 30, GA 23. Today's success rate... 56.25%.

Birthdays

Liam Tuohy born today in 1933.
Winger 1960-1963, Apps 42. Goals 9.

yed on this day

Test Match.
Blackburn Rovers (a) 3-4 Att. 30,000
Wardrope, Smith, Aitken
Division 1.
Sunderland (a) 2-1 Att. 22,000
Fraser, A. Gardner (pen)
Division 1.
Bolton Wanderers (a) 1-1 Att. 12,000
Appleyard
FA Charity Shield.
Northampton Town(n*) 2-0 Att. 7,000
Allan, Rutherford
Played at Stamford Bridge, Chelsea.
Newcastle win their first (and to date)
their only Charity Shield victory having
competed in five of its fixtures.
FA Cup Final.
Barnsley (n) 2-0 Att. 69,364
Shepherd (2)
Played at Goodison Park, Liverpool.
Having made the Final four times in the
last six years Newcastle finally win the FA
Cup for the first time.
Division 1.
Aston Villa (h) 3-0 Att. 10,000
Goodwill, Hibbert, Cooper
Division 1.
Manchester City (a) 0-0 Att. 25,000
Division 1.
Portsmouth (a) 1-0 Att. 30,000
Seymour
Division 1.
Stoke City (a) 1-2 Att. 10,000
Murray
Newcastle who had to win to stay in
Division One go down by 2-1 at the
Victoria Ground and are relegated for the
first time in the club's history.
Wartime.
Bolton Wanderers (h) 4-2 Att. 43,453
Stubbins (3), Milburn
FA Cup Final.
Blackpool (n) 2-0 Att. 100,000
Milburn (2)
Played at Wembley Stadium, London.
Division 1.
Burnley (h) 1-3 Att. 21,610
Bottom
Division 2.
Leeds United (h) 0-3 Att. 21,708
Division 1.
West Bromwich A. (h) 3-0 Att. 18,444
Young, Smith, Tudor
Division 1.
Tottenham Hotspur (a) 2-3 Att. 21,721
Tudor, McDermott
Division 2.
Stoke City (a) 0-0 Att. 23,217
Division 2.
Cambridge United (a) 0-1 Att. 7,720
Division 2.
West Ham United (h) 2-1 Att. 31,461
Kristensen, Quinn
Premier League.
Newcastle 1 **Leicester City 0**
Cort 90 Att. 50,501

record for this day is... 19 games,
1, Drawn 3, Lost 6, GF 30, GA 21.
success rate... 60.53%.

Match of the Day from 1910

FA CUP WINNERS AT LAST
Newcastle finally take home Cup after four attempts

A crowd of almost 70,000 turned out to see this FA Cup final replay between Newcastle United and Barnsley. The match was played at Goodison Park after the first game at the Crystal Palace had ended a 1-1 draw. Newcastle were lucky to have kept the scores level and gained the chance to take the cup with this replay.

The pitch was heavy after morning rain and Newcastle were without Whitson who was injured. In his place was Carr, but that was the only change for either team from the first encounter.

Half an hour before kick off, mounted police had to move some of the overexcited crowd off the pitch after they broke through the railings. During the match some 200-300 managed to get through again, but it didn't affect the game.

So, with a slippery ball and a slippery pitch the game started fast and furious. Newcastle had made it to the FA Cup final four times in the last six years and never yet managed to take the cup. This time they were hoping they would be successful.

Newcastle started the better team, and Barnsley seemed to be struggling right from the outset. They had the fighting spirit, but found it hard to convert that into action. Newcastle were skilful in every aspect of the game, and Barnsley were completely outplayed.

Wilson and Higgins were giving their all for Newcastle and throughout the entire first half most of the attacks came from them. It was just bad luck that none of their attempts managed to break through the Barnsley defence and beat the keeper. By the half-time break Newcastle could easily have been two or three goals up, but as it was they were unfortunate to still be goalless.

In the second half Rutherford and Howie both stood out for their great performances, as did Veitch, Low and McWilliam. However, it was Albert Shepherd who eventually had the opportunity to get the ball into the net and take the lead for Newcastle. It was a fine effort, well placed and expertly shot, and it gave Newcastle the long overdue goal they deserved.

The second goal of the game also fell to Newcastle in the form of a penalty. Shepherd stepped up to the spot to take the kick and fired the ball straight past a bewildered Mearns in the Barnsley goal. The keeper had no chance to save, and United were two goals up.

In contrast, Lawrence had not had much to do in goal for Newcastle. He made one good save, running way out of his goal to jump on the ball and stop the kick from Bartrop speeding over the line. He did well, as the ball looked destined for the back of the net.

By now though time had run out for Barnsley. They clearly did not have the energy or skill to make a comeback, and the game was all over. Newcastle had finally won the FA Cup.

Newcastle United
Lawrence, McCracken, Carr, Veitch, Low, McWilliam, Rutherford, Howie, Shepherd, Higgins, Wilson.
Barnsley
Mearns, Downs, Ness, Glendinning, Boyle, Utley, Bartrop, Gadsby, Lillycrop, Tufnell, Forman.

1951: Jackie Milburn scores the opening goal in the FA Cup Final against Blackpool at Wembley.

April 29

Match of the Day from 1905

FIRST DIVISION CHAMPIONS!
Magpies take title with convincing win over Boro

Newcastle United desperately needed this win away against Middlesbrough to secure their title as First Division champions. 12,000 had turned up to watch the match unfold.

The first half began with great efforts from both sides. However, it was clear from early on that Newcastle held the advantage over the home team. This was confirmed after just five minutes when Orr put his side into the lead with a fine goal.

This spurred on Newcastle to more effort and they made further attempts at goal at every opportunity. Some of their shots were dangerous enough to get the Middlesbrough keeper working hard, others just failed to get through the defence. It was all Newcastle's play, though, and Middlesbrough didn't create any chances for themselves. They're really were no threat to the Newcastle defence, or indeed the goal.

The first half ended with no further goals, and after the interval the game stayed on the same tracks. Newcastle kept up the pressure on Middlesbrough, hoping that if enough attempts were made, some were bound to be successful. They were right, and just seven minutes into the second half Newcastle doubled their lead. It was Rutherford who managed to get through the defensive wall and send the ball past the Middlesbrough keeper.

Then just a minute later Appleyard made a superb run with the ball, and soared through to score the third and final goal for Newcastle.

The final score was 3-0, and this well deserved result was enough to secure Newcastle United's status as Division One champions, beating Everton by just one point.

Middlesbrough
Williamson, McCallum, Agnew, Aitken, Jones, Davidson, Hewitt, Atherton, Common, Green, Thackeray.
Newcastle United
Lawrence, McCombie, Carr, Gardner, Aitken, McWilliam, Rutherford, Howie, Appleyard, Veitch, Gosnell.

League Champions 1904-05: (back row, l-r) Andy McCombie, Director G.T. Milne, Director J.W. Bell, director G.G. Archibald, Jimmy Lawrence; (middle row, l-r) Director R. Oliver, Director J.P. Oliver, Jack Carr, Billy McCracken, Chairman J. Cameron, Vice-Chairman Joseph Bell, Peter McWilliam, Joe McClarence, Director J. Graham, Assistant Secretary Frank Watt Jnr.; (front row, l-r) Secretary Frank Watt, Andy Aitken, Jock Rutherford, Jimmy Howie, Bill Appleyard, Ronald Orr, Albert Gosnell, Trainer James McPherson, (ground l-r) Colin Veitch, Alec Gardner.

Played on this day

1905, Division 1.
Middlesbrough (a) 3-0   Att. 12,000
Orr, Appleyard, Rutherford
The win enables Newcastle to pip Everton by one point to take the First Division Championship.

1911, Division 1.
Manchester City (h) 3-3   Att. 5,000
Metcalf, Willis, McCracken (pen)

1922, Division 1.
Manchester City (h) 5-1   Att. 34,000
Hagan (2), McDonald (3)

1933, Division 1.
Derby County (a) 2-3   Att. 6,528
Allen, J.R. Richardson

1939, Division 2.
Luton Town (h) 2-0   Att. 10,341
Pearson (pen), Clifton

1944, Wartime.
Darlington (a) 3-2   Att. 7,660
Stubbins (2), Porter

1950, Division 1.
Chelsea (a) 3-1   Att. 24,667
Milburn, Walker (2)

1959, Division 1.
Birmingham City (h) 1-1   Att. 19,776
Allchurch

1961, Division 1.
Blackburn Rovers (a) 4-2   Att. 12,700
Allchurch, McGuigan (2), Neale
Despite winning this their last game of the season the Magpies finish 21st in the Division One table and are relegated.

1967, Division 1.
Southampton (h) 3-1   Att. 42,426
Davies, Noble, B. Robson

1978, Division 1.
Leicester City (a) 0-3   Att. 11,530
This defeat brings to a close a disappointing season in which the Magpies finished 21st in the table, and were relegated.

1989, Division 1.
Wimbledon (a) 0-4   Att. 5,206

1995, Premier League.
Manchester City 0   Newcastle 0
                Att. 27,389

1996, Premier League.
Leeds United 0   Newcastle 1
Gillespie 17
                Att. 38,562

1998, Premier League.
Leicester City 0   Newcastle 0
                Att. 21,699

2000, Premier League.
Newcastle 2   Coventry City 0
Shearer 78 (pen)
Gavilan 84   Att. 36,408

Playing record for this day is... 16 games, Won 9, Drawn 4, Lost 3, GF 32, GA 21. Today's success rate... 68.75%.

Birthdays

Ralph Callachan born today in 1955
Midfield 1977-1978, Apps 11. Goals 0.

Sadly Missed

John Auld died on this day 1932, aged 70
Centre-half & Director 1896-1906, Apps 15. Goals 3.

Played on this day

1898, Test Match.
Blackburn Rovers (h) 4-0   Att. 13,324
Campbell, Harvey, Ghee, Jackson
1906, Division 1.
Blackburn Rovers (h) 3-0   Att. 24,000
Gosnell, Higgins, Raine
1909, Division 1.
Liverpool (h) 0-1   Att. 30,000
1910, Division 1.
Sheffield United (h) 0-0   Att. 40,000
1921, Division 1.
Arsenal (h) 1-0   Att. 40,000
Smailes
1927, Division 1.
Sheffield Wednesday (h) 2-1 Att. 30,000
Gallacher (2)
*Newcastle win the League Championship
for the fourth and last time in the club's
history.*
1932, Division 1.
Sheffield United (a) 3-0   Att. 12,000
Boyd, McMenemy, J.R. Richardson
1938, Division 2.
Swansea Town (a) 0-2   Att. 11,000
1949, Division 1.
Manchester United (h) 0-1   Att. 38,266
1955, Division 1.
Tottenham Hotspur (a) 1-2   Att. 37,262
R. Mitchell
1960, Division 1.
Manchester City (h) 0-1   Att. 27,812
1966, Division 1.
Leeds United (a) 0-3   Att. 29,531
1969, Division 1.
Stoke City (h) 5-0   Att. 28,015
Arentoft, Davies, B. Robson, Scott (2)
1977, Division 1.
Arsenal (h) 0-2   Att. 44,677
1983, Division 2.
Cambridge United (a) 0-1   Att. 7,591
1988, Division 1.
Oxford United (h) 3-1   Att. 16,617
Lormor, O'Neill, Goddard
1994, Premier League.
Sheffield United 2   Newcastle 0
Blake 63, 90   Att. 29,013

Playing record for this day is... 17 games,
Won 8, Drawn 1, Lost 8, GF 24, GA 15.
Today's success rate... 50%.

Match of the Day from 1927

GALLACHER SEES DOUBLE

League champions celebrate with Gallacher's brace

Newcastle celebrated at the end of this Division One game against Sheffield Wednesday as League champions yet again. Some 30,000 were there to see the game unfold, and for a time there was little separating the two sides.

Newcastle were on the attack from the outset, and Wednesday's Blenkinsop and Felton had plenty of work to do in defence. When the ball did get through for United it was down to the Owls' keeper Brown to stop the danger, and this he managed to do quite confidently.

The Newcastle forwards didn't ease off, but Wednesday were making their presence felt too. There were opportunities for the visiting side to attack, and they relished these. However, for both teams it was a frustrating time with no goals being scored in the opening skirmishes.

Then on 29 minutes things changed. Newcastle went into the lead with a super goal from Gallacher. However, Wednesday had other ideas and just a minute later and the scores were level. It was Strange who managed to beat the Newcastle keeper and his goal silenced the home crowd.

The rest of the first half passed without incident. From the start of the second half United stepped up their efforts and were soon totally outplaying the visitors.

It was Gallacher again who penetrated the Sheffield Wednesday defence and beat Brown in goal to put Newcastle into the lead for the second time for what would turn out to be the winner.

The League title was United's for the fourth and final time, and the Lord Mayor of Newcastle congratulated all the players on their fine performance in front of a joyous crowd.

Newcastle United

Wilson, Maitland, Hudspeth, MacKenzie, Spencer, Curry, Urwin, Clark, Gallacher, McDonald, Seymour.

Sheffield Wednesday

Brown, Felton, Blenkinsop, Leach, Kean, Marsden, Hooper, Strange, Trotter, Allen, Wilkinson.

Birthdays

Glyn Hodges born today in 1963.
Midfield 1987, Apps 7. Goals 0.

May 1

Match of the Day from 1926

HAT TRICK FOR GALLACHER

Newcastle beat Manchester City 3-2 in testing home game

This Division One match against Manchester City was played out in front of a crowd of 20,000. Throughout the first half both teams were playing to the best of their abilities. Every player on the field was as eager as the next and it was inevitable that the first goal would arrive early on. The question was which team would score first?

It was Newcastle who took the lead in the first minute with a super shot, well placed by Hughie Gallacher. Gallacher would feature heavily in this game, and his presence was of utmost importance to the scoreline. This first goal served to make Manchester City a little shaky, but with only six minutes on the clock they too had added a goal to the score-sheet. A fine kick from Roberts beat the Newcastle keeper and the relief in the City team could be seen on their faces.

Then followed a barren spell, and perhaps it was a case of some of the players trying a little too hard to score. There were certainly several wasted chances and the next goal could have come a lot earlier, and for either team. As it was it arrived in the second half and fell to Newcastle, Gallacher again taking the credit for a superb effort and smashing shot. This goal put him on a hat-trick and Gallacher was not one to disappoint the fans. Manchester City were again shaken and this had a severe effect on their game. Newcastle were now totally outplaying the visiting team and it was no surprise to anyone when Gallacher completed his hat-trick.

City were now struggling to maintain any sort of proper attack, and their defence was only just about strong enough to stop the Newcastle forwards from increasing their lead. Maybe Newcastle would have tried a little harder to break through if they weren't already two goals ahead, and so they were lucky that City's second goal was so late in the game. It arrived in the final minute, and it was Browell who scored. If it had come earlier for the visitors then things may have been a little different, but even though it boosted spirits and revived the visitors side, it was too late to make any significant change to the final result.

Newcastle United
Wilson, Hudspeth, Maitland, J. Harris, Curry, Gibson, Urwin, Clark, Gallacher, McDonald, Seymour.

Manchester City
Goodchild, Cookson, McCloy, Pringle, Cowan, McMullen, Austin, Browell, Roberts, Johnson, Hicks.

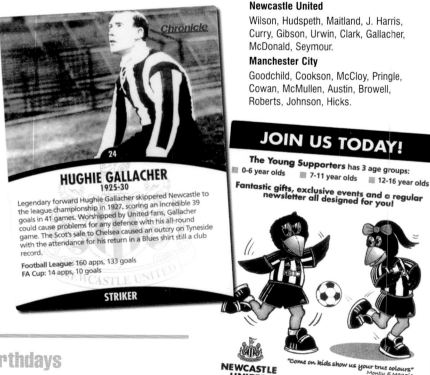

HUGHIE GALLACHER
1925-30
Legendary forward Hughie Gallacher skippered Newcastle to the league championship in 1927, scoring an incredible 39 goals in 41 games. Worshipped by United fans, Gallacher could cause problems for any defence with his all-round game. The Scot's sale to Chelsea caused an outcry on Tyneside with the attendance for his return in a Blues shirt still a club record.
Football League: 160 apps, 133 goals
FA Cup: 14 apps, 10 goals
STRIKER

Birthdays

Jimmy Crawford born today in 1973.
Midfield 1995-1998, Apps 3 (3 subs). Goals 0.

May 2

TORINO WELL BEATEN
Newcastle's convincing win gains a semi final place

Newcastle United needed this group stage win tonight in order to reach the semi finals of the Anglo-Italian Cup competition. The match took place at St. James' Park in front of a small crowd of just 9,580.

The opening stages of the game were all in Newcastle's favour, and there were plenty of chances for the forwards to break through the Torino defence. Sadly, Newcastle seemed to lack the courage to go for goal, and their early attempts all failed to get anywhere.

With the amount of opportunities they had, Newcastle really should have scored several times before the first goal eventually came. John Tudor managed to get his head to the ball with enough power to send it sailing into the net to put the home side into the lead on 21 minutes. Next to get the ball across the line was Macdonald with a lovely shot, doubling Newcastle's lead with ease.

Torino managed to scrape through the otherwise steadfast Newcastle defence and pull a goal back, but their efforts lacked the pace and skill needed to be a real threat. This was their first show of any worth, and it proved to be their last.

Smith was next in line to add his name to the score-sheet with a fine goal, and Torino decided at this point that if they couldn't increase their own score, they may as well increase Newcastle's. It was Masiello who was the 'lucky' player to be credited with the goal, and United welcomed it graciously.

Hibbitt was not one to be left out, and made sure that if there were goals going begging, one of them had his name on it. He finished off the scoring with a smashing goal to bring the score to 5-1.

Unfortunately this was not the only action to report during this game, and the last twenty minutes of play saw more than its share of bad sportsmanship. Newcastle's Jim Smith and Torino's Masiello were both sent off, and Torino's Novellino and Fosatti were booked.

With just four minutes left to play Newcastle full-back David Craig and Torino centre-half Cereser were also sent off for fighting, a sorry end to such a good game.

The win put Newcastle into the semi finals against Crystal Palace where a score of 5-1 saw them into the final. They then met AC Fiorentina and went on to take the trophy with a 2-1 victory.

Newcastle United
McFaul, Craig, Clark, McDermott, Howard, Moncur, Barrowclough, Smith, Macdonald, Tudor, Hibbitt.
Torino
Castellini, Lombardo, Fossati, Mozzini, Cereser, Masiello, Ranpanti, Madde, Bui, Crivelli, Toschi.

Played on this day

1921, Division 2.		
Manchester City (a) 1-3		Att. 25,000
Smailes		
1931, Division 1.		
Chelsea(a) 1-1		Att. 30,000
MacKenzie		
1936, Division 2.		
Plymouth Argyle (a) 0-1		Att. 12,000
1951, Division 1.		
Wolverhampton W. (a) 1-0		Att. 27,015
G. Robledo		
1973, Anglo Italian Cup, Group Stage.		
Torino (h) 5-1		Att. 9,580
Tudor, Macdonald, Smith, Hibbitt, Opponent (og)		
1979, Division 2.		
Bristol Rovers (h) 3-0		Att. 9,627
Withe, Shoulder, Bird		
1981, Division 2.		
Orient (h) 3-1		Att. 11,639
Walker, Harford, Trewick		
1987, Division 1.		
West Ham United (a) 1-1		Att. 17,844
McDonald (pen)		
1988, Division 1.		
Portsmouth (a) 2-1		Att. 12,468
Scott, Lormor		
1992, Division 2.		
Leicester City (a) 2-1		Att. 21,861
Peacock, Walsh (og)		
1996, Premier League.		
Nottingham For. 1	Newcastle 1	
Woan 75	Beardsley 32	
		Att. 28,280
1998, Premier League.		
Newcastle 3	Chelsea 1	
Dabizas 39	Di Matteo 77	
Lee 42		
Speed 59		
		Att. 36,710
2000, Premier League.		
Middlesbrough 2	Newcastle 2	
Juninho 5	Speed 10	
Festa 78	Pistone 18	
		Att. 34,744

Playing record for this day is... 13 games, Won 7, Drawn 4, Lost 2, GF 25, GA 14. Today's success rate... 69.23%.

Birthdays

Gary Megson born today in 1959.
Midfield 1984-1986, Apps 28 (4 subs). Goals 2.

Mick Quinn born today in 1962.
Centre-forward 1989-1992, Apps 140 (8 subs). Goals 71.

Alan Suddick born today in 1944.
Forward 1961-1966, Apps 152. Goals 43.

Didier Domi born today in 1978.
Defender 1998-2001, Apps 70 (15 subs). Goals 4.

Sadly Missed

Justin Fashanu died on this day in 1998, aged 37.
Centre-forward 1991, Apps 1 (1 sub). Goals 0.

Division 1.
West Ham United (h) 1-0   Att. 50,000
Devine
Wartime.
Leeds United (h) 3-2   Att. 3,187
Stubbins (2), Myers
Division 2.
Manchester City (a) 2-0   Att. 46,492
Walker, Wayman
FA Cup Final.
Arsenal (n) 1-0   Att. 100,000
G. Robledo
Played at Wembley Stadium, London.
Division 1.
West Bromwich A. (h) 4-2   Att. 18,927
Macdonald (2, 1 pen), Green,
Opponent (og)
Division 1.
Leicester City (a) 0-1   Att. 14,289
Division 2.
Luton Town (h) 2-2   Att. 13,765
Shoulder, Rafferty
Division 1.
Leicester City (a) 0-2   Att. 13,171
Division 1.
West Ham United (h) 1-2   Att. 14,445
Cormor

Premier League.

Newcastle 3	Tottenham Hotspur 3
Gillespie 7	Barmby 22
Peacock 10	Klinsman 24
Beardsley 70	Anderton 26
	Att. 35,603

Premier League.

Arsenal 0	Newcastle 1
	Elliott 44
	Att. 38,179

Premier League.

Newcastle 1	Birmingham City 0
Viana 42	
	Att. 52,146

In his last game before retirement referee David Elleray sent off Birmingham's Matthew Upson for a professional foul on the Magpies' Craig Bellamy. From the resulting free kick from 22 yards Hugo Viana curled in a magnificent winner which enabled Newcastle to qualify for the Champions' League.

record for this day is... 12 games, Drawn 2, Lost 3, GF 19, GA 14. success rate... 66.67%.

Minister Winston Churchill presents the to Newcastle United's captain Joe watched by FA Chairman Stanley Rous.

May 3

UNITED CREATE FA CUP HISTORY

Records tumble in Cup Final victory over Arsenal

Newcastle United made history by beating Arsenal 1-0 in the FA Cup final at Wembley today. They thus became the first team to win four Wembley finals, and equalled Blackburn Rovers' 61 year old record of winning the cup in successive seasons. But even the most ardent Geordie would have to concede they were a little fortunate on the day. Their gallant opponents, Arsenal, for long periods looked the better side even with the handicap of playing almost an hour with ten men. The Gunners produced the higher standard of teamwork over the 90 minutes and at times looked like they had the benefit of the extra player. But, it counted for nothing as the only goal of the game arrived in the 83rd minute from a George Robledo header and the cup was heading north again.

This was not the prettiest of games for the football purist, more a good old cup battle. At times there were two or more players left lying injured whilst the game progressed, indeed during one Newcastle attack four men in red lay hurt in thier own penalty area. First impressions of the game were Arsenal's sharpness in particular Lishman whose all-round play excelled throughout the game. It was he who almost unlocked the United defence with a spectacular overhead kick which flew just inches wide of the post with Simpson well beaten. The other noticeable early feature of the game was that the cup holders looked unsettled everywhere on the field. United were just starting to find some coordination when events took what seemed to be a decisive turn in their favour. Barnes, the Arsenal full-back, was accidentally hurt after a challenge by Milburn near the corner flag. Shortly afterwards the Welsh international collapsed with an injured right knee, and after leaving for treatment for a short while, he eventually hobbled off in the 33rd minute. The loss however, seemed to inspire the Gunners rather than hamper them, all this despite an injury to Ray Daniel who badly sprained his arm in the opening minutes. Newcastle though finished the half on top and in those final twelve minutes came close with an effort from Mitchell, who shaved the bar, and then a magnificently timed punch by Swindin took the ball from the head of Milburn as he closed in on goal. The general expectation now, was that Newcastle would be well on top after the interval once the Wembley pitch had sapped the failing strength of the ten men.

But it was Arsenal who, if anything, got stronger with the United forward line suddenly losing its shape, and the Gunners in turn were in the ascendancy. At this stage Arsenal were looking far more likely to break the deadlock. Then came the moment the 'lucky Arsenal' tag could be shed forever when Doug Lishman, whose play deserved a winning goal, rose in the penalty area to head Mercer's cross against the bar with Simpson well beaten. It seemed that fate was on Newcastle's side, and nothing was going to stop them. Their hopes of winning lay in the form of Bobby Mitchell who was both irritating yet amazing throughout, he had more of the ball than anyone, yet so often he wasted the privilege. But as is so often the case with heroes, Mitchell suddenly turned on one moment of real class to clinch the match. With seven minutes to go Mitchell sent a lovely centre to George Robledo, who got his head to the ball and sent it into the net with a little deflection off the post. The goal secured the win for Newcastle, and their place in FA Cup history.

Arsenal
Swindin, Barnes, Smith, Forbes, Daniel, Mercer, Cox, Logie, Holton, Lishman, Roper.
Newcastle United
Simpson, Cowell, McMichael, Harvey, Brennan, E. Robledo, Walker, Foulkes, Milburn, G. Robledo, Mitchell.

Sadly Missed

George Lowrie died on this day 1989, aged 69.
Centre-forward 1948-1949, Apps 12. Goals 5.

May 3

Top: George Robledo heads the winning goal with just six minutes left.

Right: Jackie Milburn is denied by Arsenal keeper George Swindin who gets his hand to a cross.

Played on this day

1929, Division 1.
Everton (h) 2-0   Att. 20,000
Gallacher (2)

1932, Division 1.
Everton (h) 0-0   Att. 40,000

1935, Division 2.
Burnley (h) 2-0   Att. 7,000
McMenemy, Pearson

1940, Wartime.
Middlesbrough (a) 2-2   Att. 10,229
Stubbins, Clifton

1946, Wartime.
Sheffield Wednesday (a) 3-2 Att. 20,000
Brown, Wayman, Stubbins

1963, Division 2.
Norwich City (a) 2-1   Att. 16,665
McGarry, McKinney

1968, Division 1.
Manchester United (a) 0-6 Att. 59,697

1974, FA Cup Final.
Liverpool(n) 0-3   Att. 100,000
Played at Wembley Stadium, London.

1983, Division 2.
Barnsley (a) 5-0   Att. 10,958
Varadi (2), McDonald (2), Keegan

1985, Division 1.
Stoke City (a) 1-0   Att. 7,088
Opponent (og)

1987, Division 1.
Charlton Athletic (h) 0-3 Att. 26,950

1991, Division 2.
West Bromwich A. (a) 1-1 Att. 16,706
Quinn

1993, Division 1.
Grimsby Town (a) 2-0   Att. 14,202
Cole, Kelly

Playing record for this day is... 13 games,
Won 7, Drawn 3, Lost 3, GF 20, GA 18.
Today's success rate... 65.38%.

FIVE FOR THE MAGPIES

Newcastle take the points in convincing win over Barnsley

Newcastle were hoping for their first league win away at Barnsley in eight visits with this match, and if they were going to win, they would do it in style. The visiting side were determined they would take the victory right from the kick off, and the game started in front of just 10,958.

From the outset it was clear that Newcastle were by far the better team. They totally outplayed Barnsley in every way. Their movements were skilful and clever, and their passes were timed to perfection.

There were many attempts at goal from Newcastle, but the home defence was able to stand its ground for a while.

It took 26 minutes for United to take the lead, and it was McDonald who finally managed to beat the Barnsley goalkeeper. The ball came from Chris Waddle on the right, and it was perfectly placed for McDonald to get his head to it and nod it into the net.

With the visitors going into the lead, Barnsley's spirit seemed to drop. More attempts from Newcastle kept up the pressure on the home defence throughout the rest of the first half, and well into the second.

It was 57 minutes into the game when Newcastle managed to increase their lead to two goals. Keegan performed a spectacular solo move and shot from fully 25 yards out to send the ball past the bewildered Barnsley keeper.

Waddle played an important role in the next goal too, sending in a lovely cross from the left for Varadi to get his head to. This he did with ease, and the ball sailed over the goal-line for number three.

Within twelve minutes of that goal Varadi scored his second, and Newcastle's fourth. He was in the right place at the right time to take advantage of a mistake by the Barnsley defence. Their goalkeeper had no chance to save as Varadi sent his powerful shot straight into the back of the net.

Then, with just a minute left on the clock, McDonald sealed the win with his second goal of the match. This brought Newcastle's tally to five, and secured a fine win for the Magpies.

The victory placed Newcastle fifth in the table with 63 points, just three points behind Leicester and Fulham, in third and fourth places respectively. With two matches left, and Newcastle's goal difference better than Fulham's, the Magpies were looking good.

Barnsley
Pierce, Joyce, Chambers, Glavin, McGuire, McCarthy, Law, Airey, Ronson, Cunningham, Barrowclough (Wilkes).

Newcastle United
Thomas, Anderson, Wharton, McCreery, Clarke, Carney, Keegan, McDonald, Varadi, McDermott, Waddle.

Referee Mr. H. Taylor (Oadby, Leics.)

Chris Waddle

Sadly Missed

Stanley Allan died on this day 1919, aged 32
Inside Forward 1908-1911, Apps 16. Goals 6.

May 5

DERBY DOWN AND OUT
Promotion bound United just too hot for County

In a sweltering cauldron with temperatures in the nineties at St. James' Park, Derby entered their worst nightmare today. With relegation staring them full in the face, they had to take on promotion-bound Newcastle United and their partisan fans relishing their inevitable rise to top-flight football for the first time in seven years.

Yet despite all this, Derby boss Roy McFarland put on the bravest of faces to heap praise on his opponents in what must have been the most difficult of circumstances. After the game he said, "It looks as if we are going down now, avoiding the drop is not in our hands anymore. But let's not take anything away from Newcastle, they have earned their success and worked hard for it, and my goodness what a superb bunch of supporters they have. "The mutual admiration of the effort both sides made to a wonderful game, played in boiling hot conditions, was summed up by United manager Arthur Cox, he said, "Even near the end when we were four goals up I couldn't help but notice their man Archie Gemmill running about and playing like a teenager. It's that sort of commitment which epitomised the Derby spirit despite their problems, their players are all a credit to their club. "Yes this was a classic game of football played in remarkable and impeccable spirit which was thoroughly enjoyed by the 35,866 fans; its hard to believe this was a Second Division game after all. It was won emphatically in the end by Newcastle who had the manpower to turn honest play into individual brilliance and one man in particular excelled in both.

Kevin Keegan, the man who has done so much to transform Newcastle in the last two years, was fittingly the player to net what proved to be the winner in the seventeenth minute of the game. His endeavour and performance was highlighted admirably in the process of his close-range headed goal. Knocked out in the collision, he eventually recovered to continue play some minutes later, and went on to produce a brilliant man-of-the-match performance.

Although Peter Beardsley added a second goal after 22 minutes the overrun Derby defence somehow knuckled down with great determination to go a further 28 minutes without conceding another. But the inevitable third Newcastle goal came just five minutes after half time and was scored by the impressive winger, Chris Waddle. Beardsley then netted his second of the match, and United's fourth, eleven minutes from time amidst amazing scenes of jubilation around the sun-drenched terraces. At the final whistle the party began as Newcastle were all but promoted and there followed a lap of honour by the United players led by Keegan. To a thunderous noise the players slipped away to the dressing room for the handshakes, the back slaps and the champagne. For Derby, at least their awful nightmare was now over.

Newcastle United
Carr, Ryan, Wharton, McCreery, Carney, Roeder, Keegan, Beardsley, Waddle, McDermott, Trewick.
Derby County
Cherry, Burns, Buckley, Gemmill, Watson, Powell, Devine, Davison, Garner (Wilson), Harbey, Robertson.

Birthdays

Andy Parkinson born today in 1959.
Forward 1978-1979, Apps 3 (3 subs). Goals 0.

Sadly Missed

George Hannah died on this day 1990, aged 61.
Midfield 1949-1957, Apps 177. Goals 43.

May 6

Played on this day

922, Division 1.
Manchester City (a) 0-1   Att. 15,000
933, Division 1.
Blackpool (h) 1-2   Att. 11,000
McMenemy
944, Wartime.
Darlington (h) 1-1   Att. 14,400
Milburn
After 90 minutes Darlington led 1-0 in this Tyne-Tees Cup Final, this meant the scores were level 3-3 on aggregate. The game went into extra time and Jackie Milburn got the winner (on aggregate), and the equaliser (on the day) after 57 minutes of extra time, the 147th minute of the game. Newcastle thus won the Cup 4-3 on aggregate.
950, Division 1.
Blackpool (h) 3-0   Att. 35,274
Milburn (2), Taylor
967, Division 1.
Leicester City (a) 2-4   Att. 13,951
Davies, Noble
985, Division 1.
Tottenham Hotspur (h) 2-3 Att. 29,652
Beardsley (2 pens)
989, Division 1.
Millwall (h) 1-1   Att. 14,731
Anderson
993, Division 1.
Oxford United (h) 2-1   Att. 29,438
Clark, Cole
1997, Premier League.
West Ham United 0 Newcastle 0
                            Att. 24,617
2000, Premier League.
Derby County 0   Newcastle 0
                            Att. 32,724

Playing record for this day is... 10 games, Won 2, Drawn 4, Lost 4, GF 12, GA 13. Today's success rate... 40%.

HOME VICTORY FOR THE CHAMPIONS

Clark and Cole goals entertain the 29,438 party goers

Newly crowned champions Newcastle United, who clinched the First Division title at Grimsby two days ago, returned to St. James' Park today and discovered exactly what their magnificent achievement means to their fanatical fans on Tyneside. They received a welcome perfectly fit for North-East football heroes from the Toon Army's 29,000 strong crowd. Second half goals from Lee Clark and the ever impressive Andy Cole proved too much for an enterprising Oxford side who deserved their late consolation goal from substitute Nick Cusack.

Oxford set the tone for a match enveloped in joyful carnival atmosphere by forming a guard of honour to applaud the Newcastle team onto the pitch following their championship triumph. Surprisingly however, it took Kevin Keegan's usually flamboyant attacking side until the 35th minute to show any desire to carve out a real goalscoring chance. Then Scott Sellars sent John Beresford clear but the normally assured full-back's first touch this time let him down, and allowed Oxford keeper Paul Reece to dash out and clear with his feet. This being the one highlight of a first half which resembled a post-season friendly game, not that anyone in the ground minded too much.

Seventeen minutes into the second half Keegan had seen enough of this stale encounter and made the significant changes, sending on Gavin Peacock for Paul Bracewell and Mark Robinson for the tired looking Robert Lee. This calculated double substitution sparked United into life almost immediately and they were rewarded with the opening goal in the 70th minute, just eight minutes after the change. A patient build up, started by Peacock at the back, was taken over by Robinson who fed Clark on the edge of the penalty area and his shot sailed past the diving Reece and into the bottom corner of the net. A relaxed Newcastle now turned on the style, much to the delight of the crowd who were rewarded again just nine minutes later when Cole struck a ferocious shot which flew into the roof of the net, a real beauty. As the ground swayed in celebration and fans began to congregate pitch side for the inevitable friendly invasion, Joey Beachamp sent in a high cross to the far post and Cusack headed in a well deserved goal for the visitors with 60 seconds of the game remaining.

Newcastle United
Srnicek, Venison, Beresford, Bracewell (Peacock 62), Scott, Kilcline, Lee (Robinson 62), Cole, Kelly, Clark, Sellars.

Oxford United
Reece, Smart, Ford, Lewis, Collins, Melville, Magilton, Beachamp, Wanless (Penney 74), Murphy (Cusack 74), Allen.
Referee Mr. A. Flood (Stockport).

May 7

UNITED CLAIM SIXTH FA CUP WIN

Scoular shines as ten-man Manchester City beaten 3-1

Every FA Cup final has its man and its moments. The man of this absorbing affair in which Newcastle scored their fifth victory at Wembley and their sixth FA Cup win in all, thus equalling Aston Villa and Blackburn's record, was United's skipper Jimmy Scoular. The inspiring leadership of Scoular was the significant factor. He was the attacking wing back who set the pattern for United's continual forward momentum which, in the end, proved crucial to their success today at Wembley. There were two moments which can be said to have had a decisive effect upon the result. The first was less than a minute after kick off when Milburn scored the first of Newcastle's three goals. The second was twenty minutes later when Meadows, the Manchester City right-back, limped away through the tunnel back to the dressing room with a twisted left knee and returned only as mere spectator for the dramatic second half. Even allowing for this handicap, under which Manchester City played for most of the match, and the devastating effect of a goal against them before they had warmed up, Newcastle were the better footballing side on the day.

Nevertheless City looked their most dangerous during the last 25 minutes of the first half, when they were only a ten-man side. Their goal, scored by Johnstone a few seconds before half-time, was a superb finish. It started with a wonderful pass inside their own half from Revie to Hayes who sent over a perfect cross for Johnson to head easily past United keeper Simpson. If Scoular was the man for Newcastle, Trautmann for Manchester City made four saves which were out of this world. There were two from point-blank range in the first half and the way in which he clutched a cross-ball out of the air one handed in the second half was the work of a magician rather than a footballer. At the other end Simpson had no such chance to show what he could do, more evidence of who was the better side on the day.

Mitchell, who also played a considerable part in this victory, was involved in Newcastle's killer second and third goals. Soon after half-time a brilliant cross from White this time was coolly converted by Mitchell who had timed his run into the area perfectly. Then at the end of the hour United effectively wrapped up the game. Mitchell flicking the ball out to Hannah who smashed a beautiful shot from the edge of the penalty area which Trautmann, either didn't see, or couldn't move quickly enough to keep out.

So once again the Wembley favourites were beaten. When it was all over the unfortunate Meadows was seen consoling his dejected team-mates, in particular keeper Trautmann. In spite of his dazzling and fantastic saves he had been beaten fairly and squarely three times. The last man to leave the awesome Wembley arena was, fittingly, Scoular, clutching the Cup. It was right and proper that the hero should take the last curtain. Except that there were many heroes in this final. This was one of those Wembley showdowns that people will talk about for many years to come; a truly great football match.

Manchester City

Trautmann, Meadows, Little, Barnes, Ewing, Paul, Spurdle, Hayes, Revie, Johnstone, Fagan.

Newcastle United

Simpson, Cowell, Batty, Scoular, Stokoe, Casey, White, Milburn, Keeble, Hannah, Mitchell.

Referee Mr. R. J. Leafe (Nottingham).

Sadly Missed

Tom Urwin died on this day in 1968, aged 72.
Winger 1924-1930, Apps 200. Goals 24.

Newcastle United captain Jimmy Scoular lifts the FA Cup as trainer Norman Smith joins in with the victory celebrations.

May 8

Played on this day

1963, Division 2.
Walsall (h) 0-2   Att. 21,797
1972, Division 1.
Stoke City (h) 0-0   Att. 21,264
1979, Division 2.
Wrexham (h) 2-0   Att. 7,134
Pearson, Shoulder
1982, Division 2.
Wrexham (h) 4-2   Att. 9,419
Waddle, Varadi, Trewick (pen), Brownlie
1995, Premier League.
Blackburn Rovers 1 Newcastle 0
Shearer 28
                          Att. 30,545
1997, Premier League.
Manchester U 0   Newcastle 0
                          Att. 55,236
1999, Premier League.
Leicester City 2   Newcastle 0
Izzet 20
Cottee 41   Att. 21,125

Playing record for this day is... 7 games,
Won 2, Drawn 2, Lost 3, GF 6, GA 7.
Today's success rate... 42.86%.

UNITED FINISH ON WINNING NOTE
Wrexham beaten at last by Shoulder and Pearson strikes

The Newcastle era of the late 1970s early 1980s brought little cheer for the dwindling support of the Black-and-White Army but, for today, this rearranged game at a sun drenched St. James' Park, this has to be one of the highlights. This was the last match of Newcastle's second season back in the old Second Division, it was to be another three seasons before they would return to the top flight. They had hovered about mid-table throughout the campaign, but this fixture, three days after the end of the regular season, now gave them the chance to finish a creditable eighth place. The game against Wrexham had been abandoned back in March at half-time when heavy rainfall gradually got worse. The score at the time was 1-1 and it was a particular blow for United striker Jim Pearson who, after a lean period, had netted his first goal in four months. To put into context the period of decline during this forgettable era - the game that night was watched by just 7,134, and today's return had eighteen fans less than that.

On a fabulously sunny afternoon on Tyneside, United got off to a great start, threatening to take the Wrexham defence apart. With little but pride to play for it was clear that United's desire in this respect was far greater than their lethargic opponents. However, despite dominating possession with some great approach play, poor finishing in front of goal kept the score goalless after the opening quarter. However a goal had to come and rather fittingly the small band of die-hard United fans were treated to a great strike by a local lad. Alan Shoulder, United's Bishop Auckland-born goal poacher, a bargain £20,000 buy from Blyth Spartans, finished off in typical fashion from inside the area following a neat four-man move, his eleventh goal of the season. It was this fine piece of opportunism that ensured the Magpies led by one goal at the half-time interval.

The second half was no different with a strong confident looking Newcastle defence keeping the visitors very quiet whilst their midfield continued to feed the forwards ample opportunities to increase the lead. But try as they might United could not find any way through the Wrexham rearguard until a late goal from Pearson wrapped up the game at 2-0. For Pearson, who was having a horrid season since his high-profile transfer from Everton at the start of the season, this was just reward for his determined effort all afternoon, and finally it was his first goal since the winner over Millwall back on November 11th. The goal came as tiredness was starting to affect the players due to the hot conditions, and effectively ended the game.

Newcastle United
Carr, Nattrass, Mitchell, Martin, Barton, Bird, Shoulder, Pearson, Withe, Hibbitt, Connolly.
Wrexham
Davies, Cegielski, Dwyer, J.Jones, J.Roberts, Giles, Lyons, Sutton, McNeil, Buxton, Fox.

Birthdays

Brian Kilcline born today in 1962.
Centre-half 1992-1994, Apps 45 (16 subs). Goals 0.
Malcom Scott born today in 1936.
Centre-half 1955-1961, Apps 26. Goals 2.
Carl Wilson born today in 1940.
Centre-forward 1958-1959, Apps 1. Goals 0.

Jack Charlton born today in 1935.
Manager 1984-1985
Laurent Charvet born today in 1973.
Defender 1998-2000, Apps 53 (3 sub). Goals 1.

Sadly Missed

Andy Cunningham died on this day in 1973, aged 83.
Midfield & Manager 1929-1935, Apps 15. Goals 2.

Harry Hardinge died on this day in 1965, aged 69.
Centre-forward 1905-1907, Apps 9. Goals 1.

May 9-10

NOW FOR THE PREMIERSHIP!

Champions Newcastle go out in sensational style

The sight of a beaming Jack Charlton summed up this wonderful true Geordie occasion on Tyneside today. The Northumbrian-born manager of the Republic of Ireland was a guest of honour and fan at the home of his first love, St. James' Park. Charlton watched as the champions bowed out of First Division football, hopefully for the last time, with a fantastic demolition job over Leicester City, the 7-1 victory sets them up for next season's task in the Premier League very nicely indeed. Today was party time for Kevin Keegan's Newcastle side and the Toon Army on the terraces. First up was Geordie pop group Lindisfarne who had St. James' Park rocking and, far from there being fog on the Tyne, the sun shone when club captain Brian Kilcline received the League Championship trophy and skipper Barry Venison took the Barclays trophy. Then the team topped everything they had achieved in Keegan's record-breaking season. They were six ahead by half-time, their biggest interval lead since being seven up in a 13-0 win over Newport County back in 1946. David Kelly, bought from Leicester City for £250,000 had his second hat-trick of the season tucked away after the first 45 minutes also.

The goal riot which makes Newcastle United the country's highest scorers this season began in the sixth minute. John Beresford's cross was chested down by Kelly, whose left-foot shot was only parried by goalkeeper Kevin Poole. Andy Cole turned in the rebound to become the fifth Newcastle player to reach double figures in goals scored over the season. His tenth goal came in only his eleventh appearance and he too, like Kelly, went on to complete a hat-trick. Robert Lee scored his thirteenth goal of the season with a superb strike for United in the thirteenth minute after a one-two with Lee Clark, who received his 'North-East Player of the Year' award. In the 28th minute Kelly took over the scoring with the first of his trio before the interval and Newcastle were coasting in the party atmosphere.

Cole completed Newcastle's scoring, with their seventh goal, in the 66th minute, incredibly United's only goal of the second half. However, by this point no one in the 30,129 crowd minded too much, the football being watched was well worth the admission fee. The seventh goal was the first time Newcastle had reached that total since the 7-2 hammering of Bury in October 1961. With eight minutes of the game remaining Leicester managed a consolation goal, headed in by Steve Walsh from Mike Whitlow's cross, and the Leicester fans had something to cheer. At the final whistle their sporting cheers grew louder when joined by the Toon Army to salute Keegan, Terry McDermott and the United squad on its triumphant lap of honour around the ground. Charlton called it a smashing day, Leicester boss Brian Little, also born in the North-East, called it a good day for Newcastle. No doubt about the United fans, to them it was a truly memorable day. Now for the Premiership!

Newcastle United
Srnicek, Venison, Beresford, Robinson, Scott, Howey (Peacock) Lee, Cole, Kelly, Clark, Sellars.

Leicester City
Poole, Mills, Whitlow, Smith, Walsh, Hill, Oldfield, Thompson, Joachim (Gee), Lowe, Lewis (Grayson).

Played on this day

May 9
1942, Wartime.
 Gateshead (h) 6-2 Att. 3,500
 Stubbins (5), Donaldson
1945, Wartime.
 Sunderland (h) 5-0 Att. 20,000
 Wayman (3), Milburn, Stubbins
1987, Division 1.
 Nottingham Forest (a) 1-2 Att. 17,788
 Gascoigne
1993, Division 1.
 Leicester City (h) 7-1 Att. 30,129
 Cole (3), Lee, Kelly (3)

May 10
1947, Division 2.
 Bradford Park Ave. (h) 5-0 Att. 33,131
 Bentley (3), Walker, Wayman
1998, Premier League.
 Blackburn Rovers 1 Newcastle 0
 Sutton 88 Att. 29,300

Birthdays

May 9
David Barton born today in 1959
Centre-half 1975-1983, Apps 110 (2 subs). Goals 6.
Frank Pingel born today in 1964.
Centre-forward 1989, Apps 14 (1 sub). Goals 1.
Bill Punton born today in 1934.
Winger 1954-1958, Apps 26. Goals 1.

Sadly Missed

May 9
Joe Devine died on this day in 1980, aged 74.
Midfield 1930-1931, Apps 22. Goals 11.

May 11

Played on this day

1940, Wartime.
Middlesbrough (h) 2-1   Att. 14,551
Clifton (2)
Newcastle won the tie 4-3 on aggregate.

1963, Division 2.
Preston North End (h) 2-2   Att. 13,502
Suddick, Hughes

1968, Division 1.
Manchester City (h) 3-4   Att. 46,492
McNamee, B. Robson, Sinclair

1973, Anglo Italian Cup Semi Final, 1st leg.
Crystal Palace (a) 0-0   Att. 12,001

1974, Division 1.
Tottenham Hotspur (h) 0-2   Att. 21,601

1985, Division 1.
Norwich City (a) 0-0   Att. 18,399

1991, Division 2.
Hull City (h) 1-2   Att. 17,940
Clark

1997, Premier League.
Newcastle 5   **Nottingham F. 0**
Asprilla 20
Ferdinand 23, 26
Shearer 36
Elliott 77   Att. 36,544

2002, Premier League.
Southampton 3   **Newcastle 1**
Svensson 17   Shearer 55
Beattie 24 (pen)
Telfer 90   Att. 31,973

2003, Premier League.
West Brom. 2   **Newcastle 2**
Dobie 57, 72   Jenas 43
   Viana 80   Att. 27,036

Playing record for this day is... 10 games,
Won 2, Drawn 4, Lost 4, GF 16, GA 16.
Today's success rate... 40%.

UNITED IN THE CHAMPIONS' LEAGUE

Forest hammered 5-0 in second place decider

The championship has frustratingly eluded a desperately hungry Newcastle since Kevin Keegan re-established them as a leading light in the English game, but today they were rewarded the next best thing, a coveted place in the European Cup. Allowing runners-up the opportunity for qualifying for the Champions' League has not been well received by the purists but there were few of those at a pulsating St. James' Park today. United achieved their aim in devastating style, steamrollering an already relegated Nottingham Forest with a vintage performance which produced four first-half goals. A splendid fifth midway through the second half by Robbie Elliott endorsed a quite brilliant victory. Finishing second represents a tremendous achievement for Kenny Dalglish, who returned to management in January when Keegan's departure left the club in turmoil. Typically, Dalglish was keen to acknowledge Keegan's contribution in leaving him with solid foundations on which to rebuild. The Newcastle boss also shared the credit with his players for coming so positively through the upheaval and was as delighted at the realisation that such a lucrative prize was coming their way. Newcastle launched their late run to glory in the aftermath of a crushing defeat by Monaco in March, further testimony to Dalglish and his men that they are unbeaten in nine matches since that nightmare in that UEFA Cup-tie.

It soon became clear that Forest would not threaten that run. They began brightly enough but from the moment Faustino Asprilla pierced their defence to score a sweet opening goal after 21 minutes there was only one winner. The Colombian striker whose eccentricity makes him a big favourite with the Toon Army, showed exceptional balance in running between two Forest defenders to finish off a move begun by Warren Barton with the most confident of flicks over the advancing Alan Fettis. Asprilla turned provider to allow Les Ferdinand his 100th Premiership goal by rounding the keeper and screwing the ball past the covering Steve Chettle, who was deceived by the lack of pace on the shot from a tight angle. The England striker then reached a Newcastle landmark of 50 goals by scoring his second from another penetrating Barton pass and his international colleague Alan Shearer quickly got in on the scoring act to complete a four-goal burst for United inside sixteen minutes.

Forest who had forced Pavel Srnicek into two important early saves in the second half, and another from Scott Gemmill which hit the fortunate John Beresford on the line, came closest to a consolation goal when sub Chris Allen struck the foot of the post. In the end however, they were grateful not to have suffered even greater embarrassment United, having threatened a fifth goal on several occasions, finally got it when Elliott lashed in a long-range shot from Shearer's lay off. Asprilla had gone close with a vicious 25 yard free kick, Ferdinand had shaved a post and Shearer had been twice denied by fantastic reaction saves from the outstanding Fettis.

Newcastle United
Srnicek, Watson, Peacock, Albert (Gillespie 68), Beresford, Barton, Batty (Beardsley 72), Elliott, Ferdinand, Asprilla (Clark 56), Shearer.

Nottingham Forest
Fettis, Cooper, Phillips, Chettle, Lyttle, O'Neill (Saunders 78), Gemmill, Bart Williams (Allen h/t), Woan, Campbell, Moore.
Referee Mr. M. Reed (Birmingham).

John Beresford

May 12-13

KEEGAN SIGNS OFF IN GLORY

Promoted Newcastle finish with 3-1 victory over Brighton

Kevin Keegan rang down the curtain on an illustrious career with a match-winning performance which again delighted a huge 36,286 crowd at St. James' Park today. The former England skipper, making his 500th and final Football League appearance, took his leave of Tyneside by scoring his 171st career goal and laying on the other two goals which put Newcastle United on the road to victory over a stubborn and tenacious Brighton side.

Keegan began and finished the move which put Newcastle into a 22nd minute lead, heading the ball through perfectly to Peter Beardsley. From his pass Chris Waddle drove in a hard, low shot which Joe Corrigan did well to palm away onto the post. The rebound fell just right for the quick thinking Keegan to score his 28th goal of the season from close range. Before this however, Brighton, urged on by their skipper Jimmy Case, had done their utmost to spoil Keegan's party, but their finishing let them down terribly. Keegan who missed Newcastle's previous game, a 2-2 draw at Huddersfield Town, with concussion showed no ill effects and thrilled the crowd with some superb touches. His trickery soon earnt a caution for Brighton defender Pearce who could do little else but bring the United forward down thus preventing more trouble for Corrigan. Then against the run of play Brighton stunned the Black-and-White Army with a neatly worked equaliser just four minutes before half time Ryan, who had already hit the underside of the bar earlier, this time getting his snap shot from distance absolutely spot on.

After the interval it was one-way traffic led by the lethal trio of Beardsley, Waddle and, of course, Keegan. It was Keegan who helped regain United's lead just five minutes into the second half. His perfectly flighted centre found Waddle at the far post who made the header look easy. With Newcastle now in exhibition mode they played some marvellous football almost trying too hard to score the most improbable goals imaginable. Finally in the 85th minute United scored their third goal of the game through Beardsley. Once again a lovely ball by Keegan put Beardsley through on goal and as Corrigan came out he lobbed the ball over the stranded keeper's head, the ball bouncing once before hitting the net. A great goal to end a fantastic promotion season, and a fitting tribute to Keegan and his service to Newcastle United.

Newcastle United

Carr, Ryan, Wharton, McCreery, Carney, Roeder, Keegan, Beardsley, Waddle, McDermott, Trewick.

Brighton & Hove Albion

Corrigan, Jones, Hutchings, Case, E. Young, Gatting, Wilson, Ryan, A. Young, Connor (sub Smillie), Pearce.

May 12

John Blackley born today in 1948.
Centre-half 1977-1979, Apps 52. Goals 0.

May 13

Jimmy Denmark born today in 1913.
Centre-half 1937-1946, Apps 105. Goals 0.

John Shiel born today in 1917.
Centre-forward 1936-1938, Apps 1. Goals 0.

Jamie McClen born today in 1979.
Midfield 1994-present day, Apps 22 (12 subs).
Goals 1.

May 12
1945, Wartime.
    Middlesbrough (h) 11-0   Att. 7,000
    Gordon, Hair (2), Stubbins (5), Carr (2),
    Milburn.
1984, Division 2.
    Brighton & Hove A. (h) 3-1   Att. 36,286
    Waddle, Beardsley, Keegan
    *Newcastle finish the season by gaining
    promotion.*

May 13
1967, Division 1.
    West Bromwich A. (a) 1-6   Att. 19,928
    Noble
1989, Division 1.
    Manchester United (a) 0-2   Att. 30,379
    *Newcastle's disastrous season finishes
    with the Magpies relegated after finishing
    bottom of Division One.*

A fitting finale for Kevin Keegan.

May 14

1969, Inter Cities Fairs Cup Semi Final, 1st leg.
Rangers (a) 0-0   Att. 75,580
1977, Division 1.
Aston Villa (h) 3-2   Att. 29,873
Cannell (2), Oates
1983, Division 2.
Wolverhampton W. (a) 2-2   Att. 22,446
Varadi, McDonald
1995, Premier League.

Newcastle 3	Crystal Palace 2
Fox 6	Armstrong 51
Lee 26	Houghton 81
Gillespie 28	Att. 35,626

2000, Premier League.

Newcastle 4	Arsenal 2
Speed 6, 59	Kanu 7
Shearer 22	Malz 53
Griffin 63	Att. 36,450

Playing record for this day is... 5 games,
Won 3, Drawn 2, Lost 0, GF 12, GA 8.
Today's success rate... 80%.

Match of the Day from 2000

SHEARER COMPLETES RESTORATION

Troubled season for Newcastle ends on a high

Alan Shearer scored the 300th goal of his career bringing up his 30th for the season against an under-strength Arsenal side preparing for their UEFA Cup final in the week. Shearer's strike was a trademark free kick from a central position 25 yards from goal. The presence of Nikos Dabizas in the Arsenal defensive wall unsettled the visitors and Shearer's bullet-like shot gave Alex Manninger no chance. Typically, Shearer was more concerned with United's victory than his own historic goal but clearly he was more than pleased to have reached the milestone before the start of this summer's Euro 2000 championships. He has completed his best season for Newcastle in terms of goals and of those who had written him off, many would now be changing their opinion.

Andy Griffin

Arsenal's teenage defender Rhys Weston could hardly have had a more demanding debut but he acquitted himself well in a totally unfamiliar side. The Premier League's decision not to allow Arsene Wenger permission to rearrange the game 'forced' the Arsenal boss into playing nine players today who will not be considered in that cup final just four days away. Ashley Cole, Julian Gray, and Brian McGovern also made their senior debuts leaving only Martin Keown and Ray Parlour who will be playing against Galatasaray. Despite this the Arsenal team still managed to include seven full internationals.

Arsenal fell behind in the sixth minute when Shearer fooled Oleg Luzhny and found Gary Speed with an overhead pass which he took first time to hit a superb volley from inside the penalty area. While the Toon Army were celebrating however, Nwankwo Kanu beat the offside trap and the challenge of Dabizas before lobbing the ball over Shay Given from the edge of the penalty area for an instantly gained equaliser. Shearer then made it 2-1 with his 199th league goal in the 23rd minute and United kept this advantage at the break.

Eight minutes after the restart Arsenal were back level, Kanu putting Stefan Malz clear and the German shrugged off Warren Barton before scoring his first Premiership goal. Speed then got his second goal of the game with a great downward header following Nolberto Solano's corner to put Newcastle ahead for a third time after 59 minutes. United then killed of any further comeback with a fourth goal just four minutes later when Andy Griffin, starting his first game for the club, scored with a delightful chip over Manninger from twenty yards out. The Austrian keeper then almost conceded what would have been the most embarrassing goal of his career. Fooled by Given's massive clearance he frantically raced back towards his own goal just managing to tip the ball over the crossbar as it bounced towards the roof of the net. So, it was, Newcastle finished comfortable and worthy 4-2 winners, making it their tenth home win of the season.

Newcastle United

Given, Griffin, Howey, Dabizas, Barton, Solano (Maric 85), Lee (McClen 89), Dyer, Speed, Ketsbaia (Gallacher 76), Shearer.

Arsenal

Manninger, Luzhny, Keown, Weston (McGovern 67), Cole, Parlour (Silvinho 46), Vernazza, Winterburn, Malz, Kanu (Gray 71), Suker.

Referee Mr. G. Poll (Tring).

Match of the Day from May 21 1969

UNITED WIN BATTLE OF BRITAIN
Scott and Sinclair see off Rangers as fans cause havoc

Amidst scenes of total chaos with thousands of drunk and disorderly Rangers fans streaming onto the pitch halting the game for seventeen minutes, Newcastle United held their nerve and found the composure to score two memorable goals in the second half of this Fairs Cup second leg tie, which puts Newcastle into their first European final. But, apart from the those glorious strikes from Jim Scott just after half-time, and Jackie Sinclair thirteen minutes from the end, the game will be forever remembered for the ugly scenes of violence and disorder which will be the subject of a major police inquiry, and brought up at a House of Commons debate. However, when all is said and done, perhaps someone will remember that the fans of Newcastle United were exceptionally well behaved, and like their heroes in Black-and-White stripes on the pitch, went about their business on the night in an exemplary manner despite the provocation. This was an honourable victory for United on a night of shame for Glasgow Rangers.

Like the entire first leg, played at Ibrox a week ago, there was nothing between these two typically determined British club sides at the half-time interval. St. James' Park had witnessed some great cup-tie battles over the years but nothing came close to this one, full of meaty tackles, plenty of stoppages, both sides willing to shed blood rather than give the opposition an inch of space. But, confined to the playing arena only, this made for a tremendous, all-British epic, watched by a huge 59,303 crowd on the night, and an unbelievable 134,883 over the two-legged semi-final.

In the 52nd minute Tommy Gibb took control of the ball and timed a superb defence-splitting ball through to Scott to create the game's first real goalscoring opportunity. Scott took the ball in his stride leaving Rangers defender Mathieson for dead as he went clear into the penalty area, as German keeper Neef came out to narrow the angle Scott sent a powerful rising drive fizzing past him and into the roof of the net. There followed a brief stoppage whilst police and stewards cleared the pitch of spectators from the field, this a small taster of what was to become an entire three-course meal later in the game. United, playing the more controlled football, settled down and this looked ominous for Rangers. Then in the 77th minute they wrapped the tie up with a second goal. A long clearance from Ollie Burton was flicked on by Wyn Davies, and before the Rangers defence had reacted, in came Sinclair to hammer a volley past Neef from close range, the keeper again having no chance. It was all over and once the game restarted after the much more prolonged stoppage caused by the third pitch invasion, the Rangers team merely ran the clock down without any real effort to try for a consolation goal.

Newcastle United
McFaul, Craig, Clark, Gibb, Burton, Moncur, Scott, Robson, Davies, Arentoft, Sinclair.

Glasgow Rangers
Neef, Johansen, Mathieson, Greig, McKinnon (Provan), Smith, Henderson, Penman, Stein, Johnston, Persson.

Referee Mr. J. Gow (Swansea).

Birthdays

May 16
Charlie Wayman born today in 1921.
Centre-forward 1941-1947, Apps 124. Goals 71.

May 17
Roy Bentley born today in 1924.
Midfield 1946-1948, Apps 54. Goals 25.
John Karelse born today in 1970.
Goalkeeper 1999-2003, Apps 3.

May 18
Howard Gayle born today in 1958.
Forward 1982-1983, Apps 8. Goals 2.
Jeff Wrightson born today in 1968.
Midfield 1985-1987, Apps 4 (1 sub). Goals 0.

May 20
Mark McGhee born today in 1957.
Forward 1977-1979 & 1989-1991, Apps 115 (13 subs). Goals 36.

May 21
Laurent Robert born today in 1975.
Forward 2001-present day, Apps 82 (7 subs). Goals 15.

Sadly Missed

May 18
Norman Smith died on this day in 1978, aged 80.
Trainer and Manager 1938-1962.

Played on this day

May 15
1982, Division 2.
Crystal Palace (a) 2-1   Att. 8,453
Waddle, Mills (pen)
2001, Premier League.
Newcastle 0   Arsenal 0
                                 Att. 50,729

May 16
1966, Division 1.
Leeds United (h) 2-0   Att. 21,669
Suddick, Robson
1998, FA Cup Final
Arsenal 2   Newcastle 0
Overmars 23
Anelka 69   Att. 79,183
Played at Wembley Stadium, London.
1999, Premier League.
Newcastle 1   Blackburn Rovers 1
Hamann 51   Wilcox 37
                                 Att. 36,623

May 17
1947, Division 2.
Bury (a) 2-2   Att. 17,298
Bentley, Wayman
1969, Division 1.
Liverpool (h) 1-1   Att. 34,927
Davies

May 18
1940, Wartime.
Bristol Rovers (h) 1-0   Att. 11,573
Cairns

May 21
1945, Wartime.
Gateshead (h) 3-1   Att. 18,000
Stubbins, Milburn, Carr
1969, Inter Cities Fairs Cup Semi Final, 2nd leg.
Rangers (h) 2-0   Att. 59,303
Scott, Sinclair
Newcastle won 2-0 on aggregate.
1973, Anglo Italian Cup Semi Final, 2nd leg.
Crystal Palace (h) 5-1   Att. 12,510
Macdonald (3), Barrowclough, Gibb

May 22-31

Played on this day

May 22
1999, FA Cup Final.
Manchester U. 2   Newcastle 0
Sheringham 11
Scholes 53   Att. 79,101
Played at Wembley Stadium, London.

May 24
1947, Division 2.
Sheffield Wednesday (a) 1-1 Att. 25,000
Hair
1977, Division 1.
Everton (a) 0-2   Att. 25,208

May 25
1940, Wartime.
Blackpool (a) 2-0   Att. 7,800
Cairns, Gordon
1942, Wartime.
Sunderland (h) 2-2   Att. 5,000
Short (pen), Walker

May 26
1947, Division 2.
West Ham United (h) 2-3   Att. 30,112
Milburn, Shackleton

May 29
1969, Inter Cities Fairs Cup Final, 1st leg.
Ujpesti Dozsa (h) 3-0   Att. 59,234
Moncur (2), Scott

FINAL COUNTDOWN

Newcastle take a three goal lead into second leg of final

Hungarian side Ujpesti Dozsa who had sent the Inter Cities Fairs Cup holders, Leeds, out of the competition in March were expected to see off Newcastle just as easily. United, however had other ideas, and they had the advantage of playing the first leg in front of 59,234 eager supporters.

The home side were dominant from the start. Davies and Robson threatened the defence, and managed to maintain the pressure throughout the first half. Yet, despite their many chances, United were thwarted by the impressive Szentmihalyi in goal for the visitors.

It was Bobby Moncur who eventually managed to get the first goal for a well deserving Newcastle. It came in the 63rd minute when a free kick from Gibb fell into the penalty area. There was a scramble for the ball, and after Davies' shot rebounded to Moncur he fired the ball into the net to get that all-important lead.

Things were made worse for the Hungarians when Moncur added his second to the score-sheet in the 72nd minute. He sent the ball speeding into the net from eighteen yards out to give Newcastle the two-goal lead they so desperately needed to take into the second leg on June 11th.

Newcastle remained in control and there were further chances from Gibb, Arentoft and Foggon. The pressure on the Ujpesti defence and goal was constant, and Newcastle were unfortunate not to score more. The visiting forwards had not been a threat all night. Newcastle, on the other hand, kept up the pace and just six minutes before the final whistle they scored their third goal. Arentoft, performed a lovely move with Scott, who received the ball and slipped it past Szentmihalyi with perfect timing. Ujpesti knew it was hopeless now, and the game ended with a joyous and confident Newcastle side looking forward to the teams' next meeting.

This was Ujpesti's first loss out of nine games in the Fairs Cup this season, but it wasn't their last. Newcastle travelled to Budapest for the next leg on June 11th where they won 3-2. Newcastle had won the Fairs Cup at their first attempt with a 6-2 win on aggregate.

Newcastle United
McFaul, Craig, Clark, Gibb, Burton, Moncur, Scott, Robson, Davies, Arentoft, Sinclair (Foggon 70).
Ujpesti Dozsa
Szentmihalyi, Kaposzta, Solymosi, Bankuti, Nosko, Dunai E., Fazekas, Gorocs, Bene, Dunai A., Zambo.

Sadly Missed

May 25
James Logan died on this day in 1896, aged 25.
Centre-forward 1895-1896, Apps 9. Goals 8.
May 26
Dave Willis died on this day in 1949, aged 67.
Midfield 1907-1913, Apps 108. Goals 4
May 27
Stan Docking died on this day in 1940, aged 25.
Midfield 1934-1938, Apps 21. Goals 3.

Birthdays

May 22
Alan Brown born today in 1959
Forward 1981-1982, Apps 5. Goals 3.
George Lackenby born today in 1931.
Right-back 1950-1956, Apps 20. Goals 0.
Paul Moran born today in 1968.
Centre-forward 1991, Apps 1. Goals 0.
David McKellar born today in 1956.
Goalkeeper 1986, Apps 10.
Roddie MacKenzie born today in 1901.
Midfield 1922-1935, Apps 256. Goals 7.
May 26
Kenny Mitchell born today in 1957.
Left-back/Centre-half 1975-1981, Apps 73
(6 subs). Goals 2.

May 27
Reg Davies born today in 1929.
Midfield 1951-1958, Apps 171. Goals 50.
Paul Gascoigne born today in 1967.
Midfield 1980-1988, Apps 109 (10 subs). Goals 25.
May 28
Henry Clifton born today in 1924
Forward 1938-1946, Apps 77. Goals 44.
William Forster born today in 1909.
Right-back 1932-1938, Apps 3. Goals 0.

July 1-15

ADVANTAGE NEWCASTLE

Belgians demolished 4-0 in United's Euro quest

Newcastle began their quest for a place in the UEFA Cup in impressive style with a comfortable first leg win in this Inter Toto Cup tie. With a three-goal advantage at half-time, Lomana LuaLua came on as a second-half substitute and sealed the win with a stunning overhead kick in the 86th minute. Sporting Lokeren were brushed aside despite United being without the injured of Alan Shearer, Kieron Dyer, Carl Cort, Rob Lee and Clarence Acuna.

It was however, a Welshman who helped settle the game in United's favour. Making his debut in silver boots, £6 million Craig Bellamy darted onto Christian Bassedas's thirteenth minute pass to pull back an inviting ball which Quinn slotted into an unguarded net from close range. Some ten minutes later Bellamy was at it again with a pass which Ameobi converted for the second after fooling the keeper with the aid of a pirouette. Shortly before the interval the teenager stroked home the third goal, ending off a clinical 70-yard, six-man move.

Bellamy was again at the heart of Newcastle's most positive work in the second half and was only denied a clear run on goal by a desperate challenge from Kimoto, an interception which saw the ball propelled upfield to present Audun Helgason with a chance, only for the Lokeren forward to pull his effort wide having done the hard work by muscling his way past Nikos Dabizas. But, by now, the game was dead as a contest, and LuaLua's impressive strike secured the well deserved 4-0 advantage.

Sporting Lokeren

Zitka, Van Dender, Kimoto, De Beule, Seyfo, Katana, Vonasek (El Bodmossi 33), Helgason, Vidarsson, Gretarsson, Mrzlecki (Zoundi h/t).

Newcastle United

Given, Barton, Dabizas, Hughes (S Caldwell 61), Elliott, Bassedas (McClen 80), Speed, Quinn, Solano, Bellamy, Ameobi (LuaLua 71).

Played on this day

July 14th
2001, Inter Toto Cup 3rd round, 1st leg.
Sporting Lokeren 0 Newcastle 4
Quinn 13
Ameobi 24, 39
LuaLua 86
Att. 2,425

Birthdays

July 1
George Heslop born today in 1940.
Centre-half 1959-1962, Apps 32. Goals 0.

July 2
Gordon Marshall born today in 1939.
Goalkeeper 1963-1968, Apps 187.
Mirandinha born today in 1959.
Centre-forward 1987-1990, Apps 69 (9 subs).
Goals 24.

July 4
John Thompson born today in 1932.
Goalkeeper 1950-1957, Apps 9.

July 5
Arthur Horsfield born today in 1946.
Forward 1969, Apps 10 (2 subs). Goals 3.
Michael O'Neill born today in 1969.
Midfield/Forward 1987-1989, Apps 60 (15 subs).
Goals 17.

July 7
Jesse Carver born today in 1911.
Centre-half 1936-1939, Apps 76. Goals 0.

July 8
Imre Varadi born today in 1959.
Centre-forward 1981-1983, Apps 90. Goals 42.

July 9
Mick Martin born today in 1951.
Midfield & Coach 1978-1983 & 1987-1990,
Apps 163 (8 subs). Goals 6.

July 10
Paul Ferris born today in 1965.
Winger & Physio 1981-1986, 1993-present day,
Apps 13 (12 subs). Goals 1.

July 12
Tony Galvin born today in 1956.
Assistant Manager 1991-1992.

July 13
Craig Bellamy born today in 1979.
Forward 2001-present day, Apps 75 (4 subs).
Goals 24.
Gordon Lee born today in 1934.
Manager 1975-1977.
Albert Stubbins born today in 1919.
Centre-forward 1936-1946, Apps 218. Goals 237.

July 14
Colin Clish born today in 1944.
Left-back 1961-1963, Apps 23. Goals 0.

July 15
Fumaca born today in 1976.
Midfield 1999-2000, Apps 6 (5 subs). Goals 0.

Sadly Missed

July 1st
Tommy Goodwill died on this day 1916, aged 22.
Winger 1913-1916, Apps 60. Goals 7.

July 5th
Bobby Ancell died on this day 1987, aged 76.
Left-back 1936-1944, Apps 155. Goals 1.

July 5th
John Little died on this day in 1988, aged 83.
Full-back 1927-1928, Apps 3. Goals 0.

July 6th
Lawrie Crown died on this day 1984, aged 86.
Left-back 1926-1927, Apps 2. Goals 0.

July 9
Ivor Allchurch died on this day in 1997, aged 67.
Midfield 1958-1962, Apps 154. Goals 51.

Played on this day

July 21st
2001, Inter Toto Cup 3rd round, 2nd leg.

Newcastle 1	Sporting Lokeren 0
Bellamy 60	Att. 29,021

July 25th
2001, Inter Toto Cup Semi Final, 1st leg.

1860 Munich 2	Newcastle 3
Agostino 55	Solano 10, 54 (pen)
Tapalovic 65	Hughes 83
	Att. 15,000

Match of the Day from July 25 2001

UNITED, BY A SHORT HEAD

Hughes nets the winner after two-goal lead wiped out

In front of a crowd of 15,000 at the Olympic Stadium, the Magpies drew first blood on ten minutes when Nolberto Solano burst into the penalty area, side-stepping defender Vidar Riseth before expertly chipping the ball over the advancing keeper. 1860 looked to respond immediately and on sixteen minutes made their first attempt. Newcastle's defence were guilty of ball watching as Thomas Hassler chipped into the path of Ned Zelic, his fierce half-volley flying inches wide. As the half wore on, Newcastle took control, but just before the break were caught by a counter attack when Weissenberger shot powerfully, Given making the save look easier than it was.

In the second half, 1860 came out with greater purpose and twice hit the woodwork during one frantic attack. Hassler fired in a free kick which smashed against the bar and from the rebound Schroth, with an instinctive header, saw his effort cannon back off the post. Just as the German side were cursing their luck, Newcastle struck an almighty blow by adding a second goal at the other end. Ameobi's long clearance found Bellamy and he raced forward only to be bundled over in the area. Solano stepped up to convert the penalty to give United a strong advantage of 2-0 after 54 minutes. However, 1860 came back within a minute as Hassler's deft cross from the left was steered beyond Given's dive by a spectacular overhead kick from Agostino. Buoyed by that strike, Munich piled on the pressure and were on level terms ten minutes later when the Newcastle defence failed to clear a cross and Topolovic scored. The thrilling tie still had one more twist and with time running out United re-established their lead. It was the 83rd minute when Solano's beautifully flighted cross into the area was met by Hughes, who, stealing in at the far post, headed decisively past Jentsch.

1860 Munich
Jentsch, Zelic, Mykland, Riseth, Hassler, Tapalovic, Weisinger, Agostino, Weissenberger, Schroth (Max 62), Dheedene (Ipova 70).

Newcastle United
Given, Barton, Elliott, Dabizas, Hughes, Quinn(Bernard 85), Solano, Bellamy, Ameobi (LuaLua 85), Bassedas (S Caldwell 85), Speed.

Referee Mr. S. Bre (France).

Sadly Missed

July 19
Harry Wake died on this day in 1978, aged 77.
Midfield 1919-1923, Apps 4. Goals 0.

Birthdays

July 16
Albert Bennett born today in 1944.
Forward 1965-1969, Apps 90 (1 sub). Goals 23.

July 19
Paul Bracewell born today in 1962.
Midfield 1992-1995, Apps 87 (12 subs). Goals 4.

July 20
Bill McKinney born today in 1936.
Right-back 1956-1965, Apps 94. Goals 8.

July 21
Jackie Sinclair born today in 1943.
Winger 1967-1969, Apps 52 (4 subs). Goals 8.

July 22
Tom Mordue born today in 1905.
Centre-forward 1925-1926, Apps 5. Goals 2.

July 24
Albert Clark born today in 1921.
Midfield 1948-1949, Apps 1. Goals 0.

July 25
Darren Jackson born today in 1966.
Forward 1986-1988, Apps 83 (16 subs). Goals 9.

July 26
Ken Leek born today in 1935.
Centre-forward 1961, Apps 14. Goals 6.

July 27
Alessandro Pistone born today in 1975.
Defender 1997-2000, Apps 63 (2 subs). Goals 1.

July 28
Derek Craig born today in 1952.
Centre-half 1969-1975, Apps 2. Goals 0.

Isaac Tate born today in 1906.
Goalkeeper 1923-1927, Apps 4.

July 30
Alex Gaskell born today in 1932.
Centre-forward 1953-1954, Apps 1. Goals 0.

July 31
Titus Bramble born today in 1981.
Defender 2002-present day, Apps 24 (3 subs). Goals 0.

Peter Manners born today in 1959.
Midfield 1977-1979, Apps 2. Goals 0.

Rob McKinnon born today in 1966.
Left-back 1984-1986, Apps 1. Goals 0.

Tommy Robson born today in 1944.
Winger 1966-1968, Apps 50 (2 subs). Goals 11.

Played on this day

August 1
2001, Inter Toto Cup Semi Final, 2nd leg.
Newcastle 3   1860 Munich 1
Speed 5   Schroth 41
LuaLua 79
Solano 89 (pen)   Att. 36,635

August 2
1975, Anglo Scottish Cup, Group Match.
Carlisle United (a) 0-2   Att. 9,209

August 3
1974, Texaco Cup Group Match.
Sunderland (a) 1-2   Att. 28,738
Tudor

August 6
1974, Texaco Cup, Group Match
Carlisle United (a) 2-2   Att. 13,560
Burns (2)
1975, Anglo Scottish Cup, Group Match
Sunderland (h) 0-2   Att. 20,088

August 7
1976, Anglo Scottish Cup, Group Match.
Sheffield United (a) 1-0   Att. 7,933
Gowling
1999, Premier League.
Newcastle 0   Aston Villa 1
             Joachim 7 Att. 36,376
2001, Inter Toto Cup Final, 1st leg.
Troyes 0   Newcastle 0
               Att. 10,414

UNITED ON COURSE FOR EURO GLORY
Newcastle just two games from UEFA Cup place

The Inter Toto Cup may be seen as something of a 'Mickey Mouse' competition, but there was absolutely nothing artificial about the excitement in today's tie at St. James' Park. Watched by a thrilled and occasionally fraught crowd of 36,635, a tournament record, Newcastle opened the scoring with a superb header from Gary Speed but then conceded the initiative to 1860 who equalised through Markus Schroth. But then Bobby Robson's side rediscovered their buoyancy and eventually went through a convincing 6-3 on aggregate following goals from Lomana LuaLua and Nolberto Solano's penalty. Newcastle now travel to France to meet Troyes in the first leg of their Inter Toto Cup final with the winner over two legs entering the UEFA Cup, the real prize of this competition. Before the game Newcastle paraded their new £9.5 million signing from Paris St Germain, Laurent Robert, he couldn't take part but should Newcastle qualify for the UEFA Cup then he will be eligible.

Newcastle started brightly with all their good work coming from the wing play of Solano and the running of Shola Ameobi. It was the latter's menace that forced Munich defender Achim Pfuderer into a foul which led to the opening goal in the fifth minute. Solano whipping in the free kick and Speed heading in from ten yards out. Buoyed by such a start, Newcastle played with complete control, particularly when the ball was in the possession of the nimble Solano. Yet the concern was the United defence which was occasionally vulnerable to Munich's quick counter attacks. So it proved to be, frustratingly, just five minutes before the interval. A clever backheel from Schroth sent Daniel Borimirov racing down the right and the Bulgarian's return pass, drilled low across the six-yard box, was comfortably despatched by Schroth, who had started the move and was not tracked back into the United danger zone.

The problems continued after the break. Newcastle were defending far too deep, allowing Erik Mykland too much space and were fortunate not to concede a second goal. Robson then, surprisingly, decided to freshen up his attack by bringing on LuaLua for Craig Bellamy. The effectiveness of the switch was swift and devastating, LuaLua rounding the keeper and scoring from an acute angle. The customary celebration which followed was just as impressive, a series of cartwheels and forward rolls, which any gold-winning Olympic gymnast would have been proud of. With the tie as good as won United settled and in the last minute Thomas Hassler handled in the area, allowing the cool-headed Solano to score Newcastle's third goal of the game from the penalty spot.

Newcastle United
Given, Barton, Dabizas, Elliott, Hughes, Solano, Lee (Caldwell 81), Speed (Acuna 78), Quinn, Ameobi, Bellamy (LuaLua 78)
1860 Munich
Jentsch, Pfuderer, Riseth, Greilich, Borimirov, Tapalovic (Agostino 78), Mykland, Tyce, Hassler, Max, Schroth.
Referee Mr. I. Baskakov (Russia).

Sadly Missed

August 5
Terry Hibbitt died on this day in 1994, aged 47. Midfield 1971-1975 & 1978-1981 Apps 292 (1 sub). Goals 18.

Birthdays

August 3
Ossie Ardiles born today in 1952.
Manager 1991-1992.
Nikos Dabizas born today in 1973.
Defender 1998-present day, Apps 176 (13 subs). Goals 13.
Gary Kelly born today in 1966.
Goalkeeper 1984-1989, Apps 64.

August 6
Ernest Hall born today in 1916.
Centre-half 1933-1937, Apps 2. Goals 0.
Ken Waugh born today in 1933.
Right-back 1952-1956, Apps 7. Goals 0.

August 7
Willie Penman born today in 1939.
Midfield 1963-1966, Apps 65 (1 sub). Goals 18.

August 8
Henry Johnson born today in 1913.
Left-back 1933-1937, Apps 5. Goals 0.
Louis Saha born today in 1978.
Forward 1999, Apps 12 (6 subs). Goals 2.

Match of the Day from August 13 1997

BERESFORD BRACE KEEPS HOPES ALIVE

United have the referee to thank, too, in crucial victory

John Beresford and Czech Republic referee Vaclav Krondl emerged as the unlikely heroes for Newcastle who were fortunate to gain a slender advantage against Croatia Zagreb today at St. James' Park. However, United will need to produce one of their finest displays in Zagreb in the second leg, on August 27th, if they are to join Manchester United in the Group Stages of the European Champions' League. The winning goal came with fifteen minutes remaining. Drazen Ladic came out to catch a looping header from Faustino Asprilla, but the keeper was arguably impeded by the Colombian, whose jump was more towards the player than the ball. When Ladic failed to collect cleanly, no surprise under the circumstances, Beresford was on hand to score his second goal of the match. Most referees would have awarded a foul, however Krondl was in sympathetic mood and merely waved play on, and to make matters worse the hapless Ladic was later cautioned for his prolonged protest. Zagreb on the day played some fantastic football and one fears for the backlash in the return leg in Croatia. It is pointless to ponder whether the injured pair of Alan Shearer or Les Ferdinand would have made a difference. The simple fact is, that Newcastle won the match and must play the return leg in positive mood.

Beresford, United's wing-back, had been the main focal point of Newcastle's attack and he supplied the game's opening goal on 22 minutes. It was a superbly crafted goal too. Steve Watson, the only Geordie on the pitch, starting the move which Asprilla and Robert Lee further developed to carve out the chance for Beresford to fire in from close range. Zagreb began to close down wing-backs Watson and Beresford and the result was Newcastle losing their cutting edge, a major turning point in the game. But, at half-time United held their single-goal advantage with some great and concentrated defending.

Seven minutes after the interval however, Silvio Maric ran at the heart of the Newcastle defence and as Alessandro Pistone came to challenge he neatly turned the ball to Digor Cvitanovic who gave Shay Given no chance with a thundering drive. The goal lifted Zagreb's spirits and their game, ominously for United, stepped up a gear. Robert Prosinecki was invariably at the heart of their attacks and Magpies' manager Kenny Dalglish may well have to consider David Batty for a man-marking role in the return leg. Twice the Croatian tested Given with long-range shots and another was blocked by Robert Lee from a free kick he had illegally encroached upon, earning him a yellow card. At the other end a well organised defence kept Asprilla relatively subdued which meant a comfortable second half for keeper Ladic. All that however changed in the 76th minute when Newcastle snatched that priceless one-goal lead, which could well prove to be crucial.

Newcastle United

Given, Pistone, Albert, (Howey 68), Pearce, Watson, Lee, Ketsbaia, Batty, Beresford, Tomasson (Gillespie 57), Asprilla.

Croatia Zagreb

Ladic, Simic, Juric, Miadinic, Saric (Tomas 83), Prosinecki, Jurcic, Maric, Kiznar, D. Cvitanovic, Viduka.

Referee Mr. V. Krondl (Czech Republic)

Played on this day

August 9
1969, Division 1.
West Ham United (a) 0-1   Att. 33,323
1975, Anglo Scottish Cup, Group Match.
Middlesbrough (h) 2-2   Att. 11,624
Hibbitt, Gowling
1997, Premier League.
Newcastle 2	Sheffield Wed. 1
Asprilla 2, 72	Carbone 8
	Att. 36,711

1999, Premier League.
Tottenham H. 3	Newcastle 1
Iverson 29	Solano 16
Ferdinand 45	
Sherwood 61	Att. 28,701

August 10
1968, Division 1.
West Ham United (h) 1-1   Att. 37,307
B. Robson
1974, Texaco Cup Group Match.
Middlesbrough (h) 4-0   Att. 11,571
Macdonald, Cassidy, Tudor, Burns
1976, Anglo Scottish Cup, Group Match.
Hull City (a) 0-0   Att. 4,715

August 12
1972, Division 1.
Wolverhampton W. (h) 2-1   Att 33,790
Tudor, Green
2001, Inter Toto Cup Final, 2nd leg.
Newcastle 4	Troyes 4
Solano 2	Leroy 25
Ameobi 65	Gousse 28
Speed 69 (pen)	Boutal 46, 61
Elliott 90	Att. 36,577
Newcastle lost on the away goals rule after the tie finished 4-4 on aggregate.

August 13
1969, Division 1.
Sheffield Wednesday (h) 3-1   Att. 41,341
Foggon, Robson (2)
1997, Champions' League 2nd Qualifying round, 1st leg.
Newcastle 2	Croatia Zagreb 1
Beresford 22, 76	Cvitanovic 52
	Att. 34,465

Birthdays

August 10
Philippe Albert born today in 1967.
Centre-half 1994-1999, Apps 138 (14 subs).
Goals 12.
Jimmy Murray born today in 1908.
Midfield 1932-1936, Apps 96. Goals 10.

August 11
Mike Jeffery born today in 1971.
Midfield 1993-1995, Apps 5 (2 subs). Goals 1.
August 13
Alan Shearer born today in 1970.
Centre-forward 1996-present day, Apps 270 (5 subs). Goals 145.

Sadly Missed

August 9
William Aitken died on this day in 1973, aged 79.
Winger 1920-1924, Apps 110. Goals 10.
August 13
Ed Dixon died on this day in 1979, aged 85.
Midfield 1914-1923, Apps 61. Goals 10.

August 14

Played on this day

1968, Division 1.
Sheffield Wednesday (a) 1-1 Att. 27,258
B. Robson
1971, Division 1.
Crystal Palace (a) 0-2 Att. 25,281
1976, Anglo Scottish Cup, Group Match.
Middlesbrough (h) 3-0 Att. 15,703
Gowling (2), Barrowclough
1993, Premier League.
Newcastle 0 Tottenham H. 1
Sheringham 36
Att. 35,216
2002, Champions' League 3rd Qualifying round, 1st leg.
Zelijeznicar 0 Newcastle 1
Dyer 55
Att. 36,000

Playing record for this day is... 5 games,
Won 2, Drawn 1, Lost 2, GF 5, GA 4.
Today's success rate... 50%.

VIBRANT NEWCASTLE ON THE BRINK OF EURO GLORY

Dyer's goal poves decisive for United

Kieron Dyer's first European goal promises to be worth a fortune to Newcastle United. The England midfielder produced his moment of brilliance after 55 minutes into today's Champions League Qualifier in Sarajevo to put Bobby Robson's team on the brink of a place in the group stages. Dyer's superbly taken goal gives Newcastle a solid platform to claim their financial jackpot at St. James' Park in two weeks time. This was Zeljo's biggest match since beaten in the UEFA Cup semi finals, but even though a packed and passionate crowd of 36,000 urged them to raise their game, a vibrant United side suffered few alarms on their way to an important victory.

Newcastle's most worrying moment came 30 seconds into the second half when they allowed striker Jure Guvo to burst into their penalty area and bring an excellent one-handed save from the diving Shay Given. The Republic of Ireland international's crucial intervention inspired Newcastle and shortly afterwards Dyer went skipping through the Bosnian defence at the other end. The Slovakian referee allowed the elusive midfielder to continue his run, despite crude attempts to stop him, and Dyer capitalised fully on the advantage rule to exchange passes with Lomana LuaLua and Alan Shearer before flicking the ball past the advancing keeper Kelian Hasagic. United, who survived a swift response when Almir Dredic's low drive skimmed inches wide of Given's far post, should have gone on to make the tie safe from there. LuaLua was particularly guilty of letting Zeljeznicar off the hook. His pace took him past Haris Alihodzic and into the penalty area, where both Nolberto Solano and Dyer were waiting for a simple tap in, but, the unpredictable striker attempted to round the keeper and

Titus Bramble

instead ran the ball out of play. Robson's response was to withdraw LuaLua and send on Shola Ameobi. That proved an inspirational change as Ameobi's first significant contribution ended with a rising shot which clipped the top of the crossbar.

Newcastle, who escaped early on in the first half when Gredic was flagged offside before shooting past an exposed Given, should have been ahead at the interval and would have been if LuaLua or Jermaine Jenas had shown greater sharpness in the penalty area with the goal at their mercy. LuaLua headed badly off target when a curling cross from Aaron Hughes found him unmarked ten yards out, while a right-wing corner found its way to Jenas, who had just as much space on the six-yard line, but again he mistimed his header horribly. In the end Newcastle were worthy winners and only an exceptionally bad performance will withdraw them from a rightful place in the latter stages of the Champions' League.

Zeljeznicar
Hasagic, Jahic (Alagic 71), Mulalic, Alihodzic, Mulaosmanovic, Gredic, Karic, Mesic (Mucrinic 82), Seferovic, Guvo, Cosic (Radonja 88).
Newcastle United
Given, Hughes, Bramble, Dabizas, Bernard (Elliott 88), Solano, Dyer, Jenas, Viana (Quinn 88), Shearer, LuaLua (Ameobi 82).
Referee Mr. L. Michel (Slovakia).

August 15

WOLVES RECOVER TOO LATE

Newcastle take 3-2 win after three-minute fight back

Wolverhampton Wanderers came to St. James' Park today to meet Newcastle in front of 38,346. The home side started out the better team in the first half, and for a good twenty minutes Wolves were hardly out of their half. It was clear that communication was the key to Newcastle's success, and that was something that the visitors were lacking.

Half way through the first period Wolves pulled together and their play improved a lot. Their few attacking attempts were quite a threat to the Newcastle defence, but the danger was averted each time by the quick thinking of the home side.

Hegan almost took the lead for Wolves when his shot headed straight for goal. McFaul managed to get a hand to the ball, and it came back to Wagstaffe. He fluffed his effort, and the Newcastle keeper had no trouble making the save.

Then, just before the half-time break, Newcastle took the lead. Wolves keeper Oldfield made a superb save from a try from Davies, but the ball came back out into the area. Robson was well placed to send the ball across the goalmouth, and Smith just flicked it into the net to put the home side ahead going into the break.

In the second half Newcastle continued the attack, and there were plenty more opportunities for both sides to grab a goal. A corner kick was awarded to United in the 54th minutes, and it was taken by Dyson. The ball came off the head of Davies straight to Foggon who took his time to plant the ball safely in the back of the net for a second goal.

The Magpies managed to increase their lead to three just ten minutes later when Gibb had two shots on target. The first one rebounded out but came back to him, and the second one was sent in so powerfully that it had no chance of missing the goal. The ball sailed past Oldfield to give the home side their third goal.

Things did not go quite so smoothly for Newcastle for the rest of the game, though. There were a few good attempts from Gould, but each one failed to hit the target. The game looked as if it was over with a 3-0 win to Newcastle, but just three minutes from the final whistle Wolves had other plans.

A centre from Wagstaffe came over to Dougan, who got his head to the ball to nod it into the net past the surprised McFaul. However, with just two minutes left on the clock, the home side thought the danger was over.

They were proved wrong, for in the dying seconds Hegan's replacement Curran also managed to get his head to a corner from Wagstaffe. The ball zoomed into the net to bring the score up to 3-2.

Had there been a few more minutes left, the scores might well have been equal, but luckily for Newcastle time ran out. Overall it was the home side who had played the better football, but it was a cracking fight back from Wolves. They had just left it too late to gain a point.

Newcastle United
McFaul, Craig, Guthrie, Gibb, McNamee, Moncur, Dyson, Robson, Davies, Smith, Foggon.
Wolverhampton Wanderers
Oldfield, Parkin, Shaw, Bailey, Holsgrove, Wilson, McCalliog, Hegan (Curran 82), Gould, Dougan, Wagstaffe.

1970, Division 1.
Wolverhampton W. (h) 3-2   Att. 38,346
Smith, Foggon, Gibb
1972, Division 1.
Birmingham City (a) 2-3   Att. 35,831
Macdonald, Barrowclough
1992, Division 1.
Southend United (h) 3-2   Att. 28,545
Bracewell, Prior (og), Clark
1998, Premier League.
Newcastle 0   Charlton Athletic 0
Att. 36,719

1999, Premier League.
Southampton 4   Newcastle 2
Kachloul 58, 68   Shearer 22 (pen)
M. Hughes 78   Speed 84
Att. 15,030

Playing record for this day is... 5 games, Won 2, Drawn 1, Lost 2, GF 10, GA 11. Today's success rate... 50%.

Stuart Alderson born today in 1948.
Winger 1965-1967, Apps 4.
Ray King born today in 1924.
Goalkeeper 1942-1946, Apps 33.

Des Hamilton born today in 1976.
Midfield 1997-2001, Apps 18 (7 subs). Goals 1.

Played on this day

1969, Division 1.
Manchester City (h) 1-0   Att. 46,860
Robson (pen)

1975, Division 1.
Ipswich Town (a) 3-0   Att. 27,680
T. Craig (pen), Macdonald (2)

1980, Division 2.
Sheffield Wednesday (a) 0-2 Att. 26,164

August 17
1968, Division 1.
Burnley (a) 0-1   Att. 13,500

1974, Division 1.
Coventry City (h) 3-2   Att. 35,950
Macdonald, Howard, Kennedy

1985, Division 1.
Southampton (a) 1-1   Att. 16,401
Beardsley (pen)

1996, Premier League.
Everton 2   Newcastle 0
Unsworth 29 (pen)
Speed 40   Att. 40,117

Match of the Day from August 17 1974

UNITED HOLD ON TO WIN

Newcastle win despite second-half fight from Coventry

Coventry travelled to St. James' Park today to play Newcastle in front of a crowd of 35,950. The home side were at full strength, but Coventry had not registered new signing Larry Lloyd in time for this game, so he was unable to take the field.

Newcastle were the better team from the start, going on the attack as early as possible, but Coventry lacked the ability to break through and cause any threat to the home defence.

United stayed in control, and the Sky Blues were constantly trying to keep up with the pace of the game. There were sixteen minutes on the clock when Newcastle netted the first goal. It was Alan Kennedy who put the ball past Ramsbottom in the Coventry goal, to give his team the lead.

Newcastle managed to hold on to their advantage for the rest of the first half, but they seemed to have lost their attacking force. They were no longer a danger to the Coventry defence, but the visitors rarely threatened either, so there seemed little to worry about for the home fans.

The start of the second half saw a change in the Newcastle side. Kennedy did not return on to the pitch as he was still recovering from a knock in the first period. David Craig took his place, and fifteen minutes into the second half United extended their lead when a mistake by Coop enabled Tommy Cassidy to send the ball to Malcolm Macdonald. Supermac slammed it into the net with confidence to put Coventry two goals behind.

Following this there were some tame attempts at goal from both sides, but none of them amounted to anything for over twenty minutes.

Then, with just seven minutes to go, a corner kick from Coop found its way to Alderson who beat Iam McFaul with style to pull a goal back for Coventry.

Three minutes later it was Newcastle's turn again. This time John Tudor was the man who got the goal, his shot perfectly timed to beat the visitors' defence and keeper. Now the score was 3-1, but it wasn't over yet.

In the dying seconds of the game the Sky Blues scored again when a super cross from Cattlin found its way to the head of Tommy Hutchison. He nodded the ball into the net to bring the score to 3-2. The visitors had left it just a little too late to stage their comeback; another couple of minutes of play might have seen snatch a point. However, Newcastle had played well and for the most part deserved all the points from this match.

Newcastle United
McFaul, Nattrass, Kennedy (Craig), Smith J, Keeley, Howard, Burns, Cassidy, Macdonald, Tudor, Hibbitt.
Coventry City
Ramsbottom, Smith W, Cattlin, Mortimer, Hindley, Carradine, Coop, Alderson, Stein, Carr, Hutchison.

Birthdays

August 16
Barry Venison born today in 1964.
Defender/Midfield 1992- 1995, Apps 133 (1 sub).
Goals 1.

Sadly Missed

August 16
Bob Foyers died on this day in 1942, aged 74.
Left-back 1895-1897, Apps 39. Goals 0.
Archie Livingstone died on this day in 1961, aged 45.
Midfield 1935-1938, Apps 33. Goals 5.

August 18

TEN MEN NOT GOOD ENOUGH
Sending off turns the game

This match stands out for Newcastle for all the wrong reasons. Coventry played host to the Magpies in front of 15,763 for this Premiership clash, and it was to be a match to remember. The home side started out the better team and Newcastle had a lot of work to do in order to match the pace of the Sky Blues side.

The visitors gradually got into the game and began to put pressure on the home defence, and they were lucky to take the lead in the 22nd minute. A free kick from Liam O'Brien from 25 yards didn't seem to be a danger to Jonathan Gould in the Coventry goal. That all changed in a split second when the ball took a deflection off Peter Atherton and sailed past the keeper into the goal to put Newcastle into the lead.

Then with 37 minutes on the clock United's luck began to change for the worse. John Beresford made a huge mistake which his side paid for immensely. He sent a pass right across his own penalty area, giving the ball away to Roy Wegerle. Wegerle attempted to evade Pavel Srnicek in the Newcastle goal, but the keeper brought him down. The referee had no option but to show Srnicek the red card and award Coventry a penalty. Before the kick was taken Newcastle took off Nicky Papavasiliou and brought on their substitute goalkeeper Tommy Wright in his place. In a strange twist of fate it was Mick Quinn who stepped up to take the spot kick, he had been sold to Coventry by Kevin Keegan the previous year. The excitement may have been too much for Quinn as his shot flew straight over Wright, and the crossbar, missing the goal by a long way. A small reprieve for Beresford, but the damage was done and Newcastle still had to pay the price.

Newcastle were struggling now with ten men. Their play was suffering and Coventry were able to take advantage. The home side outplayed the visitors for the rest of the first half, and on into the second.

Coventry eventually managed to equalise when Peter Ndlovu accepted the ball from Wegerle and slipped through the Newcastle defence to fire the ball straight past Wright from twenty yards out and bring the scores level on 57 minutes.

So, Coventry continued in control of the game, and it was a double substitution in the 73rd minute which sealed the result for the home team. Paul Williams and Mick Harford were brought on and together were responsible for the winning goal. It was Williams who was provider, and Harford, marking his debut in the team, managed to get his head to the ball to nod it powerfully into the back of the net.

Despite this, Newcastle showed plenty of promise towards the end of the match. It was too late on this occasion, but it gave the warning that they had fighting spirit and were ready for the challenges of the rest of the season.

Coventry City
Gould, Atherton, Rennie, Babb, Flynn, Sheridan (Harford 73), Ndlovu, Morgan (P. Williams 73), Wegerle, J. Williams, Quinn.

Newcastle United
Srnicek, Watson, Venison, Scott, Beresford, Lee, Clark, O'Brien, Bracewell, Papavasiliou (Wright 37), Cole.

Referee Mr J. Borrett (Harleston, Norfolk).

Played on this day

1951, Division 1.
Stoke City (h) 6-0   Att. 47,047
Crowe, Milburn (3), Mitchell, G. Robledo
1956, Division 1.
Portsmouth(h) 2-1   Att. 30,191
Crowe, Taylor
1962, Division 2.
Cardiff City (a) 4-4   Att. 26,800
Fell (pen), Kerray, Hilley, Opponent (og)
1971, Division 1.
Tottenham Hotspur (a) 0-0   Att. 42,715
1979, Division 2.
Oldham Athletic (h) 3-2   Att. 19,099
Withe, Shoulder (2 pens)
1991, Division 2.
Charlton Athletic (a) 1-2   Att. 9,322
Carr
1993, Premier League.
Coventry City 2   Newcastle 1
Ndlovu 58   Atherton (og) 22
Harford 85   Att. 15,763

Playing record for this day is... 7 games, Won 3, Drawn 2, Lost 2, GF 17, GA 11. Today's success rate... 57.14%.

Birthdays

Jimmy Harrower born today in 1935.
Midfield 1961-1962, Apps 6. Goals 0.

Sadly Missed

James Fleming died on this day in 1917, aged 33
Centre-forward 1911-1913, Apps 4. Goals 0.

Played on this day

1950, Division 1.
Stoke City (a) 2-1   Att. 22,000
Milburn (2, 1 pen)

1961, Division 2.
Leyton Orient (h) 0-0   Att. 26,638

1967, Division 1.
Southampton (h) 3-0   Att. 33,709
Bennett, T. Robson, Scott

1970, Division 1.
Stoke City (a) 0-3   Att. 15,197

1972, Division 1.
Sheffield United (a) 2-1   Att. 23,078
Tudor, Macdonald

1978, Division 2.
Millwall (a) 1-2   Att. 12,105
Barton

1987, Division 1.
Tottenham Hotspur (a) 1-3   Att. 26,261
McCreery

1989, Division 2
Leeds United (h) 5-2   Att. 24,396
Quinn (4, 1 pen), Gallacher

1992, Coca Cola Cup 1st round, 1st leg.
Mansfield Town (h) 2-1   Att. 14,083
Peacock (2)

1995, Premier League.
Newcastle 3   Coventry City 0
Lee 7
Beardsley 82 (pen)
Ferdinand 83   Att. 36,485

2001, Premier League.
Chelsea 1   Newcastle 1
Zenden 8   Acuna 76
    Att. 40,124

2002, Premier League.
Newcastle 4   West Ham 0
LuaLua 61, 72
Shearer 76
Solano 86   Att. 51,072

Playing record for this day is... 12 games,
Won 7, Drawn 2, Lost 3, GF 24, GA 14.
Today's success rate... 66.67%.

SO GOOD THEY NAMED HIM TWICE
LuaLua's double destroys West Ham

Lomana LuaLua struck two fine goals in another classy display of attacking football at St. James' Park today. Alan Shearer and Nolberto Solano got the other two, Kieron Dyer was a font of energy and ideas, but it was LuaLua's day and at the final whistle he departed to a deserved standing ovation from the Toon Army. LuaLua completely destroyed the club he supported as a child growing up in London's East End. He continually ran at West Ham's defenders, dribbling adventurously with the ball or simply charging into space to receive flighted deliveries, two of which he scored from. The DR Congo international has needed to seize his opportunity in the injury induced absence of Craig Bellamy and Carl Cort. LuaLua appears a more confident, individual than last season. Now strengthened with self belief

Lomana LuaLua

bestowed on him by the master motivator Bobby Robson. This was United's 50th Premiership win under Robson and once again Newcastle, on this evidence, will be challenging again for that elusive Premiership title.

Newcastle, through LuaLua, almost scored a spectacular goal as early as the ninth minute, jiggling the ball through and over West Ham's defence before volleying wide. When his best chance came, on the hour, LuaLua reacted well to Jermaine Jenas' flicked redirection of Solano's corner and swept the ball low under David James' body. His next goal was brilliantly conceived by Solano, who slid the ball to the left and Hugo Viana, who showed increasing flickers of class. The Portuguese teenager's clipped cross was met firmly by LuaLua, whose header was pushed onto the crossbar by James. It was a sharp reaction save by the West Ham captain but he could do nothing to prevent the ball dropping down over the goal-line. Stripping West Ham's defence of any solidity, LuaLua played an important part in United's third goal, producing neat footwork to guide the ball down to Solano on the right wing, his cut-back cross was driven in by Shearer. Shearer then repaid the compliment, squaring the ball to the far post where Solano netted Newcastle's fourth goal in 25 minutes.

Goals from a DR Congo international, a Peruvian and a retired England captain were probably not quite what the watching England manager, Sven Göran Eriksson, would have wanted. However, the real plus was Dyer, who confirmed that his most effective role was dictating forward momentum from central midfield. Before the black-and-white tide began to swamp West Ham they did manage moments of hope before being truly sunk. Jermain Defoe was twice thwarted by Olivier Bernard and Titus Bramble before Newcastle grabbed control and the goals began to flow. West Ham will not be the only side put to the sword here this season.

Newcastle United
Given, Hughes, Bramble, Dabizas, Bernard, Solano, Dyer, Jenas, Viana (Elliott 90), LuaLua, Shearer.

West Ham United
James, Pearce, Repka, Dailly, Winterburn, Schemmel (Labant 71), Cisse (Moncur 71), Carrick, Sinclair, Cole, Defoe.

Referee Mr. P. Durkin (Portland).

Birthdays

Peter Noble born today in 1944.
Forward 1964-1968, Apps 25 (3 subs). Goals 7.

Sadly Missed

Frank Houghton died on this day in 1994, aged 68.
Midfield 1948-1953, Apps 57. Goals 10.

August 20

UNITED RALLY FOR DRAW

Second-half improvement brings draw against Villa

Newcastle travelled to the Midlands for this Division One match against Aston Villa today. It was the first Saturday of the season, and the weather was lovely. Surprising then that only 17,673 made it to Villa Park to watch the game. In the Villa team Hateley had suffered from a cold in the week but was included in the side, although his performance was badly affected and Villa paid the price for his lethargy.

In the first period there was some organised play, although most of it was random. There were few attempts at goal from either side, but Villa looked the stronger team. Hateley's usual energetic heading skills were notably missing from play, and Villa lost many chances of scoring as a result.

The Villa defence was strong, and Newcastle were finding it very difficult to penetrate. Their attempts always thwarted by the back line or Withers in the Villa goal. Then, with seven minutes to go before the interval Villa took the lead. It was Chatterley who sent in the powerful shot, and Marshall in the Newcastle goal almost managed to stop the ball. He got his fingers to it, but only succeeded in pushing it into the roof of the net.

The home side were a goal ahead, and they managed to keep it that way until after the break. Within a minute of the restart Burton sent the ball back into danger from the touchline. Withers came off his line to try to stop the threat, but McGarry got up to the cross and headed the ball powerfully past the Villa keeper to draw level.

This boost gave Newcastle confidence and determination, in particular Jim Iley was responsible for getting the team to pull together. The visitors improved greatly and seemed revived after their goal. They pushed on the attack with force, and this meant Villa had to do all they could to defend.

Play continued like this for the most part, and it was only in the final ten minutes that Villa got the chance to fight back. Several attempts by Chatterley were kept out of goal by the joint efforts of the Newcastle defence and Marshall. The Newcastle keeper pulled off a great save from Chatterley when he managed to get to the ball just in time to push it round the post. Next it was the defence who kicked the ball out of danger off the goal-line when Marshall appeared to have been beaten.

It was a super display from the Newcastle side, but it came just a little too late for their efforts to make any difference to the scoreline and the game ended 1-1.

Aston Villa

Withers, Wright, Aitken, Pountney, Sleeuwenhoek, Deakin, McLeod, Hamilton (Park 80), Hateley, Chatterley, Scott.

Newcastle United

Marshall, Craig, Guthrie, Burton, Thompson, Iley, Robson, Kettleborough, McGarry, Hilley, Suddick.

Sadly Missed

Bill Curry died on this day in 1990, aged 54
Centre-forward 1953-1959, Apps 88. Goals 40.

Played on this day

1949, Division 1.
Portsmouth (h) 1-3   Att. 54,258
G. Robledo
1955, Division 1.
Sheffield United (h) 4-2   Att. 42,559
Davies (2), Hannah, Keeble
1960, Division 1.
Preston North End (a) 3-2   Att. 17,363
White (3)
1966, Division 1.
Aston Villa (a) 1-1   Att. 17,673
McGarry
1969, Division 1.
Sheffield Wednesday (a) 0-1   Att. 19,12
1975, Division 1.
Middlesbrough (h) 1-1   Att. 41,417
Macdonald
1977, Division 1.
Leeds United(h) 3-2   Att. 36,700
Burns (2), Kennedy
1980, Division 2.
Notts County (h) 1-1   Att. 17,272
Shoulder
2000, Premier League.
Manchester U. 2   Newcastle 0
Johnsen 21
Cole 70   Att. 67,47

Playing record for this day is... 9 games,
Won 3, Drawn 3, Lost 3, GF 14, GA 15.
Today's success rate... 50%.

Alan Suddick

Played on this day

1948, Division 1.
Everton (a) 3-3 — Att. 57,279
Walker, Lowrie (2)

1954, Division 1.
Arsenal (a) 3-1 — Att. 65,334
Davies, R. Mitchell (2)

1965, Division 1.
Nottingham Forest (h) 2-2 — Att. 37,230
Suddick, McGarry

1968, Division 1.
Chelsea (h) 3-2 — Att. 39,048
Gibb, B. Robson (2)

1971, Division 1.
Liverpool (h) 3-2 — Att. 39,736
MacDonald (3, 1 pen)

1974, Division 1.
Sheffield United (h) 2-2 — Att. 34,283
Macdonald, Burns

1976, Division 1.
Derby County (h) 2-2 — Att. 35,927
T. Craig (pen), Hudson

1979, Division 2.
Preston North End (a) 0-1 — Att. 12,707

1985, Division 1.
Luton Town (h) 2-2 — Att. 21,933
Roeder, Beardsley

1993, Premier League.

Manchester U. 1	Newcastle 1
Giggs 40	Cole 71
	Att. 41,829

1994, Premier League.

Leicester City 1	Newcastle 3
Joachim 90	Cole 51
	Beardsley 58
	Elliott 74
	Att. 20,048

1996, Premier League.

Newcastle 2	Wimbledon 0
Batty 3	
Shearer 88	Att. 36,385

1999, Premier League.

Newcastle 3	Wimbledon 3
Speed 7	M. Hughes 44
Domi 28	Ainsworth 68, 90
Solano 46 (pen)	Att. 35,809

Playing record for this day is... 13 games, Won 6, Drawn 6, Lost 1, GF 29, GA 22. Today's success rate... 69.23%.

Match of the Day from 1994

LEICESTER OUT FOXED

Beardsley down but not out in fine 3-1 win

Peter Beardsley sustained a fracture of his cheekbone as he and Andy Cole carried on where they left off in May, scoring goals. This paved the way for United who expected a convincing victory over newly-promoted Leicester City today. Beardsley picked up an injury in the 80th minute in an accidental collision with Steve Thompson, and Newcastle fear it is a similar fracture to the one he got a year ago in a pre-season game with Liverpool's Neil Ruddock, which kept him sidelined for seven matches. To add to their troubles United had keeper Pavel Srnicek sent off five minutes later for bringing down Julian Joachim as he raced free into the penalty area. However, Beardsley's bad luck and Srnicek's dismissal should not detract from a win that showed again that Newcastle will be up with the leaders in this season's Premiership race. It may not have been a vintage Newcastle display, but they dominated the match in terms of possession and should have turned this into at least a five-goal margin of victory which would have done them better justice.

Amongst a number of plusses in the United side was Philippe Albert, a £2.65 million signing from Anderlecht, who settled in comfortably as did Marc Hottiger United's other summer signing from Swiss side Sion. Albert oozed class as much in attack as he did in defence. His performance was marred, though, by his 47th minute booking, but overall the Belgian is a welcome addition to the Magpies' squad. Newcastle opened the scoring in the 51st minute when Scott Sellars and Beardsley set up Cole to score a typical tap-in goal from close range, his 47th league goal for the club in just 53 games now. Seven minutes later Beardsley scored the sort of goal he makes look so easy. Shuffling past Nicky Mohan as if the defender wasn't there and shooting through Gavin Ward's legs from ten yards. The game at this point looked over with Newcastle in cruise control.

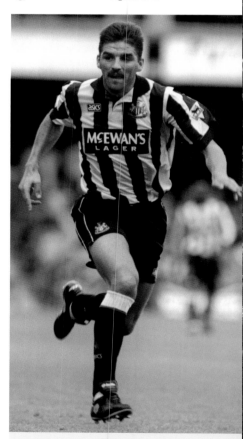
Philippe Albert

However, Leicester wasted the chance to pull one back when Albert was adjudged to have pushed Steve Walsh over in the box. Mark Draper, making his debut for the Foxes following his £1.25 million summer transfer from Notts County, probably worried about the new time wasting crackdown, hurried his penalty and Srnicek was able to save with ease. Newcastle made the game entirely safe when Robbie Elliott, who had been on as a sub for only five minutes, made it 3-0 in the 75th minute from a glorious pass by Ruel Fox. In the last minute Joachim, virtually a one-man attack and Leicester's best player by a long way, scored a consolation goal after United's substitute keeper Mike Hooper failed to hold Agnew's pile driver from 25 yards and left a simple tap-in for the remaining few City fans to have something to cheer.

Leicester City
Ward, Grayson (Thompson 65), Smith, Hill, Mohan, Whitlow, Agnew, Blake (Roberts 65), Draper, Walsh, Joachim.

Newcastle United
Srnicek, Hottiger, Peacock, Albert, Beresford, Fox, Venison, Lee, Sellars (Elliott 69), Cole, Beardsley (Mathie 82, Hooper 85)
Referee Mr. M. Reed (Birmingham).

Birthdays

Keith Mulgrove born today in 1959. Left-back 1977-1980, Apps 1 (1 sub). Goals 0.

Jim Scott born today in 1940. Midfield/Winger 1967-1970, Apps 98 (6 subs). Goals 12.

August 22

FERDINAND BRACE UNLOCKS BOLTON

Classy Newcastle just too good for the new boys

Bolton have proved themselves a match for the very best at Burnden Park in recent seasons. Newcastle today showed themselves to be amongst the best teams they will meet this season to claim a thrilling victory which brings with it early Premiership ascendancy. Two more goals from Les Ferdinand, United's record £6 million signing, and what promises to be one of many this term from the ever dangerous Robert Lee gave the team which Kevin Keegan has bought and built a crucial edge in a splendid encounter. Favourites in the eyes of the bookmakers, they will be favourite visitors to grounds all over the country if they continue to perform like they did today.

If Ferdinand's decisive goals were sparkling and simplistic, the touches of David Ginola, another purchase in Keegan's £14 million summer spending spree, were simply magnificent. Ginola's first meaningful touch, on seventeen minutes, was to supply the inch-perfect centre from which Ferdinand converted with a deft glancing header. Then Ginola, a few moments later, left Bolton full-back Scott Green stranded as the winger slipped effortlessly down the wing and came within inches of scoring a goal of his own, which would have lingered long in the memory. Proving that he is a two-footed player he let fly first time with the outside of his right foot from 30 yards out and the ball curled agonisingly just inches wide. Newcastle were unlucky not to add a second goal before the interval when Keith Gillespie, showing great pace from a run from inside his own half, was sent sprawling inside the penalty area by Chris Fairclough and inexplicably the referee failed to award the penalty. Bolton were also unfortunate not to have scored early on when Owen Coyle put the ball in the net after Mark Patterson's shot deflected off Darren Peacock. A linesman decided that he was offside when the original attempt was made. Earlier a superb run and decent shot, but lacking any power, by Jason McAteer almost crept in much to the embarrassment of Shaka Hislop.

The immense spirit which had swept Bolton into the Premiership eventually brought them on level terms, to the delight of their capacity 20,000 plus crowd, six minutes into the second half. McAteer's skill on the edge of the area produced a neat shot which was deflected for a corner. Patterson crossed the ball in and Gudni Bergsson rose unopposed to head in his first goal in England for four years. This briefly gave Bolton a chance to go on and record a famous victory. They might have done just that if Fabian De Freitas, having left his markers trailing in a race for Patterson's through ball, had been more accurate with the ensuing shot. But the greater subtlety of the better players gradually came to the fore. The warning signs for Bolton came when Ferdinand headed Peter Beardsley's cross against the bar, and the home defence were powerless to prevent Lee restoring United's advantage fifteen minutes from time. Not for the first time Gillespie broke clear and his cross on the run was brilliantly headed in by Lee with perfect placement. Ferdinand, with his second goal down to sheer strength and persistence, wrapped up United's stylish win in the 83rd minute.

Bolton Wanderers
Branagan, Green, Bergsson, Fairclough (D. Lee 77), Stubbs, Phillips, McAteer, Patterson, Thompson (Sneekes 74), Coyle, De Freitas.

Newcastle United
Hislop, Barton, Peacock, Howey, Beresford, Gillespie, R. Lee, Clark, Ginola, Ferdinand, Beardsley.

Referee Mr. S. Lodge (Barnsley).

Darren Peacock

Played on this day

1947, Division 2.
Plymouth Argyle (h) 6-1   Att. 52,642
Bentley, Pearson, Shackleton (2), Walker, Wayman
1950, Division 1.
West Bromwich A. (h) 1-1   Att. 48,720
Brennan
1952, Division 1.
Sheffield Wednesday (a) 2-2 Att. 55,000
Hannah, G. Robledo
1958, Division 1.
Blackburn Rovers (h) 1-5   Att. 52,497
Opponent (og)
1961, Division 2.
Walsall (h) 1-0   Att. 33,821
Tuohy
1966, Division 1.
Sheffield United (a) 1-0   Att. 15,188
McGarry (pen)
1967, Division 1.
Chelsea (a) 1-1   Att. 32,677
Bennett
1969, Division 1.
Leeds United (a) 1-1   Att. 40,403
Scott
1972, Division 1.
West Bromwich A. (h) 1-1   Att. 29,695
Macdonald
1975, Division 1.
Leicester City(h) 3-0   Att. 36,084
Macdonald (2), Burns
1977, Division 1.
Liverpool (a) 0-2   Att. 48,267
1978, Division 2.
West Ham United (h) 0-3   Att. 27,167
1980, Division 2.
Bolton Wanderers (a) 0-4   Att. 11,835
1986, Division 1.
Liverpool (h) 0-2   Att. 33,306
1997, Premier League.
Newcastle 1   **Aston Villa 0**
Beresford 13   Att. 36,783
2000, Premier League.
Newcastle 3   **Derby County 2**
Cort 5   Strupar 32
Cordone 46   Burton 49
Glass 55   Att. 51,327

Playing record for this day is... 16 games, Won 6, Drawn 5, Lost 5, GF 22, GA 25. Today's success rate... 53.13%.

August 23

NEW RECRUITS INSPIRE UNITED VICTORY
Ten men hold out after Cort and Cordone goals

Daniel Cordone beats Poom to score the second goal.

Newcastle manager Bobby Robson was rewarded with an instant return on his £7.5 million pound summer investments at St. James' Park today against Derby. New-comers Carl Cort, a £7 million capture from Wimbledon, and Daniel Cordone, the Argentine secured on a £500,000 year-long loan deal, scored important early goals in each half as Derby County were finally seen off in a 3-2 thrilling win. But the 77th minute dismissal of Warren Barton on his 350th league appearance, somewhat soured events as Newcastle clinched their first victory of the season in front of over 51,000 fans, their highest attendance for over 24 years.

Stephen Glass, a 32nd minute substitute for Cort who went off with a hamstring injury, rifled in a 30-yard thunderbolt which seemingly put the game beyond Derby for whom Branko Strupar, in the 32nd minute, had wiped out Cort's fourth minute opening goal. However, the dismissal of Barton for a 'professional foul', denying Strupar a clear scoring opportunity, handed the initiative to Derby and Seth Johnson notched a second for the visitors seven minutes from the end. Newcastle were then left hanging on grimly to the points that should have been easily secured. This was a memorable game for United, one that was inspired by everyone connected with the club, the players responding magnificently to the huge Toon Army support. It was indeed a great day for Tyneside.

Cort's early strike proved decisive for Newcastle as he accepted a teasing cross from Nolberto Solano to drift away from his marker and deftly head the ball past Matt Poom and into the corner with pinpoint accuracy. Derby, however, then revealed their fighting qualities and it was no surprise when Strupar drove in right-footed from Johnson's superb long-range ball.

But, just as in the first half, Newcastle resumed the second half in explosive fashion. Cordone expertly controlling then hammering a shot from just inside the area which went low into the corner under Poom's despairing dive. Glass then hit Newcastle's third goal of the game only for Derby's commendable resilience to be rewarded with their second goal late on from Johnson.

Newcastle United
Given, Barton, Dabizas (sub Goma 44), Hughes, Domi, Solano (Charvet 78), Dyer, Speed, Cort (Glass 32), Shearer, Cordone.
Derby County
Poom, Blatsis (Morris 84), Elliott, Bragstad, Higginbotham, Eranio (Sturridge 66), Valakari, Powell, Johnson, Burton, Strupar.
Referee Mr. D. Gallagher (Banbury).

Birthdays

Peter Cartwright born today in 1957
Midfield 1979-1983, Apps 69 (11 subs). Goals 4.

August 24

FUL-HAMMERED
Newcastle triumph in 7-2 win over Cottagers

There were two players making their debut for Newcastle United in this Division One match at St. James' Park against Fulham. Duncan Neale was making his league debut, and Liam Tuohy was playing his first home match for his club. Also included in the team was Bobby Gilfillan, normally a reserve centre-forward.

With this in mind, all 23,498 who witnessed the match unfold were in for a treat. What is certain is that not one of them would have predicted the scoreline given the United team that was fielded.

The two teams started reasonably well, attacks coming strong on both goals. Fulham seemed stronger, and this view seemed justified when they took an early lead through a splendid goal from Key.

However, this seemed to kick-start Newcastle into gear, and they began their fight back immediately. Their pace and determination increased noticeably, and with 22 minutes on the clock the tables were about to turn.

It was Neale who managed to penetrate the Fulham defence and beat the keeper to bring the scores level, and just seven minutes later he had added his second to the score sheet.

On the stroke of thirty minutes Gilfillan netted his first, and Newcastle's third. Then the next one also fell to the reserve player three minutes later to bring Newcastle's tally to four.

Seconds before the half-time whistle blew Tuohy scored his first, Newcastle's fifth, and it seemed there was no stopping the inspired home side.

In the second half things were not so rushed. Newcastle were well ahead, and decided that there was no need to try quite so hard. Fulham were relieved, especially the defence and the goalkeeper, and they stepped up their efforts to snatch a goal back.

Their improved fighting spirit paid off when Doherty managed to save a little pride with a goal for the Londoners, but it wasn't enough to turn the match around.

It didn't stop them trying though, but nevertheless Newcastle went on to add another to the score-sheet, Tuohy again responsible for this one.

The final insult came from White who netted the final goal to bring the score to 7-2.

Newcastle United
Harvey, Keith, McMichael, Wright, Stokoe, Bell, Hughes, Neale, Gilfillan, White, Tuohy.
Fulham
Macedo, Cohen, Langley, Mullery, Lampe, Bentley, Key, Hill, Doherty, Haynes, Leggat.

Dick Keith

1949, Division 1.
Everton (a) 1-2   Att. 49,504
Lowrie
1955, Division 1.
Birmingham City (h) 2-2   Att. 34,473
Davies, Keeble
1957, Division 1.
West Bromwich A. (a) 1-2   Att. 31,410
White
1960, Division 1.
Fulham (h) 7-2   Att. 23,498
Gilfillan (2), Neale (2), Tuohy (2), White
1963, Division 2.
Derby County (h) 3-1   Att. 35,269
Taylor, Penman, McGarry
1964, Division 2.
Charlton Athletic (h) 1-1   Att. 32,805
Hilley
1968, Division 1.
Everton (h) 0-0   Att. 38,851
1974, Division 1.
Wolverhampton W. (a) 2-4   Att. 23,526
Tudor (2)
1985, Division 1.
Liverpool (h) 1-0   Att. 29,941
Reilly
1991, Division 2.
Watford (h) 2-2   Att. 22,440
Hunt, Clark
1994, Premier League.
Newcastle 4   Coventry City 0
Lee 21, 34
Watson 26
Cole 73   Att. 34,163
1996, Premier League.
Newcastle 1   Sheffield Wed. 2
Shearer 13 (pen)   Atherton 15
Whittingham 80
Att. 36,452
2002, Premier League.
Manchester City 1   Newcastle 0
Huckerby 36   Att. 34,776

Playing record for this day is... 13 games,
Won 4, Drawn 4, Lost 5, GF 25, GA 19.
Today's success rate... 46.15%.

Colin Taylor born today in 1940.
Winger 1963-1964, Apps 36. Goals 7.

Arnold Woollard born today in 1931.
Right-back 1952-1956, Apps 10. Goals 0.

Played on this day

1923, Division 1.
Arsenal (a) 4-1   Att. 45,000
Seymour, McDonald, Harris (2)

1928, Division 1.
Cardiff City (h) 1-1   Att. 35,000
Gallacher

1934, Division 2.
Nottingham Forest (a) 1-5   Att. 22,000
Lang

1945, Wartime.
Sheffield United (h) 6-0   Att. 31,391
Milburn, Clifton, Stubbins (3), Wayman

1948, Division 1.
Chelsea (h) 2-2   Att. 59,020
Lowrie, Milburn

1951, Division 1.
Manchester United (a) 1-2   Att. 48,000
G. Robledo

1954, Division 1.
West Bromwich A. (h) 3-0   Att. 58,548
Milburn, White (2)

1956, Division 1.
Sunderland (a) 2-1   Att. 51,032
Davies, Milburn

1958, Division 1.
Blackpool (a) 0-3   Att. 25,531

1962, Division 2.
Portsmouth (h) 1-1   Att. 35,214
Thomas

1965, Division 1.
West Bromwich A. (h) 0-1   Att. 43,901

1971, Division 1.
Huddersfield Town (h) 0-0   Att. 40,989

1973, Division 1.
West Ham United (a) 2-1   Att. 28,169
Macdonald (2)

1976, Division 1.
Tottenham Hotspur (a) 2-0   Att. 24,022
Burns, Barrowclough

1979, Division 2.
Charlton Athletic (a) 1-1   Att. 6,849
Cassidy

1984, Division 1.
Leicester City (a) 3-2   Att. 18,636
McCreery, Waddle, Carney

1986, Division 1.
Tottenham Hotspur (a) 1-1   Att. 25,381
Beardsley

1990, Division 2.
Plymouth Argyle (h) 2-0   Att. 23,984
Kristensen, Quinn

1992, Coca Cola Cup 1st round, 2nd leg.
Mansfield Town (a) 0-0   Att. 6,725
Newcastle won 2-1 on aggregate.

1993, Premier League.
Newcastle 1   **Everton 0**
Allen 18   Att. 34,833
*Newcastle's first Premiership League.
victory.*

1999, Premier League.
Newcastle 1   **Sunderland 2**
Dyer 28   Quinn 64
         Phillips 75
         Att. 36,420

Playing record for this day is... 21 games,
Won 9, Drawn 7, Lost 5, GF 34, GA 24.
Today's success rate... 59.52%.

Match of the Day from 1984

KEEPER HANDS UNITED LATE VICTORY

Season kicks off with a sound 3-2 win at Leicester

Poor old Leicester, missing five first-team regulars, they were constantly left panic stricken by a slick Newcastle side, and thus slumped to a needless home defeat. The Geordies had Leicester in total disarray for long periods of this game with City's keeper Mark Wallington, in particular, having a disastrous performance. His confidence was shattered by an already substantially weakened defence which made blunders galore throughout the game. There were very few bright spots for the home side and the suspended trio of Andy Peake, Kevin MacDonald, and Ian Wilson will certainly be welcome returnees to the next team selection sheet.

Newcastle got off to a flying start when the first of Leicester's defensive lapses won United a corner within the opening two minutes. From this kick, and the subsequent half clearance, the ball fell to Steve Carney who drove home fiercely into the right-hand corner of the net. Newcastle then, allowed their shaky opponents time to show some cohesive play by backing off when really a full scale onslaught would have produced a landslide win. Shortly before half-time, they paid the penalty for it, Steve Lynex crossed long and high from the right and Alan Smith rose well to knock the ball into the centre where Gary Lineker gobbled up the simple chance.

Undeterred, Newcastle took the lead again eight minutes into the second half through David McCreery and from this point should have added many more. But, goal poacher Lineker pulled Leicester back into the game when, once more, Newcastle's concentration wandered and slipped. The Foxes' striker was left unmarked from another set-up by Lynex, this time an inch-perfect corner, to ram the ball into United's net from no more than a yard off the goal-line. Now it seemed the game had drifted away from Newcastle, despite their early domination. But Wallington's horrendous blunder just ten minutes from time settled the game in their favour. A harmless cross from Kenny Wharton should have been collected comfortably but the keeper inexplicably let the ball slip between his hands and Waddle was fortunately on hand to nod into the empty net and give Newcastle a thoroughly deserved victory.

Leicester City
Wallington, Feeley, B.Smith, Banks, Rennie, O'Neil, Lynex, Lineker, A.Smith, Ramsey.

Newcastle United
Carr, Brown, Ryan, Carney, Roeder, Saunders, McDonald, Wharton, Waddle, Beardsley, McCreery.

Referee Mr. D. Reeves
(Uxbridge).

August 26

MAGPIES SNATCH WIN
Newcastle take win from confident Coventry

12,097 were at Highfield Road for this Division One clash against Coventry City tonight. It was to be a hard slog from the beginning, and both teams become frustrated at the lack of goals in the early period.

Newcastle had the upper hand during the first half, and outplayed Coventry by a mile. The home side lacked pace and heart, and seemed to be in slow motion for the most part. United, despite being the better side, failed to create enough scoring opportunities, and when they did manage to break through, they lacked the stamina to convert their chances into goals.

It was at half time that things changed. Coventry seemed to have a stern talking to in their dressing room, and came out for the second half revived and refreshed. Newcastle were surprised at the change in the home side, and certainly hadn't been expecting such a dramatic turnaround. They had to step up their game if they wanted to be in with a chance of a win, or even a draw.

The fight continued, as Coventry kept up the pressure on Thomas in the Newcastle goal. There were several attempts, notably from Dave Bennett and Mickey Adams, but they either missed their target or were saved from danger. However, it wasn't all one way. United had more than their share of attacks. Ogrizovic was made to work hard in the Coventry goal, as was the entire home defence.

Then, with nine minutes left on the clock the Sky Blues burst into the lead. Terry Gibson leapt at the chance to score, and managed to put the ball past Thomas to score the opening goal. The home crowd were convinced that there would be no chance for Newcastle to equalise, but how wrong they were.

Peter Beardsley sent a superb free kick over to George Reilly, who evaded the tackles of Kilcline and fought his way through to slam the ball into the net, levelling the scores with just three minutes to go. The home crowd were dumbfounded that Coventry had allowed the lead to slip. The travelling Newcastle supporters, on the other hand, were willing their team to grab another goal before the end and snatch the win.

Cyrille Regis had a ball blocked by Thomas, and soon afterwards Newcastle seized the opportunity to seize control.

In the final minute another long pass from Beardsley fell to Ian Stewart, who escaped a tackle by Borrows to send a low shot into the goal, giving Ogrizovic no chance to save.

That was it, for the full-time whistle blew soon afterwards, and United had snatched a dramatic late victory.

Coventry City
Ogrizovic, Borrows, Downs, Bowman, Kilcline, Peake, Bennett, Hibbitt, Regis, Gibson, Adams.
Newcaste United
Thomas, Anderson, Wharton, Gascoigne, Clarke, Roeder, McDonald, McCreery, Reilly, Beardsley, Stewart.
Referee Mr. R. Dilkes (Lancashire).

August 27

ayed on this day

Division 1.
Huddersfield Town (a) 2-1   Att. 25,000
McDonald (2)

Division 1.
Huddersfield Town (a) 3-1   Att. 24,500
Gallacher (3)

Division 1.
Bolton Wanderers (a) 2-2   Att. 15,000
Allen, J.R. Richardson

Division 2.
Blackpool (a) 1-4   Att. 25,000
J.R. Richardson

Division 2.
Plymouth Argyle (h) 2-1   Att. 38,000
Birkett, Clifton

Division 2.
Chesterfield (a) 1-0   Att. 15,000
Wayman

Division 1.
Wolverhampton W. (a) 1-2   Att. 50,922
Milburn

Division 1.
West Bromwich A. (a) 0-1   Att. 46,206

Division 1.
Preston North End (a) 3-4   Att. 39,583
Hannah, White (2)

Division 1.
Burnley (h) 0-1   Att. 35,485

Division 1.
Tottenham Hotspur (h) 0-2   Att. 35,780

Division 1.
Manchester United (a) 0-0   Att. 53,267

Division 1.
Sheffield United (a) 1-2   Att. 17,650
Keeley

Division 1.
Derby County (a) 2-3   Att. 27,585
Macdonald, Bruce

Division 1.
Middlesbrough (a) 0-2   Att. 26,712

League Cup 2nd round, 1st leg.
Bury (h) 3-2   Att. 9,073
Rafferty (2), Shoulder

Division 2.
Leeds United (a) 1-0   Att. 30,806
Anderson

Division 1.
Sheffield Wednesday (h) 2-1   Att. 29,673
Beardsley (pen), Wharton

Division 1.
Everton (a) 0-4   Att. 41,560

Division 2.
Middlesbrough (a) 0-3   Att. 16,970

Premier League.
Newcastle 5   Southampton 1
Watson 30, 37   Banger 52
Cole 40, 70, Lee 85   Att. 34,182
Newcastle top the Premier League for the first time and stay there for two months.

Premier League.
Sheffield Wed. 0   Newcastle 2
   Ginola 53
Att. 24,815   Beardsley 75
Newcastle go top of the Premier and stay there until March before finishing second.

Champions' League 2nd Qualifying round, 2nd leg.
Croatia Zagreb 2   Newcastle 2
D. Simic 59   Asprilla 44 (pen)
Cvitanovic 90   Ketsbaia 120
   Att. 34,000
A.E.T. Newcastle won 4-3 on aggregate.

ng record for this day is... 23 games,
9, Drawn 3, Lost 11, GF 33, GA 39.
's success rate... 45.65%.

UNITED STORM TO PREMIERSHIP SUMMIT
Venison inspires another superb United win over Saints

Comparisons with the great Liverpool teams of the 70s are being lavished on Newcastle United. It is no surprise, boss Kevin Keegan has rebuilt his side on the experience gained at Anfield in those glory days. There have been suggestions that Newcastle could become the Liverpool of the 1990s. Remember, though that Terry Venables' Crystal Palace were labelled the team of the 80s, and try to recall what happened to them. Newcastle appear more durable, however. One season wonders they are not. It is no accident they lead the Premiership already, having dispatched Leicester, Coventry and today Southampton all convincingly. Southampton fully deserved their drubbing. They defended awfully, made schoolboy errors, gave away some disgraceful goals, indeed it was all far too embarrassing, and these were the descriptions used by manager Alan Ball after the game.

Barry Venison

Newcastle started brightly enough, but passes frequently went into the spaces their forwards had just vacated. Their success was built on perseverance, and a willingness to keep going even when the job was done. Their great performance was also down to the inspired utility man Barry Venison. A right back, left back, centre back, and now central midfield, he calmly sprayed around magnificent passes as if he'd played there much longer than the three games he has done so far. Even his manager, Keegan, has been completely perplexed as to which is Venison's best position. Venison was the catalyst for Newcastle's superior forward play and the team did plenty of that to convince the Saints they were lucky to get away with conceding just five.

Southampton won their solitary corner in the 82nd minute, and apart from the lone Nicky Banger goal in the 52nd minute were rarely a threat all afternoon. Even Matt Le Tissier, scorer of two goals against the Magpies when they achieved the double over United last season, never really showed and this left Darren Peacock severely underemployed. Steve Watson, after switching from right wing to a central midfield position, put United ahead after half an hour's play and then added a second seven minutes later. Newcastle then had the game wrapped up after Andy Cole made it 3-0 five minutes before half-time. Although the Saints pulled one back after the interval you always expected Newcastle to add to the score at any time. This they did through Cole, again, on 70 minutes and Robert Lee who completed the 5-1 victory with a wonderful finish five minutes from time.

Newcastle will now wait for their real test against Arsenal in mid-September but the signs are looking good when considering this victory was achieved without the injured Peter Beardsley, Paul Bracewell, Lee Clark and Steve Howey. When they are fit Keegan will have a powerful, flexible squad capable of matching the best in the land, pity the likes of Southampton then.

Newcastle United
Srnicek, Hottiger, Peacock, Albert, Beresford, Watson, Venison, Lee, Sellars (Elliott 79), Fox (Mathie 60), Cole.

Southampton
Grobbelaar, Kenna, Hall (Whiston 74), Widdrington (Heaney h/t), Benali, Charlton, Le Tissier, Allen, Magilton, Maddison, Banger.

Referee Mr. D. Elleray (Harrow).

Birthdays

Dietmar Hamann born today in 1973.
Midfield 1998-1999, Apps 31(1 sub). Goals 5.

Sadly Missed

Colin Veitch died on this day in 1938, aged 57.
Midfield & Trainer 1899-1926, Apps 322. Goals 49.

Match of the Day from 1926

GALLACHER FOUR FORCES WIN

Newcastle gain victory over Villa by four goals to nil

Newcastle met Aston Villa today at St. James' Park in front of 36,000. United were obviously hoping for a win, as were the visitors side, but no one could have predicted the outcome.

Hughie Gallacher

Newcastle started the better team, and there were many attacks on the Villa goal. It took just thirteen minutes for Gallacher to open the scoring for United, his low shot speeding past the Villa keeper. It was a fitting end to some skilful play, and the goal was well deserved. Immediately Villa started to increase their efforts, and they went all out for attack. However, they failed to create chances, and as a result all their attempts came to nothing. Villa continued to battle for the rest of the second half, and for the most part there was no separating the play between the two sides. The difference lay in the forwards - Villa struggling to make an impact, while only the one line of defence kept out United, who attacked with skill and power.

From the start of the second half Newcastle were determined not to lose their lead. Their play was refreshing, and it was only a matter of time before another goal was added to the score-sheet. It arrived with 54 minutes on the clock, and it was Gallacher again who was the scorer. Villa keeper Spiers was left reeling after the powerful shot slammed into the net for his team's second goal.

Then fifteen minutes later Gallacher completed his hat-trick. Spiers came out of his goal, determined to stop the Newcastle striker, only to suffer the indignity of having Gallacher send the ball looping over the his shoulder and straight into the back of the net.

Villa knew it was hopeless after this and for the rest of the game there was something missing in their play. They tried as hard as they could to pull back a goal, but they just didn't have enough energy and heart for it to be of any use.

With a minute to go before the end of the game Gallacher sealed the win with his, and Newcastle's, fourth. The Villa defence was not up to the challenge of stopping the super striker, and he evaded them with ease to shoot past Spiers.

Newcaste United

Wilson, Chandler, Hudspeth, MacKenzie, Mooney, Gibson, Urwin, Clark, Gallacher, McDonald, Seymour.

Aston Villa

Spiers, Smart, Mort, Johnstone, Talbot, Muldoon, York, Norris, Nicholson, Capewell, Dorrell.

Played on this day

1920, Division 1.
West Bromwich A. (h) 1-1   Att. 61,080
Seymour
1922, Division 1.
Birmingham (a) 2-0   Att. 35,000
Harris (2)
1926, Division 1.
Aston Villa (h) 4-0   Att. 36,000
Gallacher (4)
1937, Division 2.
Manchester United (a) 0-3   Att. 30,000
1943, Wartime.
Bradford City (a) 1-2   Att. 3,038
Dixon
1948, Division 1.
Preston North End (h) 2-5   Att. 63,549
Donaldson, Stobbart
1954, Division 1.
Sheffield United (h) 1-2   Att. 52,341
R. Mitchell
1965, Division 1.
Sheffield Wednesday (a) 0-1 Att. 23,391
1968, Division 1.
Nottingham Forest (h) 1-1   Att. 34,613
B. Robson
1971, Division 1.
Coventry City (a) 0-1   Att. 22,638
1976, Division 1.
Bristol City (h) 0-0   Att. 31,775
1982, Division 2.
Queens Park Rangers (h) 1-0 Att. 35,718
Keegan
2002, Champions League 3rd qualifying round, 2nd leg.
Newcastle 4   Zeljeznicar 0
Dyer 23
LuaLua 37
Viana 74
Shearer 80   Att. 34,067
Newcastle won 5-0 on aggregate.

Playing record for this day is... 13 games, Won 4, Drawn 3, Lost 6, GF 17, GA 16. Today's success rate... 42.31%.

Birthdays

Jimmy Richardson died on this day in 1964, aged 53.
Midfield 1928-1934 & 1937-1938, Apps 164.
Goals 53.

Played on this day

1923, Division 1.
 Blackburn Rovers (h) 2-1   Att. 11,000
 Seymour, Harris
1925, Division 1.
 Bolton Wanderers (a) 2-2   Att. 28,675
 Cowan (2)
1928, Division 1.
 Burnley (h) 2-7   Att. 19,648
 Chalmers (2)
1931, Division 1.
 Liverpool (h) 0-1   Att. 30,000
1936, Division 2.
 Barnsley (h) 0-1   Att. 35,000
1942, Wartime.
 Bradford Park Ave. (h) 1-4   Att. 10,000
 Short
1951, Division 1.
 Bolton Wanderers (h) 0-1   Att. 49,587
1953, Division 1.
 Manchester United (a) 1-1   Att. 25,000
 Hannah
1956, Division 1.
 Cardiff City (h) 1-0   Att. 34,859
 Keeble
1959, Division 1.
 Manchester United (a) 2-3   Att. 53,257
 Allchurch, White
1961, Division 2.
 Walsall (a) 0-1   Att. 25,453
1962, Division 2.
 Middlesbrough (h) 6-1   Att. 41,550
 Thomas (3), Hilley, Hale (2)
1964, Division 2.
 Southampton (h) 2-1   Att. 24,531
 Thomas, Hilley
1970, Division 1.
 Blackpool (h) 1-2   Att. 34,041
 Hindson
1973, Division 1.
 Southampton (h) 0-1   Att. 25,351
1978, League Cup 2nd round.
 Watford (a) 1-2   Att. 15,346
 Pearson
1979, League Cup 2nd round, 1st leg.
 Sunderland (a) 2-2   Att. 27,746
 Davies, Cartwright
1981, Division 2.
 Watford (h) 0-1   Att. 19,244
1983, Division 2.
 Shrewsbury Town (h) 0-1   Att. 29,140
1987, Division 1.
 Nottingham Forest (h) 0-1   Att. 20,111
1992, Division 1.
 West Ham United (h) 2-0   Att. 29,855
 Peacock, Kelly
1993, Premier League.
 Newcastle 1   Blackburn Rovers 1
 Cole 61   Shearer 75
                    Att. 34,272

Playing record for this day is... 22 games,
Won 5, Drawn 4, Lost 13, GF 26, GA 35.
Today's success rate...31.82%.

Match of the Day from 1992

WEST HAMMERED

Newcastle secure win with two goals

This Division One match at St. James' Park was watched by 29,855, who all witnessed a game worthy of Premiership status. Players from both sides seemed comfortable with the pace of the game, and it was clear for Newcastle manager Kevin Keegan that, despite missing several players due to injury, his side was well equipped for a match of this standard.

It was quite surprising therefore, when there was such a long period in the first half without any goals. There were plenty of attempts on goal, but none were successful.

This was the story throughout the first forty minutes of play, desperate attempts to score from both sides meeting with failure. It was inevitable that eventually a goal would be scored, and indeed the first success came with three minutes to go before the half-time whistle. The ball ended up in the West Ham penalty area, and a huge scramble for possession followed. Steve Howey was fortunate to get his toe to the ball before the visitors' defenders, and he poked it into the net to put the home side a goal up. The goal was later awarded to Gavin Peacock as the ball had crossed the line before Howey had touched it.

The joy of the home fans was increased two minutes into injury time when the lead was doubled. Lee Clark hit his shot on target, but it slammed into West Ham keeper Miklosko and came out into the area again. David Kelly was perfectly placed to hit his shot straight past the keeper and into the back of the net.

Half time arrived with the entire West Ham side protesting at the second Newcastle goal, claiming that Clark was offside.

In the second period West Ham seemed to have taken a back seat. They were well beaten already, and didn't have the fight to make a comeback.

They attempted one shot in the 51st minute, but the ball was sent wide, and there was little to worry Newcastle keeper Tommy Wright.

West Ham's Julian Dicks was shown the yellow card on 65 minutes for a foul. Nine minutes later he foolishly elbowed Franz Carr, and started to trudge off to the dressing room. The referee called him back, but only to emphasise his role with the formality of showing Dicks the red card.

Newcastle United
Wright, Venison, Ranson, O'Brien, Scott, Howey, Carr, Peacock, Kelly, Clark, Sheedy.
West Ham United
Miklosko, Breaker, Dicks, Potts, Martin, Holmes (Small h/t) Bishop, Butler, M. Allen, C. Allen, Keen.
Referee Mr. W. Burns (Scarborough)

Gavin Peacock

Birthdays

Tommy Wright born today in 1963.
Goalkeeper 1988-1993, & 1999 Apps 87 (1 sub).
Jon Dahl Tomasson born today in 1976.
Forward 1997-1998, Apps 35 (8 subs). Goals 4.

Sadly Missed

Jimmy Gordon died on this day in 1996, aged 80.
Midfield 1935-1945, Apps 254. Goals 21.

Match of the Day from 1967

CHELSEA SWEPT AWAY

Newcastle give Chelsea first defeat of season in 5-1 win

Newcastle went into this game against Chelsea with high hopes of a win after a 6-0 defeat at Liverpool. Chelsea were missing Cooke and Thomson, and their absence seemed to affect the entire side. They lacked confidence from the outset, and Newcastle were the better team starting this Division One match at home in front of a crowd of 34,809.

Fittingly for United it was ex-Chelsea winger Tommy Robson who opened the scoring on eight minutes. This further reduced the Blues' confidence and they never fully recovered from the shock. Chelsea lacked the strength to maintain attacks on the Newcastle goal, although they occasionally produced short bursts of danger for goalkeeper Marshall.

Then just two minutes after the first goal, Wyn Davies flew high into the air to get his head to a ball which was sent in by Scott from a corner. He succeeded in nodding the ball into the net past Bonetti for Newcastle's second. Shortly afterwards the referee awarded a penalty to Chelsea when Marshall seemed to push Lloyd. It was Tambling who stood up to take the spot kick, and he neatly sent the ball into the back of the net to pull a goal back.

Newcastle soon regained control of the game, and Davies made several sustained attacks on the Chelsea goal, causing Bonetti to work extremely hard to keep the ball out. There were a number of scrambles in front of the goal, and the keeper was required to pull off two great saves to keep the score down.

Tommy Robson

Then after 34 minutes Davies hit a third goal for Newcastle, and Chelsea knew that they were out of the game.

The second half continued in similar fashion and when Tambling had a good chance at goal, he fluffed his shot and the ball went wide. In the 65th minute Bennett provided a good ball for Elliott, who managed to slam his shot straight past Bonetti for the fourth.

The final goal came courtesy of a blunder from Chelsea's Osgood. He attempted a back pass, but it lacked aim and power, and Bennett seized the opportunity to take advantage of this good fortune. His kick was perfectly timed, and it had no problems crossing the goal line for a fifth Newcastle goal with just nine minutes left to play. The rest of the match passed without incident and United ran out comfortable 5-1 winners.

Newcastle United

Marshall, Burton, Clark, Elliott, McGrath, Iley, Scott, Bennett, Davies, Hilley, T. Robson.

Chelsea

Bonetti, Hinton, Houseman, Hollins, Waldron, Harris, Boyle, Tambling, Osgood, Baldwin, Lloyd.

Played on this day

1919, Division 1.
Arsenal (a) 1-0   Att. 55,000
Henderson
1924, Division 1.
Huddersfield Town (h) 1-3   Att. 47,000
Cowan
1930, Division 1.
Sheffield Wednesday (a) 1-2 Att. 25,000
Cape
1939, Wartime.
Nottingham Forest (a) 0-2   Att. 15,000
1941, Wartime.
Bradford City (h) 1-1   Att. 6,046
Birkett
1947, Division 2.
Luton Town (a) 1-2   Att. 26,000
Bentley
1950, Division 1.
West Bromwich A. (a) 2-1   Att. 29,377
Milburn, Mitchell
1952, Division 1.
Tottenham Hotspur (h) 1-1   Att. 59,629
G. Robledo
1958, Division 1.
Everton (a) 2-0   Att. 36,602
McGuigan, Wright
1967, Division 1.
Chelsea (h) 5-1   Att. 34,809
Bennett, Davies (2), Elliott, T. Robson
1969, Division 1.
Arsenal (h) 3-1   Att. 47,208
Foggon, Davies, Robson
1972, Division 1.
Tottenham Hotspur (h) 0-1   Att. 27,912
1975, Division 1.
Manchester City (a) 0-4   Att. 31,875
1980, Division 2.
Luton Town (h) 2-1   Att. 13,175
Koenan, Hibbitt
1986, Division 1.
Luton Town (a) 0-0   Att. 9,254
1995, Premier League.
Newcastle 1   Middlesbrough 0
Ferdinand 68   Att. 36,483
1998, Premier League.
Newcastle 1   Liverpool 4
Guivarc'h 28   Owen 17, 18, 32
                     Berg 45
                         Att. 36,740
1999, Premier League.
Manchester U. 5   Newcastle 1
Cole 14, 46, 65, 71 Berg (og) 31
Giggs 80   Att. 55,190

Playing record for this day is... 18 games, Won 7, Drawn 3, Lost 8, GF 23, GA 29. Today's success rate... 47.22%.

Birthdays

Aidan McCaffery born today in 1957.
Centre-half 1975-1978, Apps 71 (3 subs). Goals 5.

Peter Withe born today in 1951.
Centre-forward 1978-1980, Apps 83. Goals 27.

August 31

Division 1.
Everton (h) 3-0   Att. 40,000
Harris, Paton (2)
Division 1.
Manchester United (h) 4-1   Att. 45,000
Gallacher (3), McDonald
Division 1.
Middlesbrough (h) 5-1   Att. 35,000
Lang, McMenemy (2), Allen, Weaver (pen)
Division 2.
Bradford Park Ave. (h) 3-3   Att. 28,000
Cairns, McMenemy, Pearson
Division 2.
West Ham United (a) 2-0   Att. 23,000
McMenemy, Pearson
Division 2.
Luton Town (a) 1-2   Att. 17,689
Clifton
Wartime.
Bradford Park Ave. (h) 0-2.   Att. 5,000
Division 2.
Millwall (a) 4-1   Att. 39,187
Bentley (2), Milburn, Stubbins
Division 1.
Everton (h) 4-0   Att. 42,689
Milburn, Mitchell, G. Robledo, Walker
Division 1.
Birmingham City (a) 1-3   Att. 38,690
White
Division 1.
Tottenham Hotspur (h) 3-1   Att. 37,742
Eastham, Keeble, R. Mitchell
Division 1.
Fulham (a) 3-4   Att. 21,361
Allchurch, Hughes, Woods
Division 2.
Plymouth Argyle (a) 4-3   Att. 13,960
Taylor, Thomas (3)
Division 1.
Sheffield United (h) 1-0   Att. 21,876
Opponent (og)
Division 1.
Sunderland (a) 1-1   Att. 49,807
B. Robson
Division 1.
West Ham United (h) 2-0   Att. 30,782
Tudor, Macdonald
League Cup 2nd round.
Millwall (h) 0-2   Att. 21,861
Division 1.
Queens Park Rangers (h) 3-1 Att. 25,219
Beardsley (pen), Reilly, McDonald
Division 2.
Bristol Rovers (a) 2-1   Att. 6,334
O'Brien, Quinn
Premier League.

Ipswich Town 1	Newcastle 1
Kiwomya 77	Cole 47

Att. 19,126
Premier League.

West Ham 1	Newcastle 3
Hutchinson 87 (pen)	Potts (og) 32,
	Lee 35
	Mathie 90

Att. 18,580

record for this day is... 21 games,
, Drawn 3, Lost 5, GF 50, GA 28.
success rate... 69.05%.

NEWCASTLE BACK IN POLE POSITION

Hammers beaten, United head race for the Premiership

Newcastle continued their compelling start to the 1994/95 season by regaining top spot in the Premiership after an easy win at Upton Park today. In retaking pole position, which they had lost to Nottingham Forest, United collected their fourth successive victory. They were also able to record their best start to a season in the top flight for almost a century. Not since 1908 have Newcastle begun so positively and the manner in which they sauntered to their latest success will raise eyebrows amongst all the other realistic title contenders. In contrast, West Ham look like a side with the world on their shoulders. Goals are not something that come easily to them and though they ended their drought with a late penalty from debutant Don Hutchinson the odds are already stacked against them. Newcastle owed their success to Andy Cole, who spent the game providing rather than taking goal scoring opportunities, and now must be genuinely considered by coach Terry Venables for the England squad. Cole came desperately close to his first goal today but in truth it must officially be recognised as an own goal, but this must not cloud another highly impressive individual display. Sadly, one player who did attract the attention of Venables for the forthcoming international with the United States, Robert Lee, may not be fit to win his cap after limping out of this game after he scored United's second goal.

West Ham, searching for their first victory at Upton Park since last April, began with purpose but their options in attack seemed worryingly limited. Hutchinson, Hammers £1.5 million club record capture from Liverpool, laboured alone in the first half although midfielder Mike Marsh moved forward later on in the game. The attacking options at the other end were almost embarrassing. Cole showed articulate skills to lob a shot inches over the crossbar and then Lee's tenacity almost brought the first goal, his attempt flying across an unguarded target. The opener was eventually delivered in the 32nd minute when Cole won the ball from Alvin Martin, and although forced to the by-line, he shot from the acutest of angles and the ball spun in off Steve Potts on the line. Within three minutes Newcastle, who had scored twelve goals in their previous three games, had increased their lead. The move began ten yards inside their own half, Barry Venison and John Beresford combining. Then Cole cut inside before slipping the ball towards goal and Lee left his marker to slide home.

In the second half West Ham tried desperately to get forward with the introduction of substitute forward Steve Jones, but still they offered little. Newcastle, had they been greedy, could have eclipsed their latest win against Southampton 5-1; instead they allowed West Ham to dictate play. The home side's approach work was not bad, but too often they took one step forward, two steps back. Jones hit the crossbar and then West Ham did score, referee Brian Hill awarding them an 88th minute penalty when Jones' cross hit Beresford's hand. Hutchinson converted the spot-kick, but Newcastle responded by a quick breakaway which led to their third goal. Again Cole was the architect, his leggy run down the right leaving West Ham square. He moved inside and unselfishly laid the ball to Alex Mathie, who tapped in a simple goal to complete the 3-1 away victory.

West Ham United
Miklosko, Breaker, Martin, Potts, Burrows, Allen, Moncur, Butler, Holmes (Jones h/t), Hutchinson, Marsh.
Newcastle United
Srnicek, Hottiger, Peacock, Albert, Beresford, Watson, Lee (Elliott 59 mins), Venison, Sellars, Cole, Mathie.
Referee Mr. B. Hill (Leicester).

Birthdays

Harry Heward born today in 1910.
Midfield 1932-1934, Apps 5. Goals 0.
Alan Kennedy born today in 1954.
Left-back 1971-1978, Apps 216 (6 subs). Goals 10.
Niki Papavasiliou born today in 1970.
Midfield 1993-1994, Apps 7. Goals 0.

Sadly Missed

Jimmy Naylor died on this day in 1983, aged 82.
Midfield 1930-1932, Apps 32. Goals 0.

September

September 1

Played on this day

1894, Division 2.
Darwen (a) 0-5   Att. 5,000
1900, Division 1.
Nottingham Forest (h) 0-0   Att. 20,000
1906, Division 1.
Sunderland (h) 4-2   Att. 56,375
Appleyard, Howie, Rutherford (2)
1909, Division 1.
Bolton Wanderers (h) 1-0   Att. 25,000
Rutherford
1910, Division 1.
Sunderland (a) 1-2   Att. 30,000
Shepherd (pen)
1913, Division 1.
Blackburn Rovers (a) 0-3   Att. 20,000
1920, Division 1.
Everton(a) 1-3   Att. 45,000
Harris
1923, Division 1.
Arsenal (h) 1-0   Att. 40,000
Aitken
1924, Division 1.
Blackburn Rovers (a) 1-1   Att. 30,000
Seymour
1926, Division 1.
Burnley (h) 1-5   Att. 35,000
Hudspeth (pen)
1928, Division 1.
Sheffield United (a) 1-3   Att. 30,000
Chalmers
1934, Division 2.
Brentford (h) 2-5   Att. 24,000
Gallantree, Kelly
1937, Division 2.
Barnsley (h) 0-1   Att. 19,065
1945, Wartime.
Sheffield United (a) 0-3   Att. 15,000
1948, Division 1.
Chelsea (a) 3-2   Att. 43,840
Gibson, Milburn, Thompson
1951, Division 1.
Tottenham Hotspur (h) 7-2   Att. 52,541
Mitchell (2), G. Robledo (3), Taylor,
Walker
1954, Division 1.
West Bromwich A. (a) 2-4   Att. 36,414
Hannah, Scoular
1956, Division 1.
Sheffield Wednesday (a) 0-4   Att. 36,270
1962, Division 2.
Preston North End (a) 1-2   Att. 13,884
Hale
1964, Division 2.
Charlton Athletic (a) 1-0   Att. 22,939
Robson
1965, Division 1.
West Bromwich A. (a) 2-1   Att. 22,043
Hilley, McGarry
1971, Division 1.
Leeds United (a) 1-5   Att. 18,623
Opponent (og)
Played at Hillsborough, Sheffield.
1973, Division 1.
Arsenal (h) 1-1   Att. 30,665
McDermott
1976, League Cup 2nd round.
Gillingham (a) 2-1   Att. 11,203
Cassidy, Cannell

continued opposite

Match of the Day from 1951

CHAMPIONS HIT BY MAGNIFICENT SEVEN
Robledo nets hat-trick in superb Newcastle win

Rarely do reigning League Champions get walloped by seven goals, imagine a Manchester United or Arsenal of today getting thrashed by a score of seven! But that's exactly what Newcastle did to the great Spurs team of the fifties, one of the best post-war sides and League title winners just four months previous. This was some special performance and United achieved it without one of their own influential players Jackie Milburn, ruled out through injury.

A crowd of 52,541 greeted the teams at a sun-drenched St. James' Park, hardly expecting anything the game to unfold as it did in the next ninety minutes. From the kick off Newcastle sprung quickly into action dominating the early exchanges and they were a goal in front after just four minutes. The goal was a well taken solo effort from United left-winger Bobby Mitchell who outpaced the Spurs full-back Alf Ramsey, dribbling all the way into the penalty area before slipping the ball wide of Ditchburn and into the bottom corner of the net. Soon after, United's right-winger Tommy Walker blasted home from the edge of the box, beating the diving Ditchburn and Ramsey's despairing jump on the goal line to smash into the roof of the net. United were 2-0 up. With just seventeen minutes gone it was three, this time following an error by Ditchburn who dropped the ball from a Mitchell cross and George Robledo dashed in to poke the ball over the line from a couple of yards out. United were on fire and the normally reliable Ramsey was having a torrid time against man-of-the-match Mitchell who caused havoc in the Spurs defence all afternoon. With half-time approaching the home side went 4-0 up when a fantastic through ball from George Hannah put Mitchell away on his own and he made no mistake with the one-on-one with the keeper. Then on a rare Spurs attack Scarth pulled a goal back for the visitors, right on the half-time whistle.

Tottenham further reduced the deficit immediately after the break when Bennett scored from a spectacular overhead kick after good work from Medley. Rather than subdue the Magpies though, the goal spurred on United, urged on by a noisy Gallowgate crowd who roared their team forward. Try as they might however, Newcastle did not add to the score until the 75th minute, and this led to two more goals soon after. Robledo got the fifth, then completed his hat-trick with United's sixth five minutes later. Newcastle's seventh goal came right at the death, following enormous pressure on the Spurs goal, the ball fell nicely for Ernie Taylor to net his first goal of the season to complete a memorable 7-2 win.

The ecstatic home crowd left the ground thrilled at the magnificent result. Little did they know that on their next return to St. James' Park they were in for another seven-goal victory; Burnley this time the victims by 7-1. (See September 15.)

Newcastle United
Simpson, Cowell, McMichael, Harvey, Brennan, Crowe, Walker, Taylor, G.Robledo, Hannah, Mitchell.
Tottenham Hotspur
Ditchburn, Ramsay, Willis, Brittan, Nicholson, Burgess, Scarth, Bennett, McLellan, Murphy, Medley.
Referee Mr. A.W. Leuty (Leeds).

Birthdays

Glenn Keeley born today in 1954. Centre-half 1974-1976, Apps 73 (1 sub). Goals 4.

Ruud Gullit born today in 1962. Manager 1998-99.

September 1

Played on this day

1979, Division 2.
Chelsea (h) 2-1   Att. 25,047
Withe (2)

1982, Division 2.
Blackburn Rovers (a) 2-1   Att. 14,421
Keegan, Martin

1984, Division 1.
Aston Villa (h) 3-0   Att. 31,591
Beardsley, Waddle (2)
Under the new 3 points for a win rule for the season, Newcastle go top of Division One with 9 points from three games. They held top spot for just a week and eventually finished the season in 14th place.

1987, Division 1.
Norwich City (a) 1-1   Att. 16,636
P. Jackson

1990, Division 2.
Blackburn Rovers (a) 1-0   Att. 11,329
O'Brien

Playing record for this day is... 29 games, Won 12, Drawn 4, Lost 13, GF 42, GA 58. Today's success rate... 48.28%.

South American star George Robledo with the Chilean Ambassador, Manuel Bianchi

Division 2.
Woolwich Arsenal (a) 2-2   Att. 6,000
Crate, Sorley
In Newcastle United's first league fixture Tom Crate scores United's first ever league goal. This fixture is also the first Football League game played in London.
Division 1.
West Bromwich A. (a) 1-1   Att. 4,000
Peddie (pen)
Division 1.
Aston Villa (h) 1-1   Att. 8,000
Templeton
Division 1.
Sunderland (a) 2-3   Att. 30,000
Orr, Howie
Division 1.
Bradford City (h) 1-0   Att. 26,000
Veitch
Division 1.
Bolton Wanderers (a) 2-0   Att. 30,000
Stewart (2)
Division 1.
Bolton Wanderers (a) 2-1   Att. 30,000
McDonald, Rutherford
Division 1.
West Bromwich A. (h) 1-2   Att. 15,000
Hibbert
Division 1.
Everton (a) 2-3   Att. 35,000
Harris, McDonald
Division 1.
Birmingham (a) 1-4   Att. 20,000
Boyd
Division 1.
Leeds United (a) 0-3   Att. 18,000
Wartime.
Swansea Town (h) 8-1   Att. 14,000
Bowden (3), Pearson (2),
Hamilton, Scott, Cairns
Wartime.
Gateshead (h) 3-1   Att. 4,000
Stubbins, Porter, Carr
Division 1.
Portsmouth (a) 0-0   Att. 43,244
Division 1.
Liverpool (h) 4-0   Att. 48,439
Keeble, Milburn, Mitchell (2)
Division 1.
Birmingham City (h) 1-0   Att. 35,395
White
Division 2.
Plymouth Argyle (h) 0-2   Att. 28,235
Division 1.
Stoke City (h) 1-1   Att. 38,924
Davies
League Cup 2nd round.
Southport (a) 2-0   Att. 8,521
B. Robson (pen), Sinclair
League Cup 2nd round.
Sheffield United (a) 0-2   Att. 22,101
Division 1.
West Bromwich A. (a) 2-1   Att. 25,183
Dyson, Opponent (og)
Division 1.
Crystal Palace (a) 1-2   Att. 21,749
Tudor
Division 2.
Cambridge United (a) 0-0   Att. 8,174
League Cup 2nd round, 2nd leg.
Bury (a) 0-1....Att. 4,348
The tie finished 3-3 on aggregate, Bury went through on the away goals rule.

continued opposite

September 2

Match of the Day from 1970

OWN GOAL IS LATE BONUS FOR UNITED

First away victory of the season at the Hawthorns

An own goal by the unfortunate Ray Wilson and two magnificent saves from Newcastle's Northern Ireland international keeper Willie McFaul earnt the Magpies their first away win of the season today at the Hawthorns. Albion, with their new £30,000 signing from Carlisle George McVitie, had taken the lead through Jeff Astle but United fought back bravely against the odds thanks to man-of-the-match McFaul's second-half heroics. After Keith Dyson had put the scores level United held the home side at bay and, on the balance of play, they were lucky to get the defensive mix up late on which secured their win, Albion's first defeat at home this season.

McVitie took just fifteen minutes to show exactly why Albion manager Alan Ashman was prepared to fork out such a large transfer fee for his services. He had spent most of the game as a lone stranger as Albion, usually without a winger, struggled to get the ball out to him. But, tired of this inactivity, McVitie picked up a clearance from his defence, accelerated past Frank Clark and Bobby Moncur to cross perfectly for the well placed Astle to thump a powerful header past McFaul. This was Albion's first real threat of the game. They had been pegged well back as United tried to improve their dreadful away record. After half an hour they got the goal which thus far had eluded them all season outside of St. James' Park. A left wing corner from Dave Young, brought into the side ostensibly as a defender, was headed across goal by Wyn Davies who had been lurking at the far post. Dyson, who had missed a similar chance just three minutes before, this time rushed in to plant the ball surely past Jim Cumbes and into the back of the net.

Albion were the better starters in the second half and the ever dangerous pair of McVitie and Astle almost put the home side ahead for a second time, seven minutes after the restart. The chance came after McFaul leapt acrobatically to touch the ball over from Bobby Hope's stinging 25-yard drive. Astle, from the corner, did well to shake off Ollie Burton and reach McVitie's cross, but from close range he somehow cleared the bar with his header. Albion poured forward, Hope was just wide with another effort from distance, Clark got in the way of an on-target shot from McVitie and McFaul brought of another superb save to stop Merrick's header from point-blank range. Again in the 70th minute, McFaul saved brilliantly to stop Astle's placed shot by pushing the ball round the post with his fingertips. With United holding on grimly to a point, then came the huge bonus of a winner. Wilson just beating Tommy Gibb to a long ball, played out from the Albion defence, in the penalty area and as Gibb put him under pressure, Wilson could only knock it back to Cumbes. But the West Brom keeper had already come off his line to meet the bouncing ball and the slight deflection made him slip and unable to move quickly enough to stop the ball sailing over his right hand and into the empty net behind him. With little time left, Albion were crushed. For United and their loyal followers it was a great, and somewhat surprising victory.

Birthdays

Paul Cannell born today in 1953.
Forward 1972-1978, Apps 70 (3 subs). Goals 20.

Bob McKay born today in 1900.
Midfield 1926-1928, Apps 66. Goals 23.

Played on this day

1989, Division 2.
    Oldham Athletic (h) 2-1   Att. 21,09*
    Quinn (2, 1 pen)
1992, Division 1.
    Luton Town (h) 2-0   Att. 27,05*
    Clark, Kelly
2002, Premier League.
    Liverpool 2   **Newcastle 2**
    Hamann 53   Speed 80
    Owen 73 (pen)   Shearer 88
                           Att. 43,2

Playing record for this day is... 27 games,
Won 11, Drawn 7, Lost 9, GF 43, GA 34.
Today's success rate... 53.70%.

West Bromwich Albion

Cumbes, Hughes, Wilson, Merrick, Talbut, Kaye, McVitie, Brown, Astle, Suggett, Hope.

Newcastle United

McFaul, Craig, Clark, Gibb, Burton, Moncur, Dyson, Robson, Davies, Smith, Young.

RD ALBION ER NEWS

SEASON 1969-70 VOLUME 62 NUMBER 4 OFFICIAL MATCHDAY MAGAZINE PRICE 1/– (WITH FOOTBALL LEAGUE REVIEW 1/6)

West Bromwich Albion v Newcastle

Football League Division One/Wednesday September 2/70

Honours League Champions 1920, Runners-up 1925, 1954. F.A. Cup Winners 1888, 1892, 1931, 1954, 1968. League Cup Winners 1966. W. B. Albion have appeared in 17 Semi-Finals and 10 Finals of the F.A. Challenge Cup—a current record aggregate number of appearances.
President Major H. Wilson Keys M C, TD.   Vice-Presidents S. R. Shephard J P,   J. Gordon
Board of Directors J. W. Gaunt Chairman,   F. A. Millichip Vice-Chairman,   T. W. Glidden
L. Prichards T. H. Silk   Secretary Alan Everiss J P.   Manager Alan Ashman
               Promotions Manager Les Thorley   Publicity G. Bartram
Medical Officers J. H. Kirkham F R C S, Dr R. O. Rimmer M B, Ch B, Dr F. Bottomley M B, Ch B

Played on this day

1898, Division 1.
Wolverhampton W. (h) 2-4....Att. 20,000
Peddie (2)
The Magpies' first game in Division One, a tough away fixture against the team who finished third last season. After being 3-0 down at half time Newcastle make a spirited come back in the second half but still go down 4-2 at full time.

1904, Division 1.
Woolwich Arsenal (h) 3-0   Att. 21,897
Orr (2), Rutherford

1906, Division 1.
Sheffield Wednesday (a) 2-2   Att. 8,000
Appleyard (2)

1910, Division 1.
Bristol City (h) 0-1   Att. 26,000

1919, Division 1.
West Bromwich A. (h) 0-2   Att. 50,000

1921, Division 1.
Huddersfield Town (h) 1-2   Att. 50,000
McDonald

1927, Division 1.
Tottenham Hotspur (h) 4-1   Att. 40,000
Seymour (2) McDonald(pen), Gallacher

1930, Division 1.
Chelsea (h) 1-0   Att. 68,386
Cape
Newcastle's record attendance to date on the return of Hughie Gallacher.

1932, Division 1.
Liverpool (h) 4-3   Att. 28,000
Allen, Lang, McMenemy, Opponent (og)

1938, Division 2.
Sheffield United (a) 0-0   Att. 30,000

1947, Division 2.
Chesterfield (h) 2-3   Att. 58,334
Bentley, Milburn

1949, Division 1.
Aston Villa (h) 3-2   Att. 57,669
Milburn (3, 1 pen)

1955, Division 1.
Burnley (h) 3-1   Att. 41,272
Davies, Mitchell, Scoular

1958, Division 1.
Blackpool (h) 1-0   Att. 44,979
White

1960, Division 1.
Nottingham Forest (a) 2-0   Att. 23,806
Gibson, Opponent (og)

1966, Division 1.
Manchester United (a) 2-3   Att. 44,448
Craig, McGarry

1977, Division 1.
West Ham United (h) 2-3   Att. 26,942
Burns, Cassidy

1983, Division 2.
Oldham Athletic (h) 3-0   Att. 22,573
Waddle, McDermott, Mills

1986, Division 1.
Queens Park Rangers (h) 0-2 Att. 23,080

1988, Division 1.
Tottenham Hotspur (h) 2-2 Att. 33,508
Thorn, D. Jackson

Playing record for this day is... 20 games, Won 9, Drawn 3, Lost 8, GF 37, GA 31. Today's success rate... 52.50%.

September 3

Match of the Day from 1930

RECORD ATTENDANCE FOR THE RETURNING HERO

68,386 pack St. James' Park for Gallacher and Chelsea

When Hughie Gallacher was sold to London club Chelsea in the summer of 1930 controversy raged on Tyneside. Despite the record fee received for their Scottish international centre-forward almost every United fan was devastated to lose their star player who had netted 143 goals in 174 games for the Magpies during his five-year career at Newcastle. This game therefore had been eagerly awaited since the fixtures were produced soon after his sudden departure. United fans turned out in force to show their appreciation for his efforts, to get to the ground which was full within an hour of the turnstiles opening up. As many as 10,000 were shut outside by kick off and men clambered onto the stand roof to gain any remote glimpse of the action they could. Along Leazes Terrace the treetops were filling up with desperate fans clinging onto the smallest branches possible, if the vantage point had a view it was quickly snapped up, no matter what the danger it presented. This was by far the biggest midweek crowd for a match anywhere in Britain at the time.

Gallacher emerged from the tunnel with his Chelsea team-mates to a fantastic roar never before, and certainly never since repeated, he said afterwards, "The reception I got today was the highlight of my career." A real tribute to the fanatical Geordie following.

Chelsea's 'all star' team started the better and the home defence was soon under pressure McInroy making an important early save to deny Pearson. Thankfully United's defence held firm, Hill marshalling a subdued Gallacher, who had a quiet game. The former United forward was allowed one chance moments before half-time but again the effort was brilliantly saved by McInroy.

The real stars of the game were the Magpies' youngsters of Starling and Wilkinson, who was by far the best player on the pitch, bar the busy home goalkeeper. With the visitors still well on top in the second half, United were reduced to ten men when full-back Jimmy Nelson was carried off with a serious knee injury. This unfortunate luck spurred Newcastle on and they began to mount attacks on the Chelsea goal. The deadlock was eventually broken on 76 minutes when a desperate long clearance from Fairhurst was latched onto by Wilkinson. After skipping clear of his full-back he waited for assistance before lobbing the ball into the box; there Jackie Cape raced in to head United into a 1-0 lead. Despite intense Chelsea pressure for the final fourteen minutes United held firm and bagged both points. At the final whistle the crowd again showed a last touching tribute to Gallacher, and hailed the new star in the making, Jack Wilkinson.

Newcastle United
McInroy, Nelson, Fairhurst, Mathison, Hill, Naylor, Cape, Starling, Lindsay, McDonald, Wilkinson.
Chelsea
Millington, Smith, Law, Russell, Townrow, Bishop, Crawford, Cheyne, Gallacher, Miller, Pearson.

Jackie Cape.

Sadly Missed

Jack Peart died on this day in 1948, aged 59
Forward 1912-1913, Apps 17. Goals 6.

September 4

Match of the Day from 1996

DERBY DAY JOY FOR UNITED
Last derby at Roker won by the cream of Tyneside

It took the prospect of real humiliation in the final Tyne-Wear Roker Park derby to stir Newcastle from their early-season slumber. Trailing to Martin Scott's penalty, and initially outplayed, Newcastle came to life only after the break, settling this lively long awaited affair with goals from Peter Beardsley and Les Ferdinand. Sunderland move grounds next season where surely visiting supporters will be allowed to go. The nonsense in refusing Newcastle tickets to today's spectacle was exposed the moment Beardsley equalised. Inevitably, The Toon Army, having somehow acquired tickets, voiced their joy, leading to minor skirmishes quickly dealt with by police and stewards. Back on Tyneside, thousands watched in a fantastic party atmosphere in a city centre arena. Their relief will have been palpable, going a goal down is one thing, losing to Sunderland is a different kettle of fish altogether.

Newcastle's recovery was rooted in the half-time exhortations from Kevin Keegan, and the Peter Beardsley-David Batty combination leading the way on the field, helped by the creativity of David Ginola. Yet for some time, United looked so troubled by Sunderland, led by the impressive and eager Steve Agnew. Within twenty minutes, Agnew got his reward, tricking Robbie Elliott into conceding a penalty. The build up was awesome and a model of how to unhinge the Newcastle rearguard. Turning defence into attack with one pass, Richard Ord found Paul Stewart who knocked the ball into Kevin Ball with his chest, and he found Agnew with Newcastle now totally exposed. Racing into the area Elliott applied the lightest of trips to send the winger sprawling, and Scott's well placed penalty flew past Pavel Srnicek before he'd even flinched a muscle. Sunderland were now in command and almost increased their lead in the 23rd minute, Micheal Gray's blocked tackle spun back to Stewart whose first-time hooked shot was touched onto the post by the diving Srnicek. At the break United left for the dressing rooms relieved to still be in the game but dreading the half-time pep talk no doubt.

New half, totally new story. With Sunderland unable to maintain their punishing pace Newcastle were soon back on level terms. Ferdinand's excellent run from left to right took him past three Sunderland players, the surge indicative of United's new hunger. Then, as Beardsley darted into the box, Ferdinand crossed back in for his nippy team-mate to angle his header past the flat-footed Tony Coton. Just seven minutes into the second half Newcastle were finally buzzing, even outhustling the hustlers from Wearside, and on Sunderland's renowned Roker Park too. Alan Shearer, so often chasing down cul-de-sacs, forced a 63rd minute corner through sheer persistence which brought the victory. Ginola, running the gauntlet of jeers from the home crowd, walked coolly over to take the corner kick which was driven with renewed vigour and accuracy. In came Ferdinand all muscle, bravery and determination to thump his header past the bewildered looking Coton. Sunderland were done for, again!

Sunderland
Coton, Kubicki, Ord, Melville, Scott, Agnew (Rae 76), Bracewell, Ball, Gray, Quinn, Stewart (Russell 74).
Newcastle United
Srnicek, Watson, Howey, Peacock, Elliott, Lee, Beardsley, Batty, Ginola, Ferdinand (Clark 76), Shearer.
Referee Mr. J. Winter (Middlesbrough).

Birthdays

John Beresford born today in 1966.
Left-back 1992-1998, Apps 232 (5 subs). Goals 8.
George Dalton born today in 1941.
Midfield/Left-back 1958-1967, Apps 94. Goals 2.
Jimmy Gibson born today in 1940.
Centre-forward 1959-1961, Apps 2. Goals 1.

Sadly Missed

James Raine died on this day in 1928, aged 42.
Winger 1905-1906, Apps 4. Goals 1.

Played on this day

1897, Division 2.
Woolwich Arsenal (h) 4-1   Att. 10,000
Wardrope (3), Campbell
1907, Division 1.
Notts County (h) 1-1   Att. 25,000
Rutherford
1909, Division 1.
Blackburn Rovers (a) 0-2   Att. 16,000
1920, Division 1.
West Bromwich A. (a) 0-0   Att. 35,000
1926, Division 1.
Bolton Wanderers (a) 1-2   Att. 25,049
Seymour
1929, Division 1.
Blackburn Rovers (h) 5-1   Att. 40,000
Gallacher, Lang, J.R. Richardson, Urwin, McDonald
1935, Division 2.
Barnsley (h) 3-0   Att. 21,000
Cairns (2), Pearson
1937, Division 2.
Sheffield United (h) 6-0   Att. 22,000
Pearson (2), Livingstone (2), Imrie (pen), Gordon
1943, Wartime.
Bradford City (h) 3-2   Att. 12,000
Stubbins, Milburn, Dixon
1948, Division 1.
Burnley (a) 3-0   Att. 32,947
Donaldson (2), Milburn
1954, Division 1.
Preston North End(a) 3-3   Att. 36,600
Hannah, Milburn, White
1957, Division 1.
Sheffield Wednesday (a) 0-1 Att. 23,060
1962, Division 2.
Scunthorpe United (a) 1-2   Att. 13,953
Kerray
1963, Division 2.
Middlesbrough (h) 2-0   Att. 56,918
Penman, McGarry
1965, Division 1.
Northampton Town (h) 2-0 Att. 28,051
Suddick, Cummings
1971, Division 1.
West Ham United (h) 2-2   Att. 31,972
Tudor, Cassidy
1973, Division 1.
Ipswich Town (a) 3-1   Att. 21,696
Robson, Cassidy, Smith
1976, Division 1.
Middlesbrough (a) 0-1   Att. 26,000
1982, Division 2.
Bolton Wanderers(a) 1-3   Att. 17,707
Keegan (pen)
1984, Division 1.
Arsenal (a) 0-2   Att. 37,078
1985, Division 1.
Manchester United (a) 0-3 Att. 51,102
1991, Division 2.
Plymouth Argyle (h) 2-2   Att. 19,543
Carr, Quinn
1996, Premier League.
Sunderland 1   Newcastle 2
Scott 19 (pen)   Beardsley 52
                      Ferdinand 62
                              Att. 22,037

Playing record for this day is... 23 games, Won 10, Drawn 5, Lost 8, GF 44, GA 30.
Today's success rate... 54.35%.

...yed on this day

Division 2.
Small Heath (a) 1-3   Att. 4,000
Thompson
Division 1.
West Bromwich A. (a) 2-1   Att. 15,000
Appleyard, Rutherford
Division 1.
Leicester Fosse (h) 2-0   Att. 32,000
Howie, Veitch
Division 1.
Everton (h) 0-1   Att. 12,000
Division 1.
Notts County (h) 6-3   Att. 35,000
Mitchell, McDonald, N. Harris, Cowan,
Opponents (2 ogs)
Division 1.
Derby County (a) 1-1   Att. 21,000
Seymour
Division 1.
Grimsby Town (a) 2-1   Att. 12,000
Boyd, J.R. Richardson
Division 2.
Sheffield United (a) 1-2   Att. 20,000
McMenemy
Wartime.
Bradford Park Ave (a) 0-0   Att. 3,500
Division 2.
Nottingham Forest (a) 2-0   Att. 32,691
Bentley, Harvey
Division 1.
Blackpool (a) 0-0   Att. 25,000
Division 1.
West Bromwich A. (a) 3-3   Att. 29,311
Hannah, G. Robledo (2)
Division 1.
Bolton Wanderers (h) 2-3   Att. 61,321
Hannah, Mitchell
Division 1.
Birmingham City (a) 1-6   Att. 32,506
Keeble
Division 1.
Preston North End (h) 1-2   Att. 37,683
Eastham
Division 1.
West Bromwich A. (a) 0-6   Att. 22,661
Division 2.
Huddersfield Town (a) 1-0   Att. 8,770
McGarry
Division 1.
Derby County (a) 2-1   Att. 30,466
Dyson, Young
League Cup 2nd round.
Port Vale (a) 3-1   Att. 10,370
Macdonald, Barrowclough, Craig
League Cup 2nd round, 2nd leg.
Sunderland (h) 2-2   Att. 30,533
Shoulder, Boam
The tie finished 4-4 on aggregate and remained the same after 30 minutes extra time. Newcastle eventually lost 7-6 on penalties.
Division 2.
Queens Park Rangers (a) 0-3 Att. 14,176
Division 1.
Wimbledon (h) 1-2   Att. 22,734
McDonald (pen)
Division 1.
Bristol Rovers (a) 2-1   Att. 7,487
Sheedy, O'Brien

...record for this day is... 23 games,
...Drawn 5, Lost 9, GF 35, GA 42.
...success rate...50%.

Match of the Day from 1925

SIX OF THE BEST FOR THE MAGPIES

Newcastle beat Notts County in nine-goal thriller

Newcastle entertained Notts County at St. James' Park today in front of 35,000 for their first home league match of the season. The home side played considerably better than the visitors, and this was justified by the scoreline.

The United forwards were excellent, applying constant pressure on the County defence, while the home defence was sturdy in contrast. In particular it was Albert Chandler who seemed to be the glue that held the line together, and coupled with new goalkeeper Allan Taylor, the Newcastle goal was going to be difficult to conquor for the visitors.

It was Newcastle who opened the scoring, McDonald sending a super kick into the back of the net to put the home side a goal ahead, and this was just the beginning of the action. Newcastle also got the second goal of the game, albeit from a lovely shot from a member of the County forward line which gave his keeper no chance to save.

Before the half-time interval another own goal was gifted to Newcastle, putting them three ahead. However, County managed to pull a goal back for themselves, Staniforth beating Taylor in the Newcastle goal to bring the score to 3-1 going into the break.

In the second half things hotted up even more, and for a while it could have been anybody's game. It was Harris who was first to score his cracking shot increasing the home side's tally to four.

Next, Cowan netted with ease, bringing the score to 5-1. Newcastle seemed unstoppable, and by now they were confident of a win.

The chances of that were further increased when Mitchell sent a lovely ball into the back of the net for his team's sixth, and final, goal.

However, County hadn't finished yet and Staniforth got onto the ball, provided by Barry and Davis, to score his second of the match and give the visitors some hope of drawing level.

Staniforth then managed to complete his hat-trick before the end with a super shot which sailed past Taylor for Notts County's third.

The visitors tried as hard as they could to add more goals to their tally, but the game ended with the score at 6-3.

Newcastle United

Taylor, Chandler, Hudspeth, MacKenzie, Spencer, Curry, Urwin, Cowan, N. Harris, McDonald, Mitchell.

Notts County

Iremonger, Cornwell, Cope, Flint, Dinsdale, Kemp, Taylor, Staniforth, Widdowson, Davis, Barry.

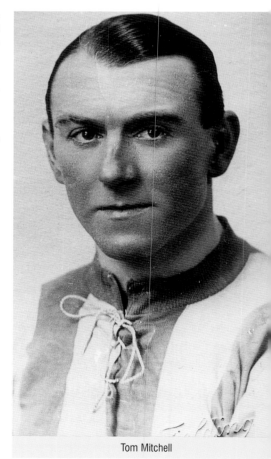

Tom Mitchell

Birthdays

Tommy Knox born today in 1939.
Winger 1965-1967, Apps 26 (1 sub). Goals 1.
Liam O'Brien born today in 1964.
Midfield 1988-1994, Apps 185 (24 subs). Goals 22.

Willie Wilson born today in 1900.
Goalkeeper 1925-1929, Apps 134.

September 6

Match of the Day from 1902

STOKE GO FOR BROKE (and fail)

Newcastle take victory in 5-0 whitewash

A crowd of 17,000 attended this Division One match against Stoke today. Right from the kick-off it was Newcastle who showed promise and ability, completely outplaying the visiting side. It was easy to predict which team was most likely to win, but no one could have guessed the score.

It took only a few minutes from the start for Newcastle to open the scoring. Bob McColl was the man to do the honours with a lovely ball straight past the Stoke keeper. It was just a taste of what was to come, but Newcastle were in for a dry spell for the rest of the first half.

Newcastle keeper Kingsley had two great saves to make from attempts by Johnson and Higginson, but he managed these with ease to keep the lead for his side.

Another super shot from McColl went into the net, but his kick was ruled offside and the goal was disallowed. So, the score remained unchanged, with Newcastle leading 1-0 going into the break.

The second half saw an improvement in play from Stoke, but their efforts still were not enough to be better than, or equal to, those of Newcastle. Orr soon scored the second goal for the home side, doubling their lead with an easy shot.

Stoke were by now beginning to flag. They were trying their hardest, but they just weren't good enough to break through the Newcastle defence and create chances.

Shortly afterwards McColl managed to net the ball again for his second, and Newcastle's third. Stoke now began to realise that time was running out if they were going to make an impact on the game.

Their misery was increased when Rutherford beat the keeper to score Newcastle's fourth, and a finishing touch was added by Orr, with a lovely flick of the ball straight into the net for the fifth and final goal of the game.

Andy Aitken

It had been a completely one-sided throughout the match, and Stoke were glad to hear the final whistle. Newcastle thoroughly deserved to win, and they had certainly done so in style today.

Newcastle United
Kingsley, Bennie, Agnew, Alex Gardner, Aitken, Carr, Stewart, Orr, McColl, Rutherford, Roberts.
Stoke
Roose, Meredith, Clark, Ashworth, Holford, Bradley, Johnson, Higginson, Watkins, Capes, Lockett.
Referee Mr. T. Helme (Farnworth)

Birthdays

Steve Hardwick born today in 1956.
Goalkeeper 1976-1983, Apps 101.
Bobby Saxton born today in 1943.
Assistant Manager 1988-1991.

Stephane Guivarc'h born today in 1970.
Forward 1998, Apps 4 (2 subs). Goals 1.

Played on this day

1902, Division 1.
  Stoke (h) 5-0   Att. 17,000
  Rutherford, McColl (2), Orr (2)
1905, Division 1.
  Manchester City (h) 2-2   Att. 20,000
  Gosnell, Orr
1909, Division 1.
  Everton (a) 4-1   Att. 30,000
  Wilson, Stewart, Howie, Rutherford
1911, Division 1.
  Everton (h) 2-0   Att. 20,000
  Low, Stewart
1913, Division 1.
  Sunderland (a) 2-1   Att. 40,000
  Hall, King
1919, Division 1.
  Arsenal (h) 3-1   Att. 45,000
  Wilson (2), Hudspeth (pen)
1922, Division 1.
  Birmingham (h) 0-0   Att. 20,000
1924, Division 1.
  Aston Villa (a) 0-0   Att. 40,000
1926, Division 1.
  Burnley (a) 3-3   Att. 28,000
  Gallacher, McDonald, Seymour
1930, Division 1.
  Grimsby Town (h) 1-2   Att. 30,000
  Lindsay
1933, Division 1.
  Blackburn Rovers (h) 3-1   Att. 18,000
  Lang (2), McMenemy
1937, Division 2.
  Barnsley (a) 0-3   Att. 9,000
1941, Wartime.
  Bradford City (a) 1-1 Att. 2,500
  Anderson
1947, Division 2.
  Brentford (h) 1-0   Att. 56,62
  Woodburn
1950, Division 1.
  Huddersfield Town (h) 6-0   Att. 34,03
  Milburn (3), Mitchell, G. Robledo, Taylor
1952, Division 1.
  Burnley (a) 1-2   Att. 35,068
  G. Robledo
1958, Division 1.
  Tottenham Hotspur (a) 3-1   Att. 41,805
  McGuigan, White (2)
1967, Division 1.
  Manchester City (a) 0-2   Att. 29,978
1969, Division 1.
  Ipswich Town (a) 0-2   Att. 18,229
1975, Division 1.
  Aston Villa (h) 3-0   Att. 35,604
  T. Craig, Macdonald (2)
1980, Division 2.
  Cardiff City (h) 2-1   Att. 15,78
  Clarke, Shoulder (pen)
1983, Division 2.
  Middlesbrough (a) 2-3 Att. 19,648
  Mills, Keegan
1986, Division 1.
  Sheffield Wednesday (h) 2-3 Att. 22,010
  Allon, Scott
2000, Premier League.
  Coventry City 0   Newcastle 2
                         Shearer 30 (pen)
                         Gallacher 58
                         Att. 22,102

Playing record for this day is... 24 games, Won 12, Drawn 5, Lost 7, GF 48, GA 29. Today's success rate... 60.42%.

September 7

Played on this day

1895, Division 2.
Loughborough Town (h) 3-0   Att. 7,000
Wardrope, Aitken, Logan
1901, Division 1.
Blackburn Rovers (a) 0-0   Att. 7,000
1907, Division 1.
Sheffield Wednesday (a) 1-3 Att. 20,000
Orr (pen)
1909, Division 1.
Bolton Wanderers (a) 4-0   Att. 18,000
Shepherd (3), Rutherford
1912, Division 1.
Sunderland (h) 1-1   Att. 54,200
Shepherd
1921, Division 1.
Everton (a) 3-2   Att. 30,000
Harris, McDonald (2)
1929, Division 1.
Grimsby Town (a) 0-4   Att. 22,000
1935, Division 2.
Tottenham Hotspur (a) 2-1 Att. 48,112
Cairns (2)
1938, Division 2.
West Bromwich A. (a) 2-5   Att. 17,016
Mooney, Stubbins
1940, Wartime.
Leeds United (h) 1-0   Att. 4,000
Dodgin
1946, Division 2.
Swansea Town (h) 1-1   Att. 54,966
Woodburn
1955, Division 1.
West Bromwich A. (a) 1-1   Att. 22,000
Davies
1957, Division 1.
Birmingham City (a) 4-1   Att. 29,784
Curry (2), Hill, R. Mitchell (pen)
1963, Division 2.
Charlton Athletic (h) 5-0   Att. 33,225
Penman (2), Thomas, Suddick (2)
1966, Division 1.
West Bromwich A. (h) 1-3   Att. 24,748
B. Robson
1968, Division 1.
Coventry City (a) 1-2   Att. 34,361
Sinclair
1974, Division 1.
Derby County (a) 2-2   Att. 21,197
Macdonald, Burns
1985, Division 1.
Tottenham Hotspur (a) 1-5 Att. 23,883
Davies
1991, Division 2.
Tranmere Rovers (a) 2-3   Att. 11,465
O'Brien, Clark
1996, Premier League.
Tottenham H. 1   Newcastle 2
Allen 28   Ferdinand 37, 61
                 Att. 32,535

Playing record for this day is... 20 games,
Won 8, Drawn 5, Lost 7, GF 37, GA 35.
Today's success rate... 52.50%.

Match of the Day from 1957

MORE BLUES IN BIRMINGHAM
Newcastle take easy win over poor City

Newcastle United travelled to St. Andrew's today for this match against Birmingham City. 29,784 were there to see the game, and Birmingham were hoping to win their first match since the opening one of the season.

Both teams started in attacking mode, and Reg Davies was a constant threat to the home side, but Birmingham had young Mike Hellawell who forced Simpson to pull off two great saves in the Newcastle goal. At the other end Schofield in the home goal managed a superb save to deny Casey from the penalty spot. The kick had been awarded when Smith brought down Curry in the box.

In the second half fortunes changed. Birmingham seemed to be lacking in enthusiasm, and provided little threat to the Newcastle defence. Just six minutes into the half United took the lead after an attempt by Hill was punched out by Schofield. The ball landed for Curry, who had no problem in sending the ball past the Birmingham keeper to put his team a goal ahead.

A few minutes later the visitors added another to their tally when Curry took advantage of the Birmingham defence, who were motionless, appealing for offside, and shot into the back of the net.

In the 61st minute Birmingham managed to claw one back when Hellawell swiped the ball from Casey, and sent a powerful shot past Simpson who couldn't stop it despite his full stretch attempt.

Although, Newcastle were now a little concerned that the home side had pulled a goal back, they pushed forward stepping up the pressure to try and secure another goal.

Birmingham tried everything they could to get the equaliser, but their efforts failed to make an impact on the strong Newcastle defence. The home side began to tire, and United seized their chance to increase their lead.

In the 74th minute a corner-kick from Mitchell was perfectly placed for Curry to get his head to the ball He nodded home his second of the game, and Newcastle's third.

Newcastle's win was sealed with three minutes left on the clock when Mitchell sent in a nice cross, which was handled by a Birmingham defender. A penalty was awarded, and Mitchell stepped up to take the kick. He fired the ball into the net for United's fourth, and the game was all over.

Birmingham City
Schofield, Hall, Green, Watts, Smith, Neal, Hellawell, Kinsey, Brown, Murphy, Govan.
Newcastle United
Simpson, Batty, McMichael, Scoular, Stokoe, Casey, Hill, Davies, Curry, Eastham, Mitchell.

Birthdays

Chris Guthrie born today in 1953.
Centre-forward 1970-1972, Apps 4. Goals 0.
Dave Turner born today in 1943.
Midfield 1960-1963, Apps 3. Goals 0.

Garry Brady born today in 1976.
Midfield 1998-2001 Apps 12 (7 subs). Goals 0.

BLUES
News
THE OFFICIAL PROGRAMME OF
BIRMINGHAM CITY
FOOTBALL CLUB
SEASON 1957-58
PRICE THREEPENCE

Division 2.
Burton Swifts (h) 6-3   Att. 6,000
Wallace (2), Smith (2), Willis (2)
Division 1.
Blackburn Rovers (a) 0-0   Att. 10,000
Division 1.
Birmingham (a) 4-2   Att. 17,000
Brown (3), Veitch (pen)
Division 1.
West Bromwich A. (a) 0-3   Att. 21,000
Division 1.
Everton (h) 2-0   Att. 35,000
Smailes, Finlay
Division 1.
Sheffield United (h) 2-2   Att. 40,000
Harris, Hudspeth (pen)
Division 1.
West Ham United (a) 0-0   Att. 23,000
Division 1.
Bury (h) 2-1   Att. 20,000
Gallacher (2)
Division 2.
Fulham (a) 2-3   Att. 30,000
.R. Richardson (2)
Wartime.
Middlesbrough (a) 6-0   Att. 18,000
Clifton (3), Stubbins (2), Milburn
Division 1.
Aston Villa (h) 2-1   Att. 56,110
Gibson, Milburn
Division 1.
Preston North End (a) 2-1   Att. 39,500
G. Robledo (2)
Division 1.
Aston Villa (h) 5-3   Att. 39,960
Milburn, White (4)
Division 1.
Manchester United (h) 1-1   Att. 50,133
Milburn
Division 2.
Plymouth Argyle (h) 3-1   Att. 34,375
Fell, Kerray (2)
Division 2.
Northampton Town (a) 0-1   Att. 15,365
Division 1.
Manchester United (h) 1-2   Att. 57,436
Hockey
League Cup 2nd round.
Bristol Rovers (a) 1-2   Att. 16,824
Dyson
League Cup 2nd round.
Halifax Town (h) 2-1   Att. 19,930
Macdonald, Cassidy
Division 1.
Sheffield United (a) 1-1   Att. 26,897
Robson
Division 2.
Orient (a) 4-1   Att. 5,700
Cartwright, Hibbitt, Withe, Shoulder (pen)
Division 2.
Middlesbrough (h) 1-1   Att. 27,984
Channon
Division 1.
Manchester United (a) 0-5   Att. 54,915
Division 2.
Millwall (h) 1-2   Att. 23,922
Quinn
Premier League.
Middlesbrough 1   Newcastle 4
Cooper 4   Shearer 34 (pen), 76
                   Dabizas 59
Att. 30,004   Robert 62
record for this day is... 25 games,
2, Drawn 6, Lost 7, GF 52, GA 38.
success rate... 60%.

Match of the Day from 1954

VILLA THRILLER

Newcastle manage 5-3 win over hard-to-beat Villa

Newcastle played host to Aston Villa at St. James' Park in front of a crowd of 39,960. The game began with plenty of excitement, Milburn scoring the opening goal with just ninety seconds on the clock to put Newcastle into the lead. The chance came from a corner kick, taken by Mitchell, and the home side were thrilled to have taken such an early lead.

However, before the cheers had subsided, Villa had equalised. Pace shot well to beat Simpson in the Newcastle goal from ten yards out. United were stopped in their tracks. The scores were level, and the home side had a fight on their hands. Newcastle proved to be the better team throughout the rest of the first half, the Villa defence struggling at time. That fact was emphasised when White got his first goal of the game on seventeen minutes. A pass from Milburn allowed him to get his head to the ball for Newcastle's second. Just four minutes later and a cross from Mitchell also came to White, and he got up to nod the ball into the net for his second, and Newcastle's third.

Things were going well for the home side, and Villa were finding it difficult to stay in the game. Their defence was under pressure, and they were finding it hard to keep the ball away from the danger zone. After 31 minutes another perfectly timed pass from Milburn allowed White to meet it and shoot it into the net straight past a despairing Parsons in the Villa goal.

Half time arrived with the home side winning 4-1. However, the dressing room talking-to that Villa received changed the game completely. Play resumed after the break with a revived Villa performance. Now the fight was back on, and Newcastle were in for a shock.

With 54 minutes on the clock the ball came for Dixon to send a lovely header past Simpson and into the back of the net for Villa's second. More attacks followed from both sides, but Newcastle just couldn't break through the revitalised Villa defence. After 70 minutes of play, Villa added another to their tally when Parkes took a free kick and his shot deflected into the net for a third goal for the visitors. The score now stood at 4-3.

The game could go either way now. There was certainly time for Villa to score again, and even take the lead given the chance, and Newcastle needed to make sure that it didn't happen.

Relief came after 77 minutes, and it was White again with his fourth of the match who managed to get through the tight Villa defence and notch the fifth goal for Newcastle. The scoring was complete and United finished up 5-3 winners.

Newcastle United

Simpson, Cowell, McMichael, Scoular, Stokoe, Crowe, Milburn, Broadis, White, Hannah, Mitchell.

Aston Villa

Parsons, Lynn, Parkes, Blanchflower, F. Moss, Baxter, Gibson, Thompson, Pace, Dixon, McParland.

Birthdays

Alan Guy born today in 1957.
Forward 1975-1979, Apps 8 (1 sub). Goals 0.

Gary Speed born today in 1969.
Midfield 1998-present day, Apps 231 (7 subs).
Goals 35.

September 9

Match of the Day from 1922

UNITED IN BATTLE

Newcastle win after struggling against Blades' defence

35,000 turned out to see this clash against Sheffield United at St. James' Park today. Conditions were difficult, with a strong wind making it hard to control the ball, but Newcastle were hoping for a win after they only managed to take a draw from their midweek meeting with Birmingham. There were a few team changes to that side, and it was hoped that it would make a difference for this game.

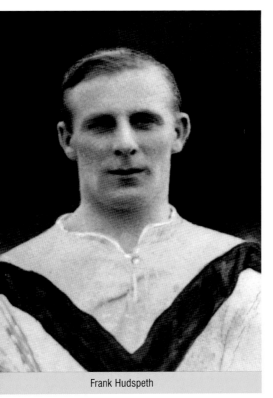

Frank Hudspeth

Despite the weather, Newcastle battled on to take control of the game right from the start. It was only the steadfast Blades' defence of Sturgess, Milton and Gough that managed to stop the home side taking the lead on several occasions.

Throughout the first half, the Magpies were frustrated at the ability of the opposition to keep their shots away from danger. Newcastle were quicker than the visitors, and had most of the possession, so it was expected that they would take an early lead, but it wasn't to be.

The second half began without the sturdy Sheffield defender Milton, who was unable to come back onto the field after suffering concussion in a clash in the first half. Newcastle seized the advantage, and began to pressure the opposition goal.

Less than three minutes into the second half the Blades' McCourt committed a foul on Harris inside the penalty area. Hudspeth stepped up to take the penalty kick and duly scored, breaking the deadlock for Newcastle.

The onslaught resumed, and this time it was more productive. Six minutes later Harris slipped through the defence and beat the visitors' keeper with a superb shot, taking the score to 2-0.

The Blades' defence continued to stand up to the pressures of the home forwards, but with so many attacks raining on them it was inevitable that they would be overwhelmed.

That is precisely what happened with the final goal for Newcastle. The visitors just couldn't cope with the effort and pace of the home side, and McDonald managed to slip through and hit a fourth for the Magpies, leaving the keeper Gough deflated and his defence shattered.

Newcastle United
Mutch, McCracken, Hudspeth, McIntosh, Spencer, Curry, J. Low, Hagan, Harris, McDonald, Mitchell.

Sheffield United
Gough, Sturgess, Milton, Pantling, McCourt, Plant, Mercer, Menlove, Johnson, Gillespie, Tunstall.

Birthdays

Kevin Brock born today in 1962.
Midfield 1988-1994, Apps 173 (11 subs). Goals 17.
Frank Clark born today in 1943.
Left-back 1962-1975, Apps 487 (2 subs). Goals 2.

Stan Keery born today in 1931.
Midfield 1952-1957, Apps 20. Goals 1.

Played on this day

1899, Division 1.
Everton (h) 2-0   Att. 25,000
Peddie, Niblo
1905, Division 1.
Birmingham (h) 2-2   Att. 23,912
Orr, Howie
1908, Division 1.
Bristol City (h) 2-1   Att. 22,000
Howie (2)
1911, Division 1.
Bradford City (h) 0-2   Att. 40,000
1914, Division 1.
Sheffield Wednesday (h) 0-0   Att. 8,000
1922, Division 1.
Sheffield United (h) 3-0   Att. 35,000
McDonald, Harris, Hudspeth (pen)
1925, Division 1.
Blackburn Rovers (h) 1-7   Att. 22,000
McDonald
1929, Division 1.
West Ham United (a) 1-5   Att. 20,000
Gallacher
1933, Division 1.
Derby County (h) 1-1   Att. 25,000
J.R. Richardson
1935, Division 2.
Barnsley (a) 2-3   Att. 13,000
Cairns, McMenemy
1936, Division 2.
West Ham United (h) 5-3   Att. 22,500
Cairns (4), McMenemy
1944, Wartime.
Bradford Park Ave. (h) 0-2   Att. 16,112
1950, Division 1.
Chelsea (h) 3-1   Att. 56,903
Milburn, Walker (2)
1953, Division 1.
West Bromwich A. (a) 2-2   Att. 40,220
Keeble, Mitchell
1959, Division 1.
West Bromwich A. (a) 2-2   Att. 28,200
Eastham, White
1961, Division 2.
Huddersfield Town (a) 1-2   Att. 18,087
White
1967, Division 1.
Nottingham Forest (a) 0-4   Att. 30,155
1972, Division 1.
Arsenal (h) 2-1   Att. 23,878
Macdonald, Craig
1978, Division 2.
Blackburn Rovers (h) 3-1   Att. 23,751
Withe (2), McGhee
1989, Division 2.
Bournemouth (a) 1-2   Att. 9,982
Quinn
1995, Premier League.
Southampton 1   Newcastle 0
Magilton 65   Att. 15,237
1998, Premier League.
Aston Villa 1   Newcastle 0
Hendrie 63 (pen)   Att. 39,241
2000, Premier League.
Newcastle 0   Chelsea 0
   Att. 51,687

Playing record for this day is... 23 games,
Won 7, Drawn 6, Lost 10, GF 33, GA 43.
Today's success rate... 43.48%.

September 10

Division 1.
Everton (a) 0-3   Att. 16,000
Division 1.
Derby County (a) 1-1   Att. 12,000
Appleyard
Division 1.
Oldham Athletic (a) 2-0   Att. 34,000
Shepherd (2)
Division 1.
Burnley (a) 0-2   Att. 30,000
Division 1.
Blackburn Rovers (h) 4-0   Att. 30,000
Harris (3), Hudspeth (pen)
Division 1.
Manchester United (a) 7-1   Att. 50,000
Seymour (2), McDonald, Gallacher,
McKay, Urwin, Harris
Division 1.
Burnley(a) 3-4   Att. 20,000
Lang, Hudspeth (2 pens)
Division 1.
Birmingham (a) 1-1   Att. 19,862
Lindsay
Division 1.
Leicester City (a) 3-0   Att. 20,000
Boyd (2), Lang
Division 2.
Burnley (h) 3-2   Att. 30,000
Bowden, Cairns, Stubbins
Division 2.
Birmingham City (a) 0-0   Att. 51,074
Division 1.
Charlton Athletic (a) 3-6   Att. 42,000
Milburn (2), Mitchell
Division 1.
Sunderland (h) 2-2   Att. 60,727
Davies, Opponent (og)
Division 1.
Luton Town (a) 2-4   Att. 25,719
Milburn (2)
Division 1.
Chelsea (a) 5-6   Att. 46,601
Wright (2), White, Davies, Franks
Division 1.
Manchester City (h) 1-3   Att. 25,904
Marshall
Division 1.
Burnley (h) 1-1   Att. 25,485
McGarry
League Cup 2nd round.
Nottingham Forest (a) 1-1   Att. 14,183
Macdonald
League Cup 2nd round.
Southport (h) 6-0   Att. 23,352
Gowling (4), Cannell (2)
*Southport were drawn at home but played
at St. James' Park by mutual agreement.*
Division 1.
West Bromwich A. (h) 0-3   Att. 22,705
Division 2.
Grimsby Town (a) 1-1   Att. 9,000
Keegan
Division 1.
Derby County (a) 0-2   Att. 16,014
Premier League.
Newcastle 4   Chelsea 2
Cole 7, 66   Peacock 15
Fox 21   Furlong 27
Lee 53   Att. 34,435
UEFA Cup 1st round, 1st leg.
Newcastle 4   Halmstads 0
Ferdinand 6, Asprilla 26
Albert 51, Beardsley 54   Att. 28,124
record for this day is... 24 games,
Drawn 7, Lost 9, GF 54, GA 45.
success rate... 47.92%.

Match of the Day from 1927

THE MAGNIFICENT SEVEN
Newcastle outplay Manchester United in 7-1 thrashing

Newcastle United travelled to Manchester United today for this Division One clash, played out in front of 50,000 eager supporters. The Reds were missing their key player Barson, and his absence really showed in the way the team played.

United were on top right from the kick off, and it was clear which way the game would go. The visitors, however, were calm and collected, and pulled together in a real team effort. Manchester United, on the other hand, seemed to be in a bit of a panic, nothing was going right for them, and they seemed to lack cohesion.

So, it was no surprise to anyone when Newcastle opened the scoring midway through the first half with a lovely ball from Gallacher. His shot beat the home keeper easily to put the Magpies ahead.

Newcastle doubled their lead shortly afterwards when McDonald slipped through the weak home defence to knock the ball into the net for the second goal.

Half time arrived, and after the break there was no change in the way the teams were playing. The dressing room talk had obviously not inspired the Reds enough for them to improve their game. Newcastle were just as energetic and confident, and it seemed they had more stamina than the home side.

However, it was Manchester United who were next to score, albeit from a scramble in the penalty area. Spence managed to slot the ball into the net more by luck than actual skill, but it was still a welcome goal for the Reds.

Newcastle were not going to let their lead slip, and they made a noticeable effort to step up the pace. Three goals in the next twelve minutes effectively decided the outcome. Urwin was next to add his name to the score-sheet, a lovely shot sailing past the home keeper to give Newcastle their fourth.

Then it was Harris who managed to get the ball into the net, rounding off a superb spell.

Twenty minutes before the end of the game the home team's luck was out once more when they lost one of their players. Wilson had to be carried off the field with an injury, and his team were now down to ten men.

Moore increased the agony for his home side when he got a touch to an Urwin pass. The ball crossed the goal-line past his own keeper, and Newcastle were awarded another goal.

Seymour finally finished the goal-fest with Newcastle's seventh, and the Red of Manchester were glad to hear the final whistle.

Manchester United
Steward, Moore, Silcock, Bennion, Hilditch, Wilson, Chapman, Hanson, Spence, Partridge, Thomas
Newcastle United
Wilson, Maitland, Hudspeth, MacKenzie, Spencer, Harris, Urwin, McKay, Gallacher, McDonald, Seymour.

Birthdays

Ian Stewart born today in 1961.
Winger 1985-1987, Apps 50 (10 subs). Goals 3.

Newcastle United squad 1927-28:

Back row (l-r): Dr E.B. Appleby, John Lee, Frank Watt Jr, Mick Burns, W. Davis, George Mathison, E. Hall, Tom Curry, Andy McCombie (trainer);

Second row (l-r): J.T. Patten, Jimmy Boyd, Bob Bradley, director G.F. Rutherford, William Carlton, J. Wilkinson, Ossie Park, T. Oliver (director), A. Brown, Tommy Lang, R.W. MacKenzie;

Third row (l-r): J.Q. McPherson (trainer), Stan Barber, Jack Little, Bob Clark, director R.W. Simpson, Charlie Spencer, Willie Wilson, J. Graham (director), Joe Harris, Tom Curry, William Gillespie, S.F. Bates (director);

Front row (l-r): Secretary Frank Watt, Tommy Urwin, Bobby McKay, Roddie MacKenzie, Frank Hudspeth, J.P. Oliver (Chairman), Hughie Gallacher, Tommy McDonald, Alf Maitland, Jimmy Low, J. Lunn (director).

, Division 2.
Walsall (a) 3-2 Att. 4,000
Wardrope, Opponents (2 ogs)
, Division 1.
Nottingham Forest (h) 1-2 Att. 25,000
Shepherd
, Division 1.
Bolton Wanderers (h) 2-1 Att. 12,000
G. Wilson, McTavish
, Division 1.
Preston North End (h) 4-2 Att. 48,000
Hagan (2), Harris, Opponent (og)
, Division 1.
Manchester United (h) 4-2 Att. 29,000
Gallacher, McDonald (2), Seymour
, Division 2.
Tottenham Hotspur (a) 2-2 Att. 26,125
Park, Imrie (pen)
, Wartime.
Bradford Park Ave. (a) 0-1 Att. 2,763
, Division 2.
Coventry City (h) 3-1 Att. 55,313
Wayman, Stobbart (2, 1 pen)
, Division 1.
Stoke City (h) 2-2 Att. 59,265
Walker, Donaldson (pen)
, Division 1.
Burnley (h) 2-1 Att. 47,346
Milburn, R. Mitchell
, Division 1.
Portsmouth (h) 2-0 Att. 39,027
Davies, R. Mitchell
, Division 2.
Southampton (h) 2-2 Att. 42,879
Thomas, McGarry (pen)
, Division 1.
Stoke City (a) 0-4 Att. 25,702
, Inter Cities Fairs Cup 1st round, 1st leg.
Feyenoord (h) 4-0 Att. 46,348
Davies, Gibb, B. Robson, Scott
, Division 1.
Manchester City (a) 1-2 Att. 32,710
Macdonald
, Divsion 1.
Manchester United (h) 2-2 Att. 39,037
Burns, Cannell
, Division 2.
Chelsea (h) 1-1 Att. 29,136
Clarke
, Premier League.
Chelsea 1 **Newcastle 0**
Leboeuf 37 (pen) Att. 35,092
, Premier League.
Newcastle 0 **Leeds United 2**
Viduka 5
Smith 87
Att. 51,730

ng record for this day is... 19 games,
8, Drawn 5, Lost 6, GF 35, GA 30.
's success rate... 55.26%.

September 11

Match of the Day from 1968

UNITED ON THEIR WAY

Newcastle beat Feyenoord to take 4-0 lead to Rotterdam

Newcastle met Feyenoord today at St James' Park in front of a crowd of 46,348 for this Inter-Cities Fairs Cup match.

United manager Joe Harvey had given his team the aims for today's game. He wanted them to score, and score well. His instructions were that a three-goal lead would be sufficient for them to take with them to Rotterdam for the return meeting.

Most would think it would be easier said than done, but this was Newcastle United, and they were capable of anything when they put their minds to it.

True to form it was Jim Scott who opened the scoring for United with a lovely shot, beating Graafland in the Feyenoord goal.

Bryan Robson

Next it was the turn of Bryan Robson to add his name to the score-sheet with a super shot. Feyenoord were reeling, and their game began to flag.

Still before the half-time break, and Newcastle were enjoying every minute of play. They knew they had the upper hand, and they were taking full advantage of their position.

Harvey's wish would be granted even earlier than expected, another effort before the end of the first half gave Newcastle their three-goal lead. Tommy Gibb was the man for the job, and he made no mistake in securing the goal, beating the Feyenoord defence and smashing the ball past the keeper.

The second half began with few expectations from either side. Feyenoord knew they had little chance of a comeback, and Newcastle were content with the way things stood.

So, it was a welcome bonus when Wyn Davies managed to break his barren spell and score Newcastle's fourth goal. It was his first goal in 22 games, and the lack of pressure must have given him the relaxed confidence to go for it.

So, the game ended 4-0 to Newcastle with winger Geoff Allen man-of-the-match following a brilliant display, and nicely set up to progress to the next round.

Newcastle United
McFaul, Craig, McNamee, Burton, Clark, Gibb, Elliott, Scott, B. Robson, Davies, Allen.
Feyenoord
Graafland, Romeijn, Israel, Laseroms, Veldhoen, Boskamp, Jansen, Van Hanegem (Geels 67), Wery, Kindvall, Moulijn.

Birthdays

Chris Holland born today in 1975.
Midfield 1994-1996, Apps 4 (2 subs). Goals 0.

Match of the Day from 1992

ANOTHER WIN FOR MAGPIES

Newcastle keep on winning, final score today: 3-1

David Kelly

This Division One match against Portsmouth in front of 29,885 could easily have graced the Premiership. Granted, it was mostly Newcastle performing well enough to be given that compliment, but there were odd bursts of good play from Portsmouth too.

Thousands had been turned away from the turnstiles today, the ground too full to cater for any more eager supporters.

Liam O'Brien and Lee Clark played exceptionally well in midfield, and it was Clark who provided the inspiration for the first two goals. The first of these came from the former Portsmouth striker Mick Quinn, who shot straight past Alan Knight in the Pompey goal.

Newcastle's second goal came shortly before the half-time break, and it was David Kelly who added his name to the score-sheet.

The second half started with Quinn missing a golden opportunity when he fluffed his shot and it went wide. Next, Kelly received a great chance - an open goal, and enough time to score. However, he decided to hurry his shot and as a result sent the ball wide too. Quinn then managed to beat Knight with a lovely header, but it was ruled offside and the goal was disallowed.

Then Kelly's shot hit the crossbar, and Steve Howey's attempt at a goal suffered the same fate. Kelly made appeals for a penalty when he was pushed by Portsmouth's Awford, but the referee wasn't convinced and the game continued. Quinn then added the third and final goal for Newcastle with a lovely ball neatly tucked into the net past Knight.

Portsmouth managed to snatch themselves a late consolation goal with five minutes left on the clock. Guy Whittingham got his head to the ball and finally beat the Newcastle keeper to bring the score to 3-1.

This was Newcastle's sixth win in a row from the start of the season, and their eighth consecutive league win altogether. Both of these facts were new club records, and it was easy to agree that they thoroughly deserved their win today.

Newcastle United
Wright, Venison, Beresford, O'Brien, Scott, Howey, Carr, Quinn, Kelly (Thompson), Clark, Sheedy.
Portsmouth
Knight, Awford, Daniel, McLoughlin, Symons, Doling (Clark), Neil, Kuhl, Powell (Murray), Whittingham, Burns.

Birthdays

Andy Graver born today in 1927.
Centre-forward 1947-1950, Apps 1. Goals 0.

Carl Serrant born today in 1975.
Defender 1998-2001, Apps 7 (2 subs). Goals 0

Steve Caldwell born today in 1980.
Defender 1997-present day, Apps 30 (10 subs).
Goals 2.

Played on this day

1896, Division 2.
Small Heath (h) 4-3 — Att. 10,853
Smellie (3), Lennox
1903, Division 1.
Small Heath (h) 3-1 — Att. 17,000
McColl, Appleyard, Howie
1908, Division 1.
Woolwich Arsenal (a) 2-1 — Att. 20,000
Rutherford, Stewart
1914, Division 1.
Chelsea (a) 3-0 — Att. 20,000
Hall (2), Hibbert
1923, Division 1.
Bolton Wanderers (h) 1-0 — Att. 25,000
Seymour
1925, Division 1.
Aston Villa (a) 2-2 — Att. 45,000
Hudspeth (pen), Opponent (og)
1931, Division 1.
Chelsea (h) 4-1 — Att. 30,000
Boyd, Lang, J.R. Richardson (2)
1934, Division 2.
Blackpool (h) 4-1 — Att. 30,000
Boyd, Lang, J.R. Richardson, Weaver
1936, Division 2.
Tottenham Hotspur (h) 0-1 — Att. 29,000
1942, Wartime.
Huddersfield Town (a) 0-4 — Att. 2,000
1945, Wartime.
Burnley (h) 0-1 — Att. 27,660
1953, Division 1.
Preston North End (a) 2-2 — Att. 35,000
Keeble, Milburn
1959, Division 1.
Leicester City (a) 2-0 — Att. 24,318
Bell (2)
1962, Division 2.
Derby County (h) 0-0 — Att. 34,465
1964, Division 2.
Coventry City (h) 2-0 — Att. 37,481
Taylor, Thomas
1970, Division 1.
Liverpool (h) 0-0 — Att. 35,595
1973, Division 1.
Ipswich Town (h) 3-1 — Att. 30,604
Macdonald (2), Opponent (og)
1981, Division 2.
Cambridge United (h) 1-0 — Att. 14,666
Trewick
1987, Division 1.
Manchester United (a) 2-2 — Att. 45,137
Mirandinha (2)
1992, Division 1.
Portsmouth (h) 3-1 — Att. 29,885
Quinn (2), Kelly
1998, Premier League.
Newcastle 4 — Southampton 0
Shearer 8, 38 (pen)
Marshall (og) 89
Ketsbaia 90 — Att. 36,454
2001, Worthington Cup 2nd round.
Newcastle 4 — Brentford 1
Ameobi 59 — Owusi 17
Bellamy
108, 117, 120 — Att. 25,633
A.E.T.

Playing record for this day is... 22 games, Won 14, Drawn 5, Lost 3, GF 46, GA 22. Today's success rate... 75%.

Played on this day

, Division 1.
Everton (a) 1-0   Att. 20,000
Stewart
, Division 1.
Sheffield Wednesday (h) 0-3 Att. 20,000
, Division 1.
Everton (h) 0-1   Att. 30,000
, Division 1.
Chelsea (a) 0-0   Att. 60,000
, Division 1.
Arsenal (h) 2-2   Att. 22,000
McDonald, Mooney
, Division 1.
Manchester United (a) 7-4   Att. 7,000
Starling (2), Lindsay, J.R. Richardson,
Cape (3)
, Wartime.
Huddersfield Town (a) 0-5   Att. 2,800
, Division 2.
Leicester City (a) 2-2   Att. 35,472
Donaldson, Shackleton
, Division 1.
Aston Villa (a) 4-2   Att. 35,824
Donaldson, Gibson, Milburn, Walker
, Division 1.
Huddersfield Town (a) 0-0   Att. 30,323
, Division 1.
Preston North End (h) 4-3   Att. 52,020
Davies (2), G. Robledo (2)
, Division 1.
Aston Villa (a) 2-1   Att. 27,330
Milburn, R. Mitchell
, Division 1.
Manchester United (h) 1-1   Att. 60,670
Davies
, League Cup 1st round.
Scunthorpe United (h) 2-0   Att. 14,372
Hale, Allchurch
, League Cup 2nd round.
Leeds United (a) 0-1   Att. 18,131
, League Cup 2nd round.
Lincoln City (a) 1-2   Att. 15,454
Burton
, Division 1.
Derby County (h) 0-1   Att. 39,382
, Texaco Cup 1st round, 1st leg.
Ayr United (a) 0-0   Att. 8,500
, Division 1.
Everton (a) 0-3   Att. 28,938
, Division 2.
Queens Park Rangers (a) 2-1 Att. 10,865
Hibbitt, Boam
, Division 1.
Coventry City (a) 0-3   Att. 11,370
, Division 2.
Oxford United (a) 1-2   Att. 7,313
Quinn
, Premier League.

Newcastle 4	Sheffield Wed. 2
Cole 21, 76	Sinton 26, 47
Mathie 81, Allen 88	Att. 33,890

, UEFA Cup 1st round, 1st leg.

Royal Antwerp 0	Newcastle 5
	Lee 1, 9, 51
	Sellars 40
Att. 19,700	Watson 78

, Premier League.

Newcastle 1	Wimbledon 3
Barton 32	Cort 2, Perry 59
Att. 36,526	Ekoku 75

...ng record for this day is... 25 games,
9, Drawn 6, Lost 10, GF 39, GA 42.
...y's success rate... 48%.

Match of the Day from 1930

ELEVEN GOALS AT OLD TRAFFORD
Newcastle work hard to take victory in 7-4 win

A superb game awaited the 7,000 supporters who attended this Division One match at Old Trafford. Manchester United were hoping to break a losing sequence of five matches.

Both teams started well, although Newcastle made it clear from early on that they were the better side in this game. The home team made several good attempts at breaking down the visitors' defence, and fought to stay in the game.

It was Reid who opened the scoring for the Reds in the first half, his shot beating Burns in the Newcastle goal with ease. So, with the home team a goal up, United tried hard to pull together and get a goal back. Their attempts worked, and it wasn't long before the first goal arrived thanks to a fine shot by Cape.

The action was just beginning and Cape again managed to get through the home defence to add a second for Newcastle. Then Starling increased the margin when his shot sailed into the net past Chesters to put the Magpies into a two-goal lead.

The score was 3-1 now, but before the half-time interval Reid grabbed another goal for the Reds to reduce the arrears once again.

After the break Starling brought Newcastle's tally to four with a super shot, but the home side fought back with a strike from Rowley, his first of the game.

Twenty minutes into the second half the home team equalised when Rowley netted his second of the game to level the scores at 4-4.

However, Newcastle had other ideas. They wanted victory themselves, and they were going to fight for it. Lindsay helped his team on their way with his first goal of the game, his powerful shot leaving Chesters reeling in the home goal.

Then another super strike from Lindsay brought Newcastle's score to six.

The home team tried desperately to get back into the game, but a comeback became impossible when Richardson flicked the ball into the back of the net for Newcastle's seventh goal.

Luckily for the Reds this was the final goal of the game, and their losing run had now been extended to five successive matches. The Magpies returned home with a well deserved victory, and a big smile.

Manchester United
Chesters, Dale, Silcock, Williams, Hilditch, McLenahan, Spence, Warburton, Reid, Rowley, McLachlan.
Newcastle United
Burns, Richardson J.R, Fairhurst, Harris, Hill, Weaver, Cape, Richardson J, Lindsay, Starling, Wilkinson.

Birthdays

Paul Bodin born today in 1964.
Left-back 1991-1992, Apps 6. Goals 0.

September 14

Match of the Day from 1938

UNITED SINK PITIFUL ALBION
Newcastle beat WBA 5-1, with four from Cairns

West Bromwich Albion made the trip to St James' Park today to meet Newcastle in this Division Two match in front of 31,054.

Several chances came Newcastle's way very early on in the game, but Adams always managed to get to the ball with ease to stop it entering the net. White and Shaw in the Albion defence also did a fine job, but with so many shots raining in from the Newcastle forwards it was inevitable that some would get through into the danger area.

On fifteen minutes United's constant bombardment finally had the desired effect. Adams missed a drive from Cairns, and the home side were in the lead. West Brom had a lot of catching up to do if they wanted to stay in the running. They had not had one shot on target yet, and things got worse for them 25 minutes into the game. McNab collapsed on the field and was carried off, only to return ten minutes later. After a short time on outside right, he went back to his own position, but the disturbance seemed to affect his team's performance.

The rest of the first half saw no more goals, but Newcastle were definitely the better team. The home forwards were strong and confident, and the defence was reliable. Albion's only saviour was Adams, and there would have been many more goals on the score-sheet if he hadn't been there.

In the second half Jones managed to slip through the Newcastle defence on 51 minutes and net the equaliser for Albion. Although the Magpies were totally outplaying the visitors, the scores were level. Things looked more hopeful just two minutes later when Newcastle were awarded a penalty for a foul on Mooney. He stepped up to take the kick himself, but Adams was perfectly placed to make the save, and United had however, lost the chance to regain the lead.

Adams continued to thwart every attempt at goal from the Newcastle forwards. The home team didn't lose heart, and they managed to keep up the pressure knowing that it would pay off at some point. They were right, and after 63 minutes Newcastle regained their lead. It was Cairns who flicked the ball past the Albion keeper for the second goal, and this gave the home team confidence that they could score more.

Stubbins was the next to score, his super shot bringing the tally to three. By now Adams was beginning to tire, as were the whole of the visitors' defence. Newcastle were on a roll, and they had no intention of easing off.

They continued to press, and Cairns added another goal shortly afterwards, securing his hat-trick with Newcastle's fourth goal. However, the super striker was not content with the three, and soon afterwards scored his fourth of the match, bringing Newcastle's final tally to five. The home fans went home happy with a 5-1 victory.

Newcastle United
Swinburne, Richardson, Ancell, Gordon, Denmark, Wright, Birkett, Stubbins, Cairns, Bowden, Mooney.

West Bromwich Albion
Adams, White, Shaw, Sankey, Tudor, McNab, Hoyland, Heaslegrave, Jones, Sandford, Johnson.

Played on this day

1895, Division 2.
Liverpool (a) 1-5   Att. 10,000
Logan
1901, Division 1.
Stoke (h) 5-1   Att. 20,000
Roberts (2), Orr (2), Niblo
1907, Division 1.
Chelsea (h) 1-0   Att. 35,000
Orr
1912, Division 1.
Oldham Athletic (a) 0-1   Att. 30,000
1927, Division 1.
Derby County (h) 4-3   Att. 36,965
Gallacher, McKay (3)
1929, Division 1.
Leicester City (h) 2-1   Att. 30,000
Gallacher (2, 1pen)
1935, Division 2.
Manchester United (h) 0-2   Att. 28,000
1936, Division 2.
Bradford Park Ave. (a) 3-0   Att. 10,000
Cairns (2), Imrie
1938, Division 2.
West Bromwich A. (h) 5-1   Att. 31,054
Cairns (4), Stubbins
1940, Wartime.
Middlesbrough (h) 3-0   Att. 3,000
Birkett (2), Nevins
1946, Division 2.
Tottenham Hotspur (a) 1-1   Att. 52,213
Harvey
1955, FA Charity Shield.
Chelsea (a) 0-3   Att. 12,802
1957, Division 1.
Chelsea (h) 1-3   Att. 44,560
R. Mitchell (pen)
1960, Division 1.
West Bromwich A. (h) 3-2   Att. 16,107
Hughes, Tuohy, White
1963, Division 2.
Grimsby Town (a) 1-2   Att. 9,828
McGarry (pen)
1968, Division 1.
West Bromwich A. (h) 2-3   Att. 35,128
Davies, B. Robson
1974, Division 1.
Carlisle United (h) 1-0   Att. 40,568
Tudor
1977, UEFA Cup 1st round, 1st leg.
Bohemians (a) 0-0   Att. 25,000
1985, Division 1.
West Bromwich A. (h) 4-1   Att. 21,902
Reilly (2), McDonald, Clarke
1991, Division 2.
Wolverhampton W. (h) 1-2   Att. 20,195
Madden (og)
1996, Premier League.
Newcastle 2   Blackburn Rovers 1
Shearer 45 (pen)   Sutton 85
Ferdinand 61   Att. 36,424
2002, Premier League.
Chelsea 3   Newcastle 0
Gudjohnsen 14, 58
Zola 26   Att. 39,746

Playing record for this day is... 22 games, Won 11, Drawn 2, Lost 9, GF 40, GA 35. Today's success rate... 54.54%.

Birthdays

George Reilly born today in 1957.
Centre-forward 1985, Apps 33. Goals 10.

September 15

1894, Division 2.
Grimsby Town (h) 0-3   Att. 4,000
1900, Division 1.
Stoke (h) 2-1   Att. 18,000
MacFarlane, Peddie
1906, Division 1.
Everton (h) 1-0   Att. 38,000
McWilliam
1923, Division 1.
Sheffield United (a) 1-2   Att. 25,000
Hudspeth (pen)
1928, Division 1.
Aston Villa (a) 1-1   Att. 34,146
Chalmers
1934, Division 2.
Bradford Park Ave. (h) 0-1   Att. 28,000
1937, Division 2.
Luton Town (h) 1-3   Att. 17,000
Livingstone
1945, Wartime.
Middlesbrough (h) 1-1   Att. 32,211
Wayman
1951, Division 1.
Burnley (h) 7-1   Att. 51,278
Hannah (2), Mitchell, G.Robledo (4)
1956, Division 1.
Arsenal (a) 1-0   Att. 46,318
Hannah
1962, Division 2.
Grimsby Town (a) 1-0   Att. 12,318
Kerray
1965, Division 1.
Manchester United (a) 1-1   Att. 30,401
McGarry (pen)
1969, Inter Cities Fairs Cup 1st round, 1st leg.
Dundee United (a) 2-1   Att. 21,000
Davies (2)
1971, Texaco Cup 1st round, 1st leg.
Hearts (a) 0-1   Att. 18,000
1973, Division 1.
Wolverhampton W. (h) 2-0   Att. 36,412
Howard, Nattrass
1976, Anglo Scottish Cup 2nd round, 1st leg.
Ayr United (a) 0-3   Att. 3,600
Newcastle were later disqualified from the competition for deliberately fielding an under strength team for this game.
1979, Division 1.
Leicester City (h) 3-2   Att. 26,443
Cartwright, Shoulder (2 pens)
1984, Division 1.
Everton (h) 2-3   Att. 29,452
Beardsley (pen), Wharton
1990, Division 2.
Port Vale (a) 1-0   Att. 10,025
Quinn
2001, Premier League.

Newcastle 4	Manchester U. 3
Robert 5	Van Nistelrooy 29
Lee 34	Giggs 62
Dabizas 52	Veron 64
Brown (og) 82	Att. 52,056

Playing record for this day is... 20 games,
Won 10, Drawn 3, Lost 7, GF 31, GA 27.
Today's success rate... 57.50%.

Match of the Day from 2001

SHEARER LANDS THE KNOCK-OUT BLOW

Keane incident fails to mar another thrilling win for United

What a pity Roy Keane, given the captaincy at Manchester United, could not take a rare Premiership defeat with a little more grace and dignity. The red mist that regularly descends on the fiery Irishman brought a thoroughly justified ninth red card of his Old Trafford career but failed to spoil a fantastic game which sported all the greatness in England's premier sport. Newcastle captain Alan Shearer was deep into stoppage time, doing exactly what the rules allow him to protect a famous and unexpected victory over the defending champions. The former England captain's blatent shielding of the ball close to the corner flag incensed Keane, who threw the ball at his counterpart's head. A caution was on the cards until Keane took a more physical swipe and referee Steve Bennett was given little option but to dismiss him. A pity, for up till that point this game was a classic thriller producing a quite breath taking spell of high class football for a full 90 minutes.

Newcastle, using the exciting options that Nolberto Solano and new signing Laurent Robert provide down the flanks, deserved their early lead secured by a magnificent Robert free kick after just five minutes. Although Ruud van Nistelrooy equalised on 29 minutes with a trademark simple finish, Newcastle earnt a two-goal cushion through Robert Lee's bizarre strike through the flailing arms of Fabien Bartez after 34 minutes, and Nikos Dabizas act of predatory finishing seven minutes into the second half.

Remarkably, however, Bobby Robson's men found themselves hanging on grimly at 3-3 after a stunning Manchester United recovery that brought sweetly struck goals for the outstanding Ryan Giggs, with his right foot on 62 minutes, and the less impressive Juan Veron two minutes later. At this point the visitors looked ominously set to snatch all three points with an almost certain winner just a matter of time away, a point even Newcastle boss Robson conceded in a post-match interview. Indeed there were so many outstanding attacking players on the field it could well have ended up 6-6 such was the pace and brilliance of the 22 players out there. But if it was to be Newcastle's day then it was inevitably scripted for Shearer, albeit with a severe deflection off Wes Brown, to net the winning goal. That decisive strike eight minutes from time exposed the limitation of Alex Ferguson's new recruit Laurent Blanc, a replacement for the controversially departed Jaap Stam. The French defender was embarrasingly outpaced by Craig Bellamy in a move which ended with Shearer, back to 75 per cent fitness after a lengthy injury, wheeling away in the manner which has become an icon in the Premiership League's nine-year history. A superb finish, a worthy winner and a great way to end this fantastic game, yes, not even Roy Keane's petulance could upstage the master's Grand Finale.

Newcastle United
Given, Griffin, Dabizas, O'Brien, Elliott, Solano, Lee (Barton 46), Acuna, Robert, Shearer, Bellamy.
Manchester United
Bartez, G. Neville, Blanc, Brown, P. Neville, Beckham, Veron, Keane, Giggs, Cole (Scholes 59), Van Nistelrooy.
Referee Mr. S. Bennett (Orpington).

Manchester United's Juan Sebastian Veron attempts to block Andrew Griffin's pass.

Sadly Missed

Tom Rowlandson died on this day in 1916, aged 36.
Goalkeeper 1905-1906, Apps 1.

September 16

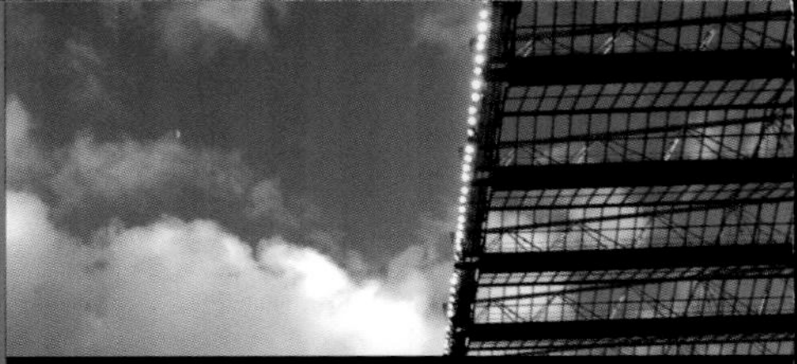

Match of the Day from 1967

UNITED FIGHTBACK STUNS COVENTRY

2-0 down, Iley goal wins a thriller for Newcastle

For half an hour Newcastle looked to be heading for almost certain defeat at St James' Park today. Coventry, who had snatched a two-goal lead, looked likely to put an end to their recent lean spell with a much needed victory, and no one would have denied them it. Then disaster struck, with an injury to inspirational forward Gibson who was withdrawn, allowing Newcastle to take control for an unlikely comeback.

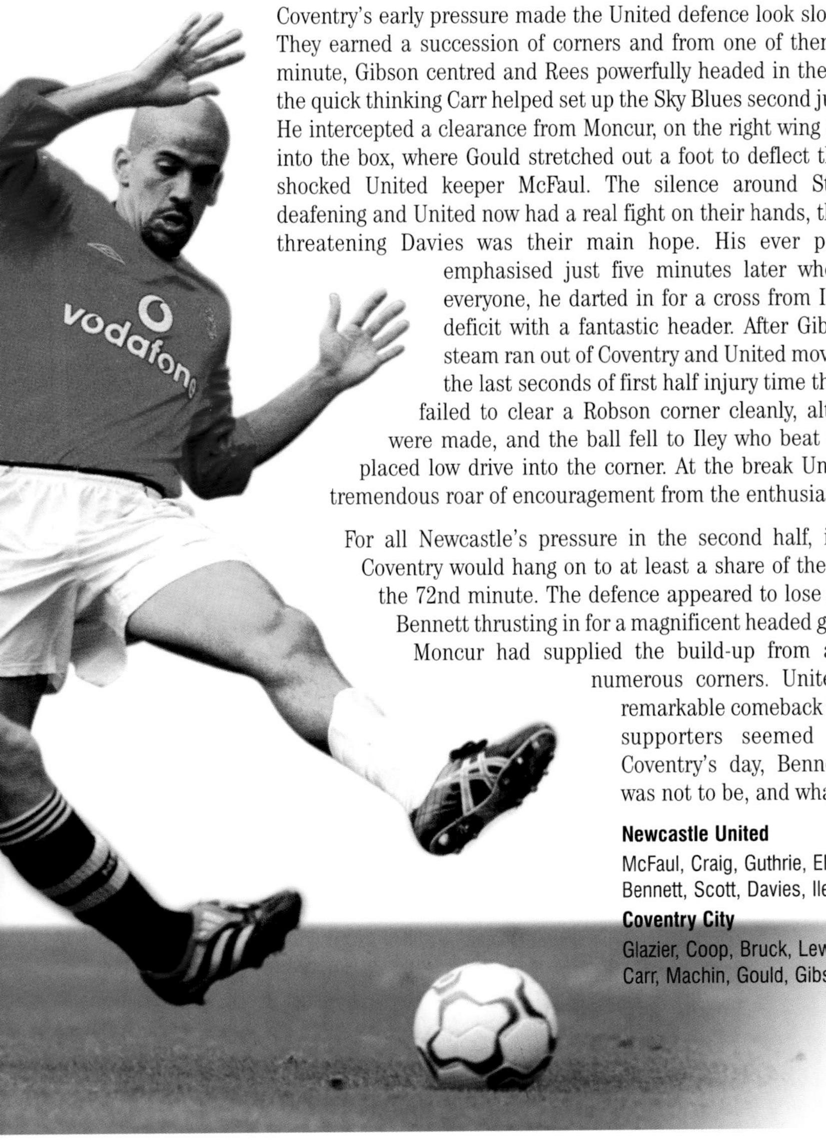

Coventry's early pressure made the United defence look slow and cumbersome. They earned a succession of corners and from one of them, in the fourteenth minute, Gibson centred and Rees powerfully headed in the opening goal. Then the quick thinking Carr helped set up the Sky Blues second just six minutes later. He intercepted a clearance from Moncur, on the right wing and curled his cross into the box, where Gould stretched out a foot to deflect the ball past a shell-shocked United keeper McFaul. The silence around St James' Park was deafening and United now had a real fight on their hands, the hard working and threatening Davies was their main hope. His ever present danger was emphasised just five minutes later when, to the relief of everyone, he darted in for a cross from Iley and reduced the deficit with a fantastic header. After Gibson's departure the steam ran out of Coventry and United moved in menacingly. In the last seconds of first half injury time the Sky Blues defence failed to clear a Robson corner cleanly, although two attemps were made, and the ball fell to Iley who beat Glazier with a well-placed low drive into the corner. At the break United walked off to a tremendous roar of encouragement from the enthusiastic crowd.

For all Newcastle's pressure in the second half, it looked as though Coventry would hang on to at least a share of the points, that is until the 72nd minute. The defence appeared to lose sight of right-winger Bennett thrusting in for a magnificent headed goal after Robson and Moncur had supplied the build-up from another of United's numerous corners. United had pulled of a remarkable comeback when even the home supporters seemed convinced it was Coventry's day, Bennett's goal proved it was not to be, and what a winner it was.

Newcastle United

McFaul, Craig, Guthrie, Elliott, McGrath, Moncur, Bennett, Scott, Davies, Iley, Robson.

Coventry City

Glazier, Coop, Bruck, Lewis, Knapp, Clements, Carr, Machin, Gould, Gibson (Farmer 37), Rees.

Played on this day

1899, Division 1.
Blackburn Rovers (a) 3-2 Att. 8,000
Fraser, Peddie, Wardrope
1905, Division 1.
Everton (a) 2-1 Att. 16,000
Orr, Howie
1911, Division 1.
Woolwich Arsenal (a) 0-2 Att. 20,000
1922, Division 1.
Sheffield United (a) 0-2 Att. 20,000
1925, Division 1.
Leeds United (a) 0-2 Att. 20,000
1929, Division 1.
Blackburn Rovers (a) 2-4 Att. 29,000
Gallacher, Opponent (og)
1933, Division 1.
West Bromwich A. (a) 1-1 Att. 25,000
Weaver (pen)
1944, Wartime.
Bradford Park Ave. (a) 0-1 Att. 8,309
1946, Division 2.
Coventry City (a) 1-1 Att. 26,024
Milburn
1950, Division 1.
Burnley (a) 1-1 Att. 33,373
Milburn
1953, Division 1.
West Bromwich A. (h) 3-7 Att. 57,838
Keeble, Mitchell (2)
1959, Division 1.
West Bromwich A. (h) 0-0 Att. 39,266
1961, Division 2.
Swansea Town (h) 2-2 Att. 23,644
Leek, Allchurch
1964, Division 2.
Plymouth Argyle (h) 2-1 Att. 29,000
Taylor, Thomas
1967, Division 1.
Coventry City (h) 3-2 Att. 28,892
Bennett, Davies, Iley
1972, Division 1.
Coventry City (a) 3-0 Att. 17,592
Macdonald (3)
1978, Division 2.
Wrexham (a) 0-0 Att. 14,091
1989, Division 2.
Portsmouth (h) 1-0 Att. 19,766
Thorn
1992, Anglo Italian Cup perliminary round.
Grimsby Town (a) 2-2 Att. 2,159
Quinn, Kelly
1995, Premier League.
Newcastle 3 **Manchester City 1**
Beardsley 17 (pen) Creaney 81
Ferdinand 36, 59 Att. 36,501
1999, UEFA Cup 1st round, 1st leg.
CSKA Sofia 0 **Newcastle 2**
Solano 51
Ketsbaia 77
Att. 20,260
2000, Premier League.
Southampton 2 **Newcastle 0**
Pahars 47, 61 Att. 15,221

Playing record for this day is... 22 games, Won 8, Drawn 7, Lost 7, GF 31, GA 34.
Today's success rate... 52.27%.

Birthdays

Paul Brayson born today in 1977.
Forward 1994-1998, Apps 2 (1 sub). Goals 0.
Albert Harris born today in 1912.
Winger 1935-1936, Apps 12. Goals 4.
David McCreery born today in 1957.
Midfield 1982-1989, Apps 273 (7 subs). Goals 2.

Sadly Missed

John Dryden died on this day in 1975, aged 67.
Winger 1932-1934, Apps 6. Goals 1.
Sandy Mutch died on this day 1967, aged 82.
Goalkeeper 1922-1958, Apps 43.

...yed on this day

Division 1.
Notts County (h) 1-2   Att. 18,000
Aitken
Division 1.
Everton (h) 3-2   Att. 21,000
Veitch (2), Rutherford
Division 1.
Tottenham Hotspur (a) 2-1   Att. 35,000
Ridley, Rutherford
Division 1.
Burnley (h) 2-1   Att. 48,000
Harris (2)
Division 1.
Blackburn Rovers (a) 1-2   Att. 26,000
Seymour
Division 1.
West Ham United (h) 4-1   Att. 30,000
Harris (3), McDonald
Division 1.
Everton (h) 2-2   Att. 50,539
McDonald, McKay
Division 1.
Birmingham (h) 2-2   Att. 30,000
Lindsay, J.R. Richardson
Division 1.
Portsmouth (h) 1-1   Att. 40,000
Allen
Division 2.
Tottenham Hotspur (a) 0-1   Att. 40,531
Division 2.
Birmingham City (h) 1-0   Att. 51,704
Hair
Division 1.
Manchester City (h) 4-2   Att. 58,141
Hannah, Milburn, G. Robledo, Walker
Division 1.
Sunderland (a) 2-0   Att. 59,665
Mitchell, G. Robledo
Division 1.
Charlton Athletic (h) 4-1   Att. 39,040
Keeble, Milburn (3)
Division 1.
Chelsea (h) 1-2   Att. 50,283
White
Division 1.
Arsenal (a) 0-5   Att. 34,885
Division 1.
Nottingham Forest (a) 0-3   Att. 21,732
Inter Cities Fairs Cup 1st round, 2nd leg.
Feyenoord (a) 0-2   Att. 45,000
Newcastle won 4-2 on aggregate.
Division 1.
Everton (h) 1-2   Att. 37,094
Elliott
Division 1.
Birmingham City (a) 0-3   Att. 18,953
Division 2.
Crystal Palace (h) 3-1   Att. 22,869
Waddle, Keegan, Ryan
Division 1.
Norwich City (h) 0-2   Att. 22,809
Division 2.
Ipswich Town (h) 1-1   Att. 16,336
Quinn (pen)
Champions' League, Group C.
Newcastle 3   Barcelona 2
Asprilla   Luis Enrique 72
22 (pen), 30, 48   Figo 88   Att. 35,274
European Cup Winners Cup
1st round, 1st leg.
Newcastle 2   Partizan Belgrade 1
Shearer 12   Rasovic 69 (pen)
Dabizas 71   Att. 26,599
...record for this day is... 25 games.
..., Drawn 4, Lost 10, GF 40, GA 42.
... success rate... 52%.

Match of the Day from 1997

BARCA BEATEN BY ACE ASPRILLA

Hat-trick sets up memorable Champions' League victory

A hat trick by Tino Asprilla ensured that this game lived up to its expectations. Newcastle's first Champions' League tie saw one of the finest performances most United fans have ever witnessed. United showed that while they have only ever been Premiership runners-up, they are not out of place among the Champions of Europe. In what used to be called the European Cup, the South American skills of Asprilla earned Newcastle a famous victory, the Colombian scoring three and almost managing a fourth. He may have grabbed the spotlight but the performance of Keith Gillespie on the right flank was a throw-back to the days when wing play ruled supreme. The Northern Ireland international gave Sergi and the rest of the Barcelona defence a torrid time, making two of Asprilla's goals and looking like a player who could make a big impact on the Champions' League.

Tino Asprilla (left, no.11) scores from the spot.

As early as the sixth minute, Jon Dahl Tomasson missed the target from fifteen yards. Then the Dane, with the goal at his mercy, miscontrolled the ball and another chance was lost. Would Barcelona punish Newcastle for such wasted opportunity? United continued to pound away at the Barcelona defence and only a perfectly timed tackle from Nadal on Asprilla inside the penalty area saved the Spanish champions in the twentieth minute. A minute later, Ruud Hesp was ruled to have fouled Asprilla as the goalkeeper dived to save at his feet. A harsh decision, perhaps, but Asprilla was coolness personified as he struck the penalty to Hesp's right for the game's opening goal. In the 31st minute, Newcastle extended their lead. Steve Watson played a free kick out to Gillespie, who gained a yard on Sergi before crossing for Asprilla to beat Albert Celades and head powerfully past Hesp.

The second half saw no let up in the United pressure as they streamed forward roared on by the passionate and noisy St James' Park crowd. Four minutes after the restart, Asprilla completed his hat-trick after Gillespie once again left Sergi trailing in his wake down the right wing. Asprilla outjumped Nadal to head home and for the third time the fans were treated to his impressive trademark somersault. Barcelona regained some poise and Shay Given made magnificent saves from Rivaldo and Nadal. Luis Enrique's chested goal in the 73rd minute from Luis Figo's cross gave them a glimmer of hope, and sensing a revival was possible, Barcelona began throw everything available at the United defence. In the 88th minute, Newcastle failed to clear a corner and Figo, Barcelona's stand-in captain, fired a low shot through a ruck of players to make the score 3-2. This ensured a nervy last two minutes for the partying crowd who to their credit roared Newcastle home to the final whistle never showing a sense of panic. Newcastle deserved this win, and the Toon Army knew it.

Newcastle United
Given, Barton, Watson, Albert, Beresford, Gillespie, Lee, Batty, Barnes (Ketsbaia 81), Tomasson (Peacock 77), Asprilla.

Barcelona
Hesp, Reiziger, Celades, Sergi, Nadal, De La Pena, Amunike (Ciric h/t), Figo, Luis Enrique, Rivaldo, Anderson (Dugarry 56).

Referee Mr. P. Collina (Italy)

September 18

Match of the Day from 1994

BEARDSLEY FIRES RED HOT UNITED

Six wins in succession now for for title favourites

For the first time in two years Manchester United have been replaced as Premiership favourites with Newcastle United now taking over; according to leading bookmakers you can get 13/8 on them for the title, even at this early stage. Who would argue? Arsenal today played their most positive football this term, dominating for long periods but failing to stifle Newcastle when it counted. The Toon Army departed with a growing feeling that the championship trophy, not witnessed at St James' Park since 1927, was on its way. The season is still young but there is impressive evidence seen today that Newcastle are, in George Graham's words, "Championship material." Kevin Keegan's team have enjoyed a straightforward start, securing wins against teams they really ought to, but a determined victory at Arsenal's citadel in North London gave notice of their intent.

The charge was sparked by the livewire Peter Beardsley making his 500th league appearance. His seventh minute shot, after Martin Keown had headed out Marc Hottiger's right-wing cross, arrowing its way past David Seaman when Keown stooped to deflect it in. But it was Beardsley's goal; 1-0 and Newcastle off and running. But Graham's teams are always resilient and they drew level within two minutes. A foul by Beardsley on Wright allowed the excellent Paul Merson to cause chaos by chipping a free kick into the Newcastle box. When Darren Peacock failed to clear, Tony Adams marched in to beat Pavel Srnicek at the second attempt. An open game of persistent excitement swung each way but, slowly, Arsenal began to take control. Wright, twice, and Alan Smith, with a splendid hooked volley, went close as Arsenal strove intelligently forward. The Gunners made particular headway down the left, where Hottiger was continually troubled by Wright and the free-ranging Merson. But for all this, it was United who went ahead again thanks to Lee Dixon's error moments before half-time. The fullback's push on the dynamic Philippe Albert was spotted and Beardsley confidently converted the spot kick, low to Seaman's left.

Ruel Fox and Andy Cole, desperate to score against a team that rejected him, emphasised Newcastle's counter-attacking danger in the second half, and they should have been awarded another penalty in the 72nd minute when Schwarz fouled Scott Sellars. Referee Holbrook this time wrongly ignored the incident. But, just two minutes later, this was forgotten when United scored their third goal. Again Beardsley involved, skipping past Keown and Ian Selly before seeing his shot deflected by Dixon to Fox at the far post. Fox's shot slammed down off the crossbar and in off the hapless Keown. Although Wright reduced the deficit in the penultimate minute with a low drive, following Peacock's poor headed clearance, nothing could deny Newcastle's fully deserved victory.

Arsenal
Seaman, Dixon, Keown, Adams, Winterburn, Parlour (Campbell 70), Jensen, (Selly 70), Schwarz, Merson, Wright, Smith.
Newcastle United
Srnicek, Hottiger, Peacock, Albert, Howey, Beresford, Lee, Beardsley, Sellars, Fox, Cole.
Referee Mr. T. Holbrook (Walsall).

Birthdays

Ken Hale born today in 1939.
Midfield 1956-1962, Apps 35. Goals 16.

September 19

, Division 2.
Notts County (a) 1-3   Att. 5,000
Stott
, Division 1.
Everton (a) 1-4   Att. 20,000
Howie
, Division 1.
Notts County (h) 1-0   Att. 31,000
Wilson
, Division 1.
Bradford City (h) 1-0   Att. 15,000
Douglas
, Division 1.
Leicester City (h) 3-2.   Att. 31,000
Loughlin (3)
, Division 1.
West Ham United (a) 1-2   Att. 25,000
Allen
, Division 2.
Blackpool (a) 0-3   Att. 26,962
, Wartime.
Huddersfield Town (h) 0-4   Att. 8,000
, Division 1.
Tottenham Hotspur (h) 1-3   Att. 53,056
Milburn
, Division 1.
Burnley (h) 1-3   Att. 38,576
Tait
, Division 2.
Derby County (a) 1-0   Att. 14,901
Fell
, Division 2.
Cardiff City (a) 1-1   Att. 12,016
Cummings
, Division 1.
West Ham United (a) 2-0   Att. 25,841
Robson (2)
, Texaco Cup 1st round, 1st leg.
Morton (a) 2-1   Att. 4,326
Tudor, Smith
, Division 2.
Norwich City (a) 1-2   Att. 14,384
Waddle
, Littlewoods Cup 2nd round, 1st leg.
Reading (a) 1-3   Att. 7,960
Gallacher
, Division 1.
Bristol City (h) 5-0   Att. 29,465
O'Brien, Peacock (2, pens), Carr, Brock
, Coca Cola Cup 2nd round, 1st leg.

Bristol City 0	Newcastle 5
	Peacock 8
	Sellars 22
	Ferdinand 30
	Gillespie 46
Att 15,592	Lee 85

, Premier League.

Coventry City 1	Newcastle 5
Whelan 4	Dabizas 14
	Shearer 42, 90
	Speed 43
Att. 22,656	Glass 58

, Premier League.

Newcastle 8	Sheffield Wed. 0
Hughes 11	
Shearer 30, 33 (pen),	
42, 81, 84(pen)	
Dyer 46	
Speed 78	Att. 36,619

ing record for this day is... 20 games,
 10, Drawn 1, Lost 9, GF 41, GA 32.
y's success rate... 52.50%.

ROBSON'S HOMECOMING GIVEN AN EIGHT GOAL SALUTE

Shearer hits five as the Owls crumble

As over 36,000 Geordies sang "walking in a Robson wonderland", Newcastle ripped apart Sheffield Wednesday with an exhibition of spirited, awesome football at St James' Park today. It was an encouraging start to the Robson reign bringing Newcastle their biggest goal tally in a game since November 1959, an 8-2 win over Everton, and the largest margin of victory since October 1946, when a debut-making Len Shackleton scored six and Jackie Milburn two in a 13-0 win over Newport County. What a homecoming for Robson. If the jubilant Toon Army had come to welcome Bobby Robson home to the ground where he once stood and marvelled at Milburn and Co., they were soon lauding a beloved No.9 of the modern era. Alan Shearer not only scored five times, equalling Andy Cole's Premiership record for Manchester United, but he gave a wonderful display of the centre-forward arts, teasing and turning defenders mercilessly. He battled bravely, passed intelligently, scored truly magnificently.

United's players were in the mood, their formation with Kieron Dyer floating behind the attack proved just too much for Wednesday. The gathering thunder of Shearer's incipient goals was initially stolen by Aaron Hughes, who headed in Dyer's eleventh minute cross for his first professional goal. Confidence swept through the whole team, as Gary Speed, Robert Lee, Dyer, and Shearer took an unshakeable grip on proceedings. On the half-hour, Shearer began his obliteration of the Owls. Temuri Ketsbaia and Nolberto Solano combined and there was Shearer, poaching brilliantly. Shearer's second came two minutes later when he thumped in a debatable penalty, given as Warren Barton had driven the ball straight at one of Thome's hands. England's captain then completed his hat-trick four minutes before the break, again profiting from good service from the flanks, this time from the irrepressible Dyer.

Dyer's neat header made it 5-0 after the break, following pressure by Speed initially and a final telling pass by Shearer. Dyer then limped off, with a twisted ankle, but Newcastle never lost their momentum. Right-wing deliveries from Solano brought goals six and seven, a firm header from Speed and a cool shot by Shearer. Substitute Paul Robinson then bustled into the box and was allegedly fouled by Gerald Sibon. Referee Neale Barry, gave it and Shearer converted the spot-kick. This was unfortunate for a dejected, under pressure Wednesday boss Danny Wilson whose side remain rooted to the bottom of the Premiership. In total contrast United's delighted new boss departed St James' Park saying "I hope the fans don't expect that every week." They don't, but once or twice a season would be nice.

Newcastle United
Harper, Barton, Hughes, Goma, Domi (Glass 81), Solano, Lee, Speed, Dyer (Robinson 63), Ketsbaia (McClen 78), Shearer.
Sheffield Wednesday
Pressman, Newsome, Thome, Walker, Nolan, Donnelly (Sibon 83), Sonner, Alexandersson, Rudi (Haslam h/t), Booth (Carbone 27), De Bilde.
Referee Mr. N. Barry (Scunthorpe)

Birthdays

Gary Brazil born today in 1962
Forward 1989-1990, Apps 27 (19 subs). Goals 3.
Arnold Grundy born today in 1919.
Midfield 1936-1944, Apps 2. Goals 0.

Eric Ross born today in 1944.
Midfield 1967-1969, Apps 4. Goals 0.
Brian Wright born today in 1939.
Midfield 1956-1963, Apps 47. Goals 1.

Sadly Missed

Jonathon Wilkinson died on this day in 1979, aged 71.
Centre-forward 1927-1929, Apps 27. Goals 11.

September 20

Match of the Day from 1975

HAT-TRICK FOR GOWLING

Newcastle fight hard to win against poor Wolves

30,876 turned out to see this clash at St James' Park against Wolverhampton Wanderers today. Newcastle were missing Malcolm Macdonald in the team, but fortunately they did have Alan Gowling, his presence was going to prove invaluable for this match.

At the beginning it seemed as if Wolves had the upper hand when both Carr and Hibbitt had their efforts saved by the energetic Mahoney in the home goal. Then the visitors caused more worry for Newcastle when they took the lead nine minutes into the game. Daley was positioned just right to get on to a low cross from Palmer. His shot slammed into the net past Mahoney to put the visitors ahead.

Newcastle took just one minute to bring the scores level. Pierce came off his line, and Gowling was on hand to nod the ball into the goal, with a little help from the post. So, now both teams had a goal, but there were already signs of weakness showing in the Wolves' defence.

The second half began with Parkin unable to continue for Wolves. He had been injured in the first half, and Farley took his place at the interval. Ten minutes into the half and things started to go badly wrong for Wolves. Bailey was booked for a crash into Burns, and then straightaway Pierce tried to get hold of a shot from Craig. The Wolves' keeper grabbed for the ball desperately, and in doing so helped it on to where Tudor was waiting to flick it into the net to put the home side into the lead.

On 60 minutes Newcastle increased their lead when Gowling won the ball from Daley and ran unchallenged past the Wolves' defence to send the ball rocketing into the net. Wolves had two good chances next, but they fluffed them both. Sunderland's shot floated into the side netting, and then a jumble in the Newcastle goal area caused concern when the ball bounced off Farley and headed goalwards. Fortunately it hit the bar and went out of danger and Newcastle took control once more.

With ten minutes to go before the end Gowling completed his hat-trick with an easy shot past Pierce to bring the score to 4-1. Newcastle weren't finished yet, though and they managed another goal before the end. On 87 minutes it was Cassidy who performed a lovely solo move from midfield and sent the ball into the back of the net past the defeated Wolves keeper.

Newcastle United
Mahoney, Nattrass, Kennedy, Nulty, Bird, Howard, Burns, Cassidy, Tudor, Gowling, Craig.

Wolverhampton Wanderers
Pierce, Palmer, Parkin (Farley h/t), Bailey, Jefferson, McAlle, Hibbitt, Carr, Richards, Sunderland, Daley.

Alan Gowling

Played on this day

1902, Division 1.
Sheffield Wednesday (h) 3-0 Att. 25,000
Roberts (2), Rutherford
Newcastle go top of Division One after this win, their first time at the top in their history.

1913, Division 1.
West Bromwich A. (a) 1-1   Att. 30,000
Hudspeth (pen)

1919, Division 1.
Chelsea (h) 3-0   Att. 40,000
Dixon (3)

1924, Division 1.
Manchester City (a) 1-3   Att. 35,000
McDonald

1926, Division 1.
Cardiff City (a) 1-1   Att. 14,000
Urwin

1930, Division 1.
West Ham United (h) 4-2   Att. 20,000
Cape, Starling, Wilkinson, Opponent (og)

1941, Wartime.
Huddersfield Town (h) 3-1   Att. 5,500
Stubbins (2), Price

1947, Division 2.
Leeds United (h) 4-2   Att. 57,275
Hair, Shackleton (2), Stobbart

1952, Division 1.
Stoke City (a) 0-1   Att. 30,000

1958, Division 1.
Wolverhampton W. (a) 3-1   Att. 39,130
Bottom, White (2)

1961, Division 2.
Liverpool (h) 1-2   Att. 38,192
Hale

1969, Division 1.
Southampton (a) 1-1   Att. 19,130
Robson

1975, Division 1.
Wolverhampton W. (h) 5-1   Att. 30,876
Gowling (3), Tudor, Cassidy

1980, Division 2.
Oldham Athletic (h) 0-0   Att. 19,786

1986, Division 1.
Wimbledon (h) 1-0   Att. 21,545
Gascoigne

1987, Division 1.
Liverpool (h) 1-4   Att. 24,141
McDonald (pen)

1997, Premier League.
West Ham 0   Newcastle 1
                    Barnes 44
                             Att. 25,884

2000, Worthington Cup 2nd round, 1st leg.
Newcastle 2   Leyton Orient 0
Cort 34
Speed 77   Att. 37,284

Playing record for this day is... 18 games, Won 10, Drawn 4, Lost 4, GF 35, GA 20. Today's success rate... 66.67%.

September 21

Played on this day

1895, Division 2.
Notts County (h) 5-1   Att. 7,000
Aitken (3), Logan, McKay
1901, Division 1.
Everton (a) 0-0   Att. 20,000
1907, Division 1.
Bristol City (a) 1-1   Att. 18,000
Orr
1912, Division 1.
Chelsea (h) 3-2   Att. 38,000
Stewart (2), Peart
1929, Division 1.
Birmingham (a) 1-5   Att. 35,000
Lang
1935, Division 2.
Port Vale (a) 0-3   Att. 9,178
1940, Wartime.
Middlesbrough (a) 2-3   Att. 3,300
English (2)
1946, Division 2.
Burnley (h) 1-2   Att. 61,255
Wayman
1957, Division 1.
Sunderland (a) 0-2   Att. 45,218
1963, Division 2.
Preston North End (h) 2-4   Att. 29,710
Kirkman, Burton
1968, Division 1.
Manchester United (a) 1-3   Att. 47,262
Gibb
1974, Division 1.
Queens Park Rangers (a) 2-1 Att. 18,594
Tudor, Burns
1985, Division 1.
Oxford United (h) 3-0   Att. 23,642
Gascoigne, Beardsley, McDonald
1991, Division 2.
Millwall (a) 1-2   Att. 9,156
Neilson
1994, Coca Cola Cup 2nd round, 1st leg.
Newcastle 2   **Barnsley 1**
Cole 25   Redfearn 20
Fox 85   Att. 27,208
1996, Premier League.
Leeds United 0   Newcastle 1
Shearer 59
Att. 36,070
2002, Premier League.
Newcastle 2   **Sunderland 0**
Bellamy 2
Shearer 39   Att. 52,181

Playing record for this day is... 17 games,
Won 7, Drawn 2, Lost 8, GF 27, GA 30.
Today's success rate... 47.06%.

Match of the Day from 2002

WEARSIDERS WORRIES GROW AFTER DERBY DEFEAT

Sunderland sunk inside 83 seconds

Today's 123rd Tyne-Wear derby finally confirmed what many have feared amongst their own supporters, Sunderland really do look doomed. Their players looked second best in all areas, particularly in the passion department so crucial in games like these. Their abject display so infuriated their manager Peter Reid he even abandoned one of his lifelong principles and publicly condemned his players for the first time in his seven-and-a-half year reign. With only two goals in seven games Sunderland have just five points from a possible 21 and it's difficult to see where the next one, goal or point, will come from. Newcastle, and Sir Bobby Robson, however, were also under pressure, albeit a contrasting sort, going into this high profile game on the back of three successive defeats. The difference though was derby passion and where Newcastle had it in abundance, Sunderland inexcusably showed none.

One man demonstrated this to the entire Sunderland squad more than any exactly what the word passion means in derby showdowns, Alan Shearer. The former England captain, his head bandaged after a wound suffered during the Champions' League game in Kiev, created Newcastle's opening goal after only 83 seconds and clinched the victory with his fourth goal of the season five minutes before half-time.

That crucial early breakthrough owed much to the perceptive refereeing of Mike Riley who watched Sunderland centre-back Joachim Bjorklund clatter into the back of Shearer but allowed the striker's brave lay-off to Kieron Dyer to develop for Craig Bellamy to celebrate in style his first home start since recovering from injury and the opening goal against the 'enemy'. The referee, who eventually cautioned Bjorklund for his challenge then ruined a great performance, by later showing a yellow card to Bellamy for diving in the penalty area in what should have been the game's deciding incident, Matthew Piper clearly pushing Bellamy in the act of shooting for goal. A penalty, at that point, would have surely killed off an already demoralised Sunderland team but it mattered little. Shearer had already dealt them the killer blow. A free kick, earnt by Shearer on the edge of the penalty area again for an illegal challenge from behind, was gently rolled out to him by Nolberto Solano and Shearer fired the ball like an arrow through the crumbling defensive wall giving Sorensen no chance.

From this point Sunderland's threats were disturbingly minimal. Tore Andre Flo, brought in by Reid to lighten the load of Kevin Phillips who was far from full fitness failed to hit the target with two close range headers. The closest Sunderland come, through good fortune, was when Flo charged down a clearance from Shay Given which the keeper still managed to stop as the ball sailed backwards, Given retrieving the ball inches from the goal-line.

Newcastle United
Given, Griffin, O'Brien, Dabizas, Hughes, Solano (Jenas 64), Dyer, Speed, Robert (Viana 77), Shearer, Bellamy (Ameobi 85).
Sunderland
Sorensen, Wright, Bjorklund (Williams 71 mins), Babb, Gray, Piper, McAteer (Quinn h/t), McCann, Reyna, Kilbane, Flo (Stewart 85).
Referee Mr. M. Riley (Leeds).

Birthdays

Bob Stokoe born today in 1930.
Centre-half 1947-1961, Apps 288, Goals 5.

September 22

Match of the Day from 1984

FIVE-STAR GAME AT LOFTUS ROAD

Newcastle lose a huge lead in a second-half turnaround by QPR

The 14,144 supporters who turned up at Loftus Road to watch this Division One match were in for a treat. QPR were hoping that today they could put behind them the humiliating 5-0 defeat they suffered last week at Spurs. Newcastle had the energetic and enthusiastic Chris Waddle in their side, and he made a huge impact on the game.

It was Waddle who provided the ball for Neil McDonald on three minutes. McDonald fired the ball into the net for Newcastle's first goal, and that was just the beginning of an exciting display of action.

Waddle then brought the tally to two with his first shot of the game, and Newcastle were growing in confidence. QPR began to worry further when Waddle again slammed the ball into the back of the net for his second, and Newcastle's third.

Waddle then completed his hat-trick with a super shot before the interval, and the visiting team had the huge advantage of being four goals up going into the break.

In the second half QPR changed their tactics, and the game was thrown open again. No one thought it was possible for the home side to pull back from their four-goal deficit, but they were going to try. Their change of approach worked, and it wasn't long before Gary Bannister shot home the first goal for QPR.

Another goal followed soon after, when Simon Stainrod sent in a lovely shot, which deflected off the nose of Kenny Wharton before entering the net. Now the home team were only two goals behind, and they were on a roll.

The Newcastle defence began to panic, and this left openings for QPR to take advantage of. John Gregory managed to slip through and send the ball past the Magpies' keeper to bring the home side's tally to three.

Now the home fans were starting to believe that the revived QPR side could draw level, while the Newcastle fans were worrying about just that too. Newcastle were given an extra boost in front when a lovely pass from Waddle came to Wharton. He made amends for his own goal and sent the ball powerfully into the net past the QPR keeper to give Newcastle five.

It looked to be all over by now, with just two minutes left on the clock. However, QPR had other ideas. They pulled together and managed to get another goal when the big defender Steve Wicks took it upon himself to charge up the field and plant the ball in the Newcastle net.

Just a goal behind, but the home team weren't happy with that. Newcastle lost out on their incredible away win in the dying seconds of the game when Gary Micklewhite slammed the ball home for QPR's fifth, securing the draw at the very end of play.

Queen's Park Rangers
Hucker, Neil, Dawes, Waddock, Wicks, Fenwick, Micklewhite, Fillery (Stewart), Bannister, Stainrod, Gregory.
Newcastle United
Carr, Brown, Saunders, Haddock, Anderson, Roeder, McDonald, Wharton, Waddle, Beardsley, McCreery.

Played on this day

1894, Division 2.
Notts County (h) 2-2   Att. 3,000
Thompson, Willis
1900, Division 1.
West Bromwich A. (a) 1-0   Att. 10,000
Peddie
1906, Division 1.
Woolwich Arsenal (a) 0-2   Att. 30,000
1923, Division 1.
Cardiff City (h) 1-1   Att. 40,000
McDonald
1928, Division 1.
Leicester City (h) 1-0   Att. 31,000
Hudspeth
1934, Division 2.
Plymouth Argyle (a) 3-1   Att. 12,000
Boyd, Leach, Smith
1945, Wartime.
Stoke City (h) 9-1   Att. 46,349
Hair, Wayman, Stubbins (5), Clifton (2)
1951, Division 1.
Charlton Athletic (a) 0-3   Att. 52,168
1956, Division 1.
Burnley (h) 1-1   Att. 36,790
Keeble
1962, Division 2.
Norwich City (h) 2-1   Att. 36,345
Fell (pen), Thomas
1965, League Cup 2nd round.
Peterborough United (h) 3-4 Att. 16,132
Hilley, Bennett, Iley
1973, Division 1.
Coventry City (a) 2-2   Att. 24,085
Tudor, Macdonald
1976, League Cup 3rd round.
Stoke City (h) 3-0   Att. 27,143
T. Craig (pen), Burns, Nattrass
1979, Division 2.
Wrexham (h) 1-0   Att. 27,904
Shoulder (pen)
1984, Division 1.
Queens Park Rangers (a) 5-5 Att. 14,144
Waddle (3), Wharton, McDonald
1990, Division 2.
West Ham United (h) 1-1   Att. 25,462
McGhee
1993, Coca Cola Cup 2nd round, 1st leg.
Newcastle 4   Notts County 1
Cole 30, 54, 63   Srnicek (og) 16
Bracewell 72   Att. 25,887

Playing record for this day is... 17 games,
Won 8, Drawn 6, Lost 3, GF 39, GA 25.
Today's success rate... 64.71%.

Birthdays

Steve Carney born today in 1957
Centre-half 1979-1985, Apps 149 (9 subs). Goals 1.

Bob Whitehead born today in 1936.
Right-back 1954-1962, Apps 20. Goals 0.

Division 2.
Burton Swifts (a) 1-3
Unknown
Division 1.
Derby County (h) 2-0   Att. 19,000
Peddie, Wardrope
Division 1.
Derby County (h) 0-1   Att. 31,600
Division 1.
Chelsea (a) 0-2   Att. 25,000
Division 1.
Manchester City (h) 1-0   Att. 11,000
Stewart
Division 1.
Preston North End (h) 3-1   Att. 35,000
Harris (2), McDonald
Division 1.
Birmingham (h) 0-0   Att. 22,000
Wartime.
Sunderland (a) 0-2   Att. 18,000
Division 1.
Arsenal (h) 2-1   Att. 66,926
Milburn, Taylor
Division 1.
Sheffield Wednesday (a) 0-3 Att. 29,271
Division 2.
Southampton (a) 0-1   Att. 20,064
League Cup 2nd round.
Blackpool (a) 0-3   Att. 13,670
Division 1.
Sheffield United (a) 1-2   Att. 16,387
B. Robson (pen)
Inter Cities Fairs Cup 1st round, 1st leg.
Internazionale (a) 1-1   Att. 14,460
Davies
Division 1.
Leeds United (h) 3-2   Att. 38,964
Tudor, Macdonald, Smith
Division 1.
Birmingham City (a) 2-3   Att. 31,166
T. Craig, Nulty
Division 2.
Orient (h) 0-0   Att. 26,361
Division 2.
Shrewsbury Town (h) 2-0   Att. 13,783
Wharton, Shinton
Littlewoods Cup 2nd round, 1st leg.
Bradford City (a) 0-2   Att. 6,384
Littlewoods Cup 2nd round, 1st leg.
Blackpool (a) 0-1   Att. 7,959
Coca Cola Cup 2nd round, 1st leg.
Middlesbrough (h) 0-0   Att. 25,814
Premier League.
Newcastle 0   Charlton Athletic 1
Stuart 8
Att. 50,866
Premier League.
West Ham United 3 Newcastle 0
Hutchinson 18
Di Canio 53
Kanoute 82   Att. 24,840

record for this day is... 23 games,
Drawn 4, Lost 13, GF 18, GA 32.
success rate... 34.78%.

September 23

Match of the Day from 1922

UNITED PREST-ON FOR WIN

Newcastle take victory over half-hearted Preston

35,000 flocked to St James' Park today to see Newcastle play host to Preston North End. The Newcastle forwards Low and Hagan had the upper hand over the Preston defence from the outset, and this gave Newcastle the edge over their opponents.

Likewise it was the Newcastle defence who held the sway over the Preston forward line, with Roberts being no match for the likes of McIntosh, McCracken and Hudspeth.

So, with the home side playing the better football, it was no surprise when they opened the scoring on nine minutes with a super shot from Harris.

Harris added a second goal for Newcastle when he managed to get his head to a lovely cross to put the home side two ahead.

Preston needed some good luck if they were going to get back into this game. They tried hard to build up their efforts, and the pace of the game picked up. Despite all their hard work, Preston's goal came from a penalty, and had nothing to do with their improved play. Rawlings stepped up to take the spot-kick, and shot past the Newcastle keeper to pull a goal back for the visitors going into the break.

After the interval Preston lacked pace and enthusiasm, but Newcastle entered the field revived and determined. The control was all Newcastle's throughout the half, and it was inevitable that they would score another goal before the game was over.

They outplayed Preston in every aspect, and a third goal was never far away. It was McDonald who got his head to the ball to nod it into the back of the net for the last goal of the game.

Newcastle United
Bradley, McCracken, Hudspeth, McIntosh, Spencer, Curry, J. Low, Hagan, Harris, McDonald, Richardson.

Preston North End
Branston, Hamilton, Doolan, Crawford, McCall, Mercer, Rawlings, Jefferis, Roberts, Woodhouse, Quantrill.

George Eastham

Birthdays

George Eastham born today in 1936. Midfield 1956-1960, Apps 129. Goals 34.

September 24

Match of the Day from 1991

PROUD PEACOCK LEADS THE FIGHT BACK

Hat trick hero stuns Crewe after leading by three

Newcastle United, who reached the final of this competition in 1976 but have not reached the third round since 1977, found themselves seemingly facing another exit today after going three goals behind to Crewe inside half an hour. Then the inspirational Gavin Peacock with his first goals of the season netted a dramatic hat-trick as United came back to win this second round, first leg tie, 4-3. It has been a great rarity in recent years for the word crisis not to appear neon-bright at least once during Newcastle's season. With an emergency board meeting to discuss the latest dire warnings of financial doom scheduled for tomorrow morning, today's troubles were confined solely to those on the pitch.

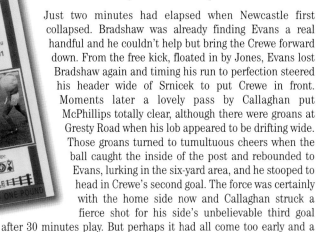

Just two minutes had elapsed when Newcastle first collapsed. Bradshaw was already finding Evans a real handful and he couldn't help but bring the Crewe forward down. From the free kick, floated in by Jones, Evans lost Bradshaw again and timing his run to perfection steered his header wide of Srnicek to put Crewe in front. Moments later a lovely pass by Callaghan put McPhillips totally clear, although there were groans at Gresty Road when his lob appeared to be drifting wide. Those groans turned to tumultuous cheers when the ball caught the inside of the post and rebounded to Evans, lurking in the six-yard area, and he stooped to head in Crewe's second goal. The force was certainly with the home side now and Callaghan struck a fierce shot for his side's unbelievable third goal after 30 minutes play. But perhaps it had all come too early and a little too easy, for by half time Newcastle had reduced the arrears from three goals to just one. A large punt by Srnicek, which keeper Greygoose flapped at like a grounded pigeon, saw Hunt run clear for a simple but very important goal moments later. Suddenly there was new heart in the Newcastle team, Peacock producing a long-range shot of real quality made it 3-2, and United were right back in the game just before half time.

Crewe however, were also still dangerous, and in the second half they hit the post twice in a vain effort to prove the opening 30 minutes was no fluke. Then they were denied what seemed a clear-cut penalty decision brushed aside by referee Dilkes. Dario Gradi's team, relegated to the Fourth Division last season, certainly deserved a fourth goal but it was not to be on the night. Instead Newcastle, always prepared to keep playing football despite adversities, equalised and then took the lead. A determined run by Clark, who refused to be shaken off the ball, allowed Peacock to make it 3-3 mid way through the half. Then a corner from the right saw the same player head the winner at close range to complete a match-ball winning trio of goals. Newcastle's sigh of relief at the end will probably be their biggest of the season, for Crewe this was by far the cruellest 90 minutes they'll endure in the decade.

Crewe Alexandra
Greygoose, Wilson, Jones, Carr, Callaghan, Walters, Garvey, (McKearney 39), McPhillips, Evans, Gardiner, Edwards.

Newcastle United
Srnicek, Neilson, Elliott, O'Brien, Scott, Bradshaw, Clark, Peacock, Quinn, Hunt (Howey 81), Roche (Appleby 88).

Referee Mr. L. Dilkes (Mossley).

Birthdays

Franz Carr born today in 1966.
Winger 1991-1993, Apps 33 (8 subs). Goals 3.

John Nesbitt born today in 1933.
Centre-half 1955-1959, Apps 3. Goals 0.

Played on this day

1898, Division 1.
Stoke (a) 0-0   Att. 12,000
In their fourth game of the season Newcastle finally earn their first top flight point at the Victoria Ground.

1904, Division 1.
Small Heath (a) 1-2   Att. 15,000
Veitch

1910, Division 1.
Middlesbrough (h) 0-0   Att. 40,000

1919, Division 1.
Derby County (h) 0-0   Att. 25,000

1921, Division 1.
Sheffield United (a) 1-1   Att. 25,000
Harris

1927, Division 1.
Cardiff City (a) 1-3   Att. 30,000
Gallacher

1928, Division 1.
Blackburn Rovers (a) 0-2   Att. 14,750

1932, Division 1.
Chelsea (a) 1-0   Att. 55,000
Boyd

1938, Division 2.
Southampton (h) 1-0   Att. 35,000
Cairns

1949, Division 1.
Fulham (a) 1-2   Att. 40,000
Milburn (pen)

1951, FA Charity Shield.
Tottenham Hotspur (a) 1-2   Att. 27,760
Milburn

1952, FA Charity Shield.
Manchester United (a) 2-4   Att. 11,381
Keeble (2)

1955, Division 1.
Tottenham Hotspur (a) 1-3   Att. 41,096
Milburn

1960, Division 1.
Leicester City (h) 1-3   Att. 21,161
McGuigan

1966, Division 1.
Fulham (h) 1-1   Att. 20,427
Noble

1977, Division 1.
Coventry City (h) 1-2   Att. 22,484
Gowling

1983, Division 2.
Barnsley (a) 1-1   Att. 14,085
Waddle

1988, Division 1.
Charlton Athletic (a) 2-2   Att. 6,088
D. Jackson, Tinnion

1989, Division 2.
Sunderland (a) 0-0   Att. 29,499

1991, Rumbelows Cup 2nd round, 1st leg.
Crewe Alexandra (a) 4-3   Att. 4,251
Hunt, Peacock (3)

1994, Premier League.
Newcastle 1   Liverpool 1
Lee 50   Rush 70 Att. 34,435

1995, Premier League.
Newcastle 2   Chelsea 0
Ferdinand 41, 57   Att. 36,225

1996, UEFA Cup 1st round, 2nd leg.
Halmstads 2   Newcastle 1
Arvidsson 74   Ferdinand 43
M. Svensson 81   Att. 7,847
Newcastle won 5-2 on aggregate

1997, Premier League.
Newcastle 1   Everton 0
Lee 87   Att. 36,705

continued overleaf

September 24

Played on this day

2002, Champions League.
Newcastle 0   **Feyenoord 1**
            Pardo 4
                      Att. 40,540

Playing record for this day is... 25 games,
Won 5, Drawn 9, Lost 11, GF 25, GA 35.
Today's success rate... 38%.

Andy Cole breaks away from West Ham United's Ian Bishop during the match played on September 25 1993 opposite.

September 25

Match of the Day from 1993

COLE HAMMERS IN TWO

Newcastle deserve victory in 2-0 win over West Ham

West Ham travelled to St James' Park today for this match, played out in front of 34,366. Newcastle were welcoming Peter Beardsley on his first home Premiership appearance since his return to the club, and spirits were high.

The game kicked off with Newcastle fully on the attack. West Ham struggled from the outset to keep up with the pace, and they failed considerably to do so. It was clear that Newcastle were the better team by far, and they were determined to win.

The first half was packed with attempts at goal, most from the home side, but none of these amounted to anything. Miklosko did well to keep the West Ham goal out of danger, but Hooper had no real chance to show his abilities, as there were no threats from the West Ham forwards.

So, the first half ended goalless and Newcastle had to step up the pressure if they were to break the deadlock in the second period.

The home side appeared revived after the interval, and seemed to have the energy needed to bring about a change in the game. Their efforts paid off in the 52nd minute when Beardsley feigned a cross and Cole leapt at the chance to slip the ball into the net for Newcastle's first goal.

Miklosko was well beaten, and West Ham were a little shaken. Now the home side were in the lead, and the visitors had plenty of work to do if they wanted to catch up.

West Ham brought on their new signing Jeroen Boere in the 63rd minute in place of Trevor Morley in the hope that this would refresh the side, but the change made little impact on the game.

Things got worse for West Ham in the 84th minute when Cole again managed to beat Miklosko for the home side's second. He got onto a pass from Lee Clark and sent the ball sailing into the corner of the net.

West Ham knew by now that they had little or no chance of making a comeback, and their misery was compounded when Boere elbowed Kevin Scott in the final minutes and was promptly shown the red card by the referee.

The game ended shortly afterwards with Newcastle content with their 2-0 win, a victory which was thoroughly deserved. The two goals from Cole brought his total for the season to ten, and 22 in 21 games for Newcastle.

Newcastle United
Hooper, Watson, Beresford, Bracewell, Scott, Venison, Lee, Allen, Cole, Clark, Beardsley.
West Ham United
Miklosko, Brown, Burrows, Potts, Gale, Marsh, Gordon, Bishop, Chapman, Holmes, Morley (Boere 63).
Referee Mr. M. Reed (Birmingham).

Birthdays

Ray Clarke born today in 1952.
Centre-forward 1980-1981, Apps 18. Goals 3

Chris Withe born today in 1962.
Left-back 1979-1983, Apps 2. Goals 0.

Played on this day

1897, Division 2.
Lincoln City (a) 3-2   Att. 3,000
Wardrope (2), Campbell
1909, Division 1.
Everton (h) 1-2   Att. 35,000
Shepherd
1920, Division 1.
Sheffield United (h) 3-0   Att. 40,000
Seymour (2), Harris
1926, Division 1.
Sheffield United (h) 2-0   Att. 30,000
Gallacher (2)
1937, Division 2.
Bury (a) 1-1   Att. 8,000
Imrie
1943, Wartime.
York City (a) 0-2   Att. 5,000
1948, Division 1.
Manchester City (h) 0-0   Att. 49,729
1954, Division 1.
Chelsea (h) 1-3   Att. 45,659
Milburn
1957, Division 1.
Sheffield Wednesday (h) 0-0 Att. 27,651
1963, League Cup 2nd round.
Preston North End (h) 3-0   Att. 14,906
McGarry (pen), Thomas, Burton
1965, Division 1.
Chelsea (a) 1-1   Att. 30,856
Bennett
1968, League Cup 3rd round.
Southampton (a) 1-4   Att. 13,840
B. Robson
1971, Division 1.
Ipswich Town (a) 0-0   Att. 18,724
1974, League Cup 2nd round, replay.
Nottingham Forest (h) 3-0   Att. 26,228
Macdonald, Burns, Keeley
1976, Division 1.
Liverpool (h) 1-0   Att. 34,813
Cannell
1982, Division 2.
Barnsley (h) 1-2   Att. 24,522
Varadi
1985, Milk Cup 2nd round, 1st leg.
Barnsley (h) 0-0   Att. 18,827
1990, Rumbelows Cup 2nd round, 1st leg.
Middlesbrough (a) 0-2   Att. 15,042
1993, Premier League.
Newcastle 2   West Ham 0
Cole 51, 84   Att. 34,366
1999, Premier League.
Leeds United 3   Newcastle 2
Bowyer 11   Shearer 42, 54
Kewell 39
Bridges 77   Att. 40,192

Playing record for this day is... 20 games,
Won 7, Drawn 6, Lost 7, GF 25, GA 22.
Today's success rate... 50%.

September 26

Played on this day

1896, Division 2.
Newton Heath (a) 0-4   Att. 7,000
1898, Division 1.
Sheffield United (a) 2-2   Att. 4,000
Peddie, Higgins
1903, Division 1.
Stoke (h) 1-0   Att. 16,000
Rutherford
1908, Division 1.
Sheffield Wednesday (a) 0-2 Att. 20,000
1914, Division 1.
Burnley (a) 0-2   Att. 15,000
1925, Division 1.
West Ham United (a) 0-1 Att. 30,000
1931, Division 1.
Sheffield Wednesday (h) 4-1 Att. 30,000
Bedford (pen), Allen, Boyd (2)
1936, Division 2.
Blackburn Rovers (h) 2-0 Att. 22,000
Cairns (2)
1942, Wartime.
Leeds United (h) 3-5   Att. 6,000
Moses, Stubbins, Carr
1953, Division 1.
Burnley (a) 2-1   Att. 33,738
Keery, Milburn
1959, Division 1.
Leeds United (a) 3-2   Att. 27,000
Allchurch, Scott (2)
1962, League Cup 2nd round.
Leyton Orient (h) 1-1   Att. 22,452
Fell (pen)
1964, Division 2.
Preston North End (h) 5-2   Att. 34,219
McGarry (2), Cummings, Hilley,
Opponent (og)
1970, Division 1.
Coventry City (h) 0-0   Att. 32,095
1981, Division 2.
Orient (h) 1-0   Att. 13,737
Trewick
1984, Milk Cup 2nd round, 1st leg.
Bradford City (h) 3-1   Att. 18,884
Wharton, McDonald, Ferris
1987, Division 1.
Southampton (h) 2-1   Att. 18,093
Mirandinha, Goddard
1992, Division 1.
Peterborough United (a) 1-0 Att. 14,487
Sheedy
1998, Premier League.
Newcastle 2   Nottingham Forest 0
Shearer 11, 89 (pen)   Att. 36,760
2000, Worthington Cup 2nd round, 2nd leg.
Leyton Orient 1   Newcastle 1
Watts 45   Gallacher 32
    Att. 9,522
Newcastle won 3-1 on aggregate
2001, Premier League.
Newcastle 1   Leicester City 0
Solano 33   Att. 49,185

Playing record for this day is... 21 games,
Won 12, Drawn 4, Lost 5, GF 34, GA 26.
Today's success rate... 66.67%.

Match of the Day from 1931

4-1 WIN FOR UNITED

Newcastle outplay Sheffield Wednesday to take win

This First Division match between Newcastle and Sheffield Wednesday drew a crowd of 30,000 at St James' Park today. Newcastle had several outstanding players in the squad, notably wingers Lang and Boyd, midfielders Weaver and Davidson, and defenders Nelson and Fairhurst. Forwards Hooper and Burgess played well for the visitors, as did Strange, Leach and Blenkinsop in midfield.

The game started well for both teams, but Newcastle were definitely the better side from the outset. However, it was Wednesday who opened the scoring with a great shot from Hooper. The ball came from a corner kick, and passed McInroy in the Magpies' goal so fast he didn't have a hope of making the save.

The rest of the first half was full of half chances for the two teams. That is until Boyd eventually managed to score the equaliser with a lovely shot, beating Brown just before the half-time whistle.

After the interval Newcastle seemed much more determined to take the win. They upped the pressure on the Owls' defence, and increased the number of shots at goal.

The second goal arrived for United, and it was Jimmy Boyd again who beat the visitors' keeper. This lead gave Newcastle the incentive to keep pushing forward, and their efforts paid off when the home side were awarded a penalty. Beeson committed a foul, and it was Bedford who stepped up to the spot to take the kick. His shot slammed into the net past Brown to give Newcastle their third goal.

The score was settled just before the end of the game when Allen slotted home his goal, bringing the result to 4-1.

Newcastle United
McInroy, Nelson, Fairhurst, Mathison, Davidson, Weaver, Boyd, Richardson, Allen, Bedford, Lang.
Sheffield Wednesday
Brown, Beeson, Blenkinsop, Strange, Leach, W. Smith, Hooper, Burgess, Ball, Stephenson, Rimmer.

Jimmy Nelson

Birthdays

'Kit' Napier born today in 1943.
Centre-forward 1965-1966, Apps 8. Goals 0.
Alan Neilson born today in 1972.
Centre-half 1989-1995, Apps 50 (7 subs). Goals 1.

Kenny Sansom born today in 1958.
Left-back 1988-1989, Apps 24. Goals 0.
Elena Marcelino born today in 1971.
Defender 1999-2003, Apps 22 (3 subs). Goals 0.

September 27

Match of the Day from 1994

COLE DEFIES THE PAIN TO PUT ANTWERP THROUGH AGONY

Hat-trick hero leads United to 10-2 aggregate victory

When Andy Cole heard Newcastle were planning to rest him for this second leg of the UEFA Cup second round tie which had been won a fortnight ago in Belgium, his insistence on taking part typified the spirit running through Kevin Keegan's team. Cole, who is suffering from shin splints, refuses to miss a single moment of the current Tyneside success story and his commitment to the Keegan cause was rewarded today with a sparkling hat-trick against Antwerp. Fielding weakened teams is as alien a concept as negative tactics to Keegan's attack minded sides. His players having earned selection are desperate not to lose it and the manager responded today by declaring he would never devalue a first-team shirt by giving it to somebody who is not ready for it. Though not fully fit, Cole led the attack with his usual aplomb and the faces around him were as familiar as ever. It was no more than Newcastle's committed supporters deserved. They filled St James' Park again and were repaid with another five-star performance which went close to matching the outstanding first-leg display in Belgium. Cole's three beautifully taken goals led the way to a 10-2 aggregate victory, a club record on their first European assignment for seventeen years.

Andy Cole is mobbed after his hat-trick.

Robert Lee, who hit a hat-trick himself in the first leg, needed just eleven minutes to inflict more misery on Antwerp, chipping the ball over keeper Yves van der Straeten after a Ruel Fox corner was not properly cleared. Peter Beardsley, who made a surprise return after breaking his cheekbone on the season's opening day, scored the third of Newcastle's goals from the penalty spot after Cole and Fox had combined to bring an illegal challenge out of Manuel Godfroid. In between those two strikes, Cole opened his account by steering home the most inviting of crosses from Scott Sellars. Just before half-time he added the best goal of the match to make it 4-0 after Philippe Albert and a brilliant cross from Beardsley set him up in the box.

It seemed a question of how many Newcastle would score in the second half, but after several reasonable chances had been squandered the proceedings took a totally unexpected turn with two goals from the visitors in as many minutes. Nobody in a 31,383 crowd begrudged the diving Wim Kierkens and the sharpshooting Francis Severeyns their moments of glory, but it was entirely appropriate that the final act should come from the indefatigable Andy Cole, who capitalised on Sellar's thrilling dribble in the penalty area to claim another hat-trick for Newcastle.

Newcastle United
Srnicek, Hottiger, Peacock, Howey, Beresford, Fox, Lee (Watson 72), Albert, Sellars, Cole Beardsley (Clark h/t)
Royal Antwerp
Van Der Straeten, Emmerechts, (Moukram h/t), Taeymans, Smidts, Godfroid, Porte, Kiekens, Kulcsar, Zohar, Severeyns, Van Gompel (Nilson).
Referee Mr. R. Pedersen (Norway).

Sadly Missed

Charles Randall died on this day in 1916, aged 34.
Midfield 1908-1911, Apps 19. Goals 6.

Played on this day

1902, Division 1.
West Bromwich A. (a) 1-6   Att. 22,160
Rutherford
1913, Division 1.
Sheffield Wednesday (h) 3-1   Att. 30,000
Hall, Hibbert, Low
1919, Division 1.
Liverpool (a) 1-1   Att. 30,000
Booth
1924, Division 1.
Bury (h) 2-2   Att. 35,000
Seymour, Urwin
1930, Division 1.
Bolton Wanderers (a) 3-0   Att. 20,000
Lindsay (2), J.R. Richardson
1941, Wartime.
York City (h) 5-3   Att. 7,900
Stubbins (3), Watters, Birkett
1947, Division 2.
Fulham (a) 0-3   Att. 41,500
1952, Division 1.
Manchester City (h) 2-0   Att. 48,961
Hannah, Milburn (pen)
1958, Division 1.
Portsmouth (h) 2-0   Att. 42,302
Bottom (2, 1 pen)
1969, Division 1.
Wolverhampton W. (h) 1-1   Att. 38,072
Robson (pen)
1972, Texaco Cup 1st round, 2nd leg.
Ayr United (h) 2-0   Att. 14,550
Smith, Tudor
Newcastle won 2-0 on aggregate.
1975, Division 1.
Queens Park Rangers (a) 0-1 Att. 22,981
1980, Division 2.
Bristol Rovers (a) 0-0   Att. 5,171
1986, Division 1.
Norwich City (a) 0-2   Att. 15,735
1988, Littlewoods Cup 2nd round, 1st leg.
Sheffield United (a) 0-3   Att. 17,900
1989, Division 2.
Watford (h) 2-1   Att. 17,008
Gallacher, Quinn
1994, UEFA Cup 1st round, 2nd leg.
Newcastle 5   Royal Antwerp 2
Cole 26, 39, 88   Kiekens 75
Beardsley 36 (pen)   Severeyns 77
               Att. 31,383
Newcastle won 10-2 on aggregate.
1997, Premier League.
Chelsea 1   Newcastle 0
Poyet 75   Att. 31,563

Playing record for this day is... 18 games,
Won 8, Drawn 4, Lost 6, GF 29, GA 27.
Today's success rate... 55.56%.

September 28

Played on this day

1895, Division 2.
Rotherham Town (a) 1-1   Att. 2,000
Logan
1901, Division 1.
Sunderland (h) 0-1   Att. 25,000
1907, Division 1.
Nottingham Forest (h) 3-0   Att. 25,000
Gardner, Hall, Speedie
1912, Division 1.
Woolwich Arsenal (a) 1-1   Att. 16,000
Stewart
1929, Division 1.
Huddersfield Town (h) 5-2   Att. 30,000
Chalmers, Gallacher (2), McCurley, Urwin
1935, Division 2.
Fulham (h) 6-2   Att. 25,000
Cairns, Harris, Pearson (3), Ware
1940, Wartime.
Barnsley (h) 1-0   Att. 3,500
Birkett
1946, Division 2.
Barnsley (a) 1-1   Att. 34,192
Stobbart
1957, Division 1.
Burnley (a) 2-0   Att. 18,405
Curry (2)
1963, Division 2.
Leyton Orient (a) 0-1   Att. 12,989
1968, Division 1.
Tottenham Hotspur (h) 2-2   Att. 30,469
Allen, McNamee
1971, Texaco Cup 1st round, 2nd leg.
Hearts (h) 2-1   Att. 24,380
Macdonald(2)
The tie finished 2-2 on aggregate.
Newcastle won 4-2 on penalties.
1974, Division 1.
Ipswich Town (h) 1-0   Att. 43,526
Howard
1977, UEFA Cup 1st round, 2nd leg.
Bohemians (h) 4-0   Att. 19,046
T. Craig (2), Gowling (2)
Newcastle won 4-0 on aggregate
1985, Division 1.
Arsenal (a) 0-0   Att. 24,104
1991, Division 2.
Derby County (h) 2-2   Att. 17,581
Hunt, Quinn
2002, Premier League.
Birmingham City 0   Newcastle 2
           Solano 34
           Ameobi 90
           Att. 29,072

Playing record for this day is... 17 games,
Won 9, Drawn 6, Lost 2, GF 33, GA 14.
Today's success rate... 70.59%.

Match of the Day from 1935

FULHAM OUTPLAYED

Newcastle get six, with both new boys scoring

Newcastle United welcomed their new right-winger Harry Ware to today's line up. He had arrived from Stoke, and joined Albert Harris, also in his first match in the side facing Fulham at St. James' Park. There was a crowd of 25,000 to see this match, and they were in for a treat.

The two new players quickly formed a good strong partnership, and vastly improved Newcastle's ability to break through Fulham's defence. They were equally to thank for the opening goal. Their moves gave the ball to Pearson, who wasted no time in scoring the first goal for Newcastle within seven minutes of the kick off.

Fulham were sparked into action by this early lead from their hosts. The visiting side quickly pulled together and a marked improvement in their play was noticeable immediately. They matched Newcastle's efforts in every way, and were just as dangerous in front of goal.

Therefore it was no surprise when Fulham managed to equal the scores with a super shot from Price. This in turn forced Newcastle to step up their efforts, and the game changed again.

The home side were not going to let the win slip away, and they increased the pressure on the Fulham goal. Their attempts were good, and Pearson managed to regain the lead for Newcastle with a lovely ball straight past Tootill in the Fulham goal.

Before the half-time break Newcastle increased their lead further when Cairns sent his shot sailing into the back of the net to bring the scores to 3-1.

In the first minute of the second half, Fulham pulled a goal back with a ball from Hammond, leaving Tapken no chance to save in the Newcastle goal.

Newcastle's fourth came from a shot by Ware, zipping through the defensive line and beating Tootill with ease. Then it was not long before a fifth was added to the score-sheet. This time it was Tommy Pearson again, netting his third for the hat-trick.

Ware had managed to score on his debut, and Harris matched his effort when he scored the sixth, and final, goal for Newcastle. It was a great start for the Magpies for both newcomers.

Newcastle United
Tapken, Richardson, Fairhurst, Imrie, Davidson, Weaver, Harris, Ware, Cairns, McMenemy, Pearson.
Fulham
Tootill, Hindson, Keeping, Clarke, Gibbons, Dennison, Johnston, Hammond, Perry, Finch, Price.

Norman Tapken

Match of the Day from 1962

SLICK UNITED HAMMER POOR WALSALL

Worst defeat for years, Newcastle should have had more

A combination of dreadful defending and slick skilful attacking football resulted in Newcastle's second six-goal haul in just twelve league matches today at Fellows Park. United, the Second Division form team, having now won five of their last six games, should have had plenty more, they had five efforts cleared off the goal-line, and squandered many more. This was the first time Walsall had conceded six on home soil since the 6-5 defeat to Millwall in November 1948, and their worst defeat since their 8-0 thrashing by Norwich back in December 1951. The Midlanders' defensive frailties knocked the stuffing out of their forwards and United keeper Hollins may well have well taken out his favourite novel to read, such was his long period of total inactivity.

United were ahead in the third minute, following a long free kick by Thompson. Partridge completely miskicked his clearance leaving Barry Thomas free to square the ball to the unmarked Jimmy Fell who tapped in from two yards. Four minutes later full-back Gregg tried to push the ball back to his keeper Boswell and it only reached eighteen-year-old Alan Suddick who had the simple task of rolling the ball into the empty net a second time for United. Newcastle's third, for once without the aid of a home player, came from a great through ball by Thomas which put Jimmy Kerray through on goal seven minutes before the interval. Kerray calmly drew the keeper out, rounded him easily and slipped the ball into another empty net.

Newcastle appeared content with a 3-0 lead and took things quietly in the opening twenty minutes of the second half until right-winger Dave Hilley added their fourth goal of the game. After the winger had crossed the ball himself, Gregg bravely stopped two shots on the line from the frustrated Suddick, Hilley chased in from the wing to smash in rebound number three into the roof of the net. Newcastle's fifth goal after 80 minutes, was by far the most comical of Walsall's afternoon of blunders. A cross, of no apparent danger, into the box had Eden attempting the most difficult of clearances, an overhead kick, which he completely made a pig's ear out of. The ball went out to Fell who crossed into the box, once again, this time the keeper rushed out and dropped the ball into the path of Thomas who couldn't miss open goal number four. United's sixth goal came three minutes from the end and again it was due mainly to some pitiful defending which allowed man-of-the-match Thomas his second goal.

The ball rolled to Partridge who seemed to panic as he dithered trying to make up his mind what to do with it. Thomas was allowed to run fifteen yards to pinch the ball off him and slam it past Boswell who remained rooted to his goal line throughout. United will never get a better chance to net six goals, and if they do it certainly won't be as easy as this game was.

Walsall

Boswell, Gregg, Partridge, Hill, Eden, Dudley, Meek, Foster, Richards, Hodgkisson, Taylor.

Newcastle United

Hollins, Keith, McMichael, Neale, Thompson, Iley, Hilley, Suddick, Thomas, Kerray, Fell.

Played on this day

1894, Division 2.
Leicester Fosse (h) 2-0   Att. 5,000
Thompson (2)
1900, Division 1.
Everton (h) 1-0   Att. 21,448
D. Gardner (pen)
1906, Division 1.
Sheffield Wednesday (h) 5-1 Att. 40,000
Appleyard, Gosnell, Kirkaldy, Speedie (2)
1923, Division 1.
Cardiff City (a) 0-1   Att. 45,000
1928, Division 1.
Manchester United (a) 0-5   Att. 25,243
1934, Division 2.
Norwich City (h) 2-0   Att. 20,000
Lang, Opponent (og)
1945, Wartime.
Stoke City(a) 1-3   Att. 20,000
Stubbins
1951, Division 1.
Fulham (h) 0-1   Att. 55,531
1956, Division 1.
Preston North End (a) 0-1   Att. 29,189
1962, Division 2.
Walsall (a) 6-0   Att. 10,336
Fell, Kerray, Thomas (2), Suddick, Hilley
1973, Division 1.
Queens Park Rangers (h) 2-3 Att. 31,402
Tudor (2)
1979, Division 2.
Birmingham City (a) 0-0   Att. 19,967
1981, Division 2.
Bolton Wanderers (a) 0-1   Att. 6,429
1984, Division 1.
West Ham United (h) 1-1   Att. 29,966
Beardsley
1990, Division 2.
Bristol City (a) 0-1   Att. 15,858

Playing record for this day is... 15 games, Won 5, Drawn 2, Lost 8, GF 20, GA 18. Today's success rate...40%.

Dave Hilley

ayed on this day

3, Division 2.
Woolwich Arsenal (h) 6-0   Att. 2,000
Wallace (3), Thompson (3)
*St. James' Park hosts its first Football
League fixture.*

9, Division 1.
Bury (a) 1-2   Att. 5,000
Niblo

5, Division 1.
Sheffield Wednesday (a) 1-1 Att. 16,000
McClarence

1, Division 1.
Everton(a) 0-2   Att. 15,000

2, Division 1.
Preston North End (a) 0-1   Att. 16,000

3, Division 1.
Sheffield Wednesday (a) 1-3 Att. 14,619
Lang

4, Wartime.
Sunderland (h) 1-5   Att. 28,693
Milburn

0, Division 1.
Sheffield Wednesday (a) 0-0 Att. 40,096

1, Division 2.
Luton Town (h) 4-1   Att. 22,452
Allchurch, White, Hale, Hughes

4, Division 2.
Plymouth Argyle (a) 1-2   Att. 21,639
McGarry

7, Division 1.
Arsenal (h) 2-1   Att. 33,377
Davies, B. Robson (pen)

0, Inter Cities Fairs Cup 1st round, 2nd leg.
Internazionale (h) 2-0   Att. 56,495
Davies, Moncur
Newcastle won 3-1 on aggregate

2, Division 1.
Everton (a) 1-3   Att. 33,028
Barrowclough

8, Division 2.
Notts County (a) 2-1   Att. 11,362
Connolly, Bird

9, Division 2.
Hull City (a) 3-1   Att. 9,629
Anderson, Brazil, McGhee

2, Anglo Italian Cup preliminary round
Leicester City (h) 4-0   Att. 14,046
Brock, Quinn (2, 1 pen), Sheedy

6, Premier League.
Newcastle 4   Aston Villa 3
Ferdinand 5, 22   Yorke 4, 59, 69
Shearer 38
Howey 67   Att. 36,400

9, UEFA Cup 1st round, 2nd leg.
Newcastle 2   CSKA Sofia 2
Shearer 36   Litera 29
Robinson 88   Simeonov 90
     Att. 36,228
Newcastle won 4-2 on aggregate.

0, Premier League.
Manchester City 0   Newcastle 1
     Shearer 74
     Att. 34,497

1, Premier League.
Newcastle 0   Liverpool 2
     Riise 3
     Murphy 86
     Att. 52,095

ing record for this day is... 20 games,
9, Drawn 3, Lost 8, GF 36, GA 30.
y's success rate... 52.50%.

Match of the Day from 1970

UNITED OVERTURN ITALIAN GIANTS
Cup success for the 'red' army at Newcastle

When the draw was made for the first round of this year's Inter Cities Fairs Cup, no one, not even on Tyneside would have given the Magpies a chance over two legs against Internazionale of Milan. Packed full of world class internationals, several having graced the World Cup finals in Mexico during the summer, Inter were a top European side. However United had gone to Milan in the first leg and outplayed their illustrious opponents, and but for a late equaliser would have snatched a shock 1-0 win at the fortress San Siro stadium. So with the aggregate score level at 1-1, everything hinged on the game at St James' Park and 56,495 packed into the ground, many expecting a Milan backlash, but more than a few hoping for a surprise home win.

Newcastle playing in an unfamiliar all-red strip started well and could, indeed should, have gone a goal up as early as the twelfth minute. United midfielder Young setting up Arentoft with a simple chance inside the area, but he snatched at his shot and the ball was launched yards over the crossbar. The home side continued to dominate the game without scoring up until the 29th minute, when finally the pressure paid off from Newcastle's tenth corner kick of the game. It was Bobby Moncur who rose unchallenged in the box to head home the inch-perfect cross from Robson. This clearly rattled the Italians and within a minute the game threatened to boil over and out of control. Davies who was proving a real handful for the Inter defence, made a move to challenge keeper Vieri from a drop goal kick. The keeper was outraged, he threw the ball at Davies and players ran from all over the place to join and help separate the fracas. During the brawl Belgium referee Joseph Minnoy was pushed then clearly punched by the irate Milan keeper. After being treated by Newcastle's physios he eventually recovered and sent off Vieri; the brawl then resumed. Police intervened as the game stopped for a full five minutes to allow the mayhem to subside; at one stage Inter almost walked off the field together.

When an attempt was made to restart the game with a dropped ball it was the Newcastle players who surrounded the poor ref, arguing he had originally awarded them a free kick. However, the game did start with a bounce up and order returned for the remaining hour. Playing a ten-man Milan side, United continued to dominate the game, twice they struck the bar in a blistering opening quarter of an hour of the second half. The killer second goal came with twenty minutes to play left and fittingly it was Davies who netted. After Dyson had headed another Robson cross onto the bar Davies dived in bravely to nod in the rebound, receiving a kick then a punch from Bellugi for his efforts. Without further incident good, or bad, United played out the remaining time comfortably to ensure a memorable and worthy win. Why did so many doubt they could?

Newcastle United
McFaul, Craig, Clark, Gibb, Burton, Moncur, Robson, Dyson, Davies, Arentoft, Young.
Inter Milan
Vieri, Righetti, Facchetti, Bellugi, Giubertoni, Cella, Jair, Fabbian, Boninsegna, Achilli (Bordon 30), Corso.
Referee Mr. J. Minnoy (Belgium).

October

October 1

...yed on this day

Division 1.
Aston Villa (h) 1-1   Att. 25,000
Rogers
Division 1.
Manchester City (h) 2-0   Att. 20,971
Veitch, Appleyard
Division 1.
Preston North End (a) 1-2   Att. 18,000
Higgins
Division 1.
Sheffield United (h) 2-1   Att. 40,000
Mooney, Smailes
Division 1.
Blackburn Rovers (h) 0-1   Att. 31,000
Division 1.
Huddersfield Town (h) 0-4   Att. 26,000
Division 2.
Coventry City (a) 0-1   Att. 18,774
Division 1.
Stoke City (h) 4-1   Att. 49,903
Houghton (2), Milburn, Thompson
Division 1.
Everton (h) 1-2   Att. 40,493
Tait
Division 1.
Cardiff City (h) 5-0   Att. 17,627
Luke (2), R. Mitchell, White (2)
League Cup 2nd round, replay.
Leyton Orient (a) 2-4   Att. 8,037
Suddick, Opponent (og)
Division 1.
Everton (a) 1-1   Att. 38,364
Bennett
Inter Cities Fairs Cup 1st round, 2nd leg.
Dundee United (h) 1-0   Att. 37,470
Dyson
Newcastle won 3-1 on aggregate.
Texaco Cup 1st round, 2nd leg.
Morton (h) 1-1   Att. 12,158
Opponent (og)
Newcastle won 3-2 on aggregate.
Division 1.
Ipswich Town (a) 1-2   Att. 21,797
McCaffery
Division 2.
Portsmouth (h) 4-2   Att. 25,488
Wharton, Waddle (2), Keegan (pen)
Division 1.
Liverpool (a) 2-1   Att. 39,139
Hendrie, Mirandinha (pen)
Zenith Data Systems Cup 1st round.
Tranmere (a) 6-6   Att. 4,056
Quinn (3, 1 pen), Peacock (2), Clark,
Newcastle lost 4-3 on penalties.
Premier League.
Aston Villa 0   Newcastle 2
Att. 29,960   Lee 66, Cole 83
Premier League.
Everton 1   Newcastle 3
Limpar 81   Ferdinand 13
   Lee 64 (pen)
Att. 33,080   Kitson 66
Champions' League, Group C.
Dynamo Kiev 2   Newcastle 2
Rebrov 3   Beresford 78, 85
Shevchenko 28   Att. 100,000
European Cup W. Cup 1st round, 2nd leg.
Partizan Belgrade 1 Newcastle 0
Rasovic 53 (pen)   Att. 24,000
2-2 aggregate, Newcastle lost - away goals.
Champions League, Group E.
Juventus 2   Newcastle 0
Del Piero 66, 81   Att. 41,424
record for this day... 23 games,
Drawn 5, Lost 9, GF 41, GA 36.
success rate... 50%.

Match of the Day from 1995

FERDINAND INSPIRES UNITED REVENGE WIN

Striker nets goal number 100 in 3-1 win at Goodison

The failure of Newcastle to claim what would have been a well-earned place in European competition can be attributed to Everton's spirited finish to their last campaign under Joe Royle. FA Cup glory over Manchester United last May, which consigned the Reds to the UEFA Cup, also sealed the fate of Kevin Keegan's United. Revenge, therefore, was most sweet today and it was exacted in the most ruthless of manners. Inspired by a magnificent exhibition of the old-fashioned art of centre-forward play by Les Ferdinand, Newcastle confirmed their right to go into October at the head of the Premiership and were unfortunate not to have done so with a goal avalanche.

Ferdinand who set them on their way with another gem of a strike, the 100th of his senior career, will feel he should have added at least one more to the thirteenth minute angled drive he rifled past Neville Southall. The £6 million striker who must surely be in the thoughts of England coach Terry Venables, will be wondering how he failed to extend that early advantage when working a defence splitting one-two with the equally impressive David Ginola and rounding Southall before inexplicably tripping over the ball in the act of shooting. One felt that miss would not matter, such was the superiority of United's all-round game and so it proved to be.

Everton, however, were justifiably aggrieved at the manner in which the second goal was conceded after 64 minutes. Ginola, seizing on Dave Watson's clearance appeared to have only a penalty in mind as he tumbled between the clumsy challenges of David Unsworth and Earl Barrett. Referee Keith Cooper obliged the Frenchman, who then departed to rest his strained thigh, safe in the knowledge the ensuing spot-kick by the outstanding Robert Lee had secured a seventh victory from eight games. It was indicative of the way things were going for Newcastle when Ginola's replacement, Paul Kitson, scored with what was his second touch of the ball, a close-range finish off head and chest from Warren Barton's cross. Everton at that 66th minute stage had been restricted to a flurry of threats inside one first-half minute when the promising Tony Grant chipped against the crossbar, Paul Rideout forced Shaka Hislop's only real save and Watson headed over when left unmarked just eight yards out. A sympathetic linesman decided Everton deserved a consolation goal which substitute Anders Limpar provided nine minutes from the end. It was not a question of whether Limpar was offside, it was by how much.

Everton
Southall, Barrett, Watson, Unsworth, Hinchcliffe, Ebbrell, Parkinson (Limpar h/t), Horne, Grant, Rideout, Stuart.

Newcastle United
Hislop, Barton, Peacock, Howey, Beresford, Gillespie (Watson 77), Lee, Clark, Sellars, Ferdinand, Ginola (Kitson 64).

Referee Mr. K. Cooper (Pontypridd).

Paul Kitson

Birthdays

Willie McFaul born today in 1943.
Goalkeeper, Coach & Manager 1966-1988, Apps 387.
Duncan Neale born today in 1939.
Midfield 1959-1963, Apps 98. Goals 12.
Alf McMichael born today in 1927.
Left-back 1949-1963, Apps 433. Goals 1.

Sadly Missed

Bob Bennie died on this day 1945, aged 72.
Right-back & Director 1901-1904, 1930-1945.
Apps 37. Goals 0.
John Fraser died on this day in 1952.
Winger 1899-1901, Apps 52. Goals 9.
Peter McWilliam died on this day in 1951, aged 73.
Midfield 1902-1911, Apps 242. Goals 12.

October 2

UNITED'S SEASON FINALLY TAKES OFF
First away win signals renewed hope in the future

There is no underestimating the style of Kevin Keegan's rejuvenated Newcastle. In securing their first away win since promotion, 2-0 at Villa, who themselves have only been beaten by Champions Manchester United, Newcastle have proved they have the mental swagger to fulfil Keegan's aim of finishing in the top six. It is one thing to take on Villa at their own attacking game, quite another to outplay them every inch of the way. There were at least three striped shirts to counter every claret-and-blue one on the run and the quick passing movements of Andy Cole, Peter Beardsley, Robert Lee and Lee Clark clearly flummoxed Ron Atkinson's prized midfield. The rampant Cole not only added to his goal-a-game tally but made Paul McGrath, Villa's heroic centre-half, look embarrassingly ordinary. If Keegan felt like the king of his castle, Atkinson looked like a landlord who had just discovered squatters in his home. Wearing the same petulant bulldog expression that had set on his face after Newcastle's first goal. That

Andy Cole scores the second goal at Villa Park.

47th minute penalty, converted by Malcolm Allen after Lee was felled by Steve Staunton, had Atkinson signalling wildly to the fans to help try to lift his team.

Villa started off defiantly enough with Dean Saunders scurrying forward with terrier-like assistance and Dalian Atkinson and Gordon Cowans attempting a few speculative shots. All to no avail. Barry Venison was exemplary in a Newcastle defence that battled magnificently in front of £550,000 signing Mike Hooper. The former Liverpool keeper was only threatened during the first half, due to his own misjudgement, when a bouncing ball caught him out which allowed Atkinson a half chance which wasn't taken. Thereafter he had little to do.

In the second half Villa, clearly in need of a change in fortunes, made the changes in personnel by bringing off Guy Whittingham and Cowans to be replaced by Tony Daley and Ray Houghton but the substitutions made little difference, barring the former missing an easy opportunity moments after coming on in the 55th minute. At the other end Beardsley epitomised United's dogged yet flamboyant spirit. The old Tyneside idol fought for every ball and, having won it, distributed it with composure and accuracy. When Lee found him with a clever through ball in the 80th minute, Beardsley's selfless pass to Cole secured Newcastle's second goal to wrap up the game. It all confirmed what a credit Newcastle United are to the top division, hopefully to stay there this time for quite a while to come.

Aston Villa

Spink, Staunton, Teale, McGrath, Richardson, Saunders, Atkinson, Townsend, Cowans (Houghton 63), Cox, Whittingham (Daley 55).

Newcastle United

Hooper, Venison, Beresford, Bracewell, Scott, Lee, Beardsley, Cole, Clark, Watson, Allen.

Referee Mr. P. Durkin (Dorset).

Played on this day

1897, Division 2.
    Burnley (a) 0-3   Att. 8,000
1909, Division 1.
    Manchester United (a) 1-1 Att. 40,000
    Rutherford
1920, Division 1.
    Sheffield United (a) 3-0   Att. 28,000
    Pyke (2), Ward
1926, Division 1.
    Arsenal (a) 2-2   Att. 45,000
    Clark, Seymour
1937, Division 2.
    Coventry City (h) 1-2   Att. 22,000
    Smith

1943, Wartime.
    York City (h) 1-1   Att. 9,877
    Milburn
1948, Division 1.
    Portsmouth (a) 0-1   Att. 44,000
1954, Division 1.
    Cardiff City (a) 2-4   Att. 36,000
    Milburn, White
1961, League Cup 2nd round.
    Sheffield United (a) 2-2   Att. 12,065
    McGuigan, McKinney
1963, Division 2.
    Portsmouth (h) 1-0   Att. 22,118
    Dalton
1965, Division 1.
    Arsenal (h) 0-1   Att. 42,841
1971, Division 1.
    Derby County (h) 0-1   Att. 31,972
1974, Texaco Cup 2nd round, 2nd leg.
    Aberdeen (h) 3-2   Att. 18,838
    Macdonald (2), Hibbitt
    Newcastle won 4-3 on aggregate.
1976, Division 1.
    Norwich City (a) 2-3   Att. 21,417
    T. Craig (pen), Gowling
1982, Division 2.
    Rotherham United (a) 5-1   Att. 12,436
    Todd, Keegan (4, 1 pen)
1993, Premier League.
    Aston Villa 0   Newcastle 2
                    Allen 46 (pen)
                    Cole 80
                    Att. 37,366

Playing record for this day....16 games, Won 5, Drawn 4, Lost 7, GF 25, GA 24. Today's success rate... 43.75%.

Birthdays

John Robertson born today in 1964.
Forward 1988, Apps 16 (7 subs). Goals 0.

October 3

1891, FA Cup Qualifying round 1.
Tow Law Town (a) 5-1   Att. 1,000
Reay (3), Thompson, Sorely

1896, Division 2.
Darwen (h) 5-1   Att. 7,000
Wardrope, Smellie (4)

1901, Division 1.
Notts County (a) 2-0   Att. 10,000
Peddie, A. Gardner

1903, Division 1.
Derby County (a) 3-1   Att. 10,000
McColl, Howie, Rutherford

1908, Division 1.
Bristol City (a) 3-3   Att. 18,000
Higgins, Veitch (2)

1914, Division 1.
Tottenham Hotspur (h) 4-0   Att. 22,000
Booth, Hall (2), Hibbert

1925, Division 1.
Arsenal (h) 7-0   Att. 35,000
Clark (3), Loughlin, Seymour (2), Urwin

1931, Division 1.
Bolton Wanderers (a) 1-2   Att. 20,000
J.R. Richardson

1936, Division 2.
Bury (a) 2-1   Att. 18,000
Cairns, Park

1942, Wartime.
Leeds United (a) 7-1   Att. 3,000
Carr (3), Dixon, Taylor (3)

1953, Division 1.
Charlton Athletic (h) 0-2   Att. 47,516

1959, Division 1.
West Ham United (h) 0-0   Att. 41,924

1964, Division 2.
Ipswich Town (a) 1-3   Att. 14,447
Burton

1970, Division 1.
Manchester City (a) 1-1   Att. 31,159
Ford

1981, Division 2.
Cardiff City (a) 4-0   Att. 5,764
Varadi (3), Davies (pen)

1987, Division 1.
Chelsea (a) 2-2   Att. 22,071
Goddard, Wharton

1990, Division 2.
Middlesbrough (h) 0-0   Att. 17,023

1999, Premier League.
Newcastle 2   Middlesbrough 1
Shearer 17, 44   Deane 89
   Att. 36,421

Playing record for this day... 18 games,
Won 10, Drawn 5, Lost 3, GF 49, GA 19.
Today's success rate...69.44%.

Match of the Day from 1925

POOR SHOW BY GUNNERS

Newcastle beat Arsenal 7-0 at St James' Park

35,000 turned up at St James' Park today to witness this incredible display by the home side. Arsenal were the visiting team, and it was clear from the beginning that they were not up to the challenge set for them by Newcastle. The home side were quick on the ball, and showed promise from the outset, whereas the visitors lacked the pace and will to be any threat at all to the Newcastle defence.

It took just nine minutes for Newcastle to open the scoring. A super shot from Loughlin sailed straight past the Arsenal keeper to put the home side into an early lead. This boosted Newcastle's morale no end, and their play improved all the more. Arsenal were already beginning to show signs of weakness in defence, and their forwards were no better either.

Newcastle were totally outplaying the London side, and it was no surprise when they increased their lead. Bob Clark got the goal, and it was a sign of things to come for the inside-right. He scored his second not long after, bringing Newcastle's tally to three, and the home side were on a roll. Clark was able to secure his hat-trick still within the first half of the match, and United were now four goals ahead of their opponents.

Urwin was next to add his name to the score-sheet with a super drive that gave the Arsenal keeper no chance to save. The visiting team were now beginning to tire, and just before the half-time whistle Seymour notched up the sixth goal for the Magpies.

The second half began with Arsenal hoping to at least prevent any further goals. However, the home side managed to deflate the Gunners once more partway through the half when Stan Seymour netted his second, bringing the score to 7-0. Arsenal were well and truly beaten. They hung their heads and left the field at the end, hoping that the supporters who had travelled all that way to see them play didn't notice them leave.

Newcastle United
Wilson, Chandler, Hudspeth, MacKenzie, Spencer, Mooney, Urwin, Clark, Loughlin, McDonald, Seymour.

Arsenal
Lewis, Mackie, Kennedy, Baker, Butler, Blyth, Hoar, Buchan, Brain, Neil, Haden.

Roddie MacKenzie

Birthdays

Scott Duncan died on this day in 1976, aged 87.
Winger 1908-1913, Apps 81. Goals 11.

Match of the Day from 1902

NOTTS NOT GOOD ENOUGH

United gain convincing 6-1 win over County

Newcastle played host to Notts County today in front of 17,000 eager supporters for this Division One clash. The weather was perfect for football, fine and dry without a strong wind, and the game began with Newcastle on the attack.

It took just three minutes of trying for United to open the scoring, Stewart being the man to get the ball past the Notts County keeper, who hadn't quite finished warming up yet.

So, with the early lead Newcastle were becoming more confident by the minute. Twelve minutes into the game the score was increased to two with a lovely shot from Orr, cleverly evading the keeper.

Notts had their first chance of the game when Ross sent a good ball goalwards, but it was saved easily by Kingsley in the home goal, and the threat was minimal.

Newcastle's confidence was unnerving for the visiting side, and things got worse for Notts when McColl shot home his first goal, and Newcastle's third.

It wasn't half-time yet, and Newcastle were already three goals ahead. The misery for Notts County was compounded further still by Rutherford. He broke through the weak Notts defence and slammed the ball into the net for Newcastle's fourth. He then added the fifth too with a lovely shot which sailed straight into the goalmouth past the keeper, who was in despair.

Half-time came, and Notts County were glad of the break in play.

The second half began with a slightly revived Notts team. They played better and seemed more confident, but they knew it would be a huge uphill struggle if they were to make an impact on this game. This task was made even harder for them just a few minutes into the half when Newcastle were awarded a penalty when Prescott fouled Rutherford. Carr stepped up to take the kick, and sent the ball effortlessly into the net for the Magpies' sixth goal.

Newcastle eased off a little after this fine show of strength, and that gave Notts County the opportunity to narrow the deficit. Green finally managed to get the ball into the Newcastle net to pull a goal back for the visiting side, but it was too late. Newcastle thoroughly deserved their win, and they had carried it off with style.

Newcastle United

Kingsley, Agnew, Davidson, Alex Gardner, Aitken, Carr, Stewart, Orr, McColl, Rutherford, Roberts.

Notts County

Pennington, Prescott, Montgomery, Mainman, Bull, McDonald, Joynes, Humphreys, Green, Ross, Gee.

Alex Gardner

Played on this day

1902, Division 1.
Notts County (h) 6-1   Att. 17,000
Rutherford (2), McColl, Orr, Stewart, Carr
A week after losing at The Hawthorns to WBA by 6-1, the Magpies bounce back immediately with a fantastic 6-1 win of their own.

1913, Division 1.
Bolton Wanderers (a) 1-3   Att. 32,000
Hall

1919, Division 1.
Liverpool (h) 3-0   Att. 45,000
Hibbert (3)

1924, Division 1.
Nottingham Forest (a) 1-1   Att. 15,000
Seymour

1930, Division 1.
Liverpool (h) 0-4   Att. 37,000

1941, Wartime.
York City (a) 2-2   Att. 4,500
Stubbins (2, 1 pen)

1947, Division 2.
Coventry City (h) 0-0   Att. 55,569

1952, Division 1.
Liverpool (a) 3-5   Att. 48,002
Prior, G. Robledo (2, 1 pen)

1958, Division 1.
Aston Villa (a) 1-2   Att. 29,335
White

1961, Division 2.
Liverpool (a) 0-2   Att. 52,419

1969, Division 1.
Crystal Palace (a) 3-0   Att. 28,407
Davies, Dyson, Robson

1972, League Cup 3rd round.
Blackpool (h) 0-3   Att. 19,810

1975, Division 1.
Tottenham Hotspur (h) 2-2   Att. 33,284
Tudor, Barrowclough

1980, Division 2.
West Ham United (h) 0-0   Att. 24,866

1986, Division 1.
Southampton (a) 1-4   Att. 14,622
A. Thomas

1989, Littlewoods Cup 2nd round, 2nd leg.
Reading (h) 4-0   Att. 15,211
Brazil (pen), Brock, Thorn, McGhee

1992, Division 1.
Brentford (a) 2-1   Att. 10,131
Kelly, Peacock

1995, Coca Cola Cup 2nd round, 2nd leg.
Newcastle 3   Bristol City 1
Barton 48   Agostino 14
Albert 55
Ferdinand 65   Att. 36,357
Newcastle won 8-1 on aggregate.

1997, Premier League.
Newcastle 1   Tottenham H. 0
Barton 89   Att. 36,708

1998, Premier League.
Arsenal 3   Newcastle 0
Bergkamp 21, 66 (pen)
Anelka 29   Att. 38,102

Playing record for this day... 20 games, Won 7, Drawn 5, Lost 8, GF 33, GA 34. Today's success rate... 47.50%.

October 5

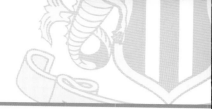

1889, FA Cup Qualifying round 1.
Shankhouse Black Watch (h) 4-0
Collins, Gibbons, Miller (2)   Att.3,000
1895, Division 2.
Liverpool (h) 1-0   Att. 10,000
Wardrope
1901, Division 1.
Small Heath (a) 1-3   Att. 12,000
Roberts
1907, Division 1.
Notts County (a) 1-0   Att. 20,000
Hall
1912, Division 1.
Bradford City (h) 1-1   Att. 35,000
Hudspeth (pen)
1929, Division 1.
Sheffield United (a) 0-1   Att. 20,000
1935, Division 2.
Burnley (a) 2-1   Att. 9,000
Cairns, McMenemy
1940, Wartime.
Barnsley (a) 0-1   Att. 2,000
1946, Division 2.
Newport County (h) 13-0   Att. 52,137
Bentley, Milburn (2), Shackleton (6),
Wayman (4)
Newcastle's record victory to date.
1957, Division 1.
Preston North End (h) 0-2   Att. 36,131
1963, Division 2.
Swansea Town (h) 4-1   Att. 23,711
Taylor, Thomas, Hilley (2)
1968, Division 1.
Leeds United (h) 0-1   Att. 41,999
1974, Division 1.
Everton (a) 1-1   Att. 40,000
McDermott
1977, Division 1.
Norwich City (a) 1-2   Att. 16,630
T. Craig
1983, Milk Cup 2nd round, 1st leg.
Oxford United (h) 1-1   Att. 21,184
McDermott
1985, Division 1.
West Ham United (h) 1-2   Att. 26,957
Reilly
1991, Division 2.
Portsmouth (a) 1-3   Att. 10,175
Quinn
1993, Coca Cola Cup 2nd round, 2nd leg.
Notts County 1   **Newcastle 7**
McSwegan 51   Allen 21, 26 (pen)
Beardsley 44
Cole 59, 61, 83
Lee 85   Att. 6,068
Newcastle won 11-2 on aggregate.
1994, Coca Cola Cup 2nd round, 2nd leg.
Barnsley 0   **Newcastle 1**
Cole 41   Att. 10,992
Newcastle won 3-1 on aggregate
2002, Premier League.
Newcastle 2   **West Bromwich A. 1**
Shearer 45,69   Balis 27   Att. 52,142

Playing record for this day... 20 games,
Won 9, Drawn 3, Lost 8, GF 42, GA 22.
Today's success rate... 52.50%.

Match of the Day from 1946

UNITED HIT RECORD SCORE
Shackleton inspires thirteen-goal rout of Newport

Len Shackleton, Newcastle's new £13,000 signing from Bradford City celebrated an amazing debut today at St. James' Park scoring a double hat-trick, breaking the club's individual scoring record for one game. On a magnificent day for the 52,137 crowd, United broke the Football League Division Two goals record in one game, as well as the record margin of victory in the Football League. It was a day Tyneside will remember for years, and has already firmly established Shackleton as a club hero. The result helps Newcastle on their way to their promotion dream, whilst for Newport, still rebuilding after the wartime break, this was the second week in a row they have been thoroughly thrashed, last week they conceded seven to West Bromwich Albion.

Newcastle's forwards played the game of their lives. They were backed up well by former England international Doug Wright who ran the midfield almost entirely on his own. For Newport only their captain Norman Low showed any determination and fight which was a pity as he deserved better from his team-mates. Low was keenly awaiting this game, and knew the Magpies very well, his father Wilf Low having appeared in 378 games for United as a centre-half.

It took just 90 seconds after kick off for United to carve out their first goal-scoring chance, and what a chance they missed. Charlie Wayman slamming his penalty kick well wide. Soon after however, Wayman made amends when he latched onto Shackleton's far post cross to start Newport's massacre. Two minutes later Shackleton's fine running dribble took him past three defenders and after a neat one-two with Brennan he placed his shot past Turner for his first goal of the afternoon. Then Wayman now eager to bury the memory of that early miss hit two goals in as many minutes to complete a hat-trick inside half an hour, both goals again created by the magical genius of Shackleton. But it was Shackleton who was about to start smashing a host of scoring records. 'Shack' scored three times inside five minutes making this one of the fastest hat-trick scored by any individual in League football. Newcastle in the eight minutes leading up to half-time had now netted five goals and the brilliant Shackleton, later dubbed 'The Clown Prince of Soccer' had had a hand in all of them.

In the second half it was the same Black and White menace that charged forward at helpless Newport. Shackleton scored again, then Milburn netted twice inside the 73rd minute to bring up double figures for the Magpies. Wayman got another, his fourth of the game, the penalty miss now truly forgotten. Roy Bentley scored the twelfth following a move of successive passes by the whole Newcastle team. The thirteenth and last goal could well have been recorded as an own goal by Wookey, but the final shot was by that man Shackleton again; who could blame him claiming a double hat-trick and yet another scoring record for his new club.

Newcastle United
Garbutt, Cowell, Graham, Harvey, Brennan, Wright, Milburn, Bentley, Wayman, Shackleton, Pearson.
Newport County
Turner, Hodge, Oldham, Rawcliffe, Low, Cabrie, Davis, Wookey, Craddock, McNab, Bowen.
Referee Mr M. Hartley (Bolton).

Birthdays

Peter Johnson born today in 1958.
Left-back 1980-1983, Apps 20. Goals 0.

Alain Goma born today in 1972.
Defender 1999-2001, Apps 41 (1 sub). Goals 1.

October 6

Match of the Day from 1934

UNITED SNATCH VICTORY

Newcastle take win in action-packed game at Swansea

Newcastle travelled to the Vetch Field today to meet Swansea in this Division Two clash. It was to be an action-packed game, and a close call right to the end. There was heavy rain throughout the game, and this made play difficult. The ball was as slippery as the pitch, but both teams started well. It was Newcastle who managed to open the scoring within the first minute of play when Murray fired a super shot which sailed past Walton in the Swansea goal to put the visitors into a very early lead.

However, Swansea proved they were a force to be reckoned with when they equalised just two minutes later. Davies was the man to get his shot past Burns, and now the fight was on.

There was little difference between the two teams, and the game could have gone either way. Both sides seemed to want the win as much as the other, but now it was Swansea's turn to take the lead. On 27 minutes a super shot from Davies sent the home side a goal ahead, but their joy was short-lived.

Weaver brought the scores level again just before the half-time break, each side now with two. The 8,000 supporters were now looking forward to a second half with as much action as the first.

They two teams didn't disappoint the crowd. There were plenty more thrills to come, and it was Warner who brought about the cheers for Swansea when he sent a lovely ball into the Newcastle net past Burns to put the home side back into the lead.

Now Newcastle had some hard work to do in order to get back into gear. Both sides were beginning to tire, and with Swansea a goal ahead, Newcastle were at a disadvantage.

McMenemy gave the visitors hope when he levelled the scores again. His shot flew past Walton into the back of the net, for Newcastle's third.

Hanford and Lloyd were weak now in midfield, and Newcastle saw this as an opportunity to try to beat Davies, who was trying to cope with the pressure. Lang kept pushing for Newcastle, and his efforts were threatening for Swansea's defence.

Lang sent a super cross over to Boyd, and he swooped the ball into the goal for the winner. It seemed Newcastle had just got enough energy and determination to bring about the win, and it was unlucky for Swansea to have lost out.

Swansea Town
Walton, T. Davies, Milne, Warner, Hanford, Lloyd, W. Davies, Martin, Bussey, Olsen, Lewis.

Newcastle United
Burns, Richardson, Russell, Imrie, Leach, Murray, Boyd, McMenemy, Smith, Weaver, Lang.

Harry McMenemy

Played on this day

1888, FA Cup Qualifying round 1.
Port Clarence (h) 3-1
Raylstone, Muir, White

1894, Division 2.
Burslem Port Vale (a) 4-4   Att. 2,000
Dickson, McNee, Thompson, Willis

1900, Division 1.
Sunderland (a) 1-1   Att. 28,688
Opponent (og)

1906, Division 1.
Bury (a) 2-3   Att. 20,000
Appleyard, Veitch (pen)

1923, Division 1.
West Ham United (a) 0-1   Att. 30,000

1928, Division 1.
Leeds United (h) 3-2   Att. 39,000
Boyd, Lang, McDonald

1934, Division 2.
Swansea Town (a) 4-3   Att. 8,000
Boyd (2), McMenemy, Murray

1945, Wartime.
Grimsby Town (a) 2-0   Att. 13,000
Woodburn, Stubbins

1951, Division 1.
Wolverhampton W. (h) 3-1   Att. 57,558
Davies, Milburn (2)

1956, Division 1.
Luton Town (h) 2-2   Att. 36,941
Hannah, Milburn

1962, Division 2.
Stoke City (a) 1-3   Att. 26,775
Thomas

1971, League Cup 3rd round.
Arsenal (a) 0-4   Att. 34,071

1973, Division 1.
Liverpool (a) 1-2   Att. 45,612
Nattrass

1976, Division 1.
West Bromwich A. (h) 2-0   Att. 28,746
Gowling, Cannell

1979, Division 2.
West Ham United (a) 1-1   Att. 23,206
Withe

1982, League Cup 2nd round, 1st leg.
Leeds United (a) 1-0   Att. 24,012
Varadi

1984, Division 1.
Ipswich Town (h) 3-0   Att. 25,677
Waddle, Heard, Opponent (og)

1990, Division 2.
Portsmouth (h) 2-1   Att. 17,682
Quinn (2)

Playing record for this day....18 games, Won 9, Drawn 4, Lost 5, GF 35, GA 29. Today's success rate...61.11%.

Birthdays

Joe Sibley born today in 1919.
Winger 1947-1950, Apps 32. Goals 6.

Harry Taylor born today in 1935.
Winger 1952-1960, Apps 29. Goals 5.

October 7

Played on this day

1893, Division 2.
Lincoln City (a) 1-2   Att. 1,000
Wallace
1899, Division 1.
Notts County (h) 6-0   Att. 20,000
Fraser (2), MacFarlane, Peddie,
Stevenson, Wardrope
1905, Division 1.
Nottingham Forest (h) 3-2   Att. 15,000
Orr, McClarence, Howie
1911, Division 1.
West Bromwich A. (h) 0-0   Att. 22,000
1922, Division 1.
Burnley (h) 0-2   Att. 38,000
1933, Division 1.
Manchester City (h) 2-2   Att. 20,000
Cape, Weaver
1944, Wartime.
Middlesbrough (h) 0-1   Att. 13,366
1950, Division 1.
Aston Villa (a) 0-3   Att. 44,240
1961, Division 2.
Charlton Athletic (h) 4-1   Att. 22,957
McGuigan (2), Allchurch, Opponent (og)
1967, Division 1.
Wolverhampton W. (a) 2-2   Att. 32,386
B. Robson, T. Robson
1972, Division 1.
Norwich City (h) 3-1   Att. 18,103
Tudor (2), Guthrie
1975, League Cup 3rd round.
Bristol Rovers (a) 1-1   Att. 17,141
Gowling
1978, Division 2.
Leicester City (h) 1-0   Att. 25,731
Walker
1980, Division 2.
Preston North End (a) 3-2   Att. 5,301
Rafferty, Shinton (2)
1981, League Cup 2nd round, 1st leg.
Fulham (h) 1-2   Att. 20,247
Barton
1987, Littlewoods Cup 2nd round, 2nd leg.
Blackpool (h) 4-1   Att. 21,228
Goddard, Mirandinha, D. Jackson,
Gascoigne
Newcastle won 4-2 on aggregate.
1989, Division 2.
Ipswich Town (a) 1-2   Att. 15,220
McGhee
1992, Coca Cola Cup 2nd round, 2nd leg.
Middlesbrough (a) 3-1   Att. 24,390
Kelly (2), O'Brien
Newcastle won 3-1 on aggregate.

Playing record for this day... 18 games,
Won 8, Drawn 4, Lost 6, GF 35, GA 25.
Today's success rate... 55.56%.

Match of the Day from 1905

FOREST OUTPLAYED

A convincing win against Nottingham Forest

Nottingham Forest travelled to Newcastle today for this Division One game in front of over 19,000 keen supporters. Newcastle started on the attack straight away, and their pace took Forest by surprise. Rutherford made the first attempt at goal, but his shot was saved by Linacre in the Forest goal.

Within seconds McClarence tried his luck, but his shot suffered the same fate as Rutherford's. Then, still less than three minutes into the game McClarence had another go, and this time managed to beat Linacre to put the home side into an early lead.

This spurred Newcastle on to keep up the pressure, and the home side soon established full control of the game.

Orr increased the lead for Newcastle with a smashing shot, perfectly placed to sail into the net, and by now Forest were feeling left out.

They battled to fight back, and it wasn't long before they had pulled a goal back just before the half-time break with a super goal from West.

The second half began with both sides in fighting spirit. Newcastle were awarded a free kick, and it was McCombie who stepped up to take it. He passed the ball on to McWilliam, who in turn sent it to Howie who fired in a super shot to increase Newcastle's tally to three goals.

Forest were now beginning to flag, and when Spouncer scored the second goal for the visiting side they wished they had pulled their efforts together earlier. By now it was too late for their play to make any more impact on this game, and the final score was 3-2 to United.

Newcastle United
Crumley, McCracken, McCombie, Gardner, Veitch, McWilliam, J. Rutherford, Howie, McClarence, Orr, Gosnell.

Nottingham Forest
Linacre, Craig, Dudley, Timmins, Wolves, Henderson, Craggs, West, Niblo, Morris, Spouncer.

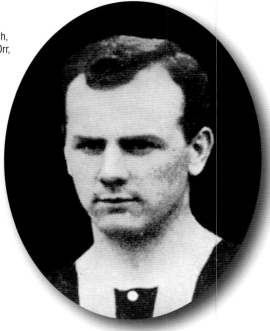

Joe McClarence

Birthdays

Pat Howard born today in 1947.
Centre-half 1971-1976, Apps 263 (2 subs).
Goals 9.

John Park born today in 1913.
Winger 1936-1941, Apps 73. Goals 14.

October 8

Match of the Day from 1974

RANGERS FLATTENED
Newcastle take four-goal win over QPR

At Loftus Road tonight in front of a crowd of 15,815 Newcastle met QPR in the third round of the League Cup. England striker Malcolm Macdonald was in the Newcastle side, and his presence in today's team would be more valuable than could be imagined.

Newcastle started well, and it took just thirteen seconds for Macdonald to open the scoring.

Willie McFaul

It was Pat Howard who started the move with a lovely long ball. Macdonald ran on to receive it and had no trouble slipping the ball past Phil Parkes in the QPR goal.

With the visitors taking such an early lead it was clear that QPR had a lot of work to do if they wanted to stay in with a chance. However Newcastle wanted this win, and just eight minutes into the game they doubled their lead. It was Macdonald who was provider for this one, a free kick was heading his way, and he helped it on to John Tudor who slammed it into the net for Newcastle's second goal.

United maintained their pressure on the QPR defence, and cracks were already starting to show. The pace of the game was too much for the home side, and Newcastle weren't going to let up.

Before the half-time break the Magpies increased their lead further. Macdonald again being the one to send the ball zooming into the net past Parkes. The visitors had the huge advantage of being three goals ahead going into the break.

Shortly after play resumed for the second half, Macdonald wrapped up the scoring with another goal, completing his hat-trick and bringing Newcastle's tally to four goals. This was Macdonald's first hat-trick in a year, his previous one coming against Doncaster in last season's League Cup.

The second half ended with no change to the score-sheet, and Newcastle happy to take home a four-goal win.

Queen's Park Rangers
Parkes, Clement, Gillard, Beck, Mancini, Hazel, Thomas, Francis, Westwood (Webb), Bowles, Givens.

Newcastle United
McFaul, Nattrass, Kennedy, McDermott, Keeley, Howard, Burns, Gibb, Macdonald, Tudor, Hibbitt (Cassidy).

Played on this day

1898, Division 1.
Burnley(a) 1-2   Att. 6,000
Rogers
1904, Division 1.
Notts County (a) 3-0   Att. 10,000
Howie, Rutherford (2)
1910, Division 1.
Notts County (h) 2-0   Att. 30,000
Shepherd, Higgins
1921, Division 1.
Chelsea (a) 1-1   Att. 35,000
Harris
1927, Division 1.
Bolton Wanderers (a) 2-1 Att. 25,000
Gallacher, McKay
1932, Division 1.
Sheffield United (a) 1-3 Att. 10,000
Allen
1938, Division 2.
Nottingham Forest (h) 4-0 Att. 31,000
Birkett, Cairns (3)
1949, Division 1.
Burnley (a) 2-1   Att. 37,319
Harvey, Walker
1955, Division 1.
Portsmouth (h) 2-1   Att. 42,320
Mitchell (2)
1960, Division 1.
Aston Villa (a) 0-2   Att. 25,336
1966, Division 1.
Arsenal (a) 0-2   Att. 24,595
1968, Division 1.
Nottingham Forest (a) 4-2 Att. 17,651
Davies, Dyson, Foggon, B. Robson
Played at Meadow Lane, Nottingham.
1969, Division 1.
Manchester City (a) 1-2 Att. 32,172
Robson
1973, League Cup 2nd round.
Doncaster Rovers (h) 6-0 Att. 15,948
Robson (2), Macdonald (3), Clark
1974, League Cup 3rd round.
Queens Park Rangers (a) 4-0 Att. 15,815
Tudor, Macdonald (3)
1977, Division 1.
Derby County (h) 1-2   Att. 26,578
Burns
1983, Division 2.
Charlton Athletic (h) 2-1 Att. 23,329
Keegan (2)
1985, Milk Cup 2nd round, 2nd leg.
Barnsley (a) 1-1   Att. 10,084
Cunningham
*The tie finished 1-1 on aggregate,
Newcastle went through to round 3 on the
away goals rule.*
1986, Littlewoods Cup 2nd round, 2nd leg.
Bradford City (h) 1-0   Att. 15,893
Roeder
Newcastle lost 2-1 on aggregate.
1988, Division 1.
Coventry City (h) 0-3   Att. 22,890

Playing record for this day... 20 games,
Won 11, Drawn 2, Lost 7, GF 38, GA 24.
Today's success rate... 60%.

Sadly Missed

Jimmy Nelson died on this day in 1965, aged 64. Right-back 1930-1935, Apps 160. Goals 0.

Jimmy Stott died on this day in 1908, aged 37. Midfield 1895-1899, Apps 131. Goals 11.

Played on this day

1897, Division 2.
Newton Heath (h) 2-0   Att. 14,000
Aitken, Harvey
1909, Division 1.
Bradford City (h) 1-0   Att. 25,000
Wilson
1920, Division 1.
Sunderland (h) 6-1   Att. 58,016
Seymour, Smailes (2), Harris (2), Ward
1926, Division 1.
Liverpool (h) 1-0   Att. 20,000
Gallacher
1937, Division 2.
Nottingham Forest (a) 0-0   Att. 28,582
1943, Wartime.
Huddersfield Town (h) 5-2   Att. 12,000
Stubbins (2), Milburn (2), Woollett
1948, Division 1.
Sunderland (a) 1-1   Att. 51,399
Hair
1954, Division 1.
Sunderland (a) 2-4   Att. 66,654
R. Mitchell (pen), Milburn
1963, Division 2.
Sunderland (a) 1-2   Att. 56,980
Taylor
1965, Division 1.
Aston Villa (h) 1-0   Att. 31,382
McGarry
1971, Division 1.
Arsenal (a) 2-4   Att. 40,509
MacDonald (2)
1982, Division 2.
Oldham Athletic (a) 2-2   Att. 11,491
Varadi (2)
1991, Rumbelows Cup 2nd round, 2nd leg.
Crewe Alexandra (h) 1-0   Att. 9,197
Howey
Newcastle won 5-3 on aggregate.
1994, Premier League.
Newcastle 1   Blackburn Rovers 1
Opponent (og) 88   Shearer 58 (pen)
                            Att. 34,334
2001, Worthington Cup 3rd round.
Barnsley 0   Newcastle 1
                   Bellamy 79
                            Att. 14,493

Playing record for this day... 15 games,
Won 8, Drawn 4, Lost 3, GF 27, GA 17.
Today's success rate... 66.67%.

Match of the Day from 1920

SUNDERLAND SMOTHERED

Newcastle outplay rivals for sensational victory at home

Newcastle United played host to Sunderland today at St James' Park in front of a crowd of over 58,000 eager supporters, keen to watch this Division One clash between the rival teams. The match promised lots of action, and it didn't disappoint. Tensions were running high on either side, and a win was desperately required by both teams.

The game started with an attack from Newcastle, but it proved fruitless. However, it was just a taste of what was to come. Both goalkeepers were made to work hard right from the outset, and there were several instances of foul play.

There was little separating the teams at this stage, and the first goal could have gone either way. It happened to fall to Newcastle, Smailes being the man to beat the Sunderland keeper. Sunderland tried frantically to snatch a goal back, but their efforts were stopped dead by the strong United defence.

A penalty was awarded to Newcastle just before the half-time break for handball. Harris took the kick, and had no problem slamming it into the net for his team's second. This was a huge advantage for the home side going into the break, and they intended to keep up the good work in the second half.

After the interval Newcastle continued in the same vein. Just two minutes into the half Seymour sent a lovely ball to Harris, who scored the third goal with ease.

Hope was given to the Sunderland supporters shortly afterwards when Buchan got his head to the ball to pull back a goal for the visitors. The score was now 3-1, and the tension was mounting.

Just a few minutes later Seymour got another great goal for Newcastle, and the home fans went wild. The lead was extended when Smailes added the fifth with a superb header, leaving the Sunderland keeper reeling in his goal.

Late attempts for Sunderland were all down to Buchan, desperately trying to retrieve some pride for his side. However his three shots at goal amounted to nothing, and the Wearsiders were now out of it.

In the dying minutes the final nail in the coffin was added with a lovely shot, confidently sent into the back of the net by Ward to secure the win. Newcastle 6, Sunderland 1.

Newcastle United

Lawrence, McCracken, Hampson, McIntosh, Low, Finlay, Aitken, Ward, Harris, Smailes, Seymour.

Sunderland

Scott, Hobson, England, Cuggy, Kasher, Poole, Best, Buchan, Travers, Shore, Martin.

NEIL HARRIS
NEWCASTLE UNITED

Birthdays

Jimmy Loughlin born today in 1905.
Centre-forward 1924-1927, Apps 12. Goals 5.

Sadly Missed

Jackie Milburn died on this day in 1988, aged 64.
Centre-forward 1943-1957, Apps 494. Goals 239.

Match of the Day from 1931

A GAME OF ONE HALF

Newcastle waste first half, but improve to take 3-1 win

45,000 flocked to St James' Park today to see Newcastle play Middlesbrough in this First Division match. Both teams were aiming for a win, but Middlesbrough had one of their star players out of the side. Cameron was brought into the team in place of Camsell, but the absence of their international player would cost them dearly.

Both teams had their good points at the start, however, it was the Middlesbrough forwards who threatened the most danger in the opening fifteen minutes of play. The Newcastle defence was tested to its limits, but luckily the visitors failed to break through and score.

Newcastle didn't seem to have much organisation to their tactics, and they changed their play constantly. Just before the break their unique style paid off. Boyd got onto a cross from Lang and managed to get through an opening in the Boro' defence to slam the ball into the net for their first goal.

So, the home side had the advantage going into the break, and it served them well in the second half. Play resumed with a revived and confident Newcastle side now playing organised and dangerous football.

Boyd had another chance for Newcastle and scored again to bring their tally to two, and that was increased further shortly afterwards when Lang added his shot to the score-sheet. Now three goals ahead, Newcastle began to relax.

Middlesbrough seized the only real opportunity they had and managed to pull back a goal with a nice shot from Pease, but ultimately they knew the game was already lost.

Newcastle United

McInroy, Nelson, Fairhurst, MacKenzie, Davidson, Weaver, Boyd, Richardson, Allen, McMenemy, Lang.

Middlesbrough

Mathieson, Jennings, Freeman, McFarlane, Elkes, Forrest, Pease, Scott, Cameron, Bruce, Warren.

Jimmy Boyd

Played on this day

1896, Division 2.
Grimsby Town (h) 3-0   Att. 5,000
Aitken (2, 1pen), Stott
1903, Division 1.
Manchester City (h) 1-0   Att. 19,730
Appleyard
1908, Division 1.
Preston North End (h) 2-0   Att. 26,000
Higgins, Stewart
1914, Division 1.
Manchester City (a) 1-1   Att. 25,000
Pailor
1925, Division 1.
Manchester United (a) 1-2   Att. 40,000
Seymour
1931, Division 1.
Middlesbrough (h) 3-1   Att. 45,000
Boyd (2), Lang
1936, Division 2.
Leicester City (h) 1-0   Att. 35,000
Cairns
1942, Wartime.
York City (a) 3-4   Att. 4,000
Carr (3)
1953, Division 1.
Wolverhampton W. (h) 1-2   Att. 39,913
Mulgrew
1959, Division 1.
Nottingham Forest (h) 2-1   Att. 33,764
White, Opponent (og)
1960, League Cup 1st round.
Colchester United (a) 1-4   Att. 9,130
Neale
Newcastle's first ever tie in the new League Cup competition.
1964, Division 2.
Leyton Orient (h) 5-0   Att. 28,454
Iley, Robson (2), Anderson (2)
1970, Division 1.
Arsenal (h) 1-1   Att. 38,024
Robson
1979, Division 2.
Preston North End (h) 0-0   Att. 25,154
1981, Division 2.
Derby County (h) 3-0   Att. 17,224
Wharton, Varadi (2)
1984, Milk Cup 2nd round, 2nd leg.
Bradford City (a) 1-0   Att. 10,210
Waddle
Newcastle won 4-1 on aggregate.
1990, Rumbelows Cup 2nd round, 2nd leg.
Middlesbrough (h) 1-0   Att. 12,778
Anderson
Newcastle lost 2-1 on aggregate.
1992, Division 1.
Tranmere Rovers (h) 1-0   Att. 30,137
Kelly

Playing record for this day... 18 games, Won 11, Drawn 3, Lost 4, GF 31, GA 16. Today's success rate...69.44%.

Birthdays

Bjorn Kristensen born today in 1963.
Centre-half 1989-1993, Apps 97 (11 subs). Goals 5.
Bill Redhead born today in 1935.
Midfield 1954-1959, Apps 1. Goals 0.

Albert Scanlon born today in 1935.
Winger 1960-1962, Apps 27. Goals 6.

October 11

1902, Division 1.
Bolton Wanderers (a) 2-0   Att. 10,000
Orr, Carr
1913, Division 1.
Chelsea (h) 1-0   Att. 22,000
McDonald
1919, Division 1.
Bradford Park Ave. (a) 1-0   Att. 12,000
Dixon
1924, Division 1.
Liverpool (h) 0-0   Att. 25,000
1930, Division 1.
Middlesbrough (a) 1-3   Att. 30,000
Cape
1941, Wartime.
Gateshead (a) 1-1   Att. 12,000
Stubbins
1947, Division 2.
West Ham United (h) 1-0   Att. 55,767
Milburn
1952, Division 1.
Wolverhampton W. (a) 0-2   Att. 45,000
1958, Division 1.
Leicester City (h) 3-1   Att. 46,686
Allchurch (2), White
1961, League Cup 2nd round, replay.
Sheffield United (h) 0-2   Att. 12,595
1969, Division 1.
Liverpool (h) 1-0   Att. 44,576
Foggon
1975, Division 1.
West Ham United (a) 1-2   Att. 30,400
Howard
1980, Division 2.
Bristol City (a) 0-2   Att. 10,539
1986, Division 1.
Manchester City (h) 3-1   Att. 21,780
McDonald (pen), Gascoigne, Cunningham

Playing record for this day... 14 games,
Won 7, Drawn 2, Lost 5, GF 15, GA 14.
Today's success rate... 57.14%.

Match of the Day from 1919

BRADFORD SUNK BY ONE GREAT GOAL
Newcastle take win with a single goal at Park Avenue

Newcastle travelled to Bradford Park Avenue today for this match, played out in front of 12,000. It was Newcastle who held the upper hand throughout, and despite the low scoreline the visitors won convincingly.

Tom Curry

It took just four minutes for Newcastle to score their only goal. Hibbert sent a lovely pass to Dixon, who slotted it into the net with ease. This was enough to cause Bradford sufficient worry to affect their game. The home side never recovered from the early lead that Newcastle had taken, and never got back into the game.

Newcastle therefore had total control over the remaining 86 minutes, and their team worked hard to pull together to maintain their lead. Ramsay, in only his second game for Newcastle, and Robinson were both outstanding on the wings and their flair made interesting watching for the crowd.

Bradford made a few attempts at goal, but rarely threatened the strong Newcastle defence. When the odd ball did slip past, Lawrence was on hand in goal to do his duty.

The efforts of the home side were few and far between, so Lawrence had an easy game.

Newcastle kept up the pace and pressure on the Bradford defence, but their attempts came to nothing, and no more goals came their way.

In the second half there was a moment of worry for Newcastle when Loughran moved into the centre-forward position and tried his luck at goal. His shot was powerful, and although it threatened the Newcastle keeper the danger was averted and the Magpies' lead remained intact.

This was the best chance Bradford had seen throughout this game, and sadly for the home side it was also their last opportunity to level the scores. Newcastle took back control of the game immediately, and Bradford rarely saw the ball for the rest of the match.

Newcastle were unable to increase their lead, but with opponents as weak as this Bradford side, it didn't really matter. The visitors knew that they were under no real threat, so they were happy with their one-goal lead. They kept their defence strong until the final whistle, and knew they deserved to take home the points.

Bradford Park Avenue
Scattergood, Blackham, Dickinson, Brown, Howie, Scott, Turnbull, Loughran, Little, Bauchop, McCandless.
Newcastle United
Lawrence, McCracken, Hudspeth, Curry, Low, Finlay, Robinson, Dixon, Hibbert, Booth, Ramsay.

Birthdays

Kevin Pugh born today in 1960.
Midfield 1976-1982, Apps 1 (1 sub). Goals 0.

Ronnie Simpson born today in 1930.
Goalkeeper 1951-1960, Apps 297.

October 12

Match of the Day from 1929

BURNLEY DEFEATED AT LAST

Newcastle pull off 2-1 win in magnificent second-half display

Burnley were the visitors today at St James' Park for this Division One match, played out in front of 30,000 eager supporters. Burnley had not lost on this ground for the previous four seasons, and were hoping to carry on the tradition. Newcastle were confident however, that the visitors would go home disappointed.

Hughie Gallacher was outstanding for the entire match, and his efforts made a huge difference to the game. He was able to think on his feet, and change course at the slightest hint of danger, and this went a long way towards saving Newcastle from another defeat.

Also superb was McInroy in the United goal. His fantastic saves helped his side take the win, and Burnley were denied goals on many occasions by the quick thinking goalkeeper.

Both teams started well enough, and Burnley got the advantage in the first half. This was not surprising as the visitors had played the better football from the start. After seventeen minutes of play, it was Wallace who opened the scoring. His shot beat McInroy, sailing into the back of the net to give Burnley the lead.

Further chances for the visitors were thwarted by McInroy, and the Newcastle keeper did well to stop the shots which were raining down on the goal. Newcastle also put up their share of the fight at the other end, and they worried the Burnley defence on a number of occasions. In the first half Burnley keeper Downs really had little to do as the visiting defence was so strong.

However, the start of the second half saw a change in fortune.

It was Chalmers who broke through and scored the equaliser for Newcastle. He sent the ball powerfully towards goal, and Downs had no chance of making the save. Now the scores were level and Newcastle's confidence was growing. Burnley began to realise that they were in danger of losing this game if they didn't pull together and fight back.

United were the ones to step up the pace, and Burnley proved unable to keep up.

It was Gallacher who managed to get the winning goal for the Magpies towards the end of the game, and this seemed to totally throw Burnley. The home side were 2-1 in front, and that's how it stayed.

This win for Newcastle broke Burnley's run of luck, and gave them their first defeat in five seasons at St James' Park. Therefore this was more than just a win for the home side, it was an inspiring victory, and a huge confidence booster.

Newcastle United
McInroy, Maitland, Thomson, Mathison, Hill, Harris, Urwin, Chalmers, Gallacher, McDonald, Lang.
Burnley
Downs, McCluggage, Waterfield, Brown, Bowsher, Steel, Bruton, Wallace, Beel, Devine, Forrest.

Played on this day

1895, FA Cup Qualifying round 2.
West Hartlepool NER (a) 8-0 Att. 3,000
Logan (2), Thompson, Collins (2), Stott, Graham, Opponent (og)
1901, Division 1.
Derby County (h) 0-1 Att. 15,000
1907, Division 1.
Manchester United (h) 1-6 Att. 30,000
McWilliam
1912, Division 1.
Manchester City (a) 1-0 Att. 35,000
Stewart
1925, Division 1.
Blackburn Rovers (a) 2-1 Att. 12,094
N. Harris, McDonald
1929, Division 1.
Burnley (h) 2-1 Att. 30,000
Chalmers, Gallacher
1932, FA Charity Shield.
Everton (h) 3-5 Att. 15,000
Boyd, McMenemy (2)
1935, Division 2.
Charlton Athletic (h) 1-2 Att. 28,000
Harris
1940, Wartime.
Chesterfield (h) 3-0 Att. 5,000
Short, Nevins, Gordon (pen)
1946, Division 2.
Southampton (a) 1-1 Att. 27,000
Shackleton
1957, Division 1.
Everton (h) 2-3 Att. 30,472
Curry, Davies
1968, Division 1.
Ipswich Town (a) 4-1 Att. 20,763
Foggon, B. Robson (2, 1 pen), Dyson
1974, Division 1.
Stoke City (h) 2-2 Att. 39,658
Tudor, Keeley
1985, Division 1.
Ipswich Town (a) 2-2 Att. 12,536
Beardsley, McDonald
1988, Littlewoods Cup 2nd round, 2nd leg.
Sheffield United (h) 2-0 Att. 14,520
Hendrie, Mirandinha
Newcastle lost 3-2 on aggregate.
1991, Division 2.
Leicester City (h) 2-0 Att. 16,966
Hunt, Clark
1996, Premier League.
Derby County 0   Newcastle 1
Shearer 76
Att. 18,092
1999, Worthington Cup 3rd round.
Birmingham City 2   Newcastle 0
O'Connor 45 (pen)
Purse 59 Att. 19,795

Playing record for this day... 18 games, Won 9, Drawn 3, Lost 6, GF 37, GA 27. Today's success rate... 58.33%.

Birthdays

Shola Ameobi born today in 1981.
Forward 1995-present day, Apps 86 (48 subs). Goals 15.

Paul Goddard born today in 1959.
Centre-forward 1986-1988, Apps 72. Goals 23.

Brian Kerr born today in 1981.
Midfield 1998-present day, Apps 13 (8 subs). Goals 0.

October 13

1894, Division 2.
Darwen (h) 3-2   Att. 6,000
Dickson (2), McNee

1900, Division 1.
Derby County (h) 2-1   Att. 18,000
Fraser, Peddie

1906, Division 1.
Manchester City (h) 2-0   Att. 20,000
Appleyard (2)

1923, Division 1.
West Ham United (h) 0-0   Att. 21,000

1928, Division 1.
Liverpool (a) 1-2   Att. 35,000
Boyd

1934, Division 2.
West Ham United (a) 2-3   Att. 29,000
Lang, Weaver

1945, Wartime.
Grimsby Town (h) 6-2   Att. 46,568
Stubbins (2), Crowe, Hair, Milburn (2)

1951, Division 1.
Huddersfield Town (a) 4-2   Att. 32,000
Hannah, Milburn (2), G. Robledo

1956, Division 1.
Aston Villa (a) 1-3   Att. 35,038
Eastham

1962, Division 2.
Sunderland (h) 1-1   Att. 62,262
Kerray

1973, Division 1.
Manchester City (h) 1-0   Att. 35,346
Macdonald

1979, Division 2.
Shrewsbury Town (h) 1-0   Att. 21,603
Shoulder

1984, Division 1.
Coventry City (a) 1-1   Att. 14,091
Beardsley (pen)

1990, Division 2.
Oxford United (a) 0-0   Att. 6,820

2001, Premier League.
Bolton Wanderers 0 Newcastle 4
     Solano 41
     Robert 62
     Shearer 72
     Bellamy 84
           Att. 25,631

Playing record for this day... 15 games,
Won 8, Drawn 4, Lost 3, GF 29, GA 17.
Today's success rate... 66.67%.

SUPERB UNITED SPELLS DOOM FOR BOLTON

Newcastle rattle in four to add to Wanderers' woes

Bolton manager Sam Allardyce, protested bitterly at what he considered a blatant offside for Newcastle's opening goal, declaring that to be the turning point of this match and not the 61st minute sending-off of his goalkeeper Jussi Jaaskelainen. While there was a certain degree of sympathy for Allardyce in his complaint, a third successive home defeat in which Bolton have remained scoreless, should be of greater concern. The bottom line is Bolton are taking on the mantle they were handed at the start of the season, favourites for relegation. Newcastle completely exposed the vulnerability of a side who are beginning to appear destined to subside further towards the foot of the table. The greater class and quality of Newcastle was evident in all departments at the Reebok Stadium and this eventually turned into superior goal-scoring advantage after an hour. Jaaskelainen had no complaints about his red card, for handling outside of his penalty area, and with injury to reserve keeper Steve Banks he left striker Bo Hansen with the impossible task of keeping out United's hungry forwards at bay for the last 29 minutes of the game. Hansen, who bravely volunteered to take the goalkeeper's position, was helpless to prevent the three goals Newcastle then plundered and thus equalled their best away victory of the season in moving up to fourth place in the Premiership.

Before Nolberto Solano's opening goal four minutes before the interval, after Alan Shearer's intelligent header, Craig Bellamy had spurned numerous opportunities to emphasise United's greater attacking potential. A half-time lead of 1-0 did the Magpies no justice whatsoever but one felt at this point the points were safely in the bag, as, a Bolton comeback just didn't seem possible.

The task, of running up a bigger margin of victory, was made simpler once Jaaskelainen had departed. Immediately, from the free kick the excellent Laurent Robert drilled the ball in for Newcastle's second goal. Ten minutes later Shearer's capable header dispatched goal number three from Robert's inch perfect running cross. Then with six minutes remaining, Bellamy was finally rewarded after good work by Gary Speed and Shearer to seal United's emphatic and well deserved 4-0 victory.

Alan Shearer gets his head to the ball to score the third goal against Bolton.

Bolton Wanderers

Jaaskelainen, Barness (N'Gotty 66), Bergsson, Whitlow, Charlton (Diawara 69), Warhurst, Gardner, Johnson, Southall (Ricketts 66), Hansen, Holdsworth.

Newcastle United

Given, Hughes, O'Brien, Dabizas (Distin 86), Elliott, Solano, Lee, Speed (Acuna 89), Robert, Bellamy (Ameobi 86), Shearer.

Referee Mr. M. Riley (Leeds).

Birthdays

John Cornwell born today in 1964.
Midfield/Full-back 1987-1988, Apps 43 (7 subs).
Goals 1.

Gordon Hodgson born today in 1952.
Midfield 1971-1974, Apps 13 (3 subs). Goals 0.

Ken Prior born today in 1932.
Winger 1952-1954 & 1956-1957, Apps 10.
Goals 3.

October 14

Match of the Day from 1995

TOP SPOT SUSTAINED THANKS TO RANGERS ERROR

Ready's mistake leads to United's late winner

Newcastle United consolidated their position at the top of the Premier League with their sixth straight league and cup victory, all thanks to a terrible blunder by QPR. With nineteen minutes of the game remaining, Karl Ready, the Rangers centre back, misplaced a back-pass to his goalkeeper with wretched consequences for the home side. Keith Gillespie seized upon his second goal of the match and Rangers were staring at their fourth home defeat in five Premiership games.

However, Queen's Park Rangers, and their hapless fans, must have been delighted with their start as Danny Dichio, the man with the responsibility of succeeding Les Ferdinand, broke the scoring deadlock in first-half stoppage time. He had already given Newcastle due warning with two headers from crosses by Ian Holloway and Simon Barker that went increasingly closer to the target, when he eventually hit it, rising high above the United defence to head home another great cross from Holloway. Newcastle for all their possession disappointed in front of goal and no one could have been more upset than David Ginola when he saw a well-drilled cross shot wriggle free of Jurgen Sommer's grasp with no one around to pounce upon it, Newcastle's best chance of the half.

However, within a minute of the restart, all was forgotten by the Frenchman as he saw his cross to the far post rewarded by Gillespie, who sent a looping header over the stranded Sommer. Ferdinand's afternoon seemed to be going from bad to worse when he completely failed to make any connection right in front of goal, from a centre from Warren Barton. But, a minute later, in the 55th, life could not have been rosier for the former Rangers striker. If his first touch may sometimes desert him, Ferdinand knows his pace is not about to. Hence Maddix had as much chance of sticking to Ferdinand as a soggy plaster when Barton's up and under clearance invited the pair to give chase. It was no contest, Ferdinand accelerating ahead to score his twelfth goal in eleven games with a flashing left-foot drive. The Toon Army's celebrations had barely died down however, when Dichio again stole his one time hero's thunder, climbing at the far post to head home Trevor Sinclair's cross after he had expertly beaten Beresford on the wing to make his cross. At this point a draw seemed likely and a fair result but for Ready and Rangers the day was yet again going to be tough on poor old Ray Wilkins' team.

Queen's Park Rangers
Sommer, Impey, Brevett, Ready, Yates, Maddix, Barker, Holloway, Osborn (Goodridge 73), Dichio, Sinclair.

Newcastle United
Hislop, Barton, Beresford, Peacock, Howey, Lee, Clark, Beardsley, Ginola(Sellars 68), Ferdinand, Gillespie.

Referee Mr. P. Durkin (Portland, Dorset).

Played on this day

1893, Division 2.
Notts County (a) 1-3   Att. 5,000
Wallace
1899, Division 1.
Manchester City (a) 0-1   Att. 25,000
1911, Division 1.
Sunderland (a) 2-1   Att. 20,000
Scott, McCracken (pen)
1922, Division 1.
Burnley (a) 0-0   Att. 25,000
1933, Division 1.
Arsenal (a) 0-3   Att. 40,000
1944, Wartime.
Middlesbrough (a) 8-2   Att. 5,000
Carr (3), Milburn (2), Wayman (2), Gordon
1950, Division 1.
Derby County (h) 3-1   Att. 54,793
Milburn, Mitchell, Walker
1961, Division 2.
Bury (a) 7-2   Att. 13,809
McGuigan, Leek (2), Hale (2), Suddick, Neale
1964, Division 2.
Manchester City (a) 0-3   Att. 10,215
1967, Division 1.
Fulham (h) 2-1   Att. 27,664
Bennett (2)
1972, Division 1.
Stoke City (a) 0-2   Att. 16,609
1978, Division 2.
Sunderland (a) 1-1   Att. 35,405
Withe
1989, Division 2.
Bradford City (h) 1-0   Att. 19,879
McGhee
1995, Premier League.
Q.P.R. 2   Newcastle 3
Dichio 44, 88   Gillespie 46, 72
Ferdinand 56
Att. 18,254

Playing record for this day... 14 games, Won 7, Drawn 2, Lost 5, GF 28, GA 22. Today's success rate... 57.14%.

Les Ferdinand battles with Danny Maddix of Queen's Park Rangers on his way to scoring.

Birthdays

Olivier Bernard born today in 1979.
Defender 2000-present day, Apps 65 (23 subs).
Goals 5.

October 15

1887, FA Cup Qualifying round.
South Bank (a) 2-3
W. Muir (2)
After extra time.
1898, Division 1.
Sheffield United (h) 1-2   Att. 6,000
Harvey
1904, Division 1.
Sheffield United (h) 1-1   Att. 23,263
Howie
1910, Division 1.
Manchester United (a) 0-2   Att. 50,000
1921, Division 1.
Chelsea (h) 1-0   Att. 40,000
Harris
1927, Division 1.
Sheffield Wednesday (h) 4-3   Att. 25,000
McDonald (2, 1 pen), Gallacher (2)
1932, Division 1.
Wolverhampton W. (h) 3-2   Att. 25,000
Boyd (2), McMenemy
1938, Division 2.
Tranmere Rovers (h) 5-1   Att. 33,000
Cairns (3), Mooney (2)
Cairns nets his second hat trick in
consecutive league matches.
1949, Division 1.
Sunderland (h) 2-2   Att. 57,999
G. Robledo, Walker
1955, Division 1.
Arsenal (a) 0-1   Att. 46,093
1960, Division 1.
Wolverhampton W. (h) 4-4   Att. 23,401
Hughes, R. Mitchell (2), White
1966, Division 1.
Manchester City (h) 2-0   Att. 16,523
McGarry, Suddick
1975, League Cup 3rd round, replay.
Bristol Rovers (h) 2-0   Att. 26,294
T. Craig (pen), Nattrass
1977, Division 1.
Manchester United (a) 2-3   Att. 55,056
Martin, Burns
1994, Premier League.
Crystal Palace 0   Newcastle 1
Beardsley 89
Att. 17,760
1996, UEFA Cup 2nd round, 1st leg.
Ferencvaros 3   Newcastle 2
Horvath 7   Ferdinand 25
Lisztes 17, 57   Shearer 35
Att. 18,000
1997, Coca Cola Cup 3rd round.
Newcastle 2   Hull City 0
Hamilton 47
Rush 83   Att. 35,856

Playing record for this day... 17 games,
Won 8, Drawn 3, Lost 6, GF 34, GA 27.
Today's success rate... 55.88%.

Match of the Day from 1927

GOOD SHOW BY UNITED

Newcastle snatch win from Sheffield Wednesday at St. James' Park

Sheffield Wednesday made the trip up to St. James' Park today to try their luck at beating the League champions on their home turf. It would be a tough job if they were to succeed. Newcastle were prepared for a battle, and in front of 25,000 eager supporters the game got under way.

There was little separating the two sides at the beginning of play. The pace was quick, and the pressure was high. The owls were doing well to keep up with the energetic Newcastle players who were constantly pressing with their skilful moves and clever play.

Wednesday gained the advantage when they opened the scoring after just four minutes of play. It was Jack Allen who was able to slip through the tight Newcastle defence and plant the ball into the back of the net to give the visitors the early lead they had hoped for.

Then with fifteen minutes on the clock Gallacher levelled the scores to the relief of the home fans. Their joy was short-lived though, as Hooper regained the lead for Wednesday after the visitors were awarded a penalty. Hooper had no trouble beating the Newcastle keeper, and United were a goal behind again.

Things got worse for the home side when Harris managed to send the ball past his own goalkeeper to give Wednesday another goal to add to their lead.

Three minutes before the half-time break, United's fortunes changed. Gallacher was brought down by Leach, and a penalty was awarded. McDonald stepped up to the spot to take the kick, and he had no trouble sending the ball straight into the net to reduce the deficit. Now Newcastle were just one goal behind, and there was still the second half to go.

The home side improved greatly after the interval, and their pace was far quicker than Wednesday expected. The visitors were quite clearly beginning to tire, and Newcastle were still ready for a challenge.

Gallacher added another goal to the score-sheet, his super shot beating the visitors' keeper and bringing the scores level at last. However, Newcastle weren't happy with a draw and went all out for victory.

It was going to be tough, but if anyone could do it Newcastle could. Their bombardment wore down the already weary Wednesday defence. McDonald saw his chance to slip through and take on the keeper, and his determination paid off. His shot sailed into the net to give Newcastle the lead they had worked so hard to gain. It was thoroughly deserved, and the visitors had to go back home to Sheffield with no return for their efforts.

Newcastle United
Wilson, Maitland, Hudspeth, Curry, Spencer, Harris, Low, McKay, Gallacher, McDonald, Seymour.
Sheffield Wednesday
Mellors, Felton, Blenkinsop, Leach, Kean, Burridge, Hooper, Seed, Trotter, Allen, Wilkinson.

Birthdays

Andy Cole born today in 1971.
Centre-forward 1993-1995, Apps 84 (1 sub).
Goals 68.

Joseph Cooper born today in 1934.
Midfield 1952-1959, Apps 6. Goals 0.

October 16

Match of the Day from 2000

BATTLE OF THE ROBSONS

Tyne-Tees derby won convincingly by Bobby's

Middlesbrough's Curtis Fleming challenges Alain Goma.

Bobby Robson outfoxed his namesake Bryan, the man he appointed as England captain, in an incident packed Tyne-Tees derby today. Newcastle climbed to third place in the title race as Robson senior insisted that the team he has rebuilt in barely a year are not yet ready to challenge for the Premiership title. But he must be confident of his expressed desire of a top-six finish and European qualification, even a place in the Champions' League must be considered a possibility after this latest victory. Alan Shearer's third goal of the season set Newcastle on their way to a win which was completed by Alain Goma's header and a simple third for Kieron Dyer two minutes from the end. Brian Deane's scrappy reply in stoppage time was scant consolation for an outclassed Middlesbrough. The Riverside continues to be an uncomfortable home for Boro and their boss Bryan Robson, who have not won a league match here in almost seven months.

Boro have conceded at least one goal in all of their matches so far this season and left the country's most prolific marksman alone near the penalty spot to make what was a thoroughly deserved 38th minute breakthrough. A high ball into the area by Nolberto Solano caused consternation in the home defence and Gary Speed again demonstrated his aerial ability by rising above his marker to head down into the path of Shearer who could afford to trap the ball before hammering it emphatically past Mark Crossley, making his home debut in the Boro goal. Many thought United had gone ahead thirteen minutes earlier when the Argentine striker Daniel Cordone stabbed the ball into the net after a jinking run into the box by Didier Domi. The Frenchman's low shot might have gone in anyway without the deflection of the offside Cordone. A disappointing Boro created one chance in a Newcastle-dominated first half, keeper Shay Given reacting well to block an unchallenged header by Gianluca Festa from a well flighted corner by Dean Gordon.

Newcastle, who at times had all ten outfield players in the opposing half, made no attempt to close down the game and were worth the cushion of a second goal which came their way after 55 minutes. The suspect Boro defence failed to deal properly with a corner by Cordone, who, when the ball was returned to him wide on the left, produced a confident volley back into the danger area. Goma reacted smartly to meet it with a powerful header past the startled Crossley. Newcastle continued to press for a third which almost came from substitute Lomana LuaLua's fierce drive. The goal finally arrived, and a real beauty too, when Dyer was allowed to take aim from fifteen yards and hammer an unstoppable shot past the hapless Boro keeper. Most of the subdued home crowd had deserted the stadium by the time Deane, moments later, salvaged a crumb of consolation for Boro by tapping in after an untidy goalmouth scramble.

Middlesbrough
Crossley, Festa, Pallister, Cooper, Fleming (Stamp 46, Marinelli 58), Ince, Karembeu, Mustoe (Deane 75), Gordon, Ricard, Boksic.
Newcastle United
Given, Charvet, Hughes, Goma, Domi, Solano, Lee, Dyer, Speed, Shearer, Cordone (LuaLua 75).
Referee Mr. S. Dunn (Bristol)

Played on this day

1897, Division 2.
    Woolwich Arsenal (a) 0-0   Att. 12,000
1909, Division 1.
    Sheffield Wednesday (a) 1-3 Att. 15,000
    Shepherd (pen)
1920, Division 1.
    Sunderland (a) 2-0   Att. 35,000
    Seymour, Harris
1926, Division 1.
    Everton (a) 3-1   Att. 45,000
    Clark, Gallacher, McDonald
1937, Division 2.
    Aston Villa (a) 0-2   Att. 50,459
1943, Wartime.
    Huddersfield Town (a) 1-1   Att. 4,268
    Milburn
1948, Division 1.
    Wolverhampton W. (h) 3-1 Att. 60,958
    Milburn (2), Opponent (og)
1954, Division 1.
    Tottenham Hotspur (h) 4-4. Att. 45,306
    Broadis (2), Crowe, White
1965, Division 1.
    Liverpool (a) 0-2   Att. 47,948
1971, Division 1.
    Crystal Palace (h) 1-2   Att. 20,711
    Dyson
1974, Division 1.
    Wolverhampton W. (h) 0-0 Att. 30,825
1976, Division 1.
    Coventry City (a) 1-1   Att. 18,083
    Gowling
1982, Division 2.
    Fulham (h) 1-4   Att. 29,647
    Keegan (pen)
1983, Division 2.
    Swansea City (a) 2-1   Att. 9,807
    Wharton, Mills
1993, Premier League.
    Newcastle 1   Q.P.R. 2
    Allen 46   Ferdinand 10
              Allen 50
                   Att. 33,926
1999, Premier League.
    Coventry City 4   Newcastle 1
    Palmer 13.   Domi 81
    Williams 21
    Keane 39
    Hadji 90   Att. 23,031
2000, Premier League.
    Middlesbrough 1   Newcastle 3
    Deane 90   Shearer 38
                   Goma 55
                   Dyer 89
                   Att. 31,436

Playing record for this day... 17 games, Won 5, Drawn 5, Lost 7, GF 24, GA 29. Today's success rate... 44.12%.

Played on this day

1896, Division 2.
Manchester City (a) 2-1 — Att. 7,000
Smellie, Auld

1903, Division 1.
Notts County (a) 2-3 — Att. 9,000
Templeton, Howie

1908, Division 1.
Middlesbrough (a) 0-0 — Att. 20,000

1914, Division 1.
Middlesbrough (a) 1-1 — Att. 18,000
Hall

1925, Division 1.
Sunderland (h) 0-0 — Att. 50,000

1931, Division 1.
Blackburn Rovers (a) 3-0 — Att. 15,000
Allen, Boyd, Lang

1936, Division 2.
Chesterfield (h) 1-2 — Att. 27,000
Cairns

1942, Wartime.
York City (h) 3-3 — Att. 4,000
Carr, Stubbins, McCormack

1953, Division 1.
Aston Villa (a) 2-1 — Att. 29,556
Davies, Milburn

1959, Division 1.
Fulham (a) 3-4 — Att. 37,200
Eastham, Hale (2)

1964, Division 2.
Bury (a) 2-1 — Att. 8,950
Cummings, Robson

1970, Division 1.
Wolverhampton W. (a) 2-3 — Att. 24,083
Davies, Opponent (og)

1981, Division 2.
Barnsley (a) 0-1 — Att. 18,477

1987, Division 1.
Everton (h) 1-1 — Att. 20,266
Mirandinha

1998, Premier League.

Newcastle 2	Derby County 1
Dabizas 13	Burton 73
Glass 17	Att. 36,750

Playing record for this day... 15 games,
Won 5, Drawn 5, Lost 5, GF 24, GA 22.
Today's success rate... 50%.

Match of the Day from 1931

BLACKBURN-ED OUT

Newcastle beat weak Rovers 3-0 at Ewood Park

Newcastle United made the trip to Ewood Park today to meet Blackburn in this Division One match in front of a crowd of 15,000. Newcastle had a strong defence, and this would prove to be invaluable throughout this entire game.

Play started well for both teams, but right from the start Blackburn were finding it difficult to create any danger for the Newcastle goalkeeper. Newcastle, on the other hand were having few problems, and provided a constant threat to the home defence.

Play continued to improve for Newcastle, the visitors rapidly gaining the upper hand in the game, as Blackburn began to get flustered.

The Blackburn forwards did not make any progress against the steadfast Newcastle back line, and the home team began to realise that they were losing the battle. United kept up the pressure, and their efforts began to pay off with eight minutes to go before the half-time break. Jack Allen scored the first goal with a lovely shot which left Crawford in the Blackburn goal no chance to save.

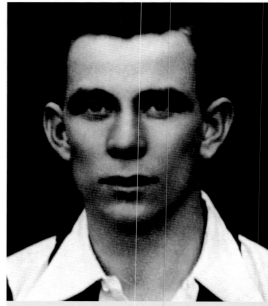
Tommy Lang

Just a few minutes later and Newcastle's lead was doubled when Tommy Lang got his head to a fine cross and nodded it into the back of the net with ease.

The second half started with a slightly improved performance from the home side, but the misery of the first half, coupled with Newcastle stepping up their game, helped to sap their enthusiasm. Blackburn's efforts soon began to dwindle, as Newcastle took control once again.

Lang got the ball past Crawford, but his shot was ruled offside and the goal didn't stand. However, it didn't really matter as there was no danger of the visitors losing their lead. Blackburn were ineffective up front, and Newcastle knew there would be more chances to add to the score-sheet, they just had to wait for them to come.

Their patience was rewarded when Boyd seized the opportunity and slammed the ball into the net with confidence, giving Newcastle a deserved third goal.

Blackburn had put on an awful performance, and even some of the home supporters praised Newcastle for their win.

Blackburn Rovers
Crawford, Gorman, Jones, Imrie, Carver, Healless, Bruton, Talbot, Thompson, McLean, Cunliffe.
Newcastle United
McInroy, Nelson, Fairhurst, MacKenzie, Davidson, Weaver, Boyd, Richardson, Allen, McMenemy, Lang.

Birthdays

Jim Smith born today 1940.
Manager 1988-1991.

Sadly Missed

George Thompson died on this day 1943, aged 65.
Winger 1903-1905, Apps 2. Goals 0.

October 18

Match of the Day from 1994

HAVE THEY BLOWN IT?

Tough game in Spain now, after United led 3-0

Newcastle's inexperience was cruelly exposed last night when they allowed a limited Athletic Bilbao side to score two goals when it seemed they were heading for a four, or even five-goal victory. The comfortable lead United appeared to be taking to the San Mames stadium in two weeks time is now only the most slender of advantages and it was no wonder the Bilbao players raised their arms in joy at the final whistle. Losing 3-2 was a moral victory for the Basques who had spent 70 minutes chasing the game. Instead of leaving St. James' Park

Scott Sellars battles with Ander Garitano of Athletico Bilbao.

demoralised Bilbao will now be full of confidence for the return leg in Spain. While Kevin Keegan's tactic of attacking from every angle at every opportunity is admirable and wonderful to watch, the United manager must know from his days at Liverpool and Hamburg that there is a time in European ties to shut up shop. If there is any consolation for Newcastle it is that they know they, too, are capable of scoring goals on opponents' grounds. However, they must show far more professionalism in the Basque country if they are to reach the third round.

The game started well for United who went ahead in the tenth minute after Scott Sellars found John Beresford on the left of the penalty area. The left back improvised and got the ball to Andy Cole who flicked it on to Ruel Fox. The winger toe-poked the ball from ten yards and Juan Jose Valencia will not be happy that the ball escaped his grasp and went into the net. In the eighteenth minute Newcastle survived a penalty appeal that should have gone against them. Steve Howey clearly pushed Jose Angel Ciganda but the German referee waved play on. Ironically Newcastle made it 2-0 from the spot with a decision that was no more valid than Bilbao's. Oscar Tabuenca tackled Cole and this time Helmut Krug decided it was a foul. Peter Beardsley did not care about the merits of the decision, he simply dispatched his kick with customary calmness.

Cole would have gone three matches without scoring, his longest drought since joining Newcastle, had he failed to strike in this game. In the 59th minute, the forward, less than 100 per cent fit because of shin-splints, put the record straight with his thirteenth goal of the season when he headed in Fox's inch-perfect cross. With the Toon Army in full flow more goals seemed inevitable. Indeed, the goals came, but surprisingly they came from the Spanish side. Bilbao made an inspired substitution when they brought on Gonzalo Suances. His presence added new dimension to Athletic and he provided the pass for Ciganda to score with a low shot from fifteen yards in the 71st minute. Worse was to come just eight minutes later. Beresford failed to jump with Suances as the sub headed a centre from Ricardo Mendiguren past Pavel Srnicek. Newcastle have only themselves to blame for slack defending. One thing is for certain, it will be one heck of a game in Bilbao for the second leg.

Newcastle United
Srnicek, Hottiger, Peacock, Howey, Beresford, Albert, Fox, Clark, Sellars, Beardsley, Cole.

Athletic Bilbao
Valencia, Tabuenca (Suances 67), Andinua, Caranca, Larrazabal, Estivariz (Corino 84), Vales, Garitano, Mendiguren, Ciganda, Alkiza.

Referee Mr. H. Krug (Germany)

Played on this day

1902, Division 1.
Middlesbrough (h) 0-1   Att. 26,000
1913, Division 1.
Oldham Athletic (a) 0-3   Att. 20,000
1919, Division 1.
Bradford Park Ave. (h) 4-0   Att. 44,000
Dixon, Hibbert (3)
1924, Division 1.
Sunderland (a) 1-1   Att. 55,642
Clark
1930, Division 1.
Derby County (h) 2-5   Att. 30,000
Lang (2, 1pen)
1941, Wartime.
Gateshead (h) 3-1   Att. 12,000
Stubbins (2), Wayman
1947, Division 2.
Bury (a) 5-3   Att. 23,827
Milburn (3), Shackleton, Opponent (og)
1952, Division 1.
Charlton Athletic (h) 3-2   Att. 41,532
Keeble (2), G.Robledo
1958, Division 1.
Preston North End (a) 4-3   Att. 25,525
Franks, White (3)
1969, Division 1.
Tottenham Hotspur (a) 1-2   Att. 33,286
Robson
1975, Division 1.
Norwich City (h) 5-2   Att. 32,799
Gowling (2), Macdonald (2), Opponent (og)
1980, Division 2.
Swansea City (h) 1-2   Att. 16,278
Rafferty
1986, Division 1.
Arsenal (h) 1-2   Att. 22,368
Stewart
1989, Division 2.
Blackburn Rovers (h) 2-1   Att. 20,702
McGhee, Quinn
1992, Division 1.
Sunderland (a) 2-1   Att. 28,098
Opponent (og), O'Brien
1994, UEFA Cup 2nd round, 1st leg.

Newcastle 3	Athletico Bilbao 2
Fox 9	Ziganda 71
Beardsley 34 (pen)	Suances 79
Cole 56	Att. 32,140

1997, Premier League.

Leeds United 4	Newcastle 1
Ribeiro 30	Gillespie 62
Kewell 38	
Beresford (og) 43	
Wetherall 47	Att. 39,834

Playing record for this day... 17 games, Won 9, Drawn 1, Lost 7, GF 38, GA 35. Today's success rate... 55.88%.

Played on this day

1895, Division 2.
  Newton Heath (a) 1-2   Att. 8,000
  Logan
1901, Division 1.
  Sheffield Wednesday (a) 0-0 Att. 15,000
1907, Division 1.
  Manchester City(a) 0-1   Att. 25,000
1912, Division 1.
  West Bromwich A. (h) 1-1   Att. 30,000
  McTavish
1929, Division 1.
  Sunderland (a) 0-1   Att. 58,519
1935, Division 2.
  Leicester City (h) 3-1   Att. 15,000
  Cairns, Harris, Ware
1940, Wartime.
  Hull City (a) 1-2.   Att. 3,000
  Gilholme
1946, Division 2.
  Bradford Park Ave. (a) 1-2 Att. 26,533
  Pearson
1957, Division 1.
  Aston Villa (a) 3-4   Att. 27,660
  Curry (2), Eastham
1963, Division 2.
  Portsmouth (a) 2-5   Att. 14,996
  McGarry, Hilley
1968, Division 1.
  Queens Park Rangers (h) 3-2 Att. 35,503
  Burton, Dyson, Gibb
1971, Texaco Cup 2nd round, 1st leg.
  Coventry City (a) 1-1   Att. 12,311
  Howard
1974, Division 1.
  Birmingham City (a) 0-3   Att. 33,339
1977, UEFA Cup 2nd round, 1st leg.
  Bastia (a) 1-2   Att. 8,500
  Cannell
1983, Division 2.
  Cardiff City (a) 2-0   Att. 9,926
  Beardsley, Keegan
1985, Division 1.
  Nottingham Forest (h) 0-3   Att. 23,304
1991, Division 2.
  Oxford United (h) 4-3   Att. 16,454
  Hunt, Peacock (3)
2002, Premier League.
  Blackburn Rovers 5 Newcastle 2
  Dunn 5 (pen)   Shearer
  Taylor 55, 74   36 (pen), 48
  Griffin (og) 65   Att. 27,307

Playing record for this day... 18 games,
Won 4, Drawn 3, Lost 11, GF 25, GA 38.
Today's success rate... 30.56%.

Match of the Day from 1935

LEICESTER LOSE OUT
Newcastle make superb comeback to take win

It was Leicester's turn today to make the journey north to St. James' Park for this Division Two match. 15,000 braved the strong winds to come and watch the game, and it was worth the effort.

Leicester started out the better team in the first half, showing more aggression and determination than the home side. Newcastle had a lot of work to do if they were to match the standard of play. Try as they might, things just weren't working for the struggling home side.

Things were looking bleak for United when Leicester took the lead after twenty minutes of play. Liggins had an easy shot into goal, his efforts totally unchallenged by the Newcastle defence.

This was not good for morale in the Magpie team, and more misery was felt when every attempt the home forwards made was thwarted by Jones and Frame in defence for Leicester. However, despite the visitors having the advantage, Newcastle managed to prevent them increasing their lead further, and the half-time break was welcome relief for the Tynesiders.

In the second half Newcastle took to the pitch revived and energetic. They clearly had more focus and team spirit, and were ready for the challenge of a comeback.

Billy Cairns

With 77 minutes on the clock, the home side finally scored the equaliser. It was Harry Ware who managed to break through the defence and beat McLaren in the Leicester goal. This super goal boosted Newcastle no end, and their game got better with every move.

Although the home side wanted the win, they didn't panic when it seemed that time was running out. Instead they pulled together and stepped up the pressure on the opposing goal.

With five minutes to go Newcastle finally took the lead they deserved. Harris was the man to get his name on the score-sheet, and his shot had no chance of being saved by McLaren.

Just to make things certain for the home side, Billy Cairns added the third for Newcastle just before the final whistle. This smashing strike brought the score to 3-1, and United were happy to finish the game on such a high.

Newcastle United
Tapken, Richardson, Fairhurst, Imrie, Davidson, Weaver, Harris, Ware, Cairns, McMenemy, Pearson.
Leicester City
McLaren, Frame, Jones, Grogan, Heywood, Grosvenor, Carroll, O'Callaghan, Liggins, Maw, Liddle.

Birthdays

Phil Leaver born today in 1961.
Centre-half 1977-1982, Apps 1. Goals 0.

Jerry Lowery born today in 1924.
Goalkeeper 1947-1952, Apps 6. Goals 0.

October 20

Match of the Day from 1996

WHAT A NIGHT!

5-0! Red Devils hammered in sensational style

Statistics rarely do justice to the size of an achievement, but they certainly do here. It was Manchester United's worst defeat since October 1984, 5-0 at Everton. Alex Ferguson got the worst defeat ever in his 22-year managerial career. The goals were the first the Reds had conceded in nine hours and nine minutes. It sure was 999 time for the visitors. Newcastle's seventh success over Manchester United in nine years propelled Kevin Keegan's side back to the top of the table. And for the Toon Army who had travelled to Wembley back in August it went a long way to erasing the memory of that heavy 4-0 defeat in the Charity Shield. Of the many statistics however, one small fact meant everything, the 5-0 scoreline. Newcastle, so often brittle at the back defended from the front, with Les Ferdinand often chasing back to help deny any space to the Reds. With Philippe Albert in exceptional form Newcastle proved so successful that it appeared Eric Cantona might lose control.

Cantona's frustration began in the thirteenth minute when the Magpies scored a scrappy first goal. A long corner by David Ginola was diverted back by Alan Shearer towards Darren Peacock. The centre half arrowed a downward header through a mass of arms and legs, the ball just crossing the line before Denis Irwin cleared. The assistant referee, his wisdom later confirmed by television, immediately signalled a goal, triggering widespread euphoria on one side and a collective annoyance from the visitors' camp. Cantona was first to inquire about the official's eyesight though it was Peter Schmeichel who was cautioned for arguing too vehemently. Mancunian protests were heard again five minutes later when Karel Poborsky's run into the box was smothered by Pavel Srnicek's brave dive at his feet, However, Poborsky went flying over the top like a gymnast going over a vault, his ambitious penalty claims were rightly ignored. The reigning Premier League champions then fell further behind on the half hour. Steve Watson transferred play from right to left towards John Beresford, who worked the ball to Ginola, cutting in down the inside-left channel. One turn and the Frenchman had foxed Gary Neville. One touch, the ball dispatched violently with his right foot, and Ginola had beaten Schmeichel emphatically. The dramas continued, an effort from Shearer struck the post, David Batty and Nicky Butt struck each other; both players were cautioned.

The second half brought no respite for Ferguson and his men. Cantona had a goalbound shot cleared off the line by Watson and his frustration soon spilled over. A growing tiff with Albert soon resulted in the Frenchman being cautioned for pushing. Newcastle kept up their terrific flowing football which soon brought them a killer third goal. Shearer muscled down the right and crossed for Ferdinand and his attacking accomplice made no mistake with a superbly timed header; brilliant stuff. Shearer, in magnificent form, started and finished the fourth after 71 minutes. After sweeping the ball out to Beardsley, Shearer accelerated into the box. Schmeichel somehow managed to block Beardsley's shot and Ferdinand's follow-up but proved helpless as Shearer played the ultimate goal poacher. Newcastle made it five in thrilling fashion. Albert, gliding through the Red Devils' defence with ease, climaxed his progress with the deftest of chips over Schmeichel from 25 yards. The partying could now officially begin.

Newcastle United

Srnicek, Watson (Barton 89), Peacock, Albert, Beresford, Lee (Clark 89), Batty, Beardsley, Ginola, Ferdinand, Shearer.

Manchester United

Schmeichel, G.Neville, May, Pallister, Irwin, Butt, Johnsen, (McClair 66), Beckham, Poborsky (Scholes 66), Cantona, Solskjaer (Cruyff 55).

Referee Mr. S. Dunn (Bristol).

Birthdays

Ian Rush born today in 1961.
Centre-forward 1997-1998, Apps 14 (5 subs).
Goals 2.

Played on this day

1894, Division 2.
Leicester Fosse (a) 4-4   Att. 8,000
Dickson, Smith (pen), Thompson, Willis
1900, Division 1.
Bolton Wanderers (a) 2-3   Att. 18,000
Peddie (2)
1906, Division 1.
Middlesbrough (a) 3-0   Att. 17,000
Appleyard (3)
1923, Division 1.
Middlesbrough (a) 0-1   Att. 25,000
1928, Division 1.
Arsenal (h) 0-3   Att. 30,000
1934, Division 2.
Manchester United (h) 0-1   Att. 25,000
1945, Wartime.
Blackpool (h) 2-2   Att. 35,299
Wayman, Clifton
1951, Division 1.
Chelsea (h) 3-1   Att. 52,168
Milburn (2, 1 pen), G. Robledo
1956, Division 1.
Manchester City (h) 0-3   Att. 34,802
1962, Division 2.
Leeds United (a) 0-1   Att. 23,250
1973, Division 1.
Chelsea (h) 2-0   Att. 32,106
Macdonald (2, 1 pen)
1979, Division 2.
Watford (a) 0-2   Att. 17,715
1984, Division 1.
Nottingham Forest (h) 1-1   Att. 28,328
Wharton
1990, Division 2.
Ipswich Town (a) 1-2   Att. 15,567
Quinn (pen)
1996, Premier League.
Newcastle 5   Manchester U. 0
Peacock 12
Ginola 30
Ferdinand 63
Shearer 75
Albert 83   Att. 36,579

Playing record for this day... 15 games,
Won 4, Drawn 3, Lost 8, GF 23, GA 24.
Today's success rate... 36.67%.

October 21

Played on this day

1893, Division 2.
Ardwick (a) 3-2   Att. 3,000
Wallace, Crate, Opponent (og)
1899, Division 1.
Sheffield United (h) 0-0   Att. 30,000
1905, Division 1.
Bury (h) 3-1   Att. 20,000
Orr, Appleyard, Veitch
1911, Division 1.
Blackburn Rovers (h) 4-2   Att. 30,000
Hay, Stewart (2), Wilson
1922, Division 1.
Arsenal (h) 1-1   Att. 30,000
J. Low
1933, Division 1.
Sunderland (h) 2-1   Att. 45,000
Weaver (2)
1939, Wartime.
Hartlepool United (a) 2-1   Att. 4,000
Pearson (pen), Meek
1944, Wartime.
Leeds United (a) 1-2   Att. 8,000
A. Donaldson
1950, Division 1.
Bolton Wanderers (a) 2-0   Att. 49,213
G. Robledo, Taylor
1961, Division 2.
Brighton & Hove A. (h) 5-0   Att. 24,408
Tuohy, Leek (3), Hale
1970, Inter Cities Fairs Cup 2nd round, 1st leg.
Pecsi Dozsa (h) 2-0   Att. 50,550
Davies (2)
1972, Division 1.
Manchester United (h) 2-1   Att. 38,214
Hibbitt, Tudor
1978, Division 2.
Charlton Athletic (a) 1-4   Att. 11,616
Walker
1989, Division 2.
Brighton & Hove A. (a) 3-0   Att. 10,756
Quinn (3)
1995, Premier League.

Newcastle 6	Wimbledon 1
Howey 31	Gayle 60
Ferdinand 35, 41, 63	
Clark 59	
Albert 84	Att. 36,434

1999, UEFA Cup 2nd round, 1st leg.

F.C. Zurich 1	Newcastle 2
Castillo 68	Maric 51
	Shearer 60
	Att. 9,600

2000, Premier League.

Newcastle 0	Everton 1
	Campbell 80
	Att. 51,625

2001, Premier League.

Newcastle 0	Tottenham H. 2
	Speed (og) 8
	Poyet 20
	Att. 50,593

Playing record for this day... 18 games,
Won 12, Drawn 2, Lost 4, GF 39, GA 20.
Today's success rate... 72.22%.

Match of the Day from 1995

FERDINAND HAT-TRICK IS TIMELY ENGLAND REMINDER

£6m striker crushes Wimbledon in United's 6-1 romp

The fans who chastised Kevin Keegan for selling goal-scoring sensation Andy Cole last season are now praising the Newcastle manager's superior wisdom. Keegan can bask in the glow of a centre-forward who can apparently score goals for fun. Les Ferdinand's first hat-trick since his £6 million transfer from QPR fanned the flames of the 'Ferdy for England' debate. Apart from bludgeoning his way into Lancaster Gate to deliver a personal letter to Terry Venables, it is hard to see what more Ferdinand can do to earn an international recall. He has scored fifteen goals in twelve appearances, equalled a post-war club record by scoring in seven successive games and established Newcastle as the new bookmakers' favourites to lift the Premiership title, their first top-flight championship for 67 years.

Keegan believes that Ferdinand should play alongside Alan Shearer in the national team. But whether Ferdinand would fit into Venables' system is hard to tell bearing in mind the England coach does not have the availability of the country's leading wingers, United have Keith Gillespie of Northern Ireland and David Ginola of France. Neither of the pair scored today, surprisingly neither did man-of-the-match Peter Beardsley, but all three were catalysts in a performance that sent injury-hit Wimbledon to a fifth straight league defeat.

The Dons were in such dire straights, that defender Vinnie Jones was forced to play the last 35 minutes in goal after regular keeper Paul Heald was sent off after receiving a second yellow card. By this time it meant very little to the result as Newcastle led 3-0, and no sooner had Jones got the gloves on he was picking the ball out of the net after Lee Clark added a fourth goal, four minutes later. Within a minute Wimbledon snatched a consolation goal through Marcus Gayle, but, the match belonged to Ferdinand and he claimed the match ball in the 63rd minute. Philippe Albert, a substitute for the game's opening scorer Steve Howey, netted the emotional sixth goal for United with six minutes remaining. The brave Belgian defender, who had been on the field for just four minutes, was making his long-awaited comeback after a knee injury threatened to end his career ten months ago, his goal was well deserved reward for such a magnificent return.

Newcastle United
Hislop, Barton, Peacock, Howey (Albert 80), Beresford, Gillespie, Lee (Sellars 80), Clark (Hottiger 80), Ginola, Beardsley, Ferdinand.
Wimbledon
Heald, Cunningham, Fitzgerald, Earle, Perry (Goodman 35 mins, Leonhardsen 50), Jones, Gayle, Reeves, McAllister (Tallboys 10), Holdsworth, Harford.
Referee Mr. G. Poll (Tring).

Steve Howey

Birthdays

Kevin Sheedy born today in 1959.
Midfield 1992-1993, Apps 48 (2 subs). Goals 6.

Match of the Day from 1910

LIVERPOOL LIFELESS

Newcastle get six against a poor Liverpool

St. James' Park was the venue today for this Division One match against Liverpool. 23,000 supporters were there to see Newcastle romp to victory with a super display of football. Anderson and Rutherford were particularly good throughout the game, making hard work for the opposing forwards.

Newcastle were on the attack from the outset, and they put enough pressure on the Liverpool defence to tire them out quickly. When the home forwards got through into the danger area, they bombarded the Liverpool goal with attempts at goal. The visiting keeper had some difficult saves to make, but did so competently.

Indeed, it was seventeen minutes into the game that Newcastle opened the floodgates with their first goal. It was Higgins who got his head to the ball and nodded it past the Liverpool keeper to give the home side the lead. This was doubled ten minutes later with a super effort from Albert Shepherd.

Then, to ensure a comfortable lead Shepherd added another goal to the score-sheet bringing Newcastle's tally to three going into the break. Now Liverpool were in a tough position. They could only hope that Newcastle were content enough with their three-goal lead to ease the pressure in the second half.

So, the second period began, and Newcastle were still on the attack. This was not what Liverpool were hoping for, although they made a brave attempt to fight back.

Surprisingly their efforts had some effect, and Peake managed to reduce the deficit with a fine goal for the visitors. However, this excitement seemed to have a negative effect on the Reds, and they lost their way again soon after.

Newcastle were on hand to take advantage of the weaknesses of the Liverpool team, and Shepherd netted another goal to bring the score to 4-1, and Shepherd notched up the fifth for the home side with his fourth of the match.

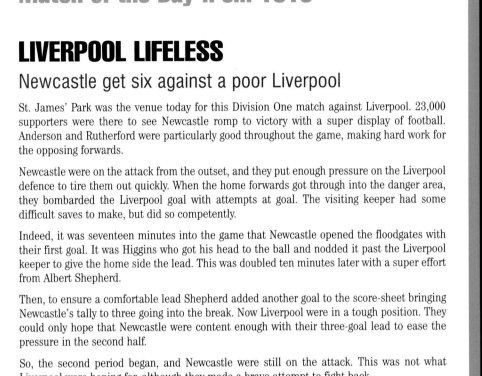

The final straw for Liverpool came when Stewart got through the defence and beat the visiting keeper to get the sixth goal for Newcastle. Disbelief and misery were on the faces of every player in the Liverpool side. They were well and truly beaten by a super performance from Newcastle.

Newcastle United

Lawrence, McCracken, Whitson, Veitch, Low, McWilliam, Rutherford, Higgins, Shepherd, Stewart, Anderson.

Liverpool

Hardy, Longworth, Crawford, Robinson, Peake, Harrop, Goddard, Brough, Parkinson, Orr, Uren.

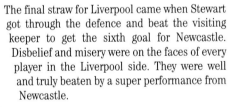

Newcastle United A.F.C.

yours truly Albert Shepherd

Played on this day

1897, Division 2.
Blackpool (h) 2-0   Att. 8,000
Aitken, Campbell

1909, Division 1.
Bristol City (h) 3-1   Att. 10,000
Anderson, Shepherd (2)

1920, Division 1.
Bradford Park Ave. (h) 2-1 Att. 48,000
Harris, Ward

1926, Division 1.
Blackburn Rovers (h) 6-1   Att. 25,000
Clark, McDonald, MacKenzie,
Seymour (3)

1937, Division 2.
Bradford Park Ave. (h) 3-0 Att. 21,000
Imrie, Mooney, J.R. Richardson

1943, Wartime.
Hartlepool United (h) 0-1   Att. 10,065

1948, Division 1.
Bolton Wanderers (a) 5-1   Att. 40,000
Gibson (2), Milburn, Sibley, Taylor

1954, Division 1.
Manchester United (a) 2-2   Att. 37,247
Broadis, R. Mitchell

1965, Division 1.
Tottenham Hotspur(h) 0-0   Att. 42,430

1971, Division 1.
Manchester United (h) 0-1   Att. 55,603

1974, Texaco Cup Semi Final, 1st leg.
Birmingham City (h) 1-1   Att. 20,559
Macdonald

1976, Division 1.
Birmingham City (h) 3-2   Att. 31,711
Burns (2), T. Craig
*Micky Burns opening goal timed at 56
seconds after kick off.*

1982, Division 2.
Crystal Palace (h) 1-0   Att. 22,616
Waddle

1996, Coca Cola Cup 3rd round.
Newcastle 1   Oldham Athletic 0
Beardsley 25 (pen)   Att. 36,314

2002, Champions' League, Group E.
Newcastle 1   Juventus 0
Griffin 62   Att. 48,370

Playing record for this day... 15 games,
Won 10, Drawn 3, Lost 2, GF 30, GA 11.
Today's success rate... 76.67%.

Match of the Day from 1926

REVENGE IS SWEET

Newcastle beat Blackburn 6-1, making up for 7-1 loss last season

25,000 turned up at St. James' Park today to see Newcastle take on Blackburn Rovers in Division One. Newcastle had an unbeaten run of eight consecutive matches, and were hoping to make it nine today. Blackburn, on the other hand, were confident after thrashing the Geordies by seven goals to one the previous season..

The visitors were understandably surprised when Newcastle started the match with determination and vigour. The entire forward line were aggressive and forceful from the outset. The defence were strong and compact, and there was a great team spirit throughout the whole home team.

Blackburn's movements were disorganised and wasteful. Their passing was random, and they seemed to be relying on pure luck to see them through.

Newcastle's forwards kept up the pressure, and the Blackburn defence began to crumble. Stan Seymour opened the scoring, being the first to beat the Blackburn keeper who fortunately had no idea of the bombardment that was to follow. Seymour's second for Newcastle started to make Blackburn realise things were going horribly wrong.

The hat-trick was completed by Seymour not long after, and a superb shot from McKenzie brought the Newcastle tally to four. Now Blackburn became even more erratic. This was not what they were expecting from the home side. Newcastle, however, seemed to be enjoying every moment. The crowd were spurring on their team, and there was a great atmosphere in the ground.

Clark added the fifth for the Tynesiders, sending the ball sailing past the deflated Blackburn goalkeeper. This was fantastic football, and the home crowd were overjoyed at the performance by the Newcastle team.

McDonald brought the tally to six for United with a super shot, and time was running out for Blackburn.

Then, just as it was looking like it was all over, Blackburn managed to pull back a goal. It was Harper who eventually beat the Newcastle keeper, and the final whistle went with the score 6-1. Newcastle had now played nine consecutive unbeaten games, and they had made amends for the thrashing they got last season from Blackburn.

Newcastle United
Wilson, Maitland, Hudspeth, MacKenzie, Spencer, Gibson, Urwin, Clark, Gallacher, McDonald, Seymour.

Blackburn Rovers
Cope, Hutton, Jones, Roscamp, Healless, McIntyre, Crisp, Puddefoot, Harper, McKay, Rigby.

J.R.CLARK:- newcastle - - United . F.C.

October 24

TRUE BRAZILIAN BLEND

Mirandinha and Gascoigne class too much for Coventry

Paul Gascoigne

A quality Newcastle performance inspired by Brazilian ace Mirandinha and aided by an English bulldog's non-stop work rate, inflicted more woes on troubled Coventry City at Highfield Road today. The Midlanders slipped to their fourth home defeat in seven, which compared with just two all last season has left them in dire trouble. For Newcastle this was only their second away win of the season and by far their best performance as they rode out the early Coventry pressure and then hit the home side with three classic counter-attacking strikes which totally demoralised the Sky Blues.

It was difficult to spot the reasons for Coventry's decline, Newcastle looked as though they were in for a roasting as they were mainly penned in their own half for much of the first quarter of an hour. However, a fifth minute Nick Pickering shot into the side netting after a good flowing move was the closest they came to breaching United's expertly marshalled defence. Slowly Newcastle began to take control and in superb winning style they scored with their first real assault on Steve Ogrizovic's goal. Paul Goddard collected a clever ball from Paul Gascoigne on the edge of the penalty area and, after a quick turn, which threw his marker, slipped a carefully placed shot past the Sky Blues keeper. The well deserved lead lasted all of a minute. Cyrille Regis, another of Coventry's many captains this season, safely putting the home side back in the game with a fiercely hit shot which bent round Gary Kelly from a wide angle just inside the penalty area. This wonder strike failed to lift Coventry and instead stung United into a rousing response led by Mirandinha. The Brazilian skilfully escaped the desperate lunge of Lloyd McGrath in a breathtaking split-second to tee-up his shot which Orgrizovic did well to palm away. The loose ball only rolled across the goalmouth where Gascoigne had chased in to tap into the unguarded net.

Newcastle then sewed up the points with a classic counter punch. Engineered by Gascoigne's pass inside Brian Borrows to Brian Tinnion his teasing cross, to the far post, was headed back across goal by John Cornwell and Darren Jackson supplied the simplest of finishing touches. A late rally by Coventry almost saw Regis add another goal, albeit by this stage a mere consolation, but Kelly pulled off a magnificent one-handed save to deny the powerful close-range header in stoppage time.

Coventry City

Ogrizovic, Borrows, Downs, McGrath, Rodger, Gynn, Bennett, Phillips, Regis, Speedie, Pickering.

Newcastle United

Kelly, McDonald, Tinnion, McCreery, P. Jackson, Roeder, D. Jackson, Gascoigne, Goddard, Mirandinha, Cornwell.

Birthdays

John Hendrie born today in 1963.
Winger 1988-1989, Apps 43. Goals 5.
Bob Thomson born today in 1905.
Left-back 1928-1934, Apps 80. Goals 0.

Sadly Missed

George Hair died on this day in 1994, aged 69.
Winger 1943-1949, Apps 77. Goals 22.

October 25

1890, FA Cup Qualifying round.
Bishop Auckland Town (a) **2-1** Att. 1,000
Young McInnes
1902, Division 1.
Derby County (a) **0-0** Att. 12,000
1913, Division 1.
Manchester United (h) **0-1** Att. 35,000
1919, Division 1.
Preston North End (a) **3-2** Att. 18,000
Hibbert, Ramsay (2)
1924, Division 1.
Cardiff City (h) **1-2** Att. 22,000
Cowan
1930, Division 1.
Sheffield United (a) **1-3** Att. 20,000
J.R. Richardson
1941, Wartime.
Sunderland (h) **1-1** Att. 13,000
Wayman
1947, Division 2.
Southampton (h) **5-0** Att. 57,184
Milburn, Pearson, Stobbart, Walker (2)
1952, Division 1.
Arsenal (a) **0-3** Att. 63,744
1958, Division 1.
Manchester City (h) **4-1** Att. 54,837
Eastham, McGuigan, White (2)
1967, Division 1.
Leeds United (a) **0-2** Att. 30,347
1969, Division 1.
Chelsea (h) **0-1** Att. 40,088
1972, Texaco Cup 2nd round, 1st leg.
West Bromwich A. (a) **1-2** Att. 7,927
Hibbitt
1975, Division 1.
Stoke City (a) **1-1** Att. 24,057
Gowling
1980, Division 2.
Chelsea (a) **0-6** Att. 22,916
1986, Division 1.
Aston Villa (a) **0-2** Att. 14,614
1989, Littlewoods Cup 3rd round.
West Bromwich A. (h) **0-1** Att. 22,619
1995, Coca Cola Cup 3rd round.
Stoke City 0   **Newcastle 4**
              Beardsley 30, 39
              Ferdinand 52
              Peacock 73
              Att 23,000
Les Ferdinand broke a post-war club scoring record for Newcastle having scored in eight successive games.
1997, Premier League.
Newcastle 1   **Blackburn Rovers 1**
Gillespie 27   Sutton 57
              Att. 36,716
1999, Premier League.
Newcastle 2   **Derby County 0**
Eranio (og) 41
Shearer 52   Att. 35,614

Playing record for this day... 20 games,
Won 6, Drawn 4, Lost 10, GF 26, GA 30.
Today's success rate... 40%.

Match of the Day from 1995

SUPER SHOW SHATTERS STOKE

Ferdinand claims scoring record in United's four-goal blitz

Two goals from Peter Beardsley and a post-war scoring record for Les Ferdinand were the outstanding highlights of this superb performance by Newcastle United today. The measure of their dominance was evident seventeen minutes from time, when central defender Darren Peacock, taking his turn to augment the attack, pivoted onto Steve Watson's pass to drive United's fourth goal high into the net past the shell-shocked Stoke keeper Mark Prudhoe.

Poor Stoke, no team should be forced to play Newcastle with ten men, a full eleven is a difficult enough task, but this is what they were condemned to when right back Ian Clarkson was sent off just before half time for the second of two clumsy fouls on his tormentor David Ginola. By then two goals from Beardsley in the 30th and 39th minute, had put Newcastle well out of Stoke's reach.

Peter Beardsley scores his and Newcastle United's second goal in this comprehensive win.

Stoke may have had the satisfaction of keeping Ferdinand quiet during the first 45 minutes but, when Prudhoe could only push out Keith Gillespie's cross-shot eight minutes into the second half, United's scoring sensation broke a club scoring record by netting in eight consecutive games. The home side who, despite everything, didn't play too badly had two great chances in the game, both coming early in each half. Unfortunately, for the majority of the 23,000 Victoria Ground crowd, Paul Peschisolido, the Stoke centre-forward, missed both of them. He could only shoot against United's keeper Shaka Hislop with the first Then, after a rare defensive error by Peacock, could only lift a straight forward lob yards wide when presented with a simpler second chance in the second half. It just wasn't Stoke City's night, but another great one for Newcastle.

Stoke City

Prudhoe, Clarkson, Overson, Sigurdsson, Sandford, Keen, Wallace, Gleghorn, Potter (Cranson 76), Peschisolido, Carruthers.

Newcastle United

Hislop, Barton, Peacock, Howey (Albert 63), Elliott, Gillespie, Lee (Watson 63), Clark, Ginola, Beardsley, Ferdinand.

Referee Mr. G. Ashby (Worcester).

Birthdays

Mick Mahoney born today in 1950.
Goalkeeper 1975-1978, Apps 138.

Grant Malcolm born today in 1940.
Winger 1957-1960, Apps 1. Goals 0.

October 26

Match of the Day from 1901

UNITED STEAL THE SHOW
Newcastle take points with 8-0 hammering of Notts

There was a crowd of 12,000 at Newcastle today to see the home team play host to Notts County in Division One. The weather for this match was perfect, and some of the players certainly found it inspiring.

Peddie was the man to open the floodgates with the first goal for Newcastle with just seconds on the clock, and Notts County began to worry. It was a lucky shot, the ball only going into the net after a slight deflection off the crossbar. Still, it was a goal, and it put the home side into an early lead, making it harder for Notts to recover.

Shortly afterwards a free kick was awarded to Newcastle, and the ball was sent into the danger area of the County goalmouth. A scramble ensued, and Peddie managed to get his head to the ball and nod it into the net with half the visitors' defence not even noticing. Newcastle were two goals ahead, and it was still early days.

Jock Peddie completed his hat-trick soon after with a super shot past the Notts' keeper, and the visiting side were already beginning to accept they were going to lose. Still in the first half, and Orr added his name to the score-sheet with Newcastle's fourth goal. The home crowd were enjoying this immensely, and there was still more to come.

Before the half-time whistle Orr scored his second, and his shot brought Newcastle's tally to five. With the second half still to be played, Notts County were starting to wish they were somewhere else. The visiting defence hung their heads in shame as they left the field for the interval, whilst the Newcastle team left the pitch to cheers and whistles from their eager supporters.

The second half began, and Notts County were only there in body. They had no spirit, and no real desire to carry on with the game. Roberts added to their misery with his goal, which brought Newcastle up to six. The Notts County team merely sighed and took up their positions to carry on.

Ronald Orr also secured a hat trick not long after. It was no shock to them that the home side were able to score again, and they were just treading water until the final whistle saved them from this agony.

And then Orr had one more nail to add to the coffin. His super shot bringing Newcastle's score to eight. The game ended to the great relief of the visiting side, and Newcastle came off the pitch with two well-earned points.

Newcastle United
Kingsley, Bennie, Davidson, Ghee, Aitken, Carr, A. Gardner, Orr, Peddie, Niblo, Roberts.
Notts County
Pennington, Prescott, Lewis, Mainman, Bull, McDonald, Spencer, Warner, Humphreys, Morris, Gee.

Played on this day

1889, FA Cup Qualifying round 2.
St Augustines (a) 1-2
Gibbons
1895, Division 2.
Newton Heath (h) 2-1   Att. 7,000
Wardrope, Opponent (og)
1901, Division 1.
Notts County (h) 8-0   Att. 12,000
Roberts, Peddie (3), Orr (4)
1907, Division 1.
Blackburn Rovers (h) 3-0   Att. 28,000
Howie, McClarence, Rutherford
1912, Division 1.
Everton (a) 6-0   Att. 10,000
Stewart (2), McTavish (2), Low (2)
1929, Division 1.
Bolton Wanderers (h) 2-3   Att. 30,000
McDonald (2)
1935, Division 2.
Swansea Town (a) 2-1   Att. 12,000
McMenemy, J. Smith
1940, Wartime
Bradford Park Avenue (a) 1-0 Att. 1,571
Billington
1946, Division 2.
Manchester City (h) 3-2   Att. 65,798
Wayman (3)
1957, Division 1.
Wolverhampton W. (h) 1-1   Att. 44,361
Curry
1963, Division 2.
Northampton Town (h) 2-3   Att. 25,943
Taylor, Iley (pen)
1968, Division 1.
Liverpool (a) 1-2   Att. 45,323
Gibb
1974, Division 1.
Leicester City (h) 0-1   Att. 34,988
1983, Milk Cup 2nd round, 2nd leg.
Oxford United (a) 1-2   Att. 13,040
Keegan
Newcastle lost 3-2 on aggregate.
1985, Division 1.
Aston Villa (a) 2-1   Att. 12,633
Beardsley, Gascoigne
1988, Division 1.
Middlesbrough (h) 3-0   Att. 23,845
Pallister (og), Mirandinha (2)
1991, Division 2.
Bristol City (a) 1-1   Att. 8,613
Clark
1994, Coca Cola Cup 3rd round.
Newcastle 2   Manchester U. 0
Albert 82
Kitson 87   Att. 34,178
1996, Premier League.
Leicester City 2   Newcastle 0
Claridge 17
Heskey 79   Att. 21,134
2002, Premier League.
Newcastle 2   Charlton Athletic 1
Griffin 37   Bartlett 30
Robert 59   Att. 51,607

Playing record for this day... 20 games,
Won 11, Drawn 2, Lost 7, GF 43, GA 23.
Today's success rate... 60%.

Birthdays

Steve Howey born today in 1971.
Centre-half 1986-2000, Apps 242 (30 subs).
Goals 7.

Sadly Missed

Dave Fairhurst died today in 1972, aged 66.
Left-back 1929-1946, Apps 285. Goals 2.

...yed on this day

FA Cup Qualifying round 2.
Stockton (h) 2-1
Hoban, unknown
Division 2.
Manchester City (h) 5-4   Att. 3,000
Dickson, Thompson (3), Graham
Division 1.
Notts County (h) 2-0   Att. 12,000
MacFarlane, A. Gardner
Division 1.
Preston North End (h) 2-1   Att. 30,000
Brown, Howie
Division 1.
Middlesbrough (h) 3-2   Att. 30,000
Seymour (2), Hampson (pen)
Division 1.
Sunderland (a) 2-5   Att. 50,519
Boyd, MacKenzie
Division 2.
Port Vale (a) 3-1   Att. 10,600
Murray, Smith (2)
Wartime.
Blackpool (a) 1-1   Att. 15,000
Clifton
Division 1.
Portsmouth (a) 1-3   Att. 39,944
Milburn
Division 1.
Charlton Athletic (a) 1-1   Att. 21,473
Curry
Division 2.
Scunthorpe United (a) 2-3   Att. 13,987
Allchurch, Suddick
Division 2.
Swansea Town (h) 6-0   Att. 24,005
Fell (2), Suddick (2), Thomas,
Opponent (og)
Division 1.
Tottenham Hotspur (a) 2-0   Att. 31,259
Barrowclough, Gibb
League Cup 4th round.
Manchester United (a) 2-7   Att. 52,002
Burns, Nattrass
Division 2.
Cambridge United (h) 2-0   Att. 24,104
Withe, Shoulder
League Cup 2nd round, 2nd leg.
Leeds United (h) 1-4.   Att. 24,984
Clarke
Newcastle lost 4-2 on aggregate
Division 1.
Watford (a) 3-3   Att. 18,753
Beardsley, Wharton, McDonald
Division 2.
West Bromwich A. (h) 1-1   Att. 14,774
O'Brien
Coca Cola Cup 3rd round.
Wimbledon 2   Newcastle 1
Barton 23   Sellars 28
Holdsworth 28   Att. 11,531
Worthington Cup 3rd round.
Tranmere Rovers 0 Newcastle 1
          Dalglish 31
          Att. 12,017
Premier League.
Everton 1   Newcastle 3
Weir 51   Bellamy 19
          Solano 49
          Acuna 86
          Att. 37,524

record for this day... 21 games,
..., Drawn 4, Lost 6, GF 46, GA 40.
.. success rate...61.90%.

GIVEN HEROICS EARNS UNITED VICTORY

3-1 scoreline 'unjust' but reward for keeper's super show

Given the good fortune (no pun intended) Newcastle had today, the supposition, that it is easier to win away from home gathered yet more conclusive proof at Goodison Park. Rarely can a side have been so overwhelmed yet still pocket the three points so conclusively. Even Bobby Robson, almost apologetically, concluded that the scoreline was unjust under the circumstances following a game in which the home side created a dozen or more excellent chances. That they were not converted was purely down to the agility of goalkeeper Shay Given and not so much Everton's profligacy. Everton enjoyed greater possession throughout and some excellent defending by Andy O'Brien and Nikos Dabizas was also good reason why Newcastle ended up the victors.

Only once were the trio beaten, when Niclas Alexandersson's corner from the right fell to the unmarked David Weir who made no mistake with his close-range header six minutes into the second half. This goal halved the advantage Craig Bellamy and Nolberto Solano had given United in the nineteenth and 49th minutes. The first, an absolute gift for Bellamy, was the result of a collision between goalkeeper Paul Gerrard and Abel Xavier as they attempted to cut out Solano's long ball. With both failing to make contact with the ball, Bellamy couldn't miss his strike inside the penalty area into the unguarded goal. Xavier was knocked out cold in the incident

Clarence Acuna scores the third goal against Everton.

and had to be stretchered off, he will now be out for a minimum of three weeks because of the rules that cover concussion injuries. While that incident was significant in gifting Newcastle the initiative, perhaps more significant was the save Given pulled off to deny Tomasz Radzinski which kept United in front at 1-0.

Given performed with equal aplomb to later deny Thomas Gravesen, David Unsworth and Duncan Ferguson who, along with Paul Gascoigne, arrived in the second half to try to salvage some reward for the relentless Everton pressure. Yet so positive was the Toffeemen's approach that they were left vulnerable to the super quick United counter-attack. With four minutes of the game remaining, Bellamy sped down the right and crossed invitingly for Laurent Robert who unselfishly set up Clarence Acuna for a simple tap in to compound Everton's anguish. United had secured an important 3-1 victory, easier because it was away from home after all.

Everton
Gerrard, Pistone, Weir, Xavier (Stubbs 22), Unsworth (Gascoigne 82), Alexandersson, Gravesen, Gemmill, Naysmith, Campbell (Ferguson 68), Radzinski.
Newcastle United
Given, Hughes, O'Brien, Dabizas, Elliott, Solano (LuaLua 89), Acuna, Speed, Robert, Shearer, Bellamy.
Referee Mr. J. Winter (Stockton-on-Tees)

Birthdays

Lee Clark born today in 1972.
Midfield 1988-1997, Apps 240 (49 subs). Goals 27.
Dennis Martin born today in 1947.
Midfield 1977-1978, Apps 11 (2 subs). Goals 2.

Sadly Missed

Willie Bertram died on this day in 1962, aged 64.
Midfield 1920-1921, Apps 3. Goals 0.
John Dowsey died on this day in 1942, aged 37.
Midfield 1924-1926, Apps 3. Goals 0.

November

November 1

Played on this day

1902, Division 1.
Wolverhampton W. (a) 0-3   Att. 8,000
1913, Division 1.
Burnley (a) 0-1   Att. 25,000
1919, Division 1.
Preston North End (h) 1-0   Att. 48,000
Robinson
1924, Division 1.
Preston North End (a) 1-0   Att. 12,000
Harris
1930, Division 1.
Leeds United (h) 4-1   Att. 10,000
Devine (2), Lindsay (2)
1941, Wartime.
Sunderland (a) 2-3   Att. 12,000
Short, Stubbins
1947, Division 2.
Doncaster Rovers (a) 3-0   Att. 28,340
Harvey, Milburn (2)
1952, Division 1.
Derby County (h) 1-0   Att. 44,571
Walker
1958, Division 1.
Arsenal (a) 2-3   Att. 62,801
McGuigan, Allchurch (pen)
1969, Division 1.
Burnley (a) 1-0   Att. 16,444
Davies
1975, Division 1.
Arsenal (h) 2-0   Att. 34,968
Gowling, Nattrass
1980, Division 2.
Watford (h) 2-1   Att. 14,590
Hibbitt, Shinton
1986, Division 1.
Oxford United (h) 0-0   Att. 19,622
1989, Division 2.
West Bromwich A. (a) 5-1   Att. 12,339
Robson (og), Brazil, Brock, McGhee,
O'Brien
1994, UEFA Cup 2nd round 2nd leg.
Athletic Bilbao 1   Newcastle 0
Ciganda 67   Att. 47,000
The tie finished 3-3 on aggregate,
Newcastle went out on the away goals
rule.
1997, Premier League.

Newcastle 3	Leicester City 3
Barnes 4 (pen)	Marshall 12, 32
Tomasson 45	Elliott 54
Beresford 90	Att. 36,754

2000, Worthington Cup 3rd round.

Newcastle 4	Bradford City 3
Shearer 22, 29	Nolan 31
Cordone 27	Ward 57, 70
Caldwell 71	Att. 41,847

Playing record for this day... 17 games,
Won 10, Drawn 2, Lost 5, GF 31, GA 20.
Today's success rate... 64.71%.

FIVE GOALS FOR UNITED AT WBA
Newcastle pack them in with help from the Baggies

Newcastle travelled to the Hawthorns to meet West Bromwich Albion who had only won at home once this season and the Magpies were confident of keeping it that way.

It took just five minutes for things to start going wrong for Albion. Mark McGhee sent the ball across the Albion goalmouth, and Gary Robson tried to clear away from danger. He totally miskicked, and the ball shot straight into his own goal past the despairing Naylor in goal.

So, a great gift to the visiting side, Newcastle were a goal ahead without even trying. This boosted their confidence no end, and they took control of the play thereafter. However, there was a surprise to come. Albion managed to get the ball into the correct net to bring the scores level in the nineteenth minute. Tony Ford provided the cross, and Don Goodman got his head to the ball to nod it past Burridge in the Newcastle goal.

Newcastle regained their control, and just four minutes later they had restored their lead. Gary Brazil beat Hodson in the air to get his head to the ball and send it into the net for Newcastle's second. Things were now getting difficult for the Albion defenders, and the United forwards were enjoying the upper hand.

The last twenty minutes of the first half passed without incident, and Albion did well to keep the scores as they were. Constant pressure from Newcastle meant a lot of hard work for the Albion side, but they rose to the challenge and played well.

The second half started with an improved performance from the home team. They upped the pace and pressure, and began with an attack straight away. It was McNally who tried his luck against Burridge, but the Newcastle keeper saved the shot with ease.

Now it was Newcastle's turn to attack, and they did it with style. The Albion defence were run ragged by the quick thinking visiting forwards, and it was only a matter of time before things slipped further out of reach for the struggling home side.

Kevin Brock scored a fabulous goal in the 67th minute after a superb solo effort. Naylor had no hope of making the save, and the goal brought Newcastle two goals ahead of their opponents.

In the 77th minute another goal was added to the score-sheet when Mick Quinn took on Stacey North in the air in a battle for the ball. Quinn won, and the ball came down to McGhee who sent a fine shot straight into the corner of the net for Newcastle's fourth.

Then with just seven minutes left on the clock, Newcastle added the final touch to an already faultless performance. Liam O'Brien had come on to the field in place of Dillon, and immediately made his presence felt. He scored the fifth goal straight away, and the entire home team were left feeling deflated.

At the start of this game Albion had been dreading facing Quinn in the Newcastle side. With fifteen goals for his team, he was a force to be reckoned with. Little did the home team know that he would be the least of their worries in this fantastic win by Newcastle.

West Bromwich Albion
Naylor, Parkin, Hodson, Talbot, Whyte, North, Ford, Goodman, Thomas (Allardyce 69), McNally, Robson (Bartlett 18).
Newcastle United
Burridge, Ranson, Stimson, Dillon (O'Brien 83), Scott, Kristensen, Fereday, Brock, Quinn, McGhee, Brazil.
Referee Mr. P. Durkin (Portland, Dorset).

Birthdays

Benny Arentoft born today in 1942.
Midfield 1969-1971, Apps 64 (5 subs). Goals 3.
George Brander born today in 1929.
Winger 1952-1954, Apps 5. Goals 2.

Carl Cort born today in 1977
Forward 2000-present day, Apps 28 (4 subs).
Goals 8.
Norman Dodgin born today in 1921.
Midfield 1940-1950, Apps 132. Goals 2.

Match of the Day from 1935

WEST HAM SHARE POINTS

Newcastle fight back to gain draw at St. James' Park

West Ham made the long journey up to Newcastle today for this match in Division Two. There were 23,000 supporters at the game, all hoping that their team would walk away with the points. Throughout the first half it seemed that the travelling fans would be the ones who went home happy.

West Ham started the game the better team by far. Their moves were perfectly timed, and things went right for them every time. They had several attempts at goal before the first ball managed to cross the line.

It was Mangnall who got the goal for West Ham, and it was a great shot which beat Tapken in the Newcastle goal with ease. The visitors were a goal ahead, and Newcastle had a lot of hard work to do in order to catch up. West Ham continued with their pressure, and their aggressiveness was causing Newcastle to falter.

Ten minutes into the second half Mangnall doubled the lead for the visitors. This brought Newcastle to their senses, and the home team stepped up their efforts and their game improved greatly. West Ham weren't expecting such a comeback from the Tynesiders, but it wasn't long before Ward had reduced the deficit for the home team with a smashing goal sent in style.

Smith brought the scores level shortly afterwards with a superbly placed ball which gave Conway no chance to save in the West Ham goal. The visiting side were now showing concern. They had been so confident of the win that they had let their guard, and their game, slip. Newcastle were improving by the minute, but their run of good play was hampered when Ruffell regained the lead for West Ham. This slightly dented United's spirits for a while, but they soon showed that they had the resolve to carry on the fight.

With just six minutes left to play Bott drew the scores level again with a cracking shot, and the West Ham keeper couldn't do anything to stop the ball.

The game ended with the scores 3-3, and it had been a fantastic comeback from the home side. Newcastle had shown that they could handle anything today, and their calmness was admirable. They never gave up, and the result showed that their ability to play as a team was second to none.

Newcastle United

Tapken, Richardson, Fairhurst, Imrie, Davidson, Weaver, Bott, Ware, Smith, McMenemy, Pearson.

West Ham United

Conway, Chalkley, Walker, Fenton, Barrett, Cockroft, Foreman, Conwell, Mangnall, Goulden, Ruffell.

Neil McDonald born today 1965.

Played on this day

1895, FA Cup Qualifying round 3.
Middlesbrough (h) 4-1   Att. 6,000
Wardrope (2), McKay, unknown
1901, Division 1.
Bolton Wanderers (a) 1-3   Att. 11,951
A. Gardner
1907, Division 1.
Preston North End (a) 0-2   Att. 12,000
1912, Division 1.
Sheffield Wednesday (h) 1-0 Att. 25,000
Higgins
1929, Division 1.
Everton (a) 2-5   Att. 30,000
Gallacher (2)
1935, Division 2.
West Ham United (h) 3-3   Att. 23,000
Bott, J. Smith, Ware
1940, Wartime.
Chesterfield (a) 1-5   Att. 1,000
Graham
1946, Division 2.
West Ham United (a) 2-0   Att. 32,000
Bentley, Shackleton
1957, Division 1.
Leicester City (a) 1-2   Att. 31,884
Batty
1963, Division 2.
Norwich City (a) 1-3   Att. 17,660
McGarry
1968, Division 1.
Leicester City (h) 0-0   Att. 20,374
1974, Division 1.
Luton Town (h) 1-0   Att. 30,141
Tudor
1977, UEFA Cup 2nd round, 2nd leg.
Bastia (h) 1-3   Att. 34,560
Gowling
Newcastle lost 5-2 on aggregate.
1985, Division 1.
Watford (h) 1-1   Att. 20,640
Gascoigne
1991, Division 2.
Swindon Town (a) 1-2   Att. 10,731
Peacock

Playing record for this day... 15 games,
Won 4, Drawn 3, Lost 8, GF 20, GA 30.
Today's success rate... 36.67%.

Birthdays

Neil McDonald born today in 1965.
Midfield/Right-back 1982-1988, Apps 208 (18 subs). Goals 28.

Sadly Missed

Bobby Templeton died on this day in 1919, aged 40.
Winger 1903-1904, Apps 52. Goals 5.

November 3

Played on this day

1894, Division 2.
Bury (a) 1-4   Att. 4,000
Thompson

1900, Division 1.
Preston North End (a) 1-0   Att. 7,000
Laidlaw

1906, Division 1.
Derby County (a) 0-0   Att. 9,000

1923, Division 1.
Manchester City (a) 1-1   Att. 25,000
Mitchell

1928, Division 1.
Huddersfield Town (h) 4-1   Att. 38,000
Boyd, Gallacher (2), Lang

1934, Division 2.
Barnsley (h) 4-1   Att. 7,959
Boyd, Murray, Smith (2)

1945, Wartime.
Liverpool (a) 0-3   Att. 35,000

1951, Division 1.
Liverpool (h) 1-1   Att. 50,132
Foulkes

1956, Division 1.
Leeds United (h) 2-3   Att. 49,034
Davies, Keeble

1962, Division 2.
Chelsea (a) 2-4   Att. 34,428
Fell, Suddick

1971, Texaco Cup 2nd round, 2nd leg.
Coventry City (h) 5-1   Att. 25,230
Macdonald, Tudor (2), Nattrass,
Opponent (og)
Newcastle won 6-2 on aggregate.

1973, Division 1.
Stoke City (h) 2-1   Att. 28,135
Gibb, McDermott

1979, Division 2.
Oldham Athletic (a) 0-1   Att. 11,486

1984, Division 1.
Luton Town (a) 2-2   Att. 10,009
Beardsley, Heard

1990, Division 2.
Hull City (a) 1-2.   Att. 8,375
McGhee

1996, Premier League.
Newcastle 3   **Middlesbrough 1**
Beardsley   Beck 88
40 (pen), 69
Lee 74   Att. 36,577

2001, Premier League.
Newcastle 3   **Aston Villa 0**
Bellamy 37, 82
Shearer 50   Att. 51,057

Playing record for this day... 17 games,
Won 7, Drawn 4, Lost 6, GF 32, GA 26.
Today's success rate... 52.94%.

BATTLE WON, UNITED GO TOP
North-East rivals find United's football far too strong

Any match that involves Juninho squaring up to Philippe Albert's waist was always going to prove captivating. A game that combined the physical and the pantomime was settled by the brilliance of Peter Beardsley and Robert Lee, two men who always keep their tempers, always focus on the scoreline rather than settling scores. Beardsley, struck twice, firstly from the penalty spot, secondly following a thrilling Newcastle break. Lee, tireless in midfield, then added a third before Mikkel Beck concluded proceedings at St. James' Park with a late consolation. This 3-1 victory swept Newcastle above Arsenal taking them to the top of the Premiership. Beardsley, Lee and the rest of the men in black and white make fitting leaders, they refuse to buckle, showing how they have learned to defend and attack as a team. Their strikers, Les Ferdinand and Faustino Asprilla, had little joy up front yet were always prepared to track back assisting their midfield to counter the very real threat posed by Juninho and Emerson. Winning a championship demands the correct blend of entertainers and enforcers, and Kevin Keegan indicated today that his side are beginning to find the right mixture. Boro boss Bryan Robson has one of the blends in abundance, the will to battle, his side were never going to lie down and this meant the skirmishing over 90 minutes was relentless. Referee, Gary Willard encouraged the game to flow, often waving play on with bodies still scattered across the ground, but, still managed to accumulate five bookings in a real derby scrap, Neil Cox, Steve Vickers and Emerson were cautioned for Boro, along with Robbie Elliott and David Batty for the Magpies.

Appropriately, it was a foul which ended the deadlock after 40 minutes. When Elliott hustled Phil Stamp into conceding possession to Asprilla the danger was obvious. The ball arrowed from the Colombian to David Ginola who was brought down by Cox. Beardsley, celebrating his 700th game as a professional, made no mistake with a firmly placed spot kick. With so many attacking avenues to delight their phenomenal support, Newcastle will always produce goals, but today's victory was down to United's new found ability to prevent them at the other end, Mark Lawrenson's input here was evident in this game. The timing of challenges was excellent, most noticeably when Albert brilliantly dispossessed Fabrizio Ravanelli after 36 minutes.

Newcastle are certainly made of sterner stuff these days and, despite the Emerson-Juninho inspired Boro charge in the second half, their defence refused to yield. With a new lock on the back door United always looked to prosper and they ventured confidently forth to add a 70th minute second goal. Albert was still smiling at Juninho's angry response to his clever defending when Pavel Srnicek launched the ball upfield. Ferdinand redirected the long ball down the middle into the penalty area arc, where Beardsley was arriving at speed. His finish, struck hard beyond Gary Walsh, was emphatic. Walsh then made a fine save to deny Beardsley a hat-trick, following a bewildering one-two with Ferdinand five minutes later. It was at the expense of a corner which Newcastle, through Ginola's kick, exploited fully. The Boro defence, in chaos, only half cleared and when Lee drove the ball back in a deflection took it past the unfortunate keeper Walsh. Middlesbrough to their credit never gave up and should have scored moments later when Srnicek could only parry Juninho's shot and Beck followed up to hit the bar from seemingly unmissable range. Beck did better two minutes from time. Everyone's attention seemed to be focused on the animated tirade by Ravanelli, who had accused Ginola of diving, which was a most watchable sideshow. Newcastle's defenders were clearly absorbed and failed to notice Stamp's dart down the right. The impressive young midfielder swiftly transferred play forward to Beck, who lifted the ball elegantly over the advanced Srnicek. But, by this stage the points were safe and all that remained was for the local hero Beardsley, and the rest of the lads, to acknowledge yet another grateful Toon Army's response at the final whistle, Newcastle were back on top.

Newcastle United
Srnicek, Peacock, Albert, Elliott, Gillespie (Barton 83), Lee, Batty, Beardsley, Ginola, Asprilla, Ferdinand.
Middlesbrough
Walsh, Cox, Whyte, Vickers, Fleming, Emerson, Stamp, Mustoe, Juninho, Beck, Ravanelli.
Referee Mr. G. Willard (Worthing).

November 3

Middlesbrough's Fabrizio Ravanelli causes anxious moments in the Newcastle goalmouth for (l-r) Pavel Srnicek, Darren Peacock and Philippe Albert.

November 4

NEWCASTLE END BLUES

The Magpies end run of bad luck with win over Birmingham City

Newcastle came down to St. Andrew's tonight to play Birmingham City in Division One in front of 14,376. It was to be a super display of football, the match filled with incidents and action. In the third minute Newcastle keeper Tommy Wright sustained a thigh injury that would result in his substitution later. For now though he had work to do, although not much at the start.

In the seventh minute Newcastle took the lead with a fine effort from Gavin Peacock. He managed to avoid being caught offside and sent a smashing shot goalwards. Sealey made the save but the ball came back out to Peacock who made sure that his second attempt didn't miss the back of the net.

So, the visitors were in front, and Birmingham were determined to fight back. Newcastle had lost their previous three games, so the Blues were hoping that things would go their way. They equalised just two minutes after Newcastle's goal thanks to a lovely move between Paul Holmes and Simon Sturridge. They provided the chance for David Speedie who got his head to the ball and nodded it past Wright to bring the scores level.

On 31 minutes the Birmingham defence allowed Steve Howey to send the ball into the danger area. Kevin Scott was on hand to flick it into the net to regain the lead for the visitors.

However, just two minutes later the scores were level again when Graham Potter slipped the ball past Wright with confidence and skill.

Half-time was approaching fast, but the action wasn't over yet. On 38 minutes Carr sent a fine ball towards goal, but Sealey managed to make the save. The ball came back out, and Trevor Matthewson couldn't stop and succeeded in sending the ball straight back, only this time it sailed past his own keeper, crossed the line and Newcastle were awarded the goal.

The second half began with a change in the Newcastle goal. Wright was unfit to carry on, so midfielder Brock was brought on in his place. This boosted Birmingham's spirits no end, and they tried hard to bring the scores level once again. Speedie came into contact with Brock, and the substitute keeper needed a lot of help from the Newcastle trainer before he could carry on. Even so, every now and then the trainer had to come back on to the pitch to refresh the substitute keeper with smelling salts after it turned out he had suffered concussion from the blow.

Luckily for Brock he only had one save to make in his time in goal. Speedie sent a fine ball towards him, but it sailed straight into his arms and out of danger.

The Newcastle forwards were making things difficult for Sealey at the other end of the field, though the Blues keeper did well to keep the ball out of the net. The final whistle went, to the relief of Brock, and the visitors took the points back home to Newcastle.

Birmingham City

Sealey, Holmes, Frain, Rennie (Rowbotham 36), Hicks, Matthewson, Rodgerson, Tait, Speedie, Sturridge, Potter (Donowa 76).

Newcastle United

Wright (Brock 45), Venison, Beresford, O'Brien, Scott, Howey, Carr, Peacock, Kelly, Clark, Sheedy (Kilcline 90).

Referee Mr. K. Hackett (Sheffield).

...yed on this day

Division 2.
Liverpool (a) 1-5   Att. 8,000
Thompson

Division 1.
Aston Villa (a) 1-2   Att. 18,000
Ghee

Division 1.
Preston North End (h) 1-0   Att. 28,000
Howie

Division 1.
Bury (h) 3-2   Att. 18,000
Hibbert, Higgins (2)

Division 1.
Sunderland (h) 2-1   Att. 60,000
Aitken, McDonald

Division 1.
Sheffield United (h) 3-1   Att. 16,000
Allen, Dennison, Lang

Wartime.
Darlington (a) 2-1   Att. 5,377
Moses, Pearson

Wartime.
Hull City (h) 7-0   Att. 9,408
Wayman, Woollett, Stubbins, Carr (2), Gordon (2)

Division 1.
Liverpool(a) 4-2   Att. 48,810
G. Robledo (3), Taylor

Division 2.
Norwich City (h) 0-0   Att. 25,895

Division 1.
Leicester City (a) 2-2   Att. 18,001
Bennett, T. Robson

Division 1.
Pecsi Dozsa(a) 0-2   Att. 25,000
After extra time scores level 2-2 on aggregate. Newcastle lost 3-0 on penalties.

Division 1.
West Bromwich A. (a) 3-2   Att. 14,379
Tudor (2), Smith

Division 2.
Bristol Rovers (a) 0-2   Att. 10,582

Division 2.
Middlesbrough (h) 2-2   Att. 23,382
McGhee, O'Brien

Division 1.
Birmingham City (a) 3-2   Att. 14,376
Peacock, Scott, Matthewson (og)

Premier League.
Newcastle 2   **Liverpool 1**
Ferdinand 2   Rush 10
Watson 89   Att. 36,547

UEFA Cup 2nd round, 2nd leg.
Newcastle 3   **F.C. Zurich 1**
Maric 33   Jamauli 17
Ferguson 58
Speed 61   Att. 34,502
Newcastle won 5-2 on aggregate.

Premier League.
Newcastle 2   **Ipswich Town 1**
Shearer   Stewart 13
22, 67 (pen)   Att. 50,922

Premier League.
Newcastle 2   **Middlesbrough 0**
Ameobi 20
Caldwell 87   Att. 51,558

record for this day... 20 games, ?, Drawn 3, Lost 4, GF 43, GA 29. success rate...72.50%.

Birthdays

Frans Koenen born today in 1958.
Midfield 1980-1981, Apps 14 (1 sub). Goals 1.

Gary Nicholson born today in 1960.
Winger 1977-1981, Apps 16 (5 subs). Goals 0.

November 5

RANGERS RALLY NOT ENOUGH

Kitson and Beardsley goals pile on the pressure for Francis

Kevin Keegan's army started like cavaliers but finished up like roundheads as Queen's Park Rangers, one of three teams to win at fortress St. James' Park last season, launched a spirited comeback in the second half in today's thrilling Premiership battle. Far from being able to build on their spectacular first-half display Newcastle were forced to hang on for long periods after young Daniele Dichio cut their lead with only the second goal of his short league career. Both clubs have had a hectic week, though in vastly different ways. Understandably, in view of manager Gerry Francis's present situation, his future in the balance, the photographers were clustered around the visitors dug-out like vultures as the under-pressure QPR boss took his seat.

Peter Beardsley, however needed just 90 seconds to make all the cameras swivel to the Rangers' goalmouth as he tested Sieb Dykstra with a drive the Dutch keeper was glad to turn round for a corner. A similar save prevented Paul Kitson scoring after Mark Hottiger put him through on ten minutes, but Rangers, who are still seeking their first away win of the season, looked far from overawed by Newcastle's awesome home record. Les Ferdinand forced Pavel Srnicek into a superb diving save seconds before Kevin Gallen hit a shot inches wide of the right-hand post. Newcastle, however, were not to be denied and went ahead after twenty minutes. Referee Gerald Ashby waved play on after Trevor Sinclair brought down Robert Lee and though Ruel Fox stumbled on the ball in his eagerness to shoot, Kitson darted in to celebrate his recall with a fine follow-up goal. Andrew Impey's speed then began to trouble Newcastle and Darren Peacock cleared a tricky situation after Impey lured Srnicek out of his goal. But Newcastle played their best football as half-time approached and should have had more than a second goal, they scored three minutes before the interval. Simon Barker's failure to stop Beardsley enabled the Newcastle captain to play a dazzling one-two with Kitson and though his first hit the post, Fox picked up the rebound and unselfishly invited Beardsley to try again., this time his shot was emphatically finished in the net. A rampant United, and Beardsley, also had another shot charged down at the last moment, and Steve Watson had cracking drive brilliantly turned away for a corner by the impressive Dykstra.

Rangers fight back started with Dichio taking over from the injured Steve Hodge in the 50th minute and Sinclair supplied the centre for the striker to reduce the deficit ten minutes later. Beardsley, not for the first time, rallied Newcastle again, sending in a great ball which the unlucky Watson this time headed against the bar. But, Sinclair kept Rangers hopes high with a spectacular drive which Srnicek sensationally dived to keep out the equaliser. It was that close a call with Newcastle now reduced to hanging onto the ball to slow the Rangers' resurgence down. Beardsley continued to toil and plot as only he can and in the end, there was only one team in it. But it was particularly demoralising for Francis and his QPR side to come away with nothing after such a terrific display.

Newcastle United

Srnicek, Hottiger, Beresford, Albert, Howey, Peacock, Fox, Lee, Kitson, Beardsley, Watson.

Queen's Park Rangers

Dykstra, Bardsley, Wilson, Barker, McDonald, Yates, Impey, Hodge (Dichio 50), Ferdinand, Gallen, Sinclair.

Referee Mr. G. Ashby (Worcester).

Played on this day

1898, Division 1.
Liverpool (h) 3-0   Att. 20,000
Peddie (2), MacFarlane
At last! In their eleventh game of the season the Magpies finally record their first top flight victory, and even sweeter, it was at St. James' Park too.

1904, Division 1.
Middlesbrough (h) 3-0   Att. 23,262
Orr, Howie, Rutherford

1910, Division 1.
Sheffield United (h) 1-1   Att. 20,000
Duncan

1921, Division 1.
Tottenham Hotspur (a) 0-4 Att. 34,448

1927, Division 1.
Sunderland (h) 3-1   Att. 45,000
McDonald, McKay, Seymour

1932, Division 1.
Everton (h) 1-2   Att. 30,000
J.R. Richardson

1938, Division 2.
Sheffield Wednesday (a) 2-0 Att. 25,358
Cairns (2)

1949, Division 1.
Bolton Wanderers (a) 2-2   Att. 35,000
Milburn, Taylor

1955, Division 1.
Blackpool (h) 1-2   Att. 54,557
Milburn

1960, Division 1.
Chelsea (a) 2-4   Att. 30,489

1966, Division 1.
Manchester City (a) 1-1   Att. 26,137
B. Robson (pen)

1977, Division 1.
Bristol City (h) 1-1   Att. 23,321
Martin

1983, Division 2.
Fulham (h) 3-2   Att. 31,660
Wharton, Keegan, Mills

1988, Division 1.
Queens Park Rangers (a) 0-3 Att. 11,013

1994, Premier League.
Newcastle 2   Q.P.R. 1
Kitson 20   Dichio 60
Beardsley 42   Att. 34,278

1997, Champions' League, Group C.
Newcastle 0   P.S.V. Eindhoven 2
Nillis 32
De Bilde 90
Att. 35,214

Playing record for this day... 16 games,
Won 6, Drawn 4, Lost 6, GF 25, GA 26.
Today's success rate... 50%.

Birthdays

Daniel Cordone born today in 1974.
Forward 2000-2001, Apps 27 (14 subs). Goals 3.

Sadly Missed

Dave Gardner died on this day in 1931, aged 58.
Left-back 1899-1902, Apps 78. Goals 2.

November 6

Played on this day

1897, Division 2.
Grimsby Town (a) 0-2   Att. 5,000
1909, Division 1.
Tottenham Hotspur (h) 1-0   Att. 26,000
Duncan
1920, Division 1.
Burnley (h) 1-2   Att. 50,000
Harris
1926, Division 1.
West Bromwich A. (h) 5-2   Att. 30,000
Gallacher (2), McKay (3)
1937, Division 2.
Southampton (h) 3-0   Att. 30,000
Park, J.R. Richardson, Smith
1943, Wartime.
Sunderland (a) 2-4   Att. 16,000
Stubbins (2)
1948, Division 1.
Blackpool (a) 3-1   Att. 30,000
Hair, Stobbart, Opponent (og)
1954, Division 1.
Blackpool (a) 0-2   Att. 20,701
1963, League Cup 3rd round.
Bournemouth (a) 1-2   Att. 11,735
McGarry (pen)
1965, Division 1.
Blackpool (h) 2-0   Att. 33,853
Robson (2)
1971, Division 1.
Southampton (h) 3-1   Att. 32,677
MacDonald (2), Green
1974, Texaco Cup Semi Final, 2nd leg.
Birmingham City (a) 4-1   Att. 17,754
Kennedy, Nattrass, Pendrey (og), Cannell
Newcastle won 5-2 on aggregate.
1976, Division 1.
Manchester City (a) 0-0   Att. 40,049
1982, Division 2.
Burnley (h) 3-0   Att. 20,961
Waddle, Varadi, Keegan
1991, Division 2.
Cambridge United (h) 1-1   Att. 13,077
Hunt
2002, Worthington Cup 3rd round.

Newcastle 3	Everton 3
Dyer 77, 78	Campbell 11
Pistone (og) 100	Watson 85
	Unsworth 112 (pen)
	Att. 34,584

A.E.T. Newcastle lost 3-2 on penalties.

Playing record for this day... 16 games,
Won 8, Drawn 3, Lost 5, GF 32, GA 21.
Today's success rate... 59.38%.

UNITED WIN PLACE IN FINAL
Newcastle into the final of the Texaco Cup after 5-2 win

Newcastle came down to the Midlands today to play Birmingham City at St. Andrew's in this semi-final second leg of the Texaco Cup. 17,754 supporters were there to witness the match, with Birmingham favourites to win. The first leg had ended in an ill-tempered 1-1 draw at St. James' Park, and the winner would be joining Southampton in the two-leg final. Newcastle welcomed young Paul Cannell into their team, and Birmingham had Malcolm Page back in the side after an injury.

Newcastle started well, and their early play showed that they should not be written off. Indeed, they were playing far better than Blues, and the visitors knew they had the advantage over their rivals.

Alan Kennedy opened the scoring for Newcastle after ten minutes with a super shot past Dave Latchford, and the Blues fans weren't happy. On 21 minutes the home side's hopes of reaching the final slipped further away when Garry Pendrey gave away the ball. Irving Nattrass took control and doubled the lead for the visitors.

This wasn't what the home crowd had been expecting, and they were not impressed with their team's performance. While the Newcastle side left the field at half-time to cheers, the Blues team got a steady, slow handclap to see them off.

The second half started well for Newcastle, but for Blues things just got worse. They were making no headway in their attempts at attacking, and Newcastle seemed to be getting stronger by the minute.

With 62 minutes on the clock the misery of the home side deepened. Latchford and Pendrey hesitated with a clearance, and Barrowclough managed a challenge for the ball. In desperation Pendrey failed to check Latchford's position, but sent the ball goalwards anyway. The Blues keeper was off his line and the ball rolled into the net. Newcastle were three goals ahead.

Blues managed to pull back a goal five minutes later with a fantastic header from Kenny Burns, but it did little to compensate the home crowd for the poor performance. Birmingham did improve slightly after this, and there were several attempts at goal which were unlucky. Bob Hatton made a super effort, but the hard work of Willie McFaul made sure that the save was well made.

With five minutes left to play Paul Cannell scored the fourth goal for Newcastle. This justified his position in the team, as the twenty-year-old had taken the place of thirteen-goal striker Malcolm Macdonald for this game.

So, the game ended with the final result 4-1. Newcastle therefore had made it into the final with an aggregate score of 5-2.

Birmingham City

Latchford, Martin, Pendrey, Kendall, Gallagher, Page, Campbell, Phillips (Taylor h/t), Burns, Hatton, Calderwood.

Newcastle United

McFaul, Nattrass (Laughton 75), Clark, Cassidy, Keeley, Howard, Barrowclough, Kennedy, Cannell, Tudor, Smith.

Birthdays

Kevin Carr born today in 1958.
Goalkeeper 1976-1985, Apps 195.

November 7

A SWEET VICTORY OVER THE TOFFEE MEN

Mitten defiant as United end poor run with stunning win

Precariously placed at eighteenth in the First Division table, Newcastle were also starting today's game on a run of three straight defeats. The usual 30,000-plus Gallowgate crowds had dwindled to 23,727 for this afternoon's kick off, all was not well on Tyneside. Manager Charlie Mitten was, however, going through a vigorous rebuilding programme that he remained confident would see improvements. Not everyone had his faith though and with just four wins in fifteen league games so far evan the most fanatical of Geordies had worries of relegation, although it was still only in November.

Mitten started United's revival plan by handing centre half George Heslop his debut for this all-important game against Everton. United started well and were 2-0 up inside six devasting minutes after kick off. The first was struck by winger George Luke, a beauty from the edge of the penalty area after four minutes. United's second was almost a repeat of the first this time Hughes giving Everton keeper Dunlop no chance with a first time shot from similar range. Now the crowd were right behind them roaring on their every move, United for the first-time in ages were playing with confidence. They were also getting some luck from the officials, White seemed marginally offside when he split the Everton back four all of whom had stopped to appeal. With no flag White was completely out on his own and rounded the exposed Dunlop for a simple tap-in, United were now 3-0 up with just eleven minutes on the clock. Newcastle were enjoying their football, people were smiling on the terraces, Mitten had allowed himself a relaxed sit on the bench, was this really St. James' Park? With half-time approaching Bramwell's clumsy challenge on Allchurch was punished by Eastham who sent Dunlop diving the wrong way from his penalty kick and at half-time United led 4-0.

There was no let up in the second half and the crowd waited just four minutes before celebrating a fifth goal, Len White netting his second of the game. Finally Allchurch managed to dribble his way through the Everton defence and convert a shooting opportunity, this had been on the cards all afternoon, United now 6-0 ahead. Then for some reason the team sat back, Everton were allowed to play, and home keeper Mitchell who for an hour had merely spectated became the most involved player on the field. Everton centre-forward Bobby Collins was creating havoc, and he laid on the inevitable goal for Thomas. Soon after Thomas bagged his second goal again after a super run and pass from Collins and fortunately this woke United up. In the final twelve minutes White completed a deserved hat-trick and Welsh international Ivor Allchurch netted his second to complete the 8-2 victory. Still United attacked to the end, and right on full time a great one-two with Scoular allowed White a shooting chance which beat Dunlop's dive but struck the outside of the post.

Newcastle's revival had started and by the season's end they had climbed the table to finish in a very creditable eighth place.

Newcastle United
Mitchell, Whitehead, McMichael, Scoular, Heslop, Bell, Hughes, Eastham, White, Allchurch, Luke.

Everton
Dunlop, Parker, Bramwell, King, Jones, B. Harris, J. Harris, Thomas, Shackleton, Collins, Laverick.
Referee Mr. J. Powell (Rotherham)

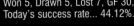

Birthdays

John Anderson born today 1959.
Right-back & Coach 1982-1992, Apps 349 (17 sub). Goals 15.
John Barnes born today in 1963
Midfield 1997-1999, Apps 40 (7 subs). Goals 7.

Marc Hottiger born today in 1967.
Right-back 1994-1996, Apps 54 (2 subs). Goals 2.
Darron McDonough born today in 1962.
Midfield 1992-1994, Apps 3 (1 sub). Goals 0.

November 8

Played on this day

1902, Division 1.
Liverpool (h) 1-2   Att. 8,000
Roberts
1913, Division 1.
Preston North End (h) 2-0   Att. 12,000
Hall, G. Wilson
1919, Division 1.
Middlesbrough (a) 1-0   Att. 30,000
Booth
1924, Division 1.
Burnley (h) 3-0   Att. 20,000
Clark (2), Cowan
1930, Division 1.
Blackpool (a) 0-0   Att. 20,000
1941, Wartime.
Bradford Park Ave. (a) 0-0   Att. 5,000
1947, Division 2.
Nottingham Forest (h) 0-2   Att. 60,244
1952, Division 1.
Blackpool (a) 2-0   Att. 30,000
Brander, G. Robledo
1958, Division 1.
Luton Town (h) 1-0   Att. 53,488
White
1969, Division 1.
Sunderland(h) 3-0   Att. 56,317
Davies, Dyson (2)
1972, Texaco Cup 2nd round, 2nd leg.
West Bromwich A. (h) 3-1   Att. 20,420
Tudor, Gibb, Hibbitt
Newcastle won 4-3 on aggregate.
1975, Division 1.
Leeds United (a) 0-3   Att. 39,304
1980, Division 2.
Cambridge United (a) 1-2   Att. 5,684
Shinton
1986, Division 1.
Leicester City (a) 1-1   Att. 9,836
McDonald (pen)
1992, Division 1.
Swindon Town (h) 0-0   Att. 28,091
1993, Premier League.
Oldham Athletic 1   Newcastle 3
Jobson 35   Cole 53, 81
                   Beardsley 74
                        Att. 13,821
1995, Premier League.
Newcastle 1   Blackburn Rovers 0
Lee 11
                        Att. 36,463

1997, Premier League.
Coventry City 2   Newcastle 2
Dublin 4, 82   Barnes 31
                   Lee 87
                        Att. 22,679
1998, Premier League.
Manchester United 0   Newcastle 0
                        Att. 55,174

Playing record for this day.... 19 games,
Won 9, Drawn 6, Lost 4, GF 24, GA 14.
Today's success rate... 63.16%.

OLDHAM OBLITERATED
United's second-half display routs Royle's men

It looks like being a long hard winter for Joe Royle's Oldham Athletic. Newcastle totally outclassed them with Peter Beardsley and Andy Cole, in particular, putting on a dazzling display. Whatever their shortcomings, Oldham generally manage to put teams under sustained pressure at Boundary Park, giving them some leeway for defensive frailties and poor away form. Today, even that was beyond them as they managed just one shot at goal over the 90 minutes. Newcastle were credited with nineteen as they dominated from start to finish to keep the 4,000-strong travelling Toon Army in full voice. Their dominance off the field is as helpful as United's stylish play is on it in winning games, a fact Royle pointed out after the game when saying Newcastle had, in effect, 42 home games in a league season.

Yet, despite the dominance, Newcastle trailed 1-0 at half-time. United keeper, Hooper, lost Brennan's free kick under pressure from both Olney and Jobson, with the latter prodding home the loose ball. Newcastle had seen half-a-dozen chances come and go by this point, on 35 minutes, and manager Kevin Keegan was seething. At half-time he laid into the over elaborate play by his midfielders and the ridiculous showboating by his forwards, as well as the collective below-par shooting at goal.

That message hit home and Newcastle in the second half were simply irresistible. Cole scored twice, one sublime, one fortunate, a combination that makes a natural goalscoring striker, as does his impeccable scoring record now eighteen goals from sixteen games this season. He could hardly have made a more pointed reply to his omission from the England squad recently. Beardsley's talent is already known but it still burns brightly and, after setting up Cole's first with a superb chip over keeper Key, Beardsley claimed the second goal for United with a cracking shot from just inside the penalty area. There was still time for Newcastle to add a third goal, this time Cole getting his deserved stroke of luck. He wriggled free in the area and saw his right-footed shot clip his left foot and slide past Key. Cole then almost completed a hat-trick, as moments later, after cutting into the area his drilled cross-shot flew past Key's despairing dive but wide of the far post by a fraction of an inch.

The only blemish on this fabulous United performance was their failure to score more goals. Key, on loan from Sheffield Wednesday, had something to do with that, showing more organised defiance than his static defenders in front of him, but it also reflected on Newcastle's early overelaboration and poor finishing. The players themselves will be aware of that; on another day this performance could have produced six or seven goals minimum. That scoreline would have been cruel on Oldham, indeed the 3-1 result leaves them now second from bottom in the Premier League, and looking favourites for the dreaded drop come next May.

Oldham Athletic
Key, Jobson, Fleming, Redmond, Makin, Palmer, Milligan, Bernard, Brennan, Olney (Adams 64), Sharp.
Newcastle United
Hooper, Watson, Venison, Scott, Elliott, Clark, Bracewell, Sellars, Lee, Beardsley, Cole.
Referee Mr. R. Gifford.

Birthdays

Aaron Hughes born today in 1979.
Defender 1995-present day, Apps 195 (15 subs).
Goals 5.
Roger Jones born today in 1946.
Goalkeeper 1976-1977, Apps 7.

Sadly Missed

Albert Shepherd died on this day in 1929, aged 44.
Centre-forward 1908-1914, Apps 123. Goals 92.

November 9

Match of the Day from 1935

LUCKY FOR UNITED

Newcastle take points after even match at Bury

This Division Two match saw Newcastle United travel to Bury today to play in front of a crowd of 12,000. Both teams were evenly matched, and it was clear from the beginning that it was going to be a close contest.

It was Bury who took the lead in the sixteenth minute when Earl sent a lovely ball which passed Tapken in the Newcastle goal with force. This set back didn't put Newcastle off their stride, it simply inspired them to keep trying. The visiting Tynesiders knew their chances would come, and they were right.

Jack Smith levelled the scores with a superb drive straight past Fairhurst in the Bury goal, and the pace increased further. Bury tried hard to regain the lead, but the Newcastle defence held fast. Another attack from the Tynesiders followed, and it was even play again.

Then, just before the half-time whistle blew, Smith put Newcastle into the lead. His powerful shot gave the Bury keeper no chance to save, and the visitors held the advantage going into the break.

The second half began the same as the first, with both teams attacking and defending in equal proportions. There was still more to come and it was Wilf Bott who managed to slip through the Bury defence and shoot past the keeper for Newcastle's third. This gave the visitors the upper hand, and Bury found it hard to fight back. They tried hard to get back into the game and score, but the Newcastle defence were keeping them away from the danger area.

Smith completed his hat-trick with the fourth for the Tynesiders, and now Bury had a lot of work to do if they were to have any sort of impact on the rest of the game. Time was running out, and the visitors were ahead by four goals to one.

Bury pulled together, and they managed to get through the tight visiting defence, Whitfield sending the ball past Tapken to pull a goal back for the home side.

The end of the game was drawing near, and Bury were still two goals behind. They put every scrap of energy into a fight back, and their attempts paid off a little more right before the end. Bagley sent a lovely shot into the Newcastle goal to reduce the deficit further, and now the score was stood at 4-3. However, it wasn't enough for the home side, and the final whistle went. The visitors, however, were lucky to be returning to Newcastle with both points.

Bury
Fairhurst, Chester, Gemmell, Jones, Matthewson, Whitfield, Bagley, Graham, Earl, Buttery, Cope.
Newcastle United
Tapken, Richardson, Fairhurst, Imrie, Davidson, Weaver, Bott, Ware, Smith, McMenemy, Pearson.

David Fairhurst

Birthdays

Mike Larnach born today in 1952.
Forward 1977-1978, Apps 14 (2 subs). Goals 0.

Played on this day

1895, Division 2.
Darwen (a) 4-4   Att. 2,000
Wardrope, Aitken, Thompson, Collins
1901, Division 1.
Manchester City (h) 3-0   Att. 8,000
Roberts, McColl (pen), Orr
1907, Division 1.
Bolton Wanderers (h) 3-0   Att. 28,000
Appleyard, Orr, Rutherford
1912, Division 1.
Blackburn Rovers (a) 0-2.   Att. 35,000
1929, Division 1.
Sheffield Wednesday (h) 1-3 Att. 30,000
McDonald
1935, Division 2.
Bury (a) 4-3   Att. 12,000
Bott, J. Smith (3)
1940, Wartime.
York City (h) 3-0   Att. 3,000
Nevins, Stubbins, Gordon (pen)
1946, Division 2.
Sheffield Wednesday (h) 4-0 Att. 46,916
Wayman(4)
1957, Division 1.
Blackpool (h) 1-2   Att. 36,410
Opponent (og)
1963, Division 2.
Cardiff City (h) 0-4   Att. 38,495
1968, Division 1.
Arsenal (a) 0-0.   Att. 34,168
1974, Division 1.
Middlesbrough (a) 0-0   Att. 39,000
1985, Division 1.
Birmingham City (a) 1-0   Att. 8,162
Reilly
1991, Division 2.
Grimsby Town (h) 2-0   Att. 16,959
Hunt, Howey
2002, Premier League.
Arsenal 1   Newcastle 0
Wiltord 24   Att. 38,12

Playing record for this day... 15 games, Won 7, Drawn 3, Lost 5, GF 26, GA 19. Today's success rate... 56.67%.

Played on this day

1894, Division 2.
Burton Wanderers (h) 3-1   Att. 6,000
Thompson, Smith, McDermid
1900, Division 1.
Wolverhampton W. (h) 3-1   Att. 16,000
MacFarlane, Peddie, Niblo
1906, Division 1.
Aston Villa (a) 0-0   Att. 30,000
1923, Division 1.
Manchester City (h) 4-1   Att. 28,000
Harris (2), Cowan, Aitken
1928, Division 1.
Manchester City (a) 4-2   Att. 15,000
Lang, Gallacher (3)
1934, Division 2.
Sheffield United (a) 1-5   Att. 18,000
Smith
1945, Wartime.
Liverpool (h) 6-2   Att. 50,833
Stubbins, Clifton (3), Wayman, Hair
1951, Division 1.
Blackpool (a) 3-6   Att. 28,611
Milburn, G. Robledo (2)
1956, Division 1.
Tottenham Hotspur (a) 1-3   Att. 51,722
White
1962, Division 2
Luton Town (h) 3-1   Att. 27,428
Fell, Thomas (2)
1973, Division 1.
Leicester City (a) 0-1   Att. 20,726
1979, Division 2.
Cardiff City (h) 1-0   Att. 22,867
Shoulder
1984, Division 1.
Chelsea (h) 2-1   Att. 24,542
Waddle, McDonald
1990, Division 2.
Wolverhampton W. (a) 1-2   Att. 18,721
Clark
*Steve Watson becomes Newcastle's
youngest ever player when making his
debut today at the age of 16 years 223
days.*

Playing record for this day... 14 games,
Won 8, Drawn 1, Lost 5, GF 32, GA 26.
Today's success rate... 60.71%.

Match of the Day from 1928

HAT-TRICK HERO GALLACHER

Three from Gallacher and one from Lang silence critics at Maine Road

Newcastle travelled to Maine Road today to meet Manchester City in front of 15,000 supporters, most of whom were expecting City to beat United hands down. There were plenty of people who had decided that the visiting side didn't stand a chance against the mighty force of the home team, but Newcastle were determined to prove them wrong.

Play was frenzied from the beginning. Newcastle went all out on the attack, and City didn't know what had hit them. Hughie Gallacher was as forceful as ever, and coupled with Tommy Lang they were frightening. The Tynesiders had a strong defence too, but it was the forwards who were particularly outstanding today.

Within minutes Gallacher had given the visitors the lead with a perfectly placed shot past the City keeper. This shook the home side a little, and their play was affected by this embarrassment.

Things were made worse for City when Gallacher doubled the lead for Newcastle with a super shot. Now the home side were beginning to worry. This was not what they had expected, and they weren't prepared for it at all.

Within thirty minutes of the start of play Gallacher completed his hat-trick, bringing the score for Newcastle to three. The visitors were truly showing their critics how wrong they were, and they were doing it in style.

City pulled a goal back soon afterwards when Johnson took advantage of a scramble in the danger area. His random shot sailed into the net past Burns to reduce the deficit for the home side.

However Newcastle were never really in any danger of losing their lead. The home forwards were no threat to the strong visiting defence. United regained their three-goal advantage with a super solo effort from Lang. He slammed the ball towards goal, and beat the City keeper with ease.

Further chances fell to Gallacher, but no more goals were added. Then, right on the final whistle City grabbed another goal back with a fine shot from Johnson again.

This effort was too late to make any difference to the outcome though, and the game ended with a win, and a moral victory to the visiting Newcastle United.

Manchester City
Gray, Ridley, McCloy, Marshall, Barrass, McMullen, Austin, Roberts, Johnson, Horne, Brook.
Newcastle United
Burns, Maitland, Thomson, MacKenzie, Hill, McDonald, Boyd, Wilkinson, Gallacher, McCurley, Lang.

Birthdays

Geoff Allen born today 1946.
Winger 1964-1974, Apps 26. Goals 1.
Faustino Asprilla born today in 1969.
Striker 1996-1998, Apps 63 (13 subs). Goals 18.
Tommy Thompson born today in 1928.
Midfield 1946-1950, Apps 20. Goals 6.

Sadly Missed

Douglas Graham died today in 1993, aged 72.
Left-back 1940-1950, Apps 164. Goals 1.

November 11

UNITED MAUL THE WOLVES

Champions on fire, Howie brilliant, Appleyard nets hat-trick

League champions Newcastle stepped up a gear in their quest to retain the title with a magnificent display against Wolves today equalling their biggest-ever league win to date.

It was United who got the game under way, kicking towards the almost complete and impressive looking new West Stand on a gloomy and cold afternoon at St. James' Park. The home side were on the attack from the first whistle and kept visiting keeper Baddeley busy throughout the game. After just seven minutes the inevitable goal came by way of some superb passing between United's fowards Orr, Appleyard and the eventual goalscorer Jimmy Howie. Then within minutes of the restart United were 2-0 up when a glorious pass from Appleyard found Howie again in acres of free space with ample time to beat Baddeley comfortably. The home side were now rampant and Ronald Orr added a third with a header from an inch-perfect cross from Rutherford, the ball fizzing past the beleaguered keeper. Then came the goal of the game when Orr, picking up a loose ball twenty yards inside the Wolves half, mesmerised the visiting defence with his dribbling skills and finished with a fierce low volley which, although Baddeley got both hands to it, was fumbled over the goal line by the unfortunate keeper. With half time just moments away the home crowd were cheering a fifth goal, this time Appleyard converting a fine cross from Gosnell from the left wing.

Newcastle continued their domination of the game in the second half thanks mainly to the form of their Scottish international Howie, who controlled everything in the middle and laid on chance after chance for his forwards. Wolves were struggling desperately and played the remaining thirty minutes with ten men when Wooldridge left the field through injury. Newcastle scored three more times before the final whistle despite playing cheeky exhibition football which thrilled the 15,000 crowd. It was a brilliant display from United and a great day for Bill Appleyard who completed his hat-trick by netting United's sixth and seventh goals. The scoring was completed by Veitch who after missing several glorious chances, smashed home a last-minute penalty kick to make it an emphatic 8-0 victory.

Newcastle United

Lawrence, McCracken, McCombie, Gardner, Veitch, McWilliam, Rutherford, Howie, Appleyard, Orr, Gosnell.

Wolverhampton Wanderers

Baddeley, Stanley, Jones, James, Goodall, Whitehouse, Breakwell, Corfield, Wooldridge, Layton, Baynham.

Referee Mr. M. McQueen (Liverpool)

Birthdays

Ollie Burton born today in 1941.
Centre-half 1963-1973, Apps 229 (9 subs). Goals 8.

Bryan Robson born today in 1945.
Forward 1962-1971, Apps 244 (1 sub). Goals 97.

Lest we forget

On Remembrance Day a tribute to the first-team players on the staff of Newcastle United FC who sadly sacrificed their lives fighting for their country.

Tom Cairns
Midfield 1914-1916, Apps 1. Goals 0.
Died in France 1917 while serving as a corporal in the Royal Field Artillery during World War I.

Tommy Goodwill aged 22
Died during the battle of the Somme whilst serving with the 16th Northumberland Fusiliers with team mates Dan Dunglinson and Stan Hardy. His name appears on a war memorial at Thiepval along with 73,412 men who have no known grave at that French village. (See also July 1st.)

Tom Hughes
Midfield 1912-1915, Apps 2. Goals 0.
Killed in action during World War I.

Richard McGough
Midfield 1914-1915, Apps 2. Goals 0.
Killed in action whilst serving as a bombardier in France during the first World War.

Played on this day

1898, Division 1.
Nottingham Forest (a) 0-2   Att. 8,000
1904, Division 1.
Wolverhampton W. (a) 3-1   Att. 6,000
Howie (2), Orr
1910, Division 1.
Aston Villa (a) 2-3   Att. 40,000
Stewart (2)
1921, Division 1.
Tottenham Hotspur (h) 0-2   Att. 30,000
1927, Division 1.
Bury (a) 4-1   Att. 21,408
Seymour, McDonald (pen), Gallacher, McKay
1932, Division 1.
Arsenal (a) 0-1   Att. 60,000
1938, Division 2.
Fulham (h) 2-1   Att. 63,962
Birkett, Bowden
1949, Division 1.
Birmingham City (h) 3-1   Att. 30,113
G. Robledo (2), Walker
1955, Division 1.
Huddersfield Town (a) 6-2   Att. 18,664
Crowe, Keeble (4), White
1960, Division 1.
Blackpool (h) 4-3   Att. 26,657
Neale (2), White (2)
1966, Division 1.
Liverpool (h) 0-2   Att. 36,920
1977, Division 1.
Wolverhampton W. (a) 0-1   Att. 16,964
1983, Division 2.
Chelsea (a) 0-4   Att. 30,638
1988, Division 1.
Arsenal (h) 0-1   Att. 23,807

Playing record for this day... 14 games,
Won 6, Drawn 0, Lost 8, GF 24, GA 25.
Today's success rate... 42.86%.

November 12

Match of the Day from 1927

UNITED BURY OPPONENTS

Bury lose 4-1 at home to on form Newcastle

Newcastle travelled to Bury today to play this Division One match in front of a crowd of 21,408. Newcastle had Urwin, McKay and Curry in outstanding form in this game, and they were by far the better team throughout the first half.

It was Bob McKay who managed to net the first goal thanks to a lovely pass from Urwin. Newcastle were one ahead early on, and Bury were already beginning to struggle. The second goal for the visiting side came from Seymour, his fine shot beat the Bury keeper with ease.

Before the half-time break another goal was added to the tally for Newcastle when Gallacher sent the ball over the line for the third.

The second half began with a renewed effort from the home team. The break seemed to have done them good, and they put up more of a fight and piled on the pressure. Their progress was hampered when Bradshaw managed to send the ball into his own net. The goal didn't stand though, as the player had handled the ball. Instead the referee awarded a penalty to Newcastle, and Tom McDonald stepped up to the spot to take the kick.

The shot was perfectly placed and sailed past the Bury keeper to put Newcastle four goals ahead of the struggling home side.

Towards the end of the game Bury's consistent efforts to fight back paid off a little when Amos finally managed to beat Wilson in the Newcastle goal to pull one back for the home side.

The score was now 4-1, and Newcastle were playing far better than their opponents. The game ended shortly afterwards with a thoroughly deserved win for the visiting Tynesiders.

Bury
Richardson, Heap, Crown, McLachlan, Bradshaw, Dutton, Gale, Davin, Bullock, Ball, Amos.
Newcastle United
Wilson, Maitland, Hudspeth, Curry, Spencer, Harris, Urwin, McKay, Gallacher, McDonald, Seymour.

Birthdays

Joe Allon born today 1966.
Centre-forward 1984-1987, Apps 10. Goals 2.
Tony Cunningham born today in 1957.
Centre-forward 1985-1987, Apps 51 (11 subs). Goals 6.

Andy Thorn born today in 1966.
Centre-half 1988-1989, Apps 43. Goals 3
David Young born today in 1945.
Midfield 1964-1973, Apps 56 (4 subs). Goals 2.

November 13

UNITED COMPLETE AMAZING COMEBACK

Bellamy strike leaves Newcastle clinging to Euro dream

Newcastle achieved the unprecedented in Holland today as the first side to qualify for the second stage of the Champions' League after starting with three defeats. Craig Bellamy's winner in the final minute at the De Kuip Stadium knocked the stuffing out of Feyenoord. It is hard to believe that United are still in the competition. they not only lost those first three games but did so without even scoring. However, they bounced back just in time to win the last three games and thus deserve their unexpected jackpot. Not only did they need to win in Rotterdam, United required a favour from Juventus in beating Dynamo Kiev in Russia. The Italian champions obliged and Newcastle, though stretching the nerve ends of their travelling Toon Army to breaking point, capitalised in thrilling fashion.

Bellamy's role as match winner was performed in demanding circumstances, not having played for nearly a month after knee surgery, his selection was a calculated risk by Bobby Robson, a gamble which has paid a multi-million pound dividend. The Welsh striker pounced in stoppage time at the end of both halves to secure Newcastle's most famous European victory ever. Hugo Viana, another surprise starter in midfield, scored what appeared to be the clinching goal four minutes after the interval. When Viana threaded his left-foot shot past the diving Patrick Lodewijks, Newcastle were pinching themselves. They appeared to be guaranteed the consolation prize of a UEFA Cup place, but prospects became brighter shortly after taking that two-goal lead when the news came through that Juventus had come from a goal behind to lead Kiev in the other important Group E game.

Feyenoord refused to accept that elimination was beckoning and hit United with a barrage of attacks, rewarded with goals for Mariano Bombarda and Anthony Lurling. The introduction of Bombarda, on 54 minutes, transformed proceedings, he scored Feyenoord's first goal in this competition since the one at St. James' Park in September. A neat finish too, after running onto a fine pass from Bonaventure Kalou he dashed into the area and placed a firm cross-shot past Shay Given.

The United keeper had moments earlier rescued his team with two instinctive saves from Brett Emerton and Paauwe, but he had no chance when his defence allowed Nurling to run on to Paauwe's cushioned header and hammer in a fierce volley from close range. It seemed only a matter of time before Feyenoord completed their victory as dangerous shots rained in on Given's goal, but Newcastle clung on and capitalised on their opponents all-out attacking to launch their own killer strike.

Kieron Dyer, who was outstanding in midfield, burst through and forced Lodewijks into a desperate save. The goalkeeper was unable to hold it, and Bellamy turned in the loose ball from another tight angle to complete Newcastle's stunning victory. The goal could not have been timed better, just as the calculations of the current group scores were confirming United's qualification, the final whistle went and Newcastle had achieved the almost impossible. A truly memorable night for all on Tyneside.

Hugo Viana wins an aerial dual with Feyenoord's Christian Gyan.

Feyenoord
Lodewijks, Gyan, Van Wonderen, Paauwe, Rzasa, Song (Bombarda 54), Bosveit, Emerton, Lurling, Buffel, Kalou.

Newcastle United
Given, Griffin, O'Brien, Dabizas, Hughes, Jenas, Dyer, Speed, Viana, (Bernard 82), Bellamy, Shearer.

Referee Mr. F. Wack (Germany)

November 13

Craig Bellamy scores the opening goal against Feyenoord on this day in 2002.

November 14

UNITED SAIL TO 7-0 WIN

Doncaster put on poor show at St. James' Park

22,000 were at St. James' Park today to see this splendid display of football by the home side. The visitors were Doncaster Rovers, and they were in for a shock. The game began in a frenzy of activity from the Newcastle team. They were by far the better team right from the kick off, and Doncaster were forced into defending at once.

Smith put Newcastle into the lead after just five minutes of play with a super shot which gave Bradshaw in the Doncaster goal no chance of saving.

Another goal fell to Newcastle shortly afterwards, with Leighton being the man to add his name to the score-sheet. The aggressive nature of the home forwards was too much for the Doncaster defence, and they gave way easily. There were no real attacks from the visiting side, and Tapken had little to do in the Newcastle goal.

The third goal came from a lovely ball by Smith. His powerful shot sailed into the net, and now Doncaster were beginning to fall apart.

Before half time Newcastle added another thanks to a fine shot from Rogers. This brought the home side's tally to four going into the break, and that gave them a huge advantage over their opponents.

The second half started much the same way as the first. Newcastle were completely in control, and Doncaster seemed to be taking a back seat.

Leighton added another to the score with a clear shot past the stationary Bradshaw.

There was plenty time left for more goals and when Jack Smith completed his hat-trick with a lovely drive into the net, Newcastle were five goals to the good.

Poor Doncaster had long since given up, and it was no surprise when Smith jumped at the chance to get his fourth goal of the game. The ball was sent perfectly into the net, and Bradshaw didn't even try to dive for the save.

The final whistle blew with the score 7-0, and Doncaster were just glad to be going home.

Newcastle United
Tapken, Richardson, Ancell, Gordon, Carver, Garnham, Rogers, Leighton, Smith, Pearson, Mooney.
Doncaster Rovers
Bradshaw, Shaw, Rodgers, Gladwin, Bycroft, McMahon, Burton, Malam, Barnes, Button, A. Turner.

Tommy Walker born on this day.

November 15

1890, FA Cup Qualifying round 1.
Shankhouse Black Watch (h) 5-0
McInnes (3), Thompson (2)   Att. 1,200
1902, Division 1.
Sheffield United (a) 1-2   Att. 14,000
Roberts
1913, Division 1.
Tottenham Hotspur (h) 2-0   Att. 25,000
Hall (2)
1924, Division 1.
Leeds United (a) 1-1   Att. 35,000
Seymour
1930, Division 1.
Portsmouth (h) 4-7   Att. 23,000
Devine, Lindsay (2), Wilkinson
1941, Wartime.
Bradford Park Ave. (h) 3-1   Att. 5,000
Short, Stubbins, Birkett
1947, Division 2.
Bradford Park Ave. (a) 3-0   Att. 24,654
Stobbart, Sibley, Opponent (og)
1952, Division 1.
Chelsea (h) 2-1   Att 37,178
G. Robledo (pen), Brennan
1958, Division 1.
Birmingham City (a) 0-1   Att. 28,720
1969, Division 1.
Nottingham Forest (h) 3-1   Att. 24,307
Dyson, Craig, Opponent (og)
1975, Division 1.
Liverpool (h) 1-2   Att. 41,145
Nulty
1980, Division 2.
Sheffield Wednesday (h) 1-0 Att. 19,145
Shinton
1986, Division 1.
Watford (h) 2-2   Att. 23,645
Anderson, McDonald (pen)

Playing record for this day... 13 games,
Won 7, Drawn 2, Lost 4, GF 28, GA 18.
Today's success rate... 61.54%.

FOUR-GOAL THRILLER ENDS IN STALEMATE

Unlucky debutant Goddard almost snatches the game for United

Four goals in an astonishing second half at St. James' Park gave the second biggest crowd of the season, 23,645, something to cheer about in a memorable game on Tyneside today.

Both teams were applauded sportingly from the field at the end of a truly nail-biting final 45 minutes which see-sawed both ways, and in the end the points that were at stake were shared out equally.

Watford went ahead on 72 minutes when Kenny Jackett coolly converted his spot kick after United full-back Kenny Wharton rashly brought down Hornets' danger man Callaghan from behind. Newcastle stormed back immediately laying siege to the Watford goal, which seemed to have an incredibly charmed life during the whole 90 minutes. Finally United prized open the tight Watford rearguard and John Anderson forced home a well deserved equaliser for the Magpies in the 78th minute. Taking advantage of yet another scramble in the Watford penalty area the ball fell kindly for Anderson to toe poke the chance past a grounded keeper Tony Coton from barely three yards out.

Newcastle were still celebrating the goal however, when Watford striker Luther Blissett broke away to score a tremendous goal within a minute of the restart. Blissett charged to the edge of the penalty area before unleashing a vicious right-foot shot which swirled and dipped over a startled Martin Thomas in United's goal. Newcastle, who had almost spent the entire game bombarding Watford's defence, now found themselves trailing again with the game now inside the last ten minutes. It seemed it just wasn't going to be United's day. This theory was further endorsed when Paul Goddard, Newcastle's record £415,000 signing from West Ham, beat the entire Watford defence on a fantastic dribble into the box. The striker making his United debut then rounded goalkeeper Coton but, his shot from an acute angle struck the bar and bounced out of play thus denying him a dream start, and capping a superb performance with a thoroughly deserved goal. However this thrill-a-minute second half was far from over and with just five minutes of the game remaining Newcastle were finally awarded some justice. The relentless pressure on the Watford goal paid off as Jackett, a forward now pulled back to become part of an eight-man defence, could only stop England striker Peter Beardsley's run with a desperate lunge and referee Breen had no hesitation in pointing to the penalty spot. St. James' Park for once during this enthralling second half fell deathly silent as full-back Neil McDonald coolly converted the kick with a well placed drive to Coton's right sending him the wrong way. Despite frantic pressure by Newcastle in the closing minutes Watford bravely held out but not a single fan left the ground complaining, this had been a truly memorable game to watch.

Newcastle United

M. Thomas, Anderson, Wharton, McCreery, Jackson, Roeder, McDonald, A. Thomas, Goddard, Beardsley, Stephenson.

Watford

Coton, Bardsley, Rostron, Richardson, Sims, McClelland, Callaghan, Blissett, Falco, Jackett, Barnes.
Referee Mr. K. J. Breen (Manchester)

Billy Pears born today in 1918.
Midfield 1936-1941, Apps 2. Goals 0.
Keith Robson born today in 1953.
Forward 1971-1974, Apps 18. Goals 6.

Neil Simpson born today in 1961.
Midfield 1990-1991, Apps 5 (4 subs). Goals 0.

November 16

COMEBACK FOR UNITED

Newcastle take points from Southampton with 2-1 win

Newcastle United played host to Southampton today for this Premiership clash in front of a crowd of 51,812 at St. James' Park. The home side were hoping to increase their run of Premiership home wins to five, and Southampton were hoping to stop them.

Newcastle fell behind very early on when Southampton managed to find the net after just 65 seconds. James Beattie was the man responsible, and his twenty yard strike left Given standing.

Despite Newcastle's obvious lethargy, Southampton weren't able to take advantage and push through to increase their lead. The scores were levelled after 40 minutes when Ameobi got onto a great pass from Kieron Dyer and netted the equaliser for Newcastle.

Dyer had persevered throughout, and his skill and determination were beginning to pay off. He was unstoppable on the field, and his energy was unmatched.

The second half saw Newcastle take to the field with a bit more pace. They needed to boost their performance if they were going to take the lead, and that's just what they managed to do.

A lovely pass from Viana came to Hughes, and the sure-footed player had no trouble getting the ball into the back of the net for Newcastle's second on 54 minutes. The home side were in the lead now, and there was no going back.

Southampton tried hard to make a comeback towards the end of the match, but Newcastle were not going to let their lead slip away. Their defence was steadfast, and Southampton had no chance to get through. Final score 2-1.

Newcastle United

Given, Griffin, O'Brien (Dabizas 78), Caldwell, Hughes, Jenas, Dyer, Speed, Viana (Bernard 82), Ameobi, Shearer.

Southampton

Niemi, Dodd (Telfer 69), M Svensson, Lundekvam, Bridge, Fernandes, Oakley, A Svensson (Pahars 82), Marsden, Beattie, Ormerod (Delgado 56).

Referee Mr. C. Wilkes (Gloucestershire)

Shay Given

November 17

1888, FA Cup Qualifying round 3.
   Sunderland (a) 0-2
   After extra time.
1894, Division 2.
   Lincoln City (a) 1-3   Att. 2,000
   Wallace
1900, Division 1.
   Aston Villa (a) 2-2   Att. 20,000
   Peddie, A.Gardner
1906, Division 1.
   Liverpool (h) 2-0   Att. 36,000
   Gardner, Speedie
1923, Division 1.
   Preston North End (a) 2-1   Att. 12,500
   Harris (2)
1928, Division 1.
   Birmingham (h) 1-0   Att. 30,000
   Wilkinson
1934, Division 2.
   Bradford City (h) 4-2   Att. 14,000
   Boyd, Leighton, Smith (2)
1945, Wartime.
   Bury (h) 4-2   Att. 43,080
   Hair, Clifton, Stubbins (2)
1951, Division 1.
   Arsenal (h) 2-0   Att. 61,192
   G. Robledo, Opponent (og)
1956, Division 1.
   Everton (h) 0-0   Att. 32,263
1962, Division 2.
   Southampton (a) 0-3   Att. 13,582
1973, Division 1.
   Manchester United (h) 3-2   Att. 42,474
   Cassidy (2), Hope
1979, Division 2.
   Bristol Rovers (a) 1-1   Att. 7,626
   Shoulder
1990, Division 2.
   Barnsley (h) 0-0   Att. 15,548
1991, Division 2.
   Sunderland (a) 1-1   Att. 29,224
   O'Brien
2001, Premier League.
   Fulham 3   **Newcastle 1**
   Saha 20   Speed 65
   Legwinski 28
   Hayles 70   Att. 21,159

Playing record for this day... 16 games,
Won 7, Drawn 5, Lost 4, GF 24, GA 22.
Today's success rate... 59.38%.

HOPE SPRINGS ETERNAL AT ST. JAMES'
Second half fightback sees off Manchester United

This was not only one of the most exciting games seen this season at St. James' Park today, but also one of the hardest fought. So keenly contested was the match that five players were cautioned: Hibbitt, McDermott, and Howard for the Magpies, and Greenhoff and Young for the Red Devils, all deservedly so for fouls that were way over the top even for this contest. When close attention was at last paid to the ball in the second half Newcastle United's superior skills cancelled out Manchester United's half-time 2-1 advantage, and in the end they came back to win 3-2 with plenty in hand. Fittingly the winning goal came from nineteen-year-old local lad George Hope, playing in his first league game at St. James' Park. In spite of Holton's considerable physical advantage, Hope gave the Manchester defence a tough time and earnt the loudest cheer of the afternoon in the 71st minute when he confidently headed in Hibbitt's precise cross to settle the game.

Tommy Cassidy

The goal also underlined once again the weakness of the visitors' defence which is becoming a concern for their manager Tommy Docherty. Their marking, covering, and clearances were still a long way removed from First Division standard. The Manchester United defence would argue that they are given far much to do because their midfield colleagues did not come to grips with the Magpies well organised middle led by Terry McDermott, he was simply every where. Only Greenhoff managed to shine briefly in the midfield department although Graham redeemed his afternoon by scoring a great goal to put United in front. Overall it's a gloomy picture for the long-suffering Manchester United supporters who now have a long hard winter ahead yet again. For Newcastle the prospects are still bright, in spite of an unfortunate run of injuries. The latest victim is Tommy Cassidy, scorer of two goals today, who after the game went into hospital for an operation that will keep him out of football for six weeks.

Cassidy's first goal came after seventeen minutes when Manchester United keeper, Stepney stopped, but failed to hold Hope's header from Hibbitt's free kick. The visitors then equalised after 34 minutes, Macari placing Greenhoff's short through pass into the corner of the net. Then right on the stroke of half time Best sprinted clear and set up a chance for Graham who took it beautifully with a shot just inside the penalty area. In a spirited rally by the Magpies in the second half Cassidy equalised, driving Gibb's low centre between Stepney's legs. Then with just nineteen minutes of the game remaining came the moment of Hope, and glory for United.

Newcastle United
McFaul, Nattrass, Craig, McDermott, Howard, Moncur, Gibb, Smith, Hope, Cassidy, Hibbitt.
Manchester United
Stepney, Buchan, Young, Greenhoff, Holton, James, Morgan, Macari, Kidd, Graham, Best.

Bobby Cummings born today in 1935.
Centre-forward 1954-1956 & 1963-1965,
Apps 45 (1 sub). Goals 14.

November 18

Match of the Day from 1905

THE CLASH OF THE TITANS

League champions meet League leaders in first game since FA Cup Final

This match, Aston Villa v Newcastle United, had been eagerly anticipated by both sets of supporters since Harry Hampton's two goals had denied United a League and Cup double in the FA Cup final at Crystal Palace seven months ago. The reigning League Champions clearly had a point to make today, and as an added spice to an already classic showpiece game, they were up against the current League leaders who themselves were out to prove April's win was no fluke.

With all the ingredients of an exciting game, it was no surprise that the early stages were nervy and scrappy as both sides knew any error would prove costly such was the pride at stake between these giant football clubs of the era. Villa had the first real chance on target when Lawrence saved brilliantly from a close-range shot by Garraty after he had skipped past McCombie in the area. At the other end a harmless cross from Rutherford was almost knocked into the net via the chest of Spencer, the Villa full-back seemed unaware of how close he was to the post and was very fortunate to put the ball behind for a corner. The incident gave United a spur of encouragement however, and on their next attack they scored the opening goal. Appleyard, having won a free kick after Leake's foul, cleverly found space in the area and when the ball arrived to him he wasted no time in slamming it past Villa's keeper George from ten yards. A minute later United almost scored a second when Gosnell rounded George in the penalty area but his acute-angled shot shaved the bar. The home side responded in sensational style, Cantrell chased and netted a pass from Hampton only to be given offside. Cantrell then set up a shot for Leake inside the area but his shot, into a virtually unguarded net, struck the back of United's defender McCracken whilst he lay on the floor and the ball bounced wide and out for a corner. A relentless five-minute burst ended with referee Gilgryst upsetting the home crowd again, waving away Villa's penalty claims after McCombie appeared to handle a shot at goal from Hampton. United survived the onslaught and then struck the sucker punch on 24 minutes. Rutherford broke on the right and his perfect cross dropped onto the head of Ronald Orr who redirected the ball wide of George's dive, scoring was that simple.

The goal ended the threat from Villa who spent the rest of the game trying to produce even a half chance against a tightened Newcastle defence. United seemed prepared to settle for frustrating Villa by denying them possession and it worked well. Villa eventually lost control and gave away needless free kicks one of which was converted for Newcastle's third goal on 66 minutes. Again Leake was the guilty man, Appleyard the victim. Gardner floated the ball into the box and Orr nipped in to head in his second goal of the game. Villa were quickly losing all their discipline and Garraty took out his frustration by wildly hacking McWilliam when shielding the ball in his own half. The Villa player was rightly cautioned and the Villa captain was seen to be spoken to by the Manchester official. United in contrast coolly saw out the last quarter of the game by keeping possession intelligently to claim a thoroughly deserved and convincing win.

Aston Villa

George, Spencer, Noon, Pearson, Leake, Hadley, Garratt, Garraty, Hampton, Cantrell, Hall.

Newcastle United

Lawrence, McCracken, McCombie, Gardner, Veitch, McWilliam, J.Rutherford, Howie, Appleyard, Orr, Gosnell.

Referee Mr. G. Gilgryst (Manchester).

Birthdays

Tommy Cassidy born today in 1950.
Midfield 1970-1980, Apps 239 (14 subs).
Goals 28.

Gavin Peacock born today in 1967.
Midfield/Forward 1990-1993, Apps 120 (3 subs).
Goals 47.

Played on this day

1898, Division 1.
Bolton Wanderers (h) 4-1   Att. 20,000
Peddie (2), MacFarlane, Rogers
1904, Division 1.
Bury (h) 3-1   Att. 18,262
Gosnell, Appleyard, Veitch
1910, Division 1.
Sunderland (h) 1-1   Att. 57,416
Shepherd
1921, Division 1.
Sunderland(h) 2-2   Att. 46,000
McDonald, McIntosh
1927, Division 1.
Burnley (h) 1-1   Att. 28,000
Gallacher
1932, Division 1.
Manchester City (h) 2-0   Att. 24,000
Cape (2)
1938, Division 2.
Blackburn Rovers (a) 0-3   Att. 21,300
1955, Division 1.
Cardiff City (h) 4-0   Att. 35,603
Milburn (2, 1 pen), Keeble, Crowe
1960, Division 1.
Everton (a) 0-5   Att. 41,123
1966, Division 1.
West Ham United (a) 0-3   Att. 31,285
1977, Division 1.
Arsenal (h) 1-2   Att. 23,679
Cassidy
1983, Division 2.
Sheffield Wednesday (a) 2-4 Att. 41,134
McDermott, Keegan (pen)
1988, Division 1.
Millwall (a) 0-4   Att. 15,767
1994, Premier League.
Wimbledon 3   **Newcastle 2**
Clarke 2   Beardsley 30
Ekoku 27   Kitson 32
Harford 36
                         Att. 14,203
1996, UEFA Cup 3rd round, 1st leg.
Metz 1   **Newcastle 1**
Traore 67   Beardsley 31 (pen)
                         Att. 23,000

Playing record for this day... 15 games,
Won 4, Drawn 4, Lost 7, GF 23, GA 31.
Today's success rate... 40%.

GOOD SHOW FOR UNITED

Newcastle take win over Bolton, great play all round

A crowd of 20,000 turned up at St. James' Park today to see a contest with Bolton Wanderers. Neither side had performed particularly well so far, but each had improved over the previous couple of weeks. Bolton had defeated the league champions last week, and Newcastle were ready for a challenge.

Within the first few minutes Newcastle made several good attempts at goal. Rogers won a corner for the home side, but Stevenson headed the ball past the goal and the chance was lost. Next Peddie missed a super opportunity to put the Tynesiders ahead, but it wasn't to be.

Then it was Bolton's turn for an attack. Kingsley had to work hard in the Newcastle goal to keep out the shots, despite the solid efforts of the home defence. However, it was one of these shots which managed to put the visiting side into the lead. Kingsley tried hard to make the save, but it was too quick for him, and Bolton had the advantage.

However, this spurred Newcastle on to step up the pace and increase the pressure on the Bolton goal. Ten minutes before the half-time break Joe Rogers scored the equaliser for Newcastle. His forceful shot had no chance of being saved by Sutcliffe, and the scores were level going into half time.

The second half started with a marked improvement in Newcastle's play. They were more relaxed and organised, and this served them well in taking control of the game for the remainder. Rogers and MacFarlane each had a good chance, but their efforts were thwarted by the Bolton defence. Next Sutcliffe had to pull off two energetic saves to keep the ball out of the goal, but it was clear that it was only a matter of time before Newcastle managed to find the back of the net again.

Stott's free kick just failed to hit its target, but the pressure was getting to the tired Bolton side. Jock Peddie was the one to put his team into the lead with a super shot which left Sutcliffe reeling in the goalmouth.

MacFarlane increased the lead for Newcastle, bringing the score to 3-1. Sutcliffe was being bombarded with shots, and he began to wilt. So, it was no surprise when Peddie scored again with five minutes left to go before the whistle. His shot sailed past the deflated Sutcliffe in the Bolton goal and the game was over. Everyone at St. James' Park had witnessed a better display of football than they had expected today, and Newcastle thoroughly deserved the win. Final score 4-1.

Newcastle United
Kingsley, Lindsay, Jackson, Ghee, Ostler, Stott, Rogers, Stevenson, MacFarlane, Wardrope, Peddie.
Bolton Wanderers
Sutcliffe, Davies R, Somerville, Freebairn, Brown, Davies W, Jack, Gilligan, Nicol, Miller, Thomson.

Birthdays

Wayne Quinn born today in 1976.
Defender 2001-present day, Apps 24 (3 subs).
Goals 1.

Sadly Missed

Jack Allen died on this day in 1957, aged 54.
Centre-forward 1931-1934, Apps 91. Goals 41.
Tom Phillipson died on this day in 1965, aged 67.
Centre-forward 1919-1921, Apps 15. Goals 4.

November 20

UNITED ADD TO BIRMINGHAM'S BLUES

Newcastle keep up their run of good luck against visiting Midlanders

Newcastle entertained Birmingham today in front of 20,000 at St. James' Park for this Division One match. The Tynesiders had done remarkably well at home against the Midland teams of Aston Villa and West Bromwich Albion. They were hoping that Birmingham would be another losing Midland side today, but Birmingham were there to fight for their pride.

Both teams started well, but it was Birmingham who showed early promise. A great ball from Briggs came to Harris, but the shot went wide and the chance was lost. Newcastle took advantage of Birmingham's disappointment, and went on the attack. The visitors' goalkeeper had a lot of work to do in the first ten minutes, but the pressure got too much for him and before long the first goal arrived.

It was Bob McKay who had managed to succeed in scoring for Newcastle, and this gave the home side a great advantage over their opponents. Then after half an hour Newcastle's lead was doubled when a lovely shot from Gallacher beat the Blues keeper with ease.

The home side went into the break, two goals to the good. The second half began with Newcastle on top. McDonald increased their lead to three with a super shot, and Birmingham were beginning to lose their way.

Things were looking hopeless for the visitors, but Briggs threw them a lifeline when he managed to beat Wilson in the Newcastle goal with a superb solo effort to reduce the deficit. With the score now 3-1, and Newcastle still in control of the game, Blues knew it was an uphill struggle for them.

Thirlaway almost scored his first goal for Birmingham shortly afterwards, but his attempt was not destined for the back of the net this time. Then Stan Seymour, who had provided the ball for the first Newcastle goal, took his turn to add his name to the score-sheet and bring the score to 4-1.

With five minutes to go before the end of the game Urwin was fouled by Barton and the referee awarded a penalty to Newcastle. Hudspeth stepped up to the spot to take the kick, and his shot sailed into the back of the net to bring the home side's tally to five.

The game ended with a well deserved win for Newcastle. They had now scored fourteen goals against the three visiting Midland teams, with only three goals being put past the home keeper in total.

Newcastle United
Wilson, Maitland, Hudspeth, MacKenzie, Spencer, Gibson, Urwin, McKay, Gallacher, McDonald, Seymour.
Birmingham
Tremelling, Smith, Barton, Liddell, Hunter, Dale, Harris, Crosbie, Briggs, Bradford, Thirlaway.

1897, FA Cup Qualifying round 2.
Stockton (a) 4-1   Att. 8,000
Campbell, Harvey, Ghee, Jackson
1909, Division 1.
Notts County (h) 1-3   Att. 18,000
Rutherford
1920, Division 1.
Liverpool (h) 2-0   Att. 50,000
Seymour, Ward
1926, Division 1.
Birmingham (h) 5-1   Att. 20,000
Gallacher, Hudspeth (pen), McDonald, McKay, Seymour
1937, Division 2.
Plymouth Argyle (h) 3-1   Att. 21,000
Mooney, Smith, Imrie (pen)
1943, Wartime.
Darlington (a) 1-4   Att. 7,838
Stubbins
1948, Division 1.
Arsenal (a) 1-0   Att. 62,000
Opponent (og)
1954, Division 1.
Bolton Wanderers (a) 1-2   Att. 27,000
Curry
1965, Division 1.
Leicester City (h) 1-5   Att. 27,603
Robson
1968, Inter Cities Fairs Cup 2nd round, 2nd leg.
Sporting Lisbon (h) 1-0   Att. 53,747
B. Robson
Newcastle won 2-1 on aggregate
1971, Division 1.
Nottingham Forest (h) 2-1   Att. 24,583
Macdonald (2)
1976, Division 1.
West Ham United (a) 2-1   Att. 21,324
Burns, Nulty
1982, Division 2.
Carlisle United (a) 0-2   Att. 16,276
1991, Division 2.
Southend United (h) 3-2   Att. 14,740
Peacock (2, 1 pen), Hunt
1999, Premier League.
Watford 1   Newcastle 1
Ngonge 53   Dabizas 59
    Att. 19,539

Playing record for this day... 15 games, Won 9, Drawn 1, Lost 5, GF 28, GA 24. Today's success rate... 63.33%.

Birthdays

Paul Robinson born today in 1978.
Forward 1998-2000, Apps 16 (14 subs). Goals 1.

Sadly Missed

Robert Roxburgh died on this day in 1974, aged 78.
Right-back 1920-1924, Apps 24. Goals 0.

Played on this day

1903, Division 1.
Liverpool (a) 0-1   Att. 9,000
1908, Division 1.
Aston Villa (h) 0-2   Att. 35,000
1914, Division 1.
Oldham Athletic (h) 1-2   Att. 12,000
Hudspeth (pen)
1925, Division 1.
Cardiff City (a) 0-0   Att. 25,000
1931, Division 1.
West Bromwich A. (h) 5-1   Att. 36,000
Allen, Boyd, J.R. Richardson (2), Weaver
1936, Division 2.
Fulham (a) 4-3   Att. 20,000
Pearson, Rogers (2), Smith
1942, Wartime.
Middlesbrough (h) 3-0   Att. 6,459
Gordon, Stubbins, Carr
1953, Division 1.
Portsmouth (h) 1-1   Att. 48,853
Milburn
1959, Division 1.
Blackburn Rovers (h) 3-1   Att. 31,368
Eastham, White (2)
1964, Division 2.
Derby County (h) 2-2   Att. 31,041
Cummings, McGarry
1970, Division 1.
Tottenham Hotspur (a) 2-1   Att. 38,873
Gibb, Craig
1981, Division 2.
Luton Town (h) 3-2   Att. 21,084
Varadi, Brown (2)
1987, Division 1.
Queens Park Rangers (a) 1-1 Att. 11,794
P. Jackson
1990, Zenith Data Systems Cup 2nd round.
Nottingham Forest (a) 1-2   Att. 9,567
Scott
1992, Division 1.
Watford (h) 2-0   Att. 28,871
Peacock, Lee
1993, Premier League.
Newcastle 3   Liverpool 0
Cole 5, 16, 30   Att. 36,374

Playing record for this day.... 16 games,
Won 8, Drawn 4, Lost 4, GF 31, GA 19.
Today's success rate... 62.50%.

Match of the Day from 1931

UNITED TAKE FIVE AT HOME
Newcastle win convincingly over poor Albion side

West Bromwich Albion travelled up to St. James' Park today to meet Newcastle in Division One. A crowd of 36,000 were there to see the game unfold, and it promised to be a great show of football for the home fans.

Pearson in the Albion goal had many saves to make in the early stages of the game, and it was

Albert McInroy

his drop of the ball in the goalmouth which enabled Boyd to knock it into the net for Newcastle's first goal.

After 23 minutes Weaver excelled himself with a throw-in, and the ball came to Jimmy Richardson. He was a long way from goal, but he sent in a shot anyway, and the ball flew straight into the net past Pearson, who only managed to touch it with his fingertips as it sailed by.

Eight minutes later Newcastle's lead was extended to three when a free kick was taken by Weaver. The Albion keeper had no chance and did not even try to make the save.

Early in the second half Newcastle's tally rose to four as Richardson again netted the ball for the home side. Albion were trying desperately hard to reduce their arrears, but it was taking its toll on the players when all their attempts proved fruitless.

It was 75 minutes into the game when Albion finally managed to put the ball past McInroy in the Newcastle goal, Glidden sending in the shot.

A good try from Raw just missed its target, but Albion knew they had no chance of keeping up with the home team. This was further proved when Jack Allen added his name to the score-sheet with the fifth and final goal for Newcastle. The Tynesiders had deserved their win, and had shown to the crowd that they were by far the better team today.

Newcastle United
McInroy, Nelson, Fairhurst, MacKenzie, Davidson, Weaver, Boyd, J.R. Richardson, Allen, McMenemy, Lang.
West Bromwich Albion
Pearson, Shaw, Trentham, Magee, W. Richardson, Murphy, Glidden, Raw, W.G. Richardson, Sandford, Wood.
Referee Mr. E. Wood (Sheffield).

Birthdays

Tommy Craig born today in 1950.
Midfield 1974-1978, Apps 157 (2 subs). Goals 29.

Mark Robinson born today in 1968.
Right-back 1993-1994, Apps 26 (11 subs).
Goals 0.

November 22

BARNES DELIVERS THE WIN

Two from Barnes snatch victory from Southampton

36,769 piled into St. James' Park today to see Newcastle play Southampton in this Premiership clash, Sir John Hall's final home game as chairman. John Barnes was in the forward line for the home side, hoping to increase his tally of goals. Southampton had young Kevin Davies in their line-up, and both strikers were to feature prominently in the game.

It took just five minutes for the first goal to be scored. It was Southampton who took the lead with a powerful and confident shot from Davies which beat Hislop in the Newcastle goal with ease.

Fortunately Newcastle were up to the challenge, and the play throughout was evenly matched. Keith Gillespie worked extremely hard to make things difficult for Francis Benali, but Jon Dahl Tomasson did not have luck on his side today. No matter how hard he tried, things just didn't go his way, and he was not going to add his name to the score-sheet this time.

The second half began with a surge of energy from Newcastle. They were still a goal behind, and they needed to up the pressure to be in with a chance of scoring. A super cross from Gillespie on 55 minutes gave Barnes the opportunity to grab the equaliser for the home side, and things were looking more hopeful.

Southampton were beginning to tire, and the Tynesiders knew how to take advantage. They kept up the pace and the attacks, and kept their patience. Fifteen minutes before the end and Newcastle earned their win with a second goal from Barnes. The cross had again come from Gillespie, and the shot was perfectly sent into the goal past Jones.

Southampton tried hard to recover but were unable to do so. Newcastle had worked hard throughout, and deserved to take the points. Barnes had now scored five goals in ten Premiership matches, and the home crowd were more than pleased with his presence in the forward line today.

Newcastle United

Hislop, Watson, Albert, Peacock, Pistone, Gillespie, Lee, Batty, Ketsbaia, Tomasson, Barnes.

Southampton

Jones, Dodd, Monkou, Lundekvam, Benali, Palmer, Richardson, Oakley (Todd 64), Le Tissier (Neilson 58), Davies, Hurst (Basham 78)

Referee Mr. D. Gallagher (Banbury).

John Barnes beats Southampton goalkeeper Paul Jones to score.

Played on this day

1895, FA Cup Qualifying round 4.
Rendal (h) **5-0**   Att. 3,000
Wardrope, Aitken (2), Logan, Thompson
1901, Division 1.
Liverpool (h) **1-0**   Att. 20,000
McColl
1907, Division 1.
Birmingham (h) **8-0**   Att. 16,000
Appleyard, Howie (2), Rutherford (3),
Veitch (2)
1912, Division 1.
Tottenham Hotspur (a) **0-1**   Att. 25,000
1929, Division 1.
Portsmouth (h) **4-1**   Att. 15,000
Gallacher (4)
1935, Division 2.
Sheffield United (a) **1-5**   Att. 32,000
Livingstone
1940, Wartime.
York City (a) **0-3**   Att. 2,000
1946, Division 2.
Bury (h) **1-1**   Att. 49,656
Bentley
1957, Division 1.
Manchester United (h) **1-2**   Att. 53,950
R. Mitchell
1963, Division 2.
Manchester City (h) **3-1**   Att. 22,557
Penman, Thomas (2)
1968, Division 1.
Wolverhampton W. (a) **0-5**   Att. 25,425
1974, Division 1.
Burnley (a) **1-4**   Att. 19,523
Barrowclough
1985, Division 1.
Manchester City (a) **0-1**   Att. 25,179
1991, Division 2.
Blackburn Rovers (h) **0-0**   Att. 23,639
1996, Premier League.
Chelsea **1**   Newcastle **1**
Vialli 24   Shearer 41
     Att. 28,401
1998, Premier League.
Everton **1**   Newcastle **0**
Ball 18 (pen)   Att. 30,357
2002, Premier League.
Manchester United **5**   Newcastle **3**
Scholes 25   Bernard 35
van Nistelrooy   Shearer 52
38, 45, 53   Bellamy 75
Solskjaer 55   Att. 67,619

Playing record for this day... 17 games,
Won 5, Drawn 3, Lost 9, GF 29, GA 31.
Today's success rate... 38.24%.

Match of the Day from 1907

PIECES OF EIGHT

Newcastle take huge win over sorry Birmingham

Birmingham made the trip up to St. James' Park today to play this Division One match in front of an eager audience of 16,000. The home crowd were in for a treat, and Birmingham would be left wondering what had hit them. The rain had been persistent all night making the pitch heavy.

At the start of play things looked to be even between the two sides. Eyre had the first chance for Blues, but his attempt went over the bar. Duffy had the next chance for Newcastle, but Cornan put a stop to his hopes of opening the scoring. However, it was Newcastle who were successful in netting the first goal, and it was merely the beginning of the great flood of goals to come their way. Howie was the man to try his luck with a long-distance shot, and the ball sailed into the back of the net past Dorrington in the Birmingham goal. Appleyard's shot just went wide, and Duffy's attempt landed in the side netting. Rutherford had a lovely shot saved by Dorrington, but the pitch was starting to take its toll on the visiting team. Thirty five minutes into play Newcastle doubled their lead with a lovely shot from Howie, the ball flew straight into the corner of the net out of reach of the diving Dorrington. Half-time came with the score 2-0, and Birmingham were glad of the rest.

King had not come back onto the field after the interval, but he made it back onto the pitch ten minutes into the second half. Appleyard fluffed his shot when faced with an open goal, and the ball went over the bar with the chance lost. The Birmingham defence was struggling hard now, and Newcastle seized the opportunity to take over the game completely. Veitch was on hand to net Newcastle's third goal, then Howie provided the ball for Appleyard to score the fourth.

It was Colin Veitch again who managed to beat Dorrington and net the fifth for Newcastle, and Birmingham were beginning to realise that they faced a hopeless task. Rutherford was next to add his name to the score-sheet, and although Blues were convinced he had been offside the referee thought otherwise and the goal was allowed.

The home side now had six, and there were still 25 minutes left to play. Birmingham made one last attempt at a fight back, but their efforts were not strong enough to get through the tight Newcastle defence. Dorrington pulled off a superb save from Duffy. Appleyard's next goal was disallowed due the referee having blown his whistle seconds before the ball crossed the line. However, it was only a minor set back, and on 80 minutes the seventh goal was added for Newcastle. It was Rutherford who scored, with his second of the game, and Blues were now praying for the final whistle.

Jackie Rutherford completed his hat-trick with a fine shot from the corner, and the goal brought Newcastle's tally to eight. The home side eased the pressure on Blues considerably after this last goal, but Blues were in no position to take advantage of the offer. Even though the game had slowed down, Dorrington still had to make two energetic saves to keep the score from increasing further for the Tynesiders. Final score 8-0.

Newcastle United
Lawrence, McCombie, Pudan, Gardner, Veitch, McWilliam, Rutherford, Howie, Appleyard, Orr, Duffy.
Birmingham
Dorrington, Kearns, Glover, Cornan, Hartwell, Beer, Eyre, Tickle, King, Green, Peplow.
Referee Mr. T.B. Campbell (Blackburn).

Birthdays

Tom Russell born today in 1909.
Left-back 1934-1937, Apps 7. Goals 0
Kevin Gallacher born today in 1966.
Forward 1999-2001, Apps 47 (13 subs). Goals 6.

Sadly Missed

Charlie Watts died on this day in 1924, aged 52.
Goalkeeper & Trainer 1896-1908, Apps 101.

November 24

MANCHESTER CITY THROW IT AWAY
Newcastle snatch deserved win at Maine Road

Newcastle United travelled to Moss Side today to face Manchester City in Division One. The crowd of 39,358 braved the pouring rain to watch a match filled with action and surprise. The Maine Road pitch was sodden and heavy, and play was going to be tough for the teams. It would be as much a test of strength and stamina as skill, and the strongest would come out the winners.

George Robledo

City defender Rigby made things difficult for Milburn throughout the game, however, the Newcastle forward's patience ensured he was not worn down.

The home team were the first to score, and it was young Meadows who took the honours after a lovely pass from Broadis. Simpson had no chance in the Newcastle goal to make the save, and City were a goal ahead.

It was beginning to look like City were in control of the play, but little did the cheering home crowd realise that Newcastle were just warming up. An attempt from Milburn was kept out of the goal by a diving Trautmann in the City goal, and Foulkes had the misfortune to hit the post with his shot. Walker had a shot stopped by Trautmann too, and City were beginning to worry.

Then, Rigby made a huge mistake that cost his team dearly. He was drawn out of position, and George Robledo was on hand to take advantage of the space created. The Newcastle striker pushed through the City defence and fired a super shot which flew past Trautmann and brought the scores level.

Almost immediately United swept into the lead when Milburn raced half the length of the pitch to send an inch-perfect shot into the back of the net to bring Newcastle to two.

Whilst the visiting fans were still celebrating their lead, Newcastle's tally increased further. Mitchell slipped through the defence and slotted the ball home for the third, and the Tynesiders were now two goals ahead.

Towards the end of the game Clarke managed to squeeze in another goal for City, but there was no time left to score again. The Tynesiders had played superbly, and had well deserved their win. They were glad to take the points back home to Newcastle, and Manchester were gutted at having lost their lead so convincingly.

Manchester City
Trautmann, Branagan, Hannaway, Paul, Rigby, McCourt, Hart, Revie, Meadows, Broadis, Clarke.
Newcastle United
Simpson, Cowell, McMichael, Harvey, Brennan, E. Robledo, Walker, Foulkes, Milburn, G. Robledo, Mitchell.

Peter Beardsley gets the ball forward despite a strong challenge from Mark Ford of Leeds.

David Ginola beats Gary Kelly of Leeds.

November 25

LEE INSPIRES UNITED VICTORY

A turnaround inside 60 seconds keeps Newcastle in the title hunt

In recent years November has signalled the start of Newcastle's annual blip which culminates in close but ultimate Premiership title failure. Last season was no exception and United's indifferent winter form eventually led to absolute catastrophe when United failed to even secure a UEFA Cup place. This season Kevin Keegan marked down the month of November as a decisive phase in his campaign to bring the Premier League title to Tyneside. After wins against Liverpool and Blackburn and a well earned draw at Villa Park, this latest home victory over Leeds, the only side to beat them last season at St. James' Park, has sent out a clear message to their title rivals, Newcastle this time have the character to go all the way.

Leeds, who took that last UEFA Cup place last season by beating United, looked capable of repeating the achievement after absorbing whatever pressure Newcastle could apply in a fascinating first-half encounter. Howard Wilkinson's team weathered the Newcastle onslaught and went into the interval deserving their 1-0 lead, courtesy of a neat Brian Deane header from Tony Dorigo's cross. The goal will certainly help him forget an earlier howler when Shaka Hislop could only parry a shot from Tony Yeboah and Deane unbelievably missed the close-range tap-in. The Toon Army were left fearing the worst during their half-time break but, and full credit to them, they responded magnificently in the second half which helped Newcastle regain the initiative.

Newcastle were indefatigable after the restart with Rob Lee, in his pivotal midfield role, showing exactly why his manager rates him as the best player in any position in the country. Recent comments that Lee is not worthy of an international place have angered Keegan and it's not surprising to see why given this clinical evidence. It was fitting that Lee's inspirational performance should include the goal that transformed the match in the 70th minute. Running on to Steve Howey's pass, which was expertly left by Peter Beardsley, he ran confidently from the halfway line to beat Jon Lukic with a powerful low drive. Newcastle were relieved but could hardly believe their dramatic turnaround, all in a matter of seconds. David Ginola broke on the right wing and sent in a terrific cross on the run which Les Ferdinand, with a mis-timed header, knocked downwards towards the Leeds' keeper. A simple take was however, uncharacteristically fumbled and the ever-alert Beardsley gobbled up the inviting rebound. The goal knocked the stuffing out of Leeds and the remaining nineteen minutes were played out comfortably for yet another November victory.

Newcastle United
Hislop, Barton, Peacock, Howey, Beresford, Gillespie, Lee, Clark, Ginola, Ferdinand, Beardsley.

Leeds United
Lukic, Kelly, Jobson, Wetherall, Dorigo (sub Bowman), Palmer, McAllister, Ford (sub Brolin), Speed, Yeboah, Deane.

Referee Mr. S. Dunn (Bristol).

Played on this day

1893, Division 2.
Liverpool (h) 0-0   Att. 2,000
1899, Division 1.
Preston North End (h) 0-0   Att. 15,000
1905, Division 1.
Liverpool (h) 2-3   Att. 32,000
Orr, McWilliam
1911, Division 1.
Tottenham Hotspur (a) 2-1   Att. 37,541
Hay, Hibbert
1922, Division 1.
Tottenham Hotspur (h) 1-1   Att. 25,000
McDonald
1933, Division 1.
Aston Villa (a) 3-2   Att. 40,000
Lang, Williams, Weaver
1939, Wartime.
Middlesbrough (a) 2-1   Att. 3,537
Stubbins, Clifton
1944, Wartime.
Bradford City (a) 2-5   Att. 5,500
Wayman, Gordon
1950, Division 1.
Charlton Athletic (h) 3-2   Att. 48,670
Milburn (2), Walker
1961, Division 2.
Stoke City (a) 1-3   Att. 22,009
Hale (pen)
1967, Division 1.
Sheffield Wednesday (h) 4-0 Att. 28,101
Bennett (2), Davies, Elliott
1978, Division 2.
Oldham Athletic (h) 1-1   Att. 20,563
McGhee
1987, Simod Cup 1st round.
Shrewsbury Town (h) 2-1   Att. 7,787
Bogie, Mirandinha
1989, Division 2.
Sheffield United (h) 2-0   Att. 27,170
Gallacher, Quinn
1995, Premier League.
Newcastle 2   Leeds United 1
Lee 70   Deane 31
Beardsley 71   Att. 36,572
1999, UEFA Cup 3rd round, 1st leg.
A.S. Roma 1   Newcastle 0
Totti 51 (pen)   Att. 45,655

Playing record for this day... 16 games, Won 8, Drawn 4, Lost 4, GF 27, GA 21. Today's success rate... 62.50%.

Birthdays

David Kelly born today in 1965.
Centre-forward 1991-1993, Apps 83. Goals 39.

Sadly Missed

Bob McColl died on this day in 1959, aged 83.
Centre-forward/Midfield 1901-1904, Apps 67. Goals 20.

November 26

1898, Division 1.
   Derby County (a) 1-3   Att. 7,000
   Wardrope
1904, Division 1.
   Aston Villa (a) 1-0   Att. 13,000
   Appleyard
1910, Division 1.
   Woolwich Arsenal (a) 2-1   Att. 13,000
   Shepherd, Duncan
1921, Division 1.
   Sunderland (a) 0-0   Att. 49,483
1927, Division 1.
   Leicester City (a) 0-3   Att. 35,000
1932, Division 1.
   Sunderland (a) 2-0   Att. 39,000
   Allen, Lang
1938, Division 2.
   Millwall (h) 2-2   Att. 37,000
   Clifton, Mooney
1949, Division 1.
   West Bromwich A. (h) 5-1   Att. 32,415
   Houghton, Milburn (2), G. Robledo,
   Walker
1955, Division 1.
   Manchester City (a) 2-1   Att. 22,860
   Hannah, Keeble
1960, Division 1.
   Blackburn Rovers (h) 3-1   Att. 22,623
   R. Mitchell, White (2)
1966, Division 1.
   Sheffield Wednesday (h) 3-1 Att. 26,873
   Bennett, Davies, B. Robson
1969, Inter Cities Fairs Cup 2nd round,
   2nd leg.
   FC Porto (h) 1-0   Att. 44,833
   Scott
   Newcastle won 1-0 on aggregate
1983, Division 2.
   Cambridge United (h) 2-1   Att. 25,065
   Beardsley, Keegan (pen)
1994, Premier League.
   Newcastle 1   **Ipswich Town 1**
   Cole 86   Thomsen 89
                   Att. 34,459
1996, Coca Cola Cup 4th round.
   Middlesbrough 3   **Newcastle 1**
   Whyte 27   Shearer 45
   Beck 61
   Ravanelli 89   Att. 29,831
1997, Championns' League, Group C.
   Barcelona 1   **Newcastle 0**
   Giovanni 17   Att. 26,000
2000, Premier League.
   Newcastle 2   **Liverpool 1**
   Solano 4   Heskey 78
   Dyer 70   Att. 51,949

Playing record for this day... 17 games,
Won 10, Drawn 3, Lost 4, GF 28, GA 20.
Today's success rate... 67.65%.

UNITED LUCKY TO TAKE WIN

Newcastle win 5-1 over WBA, but visitors lose in style

This Division One match saw West Bromwich Albion travel to St. James' Park today to meet Newcastle in front of 32,415. The home team started with confidence and organisation, whereas Albion were fidgety and random from the outset.

Newcastle were by far the better team in the first half, and the standard of football was high. Albion were playing catch-up the whole time, and this caused them to tire easily. No one in the ground was surprised when Newcastle opened the scoring with a super goal from Walker. His skilful attacking moves paying off when his shot gave Sanders no hope of making the save in the Albion goal.

This early lead gave the home side a further advantage over their opponents. Things soon got worse for the visitors when Milburn doubled the lead for Newcastle with a lovely shot straight into the back of the net.

Albion were doing all they could to keep their heads above water, but it didn't seem to be working. They had a lifeline thrown to them when Walsh managed to pull a goal back half way through the first period, but it didn't give them much hope.

Houghton restored the two-goal lead soon afterwards, his super effort bringing the score to 3-1. Albion were back to treading water again, and they were praying for the half-time break.

Before the interval George Robledo increased Newcastle's lead further with a fine shot, bringing the home side's tally to four with half a game still to play.

The second half began with a change in the attitude of the Albion players. They were far more positive and organised, and their game was all the better for it. Newcastle were taken aback by this dramatic change, and they had to alter their game to fit in with this revival.

With attacks coming more frequently for the visitors, it was surprising that they didn't manage to add another goal to their score. Good efforts were made by Elliott, Williams and Kennedy, but each one failed to hit the target.

Then Albion realised that their efforts were all in vain when Milburn took advantage of an opening in the Albion defence and slipped through to plant the ball into the back of the net for the fifth and final goal for Newcastle.

Albion were unlucky not to be able to convert their chances into goals. They made plenty of effort, but the luck just wasn't with them today. Newcastle had played better football in the first half, but had let their game slip in the second. The home side were fortunate that Albion weren't able to add any more goals to their score, and the game finished 5-1.

Newcastle United

Garbutt, Graham, Batty, Dodgin, Brennan, Crowe, Walker, Houghton, Milburn, Robledo, Mitchell.

West Bromwich Albion

Sanders, Pemberton, Millard, Kennedy, Vernon, Ryan, Elliott, Williams, Walsh, Barlow, Inwood.

Alan Shearer celebrates 100 goals for Newcastle.

November 27

QUARTER-FINALS FOR UNITED

Magpies register convincing win over Ipswich

Newcastle played host to Ipswich Town tonight for this Worthington Cup fourth round tie at St. James' Park. A good crowd of 32,576 turned out to watch the game unfold, with the winners going into the quarter-finals. The Ipswich side were missing several key players due to injury, and this was their third match in six days. Alan Shearer was hoping to achieve his 100th goal for Newcastle tonight, this being his 186th start for his team.

Laurent Robert opened the scoring after eighteen minutes play with a super shot which flew powerfully past Sereni in the Ipswich goal. Now the home side had taken the lead, they began to apply pressure was on the visiting defence the whole time, and the pace was just too quick.

In the 27th minute Newcastle extended their lead when Solano delivered a lovely pass to Shearer. He sent it on to Ameobi who slammed it into the back of the net from six yards. Two further attempts from Gary Speed almost brought the tally to three, but they both failed to hit the target.

So, it was left to Alan Shearer to add his first goal of the game on 37 minutes. It was a fine effort, and the Ipswich keeper had no chance of saving the ball. However, one goal was not enough for Shearer, and he continued to pressure the opposition. Five minutes before the half-time break Shearer got his century. It was Solano who provided him with the ball, and the confident striker made sure his shot hit the back of the net. So, Shearer had his 100th goal for Newcastle, and the score was 4-0 going into the break. Things were looking good for the home side.

In the second half, Newcastle kept control of the game. Ipswich were beginning to falter, the tiredness setting in now. Shearer was hoping to top off a great game with a hat-trick, but it wasn't to be. There were chances for Newcastle, but none of them brought about another goal.

Ipswich made one serious effort in the 77th minute when Darren Bent caught the Newcastle defence off-guard. He slipped through and tried his luck with a shot. Steve Harper saw it coming just too late, and as he came out to stop the ball it flew past him into the goal. Ipswich had pulled a goal back, and there was still time for a comeback by the visitors.

However, no more goals resulted and when the final whistle went Newcastle gained a deserved place in the quarter-finals with a 4-1 victory.

Newcastle United
Harper, Hughes (O'Brien 46), Dabizas, Distin, Elliott, Solano, Lee (Acuna 71), Speed, Robert (LuaLua 80), Shearer, Ameobi.
Ipswich Town
Sereni, Wilnis, McGreal, Hreidarsson, Makin, Wright, Holland, Miller (Gaardsoe 46), Clapham, Counago (Naylor 46), Armstrong (D. Bent 71).
Referee Mr. A. Wiley (Burntwood)

Birthdays

Dave Robinson born today in 1969.
Forward 1986-1992, Apps 10 (10 subs). Goals 1.

Scott Sellars born today in 1965.
Midfield 1993-1995, Apps 75 (6 subs). Goals 8.

November 28

Played on this day

1896, Division 2.
Loughborough Town (h) 4-1 Att. 7,000
Wardrope, Aitken, Connell, Lennox
1903, Division 1.
Bury (h) 3-2 Att. 8,000
Appleyard, Howie (2)
1908, Division 1.
Nottingham Forest (a) 4-0 Att. 8,000
Wilson, Shepherd, Higgins, Liddell
1914, Division 1.
Manchester United (a) 0-1 Att. 5,000
1931, Division 1.
Sunderland (a) 4-1 Att. 40,000
Boyd, Lang, McMenemy, J.R. Richardson
1936, Division 2.
Burnley (h) 3-0 Att. 27,000
Garnham, Leighton, Smith
1942, Wartime.
Middlesbrough (a) 6-1 Att. 3,500
Carr, Short (2), Stubbins (3)
1953, Division 1.
Arsenal (a) 1-2 Att. 62,456
Milburn
1959, Division 1.
Manchester City (a) 4-3 Att. 29,416
Allchurch, Bell, White, Opponent (og)
1964, Division 2.
Swindon Town (a) 6-1 Att. 15,866
Suddick, Penman (2), Hilley, Anderson (2)
1970, Division 1.
Burnley (h) 3-1 Att. 20,994
Ford, Robson, Moncur
1981, Division 2.
Grimsby Town (a) 1-1 Att. 9,256
Wharton
1987, Division 1.
Charlton Athletic (h) 2-1 Att. 19,453
Cornwell, Mirandinha
1989, Zenith Data Systems Cup 2nd round.
Oldham Athletic (h) 2-0 Att. 6,167
Quinn (2)
1992, Division 1.
Cambridge United (h) 4-1 Att. 27,991
Kelly (3, 1 pen), Peacock
1998, Premier League.
Newcastle 3 **Wimbledon 1**
Solano 38 Gayle 34
Ferguson 59, 90 Att. 36,623
1999, Premier League.
Newcastle 2 **Tottenham Hotspur 1**
Glass 5 Armstrong 44
Dabizas 58 Att. 36,454

Playing record for this day... 17 games,
Won 14, Drawn 1, Lost 2, GF 52, GA 18.
Today's success rate... 85.29%.

Match of the Day from 1959

McTAVISH GIFT HANDS UNITED VICTORY
Late catastrophe clinches seven-goal thriller

With only ten minutes left and despite the fact that each side had scored three times one always felt another goal was only a matter of time away. A ponderous clearance from Harvey sent the ball deep into the Manchester City half and United forward Allchurch and City defender McTavish pursued it. Trautmann came out to collect and suddenly there was a look of complete horror on his face. Twice already this month McTavish had put the ball past his hapless keeper and to further confound their misery McTavish could not resist making the deliberate knee contact with the ball to send it high over poor Trautmann's head and drop gently into the net behind him. Newcastle had won the game 4-3.

It may be some consolation to McTavish that although his generosity settled the issue, this was only the superficial cause of Manchester City's defeat. Newcastle were outstanding, despite some defensive errors of their own, Allchurch, Scoular, Eastham, and White caused the City defence trouble throughout and but for some quite brilliant goalkeeping from Trautmann, United would have had this game sewn up by a huge margin.

Newcastle played some extremely good football, as they invariably do at Moss Side, and with better finishing should have had this game in the bag before the half-time interval. White, who was generally mastered by McTavish had one header which Trautmann incredibly saved on the goal-line and Eastham and Allchurch too were denied by the inspired City keeper. Bell and Scoular attacked magnificently, and the more one sees of Scoular's imprint on the game, the more you feel for poor McTavish, if anyone deserved to be the heroic supplier of the winning goal in this game, Jimmy Scoular was the man today.

Newcastle's first goal came after 37 minutes, when from White's cross, Allchurch delivered a precise header. Straight from the kick off City attacked on the left, and McAdams headed an equaliser from Fagan's centre. In a breathtaking spell, just a minute later, McAdams put the home side in front with a curling left-foot shot which gave United keeper Harvey no chance.

In the second half there were more fumblings by City before Newcastle equalised after ten minutes. The ball had been in and out of the City goalmouth as though it were a tennis ball and when it came out a fifth time Bell raced in to hit a half-volley into the top corner. This stung City into action again and in the 63rd minute McAdams completed a hat-trick, albeit controversially, by beating the offside trap to run clear and score with a low drive. City's lead only lasted three minutes as White took advantage of more hesitancy in the City goalmouth to blast the ball past the now obviously annoyed Trautmann. As he ranted at his defenders you could only feel sorry for the man who had tried his utmost to keep City in the game.

Manchester City
Trautmann, Leivers, Sear, Cheetham, McTavish, Barnes, Barlow, Hannah, McAdams, Hayes, Fagan.
Newcastle United
Harvey, Whitehead, McMichael, Scoular, Heslop, Bell, Hughes, Eastham, White, Allchurch, Luke.
Referee Mr. M. Dixon (York).

Birthdays

Alec Betton born today 1903.
Centre-half 1931-1934, Apps 63. Goals 1.
Mick Channon born today in 1948.
Forward 1982, Apps 4. Goals 1.
Alex Tait born today in 1933.
Centre-forward 1952-1960, Apps 34. Goals 10.

Martin Thomas born today in 1959.
Goalkeeper 1983-1988, Apps 131.
Kenny Wharton born today in 1960.
Left-back/Midfield 1978-1989, Apps 335
(24 subs). Goals 27.

Sadly Missed

Len Shackleton died on this day in 2000.
Midfield 1946-1948, Apps 64. Goals 29.

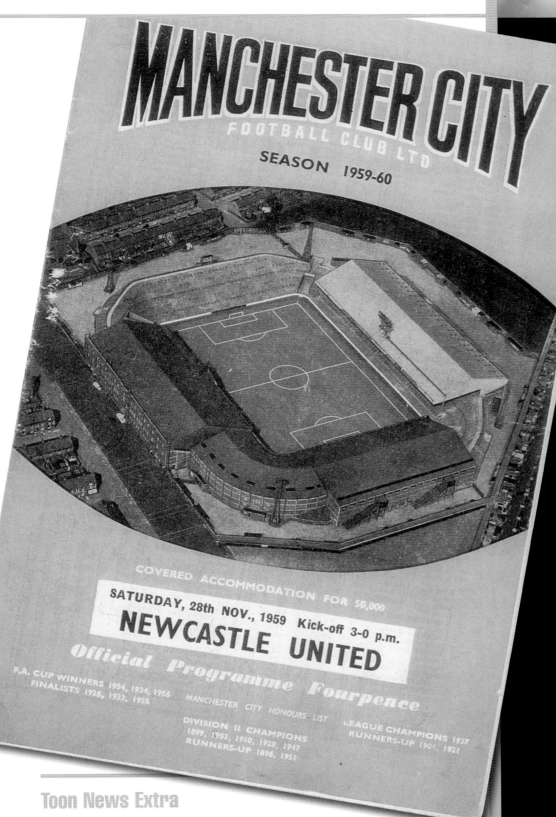

MANCHESTER CITY
FOOTBALL CLUB LTD
SEASON 1959-60

COVERED ACCOMMODATION FOR 50,000

SATURDAY, 28th NOV., 1959 Kick-off 3-0 p.m.
NEWCASTLE UNITED

Official Programme Fourpence

F.A. CUP WINNERS 1904, 1934, 1956
FINALISTS 1926, 1933, 1955

MANCHESTER CITY HONOURS LIST

DIVISION II CHAMPIONS
1899, 1903, 1910, 1928, 1947
RUNNERS-UP 1896, 1951

LEAGUE CHAMPIONS 1937
RUNNERS-UP 1904, 1921

Toon News Extra

1973... Bad light stops play
Newcastle United 1 Birmingham City 1

Despite the 2pm afternoon kick off this Texaco Cup second leg tie was abandoned when the dim light made visibility impossible. On a freezing day at St. James' Park, the match may have been abandoned anyway as snow was falling on an already frozen pitch. For the record Tudor put the Magpies 1-0 up after seventeen minutes. Blues equalised through Bowker after 63 minutes. The attendance was 5,529. The match was replayed to a conclusion on December 5th.

November 29

Played on this day

1902, Division 1.
Aston Villa (a) 0-7   Att. 10,000
1913, Division 1.
Aston Villa (h) 2-2   Att. 34,000
Low, Hudspeth (pen)
1919, Division 1.
Sunderland (h) 2-3   Att. 61,761
Hibbert, Robinson
1924, Division 1.
West Bromwich A. (a) 0-2   Att. 15,000
1930, Division 1.
Blackburn Rovers (h) 2-3   Att. 18,000
Boyd, Lindsay
1941, Wartime.
Leeds United (a) 2-5   Att. 3,000
Surtees (2)
1947, Division 2.
Sheffield Wednesday (a) 0-1 Att. 41,355
1952, Division 1.
Portsmouth (h) 1-0   Att. 46,721
G. Robledo
1958, Division 1.
Leeds United (a) 2-3   Att. 23,500
Allchurch (2)
1975, Division 1.
Manchester United (a) 0-1 Att. 52,264
1980, Division 2.
Orient (a) 1-1   Att. 5,800
Shinton
1995, Coca Cola Cup 4th round.
Liverpool 0   Newcastle 1
            Watson 77
            Att. 40,077
1997, Premier League.
Crystal Palace 1   Newcastle 2
Shipperley 67   Ketsbaia 45
          Tomasson 63
            Att. 26,085
2000, Worthington Cup 4th round.
Birmingham City 2 Newcastle 1
Adebola 31   Dyer 13
M. Johnson 90   Att. 18,520

Playing record for this day... 14 games,
Won 3, Drawn 2, Lost 9, GF 16, GA 31.
Today's success rate... 28.57%.

Temuri Ketsbaia causes problems for Crystal
Palace's keeper Kevin Miller and Marc Edworthy.

UNITED KINGS AT THE PALACE

Ketsbaia and Tomasson add to poor home record for the Londoners

Crystal Palace, still searching for their first home league win of the season, met a determined Newcastle side today eager to put their disappointing defeat by Barcelona in midweek behind them. United got the win but only after a spirited fight by Steve Coppell's Palace side who early in the game looked the better side. This was an important result for Kenny Dalglish's injury-hit Newcastle especially in the wake of that demoralising defeat, still fresh in the memory, and Champions' League exit in Spain.

This was Crystal Palace's seventh attempt to gain a home Premiership victory and it could not have started more hopefully for 26,085 fans at Selhurst Park. Newcastle had hardly ventured into the Palace half when Bruce Dyer struck the United upright. The Palace forward was a thorn in the United side early on and always looked dangerous but, typical of Palace's home 'jinx', he lasted just fourteen minutes before being forced off the field injured. It didn't end there for Palace, Michele Padovano made a big impression on his home debut but he too was withdrawn through injury early in the second half. Newcastle, who went into the game with injury problems themselves, possessed the outstanding Temuri Ketsbaia who was by far the game's best player and he gave United an important one-goal lead almost on the half-time whistle. A quickly-taken free kick caught Palace slumbering and Ketsbaia, with plenty of room to edge nearer the penalty area, finished with a beautiful left-foot drive which flew past keeper Kevin Miller.

It was Ketsbaia who set up Newcastle's second goal on 63 minutes. He charged down the left wing, then delivered an intelligent pass into the path of Jon Dahl Tomasson. Tomasson had timed his run well to meet the ball and from the distance he was from goal he required a stronger shot than the slightly mis-hit effort he produced. The 'home hoodoo' struck Palace again right on cue and somehow the ball bounced off Miller's block and trundled back into the net. Although Neil Shipperley pulled a goal back for Palace just four minutes later it was never going to be enough and in the scrappy last twenty minutes of the game the few goalscoring chances that did come were all squandered by United who deservedly claimed their second away victory of the season.

Crystal Palace

Miller, Edworthy, Gordon, Roberts (Zohar 48), Linighan, Warhurst, Shipperley, Dyer (Smith 15), Padovano (Emblem 57), Rodger, Hreidarsson.

Newcastle United

Hislop, Batty, Peacock, Barnes (Lee 64), Pearce, Ketsbaia, Tomasson, Gillespie, Watson, Hamilton, Pistone.

Referee Mr. M. A. Riley (Leeds).

Match of the Day from 1935

FOREST LOSE FIGHT

Newcastle deserve victory over sorry opponents

Nottingham Forest travelled to Newcastle today to meet at St. James' Park in Division Two. Hugh Bulloch was making his debut for Newcastle at centre-half, and 24,000 were there to see the match. It was to be a close call throughout the first half. There was little separating the two sides. However, Newcastle held the advantage as their forwards looked better at taking their chances.

Harris opened the scoring for Newcastle with a fine shot which left Ashton in the Forest goal standing. Smith was next to add his name to the score-sheet, and Newcastle were two goals up within half an hour of the start of play.

Forest maintained their pressure on the Newcastle goal, and Tapken had a few good saves to make from Dent and Simpson. Before the half-time break Forest pulled a goal back with a fine effort from Pugh, and it was going to be tough for Newcastle to stay in the lead.

In the second half things were faster and more determined for the home side. There were still opportunities for Forest to add another, but every attempt at goal failed for the visitors.

Jack Smith added a third for Newcastle, and with the widening of the gap between the teams, Forest's hopes of staying in the game slipped further. Fairhurst had taken up position on the outside-left, and he was next to score for the Tynesiders.

It was Fairhurst who netted the fifth and final goal for Newcastle, and Forest were well and truly beaten. After a close first half, the home side had by far outplayed the visitors. Final score 5-1.

Newcastle United
Tapken, Richardson, Fairhurst, Gordon, Bulloch, Weaver, Harris, Ware, Smith, McMenemy, Pearson.

Nottingham Forest
Ashton, Burton, Barrington, McKinlay, Graham, Pugh, Masters, Race, Dent, Peacock, Simpson.

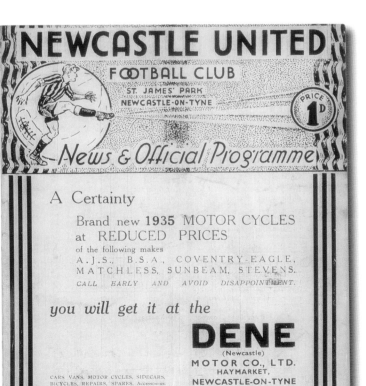

Played on this day

1901, Division 1.
Grimsby Town (h) 5-1   Att. 15,000
Roberts, Peddie (3), Orr

1907, Division 1.
Aston Villa (a) 3-3   Att. 25,000
Appleyard, Howie, Orr

1912, Division 1.
Middlesbrough (h) 3-1   Att. 25,000
G. Wilson, Peart, Hay

1929, Division 1.
Arsenal (a) 1-0   Att. 40,365
Weaver

1935, Division 2.
Nottingham Forest (h) 5-1   Att. 24,000
Fairhurst (2), Harris, J. Smith (2)

1940, Wartime.
Leeds United (a) 2-3   Att. 3,000
Billington, Gordon (pen)

1946, Division 2.
Luton Town (a) 3-4   Att. 25,410
Bentley, Shackleton, Wayman

1957, Division 1.
Arsenal (a) 3-2   Att. 41,649
Hughes, R. Mitchell (2)

1963, Division 2.
Bury (a) 2-1   Att. 9,848
Thomas, Opponent (og)

1968, Division 1.
Southampton (h) 4-1   Att. 29,515
Dyson, Foggon, B. Robson (2)

1974, Division 1.
Manchester City (h) 2-1   Att. 37,684
Macdonald, Howard

1985, Division 1.
Leicester City (h) 2-1   Att. 17,311
Clarke, Beardsley

1986, Division 1.
West Ham United (h) 4-0   Att. 22,077
McDonald, A. Thomas (2), D. Jackson

1991, Division 2.
Barnsley (a) 0-3   Att. 9,648

1994, Coca Cola Cup 4th round.
Manchester City 1   Newcastle 1
Rosler 69   Jeffrey 11
Att. 25,162

1996, Premier League.
Newcastle 1   Arsenal 2
Shearer 21   Dixon 11
Wright 60
Att. 36,565

Playing record for this day... 16 games, Won 10, Drawn 2, Lost 4, GF 41, GA 25. Today's success rate... 68.75%.

December 1

Played on this day

1894, Division 2.
    Grimsby Town (a) 1-4   Att. 1,500
    Thompson
1900, Division 1.
    Sheffield Wednesday (a) 2-2 Att. 12,000
    Peddie, Niblo
1906, Division 1.
    Notts County (h) 4-3   Att. 20,000
    Appleyard (2), Speedie, Veitch
1923, Division 1.
    Burnley (a) 2-3   Att. 8,000
    Seymour, Harris
1928, Division 1.
    Bolton Wanderers (h) 4-1   Att. 30,000
    Boyd, McCurley, MacKenzie, Wilkinson
1934, Division 2.
    Southampton (h) 1-0   Att. 16,000
    Lang
1945, Wartime.
    Blackburn Rovers (a) 2-1   Att. 14,600
    Stubbins (2)
1951, Division 1.
    Derby County (h) 2-1   Att. 49,880
    G. Robledo (2)
1956, Division 1.
    Wolverhampton W. (h) 2-1 Att. 37,562
    Curry, White
1962, Division 2.
    Bury (a) 0-0   Att. 12,633
1979, Division 2.
    Fulham (h) 2-0   Att. 23,485
    Rafferty, Withe
1984, Division 1.
    Stoke City (h) 2-1   Att. 21,564
    Waddle, Anderson (pen)
1990, Division 2.
    Leicester City (a) 4-5   Att. 11,045
    Quinn (3), O'Brien
1997, Premier League.
    Bolton Wanderers 1 Newcastle 0
    Blake 22   Att. 24,494
2001, Premier League.
    Charlton Athletic 1 Newcastle 1
    Macdonald 83   Speed 73
        Att. 24,151

2002, Premier League.
    Newcastle 2   **Everton 1**
    Shearer 86   Campbell 17
    Opponent (og) 89   Att. 51,607

Playing record for this day... 16 games,
Won 9, Drawn 3, Lost 4, GF 31, GA 25.
Today's success rate... 65.63%.

Match of the Day from 2002

SHEARER'S STUNNER SAVES UNITED
Sensational late show at St. James' Park

Everton's ascent towards the Premiership summit was halted in spectacular fashion by Alan Shearer before a deflected Craig Bellamy shot grabbed a sensational winner. David Moyes' team had seemed destined to secure victory and second position in the Premiership table, having bravely withstood the 22nd minute dismissal of Joseph Yobo until the final dramatic stages of this remarkable game. Kevin Campbell capitalised on Newcastle's defensive blunder to give Everton a lead that seemed safe until Shearer's breathtaking, 25-yard volley beat the impressive Richard Wright four minutes from time. It was the first goal Wright had conceded in the Premiership since Freddie Ljungberg's strike an incredible 62 days ago. However, three minutes later he was picking the ball out of the net again, beaten this time by Bellamy's fortuitous effort which denied Everton their seventh successive league victory.

Everton, by far the Premier League's form team, started the better and Campbell gave them a seemingly unassailable lead in the seventeenth minute when he evaded the attention of ball-watching centre halves, Andy O'Brien and Steve Caldwell. Latching onto David Unsworth's raking through-pass, he killed the ball instantly with his chest, and slipped it past a hesitant Shay Given. Yobo was then sent off just five minutes later by referee Mike Halsey when he brought down Bellamy on the edge of the penalty area as the striker careered goalwards. With Wright looking invincible, however, Yobo's intervention was probably unnecessary and the goalkeeper underlined his resurgence under Moyes' leadership when he expertly tipped over Shearer's powerful header from Laurent Robert's corner shortly before the interval.

Yobo's dismissal forced Moyes to sacrifice Lee Carsley and send on David Weir who proved a valuable stand-in. Indeed Everton, thanks to Wright's heroics, seemed to have weathered all United could throw at them, but, there was absolutely nothing Wright could do to prevent Shearer's stunning equaliser. Shearer described the goal as one of the top three strikes of his illustrious career, Bobby Robson couldn't recall him ever hitting a better strike than the "perfect shot" which was needed to beat Wright in that form. Moyes went even further by calling the Newcastle striker the best in the Premiership, the goal being all the proof needed. If the equaliser was deserved and spectacular the winner was cruel on Everton and totally bizarre. In the 89th minute Bellamy, quickly seizing on a half chance in the penalty area, hit a shot which took a deflection off Lie Tie and past the stranded Wright into the net. Newcastle had completed an amazing comeback to the tumultuous roars of an ecstatic Toon Army.

Newcastle United
Given, Griffin, O'Brien, Caldwell (Ameobi 81), Bernard, Solano, Dyer, Speed (Viana 81), Robert, Shearer, Bellamy.

Everton
Wright, Hibbert, Yobo, Stubbs, Unsworth, Carsley (Weir 25), Gravesen, Lie Tie, Pembridge, Campbell, Radzinski (Rooney 73).

Referee Mr. M. Halsey (Lancashire).

Alan Shearer scores a superb equalizing goal.

Birthdays

Arthur Frost born today in 1915.
Centre-forward 1939, Apps 5. Goals 1.

December 2

Match of the Day from 1950

VICTORY OVER MANCHESTER UNITED A STROLL, THANKS TO WALKER
Magpies pinch the points at Old Trafford

A scrappy game in rotten conditions was won by Newcastle by the odd goal in three at Old Trafford today. It was on the whole a poor game spoilt by the muddy pitch which accounted for some wayward passing and under hit defensive clearances. There were few exceptions but for the home side Carey and Allen performed well whilst Harvey and Walker starred for Newcastle.

Manchester United's problems were confounded by their continued use of the long, high ball which was easily dealt with by Frank Brennan who was head and shoulders above the Reds' forwards Rowley and Pearson. When the home side eventually played the ball forward along the ground they found it easier to beat the Newcastle defence and Rowley was able to create two fine chances. Pearson was a just a yard too late to pick up the first, but Birch darted after the second with lightening acceleration and went on to flick the ball over Fairbrother to give Manchester United the lead.

Newcastle's equalising goal scored by Hannah was equally refreshing to see coming from the out-of-position Corbett who was asked to move from left back to left wing before the game. After Corbett had forced the game's most notable save from Allen early on he laid on the perfect cross for Hannah to chase in and prod the ball home for a simple yet devastating finish.

United's second goal was the result of some comical defending in the Reds' penalty area resulting in a soft winning strike from the creator Tommy Walker. Manchester United's defence was caught in an almighty tangle and had ignored the time-honoured rule of getting the ball clear at the first opportunity. They didn't on this occasion but luckily this particular melee ended with the ball trickling wide for a corner. Walker miscued his corner kick into the centre and the stray ball travelled low towards the penalty area, again the home side did everything possible to prevent a scoring chance and when the loose ball popped back out towards Walker he delicately chipped it back over the head of the advancing Allen. No blame could be attached to the hapless keeper, on the contrary, but for him Newcastle would have sewn up this game by a far bigger margin.

Manchester United
Allen, Carey, Aston, Gibson, Chilton, Cockburn, Birkett, Pearson, Rowley, Birch, McShane.

Newcastle United
Fairbrother, Cowell, McMichael, Harvey, Brennan, Crowe, Walker, Taylor, Robledo, Hannah, Corbett.

A clinical finish by George Hannah grabbed a deserved equaliser against Manchester United.

Birthdays

David Batty born today 1968.
Midfield 1996-1998, Apps 114 (2 subs). Goals 4.
Jimmy Kerray born today in 1935.
Midfield 1962-1963, Apps 40. Goals 10.

...yed on this day

Division 1.
West Bromwich A. (h) 3-0   Att. 16,000
Aitken, Peddie, Rogers
Division 1.
Blackburn Rovers (h) 1-0   Att. 20,000
McClarence
Newcastle hit the top spot for the first time during the 1904-05 Championship winning season.
Division 1.
Bradford City (h) 6-1   Att. 18,000
Stewart, Shepherd (3), Higgins (2)
Division 1.
Middlesbrough (h) 0-0   Att. 40,000
Division 1.
Middlesbrough (h) 0-0   Att. 50,000
Division 1.
Liverpool (h) 1-1   Att. 20,000
McKay
Division 1.
Leeds United (h) 3-1   Att. 22,000
Allen (2), Lang
Division 2.
Manchester City (a) 1-4   Att. 45,000
Cairns
Division 1.
Manchester United (a) 1-1   Att. 38,000
Walker
Division 1.
Bolton Wanderers (h) 3-0   Att. 36,856
Davies, Keeble (2)
Division 1.
Bolton Wanderers (a) 1-2   Att. 12,921
White
Division 1.
Southampton (a) 0-2   Att. 21,488
League Cup 5th round.
Notts County (h) 1-0   Att. 31,114
Opponent (og)
Division 1.
Leicester City (h) 2-0   Att. 20,112
Burns, Nattrass
Division 2.
Derby County (a) 2-3   Att. 18,691
Waddle, Keegan
Full Members Cup 3rd round.
Everton (a) 2-5   Att. 7,530
A. Thomas (2)
Division 1.
Luton Town (a) 0-0   Att. 8,338
Premier League.
Tottenham H. 4   Newcastle 2
Sheringham   Fox 30, 42
5, 39, 71
Popescu 80   Att. 28,002
Premier League.
Wimbledon 3   Newcastle 3
Holdsworth 18, 65   Ferdinand 9, 29
Ekoku 21   Gillespie 35
   Att. 18,002
This was Newcastle's 100th Premier League match.
UEFA Cup 3rd round, 2nd leg.
Newcastle 2   Metz 0
Asprilla 80, 82   Att. 35,641
Newcastle won 3-1 on aggregate

record for this day... 20 games,
Drawn 6, Lost 6, GF 34, GA 27.
success rate... 55%.

Match of the Day from 1910

BRADFORD WELL BEATEN

Higgins benefit match brings 6-1 win for Newcastle

A crowd of 18,000 turned out at St. James' Park today to see Newcastle play Bradford City in Division One. It was also a benefit match for Sandy Higgins, and the home side were lacking some reliable regulars in their side. Veitch, Howie, Rutherford and Whitson were all out for various reasons, and in Tony Whitson's place was Frank Hudspeth, making his debut.

The match started well for both teams, and for a while it looked like it would be close to the end. Then Shepherd opened the scoring for the home side, and everything changed. The first goal for Newcastle boosted the team's performance, and from then on they only way was up.

The second goal for the home team who fell to Shepherd, and was perfectly placed to double the lead. The home side went into the interval two goals ahead, but there were plenty more to come in the second half.

Albert Shepherd scored the next straight after play resumed in the second period, completing his hat-trick. Then just a few minutes later Newcastle's lead was extended further when a header from Stewart brought the tally to four.

With still only 55 minutes on the clock, Higgins added his name to the score-sheet when he was fouled and the referee awarded a penalty to Newcastle. He stepped up to the spot and took the kick confidently and calmly, the ball sailing straight past the Bradford goalkeeper to put the home team five goals ahead.

Bradford finally managed to answer back, but the goal from Spiers did little to ease the misery of the visiting side. Newcastle still had the energy to run rings around the visitors side, and it was inevitable that another goal would come their way.

The sixth and final goal came from Higgins again, and the game was over for Bradford. The visitors tried hard to make a go of it at the end, but it was too little too late. Final score 6-1.

Newcastle United
Lawrence, McCracken, Hudspeth, Jobey, Low, McWilliam, Duncan, Higgins, Shepherd, Stewart, Anderson.
Bradford City
Maskrey, Campbell, Chaplin, Robinson, Taylor, Hampton, Bond, Speirs, O'Rourke, Devine, Handley.

Bill McCracken

Birthdays

John Burridge born today in 1951.
Goalkeeper 1989-1991, Apps 84.
Newcastle Coach 1993-1996.

Sadly Missed

Neil Harris died on this day in 1941.
Centre-forward 1920-1925, Apps 194. Goals 101.

December 4

Match of the Day from 1993

REAL 'ROY OF THE ROVERS' STUFF

Beardsley stunner wins thriller at Spurs

A full house today at White Hart Lane and a game of wonderful excitement and quality as the fresh faces and talents of Barmby and Anderton, Cole and Clark, ran at defenders, twisting and turning and whipping in crosses that sparked memories of the glory days of football. All this and then there was Peter Beardsley at his best, it does not get much better than this. The tone of the afternoon was set in the opening twenty minutes, when the sparkling sunshine matched the pulsating football. Tottenham's gifted midfield with Samways and Hazard probed away with accurate passes which their manager Ossie Ardilles would have been proud of. The new look United defence with makeshift centre back Barry Venison were at times in chaos, but, with Sol Campbell as a makeshift forward for the home side, Spurs never looked capable of troubling United keeper Hooper.

Indeed despite some horrendous defensive errors Spurs were handed just one genuine scoring chance when Mike Reed awarded them a penalty in the 61st minute. Barmby made no mistake from the twelve-yard shot much to the relief of the Spurs' fans who had been silenced by Beardsley's opening goal six minutes into the second half, a simple finish for the maestro this time. His second goal with just moments of the game remaining was a cracker. Andy Cole was obstructed just beyond the halfway line and, springing to his feet, released Beardsley before Spurs even clicked that a free kick had been awarded and taken. Beardsley ran at and passed a couple of dazzled defenders before sending a screaming drive wide of the despairing outstretched right hand of Thorstvedt and into the top corner, the sort of goal Roy of the Rovers only dreams of scoring.

A memorable winner by Beardsley and a performance which was described by Kevin Keegan as the best he had seen.

Tottenham Hotspur

Thorsvedt, Kerslake (Austin 75), Calderwood, Sedgley, Edinburgh, Samways, Hazard, Caskey, Anderton, Barmby, Campbell (Dozell 61).

Newcastle United

Hooper, Watson, Venison, Howey, Elliott, Lee, Bracewell, Clark, Jeffrey, Beardsley, Cole.

Referee Mr. M. Reed (Birmingham).

Peter Beardsley scores the opening goal.

Birthdays

Les O'Neil born today in 1943.
Midfield 1961-1965, Apps 1. Goals 0.

Played on this day

1897, Division 2.
Gainsborough Trinity (a) 3-1   Att. 700
Campbell, Harvey, Ostler
1909, Division 1.
Liverpool (a) 5-6   Att. 20,000
Shepherd (4), Howie
A remarkable come back by the home side after Newcastle led 5-2 at half time.
1920, Division 1.
Aston Villa (h) 2-1   Att. 25,000
Seymour, Smailes
1926, Division 1.
West Ham United (h) 2-0   Att. 36,000
Gallacher, Seymour
1937, Division 2.
Sheffield Wednesday (h) 1-0   Att. 9,500
Mooney
1943, Wartime.
Middlesbrough (a) 1-1   Att. 3,500
Stubbins
1948, Division 1.
Manchester United(a) 1-1   Att. 70,787
Stobbart
Played at Maine Road
1954, Division 1.
Sheffield Wednesday (a) 3-0 Att. 15,000
Broadis, R. Mitchell, White
1971, Division 1.
Chelsea (h) 0-0   Att. 37,586
1974, League Cup 5th round.
Chester City (h) 0-0   Att. 31,656
1976, Division 1.
Arsenal (a) 3-5   Att. 35,000
Gowling, Burns (2)
1982, Division 2.
Charlton Athletic (a) 0-2   Att. 10,381
1993, Premier League.
Tottenham H. 1   Newcastle 2
Barmby 61 (pen)   Beardsley 55, 90
Att. 30,780
1999, Premier League.
Aston Villa 0   Newcastle 1
Ferguson 65
Att. 34,531

Playing record for this day... 14 games,
Won 7, Drawn 4, Lost 3, GF 24, GA 18.
Today's success rate... 64.29%.

December 5

1891, FA Cup Qualifying round 4.
Bishop Auckland (h) 7-0   Att. 1,000
Crate, Sorely (2), Thompson (3), unknown
1896, Division 2.
Burton Wanderers (a) 1-0   Att. 2,000
Aitken
1903, Division 1.
Blackburn Rovers (a) 0-4   Att. 8,000
1908, Division 1.
Sunderland (h) 1-9   Att. 56,000
Shepherd (pen)
*United's record home defeat, and the
Magpies still lifted the championship.*
1914, Division 1.
Bolton Wanderers (h) 1-2   Att. 15,000
Hibbert
1925, Division 1.
West Bromwich A. (a) 0-4   Att. 10,000
1931, Division 1.
Portsmouth (h) 0-0   Att. 30,000
1936, Division 2.
Southampton (a) 0-2   Att. 16,038
1942, Wartime.
Sunderland (a) 5-3   Att. 7,000
Walker, Stubbins (4)
*Stubbins nets his second hat trick in
consecutive games*
1953, Division 1.
Chelsea (h) 1-1   Att. 41,728
Mitchell
1959, Division 1.
Arsenal (h) 4-1   Att. 40,031
Allchurch (2), White (2)
1964, Division 2.
Portsmouth (h) 3-0   Att. 29,135
Hockey, Iley, Anderson
1970, Division 1.
Chelsea (a) 0-1   Att. 39,413
1973, Texaco Cup 2nd round, 2nd leg.
Birmingham City (h) 3-1   Att. 9,762
Tudor (2), Clark
Newcastle won the tie 4-2 on aggregate.
1981, Division 2.
Blackburn Rovers (h) 0-0   Att. 18,775
1987, Division 1.
Oxford United (a) 3-1   Att. 8,190
McDonald (pen), O'Neill, Mirandinha
1992, Division 1.
Notts County (a) 2-0   Att. 14,840
Sheedy, Peacock

Playing record for this day... 17 games,
Won 8, Drawn 3, Lost 6, GF 31, GA 29.
Today's success rate... 55.88%.

Match of the Day from 1973

TEN MAN NEWCASTLE SHATTER BRUM'S HOPES

Smith off in the first minute but United rally to gain an emphatic victory

A game filled with incident from the kick off today at St. James' Park saw Newcastle end Birmingham City's Texaco Cup run in the second round. Within seconds of the start Birmingham full-back Tony Want, in attempting a regulation long clearance, was clattered by a terribly high and late challenge from Jimmy Smith. There was a sickening crack which resounded around the ground and immediately players and medics rushed to Want's aid, referee Ted Jolly without hesitation sent off Smith without any complaint from Newcastle at all. The game was held up for a full nine minutes whilst a splint was made for the injury, later confirmed by X-rays showing a fracture of both tibia and fibula bones in the full-back's left leg.

Within a minute of the game resuming Birmingham were hit with another blow, only this time a legitimate piece of brilliance by John Tudor. Latching onto a loose ball he raced 30 yards before unleashing a superb left-foot drive which beat keeper Dave Latchford and sailed into the top corner of the net. The ten-man Magpies were proving far too skilful for the visitors who hadn't yet mounted any serious attack on goal before it was 2-0 in the 26th minute. This time the sensational finish was supplied by Frank Clark, his wonderful curling shot from 30 yards was only his second goal for United in eleven years at St. James' Park. Newcastle were rampant and the 9,762 crowd were now, after slowly coming out of their initial shock, right behind a fabulous Newcastle display. After 43 minutes Tudor, with his second goal, made it 3-0 with another spectacular shot from twenty yards and the tie was effectively over for Birmingham.

Understandably Newcastle's attacking dominance subsided in the second half, particularly when Terry McDermott limped off four minutes after the restart. Birmingham began to fight back and on 65 minutes almost pulled a goal back with a fantastic effort by Joe Gallagher which was brilliantly turned onto the bar by Iam McFaul, but the rebound was fluffed by Gallagher's defensive partner Roger Hynd from close range. At the other end David Crosson hit the bar with a thundering drive, before the Blues eventually got their consolation fifteen minutes from the end. This too was a lovely goal scored by Trevor Francis with the game's fourth long-range strike. McFaul had little chance of saving nor too Crosson who desperately tried to clear it off the line with a brave lunge. After this United correctly closed ranks and gave Birmingham no chance of a second goal. The teams meet again in a league match in three days time with both team's managers freely admitting they are getting sick of the sight of one another.

Newcastle United
McFaul, Crosson, F. Clark, McDermott (Gibb 49), Howard, Nattrass, Barrowclough, Smith, Tudor, Robson, Hibbitt.
Birmingham City
D. Latchford, Gallagher, Want (D. Clark 1), Jenkins, Hynd, Burns, Campbell, Francis, R. Latchford, Hatton, Hendrie.
Referee Mr. T. Jolly (Manchester).

Birthdays

Ron McGarry born today in 1937.
Centre-forward 1962-1967, Apps 132
(3 subs). Goals 46.

December 6

Match of the Day from 1975

COVENTRY LOSE AGAIN
Newcastle take points in good show at St. James' Park

27,172 turned up at St. James' Park today to see Newcastle play Coventry City in Division One. Coventry were hoping to end their run of bad luck at this ground, they had not won a match here since the war, and their previous three visits cost them dearly with a total of twelve goals against them.

Newcastle were quietly confident of winning the points, and their early play certainly showed promise of what was to come. The home fans were in for a treat, and the visitors would be left wishing they hadn't bothered to turn up. Again.

Coventry's David Cross had a lot to answer for in the way this game turned out. He had several early chances, but each one of them failed to amount to anything.

Mahoney in the Newcastle goal had just one good save to make in the whole match. Again it was Cross who was disappointed when his header seemed to be going in, but Mahoney managed to touch the ball over the crossbar to safety.

Coventry's Mortimer was booked on sixteen minutes for a deliberate foul on Kennedy, then seventeen minutes into the game Newcastle took the lead with a super shot from David Craig. His header gave King no chance to make the save, and the home side were one up.

Coventry had already started to wonder if their bad luck was continuing here, and they were going to get a clear answer before the game was out. For now, Newcastle were enjoying watching their opponents struggle, and before the half-time break it was Tommy Craig's turn to add his name to the score-sheet. His inch-perfect 25-yard shot sailed into the net past King, and Newcastle were two goals ahead going into the break.

Six minutes into the second half the home side added another to their tally. Micky Burns was the man to beat the Coventry keeper this time, and the visitors were now realising that their run of poor luck was not going to end on this visit to St. James' Park.

On 67 minutes Coop brought down Tommy Craig in the penalty area, and a spot kick was awarded. Craig himself took the kick, and his sure shot flew into the net for Newcastle's fourth.

Coventry were fortunate to only lose by four goals. Macdonald and Gowling both had shots cleared off the goal-line, but Hutchison also put in several good efforts. The game ended, to Coventry's relief, with no further goals being scored.

Newcastle United
Mahoney, Nattrass, Kennedy, Nulty, D. Craig, Howard, Burns, Barrowclough, Macdonald, Gowling, T. Craig.
Coventry City
King, Coop, Brogan, Dugdale, Hindley, Holmes, Powell, Mortimer, Cross, Green, Hutchison.

Played on this day

1890, FA Cup Qualifying round 2.
Sunderland Albion (h) 2-2   Att. 4,000
Scorers unknown
1902, Division 1.
Nottingham Forest (h) 0-2   Att. 12,000
1913, Division 1.
Middlesbrough (a) 0-3   Att. 17,000
1919, Division 1.
Sheffield United (a) 1-2   Att. 35,000
Hall
1924, Division 1.
Tottenham Hotspur (h) 1-1   Att. 28,000
Seymour
1930, Division 1.
Manchester City (a) 0-2   Att. 20,000
1941, Wartime.
Middlesbrough (a) 7-0   Att. 3,000
Stubbins (5), Short, Woollett
1947, Division 2.
Tottenham Hotspur (h) 1-0   Att. 57,950
Milburn
1952, Division 1.
Bolton Wanderers (a) 2-4   Att. 41,420
Keeble, Walker
1958, Division 1.
Burnley (h) 5-2   Att. 42,561
Allchurch (2), White, Eastham, Bell (pen)
1969, Division 1.
Stoke City (a) 1-0   Att. 17,767
Robson
1975, Division 1.
Coventry City (h) 4-0   Att. 27,172
T. Craig (2, 1 pen), Burns, D. Craig
1986, Division 1.
Charlton Athletic (a) 1-1   Att. 7,333
Goddard
1997, Premier League.
Newcastle 0   Arsenal 1
   Wright 36
    Att. 36,751
1998, Premier League.
Middlesbrough 2   Newcastle 2
Townsend 13   Charvet 38
Cooper 59   Dabizas 83
    Att. 34,629

Playing record for this day... 15 games,
Won 5, Drawn 4, Lost 6, GF 27, GA 22.
Today's success rate... 46.67%.

Birthdays

Ian Bogie born today in 1967.
Midfield 1985-1989, Apps 22 (11 subs). Goals 1.
Peter Kelly born today in 1956.
Right-back 1973-1981, Apps 38 (2 subs).
Goals 0.
David Mills born today in 1951.
Midfield 1982 & 1983-1984, Apps 41 (8 subs).
Goals 9.

Sadly Missed

Ted Robledo died on this day in 1970, aged 42.
Midfield 1949-1953, Apps 47. Goals 0.

Played on this day

1895, Division 2.
Burton Swifts (a) 1-3   Att. 2,000
Wardrope
1901, Division 1.
Aston Villa (a) 0-0   Att. 20,000
1907, Division 1.
Everton (h) 2-1   Att. 30,000
Appleyard (pen), Rutherford
1912, Division 1.
Notts County (a) 1-0   Att. 10,000
Peart
1929, Division 1.
Aston Villa (h) 2-2   Att. 35,000
Gallacher (pen), Weaver
1935, Division 2.
Norwich City (a) 0-1   Att. 11,998
1940, Wartime.
Hull City (h) 3-1   Att. 3,000
Nevins, Stubbins (2)
1946, Division 2.
Plymouth Argyle (h) 3-2   Att. 47,661
Bentley (3)
1957, Division 1.
Bolton Wanderers (h) 1-2   Att. 29,886
Eastham
1963, Division 2.
Scunthorpe United (h) 3-1   Att. 24,988
Suddick, Penman, Thomas
1968, Division 1.
Stoke City (a) 0-1   Att. 11,594
1974, Division 1.
Tottenham Hotspur (a) 0-3   Att. 23,422
1985, Division 1.
Luton Town (a) 0-2   Att. 10,319
1991, Division 2.
Port Vale (h) 2-2   Att. 18,162
Makel, Peacock (pen)
2002, Premier League.
Aston Villa 0   Newcastle 1
                Shearer 81
                Att. 33,446

Playing record for this day... 15 games,
Won 6, Drawn 3, Lost 6, GF 19, GA 21.
Today's success rate... 50%.

Match of the Day from 1907

UNITED LUCKY TO TAKE WIN
Everton put up a good fight at St. James' Park

Newcastle United played host to Everton today at St. James' Park for this Division One match in front of a crowd of 30,000. The visitors had three reserves in their line-up, and Newcastle had one. This gave the home side a small, but significant advantage over their opponents.

Play was quite even throughout most of the game, and it was hard to separate the two teams in effort and skill. There were chances at both ends, and both keepers had work to do to keep the ball out of the net.

On the half-hour mark Everton were awarded a penalty and Maconnachie stepped up to the spot to take the kick. He misjudged his shot and the ball failed to hit its target and Newcastle were safe again.

The home side stepped up the pressure after this and the Everton defence were bombarded with attempts to get through.

Lawrence, in the Newcastle goal, had two super efforts to save before the half-time break, both of which he managed without too much difficulty. At half-time the score remained 0-0.

The second half began with increased pressure from the Newcastle side. A fine shot from McWilliam forced a great save from Scott in the Everton goal, but with more attempts at goal, the more likely it was that the ball would eventually cross the line at one end or the other.

Jones hoped he would be the one to break the deadlock for Everton, but his fluffed kick meant that he missed the ball completely from just six yards out. However, fifteen minutes into the half it was Everton who scored first. Settle was the man to finally get the ball past Lawrence.

Newcastle had some work to do now to get back in the game, and they managed to improve their play instantly. With fifteen minutes left on the clock the equaliser arrived after a corner from Ridley. Jackie Rutherford got to the ball, and sent it into the back of the net with ease to bring the scores level.

Newcastle had enough time left to take the win, and they stepped up their efforts even further to ensure they scored again. Everton too increased the pace of their game, and again it was evenly matched. Almost on the final whistle Newcastle were awarded a penalty and Appleyard stepped up to the spot to take the kick. His shot was perfectly placed to beat the Everton keeper, and Newcastle were in the lead in the dying minutes. Final score 2-1.

Newcastle United
Lawrence, McCombie, Pudan, Gardner, Veitch, McWilliam, Rutherford, Howie, Appleyard, Orr, Ridley.
Everton
Scott, Stevenson, Crelley, Makepeace, Maconnachie, Abbott, Sharp, Bolton, Jones, Settle, Hardman.

Colin Veitch

December 8

Match of the Day from 1923

BURNLEY BURNED OUT

Newcastle register easy win at home

Burnley were the visitors today at St. James' Park for this Division One match in front of 25,000 supporters. A strong wind was blowing, making control of the ball difficult, but the game was still a fast-paced affair.

Newcastle went on the attack immediately, and it took just nine minutes for the first goal to arrive. It was McDonald who was the man to beat the Burnley keeper and put United into an early lead, and he did it with style. The ball zipped into the net with the keeper not even having a chance to see it, let alone try to make a save.

Further attempts came from both sides, and the rest of the first half was full of half-chances that were fluffed or lost. Both keepers had a good workout, and the defences were as busy as the forwards. With the two sides so evenly matched, it was frustrating that neither had the ability to break through again.

In the second half Newcastle began to play notably better football than their opponents. Their tactics had purpose, and it showed in the way they carried on.

The growing difference between the two sides was highlighted when Seymour netted the second goal for Newcastle, and the visitors caved in. They didn't try to fight back, and the heavy pitch was taking such a toll, that they couldn't find the energy to push.

So, the game ended flatly, with no further attacks from Newcastle either. They had done enough to secure their well earned win. Final score 2-0.

Newcastle United
Bradley, Hampson, Hudspeth, Curry, Mooney, Gibson, Aitken, Cowan, Harris, McDonald, Seymour.

Burnley
Dawson, Smelt, Taylor, Bassnett, Hill, Watson, Bennie, Kelly, Beel, Cross, Waterfield.

Billy Aitken

Played on this day

1900, Division 1.
Sheffield United (a) 0-2   Att. 15,000
1906, Division 1.
Sheffield United (a) 0-0   Att. 16,000
1923, Division 1.
Burnley (h) 2-0   Att. 25,000
Seymour, McDonald
1928, Division 1.
Sheffield Wednesday (a) 1-3 Att. 25,000
Gallacher (pen)
1934, Division 2.
Bolton Wanderers (a) 0-1   Att. 21,000
1945, Wartime.
Blackburn Rovers (h) 8-1   Att. 33,092
Stubbins (5), Wayman (2), Hair
1951, Division 1.
Aston Villa (a) 2-2   Att. 32,884
Duncan (2)
1956, Division 1.
Bolton Wanderers (a) 1-3   Att. 25,131
Davies
1962, Division 2.
Rotherham United (h) 4-1   Att. 21,955
Tuohy, Kerray, Hale (2)
1971, Texaco Cup Semi Final, 2nd leg.
Derby County (h) 2-3   Att. 37,000
Macdonald, Barrowclough
Newcastle lost 4-2 on aggregate
1973, Division 1.
Birmingham City (a) 0-1   Att. 25,428
1979, Division 2.
Luton Town (a) 1-1   Att. 14,845
Rafferty
1984, Division 1.
Tottenham Hotspur (a) 1-3   Att. 29,695
Waddle
1992, Anglo Italian Cup International Stage, Group A.
Bari (a) 0-3   Att. 1,229

Playing record for this day... 14 games, Won 3, Drawn 3, Lost 8, GF 22, GA 24. Today's success rate... 32.14%.

Birthdays

Les Ferdinand born today in 1966.
Centre-forward 1995-1997, Apps 84 (2 subs).
Goals 50.

Terry McDermott born today in 1951.
Midfield & Assistant Manager 1973-1974 & 1992-1998, Apps 168 (1 sub). Goals 24.

December 9

Played on this day

1893, Division 2.
Notts County (h) 3-0   Att. 4,000
Wallace (2), Thompson

1905, Division 1.
Notts County (h) 3-1   Att. 17,073
Appleyard, J. Rutherford, Veitch

1911, Division 1.
Liverpool (a) 1-0   Att. 15,000
Stewart

1922, Division 1.
Liverpool (h) 0-1   Att. 30,000

1925, Division 1.
Sheffield United (h) 3-1   Att. 13,000
Mordue, Cowan, Hudspeth (pen)

1933, Division 1.
Wolverhampton W. (a) 1-2   Att. 17,000
J.R. Richardson

1939, Wartime.
Hull City (h) 3-0   Att. 2,500
Cairns, Clifton, Duns

1944, Wartime.
Hartlepool United (h) 3-0   Att. 12,000
Stubbins (2), Milburn

1950, Division 1.
Wolverhampton W. (h) 1-1   Att. 48,492
Walker

1967, Division 1.
Manchester United (h) 2-2   Att. 48,639
Iley, T. Robson

1972, Division 1.
Southampton (h) 0-0   Att. 20,436

1978, Division 2.
Stoke City (h) 2-0   Att. 23,459
Connolly, Withe

1989, Division 2.
Oxford United (h) 2-3   Att. 16,645
Stimson, Quinn (pen)

1995, Premier League.
Chelsea 1   Newcastle 0
Petrescu 42   Att. 31,098

1996, Premier League.
Nottingham F. 0   Newcastle 0
                              Att. 25,762

1999, UEFA Cup 3rd round, 2nd leg.
Newcastle 0   A.S. Roma 0
                              Att. 35,739
Newcastle lost 1-0 on aggregate.

2000, Premier League.
Arsenal 5   Newcastle 0
Henry 13
Parlour 16, 86, 90
Kanu 52   Att. 38,052

2001, Premier League.
Ipswich Town 0   Newcastle 1
                   Solano 20
                              Att. 24,749

Playing record for this day... 18 games.
Won 8, Drawn 5, Lost 5. GF 25, GA 17.
Today's success rate... 58.33%.

Match of the Day from 1905

TOO MUCH FOR NOTTS

United ignore the cold to pull off warm win at St. James' Park

Notts County made the trip up to St. James' Park today to meet Newcastle in Division One. A crowd of 17,073 had braved the bitterly cold weather to come and watch the match, and the home supporters would not be disappointed with their team's performance.

Newcastle were in control of the game from the very start. The forwards were faultless in their efforts, and their shots brought about several superb saves from Reilly in the Notts County goal.

The home defence was strong and confident, and there was very little chance of the visiting forwards breaking through for a good attempt at goal. Lawrence had no saves to make at all in the first half, and it was a cold day for standing around so he did all he could to keep warm.

Before the interval Newcastle finally managed to score the elusive goal they so richly deserved after all their efforts. Appleyard was the man who put the ball past Reilly to put the home side ahead, and what a relief it was for the crowd.

In the second half Newcastle were again the better side. Just four minutes into the period Rutherford netted his team's second, and the game was slipping out of Notts County's sights. Then a foul on one of the Newcastle forwards resulted in the home side being awarded a penalty. Colin Veitch stepped up to the spot to take the kick, and the ball flew straight to Reilly. The County keeper knocked the ball out of the way, but it came back to Veitch who made sure his second chance wasn't lost. The ball sailed into the net to bring Newcastle's tally to three.

With the game almost over, Notts County tried hard for one last rally. They pooled all their efforts into an attack on the Newcastle goal, and it was successful. Tarplin managing to slot the ball past Lawrence, who by now was almost frozen solid, and the goal brought the score to 3-1.

It wasn't enough though, and the visitors went back home with no return. Newcastle had earned their win, and the team soon warmed up after the final whistle.

Newcastle United
Lawrence, Tildesley, Carr, Gardner, Veitch, McWilliam, J Rutherford, Howie, Appleyard, Orr, Gosnell.

Notts County
Reilly, Jones, Montgomery, Emberton, Humphreys, Craythorne, Harrison, Dean, Green, Tarplin, Gee.

Albert Gosnell

Birthdays

Peter Haddock born today in 1961.
Centre-half 1976-1986, Apps 65 (4 subs). Goals 0.

Match of the Day from 1997

UNITED MAKE MEAL OF 'CHICKEN' KIEV

Newcastle's European adventure finishes on a high

Newcastle, ended their Champions League campaign today as they started it, with a victory, this time however against a Dynamo Kiev side who did little more than go through the motions. Credit to United for their usual committed performance and shame on the Ukrainian champions who treated this game at St. James' Park almost as a testimonial. Apart from a ten-minute period shortly before and after the half-time interval, Dynamo regarded the game with almost contempt knowing the result was academic to their progress in the competition. They were soundly beaten and deservedly so for the 33,694 partisan Geordies who turned out to witness the spectacle.

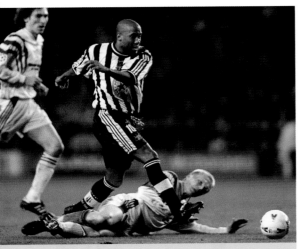

John Barnes rides the challenge of Dynamo Kiev's Andriy Gusin.

However half-hearted Dynamo were, Newcastle's two goals were sheer quality. The first, in the tenth minute, was scored by John Barnes but much credit must go to David Batty for a surging run down the right which saw him shrug off three challenges. Batty centred for Barnes, whose first touch controlled the ball while his second was an angled right-foot shot past Olexandr Shokovski from fifteen yards. Stuart Pearce made it 2-0 in the 21st minute with his first goal for United, which was a trademark shot from 25 yards. Pearce touched a free kick to Robert Lee, who stopped the ball for the centre back to curl past the diving Shokovski. Perhaps fearing a half-time blast from their manager Valery Lobanovsky, Dynamo then upped the tempo before the interval but found Shaka Hislop in inspired form. First he made a superb save from Vitaly Kossovsky's rising shot after a corner had only been partially cleared. Then the United keeper palmed away a close-range header from Sergei Rebrov, by far the best save of the night. That apart, Hislop was rarely troubled while Batty got forward more than in most games, as Dynamo's lacklustre midfield almost totally gave up.

A bonus for the Toon Army was the impressive performance of Aaron Hughes, who came on for Alessandro Pistone for the second half. Temura Ketsbaia, another second half sub, replaced the tiring Faustino Asprilla who must have set the record for the slowest walk off the field for a player being substituted. The Colombian was sadly still not match fit but still gave tremendous effort and was given a well earned standing ovation by the grateful St. James' Park crowd.

When the Champions' League began, it was thought that finishing above Barcelona would have guaranteed first place in the group. In fact, the Spanish champions finished bottom with Newcastle finishing in third spot.

Newcastle United

Hislop, Watson, Peacock, Albert, Pearce, Pistone (sub Hughes h/t), Gillespie, Batty, Lee, Barnes, Asprilla (sub Ketsbaia 57 mins).

Dynamo Kiev

Shovkovski, Volosianko (sub Nvenglinski 79 mins), Luzhny, Bezhenar, Dmitrulin, Kalitvintsev, Gusin, Mikhailenko, (sub Radchenko 79), Kossovsky, Rebrov, Shevchenko.

Referee Mr. H. Krug (Germany)

Birthdays

John Duncan born today in 1926.
Centre-forward 1950-1953, Apps 6. Goals 3.

December 11

Played on this day

1897, FA Cup Qualifying round 3.
Middlesbrough (a) 2-0   Att. 6,000
Wardrope, Harvey
1909, Division 1.
Aston Villa (h) 1-0   Att. 19,000
Higgins
1920, Division 1.
Aston Villa (a) 0-0   Att. 35,000
1926, Division 1.
Sheffield Wednesday (a) 2-3 Att. 35,000
McDonald, McKay
1943, Wartime.
Middlesbrough (h) 1-1   Att. 8,845
Dixon
1948, Division 1.
Sheffield United (h) 3-2   Att. 42,862
Milburn, Stobbart, Opponent (og)
1954, Division 1.
Portsmouth (h) 2-1   Att. 33,414
Keeble (2)
1965, Division 1.
West Ham United (a) 3-4   Att. 23,758
Robson, Bennett, Iley
1971, Division 1.
West Bromwich A. (a) 3-0   Att. 18,036
Busby, Macdonald (2)
1974, Texaco Cup Final, 2nd leg.
Southampton (h) 3-0   Att. 20,615
Tudor, Bruce, Cannell
Newcastle won 3-1 on aggregate
1982, Division 2.
Wolverhampton W. (h) 1-1   Att. 19,595
Wharton
1993, Premier League.
Newcastle 1   Manchester United 1
Cole 71   Ince 59
                             Att. 36,388
2002, Champions League, Group A.
Barcelona 3   Newcastle 1
Dani 7   Ameobi 24
Kluivert 35
Motta 58   Att. 45,100

Playing record for this day... 13 games,
Won 6, Drawn 4, Lost 3, GF 23, GA 16.
Today's success rate... 61.54%.

Match of the Day from 1974

PRICELESS TUDOR

Newcastle keep the Texaco Cup thanks to superb goal

Newcastle were hosting this Texaco Cup final second leg at St. James' Park today in front of a crowd of 20,615. The home side had a lot of catching up to do as the first leg had ended 1-0 to Southampton at the Dell. The Tynesiders were determined that they were not going to lose their hold on the cup, and they needed a huge effort if they were going to succeed.

So, the game began, and Newcastle were soon on top. They did not let the pressure get to them, and their game was tactful and patient. The first half passed by quickly with no real attacks of note from either side.

In the second half, Newcastle's efforts increased further, and their play became even more intense. Hudson was taken off the field after 63 minutes and was replaced by Tudor. This seemed to be the catalyst that finally brought about the change of fortune for the home side.

Paul Cannell

Nine minutes after his introduction Tudor gave Newcastle the goal they so richly deserved, and with it came the real hope of victory. It was a lucky shot, only coming to Tudor after Turner had knocked the ball away from goal when Macdonald had attempted to score.

Still, it was enough to bring the aggregate scores level, and Newcastle had won themselves the chance to retain the Texaco Cup. The 90 minutes ended with no further change to the score, so extra time was to be played.

Eight minutes into the extra time Southampton defender Steele was sent off for a second bookable offence, and Newcastle seized upon the advantage this gave them. Five minutes later the home side took the lead with a super shot from Bruce, the ball sailing into the net from twelve yards out.

The win was secured for Newcastle just two minutes later when a centre from Tudor came to Cannell, who got his head to the ball and nodded it home for a third.

United had done it. They had beaten Southampton against the odds to retain their hold on the Texaco Cup.

Newcastle United
McFaul, Nattrass, Clark, Hudson (Tudor), Laughton, Howard, Burns, Kennedy, Macdonald, Cannell, Bruce.
Southampton
Turner, McCarthy, Mills, Fisher, Steele, Blyth, Stokes, Channon, Osgood, Peach, O'Brien.

Toon News Extra

1937... Bad light stops play

Newcastle's Division Two fixture away at Chesterfield was abandoned today with just thirteen minutes of the game remaining. Chesterfield were ahead 1-0 at the time and when the game was replayed on April 25 they doubled that score resulting in a 2-0 defeat for the Magpies.

December 12

Match of the Day from 1936

SWANS SINK AT ST. JAMES' PARK

Newcastle beat Swansea in convincing win

Swansea were visitors to St. James' Park today for this Division Two match in front of a crowd of 14,000. Heavy rain had made the pitch soft, and play would be difficult for both teams. Despite this Newcastle started out the better side, taking control right from the kick off.

The home forwards were skilful and their efforts were far better quality than the half-hearted attempts of the visitors. Rogers and Smith both produced remarkable performances in this match, and it was no surprise when Tim Rogers opened the scoring in the first ten minutes. His goal flew past Moore in the Swansea goal, to give the home side an early lead.

Just three minutes later and that lead was doubled by Pearson. A super shot sent in with power and skill, and it gave the keeper no chance to save. Swansea had a lot to do if they were to get back into the game now they were two goals down. The pitch was also taking its toll on the players, making legs feel heavy and tired.

Before the half-time interval the lead was increased to three goals with a super shot from Rogers. Swansea were awaiting the break anxiously, hoping that they could regroup and come back onto the field fighting.

Tim Rogers

So, the second half started with a slightly tired Newcastle side, and an unimproved Swansea side.

Still, the efforts kept coming from Newcastle, and it was Jack Smith who managed to net the next goal. Now the Tynesiders were four goals ahead, and Swansea knew they had no chance of drawing level.

It was Smith again who got the next goal, bringing Newcastle's tally to five. Time was running out, and a final burst of energy from Swansea saw Mackay pull a goal back for the visitors. It was too late for it to mean anything, though, and the game ended with a deserved win for Newcastle. Final score 5-1.

Newcastle United

Tapken, Richardson, Fairhurst, Garnham, Carver, Gordon, Mooney, Pearson, Smith, Leighton, Rogers.

Swansea Town

Moore, Davies, Caldwell, Warner, Symonds, Lloyd, Mackay, T Moore, Henson, Olsen, Pears.

Played on this day

1896, Division 2.
Notts County (h) 2-2 Att. 17,000
Wardrope, Aitken

1903, Division 1.
Nottingham Forest(h) 3-1 Att. 15,000
McColl, Appleyard, Howie

1908, Division 1.
Chelsea (a) 2-1 Att. 30,000
Allan, Veitch (pen)

1914, Division 1.
Blackburn Rovers (a) 3-2 Att. 5,000
King (2), Hudspeth (pen)

1925, Division 1.
Everton (h) 3-3 Att. 36,000
Gallacher (2), Seymour

1931, Division 1.
Blackpool (a) 1-3 Att. 15,000
Lang

1936, Division 2.
Swansea Town (h) 5-1 Att. 14,000
Pearson, Rogers (2), Smith (2)

1942, Wartime.
Sunderland (h) 3-3 Att. 15,115
Carr, Stubbins (2)

1953, Division 1.
Blackpool (a) 3-1 Att. 19,896
Broadis, Hannah, Mitchell

1959, Division 1.
Luton Town (a) 4-3 Att. 14,524
Eastham (2), Hughes, Luke

1964, Division 2.
Northampton Town (h) 5-0 Att. 40,376
McGarry (3), Hockey, Opponent (og)

1970, Division 1.
Huddersfield Town (h) 2-0 Att. 21,254
Dyson, Robson

1973, Texaco Cup Semi Final, 1st leg.
Dundee United (a) 0-2 Att. 8,500

1987, Division 1.
Portsmouth (h) 1-1 Att. 20,255
Mirandinha

1998, Premier League.
Blackburn Rovers 0 Newcastle 0
Att. 27,569

1999, FA Cup 3rd round.
Tottenham H. 1 Newcastle 1
Iversen 57 Speed 77
Att. 33,116

2001, Worthington Cup 5th round.
Chelsea 1 Newcastle 0
Hasselbaink 90 Att. 27,613

Playing record for this day.... 17 games, Won 8, Drawn 6, Lost 3, GF 38, GA 25. Today's success rate...64.71%.

Birthdays

Irving Nattrass born today in 1952.
Right-back 1970-1979, Apps 313 (13 subs). Goals 22.

Lee Payne born today in 1966.
Winger 1988-1989, Apps 7 (1 sub). Goals 0.

Nolberto Solano born today in 1974.
Midfield 1998-present day, Apps 214 (15 subs). Goals 37.

December 13

Played on this day

1902, Division 1.
Bury (a) 0-1   Att. 8,000
1913, Division 1.
Sheffield United (h) 2-1   Att. 25,000
Hibbert, Hudspeth (pen)
1919, Division 1.
Sheffield United (h) 2-1   Att. 30,000
Robinson, Smailes
1924, Division 1.
Bolton Wanderers (a) 2-3   Att. 15,000
Keating, Low
1930, Division 1.
Leicester City (h) 5-2.   Att. 25,000
Bedford, Boyd, Hutchison (2),
Opponent (og)
1941, Wartime.
Middlesbrough (h) 7-4   Att. 4,000
Short (4), Woodburn (2), Stubbins
*Newcastle come back from 3-2 down at
the interval to win a thriller at St. James'
Park. Last week the Magpies thrashed
Boro 7-0 at Ayresome Park.*
1947, Division 2.
Millwall (a) 1-2   Att. 30,000
Pearson
Played at Selhurst Park
1952, Division 1.
Aston Villa (h) 2-1   Att. 38,046
Keeble, Opponent (og)
1958, Division 1.
Bolton Wanderers (a) 1-1   Att. 23,020
White
1969, Division 1.
Derby County (a) 0-2   Att. 30,057
1975, Division 1.
Leicester City (a) 0-1   Att. 18,130
1980, Division 2.
Swansea City (a) 0-4   Att. 11,672
1986, Division 1.
Nottingham Forest (h) 3-2   Att. 26,191
Wharton, A. Thomas, Beardsley
1988, Simod Cup 3rd round.
Watford (a) 1-2   Att. 6,186
McDonald
1992, Division 1.
Barnsley (a) 0-1   Att. 13,263
1997, Premier League.
Barnsley 2   **Newcastle 2**
Redfearn 9   Gillespie 44, 49
Hendrie 75   Att. 16,687

Playing record for this day... 16 games,
Won 6, Drawn 2, Lost 8, GF 28, GA 30.
Today's success rate... 43.75%.

Match of the Day from 1986

UNITED CUT DOWN FOREST

Championship hopes take a knock after St. James' Park defeat

Newcastle United midfield marksman Andy Thomas hit his seventh goal in just five matches to pave the way for this priceless victory over championship challengers Nottingham Forest in a thrilling game at St. James' Park today. Thomas, a £100,000 steel from Oxford United, took advantage of a superb defence-splitting pass from the inspirational Paul Goddard in the 68th minute to beat Forest keeper Hans Segers from close range much to the delight of the 26,191 Tyneside crowd. Then with just five minutes remaining the Black-and-White Army were sent into wild hysteria when England international striker Peter Beardsley scored a brilliant solo goal after a 40-yard run from near the halfway line which put United into a sensational 3-1 lead. However, Forest's ever dangerous winger Franz Carr severely punished a rare defensive error to reduce the arrears just two minutes later to give the visitors some hope. A nervy finish ensued but United, unbeaten in their six previous matches, held out for a well deserved victory over the high flying East Midlanders.

Newcastle got off to an absolutely fantastic start in this fiercely competitive clash when full-back Kenny Wharton gave them a sixteenth minute lead with a beautifully taken goal after a neat four-man move. Forest responded in typical fashion showing just why they are favourites for the League championship this season and within minutes Martin Thomas had saved brilliantly to deny Nigel Clough. The Forest forward helped set up the move with a quick one-two on the edge of the box before letting fly with a thumping half-volley which the United keeper just managed to reach with his fingertips to deflect the ball over the bar. Clough, however, was soon back in the action and his next telling touch set up the equaliser for the visitors midway through the first half. His run ended with an intelligent delayed through ball which fell perfectly into the path of eighteen-year-old Forest debutant Phil Starbuck, his crisp low drive beating Thomas from fifteen yards.

Newcastle United
M. Thomas, McDonald, Wharton, McCreery, P. Jackson, Roeder, Stephenson, A. Thomas, Goddard, Beardsley, Jackson (Nesbitt 76).

Nottingham Forest
Segers, Fleming, Pearce, Walker, Fairclough, Bowyer, Carr, Metgod, Clough, Starbuck, Webb.

Referee Mr. D. Phillips (Barnsley)

Birthdays

Malcom Brown born today in 1956.
Right-back 1983-1985, Apps 45. Goals 0.
Tommy Gibb born today in 1944.
Midfield 1968-1975, Apps 269 (18 subs). Goals 19.

David Roche born today in 1970.
Midfield 1986-1993, Apps 42 (15 subs). Goals 0.
Glenn Roeder born today in 1955.
Centre-half 1983-1989, Apps 219. Goals 10.

Match of the Day from 1907

WILSON NETS TWO ON DEBUT

Newcomer helps United to victory over Liverpool at Anfield

A crowd of 20,000 turned out to see Liverpool play host to Newcastle today in this Division One match at Anfield. Very heavy rain had fallen throughout the night and early morning, and the pitch was heavy and treacherous. Play would be difficult for both teams, and the strong wind didn't help matters either.

George Wilson was making his debut for Newcastle, and his presence would be hugely important to the outcome of the game. Liverpool were at full strength, and play started with Newcastle in control.

The visitors kept their hold on the game throughout the first half, and it was Rutherford who netted the ball first. Newcastle had an early lead, and this gave them a big advantage over their hosts. A few good attempts came Lawrence's way in the Newcastle goal, but the Liverpool forwards lacked the resources to gain anything from their efforts.

It was Appleyard who doubled the lead for Newcastle before the break, and this further boosted the visiting side's confidence. The interval came, and Liverpool were glad of the break.

More eager supporters flocked into Anfield during the half-time interval, and play resumed with power and control from the Newcastle side. Wilson netted his first for his new side, United's third, and Liverpool saw their game slipping away.

The home team rallied their efforts and made a strong attack on the Newcastle goal. It paid off for them when Parkinson pulled back a goal, slotting the ball past Lawrence with a confident shot.

Wilson then scored his second of the game, bringing Newcastle's tally to four, and still the attacks were coming. Right before the end the win was sealed with another goal from Jackie Rutherford. His super shot flew into the Liverpool net and brought Newcastle a deserved 5-1 victory.

Liverpool
Hardy, West, Saul, Parry, Raisbeck, Bradley, Goddard, Robinson, Hewitt, Parkinson, Cox.
Newcastle United
Lawrence, McCracken, Pudan, Gardner, Veitch, McWilliam, Rutherford, Higgins, Appleyard, Speedie, Wilson.

Played on this day

1901, Division 1.
Sheffield United (h) 1-1   Att. 18,000
Peddie (pen)
1907, Division 1.
Liverpool (a) 5-1   Att. 20,000
Appleyard, Rutherford (2), Wilson (2)
1912, Division 1.
Manchester United (h) 1-3   Att. 20,000
Rutherford
1929, Division 1.
Leeds United (a) 2-5   Att. 21,097
Gallacher (2)
1935, Division 2.
Southampton (h) 4-1   Att. 18,000
Imrie, Pearson, J. Smith (2)
1946, Division 2.
Leicester City (a) 4-2   Att. 35,262
Bentley, Pearson, Shackleton, Wayman
1957, Division 1.
Leeds United (a) 0-3   Att. 23,500
1963, Division 2.
Derby County (a) 2-1   Att. 9,237
Thomas, Hilley
1968, Division 1.
Ipswich Town (h) 2-1   Att. 26,454
Davies (2)
1974, Division 1.
Coventry City (a) 0-2   Att. 15,562
1985, Division 1.
Southampton (h) 2-1   Att. 19,340
Beardsley, Roeder
1991, Division 2.
Brighton & Hove A. (a) 2-2   Att. 7,658
Peacock, Kelly
2002, Premier League.
Southampton 1   Newcastle 1
Marsden 52   Bellamy 50
Att. 32,061

Playing record for this day... 13 games, Won 6, Drawn 3, Lost 4, GF 26, GA 24. Today's success rate... 57.69%.

Birthdays

Brian Ferguson born today in 1960.
Midfield 1979-1980, Apps 5 (1 sub). Goals 1.
Scott Sloan born today in 1967.
Forward 1990-1991, Apps 18 (5 subs). Goals 1.

Arthur Cox born today in 1939.
Manager & Coach 1980-1984 & 1994-1997.
Chris Waddle born today in 1960.
Forward 1980-1985, Apps 191 (1 sub). Goals 52.

Sadly Missed

Angus Douglas died on this day in 1918, aged 29.
Winger 1913-1918, Apps 56. Goals 2

Played on this day

1894, Division 2.
Rotherham Town (h) 5-2   Att. 4,000
Dickson (2), Willis (2), Graham

1900, Division 1.
Manchester City (h) 2-1   Att. 14,500
Laidlaw, Peddie

1906, Division 1.
Bolton Wanderers (h) 4-0   Att. 22,000
McClarence, Orr, Speedie (2)

1923, Division 1.
Sunderland (a) 2-3   Att. 45,000
Seymour, Harris

1928, Division 1.
Derby County (h) 4-1   Att. 28,000
Boyd, Chalmers, Gallacher, McCurley

1934, Division 2.
Oldham Athletic (h) 4-2   Att. 13,000
Lang, McMenemy, Smith (2)

1945, Wartime.
Bradford Park Ave. (h) 4-0   Att. 38,871
Stubbins (2, 1 pen), Clifton (2)

1951, Division 1.
Stoke City (a) 5-4   Att. 30,000
Davies (2), Duncan, G. Robledo (2)

1956, Division 1.
Portsmouth (a) 2-2   Att. 18,453
Davies (2)

1962, Division 2.
Cardiff City (h) 2-1   Att. 27,916
Fell (2)

1973, Division 1.
Derby County (h) 0-2   Att. 19,470

1979, Division 2.
Queens Park Rangers (h) 4-2 Att. 25,027
Withe (2), Shoulder, Cassidy

1984, Division 1.
Norwich City (h) 1-1   Att. 20,423
Waddle

2001, Premier League.
Newcastle 2   Blackburn Rovers 1
Bernard 65   Dunn 34
Speed 70   Att. 50,064

Playing record for this day... 14 games,
Won 10, Drawn 2, Lost 2, GF 41, GA 22.
Today's success rate... 78.57%.

Match of the Day from 1928

NO FIGHT FROM DERBY
Newcastle again 4-1 win at St. James' Park

28,000 were at St. James' Park today to see this Division One match between Newcastle and Derby County. Alf Maitland was missing from the home side, while Derby had two of their most prominent players out of the line up, their reliable strikers Bedford and Whitehouse.

It took fifteen minutes of attacking play from Newcastle before McCurley opened the scoring for the home side.

Derby then fought back and it was left to Burns in the Newcastle goal to keep the ball out, and he did a remarkable job for the most part. Unfortunately he couldn't manage to protect the goal completely, and with three minutes left to play before half-time Ruddy equalised for Derby.

Newcastle badly wanted the two points, and their return to the pitch after the half-time break brought about an improved performance from the whole team. Two minutes after the restart Chalmers put Newcastle back into the lead with a super shot past the Derby keeper.

This inspired the home side, and their game just got better by the minute.

Boyd was next to add his name to the score-sheet with a lovely confident shot to bring Newcastle's tally to three, and Derby were visibly struggling now. The game was put completely out of reach of the visitors when Gallacher rounded off the scoring with the fourth goal for the home side. Maitland's absence didn't seem to have caused any problems for the Newcastle team, and the points were well earned today.

Newcastle United
Burns, Harris, Thomson, MacKenzie, Hill, Gibson, Boyd, Chalmers, Gallacher, McCurley, Lang.

Derby County
Wilkes, Cooper, Collin, McIntyre, Davison, Storer, Crooks, Barclay, Ruddy, Stephenson, Robson.

Willie Chalmers

Birthdays

Jim Iley born today in 1935.
Midfield 1962-1969, Apps 249 (6 subs). Goals 1.

Sadly Missed

Tom Mooney died on this day in 1981, aged 71.
Winger 1936-1944, Apps 81. Goals 19.

December 16

Match of the Day from 2000

NOTHING DYER IN WIN OVER BRADFORD
Great goals in vitally important home victory

Talks of crisis in the club were emphatically silenced today at St. James' Park as Newcastle swept Bradford City to their first defeat under the leadership of Jim Jefferies. While Bradford lacked the cutting edge to complement their admirable composed football, Newcastle produced two fantastic goals and hoisted themselves up to seventh place in the Premiership. Crisis, what crisis?

Gary Speed thundered a spectacular opener and Kieron Dyer's pace exposed Robert Molenaar's inability to accelerate before dispatching what proved to be the winner. Molenaar pulled one back for Bradford, forcing United to hang on precariously in the closing stages. But, Alan Shearer should have eased the tension amongst the Toon Army when presented a simple chance, by his high standards, which he failed to convert in the closing minutes.

There remained however, obvious weaknesses throughout the United side and more ruthless opposition than Bradford would surely have exploited the uncertainty of central defender Marcelino. His woefully under-hit back pass presented a golden chance for Dean Windass who reacted too slowly and Shay Given was able to clear the danger to protect United's slender advantage.

At the other end, Gary Walsh, pulled off a well judged save to deny Dyer in Newcastle's early assault but the Bradford keeper was completely powerless to prevent Speed's opening goal in the fourteenth minute. The Welsh international's volley from fully twenty yards cannoned down from the underside of the crossbar and over the goal line. It was Dyer's speed, and his accurate finish in the 70th minute, which then carried Newcastle beyond Bradford's reach. This made Molenaar's headed goal, from Peter Beagrie's inch-perfect cross eight minutes from time, in the end purely academic.

Newcastle United
Given, Barton, Marcelino, Lee, Dyer, Bassedas (Acuna 81), Speed, Griffin, Solano, Hughes, Shearer.
Bradford City
Walsh, Nolan, McCall, Blake (Beagrie 69), Carbone (Myers 87), Molenaar, O'Brien, Windass, Atherton, Petrescu (Saunders 74), McKinley.
Referee Mr. S. Dunn (Bristol).

Kieron Dyer

Played on this day

1893, Division 2.
Small Heath (a) 4-1   Att. 2,500
Crate, Wallace, Willis, Graham
1895, FA Cup Qualifying round 5.
Tow Law Town (h) 4-0   Att. 3,000
Wardrope, Thompson, Lennox, Stott
1899, Division 1.
Stoke (a) 2-2   Att. 3,000
A. Gardner, MacFarlane
1905, Division 1.
Stoke (a) 0-1   Att. 8,000
1911, Division 1.
Aston Villa (h) 6-2   Att. 30,000
Higgins, Hibbert, Stewart, Rutherford, Hay, McCracken (pen)
1922, Division 1.
Aston Villa (a) 1-1   Att. 16,000
Harris
1933, Division 1.
Stoke City (h) 2-2   Att. 20,000
J.R. Richardson, Weaver (pen)
1944, Wartime.
Huddersfield Town (h) 1-2   Att. 22,000
Milburn
1950, Division 1.
Stoke City (h) 3-1   Att. 29,505
Hannah, Mitchell, G. Robledo
1961, Division 2.
Leyton Orient (a) 0-2   Att. 13,261
1967, Division 1.
Southampton (a) 0-0   Att. 19,498
1972, Division 1.
Derby County (a) 1-1   Att. 28,826
Tudor
1978, Division 2.
Fulham (a) 3-1   Att. 8,575
Connolly, Withe, Shoulder
1990, Division 2.
Plymouth Argyle (a) 1-0   Att. 7,845
Peacock
1992, Anglo Italian Cup, Group A.
Cesena (h) 2-2   Att. 4,609
Peacock (2)
1995, Premier League.
Newcastle 1   Everton 0
Ferdinand 17   Att. 36,557
2000, Premier League.
Newcastle 2   Bradford City 1
Speed 14   Molenaar 83
Dyer 70   Att. 50,470

Playing record for this day... 17 games, Won 8, Drawn 6, Lost 3, GF 33, GA 19. Today's success rate... 64.71%.

Birthdays

John Markie born today in 1944.
Midfield 1962-1964, Apps 2. Goals 0.
Andy Thomas born today in 1962.
Midfield 1986-1988, Apps 36 (7 subs). Goals 9.
Sylvain Distin born today in 1977.
Defender 2001-2002, Apps 35 (8 subs). Goals 0.

Sadly Missed

Thomas Blyth died on this day in 1949, aged 73.
Centre-forward 1896-1898, Apps 1. Goals 1.

December 17

Played on this day

1898, Division 1.
Sheffield Wednesday (h) 2-2 Att. 15,000
Peddie, MacFarlane
1904, Division 1.
Sheffield Wednesday (h) 6-2 Att. 18,000
Orr, Appleyard, Howie, Rutherford (2),
McWilliam
1910, Division 1.
Nottingham Forest (h) 4-1 Att. 15,000
Shepherd (4)
1921, Division 1.
Aston Villa (h) 1-2 Att. 30,000
Mooney
1927, Division 1.
Portsmouth (h) 1-3 Att. 20,000
McDonald
1932, Division 1.
Derby County (h) 0-0 Att. 23,000
1938, Division 2.
Swansea Town (a) 1-0 Att. 15,000
Clifton
1949, Division 1.
Portsmouth (a) 0-1 Att. 30,455
1955, Division 1.
Sheffield United (a) 1-2 Att. 23,000
Milburn
1960, Division 1.
Preston North End (h) 0-0 Att. 21,514
1966, Division 1.
Aston Villa (h) 0-3 Att. 25,406
1969, Inter Cities Fairs Cup 3rd round, 1st leg.
Southampton (h) 0-0 Att. 38,163
1977, Division 1.
Wolverhampton W. (h) 4-0 Att. 22,982
T. Craig, Mitchell, Cassidy, Nattrass
1983, Division 2.
Brighton & Hove A. (a) 1-0 Att. 13,896
Waddle
1988, Division 1.
Southampton (h) 3-3 Att. 20,103
Brock, O'Neill (2)
1994, Premier League.
Coventry City 0 Newcastle 0
Att. 17,237
1996, Premier League.
Coventry City 2 Newcastle 1
Huckerby 6 Shearer 61
McAllister 31 Att. 21,538
1997, Premier League.
Newcastle 0 Derby County 0
Att. 36,289

Playing record for this day....18 games,
Won 5, Drawn 7, Lost 6, GF 25, GA 21.
Today's success rate... 47.22%.

Match of the Day from 1977

UNITED BLITZ COMPOUNDS WOLVES' WOES

Newcastle record another emphatic victory at St. James' Park

Wolves' nosedive towards the foot of the First Division table continues after another impressive United display at St. James' Park today. This was the Midlanders heaviest defeat of the season and they have now conceded ten goals from three successive defeats. Their indecision and lack of understanding was severely punished by Newcastle who realistically could have produced a cricket score for the 22,982 crowd. Despite their failings in defence it would be harsh to criticise eighteen-year-old debutant Bob Hazel who on numerous times saved Wolves from total humiliation on a day Newcastle dominated the game once they had scored their opening goal.

Wolves started well with both Eves and Richards causing problems, before Newcastle eventually went ahead on sixteen minutes. A free kick was swung into the area from Cassidy and Nattrass ghosted in unmarked at the near post to head home from close range. The goal and the manner in which it came was a clear indication of what was to come with the second goal on 35 minutes almost a complete replica of the first. This time Craig pinpointed his free kick onto the head of Kenny Mitchell and the youngster, playing in only his fifth first-team game, found all the time and room he needed to head firmly past the helpless keeper Bradshaw.

The second half saw no let up from United sensing a big victory to reward the fans and just twelve minutes into the period they scored a third goal. Again from a set piece, this time Craig's inswinging corner causing confusion in the Wolves defence and no one could stop the ball floating directly into the far corner of the net. At the other end Kenny Hibbitt found the net with a shot via a deflection of Blackley but the 'goal', which was originally awarded by the referee, was ruled offside after a consultation with a linesman who had ruled an unknown Wolves player offside. It wasn't Wolves day at all and within minutes the crowd were celebrating United's fourth when in the 61st minute Cassidy, with a beautifully flighted chip, beat both Bradshaw and the desperate lunge on the line by Palmer. To their credit Wolves never gave in and only a brave diving header by Bird, from off the goal-line, kept out a cracking volley from Farley. Moments later Carr pulled off a miraculous save to push away a Kenny Hibbitt volley and the ball fell invitingly to Farley who summed up his side's afternoon by gently rolling the simple chance wide of the post.

Newcastle United
K. Carr, Nattrass, Barker, Cassidy, Bird, Blackley, Martin, Burns, Mitchell, Craig, Robinson.
Wolverhampton Wanderers
Bradshaw, Palmer, Parkin, Daley, Hazell, McAlle, Hibbitt, W. Carr, Richards, Eves, Farley.

Birthdays

George Luke born today in 1933.
Winger 1950-1953, 1959-1961, Apps 29. Goals 4
Kevin Scott born today in 1966.
Centre-half 1984-1994, Apps 275 (3 subs).
Goals 11.

Sadly Missed

Ron Starling died on this day in 1991, aged 82.
Midfield 1930-1932, Apps 53. Goals 8.

December 18

Match of the Day from 2001

UNITED'S NIGHTMARE IN THE CAPITAL OVER AT LAST

Victory puts Newcastle top of the Premiership

An enthralling match will be long remembered by the 38,012 crowd present today. For those on Tyneside they will be focusing on United's first victory in the capital in 30 attempts a result which lifts them to the top of the Premiership. Referee Poll had a controversial game, sending off Arsenal's Ray Parlour and Craig Bellamy for seemingly innocuous offences, and then awarding a late penalty against Sol Campbell for a tackle on Laurent Robert. Alan Shearer converted, registering his first goal at Highbury, and Robert added a third goal which nudged Newcastle ahead of Liverpool in the table on goal difference. At the final whistle Henry raced towards Poll and only the quick reactions of the Gunners physio prevented a worse scenario, although he required the assistance of a host of others as the confrontation continued in the tunnel.

Arsenal were by far the better team at the start, and it seemed United's dismal record in London would continue, up until Parlour departed two minutes before the half-time interval. Henry was then in more positive mood setting up the opening goal, juggling the ball brilliantly and hooking it to the far post, where Ashley Cole lurked. He quickly whipped the ball back across the Newcastle box and Robert Pires, adjusting his body well to meet the cross, neatly tucked the ball away. Then came Parlour's dismissal. His first yellow card had been understandable enough, for a push on Nikos Dabizas, but the second was very harsh. With two minutes of the half remaining, Parlour slid in on Shearer and brought him down. There seemed no malice in the obvious foul which was slightly late but over came Poll and to everyone's astonishment, off went Parlour.

Newcastle's hopes grew with the sending off particularly with Kieron Dyer running around nimbly in midfield and Bellamy and Shearer looking lively up front for the Magpies. Robson then sent on two more attackers Lomana LuaLua and Robert the effect was instantaneous. LuaLua clipped in a corner and Andy O'Brien, amazingly unmarked, headed in and United were level. Then came Bellamy's dismissal, for apparently catching Cole with his arm, again incredibly harsh as most in the ground agreed with the player's argument that he was merely shielding the ball. However, like the first red card, the second also had a great effect on the Newcastle performance. United had not finished with their scoring either and after Shearer coolly converted the penalty in the 86th minute, then Robert broke away in stoppage time to beat Stuart Taylor and wrap up an extremely valuable and convincing 3-1 victory.

Arsenal
Taylor, Lauren, Keown, Campbell, Cole, Wiltord (Bergkamp 68), Parlour, Vieira, Pires, Kanu (Van Bronckhorst h/t), Henry.

Newcastle United
Given, Hughes, O'Brien, Dabizas, Elliott (Robert 58), Solano (LuaLua 58), Dyer (Distin 86), Speed, Bernard, Bellamy, Shearer.

Referee Mr. G. Poll (Tring)

Alan Shearer strikes the penalty to put Newcastle ahead.

Played on this day

1897, Division 2.
Burton Swifts (a) 1-3   Att. 4,000
White
1909, Division 1.
Sheffield United (a) 0-4   Att. 20,000
1920, Division 1.
Manchester United (a) 0-2   Att. 30,000
1926, Division 1.
Leicester City (h) 1-1   Att. 35,702
Seymour
1937, Division 2.
Swansea Town (h) 1-0   Att. 16,000
Imrie (pen)
1943, Wartime.
Gateshead (a) 3-1   Att. 6,000
Copeland (2), Dixon
1948, Division 1.
Everton (h) 1-0   Att. 43,515
Taylor
1954, Division 1.
Arsenal(h) 5-1   Att. 35,122
R. Mitchell (2, 1 pen), Keeble (2), Milburn
1965, Division 1.
Liverpool (h) 0-0   Att. 34,153
1971, Division 1.
West Ham United (a) 1-0   Att. 21,991
Busby
1974, League Cup 5th round, replay.
Chester City (a) 0-1   Att. 19,000
1976, Division 1.
Aston Villa (a) 1-2   Att. 33,982
Gowling
1982, Division 2.
Sheffield Wednesday (a) 1-1 Att. 16,310
Varadi

1993, Premier League.

Everton 0	Newcastle 2
	Cole 14
	Beardsley 76
	Att. 25,189

1999, Premier League.

Bradford City 2	Newcastle 0
Saunders 56	
Wetherall 71	Att. 18,276

2001, Premier League.

Arsenal 1	Newcastle 3
Pires 20	O'Brien 60
	Shearer 86 (pen)
	Robert 90
	Att. 38,012

This win puts the Magpies top of the Premier League, a position they held for just two weeks, eventually finishing the 2001-02 season in fourth place.

Playing record for this day... 16 games, Won 7, Drawn 3, Lost 6, GF 20, GA 19. Today's success rate... 53.13%.

Birthdays

Micky Barker born today in 1955.
Left-back 1972-1979, Apps 29 (2 subs). Goals 0.
Ivor Broadis born today in 1922.
Midfield 1953-1955, Apps 51. Goals 18.

Kevin Dillon born today in 1959.
Midfield 1989-1994, Apps 76 (2 subs). Goals 0.

December 19

Played on this day

1903, Division 1.
Sheffield Wednesday (a) 1-1   Att. 10,000
McColl
1908, Division 1.
Blackburn Rovers (h) 2-0   Att. 22,000
Anderson, Duncan
1914, Division 1.
Notts County (h) 1-1   Att. 15,000
Hibbert
1925, Division 1.
Manchester City (a) 2-2   Att. 35,000
McDonald (pen), Gallacher
1931, Division 1.
Sheffield United (h) 5-3   Att. 27,000
Bedford (3), Boyd, Lang
1936, Division 2.
Bradford City (a) 0-2   Att. 10,000
1942, Wartime.
Gateshead (a) 1-3   Att. 5,300
Short
1953, Division 1.
Sunderland (a) 1-1   Att. 49,923
Broadis
1959, Division 1.
Tottenham Hotspur (a) 0-4   Att. 32,824
1964, Division 2.
Southampton (a) 1-0   Att. 22,365
Suddick
1970, Division 1.
Crystal Palace (h) 2-0   Att. 21,779
Robson (2, 1 pen)
1973, Texaco Cup Semi Final, 2nd leg.
Dundee United (h) 4-1   Att. 5,009
Robson, Tudor, Macdonald, Cassidy
1987, Division 1.
West Ham United (a) 1-2   Att. 18,679
Mirandinha
1998, Premier League.
Newcastle 1   Leicester City 0
Glass 66   Att. 36,718

Playing record for this day... 14 games,
Won 6, Drawn 4, Lost 4, GF 22, GA 20.
Today's success rate... 57.14%.

Match of the Day from 1931

ANYONE FOR TENNIS?

Newcastle beat Sheffield United in end-to-end thriller

Sheffield United were the visitors to St. James' Park today for this Division One match in front of a crowd of 27,000. Ex-Derby County player Harry Bedford, who had arrived at Gallowgate twelve months perviously, was included at centre-forward, and his presence would be invaluable.

Newcastle started on the attack straight away, and it was just five minutes into the game when Bedford began the scoring. It should have been Boyd's goal, but the ball had deflected off the post and run along the goal-line. Bedford was perfectly placed to knock it over the line to give the home side the advantage of an early lead.

Dunne made a good attempt at goal shortly afterwards, but his shot was not destined for the back of the net this time. However, it was only a matter of time, and his next try was successful. He sent the ball zooming home past McInroy, and the scores were level.

Next Bedford was brought down in the penalty area, and the referee awarded Newcastle the spot kick. Bedford himself stepped up to do the honours, and his confident shot sailed past Smith to restore the lead for the home side.

In a game resembling a tennis match, play again switched ends quickly as Oswald levelled the scores for the Blades once more. Then, true to form, Newcastle took back the lead when a centre from Boyd came to Bedford, who got his head to it and nodded it into the back of the net for Newcastle's third. The goal completed Bedford's hat-trick, and all before the half-time break.

In the second half the yo-yo effect carried on when Barclay evened the scores yet again. However, Newcastle were tired of losing their lead, and decided to step up the pace of the game and hope that the visitors couldn't keep up. Their tactics worked, and Lang was next to add his name to the score-sheet with a lovely ball which was perfectly placed to beat Smith.

The game was wrapped up when Boyd netted the fifth and final goal for Newcastle, and this signalled the end for Sheffield United. The match ended with the score 5-3.

Newcastle United

McInroy, Nelson, Fairhurst, Naylor, Davidson, Weaver, Boyd, Richardson, Bedford, McMenemy, Lang.

Sheffield United

Smith, Thorpe, Hooper, Gooney, Holmes, Green, Oxley, Barclay, Dunne, Pickering, Oswain.

H. BEDFORD

Birthdays

Derek Bell born today 1963.
Midfield 1981-1983, Apps 3 (1 sub). Goals 0.

December 20

Match of the Day from 1930

HIGHBURY HOPES DASHED

Newcastle take well deserved win over Arsenal

This Division One match saw Arsenal play host to Newcastle United at Highbury today in front of 32,212 eager supporters. Newcastle were fortunate to have Harry Bedford in their side, and his presence would be an inspiration for the rest of the team.

Duncan Hutchison

The first half started with Newcastle playing far better than their hosts. Bedford encouraged the other players to put in their all, and it certainly showed in their performance.

On 22 minutes the lead was taken by Newcastle, the result of hard work and a lot of patience. It was Bedford who scored, deservedly being the first to get his name on the score-sheet. This was the only goal of the first period.

In the opening minutes of the second half, things could have gone horribly wrong for the visiting Tynesiders. Jack managed to beat McInroy in the Newcastle goal to grab the equaliser for Arsenal.

However, Newcastle didn't panic, and their game was good enough to win them back the lead shortly afterwards with a super goal from Duncan Hutchison. His shot gave Harper no chance of saving the ball, and were ahead once more.

Arsenal began to lose their aim now, and Newcastle merely had to bide their time until the final whistle blew. Final score: Arsenal 1, Newcastle 2.

Arsenal
Harper, Parker, Hapgood, Seddon, Roberts, John, Williams, Jack, Lambert, James, Bastin.
Newcastle United
McInroy, Nelson, Thomson, MacKenzie, Davidson, Weaver, Boyd, Bedford, Hutchison, Starling, Wilkinson.

Played on this day

1890, FA Cup Qualifying round 2, replay.
Sunderland Albion (h) 0-2   Att. 3,000
1902, Division 1.
Blackburn Rovers (h) 1-0   Att. 12,000
Caie
1913, Division 1.
Derby County (a) 0-2   Att. 15,000
1919, Division 1.
Manchester United (a) 1-2   Att. 20,000
Hagan
1924, Division 1.
Notts County (h) 1-0   Att. 25,000
McDonald
1930, Division 1.
Arsenal (a) 2-1   Att. 32,212
Bedford, Hutchison
1941, Wartime.
Sheffield Wednesday (a) 2-4   Att. 4,000
Dixon (2)
1947, Division 2.
Plymouth Argyle (a) 0-3   Att. 25,000
1952, Division 1.
Sheffield Wednesday (h) 1-5 Att. 37,927
Mitchell (pen)
1958, Division 1.
Blackburn Rovers (a) 0-3   Att. 25,100
1969, Division 1.
Ipswich Town (h) 4-0   Att. 19,411
Ford, Dyson, Robson (2)
1975, Division 1.
Ipswich Town (h) 1-1   Att. 26,152
Nulty
1980, Division 2.
Bristol City (h) 0-0   Att. 14,131
1989, Zenith Data Systems Cup 3rd round.
Derby County (h) 3-2   Att. 6,704
O'Brien, Gallacher, Cross (og)
A.E.T.
1991, Division 2.
Plymouth Argyle (a) 0-2   Att. 5,048
1992, Division 1.
Millwall (h) 1-1   Att. 26,089
Kelly (pen)

Playing record for this day... 16 games, Won 5, Drawn 3, Lost 8, GF 17, GA 28. Today's success rate... 40.63%.

Birthdays

Alan Duffy born today in 1949.
Forward 1966-1970, Apps 4 (2 subs). Goals 0.
Dave Hilley born today in 1938.
Midfield 1962-1967, Apps 209. Goals 33.

Alex Mathie born today in 1968.
Centre-forward 1993-1995, Apps 29 (24 subs). Goals 4.

December 21

Played on this day

1895, Division 2.
Rotherham Town (h) 6-1　　Att. 5,000
Wardrope (2), McKay, Lennox (2), Stott

1907, Division 1.
Sunderland (a) 4-2　　Att. 30,000
Rutherford, Veitch, Wilson (2)

1912, Division 1.
Aston Villa (a) 1-3　　Att. 30,000
Hudspeth (pen)

1929, Division 1.
Derby County (h) 2-3　　Att. 20,000
Chalmers, Hill

1946, Division 2.
Chesterfield (h) 2-1　　Att. 53,675
Wayman (2)

1957, Division 1.
West Bromwich A. (h) 3-0　　Att. 31,699
Davies, White (2)

1963, Division 2.
Plymouth Argyle (h) 1-1　　Att. 23,572
Thomas

1968, Division 1.
Queens Park Rangers (a) 1-1　Att. 16,444
Foggon

1974, Division 1.
Leeds United (h) 3-0　　Att. 34,054
Tudor, Kennedy, Howard

1985, Division 1.
Liverpool (a) 1-1　　Att. 30,746
Beardsley

1986, Division 1.
Sheffield Wednesday (a) 0-2 Att. 28,897

1994, Coca Cola Cup 4th round, replay.
Newcastle 0　　**Manchester City 2**
　　　　　　　　Rosler 11
　　　　　　　　Walsh 80
　　　　　　　　Att. 30,156

1997, Premier League.
Newcastle 0　　**Manchester United 1**
　　　　　　　　Cole 66
　　　　　　　　Att. 36,767

2002, Premier League.
Newcastle 2　　**Fulham 0**
Solano 8
Bellamy 70　　　　Att. 51,576

Playing record for this day.... 14 games,
Won 6, Drawn 3, Lost 5, GF 26, GA 18.
Today's success rate... 46.88%.

Match of the Day from 1907

RIVALS WELL BEATEN
Victory at Roker Park an early present for fans

Newcastle United travelled to Roker Park today to meet their rivals in front of a crowd of 30,000 for this Division One clash. It was to be a closely fought game with everything at stake. Heavy rain had made the pitch hard to play on, and this was going to make things difficult for both sides.

However, the visiting Newcastle side took an early lead when Rutherford scored on the stroke of five minutes.

The joy for the Tynesiders lasted only two minutes, for Hogg was quick off the mark and netted the equaliser for Sunderland. The game was turning out like a tennis match, with play going from one end to the other, and then back again.

Newcastle regained their lead just minutes later when Veitch sent in a lovely shot which beat the Sunderland keeper easily. Then just before the half-time break Wilson managed to give Newcastle a two-goal lead with a superb shot into the back of the net. Sunderland were stunned, and they needed to work much harder if they were to have any say in the second half of the game.

The second period began, and Newcastle remained in control of play. Their defence succeeded in keeping the Sunderland forwards out of the danger zone, and the visiting forwards kept up the pressure on the home defence.

Rutherford sent a lovely cross into the area, and Wilson was there to get his head to the ball and nod it into the net for Newcastle's fourth. Sunderland mustered all their efforts and went for one last attack. It worked, and the chance created by Hogg and Foster was seized upon by Bridgett, his long shot giving Lawrence no chance to save the ball.

Still, it wasn't enough for the home team to really make their mark on the game, and the final score remained 4-2.

Sunderland
Ward, Bonthron, Daykin, Tait, Low, McConnell, Hogg, Holley, Forster, Raybould, Bridgett.
Newcastle United
Lawrence, McCracken, Pudan, Gardner, Veitch, McWilliam, Rutherford, Higgins, Appleyard, Speedie, Wilson.

George Wilson

Birthdays

Micky Burns born today in 1946.
Forward/Midfield 1974-1978, Apps 191 (2 subs).
Goals 51.

December 22

Match of the Day from 2001

YET ANOTHER SENSATIONAL FIGHTBACK FROM UNITED

3-1 down, Solano's clincher arrives in stoppage time

Lee Bowyer, fresh off the transfer list, played and scored but there was still no happy ending for Leeds. The home side played well with Bowyer netting a deserved equaliser in this astonishing and dramatic contest. However, it all counted for nothing as Newcastle came back spiritedly from 3-1 down in the second half to win with a late goal from the outstanding Nobby Solano and increase their lead at the top of the Premiership to three points. This was the Magpies' third successive away league win in the last eight days against two of the leading title candidates, Arsenal and Leeds. In each case, as Bobby Robson was quick to point out, they have had to come from behind to win. For all their perceived weaknesses, two things this United team do not lack are character and resilience. They are not exactly short of ability either. Craig Bellamy, full of pace and tricks, has proved an inspired signing in attack. The return of Alan Shearer and now Kieron Dyer has brought real class to the party and players of the quality of Gary Speed and Solano are beginning to respond to the potency of the mix.

As for Leeds, everything seemed to be going well for them until the 38th minute. They had dominated an exciting open game and it was against the run of play when United took the lead. Running on to Shearer's through pass, Dyer held off Ian Harte before offering Bellamy a low centre which the striker tucked away without fuss. But Newcastle were ahead for only a minute when Leeds struck back, Bowyer cutting inside Nikos Dabizas and driving into the penalty area before threading the ball through the legs of Shay Given. Leeds only blot, on an otherwise perfect first half, was Mark Viduka's wild challenge on Dabizas which was so late and dangerous the Greek international was carried off on a stretcher. Amazingly this assault was only punished with a yellow card.

It seemed the injustice would be doubled later when the Australian striker put Leeds ahead with a shot on the turn just five minutes into the second half. Harte made it 3-1 with a cracking left-foot drive five minutes later, following a helpful miscue by Bowyer, and the contest looked to be all over. But Newcastle were not to be denied, hitting back, they got Dyer away on the right and his cross-shot was so fierce Nigel Martyn could only palm it away. In the event, the ball fell nicely for Robbie Elliott, who dived to head United back into contention. Then, twelve minutes later, Newcastle had their stroke of luck. Eirik Bakke, on as a sub for Harry Kewell, was adjudged to have handled in the area, although it seemed to be difficult for him to get out of the way of Speed's attempted flick. The referee thought differently and Shearer dispatched the penalty with his usual coolness. Now it was Newcastle in control. Sylvian Distin, on as a sub for Dabizas, and Bellamy very nearly got the winner before Solano did so in the last of four minutes stoppage time. Bellamy sent his Peruvian team-mate away down the inside-right channel with a lovely through ball and Solano steered his shot across Martyn and into the far corner. Newcastle had come back to win another thriller 4-3.

Leeds United
Martyn, Kelly, Ferdinand, Mills, Harte, Bowyer, Batty, Johnson, Kewell (Bakke 47), Viduka, Fowler.
Newcastle United
Given, Hughes, O'Brien, Dabizas (Distin h/t), Elliott, Solano, Dyer, Speed, Robert (Bernard 78), Acuna, Harper.
Referee Mr. J. Winter (Stockton-on-Tees)

Birthdays

Alan Thompson born today in 1973.
Midfield 1989-1993, Apps 20 (3 subs). Goals 0.

Played on this day

1899, Division 1.
Sunderland (h) 2-4   Att. 21,000
MacFarlane, A. Gardner

1905, Division 1.
Bolton Wanderers (h) 2-1   Att. 20,000
Orr, McClarence

1911, Division 1.
Preston North End (a) 1-2   Att. 12,000
Hibbert

1922, Division 1.
Aston Villa (h) 0-0   Att. 20,000

1933, Division 1.
Liverpool (a) 2-1   Att. 20,000
J.R. Richardson, Williams

1939, Wartime.
Halifax Town (a) 4-3   Att. 5,000
Clifton (2), Cairns, Duns

1944, Wartime.
Huddersfield Town (a) 1-4   Att. 17,253
A. Donaldson

1950, Division 1.
Everton (a) 1-3   Att. 30,000
Taylor

1961, Division 2.
Preston North End (h) 0-2   Att. 18,775

1967, Division 1.
Liverpool (h) 1-1   Att. 46,204
Scott

1972, Division 1.
Manchester City (h) 2-1   Att. 28,274
Macdonald (pen), Barrowclough

1978, Division 2.
Burnley (h) 3-1   Att. 23,639
Withe, Shoulder, Cassidy

1995, Premier League.
Newcastle 3   **Nottingham Forest 1**
Lee 11, 74   Woan 14
Ginola 26
     Att. 36,531

1996, Premier League.
Newcastle 1   **Liverpool 1**
Shearer 28   Fowler 45
     Att. 36,570

2000, Premier League.
Derby County 2   **Newcastle 0**
Carbonari 33
Burton 73
     Att. 29,978

Playing record for this day... 15 games,
Won 6, Drawn 3, Lost 6, GF 23, GA 27.
Today's success rate... 50%.

Match of the Day from 1995

UNITED GO FROM STRENGTH TO STRENGTH

Premiership title still the goal for rampant Newcastle

Two goals from Robert Lee, and a long-awaited first home strike from Frenchman David Ginola, proved more than enough to see off yet another spirited challenge from Nottingham Forest today on Tyneside. Ginola has charmed the Toon Army for half a season now at St James' Park and, on a day of seemingly boundless quality, he revelled in more central territory to provide the extra dimension, the arrogance and subtlety to complement United's raging football. Kevin Keegan's Newcastle side, with their ten-game unblemished home record, maintain their strong advantage at the top of the Premiership with Manchester United and the rest now reduced to merely hoping for a slip up by the Magpies.

Forest for their part are renowned for their swift counter attacking and they started well in this game. Ian Woan had two chances early on which went begging then Steve Stone charged down the right and delivered a perfect cross for Jason Lee to narrowly plant his header wide, the ball smacking into the side netting. Then almost inevitably Peter Beardsley intervened and his exquisite pass sent Les Ferdinand sprinting beyond Steve Chettle only for Mark Crossley to enhance his growing reputation as one of the best Premiership keepers around with a brilliantly timed block. The Forest keeper, however was as much a spectator as the rest in the eleventh minute. Ginola's deft body swerve mesmerising two Forest defenders and his lay off to Robert Lee allowed him the chance to beat Crossley with a bending 25-yard shot.

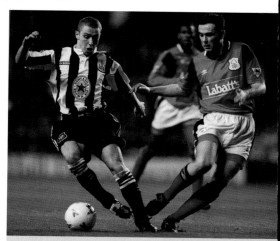

Lee Clark weaves his way past Nottingham Forest's Steve Chettle

The Newcastle lead lasted barely three minutes however. Woan accepted a return pass from Kevin Campbell, before shooting across Pavel Srnicek, inside the far post. Then came the moment the Toon Army had been waiting for as, on 25 minutes, Ginola pounced for that elusive first home goal, his balance, control and another rattling right-foot shot carrying the ball beyond Crossley's reach. Ginola was rampant. This supposedly left-footed player unleashed another scorching right-foot shot to force Crossley to save magnificently. Beardsley joined the party, as he always does, his chip clearing Crossley but, agonisingly for the fans behind the goal, also the crossbar.

Five minutes into the second half, Newcastle were relieved to see Jason Lee's shot come back off their crossbar after the towering striker turned on Stone's probing pass. Beardsley too struck the bar at the end of a tantalising dribble, before Forest broke for Stone to almost equalise. Beardsley jinked into position again and Crossley saved. Ferdinand burst through after Ginola's pass and Crossley blocked brilliantly again. It was stirring, absorbing, fast action, football at its best. Another goal just had to come and, on 74 minutes, the Magpies secured an impressive victory as Beardsley and Ferdinand played supporting roles for Lee to add his second goal of the match.

Newcastle United

Srnicek, Barton, Albert, Peacock, Howey, R Lee, Clark, Ginola, Gillespie, Beardsley, Ferdinand.

Nottingham Forest

Crossley, Lyttle, Pearce, Cooper, Chettle, Phillips, Stone, Bart-Williams, Woan, Cambell, J Lee.

Referee Mr D. Elleray (Harrow)

Birthdays

Alex Bruce born today in 1952.
Forward 1974-1975, Apps 24 (4 subs). Goals 4.

Micheal Chopra born today in 1983.
Forward 1993-present day, Apps 4 (4 subs).
Goals 0.

December 24

Match of the Day from 1898

MEMORABLE FIRST FOR UNITED

Away win at last for Newcastle, and at Roker Park too!

Newcastle and Sunderland, the big North-East rivals, had played several high profile and entertaining friendlies over the years, but had yet to meet in a league game. This was the eagerly awaited 'big one' and United in their first season in Division One travelled to Roker yet to record an away win in nine previous attempts. This was Sunderland's first season at their new ground and for the first time a match was played in front of a capacity crowd of 25,000 despite the increased admission charge.

In a nervy start it was the home side who went ahead after a terrible mix up in the United defence, Jackson, Ostler and Ghee all failed to clear a bobbling ball in the penalty area allowing Leslie to tap in from five yards, Roker Park erupted. Newcastle who were second from bottom of the league had a mountain to climb, but going behind seemed to settle their nerves. Midway through the half it was the visitors who were playing the better football and they got a deserved equaliser on the half-hour mark. A fine move involving Stevenson, Rogers and Aitken put Willie Wardrope away, and after a ten-yard sprint with defender Bach the United winger found room to shoot past Doig's outstretched dive and into the bottom corner of the net. Still Newcastle piled forward in a period of intense pressure on the Sunderland goal, a long clearance by Jackson was chased down by Jock Peddie, after taking two strides with the ball he unleashed a terrific drive from 30 yards which flew into the roof of the net.

The second half started with some fierce tackling and Wardrope became the first injury victim after a challenge from Sunderland centre-back McAllister. Thankfully he recovered after some attention to his ankle, and he then intelligently knocked a quickly taken free kick into the path of Aitken who was free on the right wing. The cross found Peddie unmarked in the area to head United into a fantastic 3-1 lead. This roused the home side and the final half hour was almost entirely played in the Newcastle half. The pressure paid off with another goal for Leslie to reduce the score to 3-2, but United held out and on the stroke of full time Peddie had a golden opportunity to complete a great hat-trick but his shot from ten yards went inches wide.

United had recorded their first away victory in the top flight of English football, and, more importantly to their passionate fans, won the first of many big North-East derbies, a Merry Christmas indeed for Newcastle United FC.

Sunderland
Doig, Bach, McNeil, Ferguson, McAllister, Jackson, Crawford, Leslie, Raisbeck, Wilson, McLatchie.
Newcastle United
Kingsley, Lindsay, Jackson, Ghee, Ostler, Stott, Rogers, Stevenson, Peddie, Aitken, Wardrope.
Referee Mr. J. Lewis

Toon News Extra

1892... East End become Newcastle United
Newcastle United 2 Middlesbrough 1

Under their new name of Newcastle United the former East End club beat rivals Middlesbrough in a thriller at St James' Park in this 'friendly' game. United led 1-0 at half-time and sealed the win with another in the second half; the goals scored by McIntosh and Reay. A crowd of 1,200 witnessed the new era for Newcastle United FC.

Sadly Missed

Stan Seymour died on this day in 1978, aged 85.
Winger, Manager & Director 1920-1929, 1938-1978. Apps 266. Goals 84.

Division 2.
Middlesbrough
Ironopolis (a) 1-1 Att. 2,000
Crate
Division 2.
Crewe Alexandra (h) 6-0 Att. 7,000
Wallace, O'Brien, Willis, Smith (3)
Division 2.
Crewe Alexandra (h) 6-0 Att. 8,000
Wardrope, Aitken, McKay (2), Collins,
Lennox
Division 2.
Blackpool (a) 3-2 Att. 4,000
Wardrope, Campbell, Stott
Division 1.
Sheffield United (a) 2-2 Att. 20,000
Appleyard, Howie
Division 1.
Woolwich Arsenal (a) 3-4 Att. 20,000
Howie (2), J. Rutherford
Division 1.
Blackburn Rovers (a) 0-4 Att. 35,000
Division 1.
Woolwich Arsenal (a) 2-2 Att. 30,000
Appleyard, Higgins
Division 1.
Manchester United (h) 2-1 Att. 40,000
Shepherd, Wilson
Division 1.
Woolwich Arsenal (a) 3-0 Att. 25,000
Shepherd (2), Rutherford
Division 1.
Oldham Athletic (a) 4-2 Att. 25,000
Hay, Hibbert (2), Low
Division 1.
Sheffield United (h) 1-2 Att. 18,000
Higgins
Division 1.
Bradford City (h) 0-0 Att. 25,000
Division 1.
Sunderland (h) 2-5 Att. 40,000
Opponents (2 ogs)
Division 1.
Tottenham Hotspur (h) 1-1 Att. 45,000
Harris
Division 1.
Middlesbrough (h) 1-1 Att. 30,000
Aitken
Division 1.
Liverpool (a) 1-0 Att. 25,000
R. Clark
Division 1.
Everton (a) 1-0 Att. 30,000
Keating
Division 1.
Liverpool (a) 3-6 Att. 35,000
Gallacher (3)
Division 1.
Cardiff City (h) 5-0 Att. 35,702
Gallacher (2), McDonald (3)
Division 1.
West Ham United (a) 0-1 Att. 30,000
Division 1.
Middlesbrough (h) 3-2 Att. 40,000
Chalmers, Gallacher, Weaver
Division 1.
Huddersfield Town (h) 2-1 Att. 44,000
Bedford, McMenemy
Division 1.
Everton (h) 1-2 Att. 34,211
Williams

continued opposite

December 25

Match of the Day from 1951

A MERRY CHRISTMAS INDEED
Sunderland hammered in wonderful Christmas panto

Christmasses just don't come much better than this one today on Wearside on a frosty Roker Park. Sunderland 1 Newcastle United 4, was thanks to a fantastic team display which the Wearsiders had absolutely no answer to all afternoon. From the kick off it was simply one way traffic as the Magpies stormed forward and, after several glorious chances went begging, they eventually got their reward. A simple ball from Milburn was finished emphatically by George Robledo. United continued to dominate for the rest of the first half and when the United forwards reversed roles Milburn scored another from Robledo's cross to put United in command with 2-0 at the half time interval.

For a brief spell Sunderland fought back giving their support, amongst the massive holiday crowd of 52,274, some encouragement, it was however short lived. Robledo adding a third goal for United to effectively finish the game. Sunderland refused to give in and were rewarded with a late consolation goal through Ford but it only seemed to spur on a second wind for Newcastle. During the closing onslaught Milburn headed down for Foulkes to bang in United's fourth goal from close range and the Wearsiders had been well and truly beaten on their home soil, what a perfect Christmas present for all on Tyneside.

December 25

Sunderland
Robinson, Stelling, Hudgell, Watson, Hall, Aitken, Bingham, Kirtley, Ford, Shackleton, McSeveney.

Newcastle United
Simpson, Cowell, McMichael, Harvey, Brennan, E. Robledo, Walker, Foulkes, Milburn, G. Robledo, Mitchell.

One goal for Jackie Milburn against Sunderland.

Birthdays

Robbie Elliott born today in 1973.
Left-back/Midfield 1989-1997 & 2001-present day, Apps 144 (18 subs). Goals 11.
William Gallantree born today in 1913.
Winger 1931-1936, Apps 9. Goals 2.

Sadly Missed

John McGrath died on this day in 1998, aged 60.
Centre-half 1961-1968, Apps 181 (1 sub).
Goals 2.

Played on this day

1934, Division 2.
Hull City (h) 6-2   Att. 26,000
Gallantree, Pearson (2), Smith (2), Wilson
1936, Division 2.
Norwich City (h) 0-1   Att. 40,000
1937, Division 2.
Stockport County (h) 0-0   Att. 29,736
1940, Wartime.
Middlesbrough (h) 1-3   Att. 4,500
Stubbins
1942, Wartime.
Gateshead (h) 6-6   Att. 15,000
Coyde, Short (2), Stubbins (3)
1943, Wartime.
Gateshead (h) 0-2   Att. 12,000
1945, Wartime.
Manchester City (a) 3-4   Att. 29,000
Clifton (2), A. Donaldson
1946, Division 2.
West Bromwich A. (h) 2-4   Att. 44,722
Shackleton, Stobbart
1948, Division 1.
Birmingham City (a) 0-2   Att. 42,000
1950, Division 1.
Middlesbrough (a) 1-2   Att. 48,000
Stokoe
1951, Division 1.
Sunderland (a) 4-1   Att. 52,274
Foulkes, Milburn, G. Robledo (2)
1952, Division 1.
Cardiff City (h) 3-0   Att. 36,143
Mitchell (pen), Foulkes (2)
1953, Division 1.
Middlesbrough (a) 3-2   Att. 28,138
Mitchell, Monkhouse, Scoular
1954, Division 1.
Manchester City (a) 1-3   Att. 26,664
Keeble
1956, Division 1.
West Bromwich A. (a) 0-1   Att. 13,730
1957, Division 1.
Nottingham Forest (h) 1-4   Att. 25,214
Hughes

Playing record for this day... 40 games,
Won 15, Drawn 8, Lost 17, GF 84, GA 76.
Today's success rate... 47.50%.

1999: A Christmas break for the cranes during St.James' Park redevelopment.

December 26

...yed on this day

Division 2.
Walsall Town Swifts(a) 2-1   Att. 5,000
Wallace (2)
Division 2.
Rotherham Town (a) 0-1   Att. 2,000
Division 2.
Grimsby Town (a) 1-2   Att. 4,000
Collins
Division 2.
Grimsby Town (a) 2-3   Att. 7,000
Wardrope, Stott
Division 1.
Aston Villa (a) 0-1   Att. 30,000
Division 1.
Derby County (a) 0-1   Att. 20,000
Division 1.
Sunderland (h) 1-3   Att. 30,000
Rutherford
Division 1.
Manchester City (a) 4-1   Att. 35,000
Gosnell, McClarence, J. Rutherford, Veitch
Division 1.
Stoke (a) 2-1   Att. 10,000
Howie, Speedie
Division 1.
Sheffield United (h) 2-3   Att. 35,000
Appleyard, Howie
Division 1.
Manchester United (a) 0-1   Att. 45,000
Division 1.
Everton (h) 1-0   Att. 40,000
Shepherd
Division 1.
Sheffield United (h) 2-2   Att. 40,000
Hibbert, Rutherford
Division 1.
Liverpool (a) 1-2   Att. 35,000
G. Wilson
Division 1.
Bradford City (a) 0-2   Att. 18,000
Division 1.
Sunderland (a) 4-2   Att. 20,000
Higgins, Hibbert (2), Hudspeth
Division 1.
Burnley (h) 0-0   Att. 45,000
Division 1.
Liverpool (a) 0-1   Att. 45,000
Division 1.
Middlesbrough (a) 1-1   Att. 40,000
Woods
Division 1.
Liverpool (h) 2-1   Att. 23,000
McDonald (2)
Division 1.
Everton (h) 1-1   Att. 25,000
Seymour
Division 1.
Liverpool (h) 3-0   Att. 50,000
Clark, Gallacher, Urwin
Division 1.
Middlesbrough (a) 1-1   Att. 35,000
Gallacher
Division 1.
West Ham United (h) 1-0   Att. 43,000
McCurley
Division 1.
Middlesbrough (a) 2-2   Att. 45,000
Scott, Hutchison
Division 1.
Huddersfield Town (a) 3-0   Att. 20,000
Boyd (2), Starling

continued opposite

Match of the Day from 1955

A REAL BOXING DAY THUMPING
United hit six in memorable Tyne-Wear derby

The large contingent of travelling United fans amongst the 55,723 Roker Park crowd were given a perfect belated Christmas present this afternoon, the biggest win over Sunderland ever: 6-1. This went a long way to avenging that infamous 9-1 beating the Wearsiders handed out to Newcastle 47 years ago. This was United's day though, both teams had so far been inconsistent during the 1955-56 season, however this win coupled with the 5-0 beating of Preston on Christmas Eve has lifted Newcastle up to sixth place in the First Division table, they were fifteenth just a week ago.

Newcastle's finishing was simply devastating throughout the 90 minutes, not once did they miss a scoring opportunity. The first chance came after just two minutes, Vic Keeble heading home a perfectly executed free kick taken by Tommy Casey. Then it was 2-0 after 12 minutes, Jackie Milburn's low left-foot drive from the edge of the penalty area arrowing into the corner. Just six minutes later United led 3-0 when a superb ball from Mitchell found Curry unmarked just six yards out, he made no mistake tapping in the simplest of chances. Newcastle's forwards were on fire and there seemed no way of keeping them at bay but some desperate defending, and a little luck, kept them out until the inevitable fourth goal on 41 minutes. The goal was another simple but clinical finish from the head of centre-forward Keeble, rising above everyone to head in Milburn's corner kick.

Sunderland could have been forgiven for looking a little shell-shocked and demoralised when walking to the dressing room at half-time, but they came back out fighting for the second half. In almost their first real threat Fleming gave the Wearsiders some hope of a comeback just three minutes after the restart. This proved to be a false dawn however, Newcastle regained control almost immediately and Sunderland were soon back again deep in their own half, defending like mad. Within ten minutes a lobbed pass from Reg Davies was neatly flicked over the reach of Fraser by the head of Milburn, his second goal of the game. Moments later Mitchell crossed for Curry who volleyed in a spectacular sixth goal. With 25 minutes of the game remaining Mitchell got a knock which virtually rendered him a passenger and he withdrew to the wings. Without his pace and crossing ability, United's chances of increasing their 6-1 advantage diminished, and with a game against the same opponents just 24 hours away Newcastle settled for the points.

The return match at St James' Park on December 27th was again dominated by United, but without the superior finishing of today, Newcastle winning by 3-1, to make it a very merry Christmas week indeed.

Sunderland
Fraser, Hedley, McDonald, Anderson, Daniel, Aitken, Shackleton, Fleming, Purdon, Chisholm, Elliott.

Newcastle United
Simpson, Batty, McMichael, Scoular, Paterson, Casey, Milburn, Davies, Keeble, Curry, Mitchell.

Referee Mr. A. W. Leuty (Leeds)

Birthdays

Terry Marshall born today in 1935.
Winger 1958-1961, Apps 5. Goals 1.

December 26

SEASON 1955-56   OFFICIAL PROGRAMME

3ᴰ

SUNDERLAND
FOOTBALL CLUB LTD · ROKER PARK

NERS — 1937
CHAMPIONS
-93 1894-95
13 1935-36
h has never
her than the

No. 23

FOOTBALL LEAGUE DIVISION I
Monday, 26th December

Sunderland
v.
Newcastle Un.

Kick-off 2 p.m.

Played on this day

1931, Division 1.
Huddersfield Town (a) 2-1   Att. 25,000
Allen, Opponent (og)

1932, Division 1.
Birmingham (h) 2-1   Att. 43,000
Boyd, J.R. Richardson

1933, Division 1.
Everton (a) 7-3   Att. 40,000
Lang, Weaver (pen), Williams (3),
J.R. Richardson, Boyd

1934, Division 2.
Hull City (a) 1-1   Att. 25,000
Pearson

1935, Division 2.
Bradford City (h) 3-2   Att. 14,000
McMenemy, J. Smith, Weaver

1936, Division 2.
Barnsley (a) 0-1   Att. 22,000

1941, Wartime.
Sheffield Wednesday (h) 2-4   Att. 10,000
Stubbins (2, 1 pen)

1942, Wartime.
Middlesbrough (h) 3-2   Att. 13,300
Short, Woollett, Opponent (og)

1944, Wartime.
Sunderland (h) 3-1   Att. 40,311
Stubbins (2), Wayman

1945, Wartime.
Manchester City (h) 1-1   Att. 54,954
Milburn

1946, Division 2.
West Bromwich A. (a) 2-3   Att. 31,794
Wayman (2)

1947, Division 2.
West Bromwich A. (a) 1-0   Att. 48,322
Opponent (og)

1949, Division 1.
Middlesbrough (h) 0-1   Att. 61,184

1951, Division 1.
Sunderland (h) 2-2   Att. 63,665
Milburn (2, 1 pen)

1953, Division 1.
Middlesbrough (h) 2-3   Att. 43,750
Broadis, Mitchell

1955, Division 1.
Sunderland (a) 6-1   Att. 55,723
Curry (2), Keeble (2), Milburn (2)

1956, Division 1.
West Bromwich A. (h) 5-2   Att. 20,319
Punton, Davies (2), Casey (pen), Scoular

1957, Division 1.
Nottingham Forest (a) 3-2   Att. 32,359
Casey, R. Mitchell, White

1958, Division 1.
Nottingham Forest (h) 1-3   Att. 49,447
Curry

1959, Division 1.
Chelsea (a) 2-2   Att. 47,462
Allchurch, White

1960, Division 1.
Birmingham City (a) 1-2   Att. 29,435
Woods

1961, Division 2.
Middlesbrough (h) 3-4   Att. 21,038
Tuohy, Allchurch, McGuigan

1963, Division 2.
Huddersfield Town (h) 2-0   Att. 37,898
Thomas, Hilley

1964, Division 2.
Middlesbrough (a) 2-0   Att. 38,184
Hilley, Opponent (og)

1966, Division 1.
Leeds United (a) 0-5   Att. 40,680

continued overleaf

December 26

ayed on this day

Division 1.
Sunderland (h) 2-1   Att. 59,579
Bennett, Davies

Division 1.
Leeds United (a) 1-2   Att. 44,995
McNamee

Division 1.
Leeds United (h) 2-1   Att. 54,517
Davies, Robson

Division 1.
Leeds United (a) 0-3   Att. 46,758

Division 1.
Leeds United (a) 0-1   Att. 45,486

Division 1.
Leeds United (h) 0-1   Att. 55,638

Division 1.
Carlisle United (a) 2-1   Att. 20,605
Tudor, Macdonald

Division 1.
Burnley (a) 1-0   Att. 22,458
T. Craig (pen)

Division 1.
Manchester City (a) 0-4   Att. 45,811

Division 2.
Sheffield United (a) 0-1   Att. 23,200

Division 2.
Burnley (a) 2-3   Att. 16,433
Shoulder, Barton

Division 2.
Grimsby Town (a) 0-0   Att. 17,623

Division 2.
Blackburn Rovers (h) 1-1   Att. 33,622
Waddle

Division 1.
West Bromwich A. (a) 1-2   Att. 20,248
Baird

Division 1.
Sheffield Wednesday (a) 2-2. Att. 30,269
Beardsley, Roeder

Division 1.
Everton (h) 0-4   Att. 35,079

Division 1.
Manchester United (h) 1-0   Att. 26,461
Roeder

Division 1.
Sheffield Wednesday (a) 2-1 Att. 25,573
McDonald, O'Neill

Division 2.
Stoke City (a) 1-2   Att. 14,878
Scott

Division 2.
Swindon Town (h) 1-1   Att. 17,003
Quinn

Division 2.
Middlesbrough (h) 0-1   Att. 26,563

Division 1.
Wolverhampton W. (h) 2-1   Att. 30,137
Kelly (2)

Premier League.
Leeds United 0   **Newcastle 0**
   Att. 39,337

Premier League.
Blackburn Rovers 1 Newcastle 0
Gallacher 75   Att. 30,398

Premier League.
Derby County 1   **Newcastle 0**
Eranio 4 (pen)   Att. 30,232

Premier League.
Newcastle 0   **Leeds United 3**
   Kewell 38
   Bowyer 62
   Hasselbaink 90
   Att. 36,783

continued opposite

2000: Nobby Solano scores the first goal against Leeds United.

2000: Clarence Acuna gets the second goal against Leeds United.

Played on this day

1999, Premier League.
Newcastle 2	**Liverpool 2**
Shearer 12	Owen 51, 52
Ferguson 67	Att. 36,445

2000, Premier League.
Newcastle 2	**Leeds United 1**
Solano 41	Dacourt 10
Acuna 44	Att. 52,118

2001, Premier League.
Newcastle 3	**Middlesbrough 0**
Shearer 29	
Speed 58	
Bernard 83	Att. 52,127

2002, Premier League.
Bolton Wanderers 4	**Newcastle 3**
Okocha 5	Shearer 8, 79
Gardner 9	Ameobi 71
Ricketts 45, 63	Att. 27,314

Playing record for this day... 81 games,
Won 30, Drawn 16, Lost 35 GF 123, GA 124.
Today's success rate... 46.91%.

Newcastle's Boxing Day record...
At St. James' Park
Played 35,
Won 16, Drawn 8, Lost 11, GF 58, GA 52.

Away from home;
Played 46,
Won 14, Drawn 8, Lost 24, GF 65, GA 72.

2001: (Left) Middlesbrough's Hamilton Ricard is beaten in the air by Sylvain Distin.

2001: (Below) Alan Shearer celebrates his goal against Middlesbrough in typical style.

layed on this day

3, Division 2.
Crewe Alexandra (a) 1-1   Att. 2,000
Graham
7, Division 1.
Burnley (h) 0-1   Att. 24,959
2, Division 1.
Sunderland (a) 0-0   Att. 24,000
9, Division 1.
Chelsea (a) 1-2   Att. 70,000
Veitch
0, Division 1.
Sheffield Wednesday (a) 2-0 Att. 20,000
Shepherd (2)
3, Division 1.
Sunderland (h) 2-1   Att. 50,000
Goodwill, Hibbert
9, Division 1.
Manchester United (h) 2-1   Att. 35,000
Hibbert, Smailes
0, Division 1.
Tottenham Hotspur (a) 0-2   Att. 54,500
4, Division 1.
Huddersfield Town (a) 0-0   Att. 15,000
6, Division 1.
Leeds United (a) 2-1   Att. 48,620
Seymour, Urwin
7, Division 1.
Middlesbrough (h) 3-3   Att. 40,000
Boyd, Gallacher, McDonald
0, Division 1.
Sheffield Wednesday (h) 1-2   Att. 38,000
Bedford
2, Division 1.
Birmingham (a) 2-1   Att. 40,000
Lang, Murray
8, Division 2.
Norwich City (h) 4-0   Att. 46,000
Mooney (2 pens), Clifton (2)
1, Wartime.
Gateshead (a) 2-2   Att. 10,000
Stubbins (2, 1 pen)
3, Wartime.
Sunderland (h) 4-2   Att. 26,272
Stubbins (2), Woollett, Opponent (og)
8, Division 1.
Birmingham City (h) 1-0   Att. 49,457
Milburn
9, Division 1.
Middlesbrough (a) 0-1   Att. 53,802
2, Division 1.
Cardiff City (a) 0-0   Att. 40,000
4, Division 1.
Manchester City (h) 2-0   Att. 52,874
R. Mitchell (2, 1 pen)
5, Division 1.
Sunderland (h) 3-1   Att. 61,058
Keeble, Milburn, White
8, Division 1.
Nottingham Forest (a) 0-3   Att. 39,907
9, Division 1.
Arsenal (a) 0-0   Att. 39,646
1, Division 1.
Sheffield United (h) 1-2   Att. 53,079
Hibbitt
5, Division 1.
Sheffield United (h) 1-1   Att. 31,762
Macdonald
6, Division 1.
Sunderland (h) 2-0   Att. 49,664
Cannell, Kennedy
0, Division 2.
Derby County (h) 0-2   Att. 20,886

continued opposite

Match of the Day from 1955

SUNDERLAND SUNK - AGAIN

Newcastle continue their joy with another win over rivals

Newcastle United met Sunderland on home turf today in front of 61,058 for this Division One clash against their rivals Sunderland. Newcastle were hoping for the win, having beaten Sunderland 6-1 at Roker Park on Boxing Day they wanted to rub salt into their wounds.

Sunderland were hoping to put that embarrassment well behind them and gain a win to restore a little bit of their dwindling pride. The game began with Newcastle on the attack from the first whistle.

Sunderland were already a little shaken by the furious start Newcastle were having, and they never seemed to recover fully. They didn't seem to be ready for this game so soon after their humiliation, and appeared reluctant to get involved.

It was a little surprising then when it was Sunderland who opened the scoring with a good goal from their new signing. They had bought Bill Holden from Burnley on Boxing Day, for £12,000, but it was money well spent just for him to score against Newcastle and put the visitors into the lead at half-time.

In the second half Keeble opened the scoring for the home side, and Sunderland lost their smiles. Newcastle were relishing their neighbours' discomfort, and Milburn worsened things for the visitors when he added a second goal with a smashing shot that left the Sunderland keeper reeling. The home crowd went wild, hoping for a repeat performance of Boxing Day.

White rounded off the scoring for Newcastle, bringing their tally to three. Sunderland tried hard to get back into the game, but the game was to finish with the score 3-1.

Over the three Christmas games Newcastle had run up a tally of fourteen goals, nine of them against Sunderland. Milburn and Keeble each scored five times, and this win brought United into sixth place in the table. They were the only First Division side to win all six points from the three Christmas matches, whereas Sunderland were one of the few teams who failed to get any points at all.

Newcastle United
Simpson, Batty, McMichael, Scoular, Paterson, Casey, Milburn, Davies, Keeble, Curry, White.
Sunderland
Fraser, Hedley, McDonald, Anderson, Daniel, Aitken, Kemp, Fleming, Holden, Elliott, Shackleton.

Toon News Extra

1937... Bad light again halts Newcastle

The Division Two fixture away for Newcastle fell victim to bad light. This afternoon's game at Stockport County was abandoned after 77 minutes with the score 2-2. Smith and Park had put Newcastle in an early command but in the gloom Stockport came roaring back to level just before the game was halted. In the rearranged game played on March 2nd Newcastle won 3-1.

Birthdays

Billy Day born today in 1936.
Winger 1962-1963, Apps 14. Goals 1.
Mark Stimson born today 1967.
Left-back 1989-1992, Apps 104 (4 subs). Goals 3.

Duncan Ferguson born today in 1971.
Centre-forward 1998-2000, Apps 41 (9 subs).
Goals 12.

Played on this day

1982, Division 2.
Derby County (h) 1-0   Att. 30,558
Gayle
1983, Division 2.
Carlisle United (a) 1-3   Att. 14,756
Waddle
1986, Division 1.
Watford (a) 0-1   Att. 18,011
1995, Premier League.
Manchester U. 2   Newcastle 0
Cole 6
Keane 53   Att. 42,024

Playing record for this day... 31 games,
Won 12, Drawn 8, Lost 11, GF 38, GA 35.
Today's success rate... 51.61%.

NEWCASTLE UNITED FOOTBALL CLUB
ST. JAMES' PARK · NEWCASTLE ·ON·TYNE.

OFFICIAL –
1955 · PRICE... **3D** **1956** PROGRAMME

Photo by Bob Edwards

TUESDAY 27th DECEMBER

NEWCASTLE U. v SUNDERLAND   DIVISION 1

Kick-off 2.0 p.m.

Programme No. 28

NEWS CHRONICLE AND DISPATCH
POCKET PORTRAIT

VIC KEEBLE
Newcastle United F.C.

Played on this day

5, Division 2.
Lincoln City (a) 0-4   Att. 1,500

6, Division 2.
Gainsborough Trinity (a) 0-2   Att. 7,000

1, Division 1.
Bury (h) 1-1   Att. 7,000
Roberts

7, Division 1.
Middlesbrough (h) 1-1   Att. 38,000
McCormack

2, Division 1.
Sunderland (a) 0-2   Att. 35,000

9, Division 1.
Manchester United (a) 0-5   Att. 10,000

1, Division 1.
Aston Villa (a) 0-3   Att. 45,000

5, Division 2.
Bradford Park Ave. (a) 2-3   Att. 12,500
Pearson (2)

6, Division 2.
Norwich City (a) 5-1   Att. 19,300
Pearson, Smith (3), Leighton

0, Wartime.
Grimsby Town (h) 5-2   Att. 4,000
Gordon (2), Birkett, Billington, Herd

6, Division 2.
Millwall (h) 0-2   Att. 53,305

7, Division 1.
Tottenham Hotspur (a) 3-3.   Att. 51,649
R. Mitchell (pen), White (2)

9, Division 1.
Chelsea (h) 1-1   Att. 43,295
Eastham

3, Division 2.
Huddersfield Town (a) 0-3   Att. 12,832

4, Division 2.
Middlesbrough (h) 2-1   Att. 54,750
Hilley (2)

7, Division 1.
Nottingham Forest (h) 0-2   Att. 41,612

2, Division 2.
Grimsby Town (a) 2-2   Att. 14,983
Varadi, Gayle

7, Division 1.
Liverpool (a) 0-4   Att. 44,637

1, Division 2.
Bristol Rovers (h) 2-1   Att. 19,329
Brock, Kelly

2, Division 1.
Oxford United (a) 2-4   Att. 9,293
O'Brien, Clark

3, Premier League.
Chelsea 1   Newcastle 0
Stein 11   Att. 22,133

6, Premier League.
Newcastle 7   Tottenham Hotspur 1
Shearer 20, 82   Nielson 89
Ferdinand 22, 59
Lee 61, 88, Albert 79   Att. 36,308

7, Premier League.
Newcastle 1   Liverpool 2
Watson 16   McManaman 31, 43
   Att. 36,702

8, Premier League.
Liverpool 4   Newcastle 2
Owen 67, 80   Solano 21
Riedle 71, 84   Andersson 53
   Att. 44,605

9, Premier League.
Leicester City 1   Newcastle 2
Zagorakis 83   Ferguson 21
Att. 21,225   Shearer 53

ing record for this day.... 25 games,
6, Drawn 5, Lost 14, GF 38, GA 56.
y's success rate... 34%.

Match of the Day from 1996

AWESOME NEWCASTLE IN SEVENTH HEAVEN

Spurs hammered by 7-1, and it could have been more

There are times when Kevin Keegan's dream team make it easy to understand why Pele called football the beautiful game. United 7 Spurs 1 is as good as it gets but, the frustrating point to this result has to be Newcastle's, after a run of seven Premiership games without a win, woeful consistency, this is what wins titles, and sadly is still not in United's make-up. Yet against Tottenham, who gave the Newcastle forwards the freedom of St James' Park with a display of non-marking and laying-off opponents rarely seen at this level, the home side were unstoppable. Had Ian Walker not made some fine saves, Spurs would have been looking at a double-digit defeat. Already this season Spurs have conceded six to lowly Bolton and manager Gerry Francis must be praying for the return of Stephen Carr and John Scales to add some stability to an awful defence in time for the visit of Leicester in three days time. Keegan, however, will remind his players that after beating Manchester United 5-0 in October, their form dipped soon afterwards and with six defeats already, history suggests Newcastle can afford to lose only one more game in the second half of the season if they are to win the Premiership title.

Today's fun started in the twentieth minute when Alan Shearer, all persistence and strength, opened the scoring. Three minutes later Les Ferdinand deflected Peter Beardsley's shot past the unfortunate Walker to make it 2-0. The full-scale rout of Tottenham was underway in the 59th minute when Ferdinand headed home John Beresford's centre. Robert Lee made it 4-0 with a low drive before Philippe Albert, as he tends to under such circumstances, joined up with the attack to score with a shot which went under Walker's body. Shearer scored his second in the 83rd minute, remarkably this is the first time he has scored twice in a game for Newcastle, before Lee made it seven following good work by man-of-the-match David Batty. With a minute remaining, Allan Nielson capitalised on Beresford's slip to score a consolation goal. But, this was still not enough to avert Spurs' worst defeat since 1978.

Keegan, who immediately had to dash off to be with his sick wife, had one word to say about the display: "Awesome!" His assistant Terry McDermott pointed out that many had been critical of the Magpies recently and that this game was "our answer to those critics." Incredibly the victory was achieved without the injured David Ginola and Faustino Asprilla, and when United lost Keith Gillespie shortly before half time they were left without any natural wide players. Food for thought for Keegan as 1996 comes to an end.

Newcastle United
Hislop, Watson, Peacock, Albert, Beresford, Gillespie (Clark 41), Batty, Beardsley, Lee, Shearer, Ferdinand,

Tottenham Hotspur
Walker, Carr, Calderwood, Campbell, Wilson, Fox, Howells, Nielson, Sinton (Dozzell 46) (Rosenthal 55), Sheringham, Iverson .

Referee Mr. A. Wilkes (Worcester)

Toon News Extra

1895... Watt arrives at Newcastle.

Frank Watt became the Newcastle FC secretary. Newcastle were in debt with an underdeveloped ground and rock bottom on the field conceding an average of three goals per game. Watt helped transform the club and over the next three decades Newcastle went on to clinch four League championships and appear in no less than six FA Cup finals, winning the coveted trophy on two occasions.

Birthdays

Lomano LuaLua born today in 1980.
Forward 2000-present day, Apps 77 (59 subs).
Goals 9.

Sadly Missed

Duggie Wright died on this day in 1992, aged 75.
Midfield 1938-1948, Apps 106. Goals 1.

December 29

Match of the Day from 2002

UNITED EARN THEIR SPURS

Late own goal adds spice to comfortable home win

Today's roller-coaster victory keeps real achievement within reach with Newcastle climbing to fourth place in the Premiership after this their sixth consecutive home win. Roller-coaster? It would not have been had the unfortunate Nikos Dabizas, a second half sub, reignited a contest effectively already decided after an hour, Spurs trailing by two goals. His spectacular full-length diving header into the wrong net with fifteen minutes of the game remaining gave Spurs fresh though thin hope.

It was swiftly apparent that the confrontation between the attacking duo, Alan Shearer and Craig Bellamy, and a rear guard of Chris Perry and Ledley King was going to pose repeated alarms for Tottenham and glee for United's gluttonous Toon Army. It took only seventeen minutes for a goal to arrive. Newcastle had already had a flurry of chances but from a throw by Laurent Robert, Shearer headed away from goal under pressure and the unmarked Gary Speed rammed the ball home from eleven yards. Now Spurs were given a roasting, though in a couple of breakaways Mauricio Taricco, their left back, forced a reflex save by Shay Given, who also parried Gus Poyet's fierce volley from ten yards. United and Bobby Robson were then forced into four changes starting with Speed who left injured on 23 minutes replaced by Jermaine Jenas. At half time the full-scale change was completed with injured Nolberto Solano and Kieron Dyer making way for Lomana LuaLua and Dabizas.

However, despite the personnel changes and the positional tinkering by Robson, Newcastle continued to have the upper hand during the second half. In the midst of which came the crucial second goal for United in the 57th minute. With Tottenham's defence once more in confusion Shearer was able to head home Craig Bellamy's perfect cross from the left. This was the veteran's thirteenth league goal of the season, on the occasion of his 250th appearance for Newcastle, his 550th in all club football, a truly great marksman proven over many years. Newcastle looked sure of victory until the moment of aberration by Dabizas as he attempted to divert a dropping cross from sub Teddy Sheringham. As Newcastle began to lose their nerve, Spurs threw everything forward, including Les Ferdinand, whose arrival was warmly greeted by his former club's generous fans. Thereafter, every run he made was mockingly cheered and booed panto-style, sadly for Tottenham he never managed to frighten anybody.

Newcastle United
Given, Hughes, O'Brien, Caldwell, Bernard, Solano (Dabizas h/t), Dyer (LuaLua h/t), Speed (Jenas 23), Robert, Shearer, Bellamy.

Tottenham Hotspur
Keller, Carr, Perry, King, Tarricco, Poyet (Sheringham 67), Davies, Freund, Bunjevcevic, Iversen (Ferdinand 67), Keane (Acimovic 77).
Referee Mr. S. Bennett (Kent)

Played on this day

1894, Division 2.
   Walsall Town Swifts (a) 3-2 Att. 2,000
   Willis (3)
1900, Division 1.
   Nottingham Forest (a) 2-1 Att. 10,000
   Peddie (2)
1923, Division 1.
   Nottingham Forest (a) 0-0 Att. 12,000
1928, Division 1.
   Cardiff City(a) 0-2 Att. 10,000
1934, Division 2.
   Nottingham Forest (h) 2-0 Att. 24,000
   Murray, Pearson
1945, Wartime.
   Burnley (a) 2-3 Att. 18,000
   Hair, Wayman
1951, Division 1.
   Tottenham Hotspur (a) 1-2 Att. 55,219
   G. Robledo
1956, Division 1.
   Sheffield Wednesday (h) 1-2 Att. 42,649
   Curry
1973, Division 1.
   Sheffield United (h) 1-0 Att. 27,943
   Tudor
1979, Division 2.
   Charlton Athletic (h) 2-0 Att. 26,225
   Shoulder, Cassidy
1984, Division 1.
   Arsenal (h) 1-3 Att. 27,828
   Beardsley (pen)
1990, Division 2.
   Notts County (h) 0-2 Att. 17,557
2001, Premier League.
   Newcastle 1   Chelsea 2
   Shearer 37   Gudjohnsen 35, 45
                  Att. 52,123
2002, Premier League.
   Newcastle 2   Tottenham Hotspur 1
   Speed 17   Dabizas (og) 73
   Shearer 58   Att. 52,145

Playing record for this day.... 14 games, Won 6, Drawn 1, Lost 7, GF 18, GA 20. Today's success rate... 46.43%.

Birthdays

Martin Gorry born today in 1954.
Left-back 1976-1978, Apps 1 (1 sub). Goals 0.
Kieron Dyer born today in 1978.
Midfield 1999-present day, Apps 139 (12 subs). Goals 19.

Played on this day

1893, Division 1.
  Burslem Port Vale (h) 2-1   Att. 3,000
  Crate, Creilly
1899, Division 1.
  West Bromwich A. (h) 4-2   Att. 12,000
  Fraser, Peddie, Stevenson (2)
1905, Division 1.
  Sunderland (h) 1-1   Att. 56,000
  Orr
1911, Division 1.
  Bolton Wanderers (h) 5-2   Att. 28,000
  Hay, Hibbert (3), Veitch
1912, Division 1.
  Sheffield United (a) 1-1   Att. 22,000
  McTavish
1922, Division 1.
  Nottingham Forest (a) 1-0   Att. 12,000
  Mitchell
1933, Division 1.
  Portsmouth (a) 0-2   Att. 15,000
1944, Wartime.
  Sunderland (a) 3-4   Att. 30,000
  Stubbins (2, 1 pen), Wayman
1967, Division 1.
  Sunderland (a) 3-3   Att. 46,030
  McNamee, Burton (2 pens)
1972, Division 1.
  Sheffield United (h) 4-1   Att. 28,620
  Macdonald, Tudor, Nattrass, Craig
1978, Division 2.
  Brighton & Hove A. (a) 0-2   Att. 25,812
1989, Division 2.
  Swindon Town (a) 1-1   Att. 11,657
  Quinn
2000, Premier League.
  Newcastle 1   **Manchester United 1**
  Glass 81   Beckham 25 (pen)
              Att. 52,134

Playing record for this day...13 games,
Won 5, Drawn 5, Lost 3, GF 26, GA 21.
Today's success rate...57.69%.

Match of the Day from 1899

YO-YO GAME WITH ALBION

Newcastle win 4-2 in back-and-forth struggle

West Bromwich Albion travelled north to meet Newcastle United in front of a crowd of 12,000 today. Newcastle were playing at full strength, but Albion were missing two of their best players, Jones and Garfield. Instead Roberts and Hadley took to the field in their places, and the match started with Albion on the attack immediately.

John Paddock managed to get through the strong Newcastle defence, but fluffed his shot and wasted a good chance.

Next it was Newcastle's turn, and they won a corner. It was well saved by Reader in the Albion goal, and the next try from United was destined for the same fate. A super effort from Paddock sent the ball to Simmons for a shot on goal, but it was Kingsley in the Newcastle goal who cleared the ball from danger.

Reader was beaten with Newcastle's next attack, but the goal from Peddie was disallowed due to his offside position. The next shot came from Fraser, but Reader was ready for that one too and the ball was saved.

Albion almost broke the deadlock when Williams stood up to take a free kick, his shot soaring into the net straight past Kingsley. However, the goal didn't stand, and it was back to square one.

Newcastle's attacking kept up the pressure on the Albion goal, and the visitors spent most of their time defending. There were few chances for Albion to try their luck at scoring, but when the opportunity arose they were a danger. Kingsley was up for the challenge though, and managed to keep the ball out for the most part, but it was just a matter of time before the first goal was scored.

It was Albion who took the lead with a lovely solo effort from Simmons, finally beating Kingsley. The visitors were a goal ahead, and it was now going to be an uphill struggle for Newcastle to come back.

The equaliser came for the home side shortly afterwards. A superb centre from Fraser fell to Stevenson, who shot with determination and power. The ball sailed past Reader to level the scores and boost Newcastle's spirit.

The game was anybody's, and both goals were attacked from all angles. Jock Peddie got the home side ahead with a fine shot which zoomed into the back of the net, and then the lead was further increased when Fraser flicked the ball into the net from close in to bring the score to 3-1.

After half-time things were much the same. Albion seemed to get the same chances as Newcastle, but they had far more difficulty in making the most of them. United looked dangerous even when they missed, and the forwards kept up the pressure on the Albion goal.

It was Stevenson who brought Newcastle's tally to four with a well-placed shot, and before the end of the game Albion also pulled back a goal to bring their total to two. It wasn't enough for the visitors, and they were relieved it was over.

Newcastle United
Kingsley, Birnie, D. Gardner, Ghee, Aitken, Carr, Rogers, Stevenson, Peddie, MacFarlane, Fraser.
West Bromwich Albion
Reader, Williams, Adams, Banks, Dunn, Hadley, Roberts, Richards, Simmons, Terry, Paddock.
Referee Mr. Boldison (Stockton).

Birthdays

Billy Rafferty born today in 1950.
Forward 1979-1980, Apps 42 (5 subs). Goals 8.

Colin Suggett born today in 1948.
Midfield & Coach 1978-1994, Apps 24 (3 subs). Goals 0.